THE COMPLETE HANDBOOK OF THE INTERNET

INTERNET

Volume I

The Complete Handbook of the Internet

Volume I

by

W.J. Buchanan
Napier University

KLUWER ACADEMIC PUBLISHERS
BOSTON / DORDRECHT / LONDON

A C.I.P. Catalogue record for this book is available from the Library of Congress.

ISBN 1-4020-7236-8 (Volume I)
ISBN 1-4020-7290-2 (Set)

Published by Kluwer Academic Publishers,
P.O. Box 17, 3300 AA Dordrecht, The Netherlands.

Sold and distributed in North, Central and South America
by Kluwer Academic Publishers,
101 Philip Drive, Norwell, MA 02061, U.S.A.

In all other countries, sold and distributed
by Kluwer Academic Publishers,
P.O. Box 322, 3300 AH Dordrecht, The Netherlands.

Printed on acid-free paper

Printed in the Netherlands.

Contents

Preface

This is one of the most exciting times in technology, ever, and the Internet has the potential to change the way that people work and play, in a way that few technological areas have ever done before. It will soon become part of the fabric of our life, in the same way that the motor car, the telephone and the television have done in the past. The greatest problem is that Internet technology is moving so fast that it is difficult to keep up with it. Thus, it is important to understand the key underlying principles of it, which allows everyone to learn new developments. This book, and the associated WWW site and CD-ROM, will hopefully help provide this foundation. It contains over 1600 pages within 74 chapters and appendices, arranged in nine main sections. These sections are:

A. **Distributed Systems**. These chapters contain information on the underlying operating systems, and how resources are shared over local systems, and also over networks.
B. **Data Communications**. These chapters contain information on the basic principles of transmitting data over an electronic connection.
C. **Networks**. The Internet could not exist without the connection of nodes to networks. These chapters discuss many of the main networking technologies, such as Ethernet, ATM, ISDN, and modem connections.
D. **Network Protocols**. These chapters outline some of the protocols that are used to transfer data from one node to another over the Internet.
E. **Routers and Security**. Routers are important devices on the Internet and allow data to be routed from one node to another. Along with routers, the main elements of security are covered in these sections. These chapters include coverage of firewalls, proxy servers, and encryption.
F. **Session Protocols**. Session layer protocols are important in the reliable transmission of data over the Internet, as they allow two nodes to negotiate a connection, and then pass information about the session. The main session protocols which are supported on the Internet are electronic mail, the WWW, and FTP/Telnet. These chapters cover the operation of thee important protocols.
G. **Networking Operating Systems**. The Internet could not really exist in its current form without an underlying network operating system which integrates the network, networking protocols, and other devices to produce an integrated system. These chapters cover the three main network operating systems: Microsoft Windows, Novell NetWare and UNIX.
H. **WWW fundamentals**. These chapters cover the key principles of WWW presentation, and the methods which are used to add extra functionality to the WWW.
I. **Multimedia and databases**. These chapters outline how multimedia can be used over the Internet, and how databases operate in a distributed system.

The appendices include reference material on related subjects, such as server configuration, and reference guides for important commands. Along with the book, the associated CD-ROM contains a fully searchable version of the book. It also contains the associated source code, and RFC documents.

Help is provided by the author from the e-mail address of:

w.buchanan@napier.ac.uk

or from the associated WWW site at:

```
http://www.soc.napier.ac.uk/~bill/hand_int.html
```

or

```
http://buchananweb.co.uk/hand_int.html
```

Dr William Buchanan,
Senior Lecturer,
School of Computing,
Napier University,
Edinburgh. UK.

A1 Introduction

A1.1 Introduction

This book contains nine main sections which relate to the main elements of the Internet. These are (as illustrated in Figure A1.1):

A. **Distributed Systems**. These chapters contain information on the underlying operating systems, and how resources are shared over local systems, and also over networks.

B. **Data Communications**. These chapters contain information on the basic principles of transmitting data over an electronic connection.

C. **Networks**. The Internet could not exist without the connection of nodes to networks. These chapters discuss many of the main networking technologies, such as Ethernet, ATM, ISDN, and modem connections.

D. **Network Protocols**. These chapters outline some of the protocols that are used to transfer data from one node to another over the Internet.

E. **Routers and Security**. Routers are important devices on the Internet and allow data to be routed from one node to another. Along with routers, the main elements of security are covered in these sections. These chapters include coverage of firewalls, proxy servers, and encryption.

F. **Session Protocols**. Session layer protocols are important in the reliable transmission of data over the Internet, as they allow two nodes to negotiate a connection, and then pass information about the session. The main session protocols which are supported on the Internet are electronic mail, the WWW, and FTP/Telnet.

G. **Networking Operating Systems**. The Internet could not really exist in its current form without an underlying network operating system which integrates the network, networking protocols, and other devices to produce an integrated system. These chapters cover the three main network operating systems: Microsoft Windows, Novell NetWare and UNIX.

H. **WWW fundamentals**. These chapters cover the key principles of WWW presentation, and the methods which are used to add extra functionality to the WWW.

I. **Multimedia and databases**. These chapters outline how multimedia can be used over the Internet, and how databases operate in a distributed system.

A1.2 History

During World War II, John Eckert at the University of Pennsylvania built the world's first large electronic computer. It contained over 19,000 electronic valves and was called ENIAC (Electronic Numerical Integrator and Computer). It was a poor acronym that just did not quite roll-off the tongue, but technically it was so innovative that it ran for over 11 years before it was switched off. Not many modern day computers will run for more than a few years before they are considered unusable. These days a computer has a typical usable age of just one or two years, before it is either cascaded onto someone who doesn't quite require the most modern computer. Alternatively, as is more typical in modern industry, they are retired to the great computer graveyard in the sky, who are well looked after by some of the great, but departed innovators of the computer, such as:

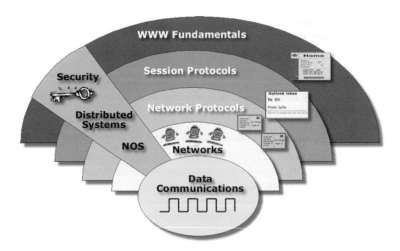

Figure A1.1 Subject areas covered

- **Gary Kildall (1942–1994).** Who, with CP/M was the innovator, and technical genius behind one of the first operating systems for microprocessor systems (and who developed many of the initial standards for the CD-ROM interface, and produced the first successful open-system architecture). If not for a blunder in arrangements with a meeting with IBM, CP/M may have become the standard operation system for the PC, rather than MS-DOS. Novell eventually bought his company, Digital Research, in 1991, and his products eventually disappeared under the weight and power of Microsoft Windows. He died in 1994 at the age of 52, after falling in a drunken state and hitting his head. Gary, unlike many others in the computer business, was always more interested in technical specifications, rather than financial statements and balance sheets.

- **John Eckert (1919–1995)** and **John von Neumann (1903-1957)**, of course, who would be totally amazed with modern computers, especially in the way that it is now possible to integrate millions of digital devices onto a single piece of silicon, which is smaller than a thumbprint. For them you could actually hold a digital device in your hand, and if it was working properly it would burn your hand. To them the invisible communications over an infrared link would seem more like magic than technology.

- **Herman Hollerith (1860–1929).** Who, at the end of the 19th century, devised a machine that accepted punch cards with information on them. These cards allowed an electrical current to pass through a hole when there was a hole present (a 'true'), and did not conduct a current when a hole was not present (a 'false'). This was one of the first uses of binary information, which represents data in a collection of one of two states (such as true or false, or, 0 or 1). He would be amazed with current transfer rates for data storage. To him a few hundred bytes a second would seem fast, but would be totally amazed with the transfer rates that give many hundred of millions of bytes every second, all from invisible magnetic fields stored on a metal disk. Also, imagine the number of punch cards that would be required to load many of our modern programs.

- **William Shockley (1910–1989).** Who, along with others at the Bell Labs, invented the electronic transistor, which allowed computers to migrate from reinforced concrete floors that occupied whole floors of a building, and need special electrical generators to power them, to ones which could be fitted onto a pin-head.

- **Grace Hopper (1906–1992).** Grace overcame one of the major problems in software development: how to write programs which could be easily understood and written by humans, and easily converted into a form which computers could understand. In the early 1950s, work had begun on assemblers which would use simple text representations of the binary operations that the computer understood (such as ADD A, B to add two numbers). The assembler would convert them into a binary form. This aided the programmer, as they did not have to continually look-up the binary equivalent of the command that they required. It also made programs easier to read. The great advance occurred around 1956 when Grace Hopper started to develop compilers for the UNIVAC computer. These graceful programs converted a language that was readable by humans into a form that a computer could understand. This work would lead to the development of the COBOL programming language (which has since survived to the present day, although it is still blamed for many of the Year 2000 problems).

By today's standards, ENIAC was a lumbering dinosaur, and by the time it was dismantled, it weighed over 30 tons and spread itself over 1,500 square feet. Amazingly, it also consumed over 25 kW of electrical power (equivalent to the power of over 400 60 W light bulbs), but could perform over 100,000 calculations per second (which, even by today's standards, is reasonable). Unfortunately, it was unreliable, and would work only for a few hours, on average, before an electronic valve needed to be replaced. Faultfinding, though, was much easier in those days, as a valve that was not working would not glow, and would be cold to touch.

While ENIAC was important in the history of the modern computer, its successor would provide a much greater legacy: the standard architecture that has been used in virtually every computer since built: the ENVAC (Electronic Discrete Variable Automatic Computer). Its real genius was due to John von Neumann, a scientific researcher who had already built up a strong reputation in the field of quantum mechanics. For computing, he used his superior logical skills to overcome the shortcomings of ENIAC: too little storage, too many valves, and too lengthy a time to program it. His new approach used the stored-program concept, which is used by virtually every computer made, ever since. With this, the storage device of the computer (its memory) is used to hold both the program instructions and also the data used by the computer and the program. His computer, as illustrated in Figure A1.2, was designed around five major elements:

- **Central control**. This reads program instructions from the memory, which are interpreted by the central control unit.
- **Central arithmetic unit**. This performs arithmetic operations, such as add/subtract, multiply/divide, binary manipulation, and so on.
- **Memory**. This holds both the program instructions and program/system data.
- **Input device**. This is used to read data into the memory. Example input devices include keyboards, disk storage, punch card reader (which were used extensively before the large-scale introduction of disk storage devices). The input device loads both program instructions and data into memory.
- **Output device**. This is used to output data from memory to an output device, such as a printer or display device.

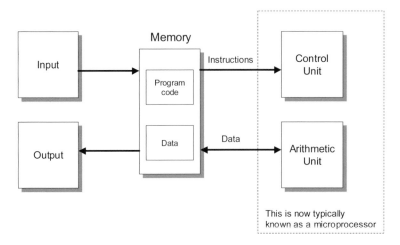

Figure A1.2 Stored-program architecture

Typically, these days, the central control unit and the central arithmetical unit have been merged into a device known as a microprocessor. The environment in which to run programs, typically known as user programs, is defined by the operating system. The von Neumann architecture made it easier to load programs into the system as the operating system can load all its associated data in the same place as it loaded the program. Previous to this architecture, a user would have to load the program into one area of memory, and all the associated data to another. The computer would then read from the program area for its instructions, and then read and write to a data area.

A1.3   System classification

Computer systems can be classified as either embedded systems or non-embedded systems. An embedded system typically has its operating system and all associated programs are integrated into the device. This allows the system to be properly tested in most operating conditions, and will thus be much more reliable, than more general-purpose devices, which cannot be properly tested for all the possible connection devices. For example the controller in a washing machine is an embedded system, and will act correctly, within given specifications, and should hardly ever crash. An embedded system also normally has a limited range of hardware that can be added to the system. Again, this makes the system more reliable, as many of the combinations of hardware can be tested for. It is thought that, in the near future, there could be as many as 10 times as many embedded systems sold than conventional computers, such as desktop PCs. The future is also likely to see the number of processing elements in devices increase, and automobiles of the future may contain hundreds of processing elements, each with their own specific function.

A non-embedded system is more general-purpose and allows operating systems and user programs to be installed as required. They are thus less reliable as the system designer cannot test for all the possible combinations of hardware and software that could be installed or run on them.

Table A1.1 outlines some of the main classifications for computer systems. These vary in size from small embedded systems which perform simple operations, to large and complex systems which control industrial plants. The classifications include:

- **Small embedded systems**. These normally include small processing elements, which have minimal input and output, and have a simple program which runs on the processor. They typically also have their own local permanent memory, which can be written to so that they can be permanently programmed. These tend to be extremely reliable, and cope reasonably well with exceptional circumstances. Normally they do not require an operating system, and the code runs directly on the processing element.

- **Large embedded systems**. These typically have a powerful processor, which can have many inputs and outputs, and perform complex operations, that cannot be typically achieved within the required specification with a more general-purpose computer. These tend to be extremely reliable, and cope well with exceptional circumstances. They are typically programmed once for their operation, and then not programmed again, until an upgrade is required. If they only run one program, they do not typically require an operating system, but if many processes are run at a time, there is normally a need for a robust operating system kernel (a basic operating system which supports the running of several programs at a time). There is typically very little need for a graphical user input for these system, as this can often adds too much of a processing overhead to the whole system.

- **Mobile devices**. These typically have medium-power processors, and have limited memory resources. In most cases, they have a remote connection to other devices, such as over an infrared link or a radio link (as with a mobile phone). As they have limited memory resources, many of their programs are embedded into the system, but some can also be downloaded from the Internet or from another device. They are typically fairly reliable, with an embedded operating system.

- **Desktop systems**. These are general-purpose computers, which can be installed with any type of operating system, and any user program which can be supported on the installed operating system. They typically do not have the same reliability as embedded systems, as they can have a large range of hardware and software installed on them. A small software or hardware bug can cause the whole system to act unreliably.

- **Server systems**. These are systems which have a definite purpose of running server programs for client computers. Typical services are for WWW services, Internet access services, file transfer services, printer services, and electronic mail services. They are fairly robust, and have large amounts of memory to run many consecutive connections. Also, they are typically not used by a single user (as this would reduce the processing time available to client computers), and access to them is typically limited to the system manager, over a network. Many servers are contained within rack-mounted units, with power supplies which have backup systems which either allow the system to be properly shut-down when there is a power failure, or will sustain the power over a given time period. A server may also have several different storage sources, which allow for one or more to fail, without a loss of data. They are not as reliable as embedded systems, as they support a wide range of hardware and software, but these tend to be more robust than the types used in a desktop system. Server programs also tend to be much more reliable than general-purpose programs. A server also typically runs a more robust operating system, which is more tolerant of incorrectly operating hardware/software, especially to network faults.

- **Supercomputer**. These are extremely fast computers, with an optimized architecture. Typically, they also have multiple processors, with a fast communications channel between them. A supercomputer will typically have a base performance speed which is at least 10 times as great as a top-of-the-range desktop computer.

Table A1.1 Computer classifications

Description	Processor power	Memory	Reliability	Input/ output/ connec-tions	Programs	Typical application
Small embedded systems	L	L	H	L	Dedicated, but upgradeable	Alarm system, car management system, mobile phones.
Large embedded systems	H	M	H	H	Dedicated, but upgradeable	Radar processing, digital TV processing, network router.
Mobile devices	L-M	L-M	M-H	L	Integrated, with some installable programs	Hand-held Computer, mobile phone with Internet access.
Desktop	M-H	M	L-M	L-M	General-purpose	Word processor, spreadsheet.
Workstation	M-H	M-H	M	L-M	Specialist programs, with other general-purpose software	Computer Aided Design, Multimedia.
Server	M-H	H	M-H	M	Server programs	WWW server, E-mail server.
Supercom-puter	H	H	H	H	Specialized programs	High-power ap-plications, such as genetic modeling, and scientific simulations
Control system	H	H	H	H	Specialized programs	Industrial control.

L – Low; L-M – Low-to-Medium; M – Medium; M-H – Medium-to-High; H-High.

- **Control systems**. These support the interfacing of many devices, normally with some form of control program. As this control must be achieved within given time limits, there must be a robust and powerful operating system to support fast response speeds. For example, it would be no good at all if the control program for a nuclear power plant crashed, just before the reactor temperature was increasing to dangerous levels. Also this type of system must also be able to prioritize signals, as the safety critical control should have a higher priority over optimization controls. The normal prioritization for an industrial plant will be (in this order):

1. **Meet safety considerations**, such as making sure that the system does not over-heat, explode, and so on. A system should not operate if it cannot meet its safety considerations. Any shutdown of the system must be carefully planned.
2. **Meet regularity/legal obligations**, such as meeting omission levels, power considerations, operating times, and so on. A system can breach its regularity obligation, only when it has to meet safety considerations.
3. **Optimize system**. Once the system has met its safety considerations and its regularity obligations, it can then be optimized in order to maximize the profit/income of the product, or in the efficiency of its production. Optimization control/data has a lower priority than regularity obligation control/data, which in turn has a lower priority than safety critical control/data.

A1.4   System definitions

A computer system consists of hardware, software and firmware, all of which interconnect. The basic definitions of each are:

- **Hardware**. These are the 'the bits that can be touched', that is, the components, the screws and nuts, the case, the electrical wires, and so on. Computer hardware can be split into different areas, such as: mechanical infrastructure (printed-circuit board, casing, screws, and so on); electrical power components (wires, electrical connectors, transformer, fuses, and so on); computer electronics infrastructure (microprocessor, memory, core components, and so on); and peripheral devices (keyboard, disk drives, video adaptor, and so on).

- **Software**. These are the programs that run on programmable hardware and change their operation depending on the inputs to the system. Inputs could be taken from a keyboard, interface hardware or from an external device. The program itself cannot exist without some form of programmable hardware such as a microprocessor or controller. Software programs typically require an operating system in which to run. This provides the program with all the necessary resources, so that it can run successfully, such as providing access to file systems, peripheral devices (such as disk drives, and printers), and access to specific hardware devices. The next chapter defines the types of operating systems that exist. An operating system, itself, is a piece of software which runs on the computer, and has a much closer level of control of the hardware, than user programs do.

- **Firmware**. These are hardware devices that are programmed using software. A good example of firmware is the serial port on a computer. With software this port can be made to operate at one of many different operating transfer rates, or with differing communication settings. Typically, a firmware device must have some local memory in which to store the updated settings. This can be achieved with some permanent memory, such as an EEPROM (Electrically Erasable Read Only Memories), or FLASH memory, where data can be stored in a permanent way, even when the power is taken away. An example is in a smart card which stores the bank details of a person. Other examples are storing the setup information for a PC (the BIOS settings), and using FLASH memory to store camera pictures. FLASH memory has many advantages over disk storage; especially that it does not require any mechanical movement of parts.

In most applications, dedicated hardware is faster than hardware that is running software, although systems running software programs tend to be easier to modify and require less development time.

Figure A1.3 shows an outline of operations that might occur in a computer system. There are many different data inputs that can occur in user programs, such as data being entered on a keyboard, or data from a network connection, or data movement on the mouse. The two main methods used to react to data input are:

- **Polling**. In this method the system scans all its input devices, at given time periods, and asks them if they have data that requires to be passed onto the system, to be processed. This is acceptable in systems which only have a few inputs, but it is very difficult to scan input devices which have a large number of data inputs. It is also inefficient as it wastes time in interrogating devices for input data when they have no data. Another major problem is that some devices may have a great deal of data, at a given time, and the system is not able to process it fast enough, as the system is too busy scanning other devices for data. Each input device typically has a temporary storage area for the data (known as a memory buffer). A typical problem in a polling system is buffer overruns. This is where the data cannot be extracted fast enough from the buffer, before it overflows, and part of the data is lost. Polling is typically only used when there is infrequent data arriving, or where the memory buffer is large enough, so that none of the data will be lost if the system cannot extract the data fast enough.
- **Event-driven**. The alternative to polling is event-driven, where programs respond to events as they occur in the system. This is more efficient for data input, and can also support other events, such as error and operating system events. It is also easier to write programs which are event-driven, as the program writer does not have to define exactly how the program scans for input data. The program basically just has to respond to specific events, such as when the user moves the cursor, or presses a key from the keyboard.

Most general-purpose systems are now event-driven; as these are more efficient, but there can also be a number of programs which are polling-based, in the way that they get data input. Typically a system event causes the system to go into a certain state, such as: a data input state; a processing and analysis state; a data output state; or a defining data requirements state. For example if the user presses a key on the keyboard, then the system goes into the data input state. The character is then read from the keyboard, and processed and/or analysed in some way. Next the results of this can be outputted; typically to the monitor. After this there can be a requirement for more data to be input (the data requirements state). There are obviously many more states in a computer, but the data input, processing/analysis, data output and defining data requirements are typical system states.

Systems events can occur for many reasons, such as:

- Movement of a mouse.
- Pressing a key on the keyboard.
- Pressing a button on a window.
- Data arriving from a network.

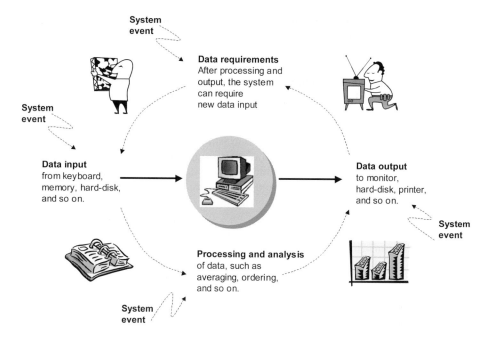

Figure A1.3 Block diagram of a simple computer system

A1.5 Computer architecture

The stored-program concept was a great revolution in computer systems, and the basic architecture of a computer has varied very little since this time. Among the many changes that have happened is the integration of devices into single units, but the concept of stored-program and shared memory for program instructions and data stays the same. Some systems have been built using Harvard architecture, as this allows for data and program instructions to be kept separately, which is a much more logical approach. This overcomes the problem of data corrupting stored program instructions. It also actually requires a simpler approach to organizing data and program instructions in memory (as they are kept apart, so there are no problems in organizing the areas which are used by program instruction, and which are used by data). Unfortunately, programmers would have to rewrite all their programs and operating system software for a different type of architecture. In addition, most system developers have been educated on systems which use von Neumann architecture, thus it now seems a more logical approach. Von Neumann architecture is much more efficient in memory than Harvard architecture, but this advantage is not so great in an era that has a large amount of memory. Von Neumann architecture was useful when memory was in short supply, but the case for it is not as strong, these days.

The main elements of a modern computer system are a CPU (central processing unit), memory, and input/output (I/O) interfacing circuitry. After von Neumann's new architecture the CPU and the arithmetic logic unit (ALU) were typically separate units. The invention of the microprocessor integrated the CPU and ALU into a single device.

A computer extracts data and instructions from memory, then processes the data, and places the results back into the memory. There must thus be some way to place a unique address tag for each element of data in memory. This tag is known as a memory address, and the address tag is passed to the memory though an address bus. A bus is a collection of common electrical connections grouped by a single name. The more connections in the address bus, the more address tags that can be used. Once the data is addressed, the data can be passed over the data bus. In order for the system to determine if the data is going to or from the processor, and whether there is valid data on the data bus, and other control definitions, a control bus is required. Thus the three main buses in computer systems are: the address bus, the control bus and the data bus.

Figure A1.4 shows a basic system (based on von Neumann architecture). External devices such as a keyboard, display, disk drives can connect directly onto the data, address and control buses or through the I/O interface circuitry. It is normally preferable that they connect to the I/O interface as devices rather than connect straight onto the address and data buses as they could do some damage to the buses, especially by corrupting the data on these.

Computers run programs which perform operations on stored data. This data can either be stored in electronic memory, or in a storage device, such as a hard disk or CD-ROM. Electronic memory normally provides a temporary storage of data, which can be accessed quickly (as compared to devices which use a mechanical method to access memory, such as hard disks, or CD-ROMs). Electronic memory consists of RAM (random access memory) and ROM (read only memory). ROM stores permanent binary information, whereas RAM is a non-permanent memory and loses its contents on a loss of power. Applications of RAM are to run programs and store temporary information. RAM is normally made up of either DRAM (Dynamic RAM) or SRAM (Static RAM). SRAM is typically much faster than DRAM, and is used when fast memory access is required. DRAM, though, is typically available in large amounts, and is cheaper for an equivalent memory size (typically a DRAM memory chip can store up to eight times the amount that a SRAM memory chip can). DRAM is typically used for the main memory of the system, and SRAM is used where fast memory is required, such as in memory for graphics devices. The other disadvantage of DRAM is that it looses its contents quickly and the system refreshes its contents many times every second. This operation causes DRAM to consume much more electrical power than SRAM.

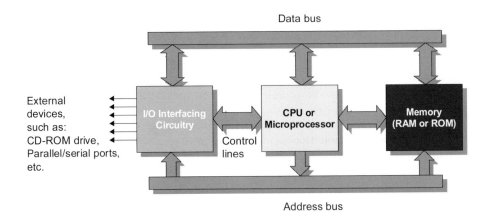

Figure A1.4 Block diagram of a simple computer system

The microprocessor is the main controller of the computer. It only understands binary information and operates on a series of binary commands known as machine code. A system clock synchronizes every operation within the computer. Thus operations, such as reading and writing data to/from memory, occur on the tick of the clock. A system clock which runs at 1MHz (one million ticks per second) will have a single tick of the clock in one millionth of a second.

As the performance of electronic devices has improved, the microprocessor has been able to multiply the system clock, and use this as its operating rate. It will thus operate at a faster speed than the rest of the system. Unfortunately, it must slow down to the rest of the system to communicate with devices outside itself. The main limitation on the speed of the system is now on the speed of the wires and interconnected circuit lines that connect the electronic devices together.

As the microprocessor is the heart of any of the operations that occur in the system, the number of bits that it can operate on at a time is an important measure of the system performance. This is knows as the classification of a microprocessor. The first microprocessor: the 4004 could only operate on 4 bits at a time, thus it was classified as a 4-bit processor. Next the Intel 8080 operated on 8 bits at a time and was classified as an 8-bit microprocessor The migration has since gone in multiples of two, from 16-bit (8086) to 32-bit (80386) and to 64-bit devices (Alpha). Table A1.2 shows some examples. Generally the more bits that a microprocessor can handle at a time, the fast the system will be. An important factor, though, is that the operating system that runs the program must also support this maximum size. If it does not, the improvement in speed may be lost, as the operating system cannot cope with the increased data size.

Table A1.2 Microprocessor classification

Classification	Microprocessor
4-bit	Intel 4004
8-bit	MOS Technologies 6502, Zilog Z80, Intel 8080, Motorola 6800
16-bit	TI TMS 9900, Intel 8086/8088, Motorola 68000, Intel 80286
32-bit	Zilog Z8000, Motorola 68020, Intel 80386/80486/Pentium
64-bit	DEC Alpha

The basic signals that we require in order to communicate between the microprocessor, memory and the I/O interface are:

- **Memory read or write**. This defines whether data is either being send from the microprocessor to the memory or I/O interface (with a memory write), or if data is being received by the microprocessor from the memory or I/O interface (with a memory read).
- **Memory or I/O interface select**. This defines whether the memory read or write is from the memory or the I/O interface.
- **Clock**. This synchronizes the events between the microprocessor and the memory or I/O interface.
- **Interrupt line**. This is used by external devices to get the attention of the processor (and thus cause an event).

The basic operation of the system is:

- Fetch binary instructions from memory.
- Decode these instructions into a series of simple actions.
- Carry out the actions in a sequence of steps.

To access a location in memory the following actions are conducted:

- The microprocessor puts the address of the location on the address bus.
- The contents at this address are then placed on the data bus.
- The microprocessor reads the data from the data bus.

To store data in memory the following actions are conducted:

- The microprocessor places the data on the data bus.
- The address of the location in memory is then put on the address bus.
- Data is read from the data bus into the memory address location.

A1.6   Bits, bytes and words

Systems can be divided into two main classifications: digital systems and analogue systems. A digital system only understands 0's and 1's (binary information), whereas an analogue system can take on many values.

A computer operates on binary digits which use a base-2 numbering system. To determine the decimal equivalent of a binary number each column is represented by two raised to the power of 0, 1, 2, and so on. For example, the decimal equivalents of `1000 0001` and `0101 0011` are:

2^7	2^6	2^5	2^4	2^3	2^2	2^1	2^0	
128	64	32	16	8	4	2	1	*Decimal*
1	0	0	0	0	0	0	1	129
0	1	0	1	0	0	1	1	83

Thus `01010011` gives:

$$(0\times128) + (1\times64) + (0\times32) + (1\times16) + (0\times8) + (0\times4) + (1\times2) + (1\times1) = 83$$

As was seen the number of different representations of the binary digits is determined by the number of bits used to represent the value. With a single binary digit we can represent two values (2^1), with two binary digits we can represent four values (2^2), and so on. For example:

- 8 bits gives 0 to 2^8-1 (255) different representations.
- 16 bits gives 0 to $2^{16}-1$ (65 535) different representations.
- 32 bits gives 0 to $2^{32}-1$ (4 294 967 295) different representations.

Just as in the decimal system (with units, tens, hundreds, and so on), the most significant bit (msb) is at the left-hand side of the binary number and the least significant bit (lsb) on the right-hand side. To convert from decimal (base-10) to binary the decimal value is divided-by-two recursively and remainder noted. The first remainder gives the least significant bit (lsb) and the last gives the most significant bit (msb). For example:

$$
\begin{array}{r|l}
2 & 54 \\
\hline
 & 27 \quad \text{r 0} <<< \text{lsb} \\
 & 13 \quad \text{r 1} \\
 & 6 \quad \text{r 1} \\
 & 3 \quad \text{r 0} \\
 & 1 \quad \text{r 1} \\
 & 0 \quad \text{r 1} <<< \text{msb}
\end{array}
$$

Thus 54 in decimal is `110110` in binary. Normally computer system use groups of 4 and 8 bits, thus it is important to memorize some of the key values for groups of 4 and 8, such as:

Binary	Decimal
0000	0
1111	15
1111 1111	255
1111 1111 1111	4095 (4k)
1111 1111 1111 1111	65,535 (64k)
1111 1111 1111 1111 1111 1111	16,777,215 (16M)
1111 1111 1111 1111 1111 1111 1111 1111	4,294,967,295 (4G)

Typical groupings of bits are:

- **Nibble**. A group of four bits. A nibble 16 (2^4) different combinations of ON/OFF, from 0000 to 1111.
- **Byte**. A group of eight bits. A byte gives 256 (2^8) different combinations of ON/OFF, from 0000 0000 to 1111 1111.
- **Word**. A group of 16 bits (2 bytes). A word gives 65 536 (2^{16}) different combinations of ON/OFF, from 00000000 00000000 to 11111111 11111111.
- **Long Word**. A group of 32 bits (4 bytes). A long word gives 4 294 967 296 (2^{32}) different combinations of ON/OFF.

A1.6.1 Binary arithmetic

Computer systems must perform arithmetic operations on binary digits. In decimal, we all know when we add a single digit (0 to 9) to another digit we get the rules of 0+0 equals 0, 0+1 equals 1, right up to 9+9 equals 18. When we perform these additions with other digits, we align them up, and then carry any values into the next column. Thus, 9+9 makes 8, with a one carried into the next column to be added with that column.

Binary addition is actually simpler as it only involves two values for each digit (but obviously, we are now more accustomed to decimal addition). There are thus four possible combinations when adding two binary digits together (with a carry from the previous column):

$$0+0 \; = 0 \qquad 1+0 \; = 1 \qquad 1+1 \; = 10 \qquad 1+1+1 = 11$$

We can then perform a binary addition as we do in decimal addition, by lining up the two values with the least significant bit at the right-hand side, and the most significant bit at the left-hand side. Any gaps in bits on the left-hand side are replaced with zero values (as we do with decimal addition, but we typically do not include preceding zeros). For example:

```
  0010001
  0001111
  0100000
   11111
```

A1.6.2 Hexadecimal

Digital computers are digital systems, and operate on binary information (base-2), that is, 0's and 1's. Unfortunately, humans have difficulties in converting binary information into a decimal format. Most of the operations within the computer do not require that the user or programmer require define binary values. Typically requirements are:

- **To specify a memory address.** Typically memory addresses in a computer are specified with their binary address, thus there must be a method to display this in a form which the user can easily convert to and from.
- **To display or set the value of a variable.** Sometimes the actual binary content of a value needs to be interrogated or set, thus there must be a form in which the user can easily read and convert it into a binary form.
- **To specify network addresses.** A network address of a computer (such as 146.176.151.140) often needs to be converted into a form which the computer understands, thus there must be a conversion between decimal and binary, or vice-versa.

These problems are solved by either converting between binary and decimal, or between binary and hexadecimal (base-16) or octal (base-8). Without the aid of a calculator, the conversion between binary and decimal is relatively difficult for large binary numbers, but hexadecimal and octal conversion make it easier, as they allow the binary digits to be split into groups of four (for hexadecimal) or three (for octal), and then converted. Hexadecimal is the conversion most often used to specify a memory address or in defining the contents of a memory address. Figure A1.5 shows an example of hexadecimal addresses.

Binary data is stored in memories which are either permanent or non-permanent. This data is arranged as bytes and each byte has a different memory address, as illustrated in Figure A1.6. The Read/Write defines whether data is read from (Read) the memory or written to (Write) the memory. In terms of size, the address bus defines the number of addressable locations, and the data bus size defines the maximum number of data bits that can be written to any addressable location. For example an 8-bit address bus can be used to access up to 256 bytes (256B), a 16-bit address bus can be used to access up to 65,636 bytes (64kB), a 24-bit address bus can be used to access up to 16,777,216 bytes (16MB), and a 32-bit address bus can be used to access up to 4,294,967,295 (4GB).

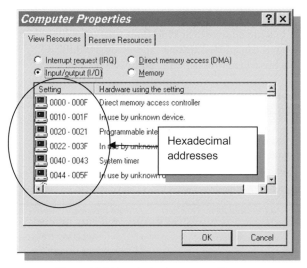

Figure A1.5 Hexadecimal memory addresses

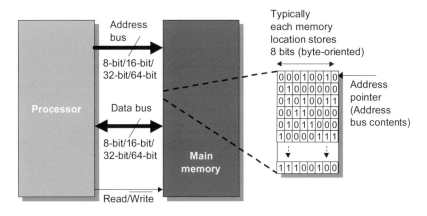

Figure A1.6 Memory storage (each address holds eight bits)

A1.6.3 Address bus

The address bus is responsible for identifying the location into which the data is to be passed. Each location in memory typically contains a single byte (8 bits), but could also be arranged as words (16 bits), or long words (32 bits). Byte-oriented memory is the most flexible as it also enables access to any multiple of 8 bits. The size of the address bus thus indicates the maximum addressable number of bytes. Table A1.3 shows the size of addressable memory for a given address bus size. The number of addressable bytes is given by:

$$\text{Addressable locations} = 2^n \; \text{B}$$

> *Addressable locations for a given address bus size*

where n is the number of bits in the address bus. For example (as defined in Table A1.3):

- A 1-bit address bus can address up to two locations (that is 0 and 1).
- A 2-bit address bus can address 2^2 or 4 locations (that is 00, 01, 10 and 11).
- A 20-bit address bus can address up to 2^{20} addresses (1 MB).
- A 32-bit address bus can address up to 2^{32} addresses (4 GB).

The units used for computers for defining memory are B (bytes), kB (kilobytes), MB (megabytes) and GB (gigabytes). These are defined as:

- Kilobyte: 2^{10} bytes, which is 1,024 B.
- Megabyte: 2^{20} bytes, which is 1,024 kB, or 1,048,576 B.
- Gigabyte: 2^{30} bytes, which is 1,024 MB, or 1,048,576 kB, or 1,073,741,824 B.

Table A1.3   Addressable memory (in bytes) related to address bus size

Address bus size	Addressable memory (bytes)	Address bus size	Addressable memory (bytes)
1	2	15	32 K
2	4	16	64 K
3	8	17	128 K
4	16	18	256 K
5	32	19	512 K
6	64	20	1 M†
7	128	21	2 M
8	256	22	4 M
9	512	23	8 M
10	1K*	24	16 M
11	2K	25	32 M
12	4K	26	64 M
13	8K	32	4 G‡
14	16K	64	16 GG

* 1K represents 1,024   † 1M represents 1,048,576 (1024 K)
‡ 1G represents 1,073,741,824 (1024 M)

A1.7   Data representation

The representation of data types is always a problem, as different computer systems use different ways to store and represent data. For example, the PC, which is based on Intel microprocessors, uses the little endian approach of representing a floating-point value. The little endian form starts with the least-significant byte in the lowest memory location, and the most-significant byte in the highest location. The big endian form, as used with Motorola-based systems, always starts with the high-order byte and ends with the lowest-order byte. For example with little endian, the value to store the 16-bit integer values of 4 (0000 0000 0000 0100b), 5,241 (0001 0100 0111 1001 b) and 26,152 (0110 0110 0010 1000b) would be:

Memory location	Contents (hex)	Contents (binary)	Value
00	04	0000 0100	4
01	00	0000 0000	
02	79	0111 1001	5,241
03	14	0001 0100	
04	28	0010 1000	26,152
05	66	0110 0110	

Whereas, in big endian, it would be stored as:

Memory location	Contents (hex)	Contents (binary)	Value
00	00	0000 0000	4
01	04	0000 0100	
02	14	0001 0100	5,241
03	79	0111 1001	
04	66	0110 0110	26,152
05	28	0010 1000	

Thus a program which has been written for a PC would incorrectly read data which has been written for a big endian program (typically for a UNIX workstation), and vice versa. Another particular problem is that different computer systems represent data (such as numeric values) in different formats. For example, an integer can be represented with either 16 bits, 32 bits, 64 bits, or even, 128 bits. The more bits that are used, the larger the integer value that can be represented.

All these problems highlight the need for a conversion technique that knows how to read the value from memory, and convert it into a standard form that is independent of the operating system or the hardware of the computer. This is the function of eXternal Data Representation (XDR), which represents data in a standard format. In XDR the basic data types are:

- **Unsigned integer and signed integer.** An unsigned and signed integer uses a 32-bit value. The unsigned value uses the range from 0 to $2^{32}-1$ (4,294,967,295), whereas the signed integer uses 2's complement which gives a range of −2,147,483,648 (1111 1111 1111 … 1111 1111) to +2,147,483,647 (0111 1111 1111 … 1111).
- **Single-precision floating point.** A single-precision floating-point value uses a 32-bit IEEE format of a floating-point value. An example is given next. The range is from $\pm 3.4 \times 10^{-38}$ to $\pm 3.4 \times 10^{38}$.
- **Double-precision floating point.** A double-precision floating-point value uses a 64-bit IEEE format of a floating-point value. The range is from $\pm 1.7 \times 10^{-308}$ to $\pm 1.7 \times 10^{308}$.
- **String.** A string is represented with a number of bytes. The first four bytes define the number of ASCII characters defined. For example, if there were four characters in the string then the first four bytes would be: 0, 0, 0, 4, followed by the four characters in the string. Note that this differs from the way that the C programming language represents strings, as C uses the NULL ASCII character to define the end of a string.

A1.7.1 Negative numbers

Signed integers use a notation called 2's complement to represents negative values. In this representation the binary digits have a '1' in the most significant bit column if the number is negative, else it is a '0'. To convert a decimal value into 2's complement notation, the magnitude of the negative number is represented in binary form. Next, all the bits are inverted and a '1' is added. For example to determine the 16-bit 2's complement of the value −65, the following steps are taken:

```
+65       00000000 01000001
invert    11111111 10111110
add 1     11111111 10111111
```

Thus, –65 is 11111111 1011111 in 16-bit 2's complement notation. Table A1.4 shows that with 16 bits the range of values that can be represented in 2's complement is from –32 768 to 32 767 (that is, 65 536 values).

Two's complement is also useful in subtraction operations, where the value to be subtracted is converted in its negative form, and then added to the value it is to be subtract from. For example to subtract 42 from 65, first 42 is converted into 2's complement (that is, –42) and added to the binary equivalent of 65. The result gives a carry into the sign bit and a carry-out (these are ignored).

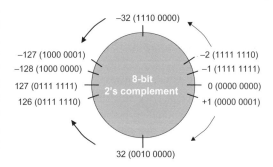

```
 65              0100  0001
-42              1101  0110
= 23         (1) 0001  0111
```

For a 16-bit signed integer can vary from –32 768 (1000 0000 0000 0000) to 32 767 (0111 1111 1111 1111).

Table A1.4 16-bit 2's complement notation

Decimal	2's complement
–32 768	10000000 00000000
–32 767	10000000 00000001
::::	::::
–2	11111111 11111110
–1	11111111 11111111
0	00000000 00000000
1	00000000 00000001
2	00000000 00000010
::::	::
32 766	01111111 11111110
32 767	01111111 11111111

A1.7.2   Hexadecimal and octal numbers

Often it is difficult to differentiate binary number from decimal numbers (as one hundred and one can be seen as 101 in binary). A typical convention is to use a proceeding b for binary numbers, for example 0101 0111 1010b and 1011 1110 1010b are binary numbers. Hexadecimal and octal are often used to represent binary digits, as they are relatively easily to convert to and from binary. Table A1.5 shows the basic conversion between decimal, binary, octal and hexadecimal numbers. A typical convention is to append a hexadecimal value with an 'h' at the end of a hexadecimal numbers (and octal number with an o). For example, 43F1h is a hexadecimal value whereas 4310o is octal.

To represent a binary digit as a hexadecimal value, the binary digits are split into groups of four bits (starting from the least significant bit). A hexadecimal equivalent value then replaces each of the binary groups. For example, to represent 0111 0101 1100 0000b the bits are split into sections of four to give:

Binary	0111	0101	1100	0000
Hex	7	5	C	0

Thus, 75C0h represents the binary number 0111 0101 1100 0000b. To convert from decimal to hexadecimal the decimal value is divided by 16 recursively and each remainder noted. The first remainder gives the least significant digit and the final remainder the most significant digit. For example, the following shows the hexadecimal equivalent of the decimal number 1103:

```
16 |  1103
        68   r F  <<< LSD (least significant digit)
         4   r 4
         0   r 4  <<< MSD (most significant digit)
```

Thus, the decimal value 1103 is equivalent to 044Fh.

Table A1.5   Decimal, binary, octal and hexadecimal conversions

Decimal	Binary	Octal	Hex
0	0000	0	0
1	0001	1	1
2	0010	2	2
3	0011	3	3
4	0100	4	4
5	0101	5	5
6	0110	6	6
7	0111	7	7
8	1000	10	8
9	1001	11	9
10	1010	12	A
11	1011	13	B
12	1100	14	C
13	1101	15	D
14	1110	16	E
15	1111	17	F

A1.7.3   Floating-point representation

A single-precision floating-point value uses 32 bits, where the most-significant bit represents the sign bit (S), the next eight bits represents the exponent of the number in base 2, minus 127 (E). The final 23 bits represent the base-2 fractional part of the number's mantissa (F). The standard format is:

$$\text{Value} = -1^S \times 2^{(E-127)} \times 1.F$$

For example:

1.23	= 3F9D 70A4h
	= 0 01111111 00111010111000010100100b

$$= -1^0 \times 2^{(127-127)} \times (1 + 2^{-3} + 2^{-4} + 2^{-5} + 2^{-9} + 2^{-10} + 2^{-11} + 2^{-16} + 2^{-18} + 2^{-21})$$

−5.67
$$= \text{C0B5 70A4h}$$
$$= 1\ 10000001\ 01101010111000010100100b$$
$$= -1^1 \times 2^{(129-127)} \times (1 + 2^{-2} + 2^{-3} + 2^{-5} + 2^{-7} + 2^{-9} + 2^{-10} + 2^{-11} + 2^{-15} + 2^{-17} + 2^{-20})$$

100.442
$$= \text{42C8 E24Eh}$$
$$= 0\ 10000101\ 10010001110001001001110b$$
$$= -1^0 \times 2^{(133-127)} \times (1 + 2^{-1} + 2^{-4} + 2^{-8} + 2^{-9} + 2^{-10} + 2^{-14} + 2^{-17} + 2^{-20} + 2^{-21} + 2^{-22})$$

A single-precision floating-point value uses 64 bits, where the most-significant bit represents the sign bit (S), the next eight bits represents the exponent of the number in base 2, minus 1023 (E). The final 52 bits represent the base-2 fractional part of the number's mantissa (F).

A1.7.4   ASCII

As we have seen, there are standard formats for integers and floating-point values. There are many standards for the representation of characters (known as character sets), but the most common one is known as ASCII. In its standard form it uses a 7-bit binary code to represent characters (letters, giving a range of 0 to 127). This is rather limited as it does not support symbols such as Greek lines, and so. To increase the number of symbols which can be represented, extended ASCII is used which has an 8-bit code.

Appendix 4 shows the standard ASCII character set (in binary, decimal, hexadecimal and also as a character). For example the 'a' character has the ASCII binary representation of 0110 0001b (61h), and the 'A' character has the binary representation of 0100 0001 (41h). One thing that can be noticed is that the upper and lower case versions of the letters ('a' to 'z') only differ by a single bit (the 6th bit, from the right-hand side).

In 1963, ANSI defined the 7-bit ASCII standard code for characters. At the same time IBM had developed the 8-bit EBCDIC code which allowed for up to 256 characters, rather than 128 characters for ASCII. It is thought that the 7-bit code was used for the standard as it was reckoned that eight holes in punched paper tape would weaken the tape. Thus the world has had to use the 7-bit ASCII standard, which is still popular in the days of global communications, and large-scale disk storage.

A2   Distributed elements

A2.1   Introduction

The following chapters cover the theory of distributing data and processing over a network, thus we need to understand the main principles involved in data distribution. The main principle is the concept of peer-to-peer systems, and client-server systems. A server is a system that provides a particular service (such as remote login, or file services) to a client. The server must wait on connections from clients. A peer-to-peer network works on co-operation, where peer computers share resources. Small networks (typically with fewer than 10 computers) normally work best with a peer-to-peer network, and larger networks work best with a client-server architecture. It must be noted that client-server and peer-to-peer architectures can easily co-exist together, and many networks operate this way. A good example is that a computer will use a client-server architecture when contacting a WWW server, but it might use a peer-to-peer architecture when it is sharing a printer with its neighbour. The Internet supports many server applications, including remote login (telnet), remote file transfer (ftp), electronic mail transfer (smtp), domain name services (dns), and so on.

A traditional method of presenting distributed elements is to define: the concept of analogue and digital data; the concept of a communications model; and the coverage of the communications channel. Thus, some of this chapter discusses these topics. These will be more important on the chapters in Data Communications and Networks, but they have been covered here in order to present distributed elements as a single entity.

Data is available in either an analogue form or in a digital form, as illustrated in Figure A2.1. Computer-generated data can be easily stored in a digital format, but if a computer is to be able to interpret analogue signals, such as speech and video, they must first be sampled at regular intervals and then converted into a digital form. This process is known as digitization and has the following advantages:

- **Less susceptible to noise**. Digital data is less affected by noise, as illustrated in Figure A2.2. Noise is any unwanted signal and has many causes, such as static pick-up, poor electrical connections, electronic noise in components, cross-talk, and so on. It makes the reception/storage of a data more difficult and can produce unwanted distortion on the received/stored data.
- **Less error prone**. Extra information can be added to digital data so that errors can either be detected or corrected.
- **Digital data tends not to degrade over time**.
- **Easier processing**. Processing of digital data is relatively easy, either in real time (on-line processing) or non real time (off-line processing).
- **Easier to store**. A single type of storage media can be used to store many different types of information (such as video, speech, audio and computer data being stored on tape, hard disk or CD-ROM). This is more difficult in an analogue media. For example in an analogue environment, images are stored on photographic paper, video and audio are stored on magnetic tape, temperatures are stored as numerical values, and so on.
- **More dependable and predictable**. A digital system has a more dependable response, whereas an analogue system's accuracy depends on its operating parameters and its

design characteristics such as its component tolerance, its operating temperature, power supply variations, and so on. Analogue systems thus produce a variable response and no two analogue systems are identical. This obviously gives analogue systems more of a personality, and they must be carefully setup in order to produce a dependable performance. Many methods, though, have been used in analogue systems to ensure that they have a more dependable performance. One of the most widely used is to provide feedback from the output and then compare this with the required output, and make some correction on the output. Unfortunately these corrections take time, and can lead to under or over compensation, which cause the system either to be too slow to respond to changes, or respond too quickly.

- **Easier to upgrade**. Digital systems are more adaptable and can be reprogrammed with software. Analogue systems normally require a change of hardware for any functional changes (although programmable analogue devices are now available). This makes upgrades and bug fixes easier, as all that is required is a change of software.

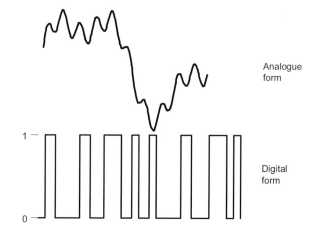

Figure A2.1   Analogue and digital format

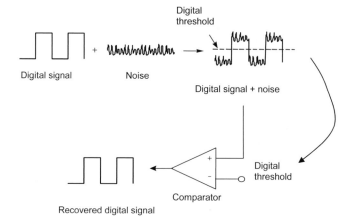

Figure A2.2   Recovery of a digital signal with noise added to it

As an analogue signal must be sampled at regular intervals, digital representations of analogue waveforms require large amounts of storage space. For example, 70 minutes of hi-fi quality music requires over 600 MB of data storage. Fortunately, we now live in a time where large amounts of digital storage are available, in a reliable form, for a modest amount of money.

The data once stored tends to be reliable and will not degrade over time. Typically, digital data is stored either as magnetic fields on a magnetic disk or as pits on an optical disk. A great advantage of digital technology is that once the analogue data has been converted to digital, it is relatively easy to store it with other purely digital data. This is known as media integration. Once stored in digital form it is relatively easy to process the data before it is converted back into analogue form. Analogue signals are relatively easy to store, such as video and audio signals as magnetic fields on tape or a still picture on photographic paper. These media, though, tend to add noise (such as tape hiss) during storage and recovery. It is also difficult preserve the data over time, and to recover the original analogue data, once it has degraded in some way (especially if it is affected in a random way). Most methods of reducing this degradation (which is due to noise) involve some form of filtering or smoothing of the data.

The accuracy of a digital system depends on the number of bits used for each sample, whereas an analogue system's accuracy depends on the specification of the components used in the system. Analogue systems also produce a differing response for different systems whereas a digital system has a more dependable response.

A2.2   Conversion to digital

Figure A2.3 outlines the conversion process for digital data (the upper diagram) and for analogue data (the lower diagram). The lower diagram shows how an analogue signal (such as speech or video) is first sampled at regular intervals of time. These samples are then converted into a digital form with an ADC (analogue-to-digital converter). The digital samples then be compressed and/or stored in a defined digital format (such as WAV, JPG, and so on). This digital form is then converted back into an analogue form with a DAC (digital-to-analogue converter). When data is already in a digital form (such as text or animation) it is converted into a given data format (such as BMP, GIF, JPG, and so on). It can be further compressed before it is stored, transmitted or processed.

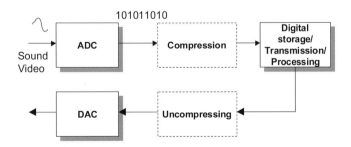

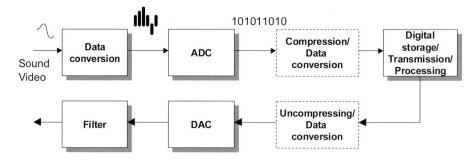

Figure A2.3 Information conversion into a digital form

A2.3   Communications model

Figure A2.4 shows a communications model in its simplest form. An information source transmits data to a destination through a transmission media. This transmission can either be with a direct communication (using a physical or wireless connection) or through an indirect communication (via a number of physical or wireless connections).

The information, itself, can either be directly sent through an electrical cable, or it can be carried on an electromagnetic wave. Electromagnetics waves act as a carrier of the data, in the same way that the postal service, or telephone providers, support channels for post and telephone information to be sent and received in a reliable way. The type of electromagnetic carrier depends on the communication media which the data is to be sent through. Each carrier has a specific frequency (which is indirectly proportional to their wavelength), which is used to tune-into the wave at the receiver. The frequency typically defines how well the carrier propagates through a media channel. Typical electromagnetic carrier types are:

- **Radio waves.** The lower the frequency of a radio wave the more able it is to bend around objects. Defense applications use low frequency communications as they can use this to transmit over large distances, and up and over solid objects (such as hills and mountains). The trade-off is that the lower the frequency of the radio wave, the less the information that can be carried. LW (MF) and AM (HF) signals can propagate large distances, but FM (VHF) requires repeaters because they cannot bend round and over solid objects such as trees and hills.

- **Microwaves.** Microwaves have the advantage over optical waves (light, infrared and ultra-violet) in that they propagate reasonably well through water and thus can be transmitted through clouds, rain, and so on. One of the first applications of microwaves was in radar, as the microwave pulses could propagate through clouds, and bounce off a metal target (normally an airplane, a missile, or a ship), and return to the transmitter. If the microwaves were of a high enough frequency they can even propagate through the ionosphere and out into outer space. This is the property that is used in satellite communications where the transmitter bounces microwave energy off a satellite, which is then picked up at a receiving station. Their main disadvantage is that they will not bend round large objects, as their wavelength is too small.

- **Infrared.** Infrared is used in optical communications, and allows for a much greater amount of data to be sent, than radio and microwaves. Infrared is extensively used for line-of-site communications (and fiber optic communication), especially in remote control applications. The amount of data that can be transmitted is normally limited by the electronics at the transmitter and the receiver, but it is possible to get many billions of bits to be transmitted, in each second.

- **Light.** Light is the only part of the electromagnetic spectrum that humans can 'see' (although we can feel the affect of infra-red radiation on the air around us). It is a very small part of the spectrum and ranges from 300 to 900 nm (a nanometer is one billionth of a meter). Colors contained are Red, Orange, Yellow, Green, Blue, Indigo and Violet (ROY.G.BIV or **R**ichard **O**f **Y**ork **G**ave **B**attle **I**n **V**ain).
- **Ultra-violet.** As with infrared, ultra-violet is used in optical communications (typically with fiber optic communications). In high enough exposures, it can cause skin cancer. Fortunately, for humans, the ozone layer blocks out much of the ultra-violet radiation from the sun. Note that you should not look directly into a fiber optic cable which is currently operating, as invisible radiation (especially infrared radiation) may damage your eye.

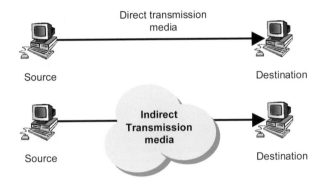

Figure A2.4 Simple communications model

A2.4   Cables

The cable type used to transmit the data over the communications channel depends on several parameters, including:

- The **reliability** of the cable, and the maximum **length** between nodes.
- The possibility of electrical **hazards**, and the **power** loss in the cables.
- Tolerance to **harsh** conditions, and **expense** and general **availability** of the cable.
- Ease of **connection** and **maintenance**, and the ease of **running** cables, and so on.
- The signal **bandwidth**. The amount of information that can be sent directly relates to the bandwidth of the system, and typically, the main limitation on the bandwidth is the channel between the transmitter and the receiver. With this, the lowest bandwidth of all the connected elements defines the overall bandwidth of the system (unless there are alternative paths for the data).

The main types of cables used for the digital communications channels are illustrated in Figure A2.5, and include:

- **Coaxial.** Coaxial cable has a grounded metal sheath around the signal conductor. This limits the amount of interference between cables and thus allows higher data rates. Typically, they are used at bit rates of 100 Mbps for maximum lengths of 1 km.
- **Fiber optic.** The highest specification of the three cables is fiber optic, and allows extremely high bit rates over long distances. Fiber optic cables do not interfere with nearby cables and give greater security. They also provide more protection from electrical damage by external equipment and greater resistance to harsh environments, as well as being safer in hazardous environments.
- **Unshielded twisted-pair (UTP) copper.** Twisted-pair and coaxial cables transmit electric signals, whereas fiber-optic cables transmit light pulses. Unshielded twisted-pair cables are not shielded and thus interfere with nearby cables. Public telephone lines generally use twisted-pair cables. In LANs, they are generally used up to bit rates of 100 Mbps and with maximum lengths of 100 m. UTP cables are typically used to connect a computer to a network. There are various standards for twisted-pair cables, such as Cat-5 cables, which can transmit up to 100 Mbps (100,000,000 bits per second), and Cat-3, which support the transmission of up to 16 Mbps (16,000,000 bits per second).

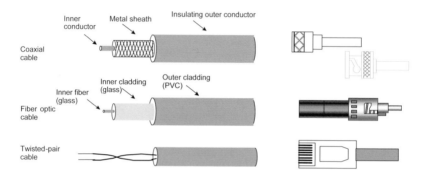

Figure A2.5 Types of network cable and their connectors

A2.4.1 Cable characteristics

The main characteristics of cables are:

- **Attenuation.** Attenuation defines the reduction in the signal strength at a given frequency for a defined distance. It is normally specified in decibels (dB) per 100 m. As a basic measure a value of 3 dB/100 m gives a reduction of half the signal power every 100 m (see Table A2.1).
- **Crosstalk.** Crosstalk is an important parameter as it defines the amount of signal that crosses from one signal path to another. This causes distortion on the transmitted signal. Shielded twisted-pair cables have less crosstalk than unshielded twisted-pair cables.
- **Characteristic impedance.** The characteristic impedance (as measured in Ω – ohms) of a cable and its connectors are important, as all parts of the transmission system need to be matched to the same impedance. This impedance is normally classified as the characteristic impedance of the cable. Any differences in the matching results in a reduction of signal power and can produce signal reflections (or ghosting). For example, twisted-pair cables have a characteristic impedance of approximately 100 Ω, and coaxial cable used in networking has a characteristic impedance of 50 Ω (or 75 Ω for TV systems).

Capacitance (pF/100 m) defines the amount of distortion in the signal caused by each signal pair. The lower the capacitance value, the lower the distortion.

The main types of cable used in networking and data communications are:

- Coaxial cable – cables with an inner core and a conducting shield having a characteristic impedance of either 75 Ω for TV signal or 50 Ω for other types.
- Cat-3 UTP cable – level 3 cables have non-twisted-pair cores with a characteristic impedance of 100 Ω (±15 Ω) and a capacitance of 59 pF/m. Conductor resistance is around 9.2 Ω/100 m.
- Cat-4 UTP cable – level 4 cables have twisted-pair cores with a characteristic impedance of 100 Ω (±15 Ω) and a capacitance of 49.2 pF/m. Conductor resistance is around 9 Ω/100 m.
- Cat-5 UTP cable – level 5 cables have twisted-pair cores with a characteristic impedance of 100 Ω (±15 Ω) and a capacitance of 45.9 pF/m. Conductor resistance is around 9 Ω/100 m.

Table A2.1 Attenuation rates as a ratio

dB	Ratio	dB	Ratio	dB	Ratio
0	1.000	10	0.316	60	0.001
1	0.891	15	0.178	65	0.000 6
2	0.794	20	0.100	70	0.000 3
3	0.708	25	0.056	75	0.000 2
4	0.631	30	0.032	80	0.000 1
5	0.562	35	0.018	85	0.000 06
6	0.501	40	0.010	90	0.000 03
7	0.447	45	0.005 6	95	0.000 02
8	0.398	50	0.003 2	100	0.000 01
9	0.355	55	0.001 8		

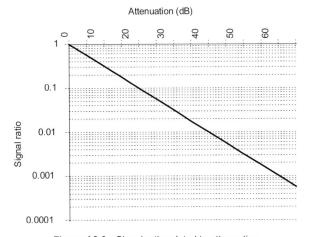

Figure A2.6 Signal ratio related to attenuation

The Electrical Industries Association (EIA) has defined five main types of cables. Levels 1 and 2 are used for voice and low-speed communications (up to 4 Mbps). Level 3 is designed for LAN data transmission up to 16 Mbps and level 4 is designed for speeds up to 20 Mbps. Level 5 cables, have the highest specification of the UTP cables and allow data speeds of up to 100 Mbps (but this can be increased using special signal processing techniques). The main EIA specification on these types of cables is EIA/TIA568 and the ISO standard is ISO/IEC11801.

Coaxial cables have an inner core separated from an outer shield by a dielectric. They have an accurate characteristic impedance (which reduces reflections), and because they are shielded they have very low crosstalk levels.

UTPs (unshielded twisted-pair cables) have either solid cores (for long cable runs) or are stranded patch cables (for shorts run, such as connecting to workstations, patch panels, and so on). Solid cables should not be flexed, bent or twisted repeatedly, whereas stranded cable can be flexed without damaging the cable. Coaxial cables use BNC connectors while UTP cables use either the RJ-11 (small connector which is used to connect the handset to the telephone) or the RJ-45 (larger connector which is used to connect LAN networks to a hub).

Table A2.2 and Figure A2.7 show typical attenuation rates (dB/100 m) for the Cat-3, Cat-4 and Cat-5 cables. Notice that the attenuation rates for Cat-4 and Cat-5 are approximately the same. These two types of cable have lower attenuation rates than equivalent Cat-3 cables. Notice that the attenuation of the cable increases as the frequency increases. This is due to several factors, such as the skin effect, where the electrical current in the conductors becomes concentrated around the outside of the conductor, and the fact that the insulation (or dielectric) between the conductors actual starts to conduct as the frequency increases.

The Cat-3 cable produces considerable attenuation over a distance of 100 m. The table shows that the signal ratio of the output to the input at 1 MHz, will be 0.76 (2.39 dB), then, at 4 MHz it is 0.55 (5.24 dB), until at 16 MHz it is 0.26. This differing attenuation at different frequencies produces not just a reduction in the signal strength but also distorts the signal (because each frequency is affected differently by the cable. Cat-4 and Cat-5 cables also produce distortion but their effects will be lessened because attenuation characteristics have flatter shapes.

Coaxial cables tend to have very low attenuation, such as 1.2 dB at 4 MHz. They also have a relatively flat response and virtually no crosstalk (due to the physical structure of the cables and the presence of a grounded outer sheath).

Table A2.3 and Figure A2.8 show typical near end crosstalk rates (dB/100 m) for Cat-3, Cat-4 and Cat-5 cables. The higher the figure, the smaller the crosstalk. Notice that Cat-3 cables have the most crosstalk and Cat-5 have the least, for any given frequency. Notice also that the crosstalk increases as the frequency of the signal increases. Thus, high-frequency signals have more crosstalk than lower-frequency signals.

Table A2.2 Attenuation rates (dB/100 m) for Cat-3, Cat-4 and Cat-5 cable

Frequency (MHz)	Cat-3	Cat-4	Cat-5
1	2.39	1.96	2.63
4	5.24	3.93	4.26
10	8.85	6.56	6.56
16	11.8	8.2	8.2

Table A2.3 Near-end crosstalk (dB/100 m) for Cat-3, Cat-4 and Cat-5 cable

Frequency (MHz)	Near end crosstalk (dB/100m)		
	Cat-3	Cat-4	Cat-5
1	13.45	18.36	21.65
4	10.49	15.41	18.04
10	8.52	13.45	15.41
16	7.54	12.46	14.17

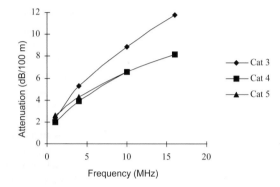

Figure A2.7 Attenuation characteristics for Cat-3, Cat-4 and Cat-5 cables

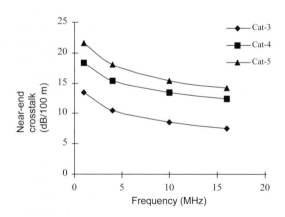

Figure A2.8 Near-end crosstalk characteristics for Cat-3, Cat-4 and Cat-5 cables

A2.5 Peer-to-peer and client/server

An important concept in Computing is the differentiation between a peer-to-peer connection and a client-server connection. With a client-server connection, servers provide services to client, and must wait for clients to connect to these services. Typical services might be to allow the printing of documents to a networked printer, or provide access to a networked file system. A peer-to-peer architecture allows two systems to actively seek connections, without involving a server. An example of a client-server network in human terms might be a travel agent, who will wait for customers (clients) to get in contact with them in order to book the best holiday for them. The clients contact the agents (servers) to book a holiday, who will then find the best holiday for them. A peer-to-peer network would be equivalent to someone phoning a friend (who is not a travel agent) and asking them of the best holiday that they could get. The friend might then go and book the holiday over the Internet. This is a peer-to-peer network, as the friend does not actively seek questions on holiday arrangements, or in booking holidays.

A peer-to-peer connection allows users on a local network to access a local computer. Typically, this might be access to:

 Local printers. Printers, local to a computer, can be accessed by other users if the printer is shareable. This can be password protected, or not. Shareable printers on a Microsoft network have a small hand under the icon.

 Local disk drives and folders. The disk drives, such as the hard disk or CD-ROM drives can be accessed if they are shareable. Normally the drives must be shareable. On a Microsoft network a drive can be made shareable by selecting the drive and selecting the right-hand mouse button, then selecting the Sharing option. User names and passwords can be set-up locally or can be accessed from a network server. Typically, only the local computer grants access to certain folders, while others are not shared.

These shared resources can also be mounted as objects on the remote computer. Thus, the user of the remote computer can simply access resources on the other computers as if they were mounted locally. This option is often the best when there is a small local network, as it requires the minimum amount of set-up and does not need any complicated server set-ups. Figure A2.9 shows an example of a peer-to-peer network where a computer allows access to its local resources. In this case, its local disk drive and printer are shareable.

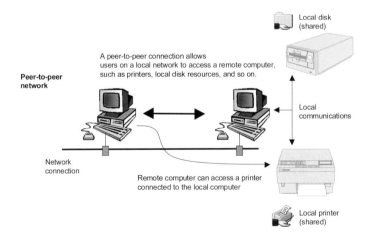

Figure A2.9   Peer-to-peer network

Normally a peer-to-peer network works best for a small office environment. Care must be taken, though, when setting up the attributes of the shared resources. Figure A2.10 shows an example of the sharing setting for a disk drive. It can be seen that the main attributes are:

- **Read-only.** This should be used when the remote user only requires to copy or execute files. The remote user cannot modify any of the files.
- **Full.** This option should only be used when the remote user has full access to the files and can copy, erase or modify the files.
- **Depends on Password.** In this mode, the remote user must provide a password to get either read-only access or full access.

If the peer-to-peer network has a local server, such as Novell NetWare or Windows NT/2000 then access can be provided for certain users and/or groups, if they provide the correct password.

A client-server network has a central server which proves services to clients, as illustrated in Figure A2.11. These clients can either be local to the network segment, or from a remote network. The server typically provides one or more of the following services:

- Store usernames, group names and passwords.
- Run print queues for networked printers.
- Allocate IP addresses for Internet accesses.
- Provide system back-up facilities, such as CD-R disk drives and DAT tape drives.
- Provide centralized file services, such as networked hard disks or networked CD-ROM drives.
- Centralize computer settings and/or configuration.
- Provide access to other centralized peripherals, such as networked faxes and dial-in network connections.
- Provide WWW and TCP/IP services, such as remote login and file transfer.

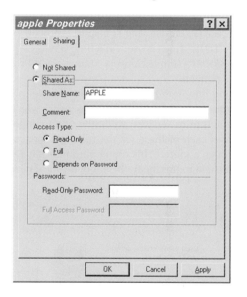

Figure A2.10   File access rights

A network operating system server typically provides file and print services, as well as storing a list of user names and passwords. Typical network operating systems are Windows NT/2000, Novell NetWare and UNIX. Internet and WWW services are typically run from an Internet server. Typical services include:

- **HTTP** (HyperText Transfer Protocol), for WWW (World-Wide Web) services. On the WWW, WWW servers and WWW clients pass information between each other using HTTP. A simple HTTP command is GET, which a WWW client (the WWW browser) sends to server in order to get a file.

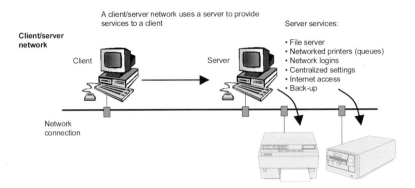

A client/server network uses a server to provide services to a client

Client/server network

Client

Server

Server services:
- File server
- Networked printers (queues)
- Network logins
- Centralized settings
- Internet access
- Back-up

Network connection

Figure A2.11   Client/server network

- **FTP** (File Transfer Protocol), which is a standard protocol and used to transfer files from one computer system to another. In order for the transfer to occur, the server must run an FTP server program.
- **TELNET**, which is used for remote login services.
- **SMTP** (Simple Mail Transport Protocol), which is used for electronic mail transfer.
- **TIME**, which is used for a time service.
- **SNMP** (Simple Network Management Protocol), which is used to analyze network components.

Figure A2.12 shows an example network which has two local network servers. One provides file and print services, while the other supports Internet services. The local computer accesses each of these for the required service. It can also access a remote Internet server through a router. This router automatically determines that the node is accessing a remote node and routes the traffic out of the local network.

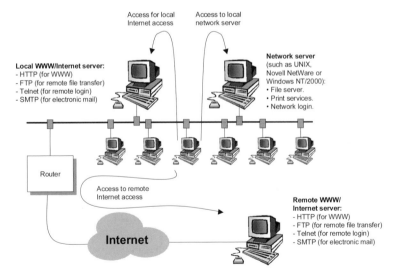

Access for local Internet access

Access to local network server

Local WWW/Internet server:
- HTTP (for WWW)
- FTP (for remote file transfer)
- Telnet (for remote login)
- SMTP (for electronic mail)

Network server (such as UNIX, Novell NetWare or Windows NT/2000):
- File server.
- Print services.
- Network login.

Router

Access to remote Internet access

Internet

Remote WWW/ Internet server:
- HTTP (for WWW)
- FTP (for remote file transfer)
- Telnet (for remote login)
- SMTP (for electronic mail)

Figure A2.12   Local and remote servers

A3 Operating systems

A3.1 Introduction

A computer system is typically made up of hardware, an operating system and a user interface, as illustrated in Figure A3.1. The hardware includes the central processing unit (CPU), memory, and input/output devices, whereas an operating system allows an easy interface between the user and the hardware. Operating systems are key components of a computer system, and they provide a foundation for programs and the user to access the resources of a computer, in an easy-to-use way. They have evolved recently into systems which can sense the hardware of the system and set it up in the required way. At one time, a computer program required to know how to access all the different types of hardware that it connected to. The user would then have to set it up in the settings of the program. These days the operating system hides much of the complexity of the hardware from user programs, and the user.

In the past, computer systems required expert user operators who understood how to add and delete devices from the computer, how to start and stop the computer, and they knew how to control the computer with the required operating system commands. These days most modern operating systems start, and shutdown, automatically and scan the connected hardware. This allows the system to configure itself when booted.

Operating systems thus provide an easy-to-use interface to the hardware. Many older operating systems, such as DOS and UNIX, used text commands which were used to control the system. Most systems, these days, provide a graphical user interface (GUI) in which the user uses Windows, Icons, Menus and Pointers (WIMPs) to run programs and organize the system.

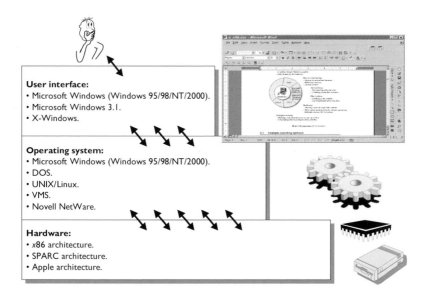

User interface:
• Microsoft Windows (Windows 95/98/NT/2000).
• Microsoft Windows 3.1.
• X-Windows.

Operating system:
• Microsoft Windows (Windows 95/98/NT/2000).
• DOS.
• UNIX/Linux.
• VMS.
• Novell NetWare.

Hardware:
• x86 architecture.
• SPARC architecture.
• Apple architecture.

Figure A3.1   User interface, operating system and hardware

The two main functions of an operating system are to provide an interface between the user and the hardware of the computer, and to provide services to application programs. As computers are designed with a maximum size of address and data bus, an operating system is designed to operate on a maximum number of bits at a time. This typically defines the classification of the operating system, such as: 16-bit, 32-bit and 64-bit operating systems (although some super computers use 128-bit operating systems). Normally the more bits that an operating system can operate on, at a time, the faster it will run application programs. The limitation on the number of bits that the operating system can operate with, limits the software that can run on the operating system. For example 32-bit software (such as Microsoft Office 2000) will not run on a 16-bit operating system (such as DOS or Windows 3.x), but 16-bit software, such as old Windows and DOS programs, can typically run on a compatible 32-bit operating system.

The main operating systems which are currently available are:

- **DOS.** This was one of the first operating systems for the PC, and quickly become a standard, not because of its technical specifications, but because of its relative cheapness against the other PC operating systems. Initially there were several different flavours of DOS, from IBM (PC-DOS) and Microsoft (MS-DOS), but MS-DOS became the standard that most systems were measured by. It eventually lived through six major version changes, before being integrated into Microsoft Windows. It still lives on today in an emulated form in modern version of Windows. It had many weaknesses: its text-based command language; its lack of integrated networking; it could only run one program at a time (single tasking); it used 16-bit software (even though the processor may be capable of running 32-bit software); it could only access up to 1MB of memory; and so on. It worked, though, and allowed the hardware to become powerful enough to support a proper multitasking operating system. For many businesses, it gave them all the functionality that they required i.e. to run a single program on a stand-alone computer. Its only real advantage, though, was its compatibility with user programs, or, in most cases, the compatibility of user programs with it. If someone wanted to sell a program, it had to work with MS-DOS; otherwise, it would be doomed to fail in the market. Thus any new operating system would have to provide exactly what MS-DOS did, and more. At the time, when DOS reined, PC hardware was not really up to running much more than a single program at a time, thus it was difficult to introduce a new operating system which properly competed with MS-DOS (IBM tried with several systems, and nearly succeeded with OS/2, but unfortunately it was too much of a compromised system). The coming wave of networking, the increased power of microprocessors (especially the 80486) and the power of graphical user interfaces would eventually kill off DOS. Luckily, for Microsoft, they released their best version of Windows, at a time when PCs could properly support the new enhanced features of graphical user interfaces. Their new version of Windows (Windows 3.1) did not properly support networking, but with Novell NetWare, for the first time PCs could communicate over a network, and users could actually *see* their programs.
- **Microsoft Windows 3.x.** This was basically a graphical user interface (GUI), which used DOS as its operating system, and thus still had all the major problems of DOS (such as only being able to run 16-bit software, only being able to access a limited amount of memory, no networking, and so on). After two failed attempts at producing a graphical user interface for the PC (Windows Version 1.0 and Windows Version 2.0), Microsoft eventually succeeded with a winner with Microsoft Windows 3.1, which included many

of the features that are standard in most modern GUIs, such as overlapping windows, menu systems, drag-and-drop, and so on. It has the advantage that it was still optional, as it built onto DOS, thus users could still use their DOS-based system, and then go into Windows when required. Some software companies who had extremely successful DOS-based versions, especially Lotus 123 and WordPerfect, failed to see the true potential of Windows, and did not create Windows versions fast enough for the market. Eventually these products were overtaken, especially with the Microsoft Office products, such as Microsoft Word for Windows, and Microsoft Excel for Windows, which incorporated the full power of the Windows interface.

- **Microsoft Windows**. In the mid-1980s, Microsoft spent a good deal of time working with IBM on OS/2. Unfortunately, the partnership broke up, and Microsoft used their experience from this project and fed it into Microsoft NT Version 3.0. This was a radical redesign of an operating system for the PC. Its aim was to provide a robust environment for programs, and also properly supported networking. As Microsoft were releasing NT, in the mid-1990s, they were also releasing a new type of graphical user interface with Windows 95. The release of the two systems was a complete success and they were the start of complete operating systems which had an enhanced graphical user interface. Both properly supported networking, and could integrate with virtually every type of network (especially with DECnet, Novell NetWare and IBM). They could also run more than one program at a time (multitasking). As they were designed to operate on 16 bits or 32 bits they could run 32-bit software. The next version of NT used the graphical user interface developed with Windows 95. Newer versions of Windows have included Windows 98, Windows ME and Windows 2000, and each has built on the robustness, networking infrastructure and GUI of its parents (Windows 95 and NT).

- **UNIX**. A powerful and robust operating system, which is typically used in high-powered workstations. It has a kernel, which interfaces to the hardware. This kernel has the advantage that it can be stripped away from the GUI and can be run on its own. This is a distinct advantage in embedded systems, which do not require user interfaces, or which might be slowed down by the extra code that is required to produce a GUI. It also has a main operating system, which runs commands, and will integrate with a GUI, typically X-Windows, to provide the interface between the user and the operating system. It typically supports either 32-bit or 64-bit software. Its greatest gift to the world has been its networking protocols, which it has nurtured over the years, and developed them so that they have become truly grown-up leaders in the worldwide Internet. Seldom has any parent been so successful in creating offspring that have truly united the world, and enhanced communication. The main contenders have been TCP/IP (for communications between computers over a network, no matter their architecture, type, operating system, or network connection), SMTP (for electronic mail), HTTP (for WWW access), TELNET (for remote login), FTP (for file transfer), RIP (for network routing) and many more.

- **Novell NetWare**. Around the time of DOS and Microsoft Windows 3.1, there was very little software which allowed computers to be connected to a network. Novell NetWare plugged this gap perfectly, with a networked operating system that provides access to networked resources, such as print queues, file services, and so on. It integrated seamlessly with DOS and Microsoft Windows, and could detect the commands which had to be run locally on the local operating system, and the ones which needed to be sent to the network server. It held a virtual monopoly on PC-based network operating systems, until Microsoft developed Windows NT.

- **VMS**. As with UNIX, a powerful and robust operating system. It is excellent at running batch processes, which are automatically started when the system is started. They then run quietly with little user input (typically described as batch processes).
- **Linux**. A version of UNIX for the PC, and one of the few PC-based operating systems to properly compete with Microsoft Windows.

Operating systems are split into two parts: the kernel component and the main operating system component, as illustrated in Figure A3.2. The operating system and kernel components can make access to user account databases, which contain the names of users who are allowed to log into the system, and their password. They also allow access to file systems and other resources, such as the scheduling of processes.

Operating systems are typically differentiated, as illustrated in Figure A3.3, by:

- **Single user** v. **Multi-user.** Single-user systems only allow a single user to login into the system at a time. They have no user account database, and have a low level of security, as users cannot protect their files from being viewed, copied or deleted. Typical single-user systems are DOS and Microsoft Windows. Multi-user operating systems have a user account database, which defines the rights that users have on certain resources. Multi-user systems are normally more secure than single user systems, as the access to resources can be limited. This security obviously protects against malicious damage, and also protects again non-malicious damage, where users cause damage to the system without actually knowing it. Most system administrators have seen users deleting files without actually meaning to. A multi-user system can guard against this, by protecting files against deletion.

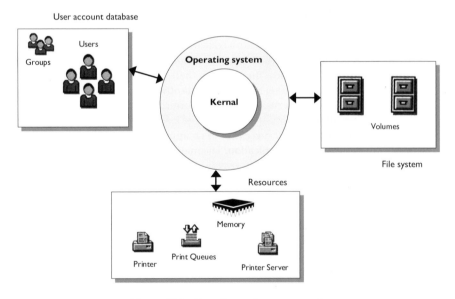

Figure A3.2 Operating system components

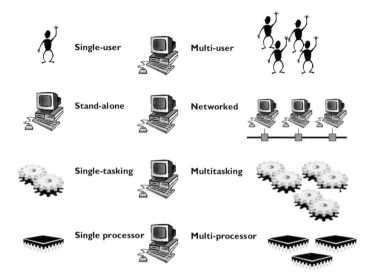

Figure A3.3 Operating system characteristics

- **Networked v. Stand-alone.** A stand-alone computer does not connect to a network, and thus cannot access any networked resources. This obviously creates a more secure environment as remote users cannot log into the computer. A networked operating system allows computers to interconnect and uses a standard communications protocol in order for them to communicate, no matter their computer type or their operating system. Typical networking protocols are TCP/IP (for UNIX networks and over the Internet) and IPX/SPX (for Novell NetWare networks). For example, the TCP part allows large chunks of data to be split into segments which can be transmitted over the network. The IP part allows computers to be addressable over interconnected networks. Networked systems are obviously less secure than stand-alone systems, and should thus be protected in some way (typically by creating user accounts). They do allow for improved system administration, as user accounts, software distribution and configuration, and system backup can be centralized over the whole network. The major problem with networked systems is that users become extremely dependent on the network, and cannot typically work without it. Typical networked operating systems are: Microsoft Windows, Novell NetWare and UNIX.
- **Multitasking v. Single-tasking.** Multitasking operating systems allow for one or more programs, or processes, to be run, at a time. Typically, this is achieved by giving each process a prioritized amount of time on the processor. Single-tasking systems only allow one program to run, at a time, and are generally faster than multitasking systems, as multitasking systems take up some time when switching between programs. Multitasking systems, though, are more efficient as they allow other tasks to run when a task is not performing any operations. Single-tasking systems are more robust, as multitasking programs often need to communicate with each other, which can cause synchronization problems (in some cases, deadlock).
- **Multiprocessor v. Single processor.** Some operating systems allow more than one processor to be used on the system. This allows more than one task to be run, at a time, on different processors. Windows server operating systems supports multiprocessors

(up to four processors). Single processor, multitasking involves running each of the processes for a given time slice on a single processor, whereas multiprocessor systems allow processes to be run at the same time, on different processors. A multiprocessor system can either use processors which are the same type and can thus run the same programs (known as homogeneous multiprocessing), or they can use processors of a different type (known as heterogeneous multiprocessing). A programming language such as Java allows programs to run over a network with different types of processor without requiring that the programs be converted to run on a different type of processor.

- **Embedded v. Non-embedded.** An embedded operating system is typically integrated into a device, and is used to perform a specific task, and support for specific applications. Embedded systems are especially written for certain applications and for a narrow range of additional hardware. These limitations allow the system to be tested for most of the conditions that can occur, and they can thus be made more robust than non-embedded systems. Generally, non-embedded systems are more general-purpose and they are open to incorrectly operating software and incorrectly configured hardware. They are thus more prone to computer crashes and incorrectly configured software. As more equipment now supports embedded computers systems, there are much more embedded operating systems in equipment than there are non-embedded. For example an automobile may have more then ten embedded systems which each communicate with each other. Typical embedded systems include car engine management systems, mobile phones and Internet routers (which direct data packets around the Internet). Typically, embedded systems are more robust, and their programs are permanently stored so that they, and their operating system, are started-up automatically when the system is started. Examples of an embedded operating system include LINUX (kernel), Windows CE and Palm OS. In an embedded system the operating system and programs are typically stored in a permanent electronic memory (know as FLASH memory), which retains its contents when the power is taken away. An embedded system can also vary widely in its computing power, from a small system, which could control a central heating system in a home, to large and complex embedded systems which process radar signals.

- **Distributed processing v. Localized processing.** Most processing is achieved locally within the computer system (localized processing), but some processing can be distributed to other computers. A good example of this is with a distributed file system where remote computers provide access to file systems which are not local to the local computer, thus any access to these is actually achieved on the remote computer rather than the local computer. In some case specialized processing is required, which could not be provided locally. This is especially relevent in high-powered applications, such as biological research, or mathematical modelling. For this a computer could initiate programs on another computer system which had enhanced facilities, such as large amounts of physical memory, enhanced processing power, or parallel processing.

Figure A3.4 lists some of the basic functions that a non-embedded operating system should implement. These functions are:

- **File system.** All operating systems create and maintain a file system, where users can create, copy, delete and move files around a structured file system. Most systems organize the files in directories (or folders). In a multi-user system these folders can have associated user ownership, and associated access rights. All files have an owner, who can define the rights of the file, some of which are defined in the box given on the right-hand side of this text.

- **Device interfacing.** Operating systems should try to hide the complexity of interfacing to devices from user programs and the user. Typically, at start-up, an operating system will try and configure devices connected, by scanning all its connected interface buses (rather than getting the user to set them up). Increasingly it is also possible to add equipment to a system while the system is still powered on (hot plugging). A device driver contains much of the methods which define how a device is operated, and the operating system should integrate this into its own environment. The user programs do not, thus, have to know how to interface to specific devices, as the operating system will deal with the detail of its control. User programs thus issue commands to the operating system, which then convert these commands into the actual control signals required to interface to the equipment. The operating system can also set up queues on devices, typically for printers, so that multiple accesses can occur when a device is busy.

- **Multi-user.** This allows one or more users to log into the system. For this, the operating system must contain a user account database, which contains user names, default home directories, user passwords, user rights, and so on. If possible the operating system should support login over a network, where users can log into any computer within the logical extent of a network (typically known as a domain), and still have the same environment as they had when they last logged into the system.

- **Multitasking.** This allows one or more tasks to run on a system, at a time. Typically this is achieved by giving each task a certain amount of time on the processor (known as a quanta time slice), and the state of the task at the end of the quanta is stored to memory, and recalled when it is next run. As far as the user is concerned the programs are all being run at the same time (and not given time slices).

- **Multiprocessing.** This allows two or more processors to be used, at a time. When running with more than one processor the operating system must decide if it can run the processes on the different processors, or it has to determine if the processes require to be run sequentially (that is, one at a time). It must also manage the common memory and common resources (such as the data and address buses) between the processors.

- **Multi-threaded applications.** Processes are often split into smaller tasks, named threads. These threads allow for smoother process operation. Threads of a program use a common area for their data. They allow smaller processes to run, as larger processes will typically get stuck waiting for resources to be freed, or data to be inputted. A thread-based approach allows other threads to continue their operation, while others wait for some form of input, or access to a certain resource.

- **Multiple access to devices.** Some devices allow many programs to access it, without causing any problems, while others require that only one program at a time can have access. Memory and disk access allow multiple access for programs, whereas modems and printers typically only allow one program to access them at a time. Thus, the operating system must put locks on devices, so that other programs cannot access them while another program is accessing it. Note that multiple accesses to a device is really a virtual thing, in that two or more programs should not be able to access the same resource, before another program has finished with it. Thus, locks are also applied to multi-access devices if they are accessing the same area of memory or the same file.

Memory:
- Creating virtual memory systems
- Disk swapping for memory

Device interfacing:
- Access to connected devices
- Multi-user access
- Device drivers

Networking:
- Remote login/file transfer
- Creating global file systems

File system:
- Creating a file system
- Copying/deleting/moving files

Multi-user
- Allowing users to loging into system
- Allow users permissions to certain resources
- Managing queues for resources

Multiprocessing
- Allowing several processes to run, at a time
- Scheduling of processing to allow priority

Figure A3.4 Operating system functions

- **Driver loading.** A device driver is a special piece of software which knows how to communicate with a specific device. For example, a mouse driver will know how to receive data from a mouse and then convert it into a form which can be used by a program. An operating system is thus responsible for loading device drivers, and making sure that they act reliably. The operating system must thus be able to handle any error message from the device, and take the required actions (such as isolating it from the rest of the system). Typically, when the computer starts-up the operating system scans all the connected hardware and loads the required device drivers. This is a more dynamic approach than was implemented in the past, where device drivers were loaded once, and then loaded every time the computer was started, no matter if the device was present, or not. Device drivers cause many of the problems in modern systems, as there is no guarantee that the loaded device drivers are reliable in their operation, and that they will not have a detrimental effect on the rest of the system. One bad device driver can cause a whole system to act unreliably. There is an increasing focus on providing operating systems which have protected areas for device drivers, so that users cannot replace existing ones, without a high level of privilege. At one time, it was possible to delete every device driver on the system, with a single command.
- **Managing memory.** This involves allocating memory to processes, and often involves creating a virtual memory for programs. Virtual memories were an invention of the VMS operating system, where programs could be given an almost infinite amount of memory, even though there was a limited physical memory. For example, in Microsoft Windows, programs are given access to several gigabytes of memory, even though there may only be a few hundred megabytes of physical memory, which is shared with other programs, and the operating system. This virtually memory is typically created by using other memory storage devices, such as the hard disk for the additional memory space. Two techniques are: paging (organizing programs so that the program data is loaded into pages of memory) and swapping (which involves swapping the contents of memory to disk storage).

- **Networking**. Typically an operating system must make provision to create a network either to connect to an external network (such as the Internet), or in a local network (or domain). This normally involves loading the required networking protocol, such as TCP/IP for communications with the Internet. An operating system can arrange for several networking protocols to be used, such as TCP/IP for the Internet and IPX/SPX for communicating with a Novell NetWare server, or NetBEUI when communicating in a Microsoft networking domain.

The concept of the operating system interfacing with devices drivers is illustrated in Figure A3.5. When the operating system starts-up it will typically scan all its interface busses for devices. Any device that can identify itself causes the operating system to load the required device driver. Newer operating systems are plug-and-play where the operating system will automatically detect a new device, and try and configure it so that it does not conflict with any other device. This allows users to add new equipment to their computer without having to worry about its configuration. New interface busses, such as USB, allow for hot plug-and-play where devices can be added and deleted to/from a system while the power is on. USB has the advantage that each USB device tells the operating system about its type (such as it being a soundcard, a printer or a video monitor), and the operating system can automatically search for the best driver for it.

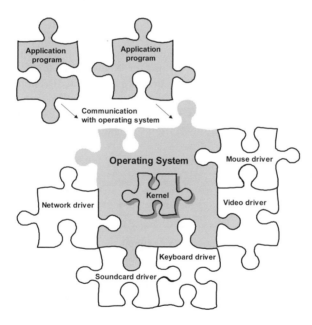

Figure A3.5   Operating system components

A3.2   Multitasking and threading

These days, networking and operating systems are almost intertwined, and most operating systems now directly support networking as part of their functionality. Without networks, operating systems could not provide the required user functionality, such as access to networked resources (printers, file systems, and so on), connection to the Internet or an Intranet, transferring of files, and so on. Typical network operating systems are Novell NetWare, Windows NT/2000/XP and UNIX.

The boundaries where processes run have now expanded from only running on local computers, to being distributed over networks. In the extreme case, it is possible to run processes over a large geographical area. This leads to the concept of distributed processing. Normally, each process must communicate with another, and there thus must be some mechanism for synchronization between them. Local computers use techniques such as hardware and software interrupts to generate events, and then signals or messages to pass the information between the processes.

Figure A3.6 shows an example of data passed between processes. These processes could be running locally on a computer, or could be run over a network on different computers. For example, initially a process on a computer sends an interrupt to the computer to identify that it is ready to transmit data. When the interrupt is received on the local computer, or a remote computer, it informs the destination process that a process wants to communicate with it. A message or a signal is then sent between the two processes to identify the type of data to be passed (if any). The data can then be passed between the processes.

Multitasking involves running several tasks at the same time. It normally involves running a process for a given amount of time, before releasing it and allowing another process a given amount of time. The two main forms of multitasking are illustrated in Figure A3.7 and Figure A3.8; and are:

- **Pre-emptive multitasking.** This type of multitasking involves the operating system controlling how long a process stays on the processor. This allows for smooth multitasking and is used in 32-bit Microsoft Windows programs and in the UNIX operating system.
- **Co-operative multitasking.** This type of multitasking relies on a process giving up the processor. It is used with Windows 3.x programs and suffers from processor hogging, where a process can stay on a processor and the operating system cannot kick it off.

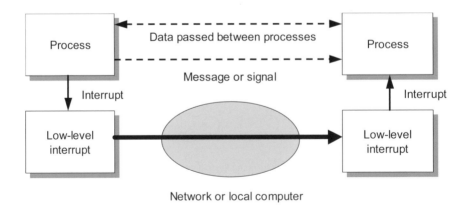

Figure A3.6 Information passed between processes

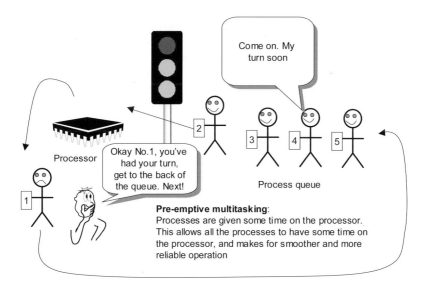

Figure A3.7 Pre-emptive multitasking

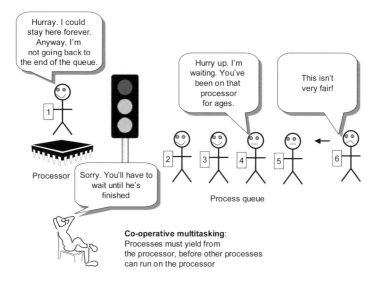

Figure A3.8 Co-operative multitasking

The logical extension to multitasking programs is to split a program into a number of parts (threads) and run each of these on a multitasking system (multi-threading). Multi-threading can be likened to splitting sequential tasks, into a number of interrelated tasks. For example, let us say that you have to cook a meal with the following recipe:

1. Put potatoes on to boil.
2. Put pie in the microwave, on HIGH for 10 minutes.
3. Wait for potatoes to become soft.

4. Take potatoes out of pan, and place on the plates.
5. Wait for pie to complete.
6. Take pie out of microwave and place on the plates.
7. Put carrots in pan, and boil.
8. Wait for carrots to become soft.
9. Take carrots out of pan, and place on the plates.

The problem with this recipe is that someone could be waiting for step 4 to complete, while they could be checking the pie to see if it has completed. An improved method would use independent subtasks, which were interrelated. In this case, the pie and the potatoes are not interrelated, but the potatoes and the carrots are (assuming that we only have one pan). Figure A3.9 shows a possible schedule using subtasks (or threads of the main task), where we now have six main threads. Each of the threads can run independently, but some cannot run until they have received something from another thread. For example it is not possible for the 'Put potatoes on plate' thread to start until it has received the potatoes from the 'Boil potatoes' thread.

A threads-based approach allows us to create specialized tasks, which have a small definitive goal. It is much easier to test a small program which has a definitive task, than to test a large and complex piece of software. It is also easier to upgrade a thread, without affecting the overall operation of the complete program.

A program that is running more than one thread at a time is known as a multi-threaded program. These have many advantages over non-multi-threaded programs, including:

- They make better use of the processor, where different threads can be run when one or more threads are waiting for data. For example, a thread could be waiting for keyboard input, while another thread could be reading data from the disk.
- They are easier to test, as each thread can be tested independently of other threads.
- They can use standard threads, which are optimized for given hardware.

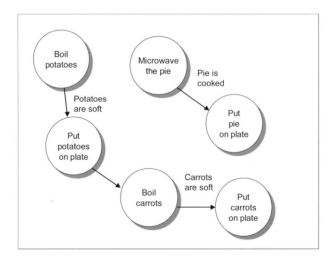

Figure A3.9   Threads in a task

They also have disadvantages, including:

- The program has to be planned properly so that threads know on which other threads they depend.
- A thread may wait indefinitely for another thread which has crashed or terminated.

The main difference between multiple processes and multiple threads is that each process has independent variables and data, while multiple threads share data from the main program, as illustrated in Figure A3.10.

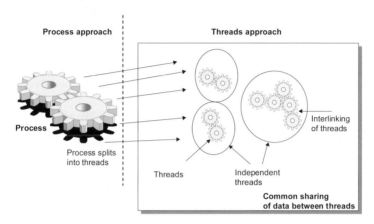

Figure A3.10 Process splitting into threads

A3.3 Example operating system components (Microsoft Windows)

The following chapters contain a theoretical study of operating systems component, before these, this section will review some of the main elements of the Microsoft Windows operating system. One of the problems for the Microsoft Windows is that it must be able to run 16-bit programs, and also 32-bit programs. These are typically referred at Win-16 or Win-32, respectively.

A3.3.1 Core system components

Applications programs use software libraries to call certain services, such as reading keys from a keyboard, or accessing the mouse. A software library contains useful routines which can either be compiled with a program (static library), or can be called up when the program is run (dynamic library), as illustrated in Figure A3.11. With a static library, the routines are added to the program by the linker, which searches the static libraries for the functions that require to be linked into the program. This extra code is included in the executable program, and remains permanently attached to the program, even though it might never be needed.

For a PC dynamic libraries are called DLLs (Dynamic Link Libraries), and are called by the user program whenever it needs the services provided by them. A typical DLL is WINSOCK.DLL, which is called whenever a computer uses the Internet, and contains the code which has the TCP/IP protocol. The functions within the dynamic library are only used when they are required, thus there is very little overhead in the actual size of the program, and the amount of space it takes up in memory.

Dynamic libraries have many advantages over static libraries, such as:

- They are only loaded when, and if, they are required.
- User programs can be kept to a minimum size, as they make use of standard dynamic libraries for many of their extra functions.
- They can be easily changed and upgraded.
- They can be standardized across all programs, so that the operating system can keep much closer control on the methods of access for certain devices.

They have several disadvantages, though, such as:

- **Easily to tamper with**. Dynamic libraries can, in certain conditions, be easily tampered with and can be easily deleted or replaced with a previous version. One well-know virus actually replaces WINSOCK.DLL with its own DLL, and thus intercepts any Internet communications (with worrying con-sequences), as illustrated in Figure A3.12. The WINSOCK.DLL dynamic library is responsible for any TCP/IP communications, thus an external hacker could make a copy of all of the Internet communication and send them to another computer, where they could be monitored. It also gives a port for an external hacker to gain access to the computer, and thus interrogate its contents, and monitor its activities.
- **Damaged or incorrectly installed dynamic library**. A common fault in a system is when the one or more of the dynamic libraries are corrupt, or replaced with an incorrect version of the library. This can cause errors, and can cause the system to crash, with very little information as to the cause of the crash. Some operating systems protect these files, so that updated versions cannot be installed, without the privilege of the network administrator.

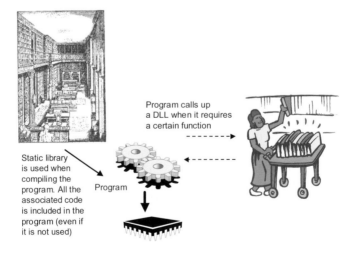

Figure A3.11   Dynamic link libraries

The core of Microsoft Windows are three components: User, Kernel, and GDI (graphical device interface), each of which has a pair of DLLs (one for 32-bit accesses; the other for 16-bit accesses). The 16-bit DLLs allow for support for 16-bit Windows programs and MS-DOS computability. A DLL contains a number of services, which can be called up when a program runs. Typical services include access to networking services, input/output functions and graphical functions.

User

The User component provides input and output to and from the user interface. Input is from the keyboard, mouse, and any other input device and the output is to the user interface. It also manages interaction with the sound driver, timer, and communications ports.

Microsoft Windows use an asynchronous input model for system input. With this, devices have an associated interrupt handler (for example, the keyboard interrupts with IRQ1) that converts the interrupt into a message. This message is then sent to a raw input thread area, which then passes the message to the appropriate message queue. Each Win32 application can have its own message queue, whereas all Win16 applications share a common message queue.

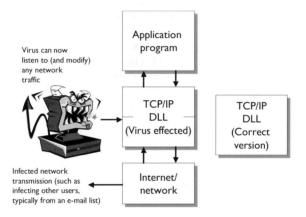

Figure A3.12 Virus attack on a DLL

Kernel

The Kernel provides for core operating system components including file I/O services, virtual memory management, task scheduling and exception handling, such as:

- **File I/O services**.
- **Exceptions**. These are events that occur as a program runs and call additional software which is outside the normal flow of control. For example, if an application generates an exception, the Kernel is able to communicate that exception to the application to perform the necessary functions to resolve the problem. An example exception is caused by a divide-by-zero error in a mathematical calculation, where an exception routine can be designed so that it handles the error and does not crash the program.
- **Virtual memory management**. This supports demand paging for the application.
- **Task scheduling**. The Kernel schedules and runs threads of each process associated with an application.

- **Provides services to both 16-bit and 32-bit applications**. This uses a thunking process which is the translation process between 16-bit and 32-bit formats. It is typically used by a Win16 program to communicate with the 32-bit operating system core.

Virtual memory allows processes to allocate more memory than can be physically allocated. The operating system allocates each process a unique virtual address space, which is a set of addresses available for the process's threads. This virtual address space appears, to the program, to be 4 GB in size, where 2 GB is reserved for program storage and 2 GB for system storage.

GDI

The Graphical Device Interface (GDI) is the graphical system that:

- Manages information that appears on the screen.
- Draws graphic primitives and manipulates bitmaps.
- Interacts with device-independent graphics drivers, such as display and printer drivers.

The graphics subsystem provides input and output graphics support. Windows uses a 32-bit graphics engine (known as DIB, Device-independent Bitmaps) which:

- Directly controls the graphics output on the screen.
- Provides a set of optimized generic drawing functions for monochrome, 16-color, 16-bit high color, 256-color, and 24-bit true color graphic devices. It also supports Bézier curves and paths.
- Support for Image Color Matching for better color matching between display and color output devices.

The Windows graphics subsystem is included as a universal driver with a 32-bit mini-driver. The mini-driver provides only for the hardware-specific instructions.

A3.3.2 Virtual Machine Manager (VMM)

One of the major problems in a computer is that it is impossible to test a program in all the conditions that it is likely to face. It would be impossible to run programs with all the other programs that could run alongside it. Thus programs are typically tested in isolation to all other user programs. The perfect environment for a user program would thus be to run it on a stand-alone, dedicated computer, which does not have any interference from any other programs and can have access to any device when it wants. This is the concept of the Virtual Machine. As much as possible an operating system should try to provide this environment for its programs.

In Microsoft Windows the Virtual Machine Manager (VMM) provides applications with the system resources when they need them. It creates and maintains the virtual machine environments in which applications and system processes run, as illustrated in Figure A3.13.

The VMM is responsible for three areas:

- **Process scheduling.** This supports process scheduling, and allows for multiple programs to run concurrently. It also provides system resources to the programs and other processes that run. Process scheduling allows multiple programs and other processes to run concurrently, using either co-operative multitasking or pre-emptive multitasking.

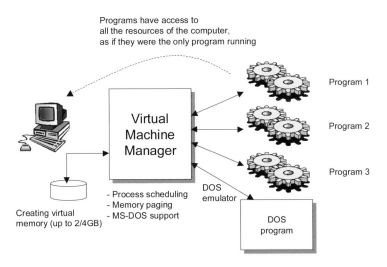

Programs have access to
all the resources of the computer,
as if they were the only program running

Virtual
Machine
Manager

Program 1

Program 2

Program 3

- Process scheduling
- Memory paging
- MS-DOS support

DOS
emulator

Creating virtual
memory (up to 2/4GB)

DOS
program

Figure A3.13 Virtual Machine Manager

- **Memory paging**. Microsoft Windows uses a demand-paged virtual memory system, which is based on a flat, linear address space accessed using 32-bit addresses. The system allocates each process a unique virtual address space of 4 GB. The upper 2 GB is shared, while the lower 2 GB is private to the program. This virtual address space is divided into equal blocks (or pages).
- **MS-DOS Mode support**. Provides support for MS-DOS-based program which must have exclusive access to the hardware. When an MS-DOS-based application runs in this mode then no other programs or processes are allowed to compete for system resources. The application thus has sole access to the resources.

Process scheduling and multitasking

This allows multiple applications and other processes to run concurrently, using either co-operative multitasking or pre-emptive multitasking (Windows 3.x, applications ran using co-operative multitasking). This method requires that applications check the message queue periodically and give up control of the system to other applications. Unfortunately, applications that do not check the message queue at frequent intervals can effectively 'hog' the processor and prevent other applications from running. As this does not provide effective multi-processing, Microsoft Windows uses pre-emptive multitasking for Win32-based applications (but also supports co-operative multitasking for compatibility reasons). Thus, the operating system takes direct control away from the application tasks.

Win16 programs need to yield to other tasks in order to multitask properly, whereas Win32-based programs do not need to yield to share resources. This is because Win32-based applications (called processes) use multi-threading, which provides for multi-processing. A thread in a program is a unit of code that can get a time slice from the operating system to run concurrently with other code units. Each process consists of one or more execution threads that identify the code path flow as it is run on the operating system. A Win32-based application can have multiple threads for a given process. This enhances the running of an application by improving throughput and responsiveness. It allows processes for smooth background processing.

A3.3.3 NT/2000 architecture

Windows NT/2000 uses two modes:

- **User mode.** This is a lower privileged mode than kernel mode. It has no direct access to the hardware or to memory. It interfaces to the operating system through well-defined API (Application Program Interface) calls.
- **Kernel mode.** This is a privileged mode of operation and allows all code direct access to the hardware and memory, including memory allocated to user mode processes. Kernel mode processes also have a higher priority over user mode processes.

Figure A3.14 shows an outline of the architecture of NT. It can be seen that only the kernel mode has access to the hardware. This kernel includes an executive services which include managers (for I/O, interprocess communications, and so on) and device drivers (which control the hardware). Its parts include:

- Microkernel. Controls basic operating system services, such as interrupt handling and scheduling.
- HAL. This a library of hardware-specific programs which give a standard interface between the hardware and software. This can either be Microsoft written or manufacturer provided. They have the advantage of allowing for transportability of programs across different hardware platforms.
- Win32 Window Manager. Supports Win32, MS-DOS and Windows 3.*x* applications.

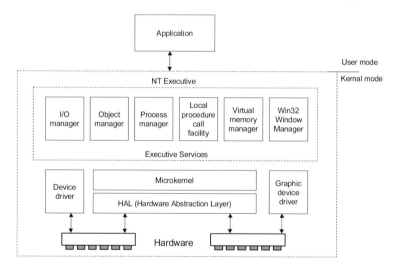

Figure A3.14   NT/2000/XP architecture

A3.4   Interrupts (on PC systems)

An interrupt allows a program or an external device to interrupt the execution of a program, and can occur by hardware (hardware interrupt) or software (software interrupt). When an interrupt occurs an interrupt service routine (ISR) is called. For a hardware interrupt, the

ISR then communicates with the device and processes any data. When it has finished the program execution returns to the original program. A software interrupt causes the program to interrupt its execution and goes to an interrupt service routine. Typical software interrupts include reading a key from the keyboard, outputting text to the screen and reading the current date and time. The operating system must respond to interrupts from external devices, as illustrated in Figure A3.15.

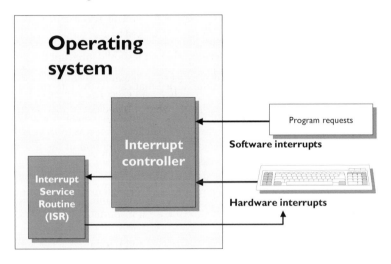

Figure A3.15 Interrupt service routine

A3.4.1 Software Interrupts

The Basic Input/Output System (BIOS) communicates directly with the hardware of the computer. It consists of a set of programs which interface with devices such as keyboards, displays, printers, serial ports and disk drives. These programs allow the user to write application programs that contain calls to these functions, without having to worry about controlling them or about which type of equipment is being used. Without BIOS the computer system would simply consist of a bundle of wires and electronic devices.

There are two main parts to BIOS. The first is permanently stored in non-volatile memory (the ROM BIOS), and is the part that starts the computer (or bootstrap) and contains programs which communicate with resident devices. The second stage is loaded when the operating system is started.

An operating system allows the user to access the hardware in an easy-to-use manner. It accepts commands from the keyboard and displays them to the monitor. The Disk Operating System, or DOS, gained its name from its original purpose of providing a controller for the computer to access its disk drives. The language of DOS consists of a set of commands which are entered directly by the user and are interpreted to perform file management tasks, program execution and system configuration. It makes calls to BIOS to execute these. The main functions of DOS are to run programs, copy and remove files, create directories, move within a directory structure and to list files. Microsoft Windows calls BIOS programs directly.

A3.4.2 Hardware Interrupts

Computer systems either use polling or interrupt-driven software to service external equipment. With polling, the computer continually monitors a status line and waits for it to become active. An interrupt-driven device sends an interrupt request to the computer, which is then serviced by an interrupt service routine (ISR). Interrupt-driven devices are normally better in that the computer is thus free to do other things while polling slows the system down, as it must continually monitor the external device. Polling can also cause problems in that a device may be ready to send data but the computer is not watching the status line at that point. Figure A3.16 illustrates polling and interrupt-driven devices.

The generation of an interrupt can occur by hardware or software, as illustrated in Figure A3.17. If a device wishes to interrupt the processor, it informs the programmable interrupt controller (PIC). The PIC then decides whether it should interrupt the processor. If there is a processor interrupt then the processor reads the PIC to determine which device caused the interrupt. Then, depending on the device that caused the interrupt, a call to an ISR is made, which then communicates with the device and processes any data. When it has finished, the program execution returns to the original program. Each PIC allows access to eight interrupt request lines. Most PCs use two PICs which gives access to 16 interrupt lines.

Hardware interrupts allow external devices to gain the attention of the processor. Depending on the type of interrupt, the processor leaves the current program and goes to the ISR. This program communicates with the device and processes any data. After the ISR has completed its task then program execution returns to the program that was running before the interrupt occurred.

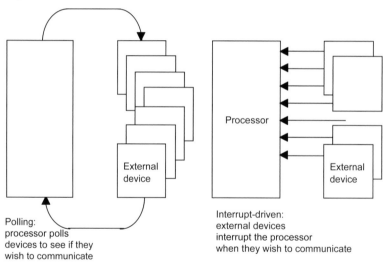

Figure A3.16 Polling or interrupt-driven communications

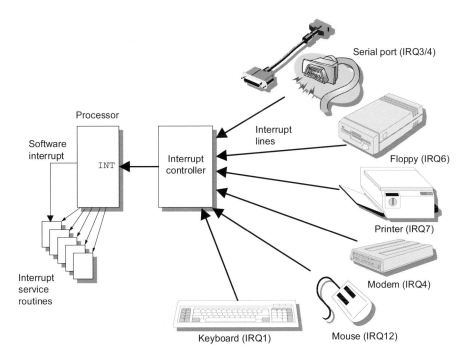

Figure A3.17 Interrupt handling

Interrupt vectors

On a PC, each device that requires to be *interrupt-driven* is assigned an IRQ (interrupt request) line. Table A3.1 outlines the usage of each of these interrupts. IRQ0 normally connects to the system timer, IRQ1 to the keyboard, and so on. The system timer interrupts the processor 18.2 times per second, and is used to update the system time. When the keyboard has data, it interrupts the processor with the IRQ1 line.

Data received from serial ports interrupts the processor with IRQ3 and IRQ4 and the parallel ports use IRQ5 and IRQ7. If one of the parallel, or serial, ports does not exist then the IRQ line normally assigned to it can be used by another device, such as for a sound card, which has a programmable IRQ line which is mapped to an IRQ line that is not being used.

Note that several devices can use the same interrupt line. A typical example is COM1: and COM3: sharing IRQ4 and COM2: and COM4: sharing IRQ3. If they do share then the ISR must be able to poll the shared devices to determine which of them caused the interrupt. If two different types of device (such as a sound card and a serial port) use the same IRQ line then there may be a contention problem as the ISR may not be able to communicate with different types of interfaces.

Figure A3.18 shows a sample window displaying interrupt usage. In this case it can be seen that the system timer uses IRQ0, the keyboard uses IRQ1, and so on. Notice that a network adapter is using IRQ7. This interrupt is normally reserved for a printer port. If there is no printer port connected then IRQ7 can be used by another device. These interrupt lines are a legacy from the original PC, and are likely to be phased-out in the coming years, as hub based technology, such as USB, allows many devices to use the same interrupt line.

Table A3.1 Interrupt handling

Interrupt name	Generated by
System timer	IRQ0
Keyboard	IRQ1
Reserved	IRQ2
Serial communications (COM2:)	IRQ3
Serial communications (COM1:)	IRQ4
Reserved	IRQ5
Floppy disk controller	IRQ6
Parallel printer (LPT1:)	IRQ7
Real-time clock	IRQ8
Math co-processor	IRQ13
Hard disk controller (primary)	IRQ14
Hard disk controller (secondary)	IRQ15

Typical uses of interrupts are:

IRQ0: System timer	The system timer uses IRQ0 to interrupt the processor 18.2 times per second and is used to keep the time-of-day clock updated.
IRQ1: Keyboard data ready	The keyboard uses IRQ1 to signal to the processor that data is ready to be received from the keyboard. This data is normally a scan code.
IRQ2: Redirection of IRQ9	The BIOS redirects the interrupt for IRQ9 back here.
IRQ3: Secondary serial port (COM2:)	The secondary serial port (COM2:) uses IRQ3 to interrupt the processor. Typically, COM3: to COM8: also use it, although COM3: may use IRQ4.
IRQ4: Primary serial port (COM1:)	The primary serial port (COM1:) uses IRQ4 to interrupt the processor. Typically, COM3: also uses it.
IRQ5: Secondary parallel port (LPT2:)	Typically, it is used by a sound card on PCs which have no secondary parallel port connected.
IRQ6: Floppy disk controller	The floppy disk controller activates the IRQ6 line on completion of a disk operation.
IRQ7: Primary parallel port (LPT1:)	Printers (or other parallel devices) activate the IRQ7 line when they become active. As with IRQ5 it may be used by another device, if there are no other devices connected to this line.
IRQ9:	Redirected to IRQ2 service routine.
IRQ12:	PS/2-style mouse.
IRQ13:	Maths co-processor.
IRQ14/IRQ15:	Hard disk (IDE0/IDE1).

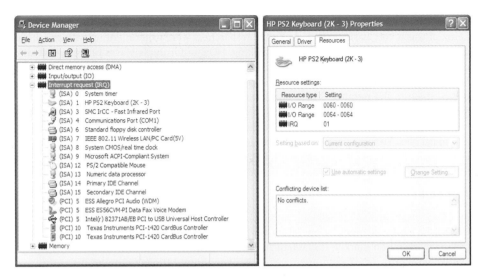

Figure A3.18 Example usage of IRQ lines

A3.5   Example operating systems

This section outlines several different types of operating systems from their historical development, and their basic system specification.

A3.5.1 DOS

Around the end of the 1970s, it was obvious that the microprocessor would drive down the cost of computer system, and make them more available to business and home users. IBM decided that they would create a system which would be attractive to businesses, and to speed its adoption, they would create it with an open architecture. As the time limits were tight, they went to other companies to create the basic operating system. For this, they first contacted Digital Research, and then a small computer company called Microsoft. At Microsoft, Bill Gates bought a program called Q-DOS (often called the Quick and Dirty Operating System) from Seattle Computer Products. Q-DOS was similar to CP/M, but totally incompatible. Microsoft paid less than $100,000 for the rights to the software, and they allowed IBM to release it on the PC as PC-DOS. Soon Microsoft released their own version called MS-DOS, which has since become the best selling software in history.

To give users some choice in their operating system, the IBM PC was initially distributed with three operating systems: PC-DOS (provided by Microsoft), Digital Research's CP/M-86 and UCSD Pascal P-System. Microsoft understood that to make their operating system the standard, that they must provide IBM with a good deal. Thus, Microsoft offered IBM the royalty-free rights to use Microsoft's operating system, forever, for $80 000. This made PC-DOS much cheaper than the other two (such as $450 for P-System, $175 for CP/M and $60 for PC-DOS). Microsoft was smart in that they allowed IBM to use PC-DOS free, but they held the control of the licensing of the software. This was one of the greatest pieces of business ever conducted. Eventually CP/M and P-System died off, while PC-DOS become the standard PC operating system.

The developed program was hardly earth shattering, but has since gone on to make billions of dollars. It was named the Disk Operating System (DOS) because of its original purpose of controlling the disk drives. Compared with work that was going on at Apple and at Xerox, it was a very basic system. At Xerox, researchers were experimenting with graphical display, mouse-driven systems, and networking. DOS, unfortunately, was little more than a mechanism to get the computer started and, once started, provide access to the disk drives. It had no graphical user interface and accepted commands from the keyboard and displayed them to the monitor. These commands were interpreted by the system to perform file management tasks, program execution and system configuration. Its function was to run programs, copy and remove files, create directories, move within a directory structure and to list files. To most people this was their first introduction to computing, but for many, DOS made using the computer difficult, and it would not be until proper graphical user interfaces, such as Windows 95, that PCs would truly be accepted, and used by the majority.

A3.5.2 UNIX

Ken Thompson, at AT&T's Bell Laboratories, developed the UNIX operating system in 1971. UNIX is an extremely popular operating system and dominates in the high-powered, multi-tasking workstation market. It is relatively simple to use and to administer, and has a high degree of security. UNIX computers use TCP/IP communications to mount disk resources from one machine onto another. UNIX's main characteristics are:

- **Multi-user.**
- **Pre-emptive multi-tasking.**
- **Multiprocessing.**
- **Multithreaded applications.**
- **Memory management with paging** (organizing programs so that the program is loading into pages of memory) **and swapping** (which involves swapping the contents of memory to disk storage).

The two main families of UNIX are UNIX System V and BSD (Berkeley Software Distribution) Version 4.4. System V is the operating system most often used and has descended from a system developed by the Bell Laboratories; it was recently sold to SCO (Santa Cruz Operation). System V was the first real attempt at unifying UNIX into a single standardized operating system, and succeeded in merging Microsoft XENIX, SunOS and UNIX 4.3 BSD. Unfortunately, after this there was still a drift by hardware manufacturers to move away from the standard (and define their standards). Although it has been difficult to standardize UNIX, it true strength is its communications protocols, especially TCP/IP, which are now world-wide standards for communicating over the Internet. The biggest challenge to UNIX has been from Windows NT, which has tried to create a hardware independent operating system. UNIX has, in the main, survived because of its simplicity and its reliability. The next threat has come from Windows 2000, which has moved towards UNIX in its network security methods.

Popular UNIX systems are:

- **AIX** (on IBM workstations and mainframes).
- **HP-UX** (on HP workstations).
- **Linux** (on PC-based systems).
- **OSF/1** (on DEC workstations).
- **Solaris** (on Sun workstations).

An initiative by several software vendors has resulted in a common standard for the user interface and the operation of UNIX. The user interface standard is defined by the common desktop environment (**CDE**), which allows software vendors to write calls to a standard CDE API (application program interface). The common UNIX standard has been defined as Spec 1170 APIs (Application Program Interfaces). Compliance with the CDE and Spec 1170 API are certified by X/Open, which is a UNIX standards organization.

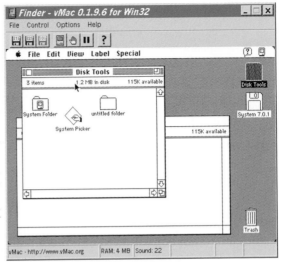

A3.5.3 Linux

Another important UNIX-like operating system is Linux, which was developed by Linus Torvalds at the University of Helsinki in Finland. It was first made public in 1991 and most of it is available free-of-charge. The most widely available version was developed by the Free Software Foundation's GNU project. It runs on most Intel-based, SPARC and Alpha-based computers, but its major problem is that it does not support as many hardware devices as Microsoft Windows does.

A3.5.4 Mac OS/System 8

Microsoft have relied on gradual improvement to their software, especially in their operating systems, while Apple got it right first time with their Mac OS system. Many reckon that MAC OS was 10 years ahead of all other systems. With the PC there were many difficulties, such as keeping compatibility with the original DOS, difficulties with the Intel 8086/88 memory model, support for a great number of peripherals, and the slowness of its internal busses (including the graphics adaptor). These all made software development of the PC difficult. Apple did not have compatibility problems to deal with when they designed the Macintosh (Mac) as started with a completely new design. They also spent as much money on the operating system and the graphical user interface as they did on developing the hardware for the Mac. This, at the time, was radical, as hardware development costs typically exceeded hardware development costs by a good factor. The Mac was designed from a user's point-of-view, and borrowed many ideas from the Xerox system used at PARC. For the first time, Mac OS actually made the computer feel friendly. Most Mac users actually enjoyed using their computer, which was not the same for the IBM PC-compatible market, which suffered from so many problems, that it is hardly worth documenting them. At the time, PCs were still DOS based, with text commands, while Mac OS had a GUI which allowed users to operate the computer with graphical images and use a mouse to guide themselves around the system. Many Mac users wondered, why, in DOS, that someone have to locate a file with the CD command, and then use the DEL command to delete it, when, with the Mac, they could simply locate it by clicking the mouse pointer though a number of folders, and then drag the file to the wastepaper basket (then undelete it if they had made a mistake). The operating system was Apple's jewel, and the Mac hardware was secondary to its success. These days it seems obvious that great amounts of profit can be made from the operating system, but it was not so obvious then. Many business analysts now acknowledge that Apple should have ported their operating system onto other systems, especially the IBM PC-compatible systems and to workstations. Apple engineers, though, thought that the Macintosh hardware could not be divorced from its beloved Mac OS. Over time, Mac OS has been caught up by other operating systems, which have typically had a more privileged place in the market. Mac OS was renamed System 7, in 1990, after a major upgrade. It is now one of many operating systems that try to do the same sort of things, in the same sort of way, rather than being the leader of the pack.

A3.5.5 VMS

In the 1970s and 1980s, DEC carved out a large market for minicomputers (which were much cheaper than mainframe computers). Their first range of computers was the PDP (Programmed Data Processor) series, which become the foundation of many scientific and engineering groups. After the PDP, DEC took a great gamble and invested a great deal of research and development into the VAX (Virtual Address eXtension) computer range. It was an instant success, and the series provided a wide range of systems from basic terminals, up to large mainframe computers. At the time, IBM was the only computer company who provided solutions for virtually every area of the industry. For the first time, DEC produced every part of the computer system: the operating system, the hardware and the software. One of the great successes of the VAX range, was not necessarily its hardware, it was its operating system: VMS (produced by David Culter). VMS allowed computer programmers to create programs which had more memory than the computer actually had (a virtual memory), and allowed several programs to run at the same time (multi-tasking). VMS is still popular in market niches, such as in the oil and gas industry (where reliability and batch processing are important). The VAX range also supported the Ethernet networking standard, which DEC had helped develop along with Intel and Xerox.

A3.5.6 Microsoft Windows

DOS had long been the Achilles heel of the PC and had limited its development. It has also been its strength in that it provides a common platform for all packages. The first two versions of Microsoft Windows were pretty poor, as they had a poor interface, and still had all of the constraints of DOS (which are, of course, great). Microsoft Windows 3.0 changed this with an enhanced usage of icons and windows, greater integration and increased memory usage. It was still 16-bit and still used DOS to boot from, but it started to make full use of the processor, and gave a hint of the forthcoming multi-tasking (it could run two processes at a time, using fixed-rate time sharing). Other enhancements were: OLE; True Type fonts; and drag-and-drop commands. After Windows 3.0, Microsoft released Windows for Workgroups which was one of their first attempts at trying to network PCs together with Windows. Unfortunately it was too complicated to set-up, and not very powerful. Soon Windows 3.1 was released, along with a 32-bit version of Microsoft Windows.

The debate about whether Microsoft Windows 95 was just a copy of the Mac operating system will continue for years, but as Windows 3.x was a quantum leap from the previous versions, so Windows 95 was to Windows 3.x. The main problems with Windows 3.x was that it still used DOS as a basic operating system, and it also used 16-bit code (which did not used the full potential of the PC as most PC, at the time, where using 32-bit processors, such as the 80386 and 80486 processors). Windows 95 was a total code rewrite using, mostly, 32-bit software, and thus used the full power of the processor, and the full memory addressing capabilities. It could now address up to 4 GB of virtual memory, and supported a great deal more devices, such as CD-ROMs and back-up resources. It also had networking properly built into it.

At the time networking was becoming one of the key elements of a computer system, and Microsoft played a massive trump card, by supporting most of the widely available network protocols, such as TCP/IP (for Internet traffic), IPX/SPX (for Novell NetWare traffic), AppleTalk and IBM DCL. It could thus be easily integrated with any type of network (and, Microsoft hoped, would eventually replace the existing network with one based on Microsoft networking, and not the existing network – which is known as gradual network migration). Microsoft created two different streams for their operating systems. For home and small business users, The Windows 95 stream allowed for a peer-to-peer network were computers can share resources, and was more tolerant with older 16-bit code, where the other stream, with Windows NT/2000/XP, was aimed at businesses and allowed for a robust environment, with enhanced security on all the networked resource. This server based approach allowed network-wide login, administration, global file systems, and so on.

A3.5.7 CP/M (Deceased)

In 1973, before the widespread acceptance of PC-DOS, the future for personal computer operating systems looked to be CP/M (Control Program/Monitor), which was written by Gary Kildall of Digital Research. One of his first applications of CP/M was on the Intel 8008, and then on the Intel 8080. At the time, computers based on the 8008 started to appear, such as the Scelbi-8H, which cost $565 and had 1KB of memory.

A3.5.8 Aegis (Deceased)

Apollo burst onto the computer market in the 1980s with high-end workstations based on the Motorola 68000 processor (as in Apple Mac). These were aimed at serious users, and their main application area was in computer-aided design (CAD). One of the first to be introduced was the DN300, which was based around the excellent Motorola 68000 processor. It had a built-in mono monitor, an external 60MB hard disk drive, an 8-inch floppy drive, built-in ATR (Apollo Token Ring) network card, and 1.5 MB RAM. It even had its own multi-user, networked operating system called Aegis. Unfortunately, for all its power and usability, Aegis never really took off, and when the market demanded standardized operating systems, Apollo switched to Domain/IX (which was a UNIX-clone). It is likely that Apollo would have captured an even larger market if they had changed to UNIX at an earlier time, as Sun (the other large workstation manufacturer) had done. The changeover of operating systems caused terrible problems for system administrators, and many users resisted the move away from their beloved Aegis. For a while, most Apollo systems ran two different operating systems.

Aegis, as does UNIX, supported a networked file system, where a global file system could be built-up with local disk resources. Thus, a network of 10 workstations, each with 50 MB hard disks allowed for a global file system of 500 MB.

A4 Processes and scheduling

A4.1 Introduction

A process is a self-contained program which has all the required elements for it to be run on a processor. It is unlikely that it will be able to run on its own, and it is likely to require the help of other processes to provide it with data, or to take data from it, and must thus have some form of communication device to signal its intentions to other processes (and vice-versa). The requirement for many processes to run, at a time, results in the need for a scheduler, which must try and be as fair as possible to all the processes, but which has the main aim of keeping the system running as smoothly as possible, without any system crashes.

The perfect environment for a process is to run on the processor, without any disturbance from any other process. Unfortunately, this would be inefficient in the usage of the system for many reasons, such as:

- **Inefficient use of the processor**. The process being run could be waiting for some input from a device, or waiting to send to an output device. This is inefficient as other processes could be run while the current process is waiting.
- **Not allowing other processes to run, at the same time**. On a general-purpose computer, the user should be able to run other processes at the same time, such as running multiple Internet sessions, and word processor programs.
- **Not running any support programs**. The system should be able to run other processes which provide support to the user's processes. Typical to these might be a process which responded to the user printing a document. This process would then take the output from a process and then store it. It would then communicate with the printer, and allow the user program to get on with other tasks, without having to communicate with the printer.
- **Not allowing the sharing of resources**. If each process was allowed dedicated access to the resources, it would not allow for sharing of resources, as they would remain fixed to the processes.

Most modern operating systems now run multiple processes and try to simulate the isolated environment with a virtual machine. This simulates the stand-alone, single-tasking environment, where other processes cannot affect the current process.

Processes, themselves, either can run locally within a computer system, or can be run over a network, such as in a distributed system. When several processes run at the same time, there must be some mechanism for them to intercommunicate and pass information. Another requirement is when processes share the same resource. This tends to be reasonably easy when the resource can be shareable, but problems can occur when the resource must be dedicated to one process at a time. This type of situation can lead to deadlock where resources, which are dedicated to processes, do not yield to other processes which are waiting on them.

The first multitasking systems were based on batch processing, which would run user programs with a high priority, but could also run background processes which required virtually no interaction with users (batch programs). Thus, batch files would typically use most of the processing time when the system was not being used by other user programs. A batch program normally involves reading data from one or more file(s), and processing it, into one or more output files. This suited many situations, especially where programs could be run overnight, without any interaction with users. Batch processing was especially important in the days before personal computers, when the cost of processing was high, and many users competed to get access to systems. In mathematical modeling, it was typical that processes would have to run for hours, days, or even weeks, on processes that would take minutes by today's standards. However, of course, the range of applications which need to be processed have also moved on, and many large-scale processing problems can take many days or weeks to complete. Thus, batch processing is still an important issue, and many batch processes are happily working in systems, and using its resources, only when the system can spare the time. One extension of this is towards using spare processing power over a network (and possibly over the Internet), as this allows the spare computing power of many computers to be used, at a time. This will be covered in more detail in a following chapter, as we look at distributed processing methods.

A4.2   Scheduling

Multitasking operating systems can run many programs at the same time, but these must be organized in some way. This is the task of the process scheduler, which must allow each process some time on the processor. A badly designed scheduler simply allows each of the processes the same period of time. Whereas a well-designed scheduler allows for priority levels, and can make decisions on which processes should be run, at a given time. Typically, system processes are more important than user programs, and need to be run at regular intervals, and will thus be given a higher priority over user programs.

The scheduler operates on a queue of processes, each of which can either be:

- **Running.** This is where the process is actually currently running on the processor.
- **Waiting.** This is where the process is waiting on another process to run and provide it with some data, or if a process is waiting to access a resource. The waiting process can sometimes turn into a zombie process, where a process terminates for some reason, but whose parent process has not yet waited for it to terminate. A zombie process is not a big problem, as it has no resources allocated to it. Normally the only way to get rid of zombie processes is to reboot the system.
- **Ready.** This is where the process is ready to be run on the processor, and is not waiting for any other processes or has terminated.
- **Terminated.** This is where a process has finished its run, and all resources that have been allocated to it must be taken away from it.

These concepts are illustrated in Figure A4.1. The scheduler must thus make a decision on when to change state, such as:

- Running to waiting.
- Waiting to ready.
- Running to ready.
- Running to terminated.

A pre-emptive scheduler uses a timer to allow each process some time on the processor and coordinates access to shared data. Along with this, it requires a kernel designed to protect the integrity of its own data structures. Kernels must be robust in the way that they are designed, as any problems in the kernel will affect the whole system.

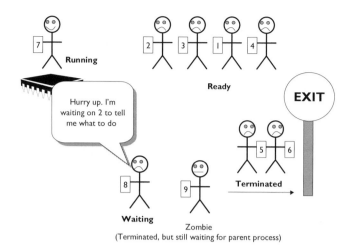

Figure A4.1 Running, ready, waiting and terminated

A4.2.1 Scheduling queues

There are three main system queues: Job Queue – incoming jobs; Ready Queue and Device Queues (blocked processes). Normally the type of scheduler chosen depends on the type of system that is required, such as:

- **Long-term (Job) scheduler.** This type of scheduler is used in batch systems.
- **Short-term scheduler.** This type of scheduler typically uses a FIFO (First In, First Out) queue, or a priority queue.
- **Medium-term scheduler.** This type of scheduler swaps processes in and out to improve the job mix. Normally it schedules on the following:
  - **Time since swapped in or out.** Swapping involves moving the running process to some temporary storage space (such as the local disk). A process which has been swapped out for a longer time than another one is more likely to be chosen by the scheduler, over the one which has waited the least time. As much as possible users should not get the feeling that their processes are not being serviced, at all.
  - **Processor time used.** In order to be fair, a scheduler might pick a process that has had a lesser time on the processor; over one that has had more time. The time that a process has spent on the processor is no guarantee that it has used its time efficiently.
  - **Size.** Typically a small process will most likely take the least amount of resources, and processing time (but this is no guarantee), thus the scheduler may pick the process which has the smallest size. An improved method is for the scheduler to make an estimate about the amount of resources that the process will require to complete, and then chose the next process on the basis of this. An efficient schedule is to try and complete processes which can be completed in the shortest time. This type of scheduling is know as shortest-first, and many busy people reckon that this is the best way to organize their work, where they tackle tasks that can be completed quickly, before the larger tasks. Unfortunately this may cause problems as the larger tasks may never get completed, as too much time is taken by completing the smaller tasks.

- **Priority**. This is possibly one of the best methods that can be used to determine which process should be run next. But who or what decides the priority of a process? It is well known that users will always believe that their process is more important than anyone else's. Thus there must be some independent method of determining the priority of a process. One of the best methods is to boost the priority of a process if it has not been on the processor for a while, and reduce the priority of a process if it has been given some time on the processor.

Processes often require different processing requirements, such as:

- **Processor I/O burst cycle**. This normally involves a large number of short bursts, along with a number of longer processor bursts.
- **Processor bound**. This involves long processor bursts.
- **I/O bound**. This involves short processor bursts.

A4.2.2   Scheduling algorithms

Every scheduler must be fair in the way that it assigns tasks, much of which should be automatic, and should not require user input. Figure A4.2 outlines some of the main objectives, which are:

Objectives	Description	Scheduler must try to:
Fairness	Each process has a fair share of the processor	Maximize
Efficiency	Efficient use of the processor	Maximize
Throughput	Number of processes completed	Maximize
Turnaround	Time taken for processes to complete	Maximize
Waiting time	Time taken in the queue	Minimize
Predictability	Allowing a dependable response	Maximize
Response time	Time to react to actions	Minimize

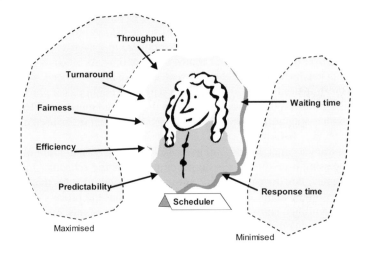

Figure A4.2   Decisions for a scheduler

The two main classifications for scheduling are:

- **Policy**. Sets priority on individual processes.
- **Mechanism**. Implements a scheduling policy.

There are various methods that the scheduler can use to implement a scheduling algorithm:

- **First-Come, First-Served** (FCFS). This type of scheduling is used with non-preemptive operating systems, where the time that a process waits in the queue is totally dependent on the processes which are in front of it, as illustrated in Figure A4.3. The response of the system is thus not dependable.
- **Round Robin** (RR). This is a first-come, first-served schedule with preemption, where each process is given a finite time slice on the processor. The queue is circular, thus when a process has been run, the queue pointer is moved to the next process, as illustrated in Figure A4.4. This is a relatively smooth schedule and gives all processes a share of the processor. As children, we would typically be assigned to things in a round-robin way, especially when there were too many demands on a certain resource, and we did not get enough time on it. A good example is when children want to get access to a bouncy castle, and there is a limit on the number that can be on the castle at any one time. An example schedule might be to allow a child onto the castle for a minute, and then they must come off, and go back to the end of the queue. The next child in the queue can then take their place on the castle, and so on.

Figure A4.3 First come, first served

Figure A4.4 Round robin

- **Shortest-Job-First** (SJF). This is one of the most efficient algorithms, and involves estimating the amount of time that a process will run for, and taking the process which will take the shortest time to complete. A problem for the scheduler is thus to determine the amount of time that the process will take to complete its task. This is not an easy task. For example, let us say that we have four tasks to complete. Task 1 will take 1 hour, task two takes 2 hours, task three will take 3 hours, and finally task four will take 8 hours to complete. We could schedule the task to each get half-an-hour of processing time. Once we have finished this time, we make a decision on what task to do next. Thus within four hours we would have the following:

ROUND ROBIN

Time slot (in half- hour blocks)	Task (remaining time to completion)
1	Task 1 (0:30)
2	Task 2 (1:30)
3	Task 3 (2:30)
4	Task 4 (7:30)
5	Task 1 (**complete**)
6	Task 2 (1:00)
7	Task 3 (2:00)
8	Task 4 (7:00)

It can be seen that we have only completed one task, but if we were to take the shortest-job first, then:

SHORTEST-JOB-FIRST

Time slot (in half-hour blocks)	Task (remaining time to completion)
1	Task 1 (0:30)
2	Task 1 (**complete**)
3	Task 2 (1:30)
4	Task 2 (1:00)

5	Task 2 (0:30)
6	Task 2 (**complete**)
7	Task 3 (2:30)
8	Task 3 (2:00)

We can see that we have now completed two tasks, and we are at the same point as the previous example with Task 3. From a user's point of view, this will be perceived as possibly the most satisfying as more tasks have actually been completed in a shorter time. From a computer system point of view, the user will perceive that the processes are running faster, as they are being completed at a perceived faster rate (although Task 4 is being starved on processing time, in order to achieve this). The only problem is that some of the processes will not make any progress until they are allowed access to the processor. The time remaining in each of the cases will be the same as the first scheme will require a further 10 hours to complete (Task 2 requires 1 hour, Task 3 requires 2 hours and Task 4 requires 7 hours), and the shortest first scheme requires a further 10 hours (Task 3 requires 2 hours and Task 4 requires 8 hours). Thus the shortest-job-first is only perceived to be running tasks faster. Shortest-job-first is very efficient on processor time with batch systems, as batch processes are less susceptible to process starvation.

- **Priority Scheduling**. This type of scheduling assigns each process a priority. It is typically used in general-purpose operating systems (such as Microsoft Windows and UNIX) and can be used with either preemptive or non-preemptive operating systems. The main problem is to assign a priority to each process, where priorities can either be internal or external. Internal priorities relate to measurable system resources, such as time limits, memory requirements, file input/output, and so on. A problem is that some processes might never get the required priority and may never get time on the processor (which leads to process starvation). To overcome this, low-priority waiting processes can have their priority increased, over time (known as ageing).
- **Multilevel Queue Scheduling**. This scheme supports several different queues, and sets priorities for them. For example, a system could run two different queues: foreground (interactive) and background (batch), as illustrated in Figure A4.5. The foreground task could be given a much higher priority over the background task, such as 80%–20%.

Each of the queues can be assigned different priorities. Microsoft Windows runs a preemptive scheme where certain system processes are given a higher priority than other non-system processes. An example priority might be (in order of priority):

1. **System processes**. Top priority. These must have a top priority as the system could act unreliably if they were not executed within a given time.
2. **Interactive processes**. These are processes which require some user input, such as from the keyboard or mouse. It is important that users feel that these processes are running with a high priority, otherwise, they may try to delete them, and try to rerun the process.
3. **Interactive editing processes**. These processes tend to run without user input for long periods, but occasionally require some guidance on how they run.
4. **Batch processes**. Lowest priority. These tend to be less important processes that do not require any user input.

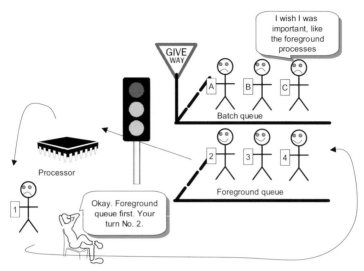

Figure A4.5 Multilevel queue scheduling

- **Multilevel Feedback Queue Scheduling.** This scheme is the most complex, and allows processes to move between a number of different priority queues. Each queue has an associated scheduling algorithm. To support this there must be a way to promote and relegate processes for their current queues.

A4.2.3   Real-time scheduling

Real-time systems normally have key processes which should be serviced before other processors. The two main classifications are:

- **Hard real time.** This is where a critical process is completed within a critical time, and cannot be stored in second memory.
- **Soft real time.** This is where critical processes receive a higher priority than less critical processes. Soft real time can lead to process starvation, and an unfair allocation of system resources. This type of real-time system is typically implemented in systems which require high-speed data transfer, especially in multimedia (such as MPEG movies) and high-speed, processor intensive graphics (such as 3D graphics).

A4.3   Higher-level primitives

Processes often need to identify that they are waiting for another process to give them data or are busy, waiting for some I/O transfer. They must thus support higher-level primitives to identify these. On shared memory systems, the following are used:

- **Semaphores.** This involves setting flags, which allow or bar other processes from getting access to certain resources. An analogy of a semaphore is where two railway trains are using a single-track railway line. When one train enters the single-track line, it sets a semaphore that disallows the other train from entering the track. Once the train on the single track has left the single track, it resets the semaphore flag, which allows the other train to enter the single track.

- **Signals.** Signals are similar to interrupts, but are implemented in software, rather than hardware. This is a primitive interrupt handler and involves a signal handler which controls process signals.

On non-shared memory systems the following are used:

- **Message passing**. Messages are sent between processes, such as SEND and RECEIVE.
- **Pipes**. Pipes allow data to flow from one process to another, in the required way.
- **Remote procedure calls** (RPC).

A4.4   Signals, pipes and task switching (UNIX)

UNIX does not implement a sharing system. In a sharing system, like Microsoft Windows and MAC OS, the operating system only changes to a different process when the current process identifies that it is ready to swap tasks. UNIX implements its scheduling using signals and pipes.

A4.4.1   Signals

UNIX uses signals in a similar way to interrupts, but they are implemented at a higher level. Events rather than hardware devices generate these interrupts. Typically, software interrupt service routines are called on certain signals. The signal handler sets the status of a process, but a process may also put itself in a sleep mode, waiting for a signal. One problem with this is that signals may get lost if they are sent before the process goes into a waiting mode. One solution is to set a flag in the process whenever it receives a signal. The process can then test this flag before it goes into the wait state, if it is set; the wait operation does not block the process.

A4.4.2   Task switching

The dispatcher receives orders from the scheduler as to the processes that are to be run. It is part of the kernel and has privileges on process information. One of its main tasks is to extracts information on the previous state of the process, such as process registers, stack pointers, and so on. It then switches the processor from kernel mode to user mode (enabling the hardware memory protection), and the process begins to run.

A4.4.3   Pipes

Pipes allow data to flow from one process to another, in the required way. Typically, they are implemented with a fixed size storage area (a buffer) in which one process can write to it, while the other reads from it (when the data is available). UNIX implements pipes with a file-like approach, and uses the same system calls to write data to a pipe and read data from a pipe; as those for reading and writing files. Each process that creates a pipe receives two identifiers: one for the reading and one for the writing. Typically, the creating process forks-off two child processes, one of which looks after one end of the pipe, and the other looks after the other end of the pipe. The two child processes can then communicate.

UNIX uses the '|' character to implement the pipe command in the command prompt. For example the 'ps -ef' command shows all the running processes with an identification of the owner of the process. The output of this command can be piped into the grep command to search for any occurrence of the word 'bill', with the following:

```
chimera:~ > ps -ef | grep bill
    bill  2319  2296  1 23:29:42 pts/2     0:00 grep bill
    bill  2296  2294  1 23:28:00 pts/2     0:01 -tcsh
```

Figure A4.6 shows an example of a pipe, and illustrates that pipes can also be implemented on two remote computers. This is normally defined as a connection, and the ends of the pipes, over a connection, are known as sockets.

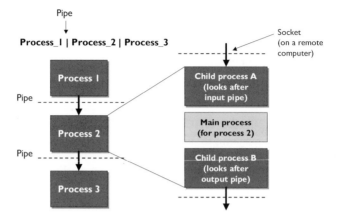

Figure A4.6 Pipes

A4.5 Messages

The best method of interprocess communication is messages, as these allow information on the actual process to be passed between processes. Messages can be of a fixed length, but are most generally of any length, and typically are unstructured. This is the method that Microsoft Windows uses to pass data between processes.

In a message system, each process communicates with a port (or message port), which is a data structure in which messages are sent to. Most systems have a single port, but others can have several message ports. In most cases, the system implements two system calls: SEND and RECEIVE, as illustrated in Figure A4.7.

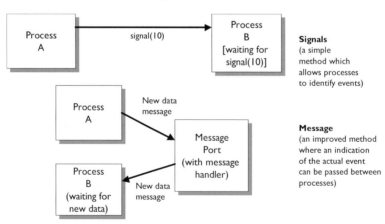

Figure A4.7 Message passing

A4.6   Microsoft Windows scheduling

Scheduling involves determining which thread should be run on the processor at a given time. This element is named a time slice, and its actual value depends on the system configuration. Each thread currently running has a base priority, which is set by the programmer who created the program. It defines how the thread is executed in relation to other system threads, and the thread with the highest priority gets use of the processor.

Microsoft Windows has 32 priority levels. The lowest priority is zero and the highest is 31. A scheduler can change a threads base priority by increasing or decreasing it by two levels, thus changing the thread's priority.

The scheduler is made up of two main parts:

- **Primary scheduler.** This scheduler determines the priority numbers of the threads, which are currently running. It then compares their priority and assigns resources to them, depending on their priority. Threads with the highest priority are executed for the current time slice. When two or more threads have the same priority then the threads are put on a stack. One thread is run and then put to the bottom of the stack, then the next is run and it is put to the bottom, and so on. This continues until all threads with the same priority have been run for a given time slice.
- **Secondary scheduler.** The primary scheduler runs threads with the highest priority, whereas the secondary scheduler is responsible for increasing the priority of non-executing threads (which are all other threads apart from the currently executed thread). It is thus important for giving low priority threads a chance to run on the operating system. Threads which are given a higher or lower priority are:

  o   A thread that is waiting for user input has its priority increased.
  o   A thread that has completed a voluntary wait also has its priority increased.
  o   Threads with a computation-bound thread get their priorities reduced. This prevents the blocking of I/O operations.

Apart from these, all threads get a periodic increase. This prevents lower-priority threads hogging shared resources that are required by higher-priority threads.

A4.7   UNIX process control

UNIX is a multitasking, multi-user operating system, where many tasks can be running at any given time. Typically there are several processes which are started when the computer is rebooted; these are named daemon processes and they run even when there is no user logged into the system, as illustrated in Figure A4.8. Only the system administrator can kill these processes.

UNIX uses special characters (called metacharacters) to define how a process runs, these are:

- **Redirect output.** The '>' operator (greater-than sign) redirects the output from the standard output (normally the user's screen) to another output, such as to a file.
- **Redirect input.** The '<' operator (less-than sign) redirects the input from the standard input (normally the keyboard) to another input, such as from a file.

- **Background task.** The '&' operator (ampersand sign) sends a process into the background. The process will execute quietly while the user conducts another task, and only the output to the console will be seen.
- **Pipe.** The '|' character (vertical bar) is used to pipe data from one process into another.

Some of these operators will be used in the following UNIX sessions.

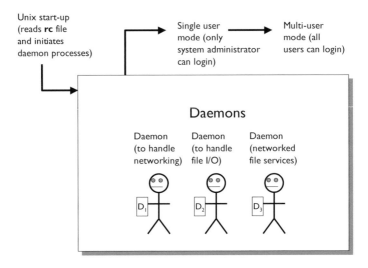

Figure A4.8 Daemon processes

A4.7.1   ps (process status)

The ps command prints information about the current process status. The basic ps list gives a list of the current jobs of the user. An example is given in Sample session A4.1.

📄 **Sample session A4.1**
```
% ps
  PID   TTY   TIME   CMD
   43    01   0:15   csh
   51    01   0:03   ls -R /
  100    01   0:01   ps
```

The information provided gives:

- **PID.** The unique process identification number.
- **TTY.** Every connected computer is identified with a unique name. The TTY name identifies the place at which the process was started.
- **TIME.** Identifies the amount of CPU time that has been used. Typically the format is HH:MM (for min:sec).
- **CMD.** Identifies the actual command line that was used to run the process.

A process can be stopped using the kill command.

A long listing is achieved using the -l option and for a complete listing of all processes on the system the -a option is used, as shown in Sample session A4.2.

Sample session A4.2

```
% ps -al
F S UID PID PPID CPU PRI NICE ADDR SZ WCHAN TTY TIME CMD
1 S 101 43    1   3  30   20   3211 12 33400 01  0:15 csh
1 S 104 44    2   2  27   20   4430 12 51400 04  0:08 sh
1 S 104 76   32   3  30   20   3223 12 33400 04  0:03 vi tmp
1 S 104 89    1   3  30   20  10324 02 44103 04  0:01 ls
1 R 101 99   55  43  52   20   4432 12 33423 01  0:01 ps
```

The main additional columns are:

- **UID.** This identifies the process owner (User ID), which is generated from the value for the user in the /etc/passwd file.
- **PRI.** This is used to define the priority of the process, where the higher the number the lower the priority it has.
- **F.** This identifies the flags that are associated with the process (0 – swapped, 1 – in core, 2 – system process, and so on).
- **STIME.** Start time for the process (the date is printed instead, if the process has been running for more than 24 hours).
- **ADDR.** Memory address of the process.
- **NI.** Nice value, which is used to determine process priority.
- **S.** This identifies the state of the process. An S identifies that the process is sleeping (the system is doing something else); W specifies that the system is waiting for another process to stop and R specifies that the process is currently running. In summary:

  - o **R.** Process is running.
  - o **T.** Process has stopped.
  - o **D.** Process is in disk wait.
  - o **S.** Process is sleeping (that is, less than 20 secs).
  - o **I.** Process is idle (that is, longer than 20 secs).

A4.7.2   kill (send a signal to a process, or terminate a process)

The kill command sends a terminate signal to a process. The general format is:

kill –*sig processid*

The *processid* is the number given to the process by the computer, which can be found by using the ps command. The *sig* value defines the amount of strength that is given to the kill process. A value of 9 is the strongest value, others are: 1 (hang up); 2 (interrupt); 3 (quit); 4 (alarm); 5 (terminate) and 6 (abort). The owner of a process can kill their own processes, but only the system administrator can kill any process.

Sample session A4.3 gives an example session.

A4.7.3   nice (run a command at a low priority)

The nice command runs a command at a low priority. The standard format is as follows:

nice *–number command [arguments]*

The lowest priority is –20 and the default is –10. Sample session A4.4 gives a sample session.

📄 **Sample session A4.3**

```
% ps
   PID   TTY   TIME   CMD
   112   01    1:15   csh
   145   01    0:05   lpr temp.c
   146   01    0:01   ps
% kill -9 145
% ps
   PID   TTY   TIME   CMD
   112   01    1:15   csh
   146   01    0:01   ps
% find / -name "*.c" -print > listing &
% ps
   PID   TTY   TIME   CMD
   112   01    1:15   csh
   177   01    0:03   find -nam
   179   01    0:01   ps
% kill -9 177
```

📄 **Sample session A4.4**

```
% nice -15 ls -al
% nice -20 find / -name "*.c" -print > Clistings &
```

A4.7.4   at (execute commands at later date)

The at command, when used in conjunction with another command, executes a command at some later time. The standard format is:

at *time [date] [week]*

where *time* is given using from 1 to 4 digits, followed by either 'a', 'p', 'n' or 'm' for am, pm, noon or midnight, respectively. If no letters are given then a 24-hour clock is assumed. A 1- or 2-digit time is assumed to be given in hours, whereas a 3- or 4-digit time is assumed to be hours and minutes. A colon may also be included to separate the hours from the minutes.

The *Date* can be specified by the month followed by the day-of-the-month number, such as Mar 31. A *Week* can be given instead of the day and month. Sample session A4.5 shows a session where a program is compiled at quarter past eight at night.

📄 **Sample session A4.5**

```
%   at 20:15
    cc - test test.c
    ^D
    520776201.a at Tue May 26 20:15:00 1997
```

---

and to send fred a message at 14:00:

📄 **Sample session A4.6**
```
%  at 14:00
    echo "Time for a tea-break" | mail fred
    ^D
    520777201.a at Mon Jun 4 14:00:00 1989
```

To remove all files with the .o extensions from the current directory on September 9th at 1 noon.

📄 **Sample session A4.7**
```
% at 1n sep 9
    rm *.o
    ^D
    520778201.a at Sat Sep 9 13:00:00 1989
```

To list all jobs that are waiting to be executed at some later time use the -l option.

📄 **Sample session A4.8**
```
% at -l
    520776201.a  Mon Jun 4 20:15:00 1989
    520778201.a  Sat Sep 9 13:00:00 1989
    520777201.a  Mon Jun 4 14:00:00 1989
```

To remove jobs from the schedule the -r option can be used, giving the job number.

📄 **Sample session A4.9**
```
% at -r 520777201.a
```

A4.8   Microsoft Windows task manager

Windows uses the Task Manager to show the currently running processes, and, if required, stopping them. It can be called by pressing Ctrl-Alt-Del and then selecting Task Manager. Figure A4.9 shows an example of some processes running. The window icon with gray indicates a program, and a window icon with white indicates a status window. The open file icon indicates an open folder.

The processes window (as shown in Figure A4.9) gives an indication of:

- **Image name.** Name of the process.
- **PID.** Process Identification.
- **CPU Time.** Total time that the process has used the processor.
- **Memory usage.** Total memory usage.

A4.9   Finite-state machines

Finite-state machines (FSM) are at the heart of most computer systems. They define the system as a finite number of states, each of which is linked by a series of events. Often complex systems can be easily modeled in this way. Figure A4.10 shows an example of a FSM for a traffic light controller. The system is started in State 1 (Red light ON, and Don't Walk ON, which is a safe starting state). After this, the system then goes from State 2 to State 3 and to State 4 (with a finite time delay between each state). When leaving State 4, the system goes back to either State 1 if the pedestrian button has not been pressed, or State 5, if it has been pressed. If the system goes into State 5, the traffic light goes to RED and the Don't Walk is still ON. Next, in State 6, the pedestrian light goes to Walk, and so on. Unfortunately, there is no state for a safe start-up (traffic lights OFF) and a shutdown state. Figure A4.11 overcomes this, with a safe shutdown from State 1. Only in State 1 can the system be shutdown (as it is unsafe to shut it down in any other state).

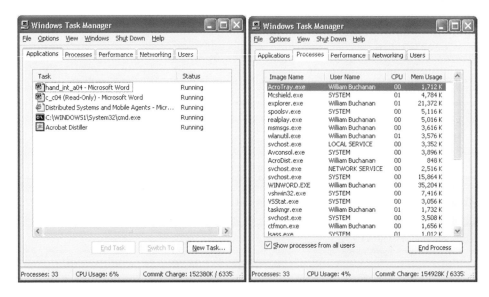

Figure A4.9 Applications and Processes

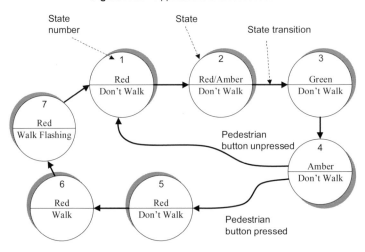

Figure A4.10 State transition for a traffic light controller

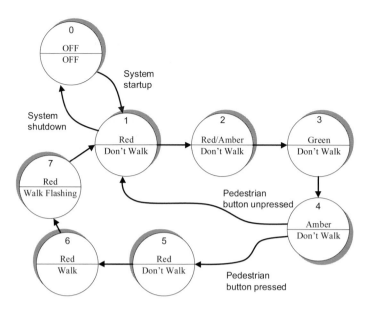

Figure A4.11 State transition for a traffic light controller with start-up/shutdown state

A5 Distributed processing

A5.1 Introduction

The previous chapter covered running processing on a local machine within a multitasking environment. With the advent of networking and the Internet, it is now possible to distribute processing over a network. An extreme example involves The National Foundation for Cancer Research (NFCR) Centre for Drug Discovery in the Department of Chemistry at the University of Oxford, England. They are working on a project that uses the CPU time of users on the Internet, when a registered computer uses their screen saver (http://www.ud.com). The program that runs on the computer is one that searches for new drugs in the treatment of cancer. By July 2001, this program had achieved 213,568,434 hours of CPU time using over 760,000 devices. This has achieved one of the world's largest computers. Most people understand the concept of not using up available local memory, or disk resources, or even network capacity, but one of the largest underutilized resources is CPU time. Many computers, especially in the office, lie idle for many hours in the day. These computers could easily be performing other tasks, such as providing solutions to state-of-the-art research projects.

A good example of a centralized system against a distributed system is in the banking industry. Figure A5.1 shows how a bank might want to organize its business. In this case, it devolves decision-making, account management and logistics to regional offices, which then devolves these to local offices. This allows for a distribution of the activities, and, for example, a holiday in one regional area will not affect the rest of the business. If the bank had a centralized model, all the customers, staff and logistics would be centralized in a single place. This would obviously be inefficient and would cause a great deal of strain on the central site. It would also not be possible to set-up an efficient system so that every customer would be able to withdraw cash from the central site. A more efficient model is to use ATMs distributed to local offices. Most governments around the world operate with this distributed model, where the central government creates the rules and policies, which are then distributed on a regional basis with regional councils. These are then passed onto local councils, which implement the policies. A centralized government would create all the policies and then decide how these would be implemented, and thus would be in total control of its implementation.

Distributed processing has many advantages over localized processing, especially in:

- **Using specialized resources**, which would not normally be accessible from a local computer, such as enhanced processing or increased amount of memory storage.
- **Using parallel processing**, where a problem is split into a number of parallel tasks, which are distributed over the network.
- **Reducing the loading on the local computer**, as tasks can be processed on remote computers.

One of the most common mechanisms for running remote processes over a network is RPC (Remote Procedure Call). With this, an RPC server waits for a request from a client. When it receives one, it runs a specified process and returns the results to the client, as illustrated in Figure A5.2.

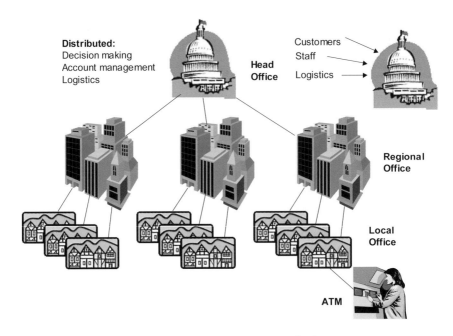

Figure A5.1 Distributed v. centralized

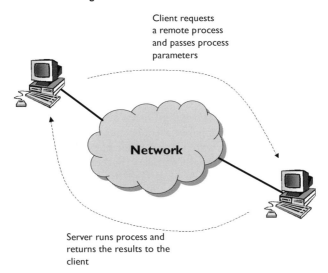

Figure A5.2 Distributed processing

Some processes can be distributed over a network, while others need to be run locally. The main criterion for determining if a process can be distributed is the communications overhead. If the communications channel is relatively slow compared with the speed of processing the task, the distribution of the processing can be inefficient. One great advantage of distributing processes is when processing moves from a server to a client. This allows the server to perform high-level operations, while the client does most of the processing. An example of distributing a process is when a user runs a word processor from a server. The files that are executed reside on the server, but the actual running of the program occurs on the client.

A5.2 Interprocess communication

Interprocess communication (IPC) is a set of interfaces that allow programmers to communicate between processes, and allow programs to run concurrently. Figure A5.3 illustrates some of the methods, these include:

- **Pipes.** Pipes allow data to flow from one process to another, and have a common process origin. Data only flows in the one direction, typically from the output of one process to the input of another. The data from the output is buffered until the input process receives it. In UNIX the single vertical bar character (|) is used to represent a pipe, and operates in a similar way to a pipe system call in a program. Two-way communication can be constructed with two pipes, one for each direction.
- **Named pipe.** A named pipe uses a pipe which has a specific name for the pipe. Unlike unnamed pipes, a named pipe can be used in processes that do not have a shared common process origin. Typically a named pipe is known as a FIFO (first in, first out), as the data written to a pipe is read in the order that it was written to.
- **Message queuing.** Message queues allow processes to pass messages between themselves, using either a single message queue or several message queues. The system kernel manages each message queue, and puts messages on the queue which identify the message (message type). Messages can vary in length and be assigned different types or usages. The queues can be created by one process and used by multiple processes that read and/or write messages to the queue. Application programs (or their processes) create message queues and can send and receive messages using an application program interface (API).
- **Semaphores.** These will be discussed later in this chapter, and are used to synchronize events between processes. Semaphores are integer values that are greater than or equal to zero. A zero value puts a process to sleep, while a non-zero value causes a sleeping process to awaken (when certain operations are performed). A signal is sent to a semaphore when an event occurs which then increments the semaphore.
- **Shared memory.** Shared memory allows processes to interchange data through a defined area of memory. For example, one process could write to an area of memory and another could read from it. To do this the writing process must check to see if the reading process is actually reading from the memory, at the same time, and vice versa. If this is occurring, the other process must wait for the other process to complete. This is implemented using semaphores, where only one process is allowed to access the memory at a time.
- **Sockets.** These are typically used to communicate over a network, between a client and a server (although peer-to-peer connections are also possible). Sockets are end points of a connection, and allow for a standard connection that is independent of the type of computer and its operating system.

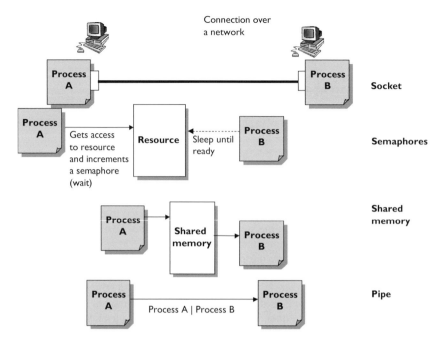

Figure A5.3 IPC methods

A5.3   Flags and semaphores

Flags are simple variables which take on a binary state (0 or a 1), and are used to identify that an event has occurred, or to pass binary information. Semaphores are positive integer values which can take on any range of values, but can also be binary values (for mutual exclusion applications). An example of using a semaphore is when a process uses a resource, and sets a semaphore flag to indicate that it is currently accessing the resource. Any device, which then accesses the resource while the semaphore flag was set, will know that the resource is still being used, and must thus wait until the flag is unset. Semaphores were initially developed by Dijkstra and are implemented in IPC. Two common uses of semaphores are:

- **Memory**. This allows processes to share a common area of memory.
- **File access**. This allows processes to share access to files.

A semaphore could simply be a memory location in which processes go to and test the value. If the semaphore is set to a given value, a process may have to sleep until the value is changed to a value which allows orderly access to the resource. Semaphores can also be used to define *critical code regions*. These are parts of a process which must wait for code in another process to complete. A practical example of this is when we imagine two trains (two processes) approaching a region of single-track rail. For safety considerations there must only be one train on the single-track line, at a time. The trains must then have some way of signaling to the other train that they are now on the track. A signal (the semaphore) could be set up so that it is set to either a red or a green light at the entrance of the track. When a train enters the track, the signal will change to red, and stops any other trains from entering the track. When it has left the track the signal will be set to green, and the other train can enter the track. In software terms, the trains could be processes which require exclusive access to a resource. When one of the processes gets access to it, all other processes must wait for the resource to be released.

Most operating systems run more than one process at a time (using time multiplexing). This can cause many problems, especially in synchronizing activities and allowing multiple processes access to shared resources. Semaphores can overcome these problems, as they are operating system variables that each process can check and change, if required. They are basically a counter value which can be zero or positive, but never negative. There are only two operations on the semaphore:

- **UP** (signal). Increments the semaphore value, and, if necessary, wakes up a process which is waiting on the semaphore. This is achieved in a single operation, to avoid conflicts.
- **DOWN** (wait). Decrements the semaphore value. If the counter is zero there is no decrement. Processes are blocked until the counter is greater than zero.

Figure A5.4 shows an example of two processes running with mutually exclusive code. Each piece of protected code is surrounded with a `wait()` at the start and a `signal()` at the end. The `wait()` operation decrements the semaphore value (which has an initial value of 1), and the `signal()` operation increments the semaphore value. Process A is the first process to execute the mutually exclusive code, and decrements the semaphore so that it is zero. When Process B tries the wait, it tests the semaphore, and since it is zero, the process will go into sleep mode. It will not waken until Process A has executed the `signal()` operation. When Process B is awoken it executes the `wait()` which sets the semaphore to 1, thus Process A cannot execute the mutually exclusive code. When finished, Process B will set the semaphore back to a 1 with the `signal()`.

A5.3.1 Semaphore values

A signal is like a software interrupt, and can be viewed as a flag, as it does not give any indication on the number of events that have occurred, it is only possible to know that it has occurred. Whereas, a semaphore can be regarded as a generalized signal, which has an integer counter to record the number of signals that have occurred. Processes can put themselves to sleep while waiting for a signal.

Semaphores are operated on by signal and wait operations. A wait operation decrements the value of a semaphore and a signal operation increments it. The initial value of a semaphore identifies the number of waits which may be performed on the semaphore. Thus:

$$V = I - W + S$$

where I is the initial value of the semaphore.

            W is the number of completed wait operations performed on the semaphore.

            S is the number of signal operations performed on it.

            V is the current value of the semaphore (which must be greater than or equal to zero).

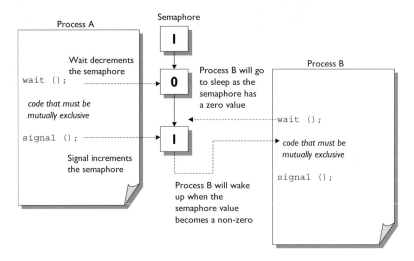

Figure A5.4 Example usage of semaphore in mutually exclusive code

As $V \geq 0$, then $I - W + S \geq 0$, which gives:

$$I + S \geq W$$

or

$$W \leq I + S$$

Thus, the number of wait operations must be less than or equal to the initial value of the semaphore, plus the number of signal operations. A binary semaphore will have an initial value of 1 ($I = 1$), thus:

$$W \leq S + 1$$

In mutual exclusion, waits always occur before signals, as waits happen at the start of a critical piece of code, with a signal at the end of it. The above equations state that no more than one wait may run to completion before a signal has been performed. Thus, no more than one process may enter the critical section at a time, as required.

A5.3.2 P and V operations

A simple process can either be in RUNNING, SLEEPING or WAKEUP mode. A process is put to sleep if it is waiting for a resource which is currently being used by another process. When the resource is released, and no other processes need to access the resource, a sleeping process can be sent a WAKEUP, where it will reactivate itself. Semaphores with a value of zero can identify that there are no processes waiting on a resource, and the process can gain access to it. A positive value can then identify that there are a number of wakeups pending.

Two operations, P and V, are generalizations of SLEEP and WAKEUP and can be used to operate on the semaphore as follows:

- P operation (the DOWN operation). This checks the semaphore, and if the value of the semaphore is greater than zero, it decrements its value. A zero value puts the process to sleep without completing the P operation.
- V operation (the UP operation). This increments a referenced semaphore, and identifies that there are one or more processes that require some processing time (as they have been put to sleep with an earlier P operation). A sleeping process is chosen at random, and is allowed to complete a P operation.

There must be no interrupts when checking a semaphore, changing a semaphore and waking up a process, and it must be done in a single indivisible operation (an atomic action). This overcomes timing hazards (see Section A5.3.3) as no other process can get access to the semaphore until the process has completed or is blocked.

A5.3.3   Producer–consumer problem

The producer–consumer problem involves two processes sharing a common, fixed-size buffer. The producer puts information into the buffer, and the consumer process reads and removes information from the buffer. This is an exclusion problem as the consumer could be reading the buffer when the producer tries to write to the buffer. The solution to this is to put the producer to sleep when the consumer is reading and removing the data from the buffer, and then is awoken when complete. When the consumer wants to read and remove the data, and the producer is writing to the buffer, it must go to sleep, and then is awoken when the producer is finished.

Program A5.1 shows an example program. There can be a number of items in the buffer, which is identified with a variable called `buffer_count`, and the maximum number of items that can be stored in the buffer is MAX_BUFF. In the program, the producer keeps filling the buffer with data. When, if ever, the buffer is full it will go to sleep (if `(buffer_count== MAX_BUFF) sleep();`). It will then wait on the consumer to wake it up when it has read at least one item from the buffer (if `(buffer_count==MAX_BUFF-1) wakeup (producer_buffer);`). The consumer goes to sleep when there are no items in the buffer (if `(buffer_count==0) sleep();`), and will be woken-up when the producer has put at least one item in the buffer (if `(buffer_count==1) wakeup(consumer);`).

Unfortunately there is a timing problem in the code. This can happen with an empty buffer and when the operating system scheduler has just run the consumer but stops it before it can check the empty buffer. The scheduler then runs the producer which then adds an item to the buffer, and thinks that the consumer should be sleeping (as the buffer was empty). This signal will be lost on the consumer, as it is not sleeping. When the scheduler runs the consumer again, it will have an incorrect count value of zero, as it has already checked the count, and will thus go to sleep. The producer will thus not wake the consumer up, as the producer will fill the buffer up, and then go to sleep. Both consumer and producer will be sleeping, awaiting the other to wake them up. One solution to this is to have a bit which defines that there is a wake up waiting, which is set by a process which is still awake. If the process then tries to go to sleep, it cannot, as the wake up-waiting bit is set. The process would thus stay awake, and reset the wake up-waiting bit.

📖 Program A5.1

```
#define MAX_BUFF 100        /* maximum items in buffer         */
int buffer_count=0;         /* current number of items in buffer  */

int main(void)
{
   /* producer_buffer();  on the producer */
   /* consumer_buffer();  on the consumer */
}
void producer_buffer(void)
{
   while (TRUE) {                        /* Infinite loop           */
   put_item();                          /* Put item                */
   if (buffer_count==MAX_BUFF) sleep(); /* Sleep, if buffer full   */
   enter_item();                        /* Add item to buffer      */
   buffer_count = buffer_count + 1;     /* Increment number of
                                           items in the buffer     */
   if (buffer_count==1) wakeup(consumer); /*was buffer empty?      */
   }
}
void consumer_buffer(void)
{
   while (TRUE) {                        /* Infinite loop           */
   if (buffer_count==0) sleep();        /* Sleep, if buffer empty  */
   get_item();                          /* Get item                */
   buffer_count = buffer_count - 1;     /* Decrement number of
                                           items in the buffer     */
   if (buffer_count==MAX_BUFF-1) wakeup(producer_buffer);
                                        /* if buffer not full
                                           anymore, wake up producer */
   consume_item();                      /*remove item              */
   }
}
```

A5.3.4 Deadlock

Deadlock is a serious problem when running processes in both a local and a distributed system. It occurs when a process is waiting for an event that will never occur. This typically occurs when:

- **Resource locking.** This is where a process is waiting for a resource which will never become available. Some resources are pre-emptive, where processes can release their access on them, and give other processes a chance to access them. Others, though, are non-pre-emptive, and processes are given full rights to them. No other processes can then get access to them until the currently assigned process is finished with them. An example of this is with the transmission and reception of data on a communication system. It would not be a good idea for a process to send some data that required data to be received, in return, to yield to another process which also wanted to send and receive data. The non-pre-emptive resources would thus be locked so that no other processes could access them. This can cause a problem when the resource which is accessing the resource never gets the event which will release the lock, or if the process crashes. Many examples of resource locking relate to the physical access for users. A good example is when a user is writing to a CD drive (with a writeable CD). It would not make any sense if the current session was interrupted, and another user was allowed to use it, as the CD would have to be changed for the new user, and then changed back again for the other user. This would continue, as the time on the resource would share.

Obviously, the reading of data from a CD-ROM drive could be shared, if the users were both using the CD-ROM disk.

- **Starvation.** This is where other processes are run, and the deadlocked process is not given enough time to catch the required event. This can occur when processes have a low priority compared with other ones, as higher priority tasks tend to have a better chance to access the required resources.

A5.3.5 Deadlock

We have all seen deadlock occurring in real life, especial with automobiles. Figure A5.5 illustrates a typical case of deadlock. In this case two cars are blocking the junction (at A and D), and do not allow any of the other cars behind them to move. Unfortunately, both automobiles cannot move as there are automobiles blocking their entry into the junction. The only way to clear the deadlock, apart from the two cars that are turning into the junctions to give up and go straight ahead, is for one of the automobiles which is blocking one of the junctions to reverse. Unfortunately, in this case, they cannot, as there are automobiles behind them. This is a deadly embrace. In resource terms, both of the car lanes of the main road has one of the junctions, and requires the other, but none of the car lanes can give their lane up.

In process terms, resource deadlock occurs when Process 1 holds Resource A, and Process 2 holds Resource B, but Process 1 wants to gain access to Resource B, and vice-versa. Each process then waits for the other to yield their exclusive access to their resource. This is a deadly embrace. A typical problem can occur when data buffers can become full. For example a print spooler can be setup so that it must receive the full contents of a print file, before it will actually send it to the printer. If print buffer is receiving print data from several sources, it can fill up the buffer before any of the print jobs have completed. The only way round this problem would be to increase the data buffer size, which can be difficult.

The four conditions that must hold for deadlock to occur are:

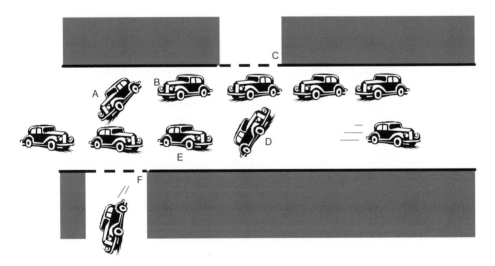

Figure A5.5 Deadlock on a road junction

- **Mutual exclusion condition.** This is where processes get exclusive control of required resources, and will not yield the resource to any other process.
- **Wait for condition.** This is where processes keep exclusive control of acquired resources while waiting for additional resources.
- **No preemption condition.** This is where resources cannot be removed from the processes which have gained them, until they have completed their access on them.
- **Circular wait condition.** This is a circular chain of processes on which each process holds one or more resources that are requested by the next process in the chain.

In our example of deadlock in Figure A5.5, we can see that this passes all of these conditions. A car blocking the junction defines mutual exclusion, and since the cars cannot move away from the junction (in the deadlock case), there will be a condition for wait and preemption. As both automobile lanes are waiting for each other, we have a circular wait. Note that deadlock may occur very infrequently, but when it does occur, it normally requires some form of user input, to try to recover the situation. In the case of the automobile deadlock, we would need someone to make directions as to the best plan to overcome the deadlock (possibly, a traffic police officer).

A5.3.6 Deadlock avoidance

If possible, processes should run without the problem of deadlock, as systems normally require a reboot to clear the problem. One of the best-known avoidance algorithms is the Banker algorithm, which tries to avoid deadlock by estimating the amount of a given resource that processes are likely to require, in order to run to completion. It is typically applied to define the amount of resources of the same type, but can be extended to resource pools with differing resource types. In our automobile deadlock, we could have applied the same principle, in that an automobile is not allowed to turn to go into the junction, unless both junctions can be cleared. Thus if one automobile could not get into the junction, then the other automobile who wants to turn into the other junction would not be allowed to enter the junction, and would have to proceed without turning into the junction. For example let's say that A is allowed to wait at the junction, while there is an automobile waiting at junction F. It will be allowed to do this, as deadlock will be avoided if there is no automobile turning at D. If this continues, but an automobile now requested to turn into C, and its path is blocked, then it will not be allowed to do this as it can cause deadlock.

In the Banker algorithm, the operating system has a number of resources of a given type (N), which are allocated a number of users (M). The operating system is told by each process the maximum number of resources that it requires (n), which must be less than N. The operating system gives access to one of the resources of a process, one at a time. Thus processes can be guaranteed access to one of the resources within a given time. A safe condition is when one of the processes can complete with the amount of resources that are left unallocated. For example, if the operating system allocated memory to processes, and the operating system has a total of 100 MB (N = 100), with four processes currently running (M = 4). Each process tells the operating system about the maximum amount of memory that it will require (n). Processes must then ask the operating system for an allocation of the resources. The algorithm then checks to see if there is enough allocation left, after the new allocation has been granted, and that at least one of the processes with allocated resources can complete, even if it asks for its maximum allocation. The best way to illustrate this is with an example:

Process A requires a maximum of 50 MB.
Process B requires a maximum of 40 MB.
Process C requires a maximum of 60 MB.
Process D requires a maximum of 40 MB.

The current state would be safe:

Process	Current allocation	Maximum allocation required
A	40	50
B	20	40
C	20	60
D	10	40
Resource unallocated	10	

This is safe as Process A can still complete, as there is still 10 MB to be allocated. This will be enough to complete this process, but no other processes would be given any more resources as all of the unallocated memory must be reserved for Process A. Process B possibly requires another 20 MB, Process C also possibly requires another 40 MB, and Process D possibly requires another 30 MB.

An unsafe condition would be:

Process	Current allocation	Maximum allocation required
A	15	50
B	30	40
C	40	60
D	10	40
Resource unallocated	5	

This is unsafe as there is only 5 MB of memory left, and this is not enough for any of the processes to complete. Thus, we can have deadlock (unless a process is willing to give up its memory allocation). The operating system would reject any allocation which took it into the unsafe region. In summary the algorithm assumes:

- Each resource has exclusive access to resources that have been granted to it.
- Allocation is only granted if there is enough allocation left for at least one process to complete, and release its allocated resources.
- Processes which have a rejection on a requested resource must wait until some resources have been released, and that the allocated resource must stay in the safe region.

The main problems with the Banker algorithm are:

- Requires processes to define their maximum resource requirement.
- Requires the system to define the maximum amount of a resource.
- Requires a maximum amount of processes.
- Requires that processes return their resources in a finite time.
- Processes must wait for allocations to become available. A slow process may stop many other processes from running as it hogs the allocation.

A5.3.7 Deadlock detection and recovery

The main technique that is used to detect a deadlocked situation is the existence of a circular wait. This detection process has a time overhead on the operation system, but the operating system can try and release deadlocked resources, rather than the user rebooting the system. A typical technique is to use resource allocation graphs, which indicate resource allocations and requests. An arrow from a process to a resource maps the request currently under consideration, and an arrow from a resource to a process indicates the resource has been allocated to that process. Squares represent processes, large circles represent classes of identical devices, and small circles drawn inside large circles indicate the number of identical devices of each class. This graph can be used to determine the processes that can complete their execution and the processes that will remain deadlocked. The graph will reduce for a process when all the requests have been granted, and will release the resources. If a graph cannot be reduced for a set of processes, deadlock occurs.

To undeadlock a system, one of the four deadlock conditions must be broken. This normally involves determining the deadlocked processes (which is often a difficult task). Once identified it is often necessary to kill one or more of the deadlocked processes, and release the resources which are allocated to it. The released resources will hopefully be released to the currently deadlocked processes, which can then complete successfully.

Memory allocation can cause a good deal of contention problems, especially if the system has a limited amount of memory that can be allocated. Most systems now operate a virtual memory system, where the storage memory of the system is used as additional memory over the physical memory. Unfortunately, many systems use up their spare capacity, and the virtual memory system become limited. Thus processes which are currently running may not be able to complete, as there is a limit on the amount of allocatable memory. Thus some prediction on the maximum requirements of a process is useful in predicting how easy it will be to complete a process.

A5.4 RPC

Remote processing has many advantages over local processing, especially as it removes the loading on the local computer. In an attempt to standardize the protocol used to communicate and initiate remote processes, Sun Microsystems Inc. developed Remote Procedure Control (RPC), which has since been standardized in the RFC1050 document. It defines:

- **Servers**. This is software which implements the network services.
- **Services**. This is a collection of one or more remote programs.
- **Programs**. These implement one or more remote procedures.
- **Procedures**. These define the procedures, the parameters and the results of the RPC operation.
- **Clients**. This is the software that initiates remote procedure calls to services.
- **Versions**. This allows servers to implement different versions of the RPC software, in order to support previous versions.

Remote Procedure Call (RPC) provides the ability for clients to transparently execute procedures on remote systems of the network. RPC fits into the session layer of the OSI model (this model will be covered in more detail in a later chapter), as illustrated in Figure A5.6. This has the advantage of being able to communicate with most transport and network layer protocols, such as TCP/IP, UDP/IP or SPX/IPX. Typically, though, it uses TCP/IP as the transport/network layer, as this allows for reliable communications. TCP/IP itself allows for a virtual connection between two hosts and the data is checked for errors, whereas UDP/IP does not setup a connection, and does not provide any guarantee that the data has been received correctly by the session layer of the OSI model.

In a local procedure call model, a calling program inserts parameters into a predefined location, and then transfers control to the procedure, which reads the parameters from the predefined location. Eventually the calling procedure will regain control, and reads from a predefined location for the results of the called procedure. An RPC is similar to this, with a calling process on the client, and a server process on the server. The operation of the client and server is illustrated in Figure A5.7, and is as follows:

- The caller process sends a call message, with all the procedure's parameters, to the server process and waits for a reply message.
- On the arrival of a call message the server process extracts the procedure's parameters, and wakes up a dormant process, which is then run with the required parameters.
- After the process has completed, the server sends a reply message with the procedure's results. Once the reply message is received, the results of the procedure are extracted, and caller's execution is resumed.
- The server process then waits, dormant, for the next call message.

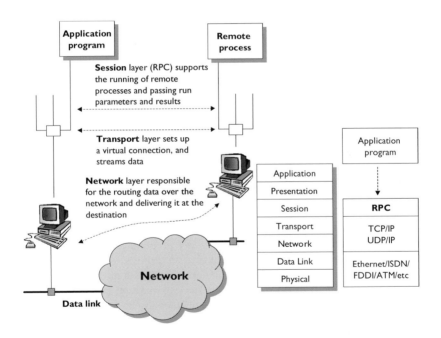

Figure A5.6 OSI model with RPC

A5.4.1 Transports, semantics and authentication

RPC does not provide any form of reliability, as it assumes that the protocol used to transmit and receive it is reliable, which is the reason that TCP/IP is typically used, as it provides for reliable transmissions. There may be several requests from a client to a server at a time, thus each client request has a transaction ID, which is used by the client to keep track of requests. Transaction IDs do not have to be unique and can be used with different requests (obviously, the previous request would have to be completed, before the same ID is used again). The server has no choice on the ID, and must only use it to identify its response to the client.

An important part of RPC is authentication, as a server would be open to abuse if any client was allowed to remotely run processes on it. This is a typical attack on a system, and, if too many processes are run on a computer, it will eventually grind to a halt, and typically requires to be rebooted. RPC supports various different types of authentication protocols.

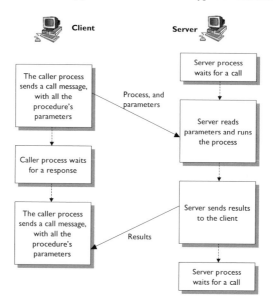

Figure A5.7   Operation of RPC

A5.4.2   RPC protocol

The RPC protocol provides:

- A unique specification of the called procedure.
- A mechanism for matching response parameters with request messages.
- Authentication of both callers and servers. The call message has two authentication fields (the credentials and verifier), and the reply message has one authentication field (the response verifier).
- Protocol errors/messages (such as incorrect versions, errors in procedure parameters, indication on why a process failed and reasons for incorrect authentication).

RPC has three unsigned fields which uniquely identify the called procedure:

- **Remote program number.** These are numbers which are defined by a central authority (like Sun Microsystems).

- **Remote program version number.** This defines the version number, and allows for migration of the protocol, where older versions are still supported. Different versions can possibly support different message calls. The server must be able to cope with this.
- **Remote procedure number.** This identifies the called procedure, and is defined in the specification of the specific program's protocol. For example, file service may define that an 8 defines a read operation and a 10 defines a write operation.

The reply message can give some indication of the cause of an error, including:

- Version number not supported. The returned message contains the upper and lower version of the version number that is supported.
- Remote program is not available on the remote system.
- Requested procedure number does not exist.
- Parameters passed are incorrect.

The RPC message has the following format:

- Message type. This is either CALL (0) or REPLY (1).
- Message status. There are two different message status fields, depending on whether it is a CALL or a REPLY. These are:
  - CALL.   Followed by a field which gives the status of: SUCCESS (executed successfully – 0), PROG_UNAVAIL (remote does not support the requested program – 1), PROG_MISMATCH (cannot support version – 2), PROC_UNAVAIL (procedure unavailable – 3).
  - REPLY.   Followed by MSG_ACCEPTED (0) and MSG_DENIED (1). If the message was denied the field following defines the reason, such as: RPC_MISMATCH (Version mismatch – 0) or AUTH_ERROR (cannot authenticate the caller – 1).

Call messages then have:

- Rpcvers. RPC version number (unsigned integer).
- Prog, vers and proc. Specifies the remote program, its version number and the procedure within the remote program (all unsigned integers).
- Cred. authentication credentials.
- Verf. authentication verifier.
- Procedure specific parameters.

A5.4.3 RPC authentication

Authentication is important as it should authenticate both the caller and the server, as this bars invalid callers from getting access to the server, and vice versa. The call message has two authentication fields (the credentials and verifier), and the reply message has one authentication field (the response verifier). This can either be:

- **No authentication** (AUTH_NULL). No authentication is made when callers do not know who they are or when the server does not care who the caller is. This type of method would be used on a system that did not have external connections to networks, and assumes that all the callers are valid.

- **Unix authentication** (AUTH_UNIX). Unix authentication uses the Unix authentication system, which generates a data structure with a stamp (an arbitrary ID which the caller machine may generate), machine name (such as 'Apollo'), UID (caller's effective user ID), GID (the caller's effective group ID) and GIDS (an array of groups which contain the caller as a member).
- **Short authentication** (AUTH_SHORT).
- **DES authentication** (AUTH_DES). Unix authentication suffers from two problems: the naming is too Unix oriented and there is no verifier (so credentials can easily be faked). DES overcomes this by addressing the caller using its network name (such as 'unix.111@mycomputer.net') instead of by an operating system specific integer. These network names are unique on the Internet. For example unix.111@mycomputer.net identifies user ID number 111 on the mycomputer.net system.

Apart from providing a unique network name, DES authentication also provides authentication of the client, and vice versa. It does this by the client generating a 128-bit DES key which is passed to the server in the first RPC call. In any communications, the client then reads the current time, and encrypts it with the key. The server will then be able to decrypt the encrypted timestamp, as it knows the encryption key. If the decrypted timestamp is close to the current time, then the server knows that the client must be valid. Thus, it is important that both the client and server keep the correct time (perhaps by consulting an Internet Time Server at regular intervals). After the initial timestamp has been validated, the server then authenticates following timestamps so that they have a later time than the previous timestamp and that the timestamp has not expired. This timestamp window is defined in the first RPC call, and thus defines the lifetime of the conversation.

The server authenticates itself to the client by sending back the encrypted timestamp it received from the client, minus one second. If the client gets anything different than this, it will reject it.

A5.4.4 RPC programming

Distributed programming is an art that should produce robust and reliable problems, as many programs provide a foundation for many other programs. The level of control depends on how well the programmer wants to control the operation of the remote process control. For this RPC defines three main layers:

- **Highest layer.** At this level the calls are totally transparent to the operating system, the computer type and the network. With this the programmer simply calls the required library routine, and does not have to worry about any of the underlying computer type, operating system or networking. For example, the `rnusers` routine returns the number of users on a remote computer (as given in Program A5.2).
- **Middle layer.** At this level the programmer does not have to worry about the network connection (such as the TCP sockets), the UNIX system, or other low-level implementation mechanisms. It just makes a remote procedure call to routines on other computers, and is the most common implementation as it gives increased amount of control over the RPC call. These calls are made with: `registerrpc` (which obtains a unique system-wide procedure identification number); `callrpc` (which executes a remote procedure call); and `svc_run`. The middle layer, in some more complex applications, does not allow for timeout specifications, choice of transport, UNIX process control, or error flexibility in case of errors. If these are required, the lower layer is used.

- **Lowest layer.** At this level there is full control over the RPC call, and this can be used to create robust and efficient connections.

At the highest layer the programmer simply uses a call to the RCP library. In UNIX, this library is typically named `librpcsvc.a`, and the program is compiled with:

```
cc progname.c -l lrpcsvc
```

📖 **Program A5.2**

```
#include <stdio.h>
int main(int argc, char *argv[])
{
  int users;
  if (argc != 2) {
    fprintf(stderr, "Use: rnusers hostname\n");
    return(1);
  }
  if ((users = rnusers(argv[1])) < 0) {
    fprintf(stderr, "Error: rnusers\n");
    exit(-1);
  }
  printf("There are %d users on %s\n", users, argv[1]);
  return(0);
}
```

Example RPC server library routines are:

- `rnusers`. Returns number of users on remote machine.
- `rusers`. Returns information about users on remote machine.
- `havedisk`. Determines if remote machine has a disk.
- `rstats`. Gets performance data from remote kernel.
- `rwall`. Writes to specified remote machines.
- `yppasswd`. Updates user password in Yellow Pages.

At the next level, the middle layer, the programmer has more control over the RPC call using `callrpc` and `registerrpc`. Program A5.3 determines the number of remote users, and uses the `callrpc` routine which has the following parameters:

argv(1)	Remote server name
RUSERSPROG	Program
RUSERSVERSION	Version
RUSERSPROCVAL	Procedure number. Together with the program and version numbers, this defines the procedure to be called.
xdr_void	Defines the data type for the next argument (which is the parameter to be sent to the remote procedure). As there are no arguments to be sent the data type is void. Other XDR types for basic data types are: `xdr_bool`, `xdr_char`, `xdr_u_char`, `xdr_enum`, `xdr_int`, `xdr_u_int`, `xdr_long`, `xdr_u_long`, `xdr_short`, `xdr_u_short` and `xdr_wrapstring`.

0	An argument to be encoded and passed to the remote procedure.
xdr_u_long	Defines the return type for next variable to be a long integer (users).
&users	Pointer to the users variable, in which the number of users is returned to.

If the routine is successful the returned value will be zero, otherwise it will contain a status value, which is defined in clnt.h.

📖 **Program A5.3**

```
#include <stdio.h>
#include <rpc.h>
#define RUSERSPROG       10002 /* Program number   */
#define RUSERSVERSION    2     /* Version number   */
#define RUSERPROCVAL     1     /* Procedure number */
int main(int argc, char *argv[]) {
unsigned long  users;
int            rtn;
  if (argc != 2) {
        fprintf(stderr, "Use: nusers hostname\n"); exit(-1);
  }
  if (rtn = callrpc(argv[1], RUSERSPROG, RUSERSVERSION, RUSERSPROCVAL,
          xdr_void, 0, xdr_u_long, &users) != 0) {
     clnt_perrno(stat); return(1);
  }
  printf("There are %d users on %s\n", users, argv[1]);
  return(0);
}
```

Typically, a server registers all its RPC calls, and then goes into an infinite wait loop. Program A5.4 shows an example of a program on a server which registers the nuser RPC call. The program assumes that the nuser routine exists in the RPC library. The svc_run routine responds to remote calls and initiates the remote procedure.

📖 **Program A5.4**

```
#include <stdio.h>
#include <rpc.h>
#define RUSERSPROG       10002 /* Program number   */
#define RUSERSVERSION    2     /* Version number   */
#define RUSERPROCVAL     1     /* Procedure number */

char  *nuser();
int    main(void)
{
  registerrpc(RUSERSPROG, RUSERSVERS, RUSERSPROC_NUM, nuser,
                              xdr_void, xdr_u_long);
  svc_run();
  fprintf(stderr, "Error: server terminated\n");
  return(1);
}
```

In UNIX the /etc/rpc file contains a listing of the RPC services (notice that 100002 corresponds to rusers). The first column defines the RPC process name, the second the procedure number, and the third defines an alias for the process (the fourth column has been added to give extra information). An example is:

```
portmapper     100000  portmap sunrpc              Port mapper
rstatd         100001  rstat rstat_svc rup perfmeter  Remote stats
rusersd        100002  rusers                      Number of users
nfs            100003  nfsprog                     Network File System (NFS)
ypserv         100004  ypprog                      Network Information Service (NIS)
mountd         100005  mount showmount             Mount daemon
ypbind         100007                              NLS binder
walld          100008  rwall shutdown              Shutdown message
yppasswdd      100009  yppasswd                    yppasswd server
etherstatd     100010  etherstat                   Ether stats
rquotad        100011  rquotaprog quota rquota     Disk quotas
selection_svc  100015  selnsvc                     Selection service
database_svc   100016                              Remote database access
rexd           100017  rex                         Remote execution
sched          100019                              Scheduling service
llockmgr       100020                              Local lock manager
nlockmgr       100021                              Network lock manager
```

A5.5 Multi-processor systems

Computer systems have generally evolved around a single centralized processor with an associated area of memory. This main processor performs most of the operations within the computer and also controls reads and writes to and from memory. This type of arrangement is useful in that there is little chance of a conflict when addressing any peripheral as only the single processor can access it. With the evolution of microelectronics, it is now possible to build computers with many processors. This has the advantage over a distributed system over a network, as the communications can be faster, as the distances involved are smaller.

It is typical on modern computers to have several processors, apart from the central processor. For example, many computers now have dedicated processors to control the graphical display, processors to control the input/output functions of the computer, processors to control the hard-disk drive, and so on.

Computer systems, especially servers, are also now being designed with several processors that can run application programs, at a time. Each of these processors can access its own localized memory and/or a shared memory. This type of multi-processor system, though, leads to several problems, including device conflicts and processor synchronization. Figure A5.8 illustrates the two types of systems.

A memory conflict occurs when a process tries to read from or write to an area of memory at the same time as another is trying to access it. Normally, multi-processor systems have mechanisms that lock areas of memory when a processor is accessing it. This is known as bus mastering, and there must be some arbitration mechanism between the processors to synchronize the access to the system buses.

Parallel systems require processor synchronization because one or more processors may require data from other processors. This synchronization can either be hard-wired into the system using data and addressing buses, or by a master controlling processor that handles the communication among slave processors (processor farms). They may also be controlled by the operating system software.

The two main classifications of parallel systems are:

- **Small-scale parallelized systems**. This normally involves just a few processors, and typically used on server systems. As many programs on general-purpose servers cannot run totally in parallel there will not be a direct scaling between the number of processors and the processing power of the system. Small-scale parallelization is normally used to overcome the limitations in maximum processing power of current systems. For example, a system may require a processing power of 1 billion operations, but current systems may only give 50% of this power. Thus, a four-processor array may give the required processing power.

- **Large-scale parallelized systems.** This normally involves a massive number of processors running in parallel in specialized applications, and typically has a specialized architecture which runs specialist software. Only certain applications scale well with large-scale parallelization. These tend to be the ones which do not require a great deal of processor intercommunication (as relative to processing time per processor). Searching and permutation programs are good examples of large-scale parallelization, such as decryption programs and biological gene searching.

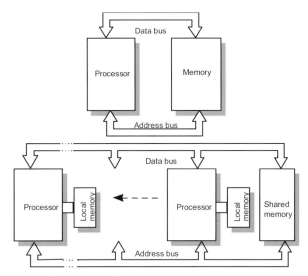

Figure A5.8   Single and multi-processor systems

A5.5.1   Parallel techniques

There are two main methods used when dividing computational tasks to individual processors. These are either to divide the task into stages in a pipeline or to divide them into parallel streams, as illustrated in Figure A5.9. A mixed method uses a mixture of pipelines and parallel streams.

The pipeline method is preferable when there is a large number of computations on a small amount of data. Distributing data between streams can be awkward, since calculations often involve two or more consecutive items of data. Parallel streams are preferable for simple operations on large amounts of data, such as mathematical processing operations.

A major problem with pipelines is that it is difficult to ensure that all the processors have an equal loading. If one processor has a heavier workload than its neighbors then this processor holds-up the neighbors while they are waiting for data from the burdened processor.

It is always important to recognize the inherent parallelism in the problem and whether to allocate fast processors to critical parts and slower ones for the rest, or to equalize the workload, called load balancing.

A5.5.2 Processor Farms

Processor farming is a technique for distributing work with automatic load balancing. It uses a master processor to distribute tasks to a network of slaves. The slave processors only get tasks when they are idle.

It is important in a parallel system that processor tasks are large enough because each task has its overheads. These include the handling overhead of the master controller and also the inter-processor communication. If the tasks are too small then these overheads take a significant amount of time and cause bottlenecks in the system. The major problem in distributing tasks to an increasing number of processors is that as the actual processing time reduces, the amount of time spent passing the results between the processors increases.

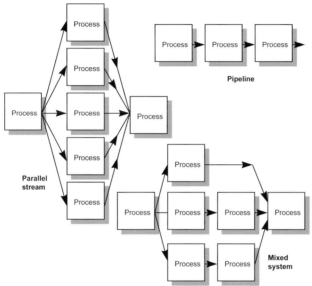

Figure A5.9 Pipeline, parallel stream and mixed systems

A5.5.3 Multi-processor scheduling

The two main classifications of multiprocessor scheduling are:

- **Heterogeneous.** This is where there are a number of different types of processors, each with their own instruction set. This is typically the case in distributed computing, where a process is run over a number of computers on a network. For it to work there must be a high-level protocol that allows communication between the computers. Java is an excellent programming language for this, as it can produce machine-independent code.
- **Homogeneous.** This is where all the processors can run the same code. In the scheduler there is either a common queue for all processors (and they take processes from the queue once they have completed a process) or there is a separate queue for each process (this involves a scheduler deciding on what processes should be given to each of the processors). The processing can either be asymmetric multiprocessor where a single processor looks after scheduling, I/O processing and other system activities, or sym-

metric multiprocessing, where each processor is self-scheduling or has a master-slave structure.

The problem with multiprocessor systems is segmenting a problem up so that it can be run on the individual processors. For example, if a program was to compute the result of:

$z = (a+3) \times (a-4)$; where $a=10$;

Then this can be broken down to the following:

$a=10$;
$x= a + 3$;
$y = a - 4$;
$z = x \times y$;

Then both processors could be passed the value of a, and one processor could run the operation $a+3$, and the other $a-4$, in parallel. Next, one of the processors would tell the other processor its result, and the processor that receives the value could then multiply the two results together. This has resulted in **three** consecutive operations, as apposed to **four** consecutive operations in the non-parallel method (1. Pass value of 10; 2. Compute $(a+3)$; 3. Compute $(a-4)$; 4. Multiply the results of Step 2. and Step 3.).

Another example is for matrix multiplication. For example if a parallel system was to compute the result of the multiplication of two 3×3 matrices. The result would be:

$$Arr = \begin{bmatrix} a & b & c \\ d & e & f \\ g & h & i \end{bmatrix} \begin{bmatrix} j & k & l \\ m & n & o \\ p & q & r \end{bmatrix} = \begin{bmatrix} aj+bm+cp & ak+bn+cq & al+bo+cr \\ dj+em+fp & dk+en+fq & dl+eo+fr \\ gj+hm+ip & gk+hn+iq & gl+ho+ir \end{bmatrix}$$

For example:

$$Arr = \begin{bmatrix} 1 & 2 & 3 \\ 4 & 5 & 6 \\ 7 & 8 & 9 \end{bmatrix} \begin{bmatrix} 1 & 2 & 1 \\ 2 & 5 & 3 \\ 1 & 2 & 3 \end{bmatrix} = \begin{bmatrix} 8 & 18 & 16 \\ 20 & 45 & 37 \\ 32 & 72 & 58 \end{bmatrix}$$

This would normally take nine mathematical operations, with a mixture of addition and multiplication. To run it in parallel, we need to partition the problem so that the processors can run the problem in parallel. Thus for example if we have a system with three processors, we could do the following:

- **Processor 1**. Pass the values of **first** column of the second matrix {j,m,p}, and all the values of the first matrix {$a,b,c;d,e,f;g,h,i$}.
- **Processor 2**. Pass the values of **second** column of the second matrix {k,n,q}, and all the values of the first matrix {$a,b,c;d,e,f;g,h,i$}.
- **Processor 3**. Pass the values of **third** column of the second matrix {l,o,r}, and all the values of the first matrix {$a,b,c;d,e,f;g,h,i$}.

Next each of the processors can calculate using the column from the second matrix and the values from the first matrix, in parallel:

- **Processor 1**. Calculate element 1 as $aj+bm+cp$; element 2 as $dj+em+fp$; element 3 as $gj+hm+ip$. Operations = 12 (nine multiply and three summations).
- **Processor 2**. Calculate element 4 as $ak+bn+cq$; element 5 as $dk+en+fq$; element 6 as $gk+hn+iq$. Operations = 12 (nine multiply and three summations).
- **Processor 3**. Calculate element 7 as $al+bo+cr$; element 8 as $dl+eo+fr$; element 9 as $gl+ho+ir$. Operations = 12 (nine multiply and one summation).

The results from each of the processors can then be collated in the complete matrix. Thus on a single processor it would have taken **nine** mathematical calculations (**36** mathematical operations: 27 multiply and nine summations). This has been reduced to **three** parallel processing calculations (**12** mathematical operations). The only overhead is that we must communicate a single column of the second array, and the values of the first array. This does not typically have a great overhead when there are just a few processors, but with many processes it can have a relatively large overhead.

If we had nine processors, then we could partition the problem as follows:

- Processor 1: Compute $aj+bm+cp$. Operations = 4 (three multiple and one summation).
- Processor 2: Compute $dj+em+fp$. Operations = 4 (three multiple and one summation).
- Processor 3: Compute $gj+hm+ip$. Operations = 4 (three multiple and one summation).
- Processor 4: Compute $ak+bn+cq$. Operations = 4 (three multiple and one summation).
- Processor 5: Compute $dk+en+fq$. Operations = 4 (three multiple and one summation).
- Processor 6: Compute $gk+hn+iq$. Operations = 4 (three multiple and one summation).
- Processor 7: Compute $al+bo+cr$. Operations = 4 (three multiple and one summation).
- Processor 8: Compute $dl+eo+fr$. Operations = 4 (three multiple and one summation).
- Processor 9: Compute $gl+ho+ir$. Operations = 4 (three multiple and one summation).

Which will only take **one** mathematical calculation (**four** mathematical operations). Unfortunately this mathematical calculation takes three multiplications and a summation. Thus if we optimize the system with 27 processors, we could partition the problem as:

- Processor 1: Compute aj.   Processor 2: Compute bm.   Processor 3: Compute cp.
- Processor 4: Compute dj.   Processor 5: Compute em.   Processor 6: Compute fp.
- Processor 7: Compute gj.   Processor 8: Compute hm.   Processor 9: Compute ip.
- Processor 10: Compute ak. Processor 11: Compute bn. Processor 12: Compute cq.
- Processor 13: Compute dk. Processor 14: Compute en. Processor 15: Compute fq.
- Processor 16: Compute gk. Processor 17: Compute hn. Processor 18: Compute iq.
- Processor 19: Compute al. Processor 20: Compute bo. Processor 21: Compute cr.
- Processor 22: Compute dl. Processor 23: Compute eo. Processor 24: Compute fr.
- Processor 25: Compute gl. Processor 26: Compute ho. Processor 27: Compute ir.

Next:

- **Processor 1:** Gets results from Processor 1, Processor 2 and Processor 3, and then summates the result to get element 1.
- **Processor 4:** Gets results from Processor 4, Processor 5 and Processor 6, and then summates the result to get element 2.

- **Processor 7:** Gets results from Processor 7, Processor 8 and Processor 9, and then summates the result to get element 3.
- **Processor 10:** Gets results from Processor 10, Processor 11 and Processor 3, and then summates the result to get element 4.
- **Processor 13:** Gets results from Processor 13, Processor 14 and Processor 15, and then summates the result to get element 5.
- **Processor 16:** Gets results from Processor 16, Processor 17 and Processor 18, and then summates the result to get element 6.
- **Processor 19:** Gets results from Processor 19, Processor 20 and Processor 21, and then summates the result to get element 7.
- **Processor 25:** Gets results from Processor 25, Processor 26 and Processor 27, and then summates the result to get element 8.

Thus with 27 processors we now get down to **two** mathematical operations. We cannot get it down to one mathematical operation as the summation process must **wait** for the multiply operation to complete. Thus, in summary:

Processors	Mathematical operations
1	36
3	12
9	4
27	2

Thus it can be seen, in this case, that the best saving in mathematical operations possibly occurs between 1 and 3 processors. An increasing number of processors does not really help to reduce the number of mathematical operations by a great deal. There is also, for an increased number of processor, an increase in the time that it takes to communicate the parameters to each of the processors, and then the intercommunications of their results. Thus in some cases it is possible for the processing time to actually increase with an increasing number of processors.

2.5.3.1 Timing

To simulate the time taken, we can estimate each of the timings, such as:

Time taken for 3-by-3 problem

Processors	Time taken	Computation
1	279	100%
3	123	44%
9	71	25%
27	145	52%

- Time to transmit one value over the network is five time units.
- Time for a two-value multiplication is eight time units.
- Time for a three-value summation is two time units.

Let us assume that the model uses a server which receives values from client processors. Also assume that the processors already know the values from both matrices.
For a one-processor system, there will be:

- 27 multiply operations (216 time units).
- 9 summations (18 time units).
- 9 transmissions of the result (45 time units).

which gives 279 time units.

For a three-processor system, there will be:

- 9 multiply operations (72 time units).
- 3 summations (6 time units).
- 9 transmissions of the result (45 time units).

which gives 123 time units. Thus, the communications of the parameters is starting to have a large effect on the total time.

For a nine-processor system, there will be:

- 3 multiply operations (24 time units).
- 1 summation (2 time units).
- 9 transmissions of the result (45 time units).

which gives 71 time units. Thus, we have increased the number of processors by a factor of three but we've only reduced the processing time by about 25% on the total time for three-processors.

Finally for 27 processors, there will be:

- 1 multiply operation (8 time units).
- 1 summation (2 time units).
- 27 transmissions of the result (135 time units). This is because two out of three of the processors must report their result to another processor in order to inform them of the result. Thus for example Processor 1 would calculate *aj*; Processor 2 would calculate *bm* and Processor 3 would calculate *cp*. Next Processor 2 and Processor 3 would send their results to Processor 1, who would then perform the summation. After which it would send the result to the server. The transmission of the intermediate results gives 18 transmissions, and the transmission of the results gives nine transmissions. Thus, the total number of transmissions is 27.

which gives 145 time units. This is actually an increase in time over the nine-processor system.

A5.5.4 Problem segmentation and processing time

A major problem with parallel processing, in some cases, is that the communication overhead increases as the number of processors increase. The computation time is likely to reduce as the number of processing elements increases, but the communication time will increase. An example is shown in Figure A5.10, which shows a system which determines the average value for a number of adjacent pixels. In this case, we could segment the problem into four physical domains and assign a 2×2 processor array to the problem. The problem that we have is that at the end of the calculations, the processors must communicate the values of the pixels at their boundary to their adjacent neighbor. For a 2×2 processor array there will be two interfaces. If we increase the array to a 3×3 processor array then there will be four interfaces, and with a 4×4 processor array there will be six interfaces. In general, an $n×n$ array will have $2(n–1)$ interfaces. The total computation time is thus the addition of the processing time plus the communication time.

In this case the computation time for the problem will reduce as the number of processors increase, but the communication time between the physical domains will increase, as the number of interfaces increase. Figure A5.11 shows a typical characteristic for total computation time. It can be seen that there is likely to be an optimal number of processors which minimizes the total computation time.

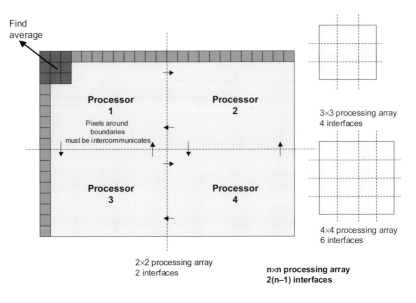

Figure A5.10   Segmentation of a problem for parallel processing

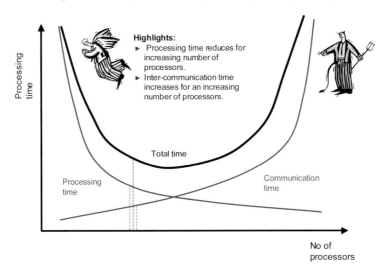

Figure A5.11   Computation time

A5.5.5 Processor arrays

Typically, in parallel processing the problem involves processors communicating with their adjacent neighbor (as illustrated in Figure A5.10). In the matrix multiplication, we assumed that we were using a single bus to connect on the processors. An improved method could use an array structure, as illustrated in Figure A5.12. With this, the column of the matrix is passed to the array elements from the north to south, and the results are computed from east to west. Each of the processors knows one of the matrices and then waits for the column data to be passed to them from the north. They then pass then data to the south to the next processor in the line. After this, they can calculate their value, after the partial result has been received from the east, as illustrated in Figure A5.13. The Sink basically does not do anything but receive data from the processing element, and the Zero passes three zero values to the next processing element. The operation for the top row will be:

1. Send column Col1 data to P_1, send Col2 data to P_2 and Col3 data to P_3. P_1, P_2 and P_3 will then pass this data onto P_4, P_5 and P_6, respectively. P_4, P_5 and P_6 will then pass this data onto P_7, P_8 and P_9, respectively.
2. P_3 receives a zero value, and computes its value ($al+bo+cr$) and passes it to P_2;
3. P_2 receives a partial vector from P_3, adds its computed value ($ak+bn+cq$). It then adds it to the partial vector, and passes this to P_1.
4. P_1 receives a partial vector for P_2 and adds its computed value ($aj+bm+cp$) and adds it to the partial vector, which will now be the completed row of the calculation, and passes this onto the Result {$aj+bm+cp$; $ak+bn+cq$; $al+bo+cr$}.

There will be a similar parallel action for P_4, P_5 and P_6, and also P_7, P_8 and P_9.

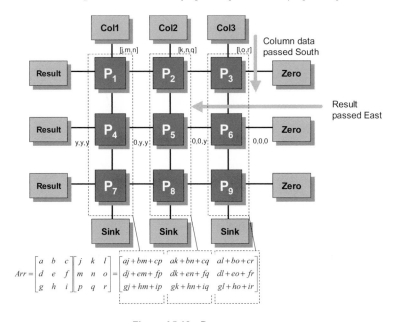

Figure A5.12 Processor array

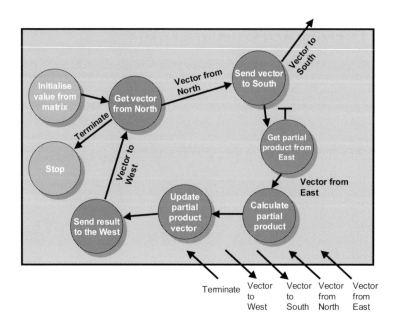

Figure A5.13   Modelling of the processes run on each of the processors

A6   Distributed file systems

A6.1   Introduction

Files systems typically use a directory structure which is based on folders which contain files and/or subfolders. They store three main types of files:

- **Information**. This will typically be user files, such as word processor files, spreadsheets, and e-mail messages.
- **Program files**. These will typically be application programs, such as a WWW browser program, word processor program, spreadsheet program, and so on.
- **Configuration data**. These will be important data which define the configuration of the user's computer. Typical storage will be hardware configuration data for the computer, the setup of user's desktop, and so on.

In the past, most information was stored locally on a computer, or centrally on a mainframe computer, but there is now a trend to distribute information around networks. This has many advantages over traditional localized information (Figure A6.1):

- **File system mirrors the corporate structure**. File systems can be distributed over a corporate network, which might span cities, countries or even continents. The setup of a complete network file system over a corporation can allow the network to mirror the logical setup of the organization, rather than its physical and geographical organization. For example, the Sales Department might be distributed around the world, but the network in which they connect to is identical to the way that the Sales Department is organized.
- **Easier to protect the access rights on file systems**. In a distributed file system, it is typical to have a strong security policy on the file system, and each file will have an owner who can define the privileges on this file. File systems on user computers tend to have limited user security.
- **Increased access to single sources of information**. Many users can have access to a single source of information. Having multiple versions of a file can cause a great deal of problems, especially if it is not known as to which one is the most up to date.
- **Automated updates**. Several copies of the same information can be stored, and when any one of them is updated, they are synchronized to keep each of them up-to-date. Users can thus have access to a local copy of data, rather than accessing a remote copy of it. This is called mirroring files.
- **Improved backup facilities**. A user's computer can be switched-off, but their files can still be backed up from the distributed file system.
- **Increased reliability**. The distributed file system can have a backbone which is constructed from reliable and robust hardware, which are virtually 100% reliable, even when there is a power failure, or when there is a hardware fault.
- **Larger file systems**. In some types of distributed file systems, it is possible to build-up large file systems from a network of connected disk drives.
- **Easier to administer**. Administrators can easily view the complete file system.
- **Interlinking of databases**. Small databases can be linked together to create large data-

bases, which can be configured for a given application. The future may also bring the concept of data mining, where agent programs will search for information with a given profile by interrogating databases on the Internet.

- **Limiting file access**. Organizations can setup an organization file structure, in which users can have a limited view of the complete file system.

in the past, the structure of file systems has been based on the physical connection of file systems to the network. An enhanced method of organizing file systems is to setup a structure which mirrors the organizational structure of the organization. This makes it easier for users to view the file system, as it is more logical in its structure. This is important because for most users the organizational structure makes more sense to them than the structure of files on a computer system. Figure A6.2 shows two file structures. The one on the left-hand side is possibly easier for an experienced user to use, and the one on the right-hand side is more intuitive to someone who understands the organizational structure of the organization. File systems, such as Novell NDS and Microsoft Active Directory try to setup file systems that have a global file structure which try to mirror the structure of the organization. In these systems, resources, other than files such as printers, and file servers can be mapped onto the file system.

Most file systems have a hierarchical file structure, which has directories that contain subdirectories files and devices. The file system, itself, is a tree on a single server (normally a single disk or a physical partition) which has a specified root. Some systems use a mount system that mounts file systems onto a single tree, while others use a forest of file systems, where the file systems appear individually. If possible, the mounting of a drive system should be transparent to the user, and should be done automatically so that the user treats the mounted drive just as a local resource. A major problem, though, is the security of the remotely connected drive, thus each mounted drive must have strict rules on the access rights for the local user.

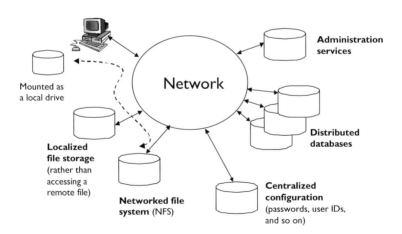

Figure A6.1 Distributed file system

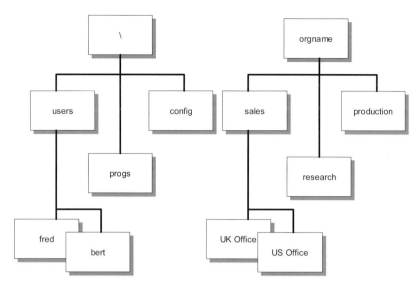

Figure A6.2 Traditional file structure v. corporate structure

Drives can either be mounted locally to a computer as a single tree (as UNIX) or as a forest of drives (as used with Microsoft Windows). In Figure A6.3, one of the computers has created a single tree that uses its local drives to create the /etc and /user directories, and then mounts two networked drives to give /progs and /sys. The global file system will then be mounted onto the common tree, with four subdirectories below the top-level directory (/). The advantages of this type of system are:

- The structure of the file system and the drives that are mounted are transparent to the user. As far as the user is concerned the complete file system is viewable.
- Every user can view the complete file system, if required.
- The file system is consistent around the network, and can be setup on a per computer basis.

With the forest of disks, a disk drive is mounted locally as if it is a local drive. In the example in Figure A6.3, the remote drives have been mounted as E: and F:. Its main advantage over the global file system is that:

- It is easier to determine if the remote drive is mounted, as it will appear as a mounted resource. With a single tree it is often difficult to determine if a drive is loaded onto the global file system as the basic structure still exists.
- Less complex than a global file, and easier to mount drives, but can become complex to setup if there are many remote drives to be mounted.

Its main disadvantage is it is more difficult to setup than the single tree system as the local mount drive must be specified, along with the path. In the global file system, files are mounted on the system in a consistent way, such as with E:\FREDS_DRIVE. If the local system does not mount the remote drive onto the required disk partition, there may be problems in the configuration of the system.

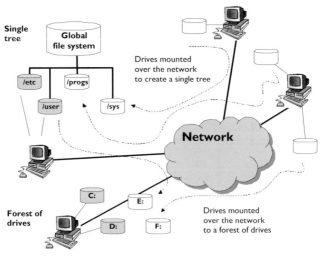

Figure A6.3 Distributed file system

A6.2 NFS

The Network File System (NFS) is defined in RFC1094 and allows computers to share the same files over a network. It was originally developed by Sun Microsystems, and has the great advantage that it is independent of the host operating system and can provide data sharing among different types of systems (heterogeneous systems). This is achieved using Remote Procedure Call (RPC), on top of XDR, which provides a standard method of representing data types. RPC is defined in RFC1057, and XDR is RFC1014.

NFS uses a client-server architecture where a computer can act as an NFS client, an NFS server or both. An NFS client makes requests to access data and files on servers; the server then makes that specific resource available to the client. NFS servers are passive and stateless. They wait for requests from clients and do not maintain any information on the client. One advantage of servers being stateless is that it is possible to reboot servers without adverse consequences to the client. Servers do not preserve the current status of any of their clients, which means that a client can simply retry a request from a server, if it fails to get a response (in the event of a failure of the network or the server). If the server was stateful, the client would have to know that a server had crashed or that the network connection had broken, so that it knew which state is should be in, when the connection was returned, or when the server came back on-line.

The server grants remote access privileges to a restricted set of clients, which allows clients to mount remote directory trees onto their local file system. The components of NFS are as follows (Figure A6.4 shows how the protocols fit into the OSI model):

- **NFS** remote file access may be accompanied by network information service (NIS).
- External data representation (**XDR**), which is a universal data representation, used by all nodes, and provides a common data representation if applications are to run transparently on a heterogeneous network or if data is to be shared among heterogeneous systems. Each node translates machine-dependent data formats to XDR format when sending and translating data. XDR enables heterogeneous nodes and operating systems to communicate with each other over the network.

- Remote Procedure Call (**RPC**) allows clients to transparently execute procedures on remote systems of the network. NFS services run on top of the RPC, which corresponds to the session layer of the OSI model.
- Network lock manager (`rpc.lockd`) allows users to coordinate and control access to information on the network. It supports file locking and synchronizes access to shared files.

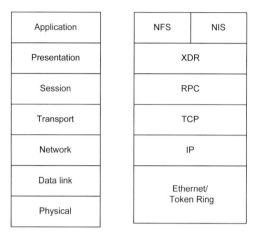

Figure A6.4   NFS services protocol stack

A6.2.5   NFS protocol

NFS assumes a hierarchical file structure. It can be used to mount file systems which map into a single tree (as the UNIX file system), or it can be used to add a file system as one of a forest of drives (as Microsoft Windows). NFS looks up one component of a pathname, at a time, as different file systems use different separators to identify a pathname (for example, UNIX uses '/' and Microsoft Windows uses '\', while others use periods).

The main NFS protocol is defined as a set of procedures with arguments and results defined using the RPC language. Each of the procedures is synchronous, and the client can assume that a response from a request completes the operation. The procedures used are:

No.	Procedure	Name	Description
0	void NULL(void)	No operation	Used for server testing.
1	attrstat GETATTR(fhandle)	Get file attributes	Returns the attributes of the file specified by fhandle.

2	attrstat SETATTR(sattrargs)	Set file attributes	The sattrargs contains fields which are either –1 or are the new value for the file attributes. The sattargs structure is:
			
			struct sattrargs {
			   fhandle file;
			   sattr attributes;
			};
			
			where fhandle is the file handle that is passed between the client and the server. The structure of the sattr is:

			struct sattr {
			        unsigned int mode; // file mode
			        unsigned int uid;
			                // user identification number
			        unsigned int gid; // group identification num-
			ber
			        unsigned int size; // size of the file
			        timeval atime; // time file last accessed
			        timeval mtime; // time file last modified
			        };

6	readres READ(readargs)	Read from file	Reads a number of bytes of data (given by count), from a given file offset. The format of the readargs structure is:
			
			struct readargs {
			        fhandle file; // used to represent file
			        unsigned offset; // starting position
			        unsigned count; // number of bytes to be read
			        unsigned totalcount; // not used
			        };

8	attrstat WRITE(writeargs)	Write to file	Writes data to a file starting at a given offset. The format of writeargs structure is:
			
			struct writeargs {
			        fhandle file; // used to represent file
			        unsigned beginoffset; // not used
			        unsigned offset; // starting position
			        unsigned totalcount; // not used
			        nfsdata data; // data to be written
			        };

9	diropres CREATE(createargs)	Create file	Creates a file in the given directory, with a given set of attributes. The format of the createargs structure is:
			
			struct createargs {
			        diropargs where;
			        sattr attributes;
			        };
			
			The format of the diropags structure is:
			
			struct diropargs {
			        fhandle dir; // used to represent direc-tory
			        filename name; // name of file
			        };

10	stat REMOVE(diropargs)	Remove file	See above.

11	stat RENAME(renameargs)	Rename file	The format of the renameargs structure is:
			
			struct renameargs {
			        diropargs from;
			        diropargs to;
			        };
			For example, from.name is changed to to.name.

12	stat LINK(linkargs)	Create link to file	The format of the linkargs structure is:
			
			struct linkargs {
			        fhandle from;
			        diropargs to;

13	stat SYMLINK(symlinkargs)	Create symbolic link	The format of the aymlinkargs structure is:
			
			struct symlinkargs {
			    diropargs from;
			    path to;
			    sattr attributes;
			};

14	diropres MKDIR(createargs)	Create directory	The format of the createargs structure is:
			
			struct createargs {
			    diropargs where;
			    sattr attributes;
			};

15	stat RMDIR(diropargs)	Remove directory	

16	readdirres READDIR(readdirargs)	Read from directory	The format of the readdirargs structure is:
			
			struct readdirargs {
			    fhandle dir;
			    nfscookie cookie; // Used to get the entries
			        // starting at the beginning of the directory
			    unsigned count;
			        // maximum number of entries
			};

Figure A6.5 shows a client sending RPC procedures to the server, which responds back with the required data, parameters or with a status flag. Typical status flags are: NFS_OK (success), NFSERR_PERM (not owner), NFSERR_NOENT (no such file or directory), NFSERR_IO (some sort of hard error occurred), NFSERR_NXIO (no such device or address), NFSERR_ACCES (permission denied), NFSERR_EXIST (the file specified already exists), NFSERR_NODEV (no such device) and NFSERR_NOTDIR (not a directory).

A6.2.5 Network Information Service (NIS)

As networks grow in size, it becomes more difficult for the system administrator to maintain the security of the network. An important factor is the maintenance of a passwords file, where new users are added with the group, and any other information (such as their default home directory). In most networks, a user should be able to log into any computer within a domain. Thus, a global password and configuration files are required. This can be achieved with NIS, which is an optional network control program which maintains the network configuration files over a network. NIS allows the system manager to centralize the key configuration files on a single master server. If anyone wants to log into the network the master server is consulted (or one of its slave servers). Figure A6.6 illustrates some of the files that the server maintains; these include password (which contains the passwords for all the users within the domain), and groups (the group that the user is associated with). It is thus easy for the system administrator to add and delete users from the NIS server, and these changes will be reflected over the domain. A user cannot log into any of the clients, without the client checking with the server to see if they have a valid login and password.

Previously NIS was named *Yellow Pages* (**YP**), but has changed its name as this is a registered trademark of the British Telecommunications company. NIS normally administers the network configuration files such as /etc/group (which defines the user groups), /etc/hosts (which defines the IP address and symbolic names of nodes on a network), /etc/passwd (which contains information, such as user names, encrypted passwords, home directories, and so on). An excerpt from a `passwd` file is:

```
root:FDEc6.32:1:0:Super user:/user:/bin/csh
fred:jt.06hLdiSDaA:2:4:Fred Blogs:/user/fred:/bin/csh
fred2:jtY067SdiSFaA:3:4:Fred Smith:/user/fred2:/bin/csh
```

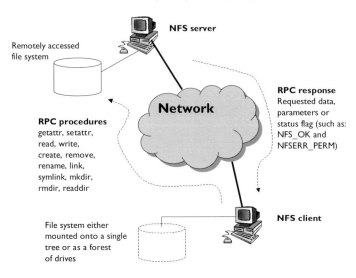

Figure A6.5   RPC procedures and responses

This `passwd` file has three defined users; these are `root`, `fred` and `fred2`. The encrypted password is given in the second field (between the first and second column), and the third field is a unique number that defines the user (in this case `fred` is 2 and `fred2` is 3). The fourth field in this case defines the group number (which ties up with the `/etc/groups` file). An example of a `groups` file is given next. It can be seen from this file that group 4 is defined as `freds_grp`, and contains three users: `fred`, `fred2` and `fred3`. The fifth field is simply a comment field and in this case it contains the user's names. In the next field each user's home directory is defined and the final field contains the initial UNIX shell (in this case it is the C-shell).

```
root::0:root
other::1:root,hpdb
bin::2:root,bin
sys::3:root,uucp
freds_grp::4:fred,fred2,fred3
```

A sample listing of a directory shows that a file owned by `fred` has the group name `freds_grp`.

```
> ls -l
-r-sr-xr-x   1 fred      freds_grp   24576    Apr 22   2000 file1
-r-xr-xr-x  13 fred      freds_grp   40       Apr 22   2000 file2
dr-xr-xr-x   2 fred      freds_grp   1024     Aug  5 14:01 myfile
-r-xr-sr-x   1 fred      freds_grp   24576    Apr 22   2000 text2.ps
-r-xr-xr-x   2 fred      freds_grp   16384    Apr 22   2000 temp1.txt
```

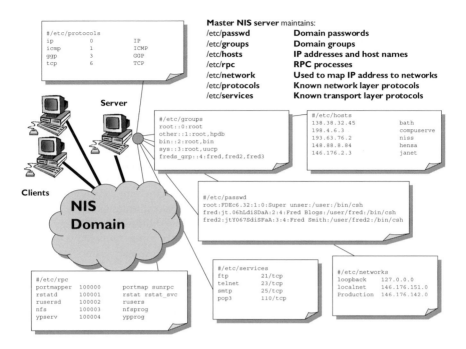

Figure A6.6 NIS domain

An excerpt from the `/etc/hosts` file is shown next.

```
138.38.32.45      bath
198.4.6.3         compuserve
193.63.76.2       niss
148.88.8.84       hensa
146.176.2.3       janet
146.176.151.51    sun
```

The `/etc/protocols` file contains information with known protocols used on the Internet.

```
# The form for each entry is:
# <official protocol name> <protocol number> <aliases>
# Internet (IP) protocols

ip        0  IP       # internet protocol, pseudo protocol number
icmp      1  ICMP     # internet control message protocol
ggp       3  GGP      # gateway-gateway protocol
tcp       6  TCP      # transmission control protocol
egp       8  EGP      # exterior gateway protocol
pup      12  PUP      # PARC universal packet protocol
udp      17  UDP      # user datagram protocol
hmp      20  HMP      # host monitoring protocol
xns-idp  22  XNS-IDP  # Xerox NS IDP
rdp      27  RDP      # "reliable datagram" protocol
```

The `/etc/netgroup` file defines network-wide groups used for permission checking when doing remote mounts, remote logins, and remote shells. Here is a sample file:

```
# The format for each entry is: groupname  member1  member2 ...
#  (hostname, username, domainname)
engineering hardware software (host3, mikey, hp)
hardware (hardwhost1, chm, hp)   (hardwhost2, dae, hp)
software (softwhost1, jad, hp)   (softwhost2, dds, hp)
```

NIS master server and slave server

With NIS, a single node on a network acts as the NIS master server, with a number of NIS slave servers, which receive their NIS information from the master server. The slaves are important in that they hold copies of the most up-to-date version of the NIS database, so if the master were to crash, or become uncontactable, the slaves could still provide password, group, and other NIS information to the clients in the domain. The slaves also relieve the workload on the master, as it may become busy responding to many NIS requests. When a client first starts up it sends out a broadcast to all NIS servers (master or slaves) on the network and waits for the first one to respond. The client then binds to the first that responds and addresses all NIS requests to that server. If this server becomes inoperative then an NIS client will automatically rebind to the first NIS server which responds to another broadcast. Figure A6.7 illustrates this.

Table A6.1 outlines the records which are used in the NIS database (or NIS map). This file consists of logical records with a search key and a related value for each record. For example, in the `passwd.byname` map, the users' login names are the keys and the matching lines from `/etc/passwd` are the values.

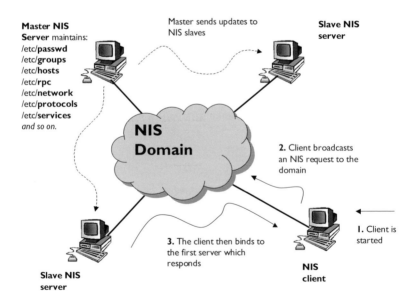

Figure A6.7   NIS domain

Table A6.1 NIS database components

NIS map	File maintained	Description
group.bygid group.byname	`/etc/group`	Maintains user groups.
hosts.byaddr hosts.byname	`/etc/hosts`	Maintains a list of IP addresses and symbolic names.
netgroup.byhost netgroup.byuser	`/etc/netgroup`	Contains a mapping of network group names to a set of node, user and NIS domain names.
networks.byaddr networks.byname	`/etc/network`	Defines network-wide groups used for permission checking when doing remote mounts, remote logins, and remote shells.
passwd.byname passwd.byuid	`/etc/passwd`	Contains details such as user names and encrypted passwords.
protocols.byname protocols.bynumber	`/etc/protocols`	Contains information with known protocols used on the Internet.
rpc.bynumber rpc.byname	`/etc/rpc`	Maps the RPC program names to the RPC program numbers and vice versa. This file is static; it is already correctly configured.
services.byname servi.bynp	`/etc/services`	
mail.byaddr mail.aliases	`/etc/aliases`	

NIS domain

An NIS domain is a logical grouping of the set of maps contained on NIS servers. The rules for NIS domains are:

- All nodes in an NIS domain have the same domain name.
- Only one master server exists on an NIS domain.
- Each NIS domain can have zero or more slave servers.

An NIS domain is a subdirectory of `/usr/etc/yp` on each NIS server, where the name of the subdirectory is the name of the NIS domain. All directories that appear under `/usr/etc/yp` are assumed to be domains that are served by an NIS server. Thus to remove a domain being served, the user deletes the domain's subdirectory name from `/etc/etc/yp` on all of its servers.

The start-up file on most UNIX systems is the `/etc/rc` file. This automatically calls the `/etc/netnfsrc` file which contains the default NIS domain name, and uses the program `domainname`.

A6.2.5 NFS remote file access

To initially mount a remote directory (or file system) onto a local computer the superuser must do the following:

- On the server, export the directory to the client.
- On the client, mount (or import) the directory.

For example suppose the remote directory `/user` is to be mounted onto the host `miranda` as the directory `/win`. To achieve this operation the following are setup:

1. The superuser logs on to the remote server and edits the file `/etc/exports` adding the `/user` directory.
2. The superuser then runs the program `exportfs` to make the `/user` directory available to the client.

   ```
   % exportfs -a
   ```

3. The superuser then logs into the client and creates a mount point `/win` (empty directory).

   ```
   % mkdir /mnt
   ```

4. The remote directory can then be mounted with:

   ```
   % mount miranda:/user /win
   ```

NFS maintains the file `/etc/mnttab` which contains a record of the mounted file systems. The general format is:

special_file_name dir type opts freq passno mount_time cnode_id

where *mount_time* contains the time the file system was mounted using mount. Sample contents of `/etc/mnttab` could be:

```
/dev/dsk/c201d6s0    /                 hfs    defaults 0 1 850144122 1
/dev/dsk/c201d5s0    /win              hfs    defaults 1 2 850144127 1
castor:/win          /net/castor_win   nfs    rw,suid  0 0 850144231 0
miranda:/win         /net/miranda_win  nfs    rw,suid  0 0 850144291 0
spica:/usr/opt       /opt              nfs    rw,suid  0 0 850305936 0
triton:/win          /net/triton_win   nfs    rw,suid  0 0 850305936 0
```

In this case there are two local drivers (`/dev/dsk/c201d6s0` is mounted as the root directory and `/dev/dsk/c201d5s0` is mounted locally as `/win`). There are also four remote directories which are mounted from remote servers (`castor`, `miranda`, `spica` and `triton`). The directory mounted from `castor` is the `/win` directory and it is mounted locally as `/net/castor_win`.`hfs` defines a UNIX format disk and `nfs` defines that the disk is mounted over NFS.

A disk can be unmounted from a system using the umount command, e.g.

```
% umount miranda:/win
```

A6.2.5 NIS commands

NIS commands allow the maintenance of network information. The main commands are as follows:

- `domainname` which displays or changes the current NIS domain name.
- `ypcat` which lists the specified NIS map contents.
- `ypinit` which, on a master server, builds a map using the networking files in `/etc`. On a slave server the map is built using the master server.
- `ypmake` which is a script that builds standard NIS maps from files such as `/etc/passwd`, `/etc/groups`, and so on.
- `ypmatch` which prints the specified NIS map data (values) associated with one or more keys.
- `yppasswd` which can be used to change (or install) a user's password in the NIS `passwd` map.
- `ypwhich` which is used to print the host name of the NIS server supplying NIS services to an NIS client.
- `ypxfr` which transfers the NIS map from one slave server to another.

For example the command:

```
ypcat group.byname
```

lists the group name, the group ID and the members of the group. Here is an example of changing a user's password for the NIS domain. In this case, the user `bill_b` changes the network-wide password on the master server `pollux`.

```
% yppasswd
Changing NIS password for bill_b...
Old NIS password: ********
New password: *******
Retype new password: *******
The NIS passwd has been changed on pollux, the master NIS passwd
server.
```

The next example uses the `ypcat` program.

```
% ypcat group
students:*:200:msc01,msc02,msc03,msc04
nogroup:*:-2:
daemon::5:root,daemon
users::20:root,msc08
other::1:root,hpdb
root::0:root
```

The next example shows the `ypmake` command file which rebuilds the NIS database.

```
# ypmake
For NIS domain eece:
The passwd map(s) are up-to-date.
Building the group map(s)... group build complete.
    Pushing the group map(s): group.bygid  group.byname
```

```
The hosts map(s) are up-to-date.
The networks map(s) are up-to-date.
The rpc map(s) are up-to-date.
The services map(s) are up-to-date.
The protocols map(s) are up-to-date.
The netgroup map(s) are up-to-date.
ypmake complete:
```

A6.2.5 Network configuration files

The main files used to setup networking are as follows:

`/etc/checklist`	is a list of directories or files that are automatically mounted at boot time.
`/etc/exports`	contains a list of directories or files that clients may import.
`/etc/inetd.conf`	contains information about servers started by `inetd` (the Internet daemon). Listing A6.1 shows an example of the inetd.conf file. It can be seen that it includes the service name, socket type (stream or datagram), the protocol (TCP or UDP), flags, the owner, the server path, and any other arguments. Lines which begin with the '#' character are ignored by `inetd`. It can be seen that many of the Internet-related programs, such as FTP and TELNET are started here, as well as the login program (LOGIN).
`/etc/netgroup`	contains a mapping of network group names to a set of node, user, and NIS domain names.
`/etc/netnfsrc`	is automatically started at run time and initiates the required daemons and servers, and defines the node as a client or server.
`/etc/rpc`	maps the RPC program names to the RPC program numbers and vice versa.
`/usr/adm/inetd.sec`	checks the Internet address of the host requesting a service against the list of hosts allowed to use the service.

📖 Listing A6.1 (inetd.conf)

```
# <service_name> <sock_type> <proto> <flags> <user> <server_path> <args>
# Echo, discard and daytime are used primarily for testing.
echo       stream   tcp    nowait    root   internal
echo       dgram    udp    wait      root   internal
discard    stream   tcp    nowait    root   internal
discard    dgram    udp    wait      root   internal
daytime    stream   tcp    nowait    root   internal
daytime    dgram    udp    wait      root   internal
time       dgram    udp    wait      root   internal
#
# These are standard services.
ftp        stream   tcp    nowait    root   /usr/sbin/tcpd /usr/sbin/wu.ftpd
telnet     stream   tcp    nowait    root   /usr/sbin/tcpd /usr/sbin/in.telnetd
#
# Shell, login, exec and talk are BSD protocols.
shell      stream   tcp    nowait    root   /usr/sbin/tcpd /usr/sbin/in.rshd
login      stream   tcp    nowait    root   /usr/sbin/tcpd /usr/sbin/in.rlogind
talk       dgram    udp    wait      root   /usr/sbin/tcpd /usr/sbin/in.ntalkd
ntalk      dgram    udp    wait      root   /usr/sbin/tcpd /usr/sbin/in.ntalkd
#
# Pop mail servers
pop3       stream   tcp    nowait    root   /usr/sbin/tcpd /usr/sbin/in.pop3d
```

```
#
bootps    dgram    udp    wait     root      /usr/sbin/tcpd /usr/sbin/in.bootpd
#
finger    stream   tcp    nowait   daemon    /usr/sbin/tcpd /usr/sbin/in.fingerd
systat    stream   tcp    nowait   guest     /usr/sbin/tcpd /usr/bin/ps -auwwx
netstat   stream   tcp    nowait   guest     /usr/sbin/tcpd /bin/netstat -f inet
```

Daemons

Networking programs normally initiate networking daemons which are background processes and are always running. Their main function is to wait for a request to perform a task.
Typical daemons are:

biod	which is asynchronous block I/O daemons for NFS clients.
inetd	which is an Internet daemon that listens to service ports. It listens for service requests and calls the appropriate server. The server it calls depends on the contents of the /etc/inetd.conf file.
nfsd	which is the NFS server daemon. It is used by the client for reading and writing to a remote directory and it sends a request to the remote server nfsd process.
pcnfsd	which is a PC user authentication daemon.
portmap	which is an RPC program to port number conversion daemon. When a client makes an RPC call to a given program number, it first contacts portmap on the server node to determine the port number where RPC requests should be sent.

Here is an extract from the processes that run a networked UNIX workstation:

```
 UID    PID  PPID  C    STIME TTY       TIME  COMMAND
root    100     1  0  Dec  9  ?        0:00  /etc/portmap
root    138     1  0  Dec  9  ?        0:00  /etc/inetd
root    104     1  0  Dec  9  ?        9:20  /usr/etc/ypserv
root    106     1  0  Dec  9  ?        0:00  /etc/ypbind
root    122   120  0  Dec  9  ?        0:00  /etc/nfsd 4
root    116     1  0  Dec  9  ?        0:00  /usr/etc/rpc.yppasswdd
root    123   120  0  Dec  9  ?        0:00  /etc/nfsd 4
root    128     1  0  Dec  9  ?        0:02  /etc/biod 4
root    131     1  0  Dec  9  ?        0:00  /etc/pcnfsd
root    133     1  0  Dec  9  ?        0:00  /usr/etc/rpc.statd
root    135     1  0  Dec  9  ?        0:00  /usr/etc/rpc.lockd
root   4652     1  0  14:33:15 ?       0:00  /etc/pcnfsd
root   4649     1  0  14:33:15 ?       0:00  /usr/etc/rpc.mountd
```

A6.3   Other distributed file systems

Active Directories, and Novell NDS will be discussed in the NOS section.

A7 Agents

A7.1 Introduction

The future is likely to see an increase in the use of agents. These are programs which automate user tasks, and are the next natural step in the development of distributed systems. Their great advantage is that they are designed to run over distributed computing systems, whereas traditional utility programs typically run on a peer-to-peer type connection. Figure A7.1 shows some of the applications of agents. They are particularly useful when working remotely from a server (especially when there is no current network connection), and for processing data that can be presented in a convenient form. For example, an agent could monitor the prices of stocks and shares, and then automatically buy and sell shares when a certain level is reached, or when the market behaves in a certain way. Another agent might seek the best price of an airline flight. This could involve the agent contacting server databases for airline prices and making requests for further details. The agent could then make a decision on which of the airline flights would be the best, for a given set of attributes (such as cost of flight, timing of flight, seat positions, airport locations, and so on).

At present, most agents are fixed in their programming, and cannot really change their operation without human input (mainly because many humans do not quite trust computer programs which change their operation and learn from their mistakes). Once artificial intelligence techniques become more reliable, agents will acquire the ability to learn their task, and, especially, learn from their mistakes. For example, a stock market agent could monitor how the market changed over time, and identify trends. They could also monitor stock market announcements, and determine the elements which trigger stock market movements (such as changes relating to interest rates, inflation rates, and taxes). The agent would thus learn the best time to buy and sell (just as a human would learn to look for trends).

Great gains will come from *intelligent* agents, which use complex artificial intelligence (AI) methods to learn their tasks. Actually defining a task is not easy, as it typically requires a complete outline of the main objectives of the task (which are often difficult to define), and the weighting that each of these should be given. For example, an agent could control a small area of industrial plant. The agent would have to be told that safety was the most critical area, and should overrule everything else. After safety was accounted for, the agent must then try to run the plant within statutory requirements (emissions, fuel consumptions, and so on). Once these have been met then the plant should run as optimally as possible, and produce a profit. All these requirements are difficult to define, and often humans do not understand the overall requirements of a system.

A typical usage of agents, in the future, will be for security purposes. One of the most prevalent attacks on a network is when a person logs into a valid user account that is not theirs. This can be difficult to overcome as the non-authorized user uses both the correct login name and correct password, which is then authenticated by the system. Biometrics could obviously be used to overcome this, such as using fingerprinting, or retina images, but these are normally too expensive to implement. It is also difficult to bar remote connections that do not have any biometric security. An improved method is to build up a profile of the user; the agent can then check the current usage against a standard profile for the user. With this, the local agent makes a request for a specific user profile to the server when the user logs in. The server then sends the user profile to the agent. This profile might include information on which application programs that the user would normally run, the types of files the user normally accesses, the type of networked resources the user uses, the times the user normally logs in, and so on. There can be even more specific information that clearly identifies the user, such as the speed at which the user normally types, the amount of usage of the mouse, and so on. The agent can then check the current usage against the user's normal usage. Any differences in behaviour can be reported to the server, which can then be checked by the system administrator. In an extreme case, the agent could use data mining, where information on the user is found from sources around the Internet. For example, the agent could find out that the user normally shops at a certain high street store, and their normally monthly phone bill.

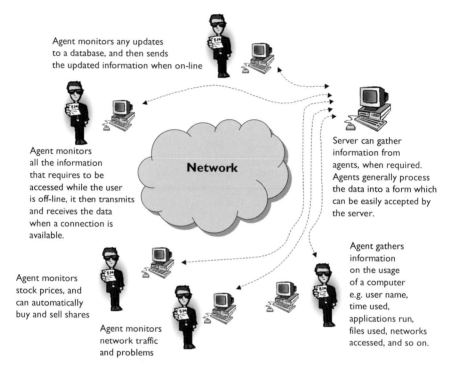

Agent monitors any updates to a database, and then sends the updated information when on-line

Agent monitors all the information that requires to be accessed while the user is off-line, it then transmits and receives the data when a connection is available.

Network

Server can gather information from agents, when required. Agents generally process the data into a form which can be easily accepted by the server.

Agent monitors stock prices, and can automatically buy and sell shares

Agent monitors network traffic and problems

Agent gathers information on the usage of a computer e.g. user name, time used, applications run, files used, networks accessed, and so on.

Figure A7.1 Agent applications

For security, the agent thus reduces the loading on the server, as the agent monitors the fine detail of the user's behavior. The agent is also responsible for updating the profile of the user, and will thus resend the updated profile when the user has completed their tasks. This has minimized the communications with the server, as the agent only requires to send/receive data at log-in, when a problem occurs, or with an updated user profile, as user profiles are dynamic, and change over time (but they tend to change slowly, thus sharp changes normally indicate a breach of security).

The requirement for agents increases for many reasons, such as:

- Increased requirement for management information for system administrators.
- Increased requirement for reliability for networked applications.

- Increased requirement for a certain quality of service from the network.
- Increased usage of many different types of computer systems, operating systems, networked operating systems, network technologies, and networking protocols.

Mobile agents are a further enhancement on agent technology. These can move around the network, and can actually migrate themselves so that they communicate with the server, on the server. This can have advantages in certain applications, as it reduces the command overhead of handshaking with the server over the network.

Traditional client-server architectures are typically wasteful in their usage of bandwidth. Agent mobility overcomes this by minimizing bandwidth consumption, as they:

- Support adaptive network load balancing.
- Solve problems caused by intermittent or unreliable network connections.

The main area that agents will bring benefits is where autonomy and mobility are required, such as in network management applications. The aim of mobile agent research is to adopt mobile agent architecture and to provide the framework on which to build a variety of network management tasks, as well as investigating the advantages of mobile agent architecture over client/server architecture. Most software development systems use object-oriented methods, and a mobile agent can be viewed as the next step in the evolution of the object-oriented design, where an agent object is also given a location.

A7.2   Agent types

Agents are commonly used in other technological areas, such as:

- **Artificial intelligence**. For improving collaborative on-line social environments.
- **Distributed systems**. Enhancements to the client/server architecture.
- **Electronic gophers**. These can monitor the stock market and purchase shares, locate and purchase cheap flights, notify a network administrator of a network fault (and even execute fault rectifying procedures), or monitor a website.

Accurate definitions for agents are:

"An agent is anything that can be viewed as perceiving its environment through sensors and acting upon that environment through effectors"
"Autonomous agents are computational systems that inhabit some complex dynamic environment, sense and act autonomously in this environment, and by doing so realize a set of goals or tasks for which they are designed"
"Intelligent agents are software entities that carry out some set of operations on behalf of a user or another program with some degree of independence or autonomy and in so doing, employ some knowledge or representation of the user's goals or desires."

These definitions, whilst informative, result from specific examples of agents, but are not truly representative as a global definition. Franklin and Graesser who have classified agents with the characteristics given in Figure A7.2 provide the best definition.

In order to be useful, an agent must respond quickly to changes in the environment, as the information would arrive too late to be acted on. In addition, the great benefit of agents is that they act autonomously and do not need to communicate with other agents or with the server for their operation. Thus, all agents are autonomous, and should run continuously. Every agent satisfies the first four properties (reactive, autonomous, goal-oriented and temporally continuous), and the others are added as they are required for the application.

Many software packages already use agents, such as Office Assistants in Microsoft Office, which match the properties of agents (that is, reactive, autonomous, goal-oriented and temporally continuous). For example, a spell-checking agent continuously monitors the typing of a user and makes corrections on the fly. Spell and grammar checking agents are complex, and rely on AI for their functionality, as they display some characteristics of intelligence (in fact, in relation to grammar, they are often better than humans). However, these agents do not possess mobility, and are, at present, unable to operate in a distributed environment.

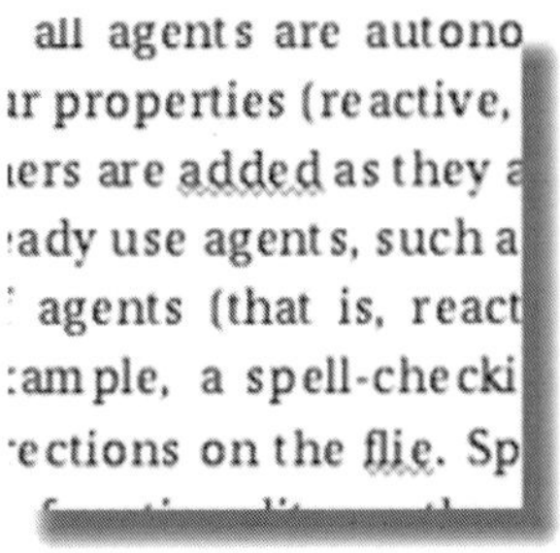

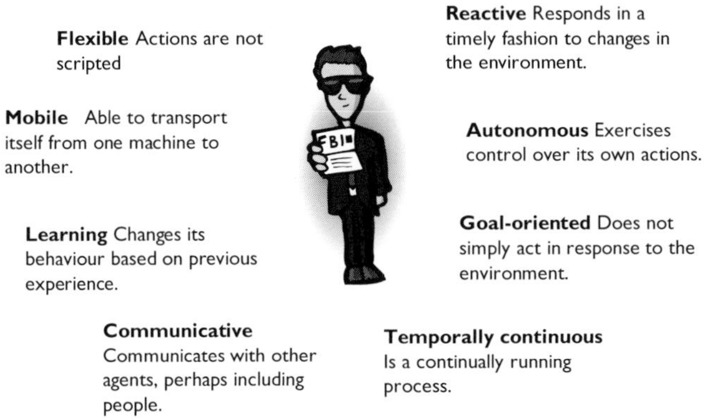

Flexible Actions are not scripted

Mobile Able to transport itself from one machine to another.

Learning Changes its behaviour based on previous experience.

Communicative Communicates with other agents, perhaps including people.

Reactive Responds in a timely fashion to changes in the environment.

Autonomous Exercises control over its own actions.

Goal-oriented Does not simply act in response to the environment.

Temporally continuous Is a continually running process.

Figure A7.2 Agent properties

In a distributed system, mobility is a key property when considering the implementation of mobile agent architectures against traditional client/server architectures. In a client/server application, the client and the server programs normally exist on different systems, and communicate over the network. When the client requires data or access to resources from the server, the client sends a request to the server. The server then responds with a response to the client. This handshaking operation has a communications overhead, and will use some of the bandwidth of the interconnection. The main difference in mobile agent architecture is the place at which the communication takes place; as, in mobile agent architecture, the client does not talk to the server over the network. It does it at the server. It is the agent which moves itself over the network, than that the data passed between the agent and the server.

Mobile agents offer several advantages over traditional client/server models, such as:

1. Possibly reduce bandwidth requirements, as the handshaking between the client and the server does not occur over the interconnected network. Normally this response is a query or a transaction from the client to the server; this eliminates repetitive re-

quest/response handshakes.

2. They allow decisions about the location of code (client against server) to be made at the end of the development cycle when more is known about how the application will perform. This reduces the design risk.

3. They solve the problems created by intermittent or unreliable network connections. Agents can be easily created to work *off-line* and communicate their results when the application is back *on-line*.

Mobile agents have great advantages in network management applications, and solve several problems:

1. **Network bandwidth**. Client/server transactions use some of the available bandwidth, would could be reduced when the agent migrates itself onto the server (or, if it is off-line, when a connection can be made). The agent can also compile the required information from the collected data, and bring this information to the server, rather than the server communicating back and forth with the client.

2. **Protocol communications**. In developing traditional client/server applications, at an early stage the programmer must clearly define the roles, and the intent, of a client and server. As the client and server communicate using a well-structured protocol, there is little scope for modifications or enhancements. By contrast, mobile agent architecture allows more flexibility, as the agent can be allowed to visit several nodes on the network in succession, carrying out some task. The only requirement is that the node must accept the mobile agent and provide it with an operation environment. The communication occurs at a high level, normally with message passing (such as GET and PUT), is clearly defined and the programmer only requires to concentrate on the tasks of the agent (and not the communications mechanism).

3. **Intermittent connections**. Agent technology helps with unreliable network connections. With traditional methods a good reliable connection must be present for the complete time of a conversation. An agent can be dispatched to a node so that it can collect some data, process it, and send the information back to the server when connection becomes active. A good example of this is with a notebook computer which creates a dial-up connection with the server, where the server would send an agent to perform a remote monitoring task, and the results communicated to the server when the notebook next connects back onto the network.

4. **Load balancing**. Large computations can be split up into a number of smaller parallel tasks which can be executed by agents on different hosts. Agents perform the lower-level tasks, such as collecting data and processing it into a form that the server requires. The server is thus not burdened with major processing and is involved with the high-level management of the information.

5. **Real-time notification**. This is where an agent on a remote site can notify a server when events occur on the remote node.

6. **Heterogeneous networks**. Many networks contain a mixture of different operating systems, and computer types. Agents cope with this as they can reside within any type of system, and hide the computer type and operating system from the server.

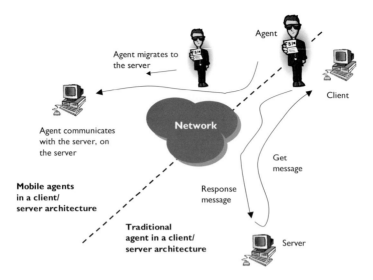

Figure A7.3 Mobile agents

A7.2.1 Agent definitions

Simple agent definitions include:

- **Co-operative agents**. Co-operative agent can communicate with, and react to its environment. An agent's view of its environment would be very narrow due to its limited sensors. Co-operation exists when the actions of an agent achieves not only the agent's own goals, but also the goals of agents other than itself.
- **Reactive agents**. These are a special type of agent, which do not possess internal symbolic models of their environment. Instead, they react to a stimulus or input that is governed by some state or event in its environment. This environmental event triggers a reaction or response from the agent.
- **Weak agents**. Wooldridge suggests that weak agents are autonomous (where they have control over their own actions and states) and have social interaction (agents interact with each other or humans via an agent-communication language). Agents of this type also react and respond to their environment through sensing and perceiving the changes in the physical world, and also display active knowledge of their goal through their actions.
- **Strong agents**. Maes' defines interface agents as "computer programs that employ Artificial Intelligence techniques to provide active assistance to a user with computer-based tasks." Maes' research utilized existing applications and connected them to a learning interface agent, which gradually built a knowledge base of what the human operator may do in certain situations. It is desirable that an agent should exhibit a learning potential to improve its decision-making methods.
- **Mobile agents**. Mobile Agents are software processes capable of moving around networks such as the Internet, interacting with other hosts, gathering information on behalf of their owner and returning with any information it found that was requested by the owner. Mobility is another way that agents can be classified, that is static or mobile.

Mobile agents have to stop execution in order to move around a network, and only continue executing when they arrive at a host that is capable of re-starting and running the code. The suspension of execution is a serious disadvantage of mobile agents. A static agent on the other hand has the ability to execute other tasks while it is communicating with other static agents. Its execution never has to stop.

A7.2.2   Agents characteristics

Agent characteristics can be further grouped into a number of characteristics:

- **Tactile**. Mobility and persistence.
- **Social**. Communication and collaboration with other agents and/or server.
- **Cognitive**. Adaptation, learning and goal orientation.

With current technology, agents can be easily made tactile and social. Mobility of code and computation towards the location of the data and the resources is not new to the WWW, as this is how Java and applets operate, as these allow portable components to be distributed over a network. This mobile code is dynamically loaded and executed by standalone programs. For an applet, this is a WWW browser. Unlike the applet however:

- An agent travels with its state of execution.
- An agent's characteristic of autonomy allows the agent to decide where it can go and what it will do.
- Agents can receive requests from external sources, follow a predetermined itinerary or make decisions such as to travel across the network to a particular host, all independently of any external influences.

Security, though, is a concern in any network. As more applications use connections over a network, the potential of attack also increases, especially with mobile code. Security is a problem with mobile agents, as agent architecture allows agents to move wherever they like over the network and which resources they can have access to. This can allow viruses to spread through a network, where virus agents pretend to be valid agents, and virus servers communicate with valid agents. A security mechanism must thus be developed to handle both trusted code, which is safe, and untrusted code, which is not safe.

Every WWW browser implements security policies to keep applets from compromising system security. The following restrictions apply:

- An applet cannot read from or write to files on the executing host.
- An applet cannot make network connections except to the host it came from.
- An applet cannot read certain system properties.
- An applet cannot start any program on the executing host.
- An applet cannot load libraries or define native methods.

Such security measures are very necessary, but inhibiting. When considering mobile agent architecture we have to address some of these concerns whilst allowing greater flexibility to enable a mobile agent to carry out its work. Java provides a highly customizable security model, which allows us to go some way in achieving this aim. Thus, just as the applet requires a WWW browser in which to execute, so an agent needs a safe environment in which to be hosted. Figure A7.4 illustrates how an agent virus could inhabit a network, either as a virus agent which operates as a valid agent and either send incorrect information to the server, or sends information to a remote server (the virus maker's server), or even causing damage to the host by deleting or moving files or running network or process intensive tasks. A server virus can also exist which receives valid agent information from valid agents. This information can then be used by the virus maker to view network activity, file usage, file information, and so on. The virus server can also get the valid agents to perform certain task (such as viewing or editing files).

To overcome these problems, as a minimum, an agent operating within its host must have:

- A unique identity.
- A means of identifying itself to other agents who are also operating within the host.
- A means of determining what messages other agents accept and send.

The host that is accepting an agent must:

- Allow multiple agents to co-exist and execute simultaneously.
- Allow agents to communicate with each other and with the host.
- Provide a transport mechanism to transfer agents to another host and to accept agents from other hosts.
- Offer a way of 'freezing' an agent's state of execution prior to transfer and conversely 'thawing' it to allow its execution to continue after transfer.
- Inhibit agents from directly interfering with each other.

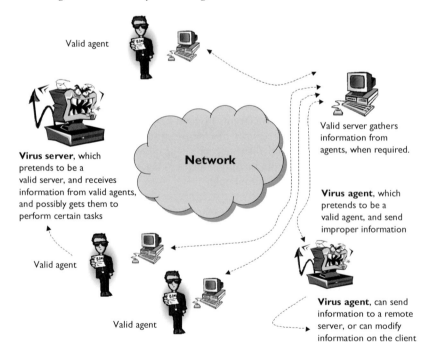

Figure A7.4 Virus agents

As well as giving the agent mobility, the agent must also be given a workplace (a context), where it gets access to only the resources and data that it requires. The context is a stationary object residing on the host computer, and:

- Maintains and runs agents in a uniform execution environment, in a way which secures the host against malicious agent attacks.
- Prevents an untrusted agent from having access to sensitive data or resources, whilst ensuring that a trusted agent has correct rights access to the resources that it requires.

It is relatively easy to create a security model to protect hosts against malicious agents; it is not so easy to protect agents against malicious hosts. If no protection is given against malicious hosts; a host could implant its own tasks into the agent or modify the agent's state. This could lead to the theft of the agent's resources, as a host could upload an agent's class file and state of execution, and then have access to such sensitive information. Thus, the agent's context must have some mechanism where rules can be set stating which privileges an agent has within its context. These privileges are likely to be based on knowledge of the agent's origin.

Agents interact with each other and applications through message passing. Message handling must be able to support both synchronous messages and asynchronous messages. The three types of messages are:

- **Now-type message**. These are synchronous and block the execution until the receiver has completed the handling of the message.
- **Future-type message**. These are asynchronous and do not block the current execution. The sending agent can then either waits for a reply from the recipient or continues processing its task and get a reply later.
- **Multicast**. These are messages which are simultaneously sent to all agents within a context. Only those agents who have subscribed to the message will receive it.

A7.3   Why Java for mobile agents?

Mobile agents can use one of two fundamental development technologies: *mobile code* or *remote objects*. Java is well suited to these environments as it supports both of these through Object Serialization Remote Method Invocation (RMI).

Java has become the development language of choice for building distributed application components. It offers:

- Modular, dynamic, class-orientated compilation units.
- Portability and mobility of compiled code (class files).
- On-demand loading of functionality.
- Built-in support for low-level network programming.
- Fine grained and configurable security control.

The main sections of code required for a Java agent are:

- **Sockets**. In Java, the `java.net` package provides classes for communications and working with networked resources. The socket interface provides access to standard network protocols used for communications between nodes on a network. TCP/IP communications provides for the usage of a socket where applications transmit though a data stream, that may or may not be on the same host. Java supports a simplified object-oriented interface to sockets making their use considerably easier. Reading from and writing to a socket across a network is as easy as reading and writing any standard I/O stream.

- **Threads**. Multitasking involves running several processes at a time. Multitasking programs split into a number of parts (threads) and each of these is run on the multitasking system (multithreading). A program that is running more than one thread at a time is known as a multithreaded program. These threads allow for smoother operation. A server application that could only handle a request from one client would be of limited use. Threads provide a means to allow an application to perform multiple tasks simultaneously. Java makes creating, controlling, and co-coordinating threads relatively simple.

- **RMI**. RMI supports the information interchange between the server and client. It uses a distributed object application, where Java objects may be accessed and their methods called remotely to take advantage of a distributed environment and thus spread a workload over a number of network nodes. It also provides a means in which agents may communicate with each another.

- **Object serialization**. This is a process which enables the reading and writing of objects, and has many uses, such as RMI and object persistence. In developing agent applications it is serialization that can provide *mobility*. An object (an agent) may be serialized (converted to a bit stream), and moved (passed over the socket) to another host where it continues its execution. Thus, the agent is no longer bound to the host, but has the whole network as a resource. Through this process an agent object may be serialized, that is converted to a stream of bytes, then written to any opened standard output stream (a file, memory, or a socket). Reading from and writing to a socket across a network is as easy as reading and writing any standard I/O stream. Prior to its imminent serialization the agent must be informed so allowing it to write to the heap all information necessary for its reconstruction. The agent, complete with its state, may then be reconstructed from the stream of bytes at its new location by reversing the process. In adopting this serialization technique, we also encompass persistence, both mobility and persistence being properties in the first of the characteristics required in a mobile agent architecture.

Java thus supports sockets, threads, RMI and object serialization, and is thus the ideal development environment for mobile agents, and any distributed application.

One important area is security. Agent architecture ultimately allows agents to move around a network, where the boundaries of hosts become blurred and access to local resources is available, security becomes a major concern. It could be easy to write agents which could corrupt the data on the systems connected to a network. Java offers a fine-grained and highly configurable security control that provides acceptable levels of security to protect hosts from malicious agents. A more difficult question, which is not so straightforward to address, is that of malicious hosts. As hosts upload an agent's class files and state of execution, it could potentially have access to sensitive information. Agent architecture must then include an environment in which agents can operate (known as a context). Rules can be adopted on what privileges an agent may be granted within this context based on knowledge of its origin. These rules are of considerable interest, and are currently being investigated as part of this research.

The original security model provided by Java (the *sandbox* model) allowed a very restricted environment in which to run untrusted code obtained from the open network. In this, local code is trusted to have full access to vital system resources, whereas downloaded code (an applet or agent) is not trusted and can only access limited resources provided inside the sandbox. A security manager is responsible for this. Security has changed over the versions of Java with:

- **Signed applet.** JDK 1.1 introduced this, where a digitally signed applet is treated like local code, with full access to resources, only if the public key used to verify the signature is trusted. Unsigned applets are still run in the sandbox.
- **Security policy.** JDK 1.2 introduced this in an attempt to integrate all aspects of security into a consistent approach. All code, regardless of whether it is local or remote, can now be subject to a security *policy*. This policy defines the set of *permissions* available for code from various signers or locations and can be configured by a user or a system administrator. Each permission specifies a permitted access to a particular resource, such as read and write access to a specified file or directory or connect access to a given host and port. The runtime system organizes code into individual *domains*, each of which encloses a set of classes whose instances are granted the same set of permissions. This fine-grained level of security will provide a highly customizable security mechanism necessary in mobile agent architecture.

A7.4   Agents and security

Computer network security mainly involves preventing intrusion of an unauthorized person onto a computer network. The number of users who connect to networks increases, thus the task of preventing unauthorized access also increases. Intrusion includes any action that attempts to compromise the integrity, confidentiality or availability of a computer system resource (for example, unauthorized distribution of sensitive material over the Internet).

The most commonly used security-enhancement method is a simple user name and a password, which is a simple and robust system, but suffers from many problems. The main drawbacks are:

- Once the password barrier has been breached, there are few means of preventing the system being modified or destroyed.
- Once the security system has been setup (proactively), it is often difficult to anticipate every possible case of abnormal behaviour.

One solution to these problems is to create and maintain historical user profiles of normal usage and compare them with current usage, and monitor the differences. These can be used as most users do not vary the way that they use the system. A historical user profile is built up over a defined time, and includes a mixture of:

- **System wide level.** For example, the type and mix of jobs being run.
- **User level.** This relates to specific user profiles, such as applications program types, process durations, user working times, typing speed, types of files accessed, and so on.

It can then be the task of the agent to gather this information, and report back its results to the server.

A7.5 Monitoring software quality

The quality of many products has increased over the years, especially due to the application of quality assurance practices. In the car industry, surveys are completed each year which monitors how reliable a make of car has been. This has had a great effect on car sales. The software industry still produces unreliable software, and it is not uncommon for a computer to crash several times a day. This is typically because it is impossible to test a software program in every possible combination. Thus, a solution is to run agents on computers which monitor the operation of a specific software program. Any time that a program crashed the agent could gather details on it and the current environment. This information could then be sent back to the software producers, for them to investigate the crash, and hopefully find a method to make the software more reliable.

Another possible extension of this is for the software industry to be monitored in the same way as the car industry. For this, the agent would send information on crashes to an independent organization, who would then compile details on the reliability of various software packages, and publish their results each year. This would have a great effect on software producers, and would give them a great motivation on improving software quality, and not as many do, increase the number of user facilities (Figure A7.5).

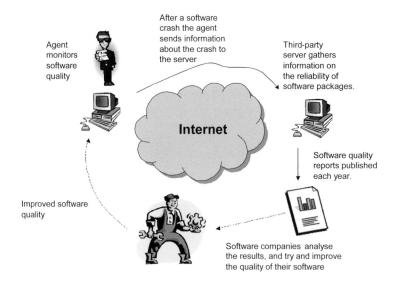

Figure A7.5 Agent monitoring software quality

A7.6 Mobile agents and network management

Distributed network management is an important task as networks have grown in their importance and the number of users who depend on them. Network managers face a difficult task in collating information. Agents may be one answer that could help in getting this information.

Typically, networks and information on those networks are managed in a centralized manner, with a client-server-based architecture. With this, a server advertises a set of *services* which provide access to *resources* (such as databases). The executable code that implements these services is hosted locally by the server. The server, itself, executes the service, and thus has the *processor* capability. If the client needs to access a resource which is hosted by the server, it will simply use one or more of the services provided by the server. The client needs some limited 'intelligence' to decide which of the services it should use. The server then holds, in one central location, all of the facilities required: the services, the resources and the processing capability.

With mobile agents, the roles of client and server are less defined, as the agent can migrate to the server directly, taking with it the code that implements the service; thus the resources and services need no longer reside at the same host. This leads to a potentially more flexible and distributed system where computation migrates toward resources. Applications which could have advantages with migrating computation and mobile agents toward resources include:

- **Data backup management**. As networks grow in size and complexity, managing a consistent backup procedure becomes increasingly difficult. Agents could be allowed to roam around the network and check or confirm the backup status for every disk locally.
- **Software deployment**. Normally software deployment on a static network is relatively simple (that is, users do not physically move). Where users are mobile (perhaps use laptops which connect to a network) and only occasionally connect to the network, tracking software upgrades becomes difficult. Agents could be used to inform a user, when they connect to the network, of any recent software upgrades. This makes the task of tracking and informing all network users simpler.
- **Software acceptance trials**. In a trails network, an agent could be used to monitor how often a certain application gets accessed. The data could then be relayed to another agent responsible for collecting and collating this data. These results could then be communicated to the network manager on a daily, weekly or monthly basis and could form the basis for software acceptance trials.
- **Accessing databases**. Typically data may be spread over a number of databases. An agent may be given an itinerary in which it is instructed to visit a number of database servers to collect information. The agent could then perform computationally intense retrieval tasks. This will not have any problems with network delay (latency) as the data is accessed locally.
- **Network usage**. Where network usage is heavy at certain key times, agents could be used to visit nodes locally and gather information relevant to network use. The agents could return to a common point of origin at a more appropriate time so relieving the network of extra traffic.
- **Intranet web site monitor**. Increasingly organizations use local web sites on their intranets as a means of sharing and distributing information. A monitoring agent could be used which could monitor specific documents for updates. When such an update occurs the agent could inform interested parties.

A7.7   User agents

The future could see an increase in personal agents, which perform specific task for the user. As Figure A7.6 illustrates, an agent could be programmed by an agent programming station, where generic agents are given tasks by the user, such as searching the best airline ticket, or determining if there are any problems on a route for a journey. It may even be possible to create hi-fi agents who determine the tastes of the person who is listening. This type of approach should make computer programs less complex, as the agent only has a small task to achieve. The trend recently has been towards large and multifunction programs which typically are unreliable.

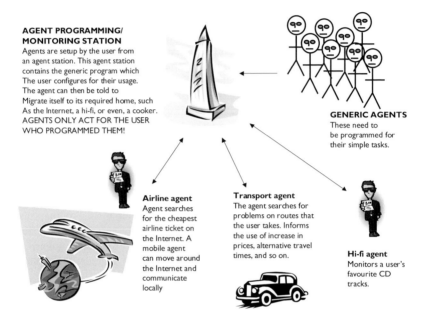

AGENT PROGRAMMING/ MONITORING STATION
Agents are setup by the user from an agent station. This agent station contains the generic program which The user configures for their usage. The agent can then be told to Migrate itself to its required home, such As the Internet, a hi-fi, or even, a cooker. AGENTS ONLY ACT FOR THE USER WHO PROGRAMMED THEM!

GENERIC AGENTS
These need to be programmed for their simple tasks.

Airline agent
Agent searches for the cheapest airline ticket on the Internet. A mobile agent can move around the Internet and communicate locally

Transport agent
The agent searches for problems on routes that the user takes. Informs the use of increase in prices, alternative travel times, and so on.

Hi-fi agent
Monitors a user's favourite CD tracks.

Figure A7.6 Agent monitoring software quality

A7.8   Agent development tool

Java is an excellent choice for a development language, but it is not so easy to determine an environment in which to develop mobile agents. It would of course be possible to develop from scratch a suitable environment, as Java supports all the necessary requirements, but this would be a massive undertaking. Instead, it is necessary to examine what is already available. There are a host of agent development environment, such as:

- **JATLite** [1]. This allows the development of agents that exchange messages and agent router functionality. Agent routing allows any registered agent to send messages to any other registered agent by making a single socket connection to the agent router – messages are forwarded without the sending agent having to know the receiving agent's address and make a separate socket connection. All messages are buffered avoiding losses due to intermittent network problems. This provides a robust message passing system, in which agents communicate through passing messages. It does not however benefit from allowing agent mobility.
- **Object Space Voyager** [2]. This provides a system which takes existing Java class and *treat* them it to create a new class with an identical interface, known as a proxy. The

proxy is an image of another class and operates just as the original to using it. A proxy, however, uses network communications to create and control an instance of the real class it represents. It offers an extension to RMI, and its strength mainly lies in the integration and support of other distributed technologies, such as CORBA.

- **IBM Aglets** [3]. This allows for the development of its mobile agent, called aglets, which are Java objects which can move from one host to another, over a network. When the aglet moves, it takes the program code as well as all the objects it is carrying.

Distributed applications can be classified into two groups: those where applications are partitioned among participating nodes and the other computation is partitioned towards resources. JATLIte and Object Space Voyager use the first type, whereas aglets migrate computation toward resources. This mobility offers an evolution of the OO paradigm where an object can be given a location, and for this reason, the Aglet Workbench has been chosen as the one of the best choices of development system.

The aglet framework provides useful generic aglet pairs from which development of network management tasks may evolve. These are:

- Messenger – receiver.
- Master – slave.
- Notifier – notification.

Using the aglet framework is a convenient way for user-defined agent to inherit default properties and functions for mobile agents.

References:

[1]   JATLite [http://java.stanforrd.edu]
[2]   ObjectSpace: Voyager Overview [http://www. objectspace.com/ products/vgrOverview.htm]
[3]   IBM Aglets SDK (1998). [http://www.trl.ibm.co.jp/aglets/]

A7.9   Practical agent implementation

Rather than having a client/server type communication, an aglet (a mobile agent) is deployed which actually travels to the server, from the client and carries out some action on the machine where the server resides.

The infoserver class handles multiple requests from any client. It responds to a PUT or GET message by collecting local information sent by the client, or by sending all the information gathered so far.

```
import java.net.* ;
import java.io.*;

import java.util.Vector;
import java.util.Enumeration;

class infoClient {
   private Socket theclient=null ;
   private InetAddress host ;
   //private PrintWriter out ;
```

```java
//private BufferedReader in ;

infoClient (int port) throws IOException {
   InetAddress local=InetAddress.getLocalHost();
   theclient=this.createsocket(local,port) ;
   this.Do(null) ;
}

infoClient (String hostString, int port)
               throws IOException {
   InetAddress host =
          InetAddress.getByName(hostString);
   theclient=this.createsocket(host,port);
   this.Do(null) ;
}

private Socket createsocket(InetAddress host,
               int port) throws IOException {
   Socket client = null ;
   try {
      client= new Socket(host,port) ;
      out= new PrintWriter(
             client.getOutputStream(), true) ;
      in= new  BufferedReader(
        new InputStreamReader(
               client.getInputStream()))) ;
   } catch (UnknownHostException e) {
      System.err.println("Can't find host") ;
   }  catch (IOException e) {
      System.err.println("Error : " + e) ;
   }
   System.out.println("Running infoCLIENT") ;
   System.out.println("Created socket : " +
               client.toString() + "\n") ;
   return client ;
}

private void Do(String action)
               throws IOException {
   PrintWriter out=new PrintWriter(
       theclient.getOutputStream(), true) ;
   BufferedReader in=new BufferedReader(
       new InputStreamReader(
         theclient.getInputStream())) ;
   BufferedReader userin=new BufferedReader(
       new InputStreamReader(System.in)) ;
   Vector info=new Vector() ;
   String userInput;

   System.out.println(in.readLine()) ;
   // get welcome message
   action=userin.readLine() ;
   out.println(action) ;                   // send client request
   System.out.println(in.readLine()) ;
   // get sever response

   if (action.equalsIgnoreCase ("PUT")) {
      // write object
      ObjectOutputStream infoOut=
         new ObjectOutputStream(
            theclient.getOutputStream()) ;
      infoOut.writeObject(new LocalInfo());
   }
```

```
        if (action.equalsIgnoreCase ("GET")) {
            // or read object(s)
            ObjectInputStream infoIn=new
                ObjectInputStream(
                    theclient.getInputStream()) ;
            try {
                info=(Vector)infoIn.readObject() ;
                System.out.println(
                    "Data returned from Server ....\n") ;
            } catch (ClassNotFoundException Ce) {
                System.out.println("Error :" +Ce) ;
            }

            Enumeration e=info.elements() ;
            while (e.hasMoreElements()) {
                LocalInfo i=(LocalInfo)e.nextElement() ;
                System.out.println(i.getAll()) ;
                System.out.println() ;
            }
        }
        userin.close() ;
        out.close() ;            // cleanup
        in.close() ;
        theclient.close() ;
    }
}
```

The infoClient class is the client side of the application. When the user issues a PUT command the local info is obtained and sent to the server as a LocalInfo object. A GET command receives an array (a Java vector) of LocalInfo objects gathered so far.

```
import java.net.* ;
import java.io.* ;

import java.util.Vector;
import java.util.Enumeration;

class infoClient {
    private  Socket theclient=null ;
    private  InetAddress host ;
    private  PrintWriter out ;
    private  BufferedReader in ;

    infoClient (int port) throws IOException {
        InetAddress local=InetAddress.getLocalHost() ;
        theclient=this.createsocket(local,port) ;
        this.Do(null) ;
    }

    infoClient (String hostString, int port)
            throws IOException {
        InetAddress host =
            InetAddress.getByName(hostString) ;
        theclient=this.createsocket(host,port) ;
        this.Do(null) ;
    }

    private Socket createsocket(InetAddress host,
            int port) throws IOException {
        Socket client = null;
        try {
            client= new Socket(host,port) ;
```

```
        out= new
            PrintWriter(
                client.getOutputStream(), true) ;
        in= new
            BufferedReader(new
                InputStreamReader(
                    client.getInputStream()));
    } catch (UnknownHostException e) {
        System.err.println("Can't find host") ;
    } catch (IOException e) {
        System.err.println("Error : " + e) ;
    }
    System.out.println("Running infoCLIENT") ;
    System.out.println("Created socket : " +
        client.toString() + "\n") ;
    return client;
}

private void Do(String action)
                    throws IOException {
    PrintWriter out=new
        PrintWriter(
            theclient.getOutputStream(), true) ;
    BufferedReader in=new BufferedReader(
        new InputStreamReader(
            theclient.getInputStream())) ;
    BufferedReader userin=new
        BufferedReader(
            new InputStreamReader(System.in)) ;
    Vector info=new Vector() ;
    //String userInput ;

    System.out.println(in.readLine()) ;
    // get welcome message
    action=userin.readLine() ;
    out.println(action) ;                          // send client request
    System.out.println(in.readLine()) ;
    // get sever response

    if (action.equalsIgnoreCase ("PUT")) {
    // write object
    ObjectOutputStream infoOut=new
            ObjectOutputStream(
                theclient.getOutputStream()) ;
        infoOut.writeObject(new LocalInfo());
    }

    if (action.equalsIgnoreCase ("GET")) {
    // or read object(s)
        ObjectInputStream infoIn=new
            ObjectInputStream(
                theclient.getInputStream()) ;
        try {
            info=(Vector)infoIn.readObject();
            System.out.println(
                "Data returned from Server ....\n");
        } catch (ClassNotFoundException Ce) {
            System.out.println("Error :" +Ce) ;
        }

        Enumeration e=info.elements() ;
        while (e.hasMoreElements()) {
            LocalInfo i=(LocalInfo)e.nextElement();
            System.out.println(i.getAll()) ;
```

```
                System.out.println() ;
            }
        }
        userin.close();
        out.close();        // cleanup
        in.close();
        theclient.close();
    }
}
```

The LocalInfo class handles the information local to a host.

```
package myAglets;

import java.util.Date;
import java.io.*;
import java.net.*;
import java.lang.System ;

class LocalInfo implements Serializable {

    private String _hostName="Unknown" ;
    private String _userName="Unknown" ;
    private String _osName="Unknown" ;
    private String _osVersion="Unknown" ;
    private String _javaVersion="Unknown" ;
    private Date _localTime ;

  LocalInfo() {
   try {
      InetAddress localHost=
                  InetAddress.getLocalHost() ;
      _hostName=localHost.toString() ;
   } catch (Exception e) {
        System.err.println("Error : " + e) ;
   }

   _userName=System.getProperty("user.name") ;
   _osName=System.getProperty("os.name") ;
   _osVersion=System.getProperty("os.version") ;
   _javaVersion=System.getProperty("java.version");
   _localTime=new Date() ;
   }

   String getHostName() {
   return _hostName;
   }

   String getUserName() {
   return _userName;
   }

   String getOsName() {
   return _osName;
   }

   String getOsVersion() {
   return _osVersion;
   }

   String getJavaVersion() {
   return _javaVersion;
   }
```

```
Date getLocalTime() {
return _localTime;
}

String getAll() {
   String str =
   "Host Name    :" + _hostName + "\n" +
   "User Name    :" + _userName + "\n" +
      "OS Name     :" + _osName + "\n" +
      "OS Version  :" + _osVersion + "\n" +
      "Java Version:" + _javaVersion + "\n" +
   "Local Time   :" + _localTime ;
   return str;
}
}
```

A7.10   Mobile agent development tool

The Aglets Software Development Kit (ASDK) from IBM's Tokyo Research Laboratory is a mobile agent framework written in pure Java that allows the development of distributed applications using mobile agent architecture.

"Aglets are Java objects that can move from one host on the network to another. That is, an aglet that executes on one host can suddenly halt execution, dispatch to a remote host, and start executing again. When the aglet moves, it takes along its program code as well as the states of all the objects it is carrying. A built-in security mechanism makes it safe to host untrusted aglets." (IBM Corp, 1998)

Aglets derive their name from a combination of agent and applet. Applets are event-driven and provide methods that the programmers may override in order to control their life cycle, whereas, ASDK provides a mobility orientated and mobility triggered framework. To create an aglet the programmer creates a subclass of the class aglet. The onCreation() method may then be used to initialize the aglet in a similar way the init() method is the starting point for any applet. The other major methods the programmer may override to customize the behaviour of the aglet are:

onDispatch()   called before an aglet is dispatched
onCloning()   called before an aglet is cloned
onDisposing()   called before an aglet is disposed (killed)

Each of these callback methods corresponds to a triggering action dispatch(), clone() and dispose() which is invoked by the aglet host. Each time an aglet begins execution at a host, the host invokes an initialisation method that will depend on the preceding event:

onCreation()   called the first time an aglet is born
onClone()   called on a clone after a cloning operation
onArrival()   called after a dispatch (or retract) action, where the aglet arrives at a
                new host

The run() method is reserved as the entry point for the aglets main thread and is invoked each time an aglet arrives at a new host, directly after the onCreation() or onArrival()

methods have been called to initialize the aglet.

Aglets communicate by message passing. An aglet wishing to communicate with another aglet first creates a message object, declaring its intent to subscribe to a particular message. The receiving aglet then uses the method `handleMessage()` to process incoming messages. A Boolean value is returned indicating whether that message is subscribed to. Messages may be synchronous or asynchronous.

The agent host supplied in the ASDK is called Tahiti. It offers a graphical user interface in which to run aglets and provides a customizable security interface configurable at each aglet host. It provides a highly customizable security environment. Within each host, the aglet is given a unique identity based on its class name and code base. The owner of the aglet may also be identified by his/her name and e-mail address. Aglets are further categorized as *trusted*, where their code base is local or *untrusted* where the code base originated elsewhere. Security options are defined for each category (trusted or untrusted) and include:

- *File access control.* Defines the parts of a file system that are accessible in either read or write mode.
- *Network access control.* Reserves ports on which network connections may be made .
- *Properties.* Defines which system properties are made available.

A7.11 Tracy

An alternative to Aglets is the Tracy development system which was developed by the Friedrich Schiller University Jena, in Germany. It uses the Java programming language and is thus not platform dependant. Its initial objectives were to provide:

- An open agent migration model.
- A mobile agent system suitable for developing applications using mobile agents.

Mobile agent architecture allows for distributed applications, which allows for simpler to manage and programming. The architecture of Tracy is shown in Figure A7.7. It can be seen that the programming that Tracy deals with transport, session and presentation layers, which means that the developer only has to build his application on top of it. Traditional network programming would require covering all the layers from the network layer, up.

A7.11.1 Management of the logical network and agent servers

In Tracy, an agent server is referred as a node, where a node has a hostname, and a server name. These are the value specified in the property file. An agent server can either be a domain manager, or a single node. On staring an agent server, it first scans its neighborhood for a manager. If it finds one, it registers itself with the manager, and acts after as a single node. If it does not find one, it will become an agent server. In Tracy, a neighborhood is defined as the subnet on which the agent server is started. This is an area confined by a router, as routers do not broadcast TCP or UDP data segments. In general, domains are dynamic, and if a domain manager goes offline, another node will relay it. The domain manager keeps records of all the nodes registered to it, and pings them at regularly intervals. A newer version of Tracy (Version 0.6) has a master node, which acts as global domain manager for local subnetwork managers. It removes any domain limit for the Tracy network.

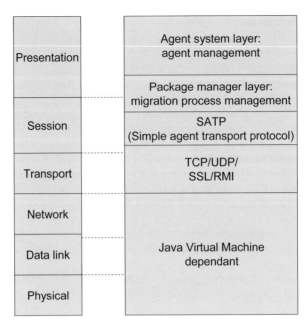

Figure A7.7 Tracy architecture

Tracy supports two types of agents:

1. **Stationary agents:** These agents provide access to additional resources that mobile agents are not allowed to access, and they do not migrate from their home. They are typically used to communicate with mobile agents. Tracy defines these agents as:

   - **Gateway agents.** These are used to interface with host's applications.
   - **System agents.** These are used to interface with host's operating system, and can achieved this by reading or writing to a system entity using the blackboard.

2. **Mobile agents.** These support mobility and dock with agent servers, and can only communicate with an agent server. To reduce security problem, the cannot execute any processes by themselves on the migrated system, and must communicate with other agents to achieve their aims. A mobile agent is transferred by agent server, on their own request or by the request of the agent server. The migration strategy, which the agent server takes into consideration to transfer for the mobile agent, is defined in the mobile agent code. This is referred by a name, and the home platform and they can kill themselves, or by an agent server, that hosts them.

Agents in Tracy can communicate with other agents using:

- **Message passing**. This is a synchronous communication channel between agents, where the sender can be either the agent server or an agent, and the recipient is an agent. The recipient agent must be present on the system to get this message (defined as a mail message). An exception is thrown if a message is sent, and no recipient agent is present. An agent can often go into a waiting state, until it receives the message, after which it can go back into a running state.

- **Blackboard**. This is an asynchronous communication channel, which is maintained by the agent server, and acts as a mailbox for agents. Agents must check the blackboard at regular intervals, as the delivery of the message is not automated.

In Tracy the migration strategy and transmission strategy are open. The main migration strategies are: push and pull. With a push strategy, two agent servers connect to each other and transfer the mobile agent's code (an upload from the source to destination). With a pull strategy, the recipient initiates the connection, and loads mobile agent to its system (a download from the source to the destination).

B1   Data communications

B1.1   Introduction

Communication has always been important to mankind, and lack of communication in the past has resulted in terrible wars and tragedies. It could be said that the reason that we have had world peace for so long is more to do with global communications, than it has to do with diplomacy. The great growth of communications has revolved around three main technologies: the telephone, television and radio. All three initially involved the transmission of analogue signals over wires or with radio waves. On an analogue telephone system, the voltage level from the telephone varies with the voice signal. Unwanted signals from external sources easily corrupt these signals. In a digital communication system, a series of digital codes represents the analogue signal, which are then transmitted as 1's and 0's. These digit forms are less likely to be affected by noise and thus have become the predominant form of communications.

Digital communication also offers a greater number of services, greater traffic and allows for high-speed communications between digital equipment. The usage of digital communications includes cable television, computer networks, facsimile, mobile digital radio, digital FM radio and so on.

B1.2   History

Communications, whether from smoke signals or pictures in the written word, is as old as mankind. Before electrical communications, man has used fire, smoke and light to transmit messages over long distances. For example, Claude Chappe developed the semaphore system in 1792, which has since been used to transmit messages with flags and light.

The history of communication can be traced to four main stages:

- **Foundation.** The foundation of electrical engineering and radio wave transmission which owes a lot to the founding fathers of electrical engineering who were Coulomb, Ampère, Ohm, Gauss, Faraday, Henry and Maxwell, who laid down the basic principles of electrical engineering.
- **Electronics revolution.** This brought increased reliability, improved operations, improved sensitization and increased miniaturization.
- **Desktop computer revolution.** This accelerated the usage of digital communication and has finally integrated all forms of electronic communications: text, speech, images and video.
- **Modern communication.** This increased the ways of connections, and has steadily increased the speed of the connection, such as from satellite communications, local area networks and digital networks.

B1.2.1   History of electrical engineering

The Greek philosopher Thales appears to have been the first to document the observations of electrical force. From this, he noted that rubbing a piece of amber with fur caused it to attract feathers. It is interesting that the Greek name for amber was *elektron* and the name has since been used in electrical engineering.

An important concept in electrical systems is that electrical energy is undoubtedly tied to magnetic energy. Thus when there is an electric force, there is an associated magnetic force. The growth in understanding of electrics and magnetics began during the 1600s when the court physician of Queen Elizabeth I, William Gilbert, investigated magnets and found that the Earth had a magnetic field. From this he found that a freely suspended magnet tends to align itself with the magnetic field lines of the Earth. From then on, travelers around the world could easily plot their course because they knew which way was North.

Much of the early research in magnetics and electrics was conducted in the Old World, mainly in England, France and Germany. However, in 1752, Benjamin Franklin put the USA on the scientific map when he flew a kite in an electrical storm and discovered the flow of electrical current. This experiment is not recommended and resulted in the premature deaths of several scientists.

In 1785, the French scientist Charles Coulomb showed that the force of attraction and repulsion of electrical charges varied inversely with the square of the distance between them. He also went on to show that two similar charges repel each other, while two dissimilar charges attract.

Two scientists who would be commemorated by electrical units made most of their major findings in the 1820s. The French scientist André Ampère studied electrical current in wires and the forces between them, and then, in 1827, the German scientist Georg Ohm studied the resistance to electrical flow. From this, he determined that resistance in a conductor was equal to the voltage across the material divided by the current through it. Soon after this, English scientist Michael Faraday produced an electric generator when he found that the motion of a wire through an electric field generated electricity. From this, he mathematically expressed the link between magnetism and electricity.

The root of modern communication can be traced back to the work of Henry, Maxwell, Hertz, Bell, Marconi and Watt. American Joseph Henry produced the first electromagnet when he wrapped a coil of insulated electrical wire around a metal inner. Henry, unfortunately, like many other great scientists, did not patent his discovery. If he had he would have enjoyed his retirement years as a very wealthy man, rather than on his poor pension. The first application of the electromagnet was in telegraphy, which was the beginning of the communications industry. Henry sent coded electrical pulses over telegraph wires to an electromagnet at the other end. It was a great success, but it was left to the artist Samuel Morse (the American Leonardo, according to one of his biographers) to take much of the credit. Morse, of course, developed Morse Code, which is a code of dots and dashes. He used Henry's system and installed it in a telegraph system from Washington to Baltimore. The first transmitted message was 'What hath God wrought'. It received excellent publicity and after eight years there were over 23,000 miles (37,000 km) of telegraph wires in the USA. Several of the first companies to develop telegraph systems went on to become very large corporations, such as the Mississippi Valley Printing Telegraph Company which later became the Western Union. One of the first non-commercial uses of telegraph was in the Crimean War and the American Civil War, where a communications line from New York to San Francisco was an important mechanism for transmitting information to and from troops.

Other important developers of telegraph systems around the world were P.L. Shilling in Russia, Gauss and Weber in Germany, and Cooke and Wheatstone in Britain. In 1839, Cooke and Wheatstone opened a telegraph system alongside the main railway route running west from London.

One of the all-time greats was James Clerk Maxwell, who was born in Edinburgh in 1831. His importance to science puts him on par with Isaac Newton, Albert Einstein, James Watt and Michael Faraday. Maxwell's most famous formulation was a set of four equations that define the basic laws of electricity and magnetism (Maxwell's equations). Before Maxwell's work, many scientists had observed the relationship between electricity and magnetism. However, it was Maxwell, who finally derived the mathematical link between these forces. His four short equations described exactly the behaviour and interaction of electric and magnetic fields. From this work, he also proved that all electromagnetic waves, in a vacuum, travel at 300,000 km per second (or 186,000 miles per second). This, Maxwell recognized, was equal to the speed of light and from this, he deduced that light was also an electromagnetic wave. He then reasoned that the electromagnetic wave spectrum must contain many invisible waves, each with its own wavelength and characteristic. Other practical scientists, such as Hertz and Marconi soon discovered these 'unseen' waves. The electromagnetic spectrum was soon filled with infrared waves, ultraviolet, gamma ray, X-rays and radio waves (and some even proposed waves which did not even exist).

While Maxwell would provide a foundation for the transmission of electrical signals, another Scot, Alexander Graham Bell, would provide a mechanism for the transmission and reception of sound: the telephone. From his time in Scotland, he always had a great interest in the study of speech and elocution. In the USA, he fully developed his interest and opened the Boston School for the Deaf. His other interest was in multiple telegraphy and he worked on a device which he called a harmonic telegraph, which he used to aid the teaching of speech to deaf people. In 1876, out of this research he produced the first telephone with an electromagnet for the mouthpiece and the receiver. Alexander Graham Bell actually made the telephone call to his assistant with the words 'Mr Watson, come here, I want you.' Unlike many other great inventions, it got good press coverage. 'It talks' was one of the headlines (it has not stopped since). Even the great Maxwell was amazed that anything so simple could reproduce the human voice and, in 1877, Queen Victoria acquired a telephone. Edison then enhanced it by using carbon powder in the diaphragm, to create a basic microphone. This produced an increased amount of electrical current. To fully commercialize his invention, Bell along with several others formed the Bell Telephone Company which fully developed the telephone so that, by 1915, long-distance telephone calls were possible. Bell's patent number 174465 is the most lucrative ever issued. At the time, a reporter wrote, about the telephone, 'It is an interesting toy … but it can never be of any practical value.'

Around 1851, the brothers Jacob and John Watkins Brett laid a cable across the English Channel between Dover and Cape Griz Nez. It was the first use of electrical communications between England and France (unfortunately, a French fisherman mistook it for a sea monster and trawled it up). The British maintained a monopoly on submarine cables and laid cables across the Thames, Scotland to Ireland, England to Holland, as well as cables under the Black Sea, the Mississippi River and the Gulf of St Lawrence. Submarine cables have since been placed under most of the major seas and oceans around the world.

Around 1888, German Heinrich Hertz detected radio waves (as predicted by Maxwell) when he found that a spark produced an electrical current in a wire on the other side of the room. Then, Guglielmo Marconi, in 1896, succeeded in transmitting radio waves over a distance of two miles. From this humble start, he soon managed to transmit a radio wave across the Atlantic Ocean.

Scot Robert Watson-Watt made RADAR (radio detection and ranging) practicable in 1935, by transmitting microwave electromagnetic pulses which were reflected by metal objects (normally planes or ships) and were detected by a receiver. Today it is used in many applications from detect missiles and planes, to detecting rain clouds and the speed of motor cars. Microwave signals have been important in the development of satellite communications.

B1.2.2 History of modern communications

The main developments of modern communications have been:

- **Automated telephone switching**. After the telephone's initial development, call switching was achieved by using operators. This tended to limit the range of the calls, and was particularly unreliable (and not very secure, as operators would often listen to the telephone conversation). However, in 1889, Almon Strowger, a Kansas City undertaker, patented an automatic switching system. In one of the least catchy advertising slogans, it was advertised as a 'girl-less, cuss-less, out-of-orderless, wait-less telephone system.' His motivation for the invention was to prevent his calls being diverted to a business competitor by his local operator. It used a pawl-and-ratchet system to move a wiper over a set of electrical contacts. This led to the development of the Strowger exchange, which was used extensively until the 1970s. Another important improvement came with the crossbar, which allowed many inputs to connect to many outputs, simply by addressing the required connection. The first inventor is claimed to be J.N Reynolds of Bell Systems, but it is normally given to G.A. Betulander.
- **Radio transmission**. One of the few benefits of war (whether it be a real war or a cold war) is the rapid development of science and technology. Radio transmission benefited from this over World War I. A byproduct of this work was frequency modulation (FM) and amplitude modulation (AM). In these, signals to be carried on (modulated) high frequency carrier waves which travelled through the air better than unmodulated waves. Another by-product of the war effort was frequency division multiplexing (FDM) which allowed many signals to be transmitted over the same channel, but with a different carrier frequency.
- **Trans-continental cables**. After World War II, the first telephone cable across the Atlantic was laid from Oban, in Scotland to Clarenville in Newfoundland. Previously, in 1902, the first Pacific Ocean cable was laid. A cable, laid in 1963, stretches from Australia to Canada. These trans-continental cables are now important trunk routes for the global Internet. Their capacity has increased over the years, especially with the introduction of fiber-optic cables.
- **Satellites**. The first artificial satellite was Sputnik 1, which was launched by the USSR in 1957. This was closely followed in the following year by the US satellite, Explorer 1. The great revolution when the ATT-owned Telstar satellite started communicating over large distances using microwave signals. It used microwave signals which could propagate through rain and clouds and bounce off the satellite. The amount of information that can be transmitted varies with the bandwidth of the system, and is normally limited by the transmission system. A satellite system can carry as much as 10 times the amount of information that a radio wave can carry. This allows several TV channels to be transmitted simultaneously and/or thousands of telephone calls. Satellite TV stations are popular in transmitting TV stations over large areas.
- **Digital transmission and coding**. Most information transmitted is now transmitted in the form of digital pulses. A standard code for this transmission, called pulse code modulation (PCM), was invented by A.H. Reeves in the 1930s, but was not used until the 1960s. A major problem in the past with computer systems was that they used dif-

ferent codes to transmit text. To overcome this Baudot developed a 5-unit standard code for telegraph systems. Unfortunately, it had a limited alphabet of upper-case letters and had only a few punctuation symbols. In 1966, ANSI defined a new standard code called ASCII. This has since become the standard coding system for text-based communications. It has only recently been upgraded with Unicode (which uses 16 bits). In its standard form it uses 7 bits and can thus only represent up to 128 characters. It has since been modified to support an 8-bit code (called Extended ASCII).

- **Fiber-optic transmissions.** Satellite communications increased the amount of data that could be transmitted over a channel, but in 1965, Charles Kao laid down the future of high-capacity communication with the proof that data could be carried using optical fibers. Optical fibers now provide the backbone to many networks, including the Internet. Satellites supported the transmission of many hundreds of bits per second, but fibre optics could support billions of bits per second over a single fiber. They are reliable, and have excellent capacity for future upgrading with a new transfer rate.

B1.3   Background

The communications industry has moved from transmitting a single character every second, to transmission of many billions of characters every second. The great breakthrough was to communicate faster than someone could type. One of the most basic communications rate is actually based on the speed of a typist. For this, a good typist will type at around 75 words per minute. If we assume that there are five characters on average in every word (with an extra character for a space). Thus, the typist will type, on average, 450 characters per minute. This will give 7.5 characters ever second. Thus, as each character is represented, in ASCII, with 8 bits. The maximum transfer rate will be:

Transfer rate = 7.5 (characters per second) x 8 (bits per character) = **60 bps**

This was the basic bit rate that a communications link would have to support if it were to receive the speed of a fast typist. When a faster rate was required, the basic rate was doubled to 120 bps (although the standard rate was typically set at 110 bps). The speed then jumped to 300 bps, and multiples of this followed with 1200 bps, 2400 bps, 9600 bps, 19,200 bps (19 bkps), 38,400 bps (37 kbps), 57,600 bps (56 kbps), 115,200 bps (112 kbps), and so on. Most serial communications ports for computers and modems support many of these rates.

From the starting rate of 60 bps, the rates have increased over the years, as more people have used communications links, and backbone data traffic can have a capacity of tens of billions of bits per second (a 166,666,667 fold increase). For example, this chapter contains over 84,000 characters. With a 60 bps transfer rate it would take over **3 hours** to transmit it, while at 10 billion bits per second it would be transmitted in less than **100 millionth of a second** (assuming a transfer rate of 10,000,000,000 bps for 672,000 bits). The basic bit rate of transmission will increase over the years as the demand for data communications increases, and the number of applications for it increases.

The growth in data communications is creating one of the largest and most important industries in the world. It is a technology that brings benefits to virtually all individuals. Without it many organizations could not work efficiently. They are also creating industries that never existed before, such as digital TV, electronic commerce, electronic delivery of video and music, and, best of them all, electronic mail. The trend for transmitting data is to transmit digital information, thus if the original information is in the form of an analogue signal, it must first be converted into a digital form. This can then be transmitted over a digital network. At one time computer type data was sent over a network which was matched to transmitting this type of data, such as Ethernet and Token Ring, and speech was sent over a telephone-type network. The future will see the total integration of both real time (such as speech) and non-real time (such as computer-type data) into a single integrated digital network (IDN), as illustrated in Figure B1.1. The true integrator is ATM, which is covered in one of the WWW-based chapters. Networking technologies such as Ethernet are likely to remain a standard network connection onto a network, as they have become de facto standards.

The communications channel normally provides the main limitation on the amount of data that can be transmitted. This normally relates to its bandwidth, which can either be dedicated to the transmission of data from one source to a destination, or can be shared between more than one source, to more than one destination. Communications systems vary a great deal in the way they setup a connection, such as:

- **Bandwidth contention, bandwidth sharing or reserved bandwidth.** Some communication systems reserve bandwidth for a connection (such as ISDN and ATM), while others allow systems to contend for it (such as Ethernet). Normally the most efficient scheme is to allow systems to share the bandwidth. In this, some nodes can have more of the available bandwidth, if they require, while others can have a lesser share.

- **Virtual path, dedicated line or datagram.** Some communication systems allow a virtual path to be setup between the two connected systems, while others support a dedicated line between the two systems. A dedicated line provides a guaranteed bandwidth for the length of the conversation, while a virtual path should support a certain amount of bandwidth, as a connection has been setup to support the data being transmitted. In a datagram-based system, there is no setup for the route and all of the transmitted datagrams (data packets) take an independent path from the source to the destination.

- **Global addressing, local addressing or no addressing.** An addressing structure provides for individual data packets to have an associated destination address. Each of the devices involved in the routing of the data read this address and send the data packet off on the optimal path. This type of addressed system normally uses datagrams. A typical global addressing structure is IP addressing, which is the standard addressing scheme for the Internet. In a non-addressed system, the data is not tagged with the destination address, and only contains enough information to get it from one device to another. This technique is typically used in setting up a virtual path. No addressing is used when circuit connection is setup, as all the data takes the same route.

Most communication channels are sequential in their nature, where the data from one connection goes straight into another channel. Each of the channels has their own bandwidth limitation, thus the bandwidth of a complete system is limited to the bandwidth of the element of the system which has the least bandwidth (unless there are parallel paths around this element). This is similar to hi-fi systems where the performance of the system is limited by the worst element in the system, as illustrated in Figure B1.6.

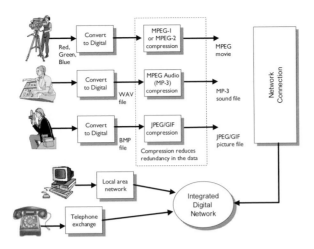

Figure B1.1 Conversion of information into an integrated digital network

B1.4 Data transfer

Data is transferred from the source to the destination through a data path. This data can either be passed in a serial manner (one bit at a time) or in parallel (several bits at a time). In a parallel system, the bits are normally passed in a multiple of eight bits at a time. Typical parallel data transmissions are 8 bits, 16 bits, 32 bits, 64 bits or 128 bits wide.

Parallel transmission is normally faster than serial transmission (as it can transmit more bits in a single operation), but requires many more lines (thus requiring more wires in the cable). A parallel data transmission system normally requires extra data handshaking lines to synchronise the flow of data between devices. Serial data transmission normally uses a start and end bit sequence to define the start and end of transmission, as illustrated in Figure B1.2.

Parallel busses are typically used for local transmission systems, or where there are no problems with cables with a relatively large number of wires. Typically, parallel communication systems are SCSI and the parallel port, and typical serial transmission systems are RS-232 and Ethernet, and most communication systems.

Serial communications can operate at very high transmission rates; the main limiting factor is the transmission channel and the transmitter/receiver electronics. Gigabit Ethernet, for example, uses a transmission rate of 1 Gbps (125 MB/s) over high-quality twisted-pair copper cables, or over fiber-optic cables (although this is a theoretical rate as more than one bit is sent at a time). For a 32-bit parallel communication system, this would require a clocking rate of only 31.25 MHz (which requires much lower quality connectors and cables than the equivalent serial interface).

The main types of communication are:

- **Simplex communication.** Only one device can communicate with the other, and thus only requires handshaking lines for one direction.
- **Half-duplex communication.** This allows communications from one device to the other, in any direction, and thus requires handshaking for either direction.

- **Full-duplex communications.** This allows communication from one device to another, in either direction, at the same time. A good example of this is in a telephone system, where a caller can send and receive at the same time. This requires separate transmit and receive data lines, and separate handshaking for either direction.

Often the transmitter and receiver are operating at different speeds, where the transmitter can send faster than the receiver can receive the data, or vice-versa. To stop too much data being transmitted before it can be processed, there must be an orderly transfer of data. This is normally achieved with handshaking, either with special handshaking lines, or by using software methods (such as sending special data characters to start and stop the flow of data).

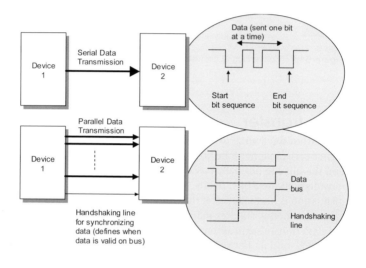

Figure B1.2 Serial and parallel data transmission

B1.5   Data transfer rates

The amount of data that a system can transfer at a time is normally defined either in bits per second (bps) or bytes per second (B/s). The more bytes (or bits) that can be transferred the faster the transfer will be. Typically, serial busses are defined in bps, whereas parallel busses use B/s.

The transfer of the data occurs at regular intervals, which are defined by the period of the transfer clock. This period is either defined as a time interval (in seconds), or as a frequency (in Hz). For example, if a clock operates at a rate of 1 000 000 cycles per second, its frequency is 1 MHz, and its time interval will be one millionth of a second (1×10^{-6} s).

In general, if f is the clock frequency (in Hz), then the clock period (in seconds) will be

$$T = \frac{1}{f} \text{ sec}$$

Conversion from clock frequency to clock time interval

For example, if the clock frequency is 8 MHz, then the clock period will be:

$$T = \frac{1}{8\times10^6} = 0.000000125 \text{ sec}$$
$$= 0.125\,\mu s$$

> Example of a calculation of clock time interval from clock frequency

The data transfer rate (in bits/second) is defined as:

$$\text{Data transfer rate (bps)} = \frac{\text{Number of bits transmitted per operation (bits)}}{\text{Transfer time per operation (s)}}$$

If operated with a fixed clock frequency for each operation then the data transfer rate (in bits/second) will be

$$\text{Data transfer rate (bps)} = \text{Number of bits transmitted per operation (bits)} \times \text{Clocking rate (Hz)}$$

For example, the ISA bus uses an 8 MHz (8×10^6 Hz) clocking frequency and can transfer 16 bits at a time. Thus the maximum data transfer rate (in bps) will be:

$$\text{Data transfer rate} = 16\times8\times10^6 = 128\times10^6 \text{ bps} = 128 \text{ Mbps}$$

Often it is required that the data rate is given in B/s, rather than bps. To convert from bps to B/s, the bps value is divided by eight. Thus to convert 128 Mbps to B/s

$$\text{Data transfer rate} = 128 \text{ Mbps}$$
$$= \frac{128}{8} \text{ Mbps} = 16 \text{ MB/s}$$

> Example conversion from bps to B/s

For serial communication, if the time to transmit a single bit is 104.167 μs then the maximum data rate will be

$$\text{Data transfer rate} = \frac{1}{104.167\times10^{-6}} = 9600 \text{ bps}$$

> Example conversion to bps for a serial transmission with a given transfer time interval

B1.6   Electrical signals

Any time-varying quantity can either be represented as a time-varying signal, or in terms of frequencies. For example when we describe sound we typically refer to it in terms of frequencies, such as an A is described as 440 Hz. Table B1.1 illustrates some of the frequencies for notes for given octaves. It can be seen that an A is taken, in the middle C octave, has a frequency of 440Hz. One octave down from this it is half the frequency (220Hz), and in the octave above this it is double this (880Hz).

Any electrical signal can be analysed either in the time domain or in the frequency domain. A time-varying signal contains a range of frequencies. If the signal is repetitive (that is, it repeats after a given time) then the frequencies contained in it will also be discrete.

Table B1.1 Note frequencies (Hz) for different octaves

	Octave 1	Octave 2	Octave 3	Octave 4	Octave 5	Octave 6	Octave 7
C	32.70	65.41	130.81	261.63	523.25	1046.50	2093.00
C#,Db	34.65	69.30	138.59	277.18	554.36	1100.73	2217.46
D	36.71	73.42	146.83	293.66	587.33	1174.66	2349.32
D#,Eb	38.89	77.78	155.56	311.13	622.25	1244.51	2489.02
E	41.20	82.41	164.81	329.63	659.26	1318.51	2367.02
F	43.65	87.31	174.61	349.23	698.46	1396.91	2637.02
F#,Gb	46.25	92.45	185.00	369.99	739.99	1474.98	2959.96
G	49.00	98.00	196.00	392.00	783.99	1567.98	3135.96
G#,Ab	51.91	103.83	207.65	415.30	830.61	1661.22	3322.44
A	55.00	110.00	220.00	440.00	880.00	1760.00	3520.00
A#,Bb	58.27	116.54	233.08	466.16	932.33	1664.66	3729.31
B	61.74	123.47	246.94	493.88	987.77	1975.53	3951.07

The standard form of a single frequency signal is:

$$V(t) = V \sin(2\pi f t + \theta)$$

where $v(t)$ is the time-varying voltage (V), V is the peak voltage (V), f the signal frequency (Hz) and θ its phase (°).

A signal in the time domain is a time-varying voltage, whereas in the frequency domain it is voltage amplitude against frequency. Figure B1.3 shows how a single frequency is represented in the time domain and the frequency domain. It shows that for a signal with a period T the frequency of the signal is $1/T$ Hz. The signal frequency is represented in the frequency domain as a single vertical arrow at that frequency, where the amplitude of the arrow represents the amplitude of the signal.

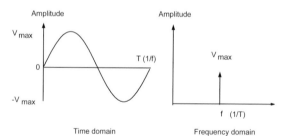

Figure B1.3 Representation of signal in frequency and time domains

B1.7   Bandwidth

In general, in a communication system, bandwidth is defined as the range of frequencies contained in a signal. As an approximation, it is the difference between the highest and the lowest signal frequency, as illustrated in Figure B1.4. For example, if a signal has an upper frequency of 100 MHz and a lower of 75 MHz then the signal bandwidth is 25 MHz. Normally, the larger the bandwidth the greater the information that can be sent. Unfortunately, normally, the larger the bandwidth the more noise that is added to the signal. The bandwidth of a signal is typically limited to reduce the amount of noise and to increase the number of signals transmitted. Table B1.2 shows typical bandwidths for different signals.

The two most significant limitations on a communication system performance are noise and bandwidth. In a data communications system the bandwidth is normally defined in terms of the maximum bit rate. As will be shown this can be approximated to twice the maximum frequency of transmission through the system.

Table B1.2 Typical signal bandwidths

Application	Bandwidth
Telephone speech	4 kHz
Hi-fi audio	20 kHz
FM radio	200 kHz
TV signals	6 MHz
Satellite comms	500 MHz

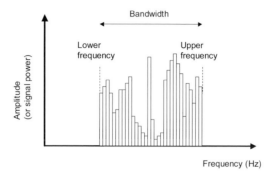

Figure B1.4   Signal bandwidth

B1.8   Bandwidth requirements

The greater the rate of change of an electronic signal the higher the frequencies that will be contained in its frequency content. Figure B1.5 shows two repetitive signals. The upper signal has a DC component (zero frequency) and four frequencies, f_1 to f_4. The lower signal has a greater rate of change than the upper signal and it thus contains a higher frequency content, from f_1 to f_6.

Typically, in a cascaded system, the overall bandwidth of the system is defined by the lowest bandwidth of the cascaded elements. Digital pulses have a very high rate of change around their edges. Thus, digital signals normally require a larger bandwidth than analogue signals. In a digital system made up of cascaded elements, each with its own bandwidth, the overall bandwidth will be given by the lowest bandwidth element (as defined in bps), as illustrated in Figure B1.6. This changes if there are parallel channels, as the bandwidth capacity of a parallel route is equal to the sum of the two parallel routes. For example if data could take two channels, each with a bandwidth of 1 Mbps. Then the total bandwidth would be 2 Mbps, as 1 Mbps could flow over each channel (assuming that the data can be split between the two streams). Typically also bandwidth is not dedicated to a single connection, and must thus be divided by several connections. For example, if the maximum bandwidth of a channel is 10 Mbps, and that this is split between 10 users. If each of the users were equally using the channel then the bandwidth available to each user will be 1 Mbps. This type of equal sharing may not be the best solution, thus in some cases users may be allocated a given share of the allocation.

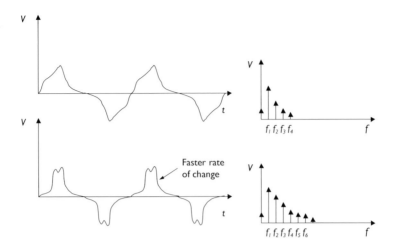

Figure B1.5 Frequency content of two repetitive signals

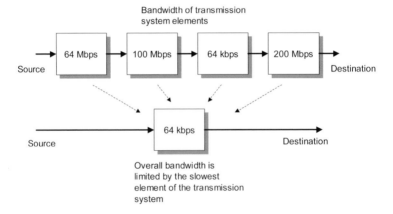

Figure B1.6 Overall bandwidth related to the system bandwidth elements

B1.9   Noise and signal distortion

Noise is any unwanted signal added to information transmission. The main sources of noise on a communication system are:

- **Thermal noise.** Thermal noise occurs from the random movement of electrons in a conductor and is independent of frequency. The noise power can be predicted from the formula:

$$N = k\,T\,B$$

where N is the noise power in watts, k is Boltzman's constant (1.38×10^{-23} J/K), T is the temperature (in K) and B the bandwidth of channel (Hz). Thermal noise is predictable and is spread across the bandwidth of the system. It is unavoidable but can be reduced by reducing the temperature of the components causing the thermal noise. Many receivers which detect very small signals require to be cooled to a very low temperature in order to reduce thermal noise. A typical example is in astronomy where the temperature of the receiving sensor is reduced to almost absolute zero. Thermal noise is a fundamental limiting factor of any communications system.

- **Cross-talk.** Electrical signals propagate with an electric and a magnetic field. If two conductors are laid beside each other then the magnetic field from one couples into the other. This is known as crosstalk, where one signal interferes with another. Analogue systems tend to be affected more by crosstalk than digital ones, but noise in a digital system can could severe errors, if the noise is large enough to change a 0 to a 1, or a 1 to a 0.

- **Impulse noise.** Impulse noise is any unpredictable electromagnetic disturbance, such as from lightning or from energy radiated from an electric motor. It is normally characterized by a relatively high energy, short duration pulse. It is of little importance to an analogue transmission system as it can usually be filtered out at the receiver. However, impulse noise in a digital system can cause the corruption of a significant number of bits.

A signal can be distorted in many ways, especially due to the electrical characteristics of the transmitter and receiver and also the characteristics of the transmission media. An electrical cable contains inductance, capacitance and resistance. The inductance and capacitance have the effect of distorting the shape of the signal whereas resistance causes the amplitude of the signal to reduce (and also to lose power).

B1.10 Capacity

The information-carrying capacity of a communications system is directly proportional to the bandwidth of the signals it carries. The greater the bandwidth, the greater the information-carrying capacity. An important parameter for determining the capacity of a channel is the *signal-to-noise ratio* (SNR). This is normally defined in decibels as the following:

$$\frac{S}{N}(dB) = 10\log_{10}\frac{Signal\ Power}{Noise\ Power}$$

For example, if the signal power is 100 mW, and the noise power is 20 nW, then:

$$\frac{S}{N}(dB) = 10\log_{10}\frac{100\times10^{-3}}{20\times10^{-9}}\,dB$$

$$\frac{S}{N}(dB) = 10\times\log_{10}\left[5\times10^{6}\right]dB$$

$$\frac{S}{N}(dB) = 6.7\ dB$$

In a digital system, Nyquist predicted that the maximum capacity, in bits/sec, of a channel subject to noise is given by:

$$Capacity = B.\log_{2}\left[1+\frac{S}{N}\right]\quad bits/sec$$

where B is the bandwidth of the system and S/N is the signal-to-noise ratio. For example if the signal-to-noise ratio is 10 000 and the bandwidth is 100 kHz, then the maximum capacity is:

$$Capacity = 10^5.\log_2\left(1+10^4\right) \text{ bits/sec}$$

$$\approx 10^5.\frac{\log_{10}\left(10^4\right)}{\log_{10}(2)} \text{ bits/sec}$$

$$= 13.3 \times 10^5 \text{ bits/sec}$$

$$\log_x(y) = \frac{\log_{10}(y)}{\log_{10}(x)}$$

Attenuation is the loss of signal power and is normally frequency dependent. A low-pass channel is one which attenuates, or reduces, the high frequency components of the signal more than the low frequency parts. A band-pass channel attenuates both high and low frequencies more than a band in the middle.

The bandwidth of a system is usually defined as the range of frequencies passed which are not attenuated by more than half their original power level. The end points in Figure B1.7 are marked at 3 dB (the –3 dB point) above the minimum signal attenuation.

Bandwidth is one of the most fundamental factors as it limits the amount of information which can be carried in a channel at a given time. It can be shown that the maximum possible symbol bit rate of a digital system on a noiseless, band-limited channel is twice the channel bandwidth, or:

Maximum symbol rate (symbols/sec) $= 2 \times$ Bandwidth of channel

If a signal is transmitted over a channel which only passes a narrow range of frequencies than is contained in the signal then the signal will be distorted. This is illustrated in Figure B1.8, where the maximum frequency content occurs when the 10101... bit sequence occurs. The minimum frequency content of this bit pattern will be B Hz. The symbol bit rate will thus be twice the highest frequency of the channel. The reason that the rate is referred to as a symbol rate, and not a bit rate, is that the symbol rate can differ from the bit rate. This is because more than one bit can be sent for each symbol. This typically happens with modems, where more than one bit is sent for every symbol. For example, several amplitudes of symbols are to be sent, such as four amplitudes can be used to represent two bits. The symbol rate for speech limited channels will be 8,000 symbols per second (as the maximum frequency is 4 kHz). As four bits can be sent for every symbol, the bit rate will be 32 kbps.

If the frequency characteristics of the channel are known then the receiver can be given appropriate compensatory characteristics. For example, a receiving amplifier could boost higher frequency signals more than the lower frequencies. This is commonly done with telephone lines, where it is known as channel equalization.

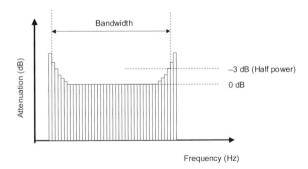

Figure B1.7   Bandwidth of a channel

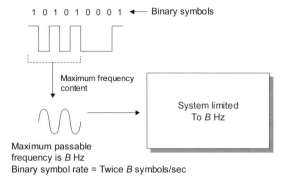

Figure B1.8 Maximum binary symbol rate is twice the frequency of the bandwidth

B1.11   Modulation

Modulation allows the transmission of a signal through a transmission medium by carrying it on a carrier wave (which can propagate through a given media). It also adds extra information that allows the receiver to pick-up the signal (allowing the modulated signal to be 'tuned-into'). For example, audio signals do not propagate well through air for any great distances. If they are added onto radio waves, the waves can propagate for vast distances. With long waves they can actually even transverse the planet. The other advantage of using a radio wave to carry the audio signal is that each audio signal can be transmitted using a different radio frequency. This then allows for many audio signals to be transmitted at the same time. This is known as frequency division multiplexing (FTM). Anyone who tunes to the correct carrier frequency can receive the signal, thus there can be one transmitter of the signal and many receivers. This is similar to the transmission of radio signals, where each radio station has its own carrier frequency, and receivers are tuned into these. This is also known as broadband communications, where a wide band is used to transmit the signals.

There are three main methods used to modulate: amplitude, frequency and phase modulation. With amplitude modulation (AM) the information signal varies the amplitude of a carrier wave. In frequency modulation (FM) it varies the frequency of the wave and with phase modulation (PM) it varies the phase.

B1.11.1 Amplitude modulation (AM)

AM is the simplest form of modulation where the information signal modulates a higher frequency carrier. The modulation index, m, is the ratio of the signal amplitude to the carrier amplitude, and is always less than or equal to unity. It is given by:

$$m = \frac{V_{signal}}{V_{carrier}}$$

Figure B1.9 shows three differing modulation indices. In Figure B1.9 (a) the information signal has a relatively small amplitude compared with the carrier signal, giving a relatively small modulation index. In Figure B1.9 (b) the signal amplitude is approximately half of the carrier amplitude, and in Figure B1.9 (c) the signal amplitude is almost equal to the carrier's amplitude (giving a modulation index of near unity).

AM is generally susceptible to noise and fading as it is dependent on the amplitude of the modulated wave. Binary information can be transmitted by assigning discrete amplitudes to bit patterns.

B1.11.2 Frequency modulation (FM)

Frequency modulation involves the modulation of the frequency of a carrier. FM is preferable to AM as it is less affected by noise because the information is contained in the change of frequency and not the amplitude. Thus, the only noise that affects the signal is limited to a small band of frequencies contained in the carrier. The information in an AM waveform is contained in its amplitude which can be easily affected by noise.

Figure B1.10 shows a modulator/demodulator FM system. A typical device used in FM is a Phased-Locked Loop (PLL) which converts the received frequency-modulated signal into a signal voltage. It locks onto frequencies within a certain range (named the capture range) and follows the modulated signal within a given frequency band (named the lock range). Typically, binary information can be sent by using two frequencies, the upper frequency representing a zero, and the lower frequency representing a one. Modems can transmit binary information by using different frequencies to represent bit patterns.

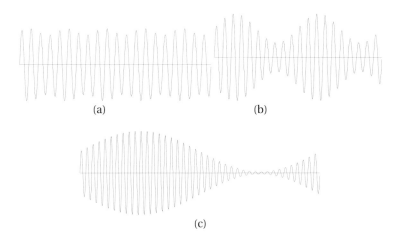

(a) (b)

(c)

Figure B1.9 AM waveform

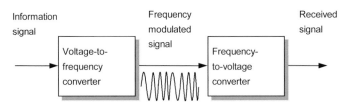

Figure B1.10 Frequency modulation

B1.11.3 Phase modulation (PM)

Phase modulation involves modulating the phase of the carrier. PM is less affected by noise than AM because the information is contained in the change of phase and, like FM, not in its amplitude. As with FM, binary information can be transmitted by assigning discrete phases to bit sequences. For example, a zero phase could represent a zero, and a 180° phase shift could represent a one.

B1.12   Digital modulation

Digital modulation changes the characteristic of a carrier according to binary information. With a sine wave carrier the amplitude, frequency or phase can be varied. Figure B1.11 illustrates the three basic types: amplitude-shift keying (ASK), frequency-shift keying (FSK) and phase-shift keying (PSK).

B1.12.1 Frequency-shift keying (FSK)

FSK, in the most basic case, represents a 1 (a mark) by one frequency and a 0 (a space) by another. These frequencies lie within the bandwidth of the transmission channel. On a V.21, 300 bps, full-duplex modem the originator modem uses the frequency 980 Hz to represent a mark and 1180 Hz a space. The answering modem transmits with 1650 Hz for a mark and 1850 Hz for a space.

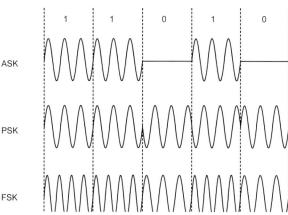

Figure B1.11   Waveforms for ASK, PSK and FSK

These four frequencies allow the caller originator and the answering modem to communicate at the same time; that is, full-duplex communication.

FSK modems are inefficient in their use of bandwidth, with the result that the maximum data rate over normal telephone lines is 1800 bps. Typically, for rates over 1200 bps, other modulation schemes are used.

B1.12.2 Phase-shift keying (PSK)

In coherent PSK a carrier gets no phase shift for a 0 and a 180° phase shift for a 1, such as:

$$0 \quad \Rightarrow \quad 0° \qquad\qquad 1 \quad \Rightarrow \quad 180°$$

Its main advantage over FSK is that as it uses a single frequency it uses much less bandwidth. It is thus less affected by noise, and has an advantage over ASK because its information is not contained in the amplitude of the carrier, thus again it is less affected by noise.

B1.12.3 *M*-ary modulation

With *M*-ary modulation a change in amplitude, phase or frequency represents one of *M* possible signals. It is possible to have *M*-ary FSK, *M*-ary PSK and *M*-ary ASK modulation schemes. This is where the baud rate differs from the bit rate. The bit rate is the true measure of the rate of the line, whereas the baud rate only indicates the signalling element rate, which might be a half or a quarter of the bit rate.

For four-phase differential phase-shift keying (DPSK) the bits are grouped into two and each group is assigned a certain phase shift. For two bits, there are four combinations: a 00 is coded as 0°, 01 coded as 90°, and so on:

$$00 \Rightarrow \quad 0° \qquad 01 \Rightarrow \quad 90°$$
$$11 \Rightarrow \quad 180° \qquad 10 \Rightarrow \quad 270°$$

It is also possible to change a mixture of amplitude, phase or frequency. *M*-ary amplitude-phase keying (APK) varies both the amplitude and phase of a carrier to represent *M* possible bit patterns.

M-ary quadrature amplitude modulation (QAM) changes the amplitude and phase of the carrier. 16-QAM uses four amplitudes and four phase shifts, allowing it to code four bits at a time. In this case, the baud rate will be a quarter of the bit rate.

Typical technologies for modems are:

FSK	– used up to 1200 bps
Four-phase DPSK	– used at 2400 bps
Eight-phase DPSK	– used at 4800 bps
16-QAM	– used at 9600 bps

Most modern modems operate with V.90 (56 kbps), V.22bis (2400 bps), V.32 (9600 bps), V.32bis (14 400 bps); some standards are outlined in Table B1.3. The V.32 and V.32bis modems can be enhanced with echo cancellation. They also typically have built-in compression using either the V.42bis standard or MNP level 5.

Table B1.3   Example modems

Type	*Bit rate (bps)*	*Modulation*
V.21	300	FSK
V.22	1,200	PSK
V.22bis	2,400	ASK/PSK
V.27ter	4,800	PSK
V.29	9,600	PSK
V.32	9,600	ASK/PSK
V.32bis	14,400	ASK/PSK
V.34	28,800	ASK/PSK

B1.12.4 V.42bis and MNP compression

There are two main standards used in modems for compression. The V.42bis standard is defined by the ITU and the MNP (Microcom Networking Protocol) has been developed by a company named Microcom. Most modems will try to compress using V.42bis but if this fails, they try MNP level 5. V.42bis uses the Lempel-Ziv algorithm, which builds dictionaries of code words for recurring characters in the data stream. These code words normally take up fewer bits than the uncoded bits. V.42bis is associated with the V.42 standard which covers error correction.

B1.12.5 V.22bis modems

V.22bis modems allow transmission at up to 2400 bps. It uses four amplitudes and four phases. Figure B1.12 shows the 16 combinations of phase and amplitude for a V.22b is modem. It can be seen that there are 12 different phase shifts and four different amplitudes. Each transmission is known as a symbol, thus each transmitted symbol contains 4 bits. The transmission rate for a symbol is 600 symbols per second (or 600 baud), thus the bit rate will be 2,400 bps.

Trellis coding tries to ensure that consecutive symbols differ as much as possible.

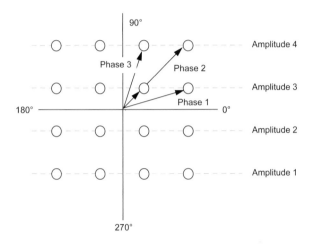

Figure B1.12   Phase and amplitude coding for V.32

B1.12.6 V.32 modems

V.32 modems include echo cancellation which allows signals to be transmitted in both directions at the same time. Previous modems used different frequencies to transmit on different channels. Echo cancellation uses DSP (digital signal processing) to subtract the sending signal from the received signal.

V.32 modems use trellis encoding to enhance error detection and correction. They encode 32 signaling combinations of amplitude and phase. Each of the symbols contains four data bits and a single trellis bit (for error detection). The basic symbol rate is 2400 bps; thus the actual data rate will be 9600 bps. A V.32bis modem uses seven bits per symbol; thus the data rate will be 14 400 bps (2400 × 6).

B1.13   Multiplexing

Multiplexing is a method of sending information from many sources over a single transmission media. For example, satellite communications and optical fibers allow many information channels to be transmitted simultaneously. There are two main methods of achieving this, either by separation in time with time-division multiplexing (TDM) or separation in frequency with frequency-division multiplexing (FDM).

B1.13.1 Frequency-division multiplexing (FDM)

With FDM each channel uses a different frequency band. An example of this is FM radio and satellite communications. With FM radio, many channels share the same transmission media but are separated into different carrier frequencies. Satellite communication normally involves an earth station transmitting on one frequency (the up-link frequency) and the satellite relays this signal at a lower frequency (the down-link frequency).

Figure B1.13 shows an FDM radio system where each radio station is assigned a range of frequencies for their transmission. The receiver then tunes into the required carrier frequency.

B1.13.2 Time-division multiplexing (TDM)

With TDM different sources have a time slot in which their information is transmitted. The most common type of modulation in TDM systems is pulsed code modulation (PCM). With PCM, analogue signals are sampled and converted into digital codes. These are then transmitted as binary digits.

In a PCM-TDM system, several voice-band channels are sampled and converted into PCM codes. Each channel gets a time slot and each time slot is built up into a frame. The complete frame has extra data added to it to allow synchronization. Figure B1.14 shows a PCM-TDM system with three sources.

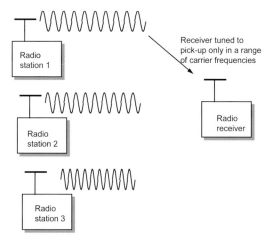

Figure B1.13 FDM radio system

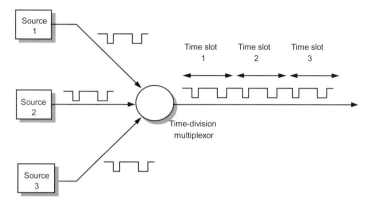

Figure B1.14 TDM system

B1.14 Frequency carrier

Often a digital signal cannot be transmitted over channel without it being carried on a carrier frequency. The frequency carrier of a signal is important and is chosen for several reasons, such as the:

- Signal bandwidth.
- Signal frequency spectrum.
- Transmission channel characteristics.

Figure B1.15 shows the frequency spectrum of electromagnetic (EM) waves. The microwave spectrum is sometimes split into millimetre wave and microwaves and the radio spectrum splits into seven main bands from ELF (used for very long distance communications) to VHF (used for FM radio).

Normally, radio and lower frequency microwaves are specified as frequencies. Whereas, EM waves from high frequency (millimeter wavelength) microwaves upwards are specified as a wavelength.

The wavelength of a signal is the ratio of its speed of propagation (u) to its frequency (f). It is thus given by:

$$\lambda = \frac{u}{f}$$

In free space an electromagnetic wave propagates at the speed of light ($300,000,000\,\text{m s}^{-1}$ or $186,000$ miles s^{-1}). For example, if the carrier frequency of an FM radio station is $97.3\,\text{MHz}$ then its transmitted wavelength is $3.08\,\text{m}$. If an AM radio station transmits at $909\,\text{kHz}$ then the carrier wavelength is $330\,\text{m}$. Typically, the length of radio antenna is designed to be half the wavelength of the received wavelength. This is the reason why FM aerials are normally between 1 and $2\,\text{m}$ in length whereas in AM and LW aerials a long coil of wire is wrapped round a magnetic core. Note that a $50\,\text{Hz}$ mains frequency propagates through space with a wavelength of $6,000,000\,\text{m}$.

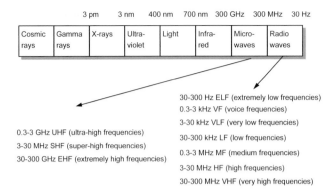

Figure B1.15 EM frequency spectrum

If an EM wave propagates through a dense material then its speed slows. In terms of the dielectric constant, ε_r of a material (which is related to density) then the speed of propagation is:

$$u = \frac{c}{\sqrt{\varepsilon_r}}$$

Each classification of EM waves has its own characteristics. The main classifications of EM waves used for communication are:

- **Radio waves.** The lower the frequency of a radio wave the more able it is to bend around objects. Defence applications use low frequency communications, as they can be transmitted over large distances, and over and round solid objects. The trade-off is that the lower the frequency the less the information that can be carried. LW (MF) and AM (HF) signals can propagate over large distances, but FM (VHF) requires repeaters because they cannot bend round and over solid objects such as trees and hills. Long wave radio (LW) transmitters operate from approximately 100 to 300 kHz, medium wave (AM) from 0.5 to 2 MHz and VHF radio (FM) from 87 to 108 MHz.
- **Microwaves.** Microwaves have the advantage over optical waves (light, infrared and ultraviolet) in that they can propagate well through water and thus can be transmitted through clouds, rain, and so on. If they are of a high enough frequency, they can propagate through the ionosphere and out into outer space. This property is used in satellite communications where the transmitter bounces microwave energy off a satellite, which is then picked up at a receiving station. Radar and mobile radio applications also use these properties. Their main disadvantage is that they will not bend round large objects, as their wavelength is too small. Included in this classification is UHF (used to transmit TV signals), SHF (satellite communications) and EHF waves (used in line-of-sight communications).
- **Infrared.** Infrared is used in optical communications. When it is used as a carrier frequency the transmitted signal can have a very large bandwidth because the carrier frequency is high. It is extensively used in fiber optic communications and for line-of-site communications, especially in remote control applications. Infrared radiation is basically the propagation of heat, and heat received from the sun propagates as infrared radiation.

- **Light.** Light is the only part of the spectrum that humans can 'see'. It is a very small part of the spectrum and ranges from 300 to 900 nm. Colors contained are red, orange, yellow, green, blue, indigo and violet.
- **Ultraviolet.** As with infrared it is used in optical communications. In high enough exposures it can cause skin cancer. Luckily, the ozone layer around the Earth blocks much of the ultraviolet radiation from the sun.

B1.15   Routing of data

Data communications involves the transmission of data from a transmitter to a receiver, over some physical distances. This could involve short distances, such as within a computer system, or a building, or could involve large distances, such as countrywide or even worldwide (or in the extreme case, planet-wide). In order for data to be delivered to a recipient, a path must exist for it. Normally this path is setup by either mechanical switching, electronic switching (where the mechanical switch is replaced by an electronic switch) or virtual switching (where no physical or electronic connection exists between the sender and the receiver, but data is routed over virtual paths). The different types of switching include:

- **Circuit switching.** This type of switching uses a dedicated line to make the connection between the source and destination, just as a telephone line makes a connection between the caller and the recipient. As the connection is dedicated to the connection, the bit rate can vary as required, and possibly underutilized, but there tends to very little delay in transmitting the data.
- **Packet switching.** This type of switching involves splitting data into data packets. Each packet contains the data and a packet header which has the information that is used to route the packet through the network. Typical information contained in the packet header are source and destination addresses. These addresses may only have local significance (such as the address of the next switching device) or could have global significance (such as the Internet address of the source and destination devices). If the addresses have local significance it is likely that they will change as the data packet is passed from place to place, whereas global addresses will stay fixed. With packet switching each switching device on the path reads the data packet and sends it onto the next in the path. The transport can either be:

  o **Datagram.** This is where the data packets travel from the source to the destination, and can take any path through the interconnected network. This technique has an advantage, over setting up a fixed path, that data packets can take alternative paths. This is important when there is heavy traffic on parts of the network, or when links become unavailable. It also does not require a call setup.
  o **Virtual circuit.** This is where all the data packets are routed along the same path. It differs from circuit switching in that there is no dedicated path for the data. Virtual circuits must be setup before any data can be transmitted, and normally the route taken by the data can be chosen so that it gives the required link quality. This quality typically relates to propagation delay (latency), error rate and bandwidth limitations. Data packets in a virtual circuit also normally have some information in the header which identifies the virtual circuit, and this is likely only to have significance to the actual circuit setup.
- **Multirate circuit switching.** Traditionally TDM (time division multiplexing) is used to

transmit data over a PSN (public switched network). This uses a circuit switching technology with a fixed data rate, and has fixed channels for the data. Multirate rates allow transmitters to transmit to different destinations over a single physical connection. For example, in ISDN a node can transmit to two different destinations with a single connection (each of 64 kbps). The bit rate, though, is fixed at 64 kbps, and it is difficult to achieve a variable bit rate (VBR).

- **Frame relay.** This method is similar to packet switching, but the data packets (typically known as data frames in frame relays) have a variable length and are not fixed in length. This allows for variable bit rates. As the data packets are of variable length there must be some way of defining the start and end of the data packet. For this, the special bit sequence of 01111110 is typically used at the start and the end of the frame. A special technique, known as bit stuffing, is then used to stop the start and end sequence from occurring at any other place, apart from at the start and the end of the data frame.
- **Cell relay.** This method uses fixed packets (cells), and is a progression of the frame relay and multirate circuit switching. Cell relay allows for the definition of virtual channels with data rates dynamically defined. Using a small cell size allows almost constant data rate even though it uses packets.

Local connections are typically either made with a direct connection, or over a local area network (LAN). For a connection over a large area, the connection is typically made over a wide area network (WAN) which connects one node to another over relatively large distances via an arbitrary connection of switching nodes. Typically the WAN can use the public data network (PDN) or through dedicated company connections. Figure B1.16 illustrates the two main types of connection over the public telephone network: circuit switching and packet switching.

With circuit switching, a physical, or a reserved multiplexed, connection exists between two nodes. This type of connection is typical in a public-switched telephone network (PSTN), as telephone connections have been made, in the past, with this method. As with a telephone call, the connection must be made before transferring any data. Until recently this connection took a relatively long time to setup (typically over 10 seconds), but with the increase in digital switching it has reduced to less than a second. The usage of digital switching has also allowed the transmission of digital data, over PSTNs, at rates of 64 kbps and greater. This type of network is known as a circuit-switched digital network (CSDN). Its main disadvantage is that a permanent connection is setup between the nodes, which is wasteful in time and can be costly. Another disadvantage is that the transmitting and receiving nodes must be operating at the same speed. A CSDN, also, does not perform any error detection or flow control.

Packet switching involves segmenting data into packets that propagate within a digital network. They either follow a predetermined route or are routed individually to the receiving node via packet-switched exchanges (PSE) or routers. These examine the destination addresses and based on an internal routing directory pass, it to the next PSE on the route. As with circuit switching, data can propagate over a fixed route. This differs from circuit switching in that the path is not an actual physical circuit (or a reserved multiplexed channel). As it is not a physical circuit, it is normally defined as a virtual circuit. This virtual circuit is less wasteful on channel resources as other data can be sent when there are gaps in the data flow. Table B1.4 gives a comparison of the two types.

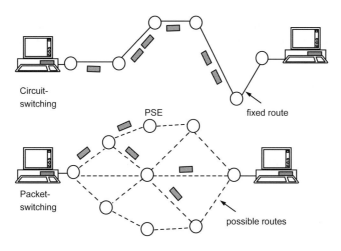

Circuit-
switching

PSE

fixed route

Packet-
switching

possible routes

Figure B1.16   Circuit and packet switching

Table B1.4   Comparison of switching techniques

	Circuit-switching	*Packet-switching*
Investment in equipment	Minimal as it uses existing connections	Expensive for initial investment
Error and flow control	None, this must be supplied by the end users.	Yes, using the FCS in the data link layer
Simultaneous transmissions and connections	No	Yes, nodes can communicate with many nodes at the same time and over many different routes
Allows for data to be sent without first setting up a connection	No	Yes, using datagrams
Response time	Once the link is setup it provides a good reliable connection with little propagation delay	Response time depends on the size of the data packets and the traffic within the network

B2 Real-time data and compression

B2.1 Introduction

Very few things in life are 100% efficient. Just think how wonderful it would be if a car engine could covert the fuel straight into engine power, and not even get hot. This would, of course, use much less fuel, and the reliability of the engine would improve. With computer data the key to efficiency typically relates to the amount of bandwidth that it uses, the size of the data, and the delay in the transmission. The optimum efficiency would be to make every single bit of data count for some information. This would be very difficult, but where resources are low, data must be optimized in the amount of the resources that it uses.

The key factors in reducing the amount of data storage are:

- **Getting rid of redundant data**. This involves determining the parts of the data that are not required. For example, a database could hold data on one hundred people. Each person could have their time and date of birth stored in the database, but if the system simply displayed the person's age, then there is no need for the time of their birth to be stored, in this case, as their age does not depend on the time of birth. Thus, the time of birth could be deleted from the database, as, in this example, it is not required.

- **Identifying irrelevant data**. This involves identifying the parts of the data which are perceived to be irrelevant. A good example of this in music, where a loud instrument, such as a trombone, will often drown-out the sound of a quiet instrument, such as a triangle. Thus, the sound of the triangle can be reduced when there are loud sections of trombone, and brought back to normal in quieter sections. This technique is often used in modern digital music compression. In the days of analogue tape recording a perceivable hiss would be heard when there were quiet sections of music, but it couldn't be perceived when there were loud sections (even though it was still there).

- **Converting the data into a different format**. This will typically involve changing the way that the data is processed and stored. A good example is to change a graphics image from a bitmap, where the color of each pixel is stored, to a metafile, where shapes and sizes are stored. This type of conversion is also used in music files, where the time-varying musical signal is converted into sound frequencies, and then processed. This conversion makes compression much simpler.

- **Reducing the quality of the data**. Often the user does not require the specified quality of the data. For example if an image is stored with 1200 pixels by 1200 pixels, and the user can only view a 800 pixel by 600 pixel size, then the high resolution is not required. There can thus be a saving of 400% of the data size, if the image was reduced to 600 by 600 pixels. If this image was downloaded over the Internet in its raw format, the larger format would take four times longer to download than the small version (360,000 pixels as apposed to 1,440,000 pixels). In addition, the number of colors used can also be much greater than can actually be viewed on a graphics display. For example, a 24-bit color image uses 16,777,216 colors, which may be too many colors for some displays. A reduction to 65,536 colors would reduce the number of bits used to store the color down to 16 bits. This would bring a 50% saving in data size (if it was stored in its raw format).

A key factor in improving the efficiency of the data is to determine the information that is required, and the parts of it that could be lost. Often computer data, in its raw form, is typically stored in an inefficient way, where the data contains a great deal of redundant information.

Computer-type data on the Internet is typically already stored in a fairly efficient manner (especially if it is a large file, as, in the past, disk storage was a precious resource). Computer networks and the Internet have also grown up transmitting computer-type data. These files are relatively easy to transmit as they are already in a digital format, and, in most cases, do not have a large requirement in the amount of data transmitted from each user. The next great wave of usage of networks is from the transmission of video, audio and speech. Each of these types of data, in their raw form, contains a great amount of data, and will generally swamp the rest of the network. Thus, a key to their acceptance will be compression, which tries to reduce the size of the stored/transmitted data, while retaining the required information.

Information must be converted into a digital format before it can be stored on a computer or transmitted over a network. This is achieved by:

- **Images.** Images are converted into digital data by converting each of the pixels in the image into a digital value which represents the color of the pixel. The more colors that are used, the greater the amount of data that is required to store the image.
- **Motion video.** Motion video is basically a series of stored images, which are updated at a constant rate (often known as the scanning rate). For TV signals this rate is 50 times per second for UK-type TV quality (PAL) and 60 times per second for US-type TV quality (NSTC). Often the overall scan rate is reduced to half of this with interlaced updates, where every second scanned line is sent in every screen update.
- **Audio.** An audio file is converted by sampling the audio waveform at a constant rate (8000 times per second for telephone quality speech, and 44,100 times per second for hi-fi audio).

The basic conversion of this data into a digital form creates extremely large amounts of digital data. For example:

Content	Description	Storage requirement
Bitmapped image	1024×800, 65,536 colors	1.5 MB
Motion video	20 frames per second, 1024×800, 65,536 colors, 10 seconds	300 MB
Audio	60 minutes, hi-fi, stereo	600 MB

Cameras contain a red, a green, and a blue sensor. The output from this is typically known as RGB, where the intensities of each of the primary colors are stored. This type of image is known as a bit-map, where the color of each pixel is stored in RGB format. Typically, these values are packed into a single value. For example if 8 bits is used for each of the primary colors then the number of bits used to store each of the colors will be 24 bits. This type of format is typically known as True color. With 8 bits for each of the primary colors there will be 256 different intensities hues, and the total number of colors will be 16.7 million colors (256×256×256). A typical format is to show the color as a hexadecimal value, with the three primary colors (in RGB format). For example:

#2016F1

defines 20h (32, in decimal) for the red intensity, 16h (22, in decimal) or the green intensity, and F1 (241, in decimal) for the blue intensity. Thus the color has a strong blue element, and a lesser red and green intensity. The graphic on the right-hand side illustrates the different intensities.

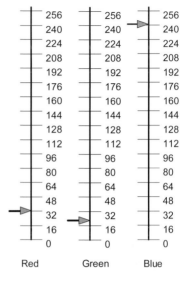

The raw form of image, video and audio contains massive amounts of redundant information, as there tends to be very little changes between one data sample and the next (Figure B2.1). One method used to compress the data is to store the changes between one data sample and the next. For example, in motion video, there are very few changes between one frame and the next (maybe just a few pixels). Thus, all that is required is to store the initial image, and then store the changes between the stored frame and the next, and so on. Occasionally it is important to store the complete frame, as the user may want to scan through the video, and start at any given point.

Motion video image compression relies on two facts:

- Images have a great deal of redundancy (repeated images, repetitive, superfluous, duplicated, exceeding what is necessary, and so on).
- The human eye and brain have limitations on what they can perceive.

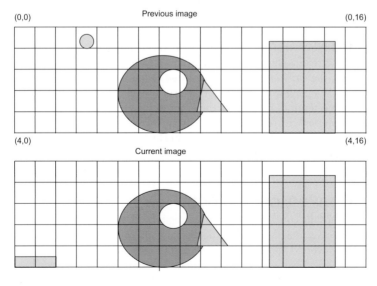

Figure B2.1 Information conversion into a digital form

The main forms of compression for images, video and audio are:

- **JPEG/GIF.** The JPEG (Joint Photographic Expert Group) compression technique is well matched to what the human eye and the brain perceive. For example, the brain is more susceptible to changes in luminance (brightness) and not so susceptible to color changes. Thus to save storage space, more information on luminance can be stored, as apposed to information on color changes. JPEG can compress a photograph which is over 1 MB to less than 20 KB. Another typical image compression standard is GIF. GIF and JPEG operate in different ways, and GIF is aimed at compressing images, while JPEG is focused on photographs. A major limitation with GIF is that it can only display up to 256 colors at a time (but these colors can be virtually any color).

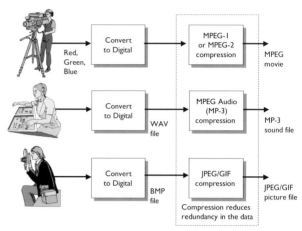

- **MPEG.** MPEG (Motion Picture Experts Group) uses many techniques to reduce the size of the motion video data. It uses the techniques that JPEG uses, to compress each of the images in the motion video. It also compresses between frames by only storing the information that is changing between frames. Typical compression rates are 130:1. Another typical video compression standard is AVI.

- **MPEG (MP-3).** The digital storage of audio allows the data to be compressed. Typically, on an audio CD, a stereo, hi-fi quality song uses about 10 MB for every minute of music (600 MB for 1 hour). The storage requirements are thus extremely large, as a few hours of music would fill many currently available hard disk drives. MP-3 audio uses a compression technique that understands the parts of the music that the human brain perceives, and retains this information, while discarding parts that it does not perceive. For example, the ear will generally only listen to loud instruments, and ignore instruments which are playing quietly. MP-3 is so successful that it can compress hi-fi quality audio into one-tenth of its normal, uncompressed, size. A standard, 60 min music CD can be compressed to around 60 MB. With the increasing size of electronic memory, it is now possible to store a whole music CD in electronic memory, rather than storing it on a CD or a hard disk. Another typical audio compression standard is Dolby AC-3.

B2.2   Conversion to digital

Figure B2.2 outlines the conversion process for digital data (the upper diagram) and for analogue data (the lower diagram). When data is already in a digital form (such as text or animation) it is converted into a given data format (such as BMP, GIF, JPG, and so on). It can be further compressed before it is either stored, transmitted or processed. The lower diagram shows how an analogue signal (such as speech or video) is first sampled at regular time intervals. These samples are then converted into a digital form with an ADC (analogue-to-digital converter). They can then be compressed and/or stored in a defined digital format (such as WAV, JPG, and so on). This digital form is then converted back into an analogue form with a DAC (digital-to-analogue converter).

B2.3 Sampling theory

As an analogue signal may be continually changing, a sample of it must be taken at given time intervals. The rate of sampling depends on its rate of change. For example, the temperature of the sea will not vary much over a short time but a video image of a sports match will. To encode a signal digitally it is normally sampled at fixed time intervals. Sufficient information is then extracted to allow the signal to be processed or reconstructed. Figure B2.3 shows a signal sampled every T_s seconds.

The faster that the signal is sampled, the larger the amount of data that will be used. Thus, it is important that the sampling rate is kept to a minimum, in order to reduce the amount of data required. Luckily, Nyquist came up with a criterion which defines that if a signal is to be reconstructed as the original signal it must be sampled at a rate which is **twice** the highest frequency of the signal.

For telephone speech channels, the maximum signal frequency is limited to 4 kHz and must thus be sampled at least 8000 times per second (8 kHz). This gives one sample every 125 µs. Hi-fi quality audio has a maximum signal frequency of 20 kHz and must be sampled at least 40,000 times per second (many professional hi-fi sampling systems sample at 44.1 kHz). Video signals have a maximum frequency of around 6 MHz, thus a video signal must be sampled at 12 MHz (or once every 83.3 ns).

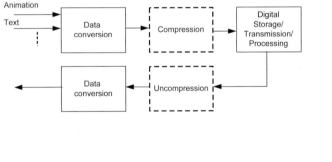

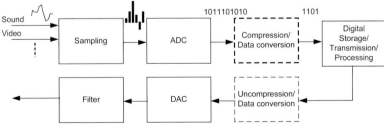

Figure B2.2 Information conversion into a digital form

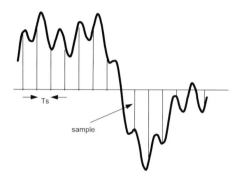

Figure B2.3   The sampling process

B2.4   Quantization

Quantization involves converting an analogue level into a discrete quantized level. Figure B2.4 shows the conversion of an example waveform into a 4-bit digital code. In this case, there are 16 discrete levels which are represented with the binary values 0000 to 1111. Value 1111 represents the maximum voltage level and value 0000 the minimum. It can be seen, in this case, that the digital codes for the four samples are 1011, 1011, 1001, 0111.

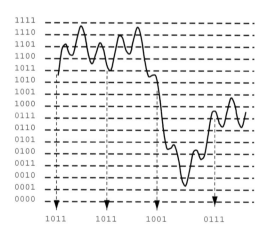

Figure B2.4   Converting an analogue waveform into a 4-bit digital form

The quantization process approximates the level of the analogue level to the nearest quantized level. This approximation leads to an error known as quantization error. The greater the number of levels the smaller the quantization error. Table B2.1 gives the number of levels for a given number of bits.

The maximum error between the original level and the quantized level occurs when the original level falls exactly halfway between two quantized levels. The maximum error will be half of the smallest increment or:

$$\text{Max error} = \pm\frac{1}{2} \cdot \frac{\text{Full Scale}}{2^N}$$

Table B2.1 states the quantization error (as a percentage) of a given number of bits. For example, the maximum error with 8 bits is 0.2%, while for 16 bits it is only 0.00076%.

Table B2.1 Number of quantization levels as a function of bits

Bits (N)	Quantization levels	Accuracy (%)	Bits (N)	Quantization levels	Accuracy (%)
1	2	25	8	256	0.2
2	4	12.5	12	4 096	0.012
3	8	6.25	14	16 384	0.003
4	16	3.125	16	65 536	0.000 76

B2.5   Compression methods

Most transmission channels have a restricted bandwidth, either because of the limitations of the channel or because the bandwidth is shared between many users. Many forms of data have redundancy, thus if the redundant information was extracted the transmitted data would make better use of the bandwidth. This extraction of the information is normally achieved with compression.

When compressing data it is important to take into account three important characteristics: whether it is possible to lose elements of the data; the type of data that is being compressed; and how it is interpreted by the user. These three factors are normally interrelated. For example, the type of data normally defines whether it is possible to lose elements of the data. For computer data, normally if a single bit is lost, then all of the data is corrupted, and cannot be recovered. In an image, it is normally possible to loose data, but it could still contain the required information. For example, when we look at a photograph of someone, do we really care that every single pixel displays the correct color. In most cases the eye is much more sensitive to changes in brightness, and less sensitive to changes in color. Thus in compressing an image, we could actually reduce the amount of data in an image, by actually losing some of the original data. Compression that loses some of the elements of the data is defined as lossy compression, while lossless compression defines compression which does not lose any of the original data. Video and sound images are normally compressed with a lossy compression whereas computer-type data has a lossless compression. The basic definitions are:

- **Lossless compression.** Where the data, once uncompressed, will be identical to the original uncompressed data. This will obviously be the case with computer-type data, such as data files, computer programs, and so on, as any loss of data may cause the file to be corrupted.
- **Lossy compression.** Where the data, once uncompressed, cannot be fully recovered. It normally involves analyzing the data and determining which data has little effect on the perceived information. For example, there is little difference, to the eye, between an image with 16.7 million colors (24-bit color information) and an image stored with 1024 colors (10-bit color information), but the storage will be reduced to 41.67% (many com-

puter systems cannot even display 24-color information in certain resolutions). Compression of an image might also be achieved by reducing the resolution of the image. Again, the human eye might compensate for the loss of resolution (and the eye might never require the high resolution, if the image is viewed from a distance).

Apart from lossy and lossless compression, an important parameter is the encoding of the data. This is normally classified into two main areas:

- **Entropy coding.** This does not take into account any of the characteristics of the data and treats all the bits in the same way. As it does not know which parts of the data can be lost, it produces lossless coding. As an example, imagine that you had a system which received results from sports matches, around the world. With this, there would be no way of knowing the scores that would be expected, and the maximum size of the name that is stored for the result. For example, a UK soccer match might have a result of **Mulchester 3 Madchester 2**, and the results of an American football match might be **Smellmore Wanderers 60 Drinksome Wanderers 23**. Thus, all the information would have to be stored as characters, where each character is stored in an ASCII format (such as with 8 bits for each character), with some way to delimit the end of the score. We could compress this, though, even not knowing the content of the result. For example there are repeated sequences in the scores: *chester* and *Wanderers.* These we could store each of these once, and then just refer to it in some way. This technique of finding repeated sequences is a typical one in compression, and is used in ZIP compression (which is a general-purpose compression technique).

    Typically entropy coding uses:

    - Statistical encoding – where the coding analyses the statistical pattern of the data. For example if a source of text contains many more 'e' characters than 'z' characters then the character 'e' could be coded with very few bits and the character 'z' with many bits.
    - Suppressing repetitive sequences – many sources of information contain large amounts of repetitive data. For example, this page contains large amounts of 'white space'. If the image of this page were to be stored, a special character sequence could represent long runs of 'white space'.

- **Source encoding.** This normally takes into account characteristics of the information. For example, images normally contain many repetitive sequences, such as common pixel colors in neighboring pixels. This can be encoded as a special coding sequence. In video pictures, also, there are very few changes between one frame and the next. Thus typically the data encoded only stores the changes from one frame to the next. In our example of sports matches, we could identify the type of sport, and then compress the data based on this. For example in a UK soccer match, we could have a table of all the names of the sports clubs that we were storing the results for. Thus, for example, we may have 256 professional clubs, which would require 8 bits to store a reference value for each of these (number 0 to 256). So that 0 could be Mudchester, 1 could be Malchester, 2 could be Readyever United, and so on. We can also compress the scores, as we know that the goals scored for a team is very unlikely to be more than 31, thus we could use 5 bits to encode the score (0 to 31). Thus each score could be sent as an 8-bit reference for the home team, followed by a 5-bit value for their score, followed by an 8-bit reference for the away team, and finally by a 5-bit value for their score. Thus, we only need 26 bits to store each of the scores, which is a large saving. In fact we could compress the data even more, as we know that the most probable goals scored will be 0, 1 or 2. Thus we could store zero goals as 00 (in binary), one goal as 01 (binary), two goals as 10 (in binary), three goals as 110 (in binary), four goals as 1110 (in binary), and so on. Thus, as most scores will only have between zero and two goals scored for each team, the average number of bit will be just over 2 bits. For example if the scores were: 0, 1, 0, 2, 3, 2, 2, 1 and 1 (which would be stored as 00, 01, 00, 10, 110, 10, 10, 01 and 01), this would require 19 bits, which is an average of 2.11 bits. This is a reduction from 5 bits for each score.

B2.6   Entropy encoding

Normally, general data compression does not take into account the type of data which is being compressed and is lossless. As it is lossless, it can be applied to computer data files, documents, images, and so on. The two main techniques are statistical coding and repetitive sequence suppression. This section discusses two of the most widely used methods for general data compression: Huffman coding and Lempel-Ziv coding.

B2.6.1   Huffman coding

Huffman coding uses a variable length code for each of the elements within the data. This normally involves analyzing the data to determine the probability of its elements. The most probable elements are coded with a few bits and the least probable coded with a greater number of bits. This could be done on a character-by-character basis, in a text file, or could be achieved on a byte-by-byte basis for other files.

The following example relates to characters. First, the textual data is scanned to determine the number of occurrences of a given letter. For example:

Letter:	'b'	'c'	'e'	'i'	'o'	'p'
No. of occurrences:	12	3	57	51	33	20

Next the characters are arranged in order of their number of occurrences, such as:

'e'	'i'	'o'	'p'	'b'	'c'
57	51	33	20	12	3

After this the two least probable characters are assigned either a 0 or a 1. Figure B2.5 shows that the least probable ('c') has been assigned a 0 and the next least probable ('b') has been assigned a 1. The addition of the number of occurrences for these is then taken into the next column and the occurrence values are again arranged in descending order (that is, 57, 51, 33, 20 and 15). As with the first column, the least probable occurrence is assigned a 0 and the next least probable occurrence is assigned a 1. This continues until the last column. When complete, the Huffman-coded values are read from left to right and the bits are listed from right to left.

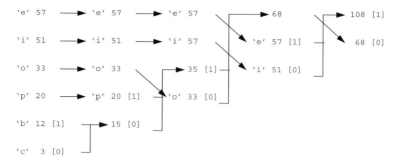

Figure B2.5 Huffman coding example

The final coding will be:

'e'	11	'i'	10
'o'	00	'p'	011
'b'	0101	'c'	0100

The great advantage of Huffman coding is that, although each character is coded with a different number of bits, the receiver will automatically determine the character whatever their order. For example, if a 1 is followed by a 1 then the received character is an 'e'. If it is then followed by two 0s then it is an 'o'. Here is an example:

    11 00 011 0100 10 011 0100

will be decoded as:

    'e'   'o'   'p'   'c'   'i'   'p'   'c'

When transmitting or storing Huffman-coded data, the coding table needs to be stored with the data (if the table is generated dynamically). It is generally a good compression technique but it does not take into account higher order associations between characters. For example, the character 'q' is normally followed by the character 'u' (apart from words such as Iraq). An efficient coding scheme for text would be to encode a single character 'q' with a longer bit sequence than a 'qu' sequence.

In a previous example, we used soccer matches as an example of how data could be compressed. In a small sample of UK soccer matches the following resulted:

0 goals – 21 times;   1 goal –34 times;   2 goals- 15 times;   3 goals– 14 times;
4 goals – 5 times;   5 goals – 2 times;   6 goals – 1 time.

We could then order them as follows:

1 goal – 34 times;   0 goals – 21 times;   2 goals - 15 times;   3 goals – 14 times;
4 goals – 5 times;   5 goals – 2 times;   6 goals – 1 time.

This is obviously a small sample, and there are thus no codes for 7 goals or more. With a larger sample, there would be an associated number of occurrences. Figure B2.6 shows the resulting Huffman coding for these results. Thus, for example, a binary value of 01 will represent zero goals scored, and so on. This code could be combined with a table of values that represent each of the soccer teams. So, if we have 256 different teams (from 0 to 255), and use 00000000b to represent Mulchester, and 00000001b to represent Madchester, then the result:

Mulchester 2 Madchester 0

would be coded as:

00000000 **00** 00000001 **01**

where the bold digits represent the score. If the next match between the two teams resulted in a score of 4–1 then the code would be:

00000000 **1001** 00000001 **11**

Notice that the number of bits used to code the score can vary in size, but as we use a Huffman code, we can automatically detect the number of bits that it has.

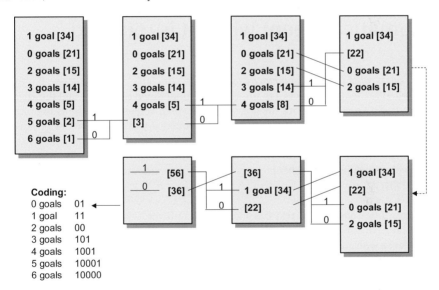

Figure B2.6 Huffman coding example

B2.6.2 Adaptive Huffman coding

Adaptive Huffman coding was first conceived by Faller and Gallager and then further refined by Knuth (so it is often called the FGK algorithm). It uses defined word schemes which determine the mapping from source messages to code words. These mappings are based upon a running estimate of the source message probabilities. The code is adaptive and changes to remain optimal for the current estimates. In this way, the adaptive Huffman codes respond to locality and the encoder thus learns the characteristics of the source data. It is thus important that the decoder learns the encoding along with the encoder. This will be achieved by continually updating the Huffman tree to stay in synchronization with the encoder.

A second advantage of adaptive Huffman coding is that it only requires a single pass over the data. In many cases, the adaptive Huffman method actually gives a better performance, in terms of number of bits transmitted, than static Huffman coding.

B2.6.3   Lempel–Ziv coding

Around 1977, Abraham Lempel and Jacob Ziv developed the Lempel–Ziv class of adaptive dictionary data compression techniques (also known as LZ-77 coding), which are now some of the most popular compression techniques. The LZ coding scheme is especially suited to data which has a high degree of repetition, and makes back references to these repeated parts. Typically a flag is normally used to identify coded and unencoded parts, where the flag creates back references to the repeated sequence. An example piece of text could be:

'The **recei**ver **requi**re**s** a **recei**pt for **it**. This **is**
            1   1

automatically s**en**t wh**en it is recei**ved.'
                                  1

This text has several repeated sequences, such as ' is ', 'it', 'en', 're' and ' receiv'. For example the repetitive sequence 'recei' (as shown by the underlined highlight), and the encoded sequence could be modified with the flag sequence #*m*#*n* where *m* represents the number of characters to trace back to find the character sequence and *n* the number of replaced characters. Thus, the encoded message could become:

'The   receiver#9#3quires   a#20#5pt   for   it.   This   is   automatically   sent   wh#6#2   it   #30#2#47#5ved.'

Normally a long sequence of text has many repeated words and phases, such as 'and', 'there', and so on. Note that in some cases this could lead to longer files if short sequences were replaced with codes that were longer than the actual sequence itself.

Using the previous example of sport results:

Mulchester 3 Madchester 2
Smellmore Wanderers 60 Drinksome Wanderers 23

we could compress this with:

Mulchester 3 Mad#13#7 2
Smellmore Wanderers 60 Drinksome#23#1123

B2.6.4   Lempel–Ziv–Welsh coding

The Lempel–Ziv–Welsh (LZW) algorithm (also known LZ-78) builds a dictionary of frequently used groups of characters (or 8-bit binary values). Before the file is decoded, the compression dictionary must be sent (if transmitting data) or stored (if data is being stored). This method is good at compressing text files because text files contain ASCII characters (which are stored as 8-bit binary values) but not so good for graphics files, which may have repeating patterns of binary digits that might not be multiples of 8 bits.

A simple example is to use a six-character alphabet and a 16-entry dictionary, thus the resulting code word will have 4 bits. If the transmitted message is:

    ababacdcdaaaaaaef

Then the transmitter and receiver would initially add the following to its dictionary:

0000	'a'	0001	'b'
0010	'c'	0011	'd'
0100	'e'	0101	'f'
0110–1111	empty		

First the 'a' character is sent with 0000, next the 'b' character is sent and the transmitter checks to see that the 'ab' sequence has been stored in the dictionary. As it has not, it adds 'ab' to the dictionary, to give:

0000	'a'	0001	'b'
0010	'c'	0011	'd'
0100	'e'	0101	'f'
0110	'ab'	0111–1111	empty

The receiver will also add this to its table (thus, the transmitter and receiver will always have the same tables). Next, the transmitter reads the 'a' character and checks to see if the 'ba' sequence is in the code table. As it is not, it transmits the 'a' character as 0000, adds the 'ba' sequence to the dictionary, which will now contain:

0000	'a'
0001	'b'
0010	'c'
0011	'd'
0100	'e'
0101	'f'
0110	'ab'
0111	'ba'
1000–1111	empty

0000 0001 0000 0111 0010
 ↑   ↑   ↑   ↑   ↑
 'a' 'b' 'a' 'ba' 'c'

Next the transmitter reads the 'b' character and checks to see if the 'ba' sequence is in the table. As it is, it will transmit the code table address which identifies it, i.e. 0111. When this is received, the receiver detects that it is in its dictionary and it knows that the addressed sequence is 'ba'.

Next the transmitter reads a 'c' and checks for the character in its dictionary. As it is included, it transmits its address, i.e. 0010. When this is received, the receiver checks its dictionary and locates the character 'c'. This then continues with the transmitter and receiver maintaining identical copies of their dictionaries. A great deal of compression occurs when sending a sequence of one character, such as a long sequence of 'a'.

Typically, in a practical implementation of LZW, the dictionary size for LZW starts at 4 K (4096). The dictionary then stores bytes from 0 to 255 and the addresses 256 to 4095 are used for strings (which can contain two or more characters). As there are 4096 entries then it is a 12-bit coding scheme (0 to 4096 gives 0 to $2^{12}-1$ different addresses).

B2.6.5 Statistical encoding

Statistical encoding is an entropy technique which identifies certain sequences within the data. These 'patterns' are then coded so that they have fewer bits. Frequently used patterns are coded with fewer bits than less common patterns. For example, text files normally contain many more 'e' characters than 'z' characters. Thus, the 'e' character could be encoded with a few bits and the 'z' with many bits. Statistical encoding is also known as arithmetic compression.

A typical statistical coding scheme is Huffman encoding. Initially the encoder scans through the file and generates a table of occurrences of each character. The codes are assigned to minimize the number of encoded bits, and then stored in a codebook which must be transmitted with the data.

Table B2.2 shows a typical coding scheme for the characters 'a' to 'z'. It uses the same number of bits for each character. Morse code is an example of statistical encoding. It uses dots (a zero) and dashes (a one) to code characters, where a short space in time delimits each character. It uses short codes for the most probable letters and longer codes for less probable letters. In the form of zeros and ones, it is stated in Table B2.3.

Thus:

```
this an
```

would be encoded as:

```
Message:     t        h        i        s                        a        n
Simple code: 10011    00111    01000    10010    11010    00000    01101
Morse code:  1        0000     00       000          0011     01       10
```

This has reduced the number of bits used to represent the message from 35 (7×5) to 18.

Table B2.2 Simple coding scheme

a	00000	b	00001	c	00010	d	00011	e	00100
f	00101	g	00110	h	00111	i	01000	j	01001
k	01010	l	01011	m	01100	n	01101	o	01110
p	01111	q	10000	r	10001	s	10010	t	10011
u	10100	v	10101	w	10110	x	10111	y	11000
z	11001	SP	11010						

Table B2.3 Morse coding scheme

a	01	b	1000	c	1010	d	100	e	0
f	0010	g	110	h	0000	i	00	j	0111
k	101	l	0100	m	11	n	10	o	111
p	0110	q	1101	r	010	s	000	t	1
u	001	v	0001	w	011	x	1001	y	1011
z	1100	SP	0011						

B2.6.6 Repetitive sequence suppression

Repetitive sequence suppression involves representing long runs of a certain bit sequence with a special character. A special bit sequence is then used to represent that character, followed by the number of times it appears in sequence. For example typically 0's (zero) and ' ' (spaces) occur repetitively in text files. For example the data:

```
8.3200000000000
```

could be coded as:

```
8.32F11
```

where F represents the flag. In this case the number of stored characters has been reduced from 16 to 7.

Graphics images typically have long sequences of the same pixel color, thus a technique called run-length encoding (RLE), has been developed to compress long sequences of the same value. RLE uses a special flag to encoded repeated character sequences. For example:

```
Fred      has     when.........
```

could be coded as:

```
FredF7 hasF7 whenF9.
```

where F represents the flag. In this case the number of stored characters has been reduced from 32 to 20. The 'F7 ' character code represents seven ' ' (spaces) and 'F9.' represents nine '.' characters.

B2.7   Source compression

Source compression takes into account the type of information that is being compressed, and is typically used with image, video and audio information. All these data sources have a great deal of redundant data in their raw form, either in that they have little relevance on the perceived media form, or contain no information at all. The main compression techniques for these are JPEG, MPEG and MP-3.

An example of the redundancy is contained in audio samples, where high-quality audio compression involves sampling the audio signal 44,000 times per second. The audio signal does not change much between samples, and will definitely not change outside a given range, thus it is possible to code the difference between samples, rather than coding for the complete range of the samples. For example, the following might be integer values for the samples:

321, 322, 324, 324, 320, 317, 310, 311

This could be coded as difference values as:

320, +1, +2, 0, −4, −3, −7, +1

where the first value is stored, and then only the change is then coded. The advantage with this technique is that the maximum value of change can be defined, and this is likely to reduce the number of bits required to code the samples. For example, in this case, the sample difference ranges between −7 and +7, thus we only require 4 bits for each difference sample (7 could be represented by 0111, 6 by 0110, 5 by 0101, ... 0 by 0000, −1 by 1111, −2 by 1110, ... −6 by 1001 and −7 by 1000). This would only take 4 bits per sample (after the initial sample), as apposed to at least 8 bits for the non-difference system.

B2.7.1 Image compression

Data communication increasingly involves the transmission of still and moving images. Most of these images are compressed using standard compression format. Some of these forms are outlined in Table B2.4. The main parameters in a graphics file are:

- **Picture resolution**. This is defined by the number of pixels in the x- and y-directions.
- **Number of colors per pixel**. If N bits are used for the pixel color then the total number of displayable colors will be 2^N. For example an 8-bit color field defines 256 colors, a 24-bit color field gives 2^{24} or 16.7 M colors.
- **Palette size**. Some systems reduce the number of bits used to display a color by reducing the number of displayable colors for a given palette size. Typically each color in the palette is defined in a relatively large number of bits (such as 24-bit or 32-bit color), but there is only a limited number of colors which can be displayed. For example, the GIF format uses 24-bit color, within an 8-bit palette.

Table B2.4 Typical standard compressed graphics formats

File	Compression type	Max. resolution or colors	
TIFF	Huffman RLE and/or LZW	48-bit color	TIFF (tagged image file format) is typically used to transfer graphics from one computer system to another. It allows high resolutions and colors of up to 48 bits (16 bits for red, green and blue).
GIF	LZW	65,536×65,536 (24-bit color, but only 256 displayable colors)	Standardized graphics file format which can be read by most graphics packages. It has similar graphics characteristics to PCX files and allows multiple images in a single file and interlaced graphics.
JPG	JPEG compression (DCT, quantization and Huffman)	Depends on the compression	Excellent compression technique which produces lossy compression. It normally results in much greater compression than the methods outlined above.

Comparison of the different methods

This section uses example bitmapped images and shows how much the different techniques manage to compress them. The left-hand side of Figure B2.7 shows an image and Table B2.5 shows the resultant file size when it is saved in different formats. It can be seen that the BMP file format has the largest storage. The two main forms of BMP files are RGB (red, green, blue) encoded and RLE encoded. RGB coding saves the bitmap in an uncompressed form, whereas the RLE coding will reduce the total storage by compressing repetitive sequences. The GIF format manages to compress the file to around 40% of its original size and the TIF file achieves similar compression (mainly because both techniques use LZH compression). It can be seen that by far the best compression is achieved with JPEG which in both forms has compressed the file to under 10% of its original size.

The reason that the compression ratios for GIF, TIF and BMP RLE are relatively high is that the image on the left-hand side of Figure B2.7 contains a lot of changing data. Most images will compress to less than 10% because they have large areas which do not change much. The right-hand side of Figure B2.7 shows a simple graphic of 500×500, 24-bit, which has large areas with identical colors. Table B2.6 shows that, in this case, the compression ratio is low. The RLE encoded BMP file is only 1% of the original as the graphic contains long runs of the same color. The GIF file has compressed to less than 1%. Note that the PCX, GIF and BMP RLE files have saved the image with only 256 colors. The JPG formats have the advantage that they have saved the image with the full 16.7 M colors and give compression rates of around 2%.

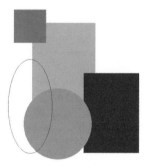

Figure B2.7 Sample graphics image

Table B2.5 Compression on a graphics file

Type	Size(B)	Compression (%)	
BMP	308 278	100.0	BMP, RBG encoded (640×480, 256 colors)
BMP	301 584	97.8	BMP, RLE encoded
GIF	124 304	40.3	GIF, Version 89a, non-interlaced
GIF	127 849	41.5	GIF, Version 89a, interlaced
TIF	136 276	44.2	TIF, LZW compressed
TIF	81 106	26.3	TIF, CCITT Group 3, MONOCHROME
JPG	28 271	9.2	JPEG – JFIF Complaint (Standard coding)
JPG	26 511	8.6	JPEG – JFIF Complaint (Progressive coding)

Table B2.6 Compression on a graphics file with highly redundant data

Type	Size (B)	Compression (%)	
BMP	750 054	100.0	BMP, RBG encoded (500×500, 16.7 M colors)
BMP	7 832	1.0	BMP, RLE encoded (256 colors)
PCX	31 983	4.3	PCX, Version 5 (256 colors)
GIF	4 585	0.6	GIF, Version 89a, non-interlaced (256 colors)
TIF	26 072	3.5	TIF, LZW compressed (16.7 M colors)
JPG	15 800	2.1	JPEG (Standard coding, 16.7 M colors)
JPG	12 600	1.7	JPEG (Progressive coding, 16.7 M colors)

JPEG compression

The GIF format is an excellent format for compressing images which have a limited range of colors. This is fine for simple images, but it does not suit the compression of photographs, thus the JPEG standard was developed by the Joint Photographic Expert Group (JPEG), which is a subcommittee of the ISO/IEC. It was based on research into compression ratios on images and their resulting image quality. The standards produced can be summarized as follows:

It is a compression technique for grey-scale or color images and uses a combination of discrete cosine transform, quantization, run-length and Huffman coding.

JPEG is an excellent compression technique which produces lossy compression (although in one mode it is lossless). As seen from the previous section it has excellent compression ratios when applied to a color image. The main steps are:

- Data blocks   Generation of data blocks
- Source encoding   Discrete cosine transform and quantization
- Entropy encoding   Run-length encoding and Huffman encoding

Unfortunately, compared with GIF, TIFF and PCX, the compression process is relatively slow. It is also lossy in that some information is lost in the compression process. This information is perceived to have little effect on the decoded image.

GIF files typically use 24-bit color information (8 bits for red, 8 bits for green and 8 bits for blue) and convert it into an 8-bit color palette (thus reducing the number of bits stored to approximately one-third of the original). It then uses LZW compression to further reduce the storage. JPEG operates differently in that it stores changes in color. As the eye is very sensitive to brightness changes it is particularly sensitive to changes in brightness. If these changes are similar to the original then the eye will perceive the recovered image as similar to the original.

Color conversion and subsampling

In the first part of the JPEG compression, each color component (red, green and blue) is separated in luminance (brightness) and chrominance (color information). JPEG allows more losses on the chrominance and less on the luminance. This is because the human eye is less sensitive to color changes than to brightness changes. In an RGB image, all three channels carry some brightness information but the green component has a stronger effect on brightness than the blue component.

A typical scheme for converting RGB into luminance and color is known as CCIR 601, which converts the components into Y (can be equated to brightness), C_b (blueness) and C_r

(redness). The *Y* component can be used as a black and white version of the image. The components are computed from the RGB components:

$$Y = 0.299R + 0.587G + 0.114B$$
$$C_b = 0.1687R - 0.3313G + 0.5B$$
$$C_r = 0.5R - 0.4187G + 0.0813B$$

For the brightness, it can be seen that green has the most effect and blue has the least. For the redness, the red color (of course) has the most effect and green the least, and for the blueness, the blue color has the most effect and green the least. Note that the YC_bC_r components are often known as *YUV*.

A subsampling process is then conducted which samples the C_b and C_r components at a lower rate than the *Y* component. A typical sampling rate is four samples of the *Y* component to a single sample on the C_b and C_r component. This sampling rate is normally set with the compression parameters. The lower the sampling, the smaller the compressed data and the shorter the compression time. All the required information on how to decode the JPEG data is contained in the JPEG header.

DCT coding

The DCT (discrete cosine transform) converts intensity data into frequency data, which can be used to tell how fast the intensities vary. In JPEG coding the image is segmented into 8×8 pixel rectangles, as illustrated in Figure B2.8. If the image contains several components (such as Y,C_b,C_r or R,G,B), then each of the components in the pixel blocks is operated on separately. If an image is subsampled, there will be more blocks of some components than of others. For example, for 2×2 sampling there will be four blocks of *Y* data for each block of C_b or C_r data.

The data points in the 8×8 pixel array start at the upper right at (0,0) and finish at the lower right at (7,7). At the point (x, y) the data value is $f(x,y)$. The DCT produces a new 8×8 block $(u \times v)$ of transformed data using the formula:

$$F(u,v) = \frac{1}{4}C(u)C(v)\left[\sum_{x=0}^{7}\sum_{y=0}^{7} f(x,y)\cos\frac{(2x+1)u\pi}{16}\cos\frac{(2y+1)v\pi}{16}\right]$$

$$\text{where} \quad C(z) = \frac{1}{\sqrt{2}} \text{ if } z = 0$$
$$\text{or} \qquad = 1 \quad \text{ if } z \neq 0$$

This results in an array of space frequency $F(u, v)$ which gives the rate of change at a given point. These are normally 12-bit values which give a range of 0 to 4095. Each component specifies the degree to which the image changes over the sampled block. For example:

* $F(0,0)$ gives the average value of the 8×8 array.
* $F(1,0)$ gives the degree to which the values change slowly (low frequency).
* $F(7,7)$ gives the degree to which the values change most quickly in both directions (high frequency).

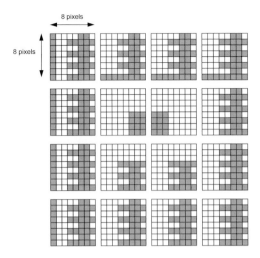

Figure B2.8 Segment of an image in 8 x 8 pixel blocks

The coefficients are equivalent to representing changes of frequency within the data block. The value in the upper left block $(0,0)$ is the DC or average value. The values to the right of a row have increasing horizontal frequency and the values to the bottom of a column have increasing vertical frequency. Many of the bands end up having zero or almost zero terms, which is useful when we compress long runs of zero values.

B2.7.2 Motion video compression

Motion video contains massive amounts of redundant information. This is because each image has redundant information and because there are very few changes from one image to the next.

Motion video image compression relies on two facts:

- Images have a great deal of redundancy (repeated images, repetitive, superfluous, duplicated, exceeding what is necessary, and so on).
- The human eye and brain have limitations on what they can perceive.

As with JPEG, the Motion Picture Experts Group (MPEG) was setup to develop an international open standard for the compression of high-quality audio and video information. At the time, CD-ROM single-speed technology allowed a maximum bit rate of 1.2 Mbps and this was the rate that the standard was built around. These days, ×12 and ×20 CD-ROM bit rates are common, which allow for smoother and faster animations.

MPEG's main aim was to provide good quality video and audio using hardware processors (and in some cases, on workstations with sufficient computing power, to perform the tasks using software). Figure B2.9 shows the main processing steps of encoding:

- **Image conversion** – normally involves converting images from RGB into YUV (or YC_rC_b) terms with optional color subsampling.
- **Conversion into slices and macro-blocks** – a key part of MPEG's compression is the detection of movement within a frame. To detect motion a frame is subdivided into slices

then each slice is divided into a number of macroblocks. Only the luminance component is then used for the motion calculations. In the subblock, luminance (Y) values use a 16×16 pixel macroblock, whereas the two chrominance components have 8×8 pixel macroblocks.

- **Motion estimation** – MPEG uses a motion estimation algorithm to search for multiple blocks of pixels within a given search area and tries to track objects which move across the image.
- **DCT conversion** – as with JPEG, MPEG uses the DCT method. This transform is used because it exploits the physiology of the human eye. It converts a block of pixels from the spatial domain into the frequency domain. This allows the higher-frequency terms to be reduced, as the human eye is less sensitive to fast changes of color, or luminance.
- **Encoding** – the final stages involve organizing the data into a pattern which will tend to produce long runs of zero value. These are then compressed with run-length encoding and then finally with fixed Huffman code to produce a variable-length code.

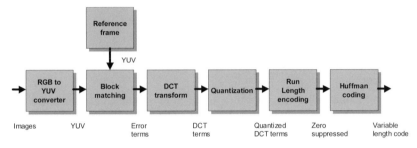

Figure B2.9   MPEG encoding with block matching

Color space conversion

The first stage of MPEG encoding is to convert a video image into the correct color space format. In most cases, the incoming data is in 24-bit RGB color format and is converted in 4:2:2 YC_rC_b (or YUV) form. Some information will obviously be lost in the conversion of the color components, as there will only be half the number of samples for the redness and the blueness as there is for the luminance, but it results in some compression.

Slices and macroblocks

MPEG compression tries to detect movement within a frame. This is done by subdividing a frame into slices and then subdividing each slice into a number of macroblocks. For example, a PAL format which has:

352×288 pixel frame (101 376 pixels)

can, when divided into 16×16 blocks, give a whole number of 396 macroblocks. Dividing 288 by 16 gives a whole number of 18 slices, and dividing 352 gives 22. Thus the image is split into 22 macroblocks in the x-direction and 18 in the y-direction, as illustrated in Figure B2.10.

Luminance (Y) values use a 16×16 pixel macroblock, whereas the two chrominance components have 8×8 pixel macroblocks. Note that only the luminance component is used for the motion calculations.

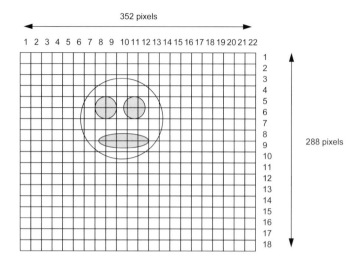

Figure B2.10 Segmentation of an image into subblocks

Motion estimation

MPEG uses a motion estimation algorithm to search for multiple blocks of pixels within a given search area and tries to track objects which move across the image. Each luminance (*Y*) 16×16 macroblock is compared with other macroblocks within either a previous or future frame to find a close match. When a close match is found, a vector is used to describe where the block is to be located, as well as any difference information from the compared block. As there tend to be very few changes from one frame to the next, it is far more efficient than using the original data.

Figure B2.10 shows two consecutive images of 2D luminance made up into 16×5 megablocks. Each of these blocks has 16×16 pixels. It can be seen that, in this example, there are very few differences between the two images. If the previous image is transmitted in its entirety then the current image can be transmitted with reference to the previous image. For example, the megablocks for (0, 0), (0, 1) and (0, 2) in the current block are the same as in the previous blocks. Thus they can be coded simply with a reference to the previous image. The (0, 3) megablock is different to the previous image, but the (0, 3) block is identical to the (0, 2) block of the previous image, thus a reference to this block is made. This can continue, as most of the blocks in the image are identical to the previous image. The only other differences in the current image are at (4, 0) and (4, 1); these blocks can be stored in their entirety or specified with their differences to a previous similar block.

A major objective of the MPEG encoder is to spend a much greater time compressing the video information into its most efficient form. Each macroblock is compared mathematically with other blocks in a previous frame, or even in a future frame. The offset information to another block can be over a macroblock boundary or even over a pixel boundary. This comparison then repeats until a match is found or the specified search area within the frame has been exhausted. If no match is available, the search process can be repeated using a different frame or the macroblock can be stored as a complete set of data. As previously stated, if a match is found, the vector information specifying where the matching macroblock is located is used along with any difference information.

As the technique involves very many searches over a wide search area and there are many frames to be encoded, the encoder must normally be a high-powered workstation. This has several implications:

- **Asymmetrical compression**. MPEG uses an asymmetrical compression process, where a relatively large amount of computing power is required for the encoder and much less for the decoder. The encoding process is normally achieved in non-real time whereas the decoder reads the data in real time (as the user requires viewing the video, without having large pauses, while the decoder processes the compressed data). As processing power and memory capacity increase, more computers will be able to compress video information in real time. Even mobile devices will have the processing power and memory to be able to process MPEG in real time.
- **Compression quality**. Encoders influence the quality of the decoded image dramatically. If the encoder takes shortcuts, such as limited search areas and macroblock matching, it can result in poor picture quality, irrespective of the quality of the decoder.
- **Memory requirements**. The decoder normally requires a large amount of electronic memory to store past and future frames, which may be needed for motion estimation.

With the motion estimation completed, the raw data describing the frame is now converted by DCT algorithm to be ready for Huffman coding.

I, P and B-frames

As video frames tend not to change much between frames, MPEG video compression uses either full frames (which contain all the frame data), or partial frames (which refer back to other frames). The three frames types are defined as:

- **Intra frame (I-frame)**. An intra frame, or I-frame, is a complete image and does not require any extra information to be added to it to make it complete. As it is a complete frame, it cannot contain any motion estimation processing. It is typically used as a starting point for other referenced frames, and is usually the first frame to be sent.
- **Predictive frame (P-frame)**. The predictive frame, or P-frame, uses the preceding I-frame as its reference and has motion estimation processing. Each macroblock in this frame is supplied as referenced to an I-frame as either a vector and difference, or if no match was found, as a completely encoded macroblock (called an intracoded macroblock). The decoder must thus retain all I-frame information to allow the P-frame to be decoded.
- **Bidirectional frame (B-frame)**. The bidirectional frame, or B-frame, is similar to the P-frame except that it references frames to the nearest preceding or future I- or P-frame. When compressing the data, the motion estimation works on the future frame first, followed by the past frame. If this does not give a good match, an average of the two frames is used. If all else fails, the macroblock can be intracoded. As B-frames reference preceding and future frames, it requires that many I- and P-frames are retained in memory, which will require a relatively large amount of memory, as apposed to using I-frames, and P-frames, only.

Other enhancements include:

- **Any order of frames**. MPEG also allows frames to be ordered in any sequence. Unfortunately a large amount of reordering requires many frame buffers that must be stored until all dependencies are cleared.
- **Random access**. MPEG allows random access to a video sequence, thus the file must contain regular I-frames. Regular I-frames also allow enhanced modes such as fast forward, which means that an I-frame is required every 0.4 seconds, or 12 frames between each I-frame (at 30 fps).

At 30 fps, a typical sequence starts with an I-frame, followed by two B-frames, a P-frame, followed by two B-frames, and so on. This is known as a group of picture (GOP):

$$I{\Rightarrow}B{\Rightarrow}B{\Rightarrow}P{\Rightarrow}B{\Rightarrow}B{\Rightarrow} \quad I{\Rightarrow}B{\Rightarrow}B{\Rightarrow}P{\Rightarrow}B{\Rightarrow}B{\Rightarrow} \quad I{\Rightarrow}B{\Rightarrow}B{\Rightarrow}P{\Rightarrow}...$$

When decoding, the decoder must store the I-frame, and the next two B-frames until the B-frame arrives. The next two B-frames have to be stored locally until the P-frame arrives. The P-frame can be decoded using the stored I-frame and the two B-frames can be decoded using the I- and P-frames. One solution of this is to reorder the frames so that the I- and P-frames are sent together followed by the two intermediate B-frames. Another more radical solution is not to send B-frames at all, simply to use I- and P-frames.

On computers with limited memory and limited processing power, the B-frames are difficult to process as they:

- Increase the encoding computational load and memory storage. The inclusion of the previous and future I- and P-frames as well as the arithmetic average greatly increases the processing needed. The increased frame buffers to store frames allow the encode and decode processes to proceed. This argument is again less valid with the advent of large and high-density memories.
- They do not provide a direct reference in the same way that an I- or P-frame does.

The advantage of B-frames is that they lead to an improved signal-to-noise ratio because of the averaging out of macroblocks between I- and P-frames. This averaging effectively reduces high-frequency random noise. It is particularly useful in lower bit rate applications, but is of less benefit with higher rates, which normally have improved signal-to-noise ratios.

Practical MPEG compression

Most MPEG encoders typically have a range of parameters which can be changed to give the required quality. The following outline some of the main parameters.

Frame rate and data rate
The frame rate and data rate are two parameters which greatly affect the quality of the encoded bitstream. The frame rate is normally set by the frame rate of the input format, such as 23.976, 24, 25, 29.97, 30, 50, 59.94, and 60 frames/sec. Many encoders do not support all of these rates for the output so there are two modes which can be used to reduce or increase the frame rate, these are:

- Keep original number of frames. In this mode, the frames are encoded frames as they are ordered in the input file, but the MPEG decoder plays these files at the wrong speed, such as slowing them down with a lower frame rate or faster to give a faster frame rate.

- Keep original duration. In this mode the encoder either duplicates (to increase rate) or skips some of the input frames (to reduce the rate) to provide the correct playback frame rate.

Most encoding systems allow the user to specify the data rate of the encoded bitstream, and the encoder then tries to keep to this limit when it is encoding the input bitstream. For example, a single-speed CD-ROM requires a maximum data rate of 150 KB/sec. This rate is relatively low and there may be some degradation of quality to produce this. Reasonable quality requires at least 300 KB/sec.

DCT conversion

As with JPEG, MPEG uses the DCT, and transforms macroblocks of luminance (16×16) and chrominance (8×8) into the frequency domain. This allows the higher-frequency terms to be reduced as the human eye is less sensitive to high-frequency changes.

Frames are broken up into slices 16 pixels high, and each slice is broken up into a vector of macroblocks having 16×16 pixels. Each macroblock contains luminance and chrominance components for each of four 8×8 pixel blocks. Color decimation can be applied to a macroblock, which yields four 8×8 blocks for luminance and two 8×8 blocks (C_b and C_r) of chrominance, using one or two chrominance values for each of the four luminance values. This is called the 4:1:1 or 4:2:2 format, respectively.

For each macroblock, a spatial offset difference between a macroblock in the predicted frame and the reference frame(s) is given if one exists (a motion vector), along with a luminance value and/or chrominance difference value (an error term) if needed. Macroblocks with no differences can be skipped except in intra frames. Blocks with differences are internally compressed, using a combination of a discrete cosine transform (DCT) algorithm on pixel blocks (or error blocks) and variable quantization on the resulting frequency coefficient (rounding off values to one of a limited set of values).

The DCT algorithm accepts signed, 9-bit pixel values and produces signed 12-bit coefficients. The DCT is applied to one block at a time, and works much as it does for JPEG, converting each 8×8 block into an 8×8 matrix of frequency coefficients. The variable quantization process divides each coefficient by a corresponding factor in a matching 8×8 matrix and rounds to an integer.

Quantization

As with JPEG the converted data is divided, or quantized, to remove higher-frequency components and to make more of the values zero. This results in numerous zero coefficients, particularly for high-frequency terms at the high end of the matrix. Accordingly, amplitudes are recorded in run-length form following a diagonal scan pattern from low frequency to high frequency.

Encoding

After the DCT and quantization state, the resultant data is then compressed using Huffman coding with a set of fixed tables. The Huffman code not only specifies the number of zeros, but also the value that ended the run of zeros. This is extremely efficient in compressing the zigzag DCT encoding method.

B2.7.3 Audio compression

Initially when audio was converted to digital information (using PCM), no one actually knew how many bits would be required to code each of the sample. The greater the number of bits used, the more accurate the decoded value will be. For every sample, an error results, which will result in noise. This noise is known as quantization noise, and it can become noticeable when it becomes relatively large, as compared with the signal. Thus, as no-one knew how this noise would be perceived, it was decided that the best test would be to let users listen to the digitized audio for differing sample sizes, and decide the one which gave the required quality. For telephone quality speech it was found that 8 bits are required, and for hi-fi quality it was found that at least 14 bits are required. Any increase in the number of bits used will improve the quality, and reduce any noise in the digitized bit stream. Unfortunately this increases the amount of bits used to encode the audio.

Audio signals normally use PCM (pulse-coded modulation) codes which can be compressed to reduce the number of bits used to code the samples. For high-quality monochannel audio, the signal bandwidth is normally limited to 20 kHz, thus it is sampled at 44.1 kHz. If each sample is coded with 16 bits then the basic bit rate will be:

Digitized audio signal rate = 44.1×16 kbps = 705.6 kbps

For stereo signals, the bit rate would be 1.4112 Mbps. Many digital audio systems add extra bits from error control and framing, which increases the bit rate, but results in a more robust signal.

Digital audio normally involves the processes of:

- Filtering the input signal.
- Sampling the signal at twice the highest frequency.
- Converting it into a digital form with an ADC (analogue-to-digital converter).
- Converting the parallel data into a serial form.
- Storing or transmitting the serial information.
- When reading (or receiving) the data the clock information is filtered out using a PLL (phase-locked loop).
- The recovered clock is then used with a SIPO (serial-in parallel-out) converter to convert the data back into a parallel form.
- Converting the digital data back into an analogue voltage.
- Filtering the analogue voltage.

These steps are illustrated in Figure B2.11. The clock recovery part is important; and there is no need to save or transmit separate clock information because it can be embedded into the data. It also has the advantage that a fixed clock becomes jittery when it is affected by noise, thus if the clock information is transmitted separately over relatively long distances it will be jittery.

CD-quality stereo audio requires a bit rate of 1.411200 Mbps (2×16 bits $\times 44.1$ kHz). A single-speed CD-ROM can only transfer at a rate of 1.5 Mbps, and this rate must include both audio and video. Thus, there is a great need for compression of both the video and audio data. The need to compress high-quality audio is also an increasing need as consumers expect higher-quality sound from TV systems and the increasing usage of digital audio radio.

A number of standards have been put forward for digital audio coding for TV/video systems. One of the first was MUSICAM, which is now part of the MPEG-1 coding system. The FCC Advisory Committee considered several audio systems for advanced television systems, but there was generally no agreement on the best technology. As it is often difficult to determine the performance of an audio system purely by its technical performance, it was finally decided to conduct a side-by-side test. The winner was Dolby AC-3, and in second place was MPEG coding. Many cable, cinemas and satellite TV systems now use either MPEG or Dolby AC-3 coding.

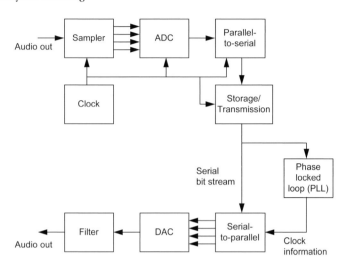

Figure B2.11   A digital audio system

Psycho-acoustic model

MPEG and Dolby AC-3 use the psycho-acoustic model to reduce the data rate, which exploits the characteristics of the human ear. This is similar to the method used in MPEG video compression which uses the fact that the human eye has a lack of sensitivity to the higher-frequency video components (that is, sharp changes of color or contrast). The psycho-acoustic model allows certain frequency components to be reduced in size without affecting the perceived audio quality as heard by the listener.

A well-known audio effect is the masking effect, where noise is only heard by a person when there are no other sounds to mask it. A typical example is in high-frequency hiss from a compact cassette when there are quiet passages of music. When there are normal periods of music the louder music masks out the quieter hiss and it is not heard. In reality, the brain is masking out the part of the sound it wants to hear, even though the noise component is still there. When there is no music to mask the sound, the noise is heard.

Noise, itself, tends to occur across a wide range of frequencies, but the masking effect also occurs with sounds. A loud sound at a certain frequency masks out a quieter sound at a similar frequency. As a result, the sound heard by the listener appears only to contain the loud sounds, which masks out the quieter one. The psycho-acoustic model tries to reduce the levels to those that would be perceived by the brain.

Figure B2.12 illustrates this psycho-acoustic process. In this case, a masking level has been applied and all the amplitudes below this level have been reduced in size. Since these frequencies have been reduced in amplitude, and any noise associated with them is also significantly reduced. This has the effect of limiting the bandwidth of the signal to the key frequency ranges.

The psycho-acoustic model also takes into account non-linearities in the sensitivity of the ear. The ear's peak sensitivity is between 2 and 4 kHz (the range of the human voice) and it is least sensitive around the extremes of the frequency range (that it, high and low frequencies). Any noise in the less sensitive frequency ranges is more easily masked, but it is important to minimize any noise in the peak range because it has a greater impact.

Masking can also be applied in the time domain, where it can be applied just before and after a strong sound (such as a change of between 30 and 40 dB). Typically, premasking occurs for about 2–5 ms before the sound is perceived by the listener and the postmasking effect lasts for about 100 ms after the end of the source.

For audio, MPEG basically has three different levels:

- MPEG-Audio Level I – This uses the psycho-acoustic model to mask and reduce the sample size. It is basically a simplified version of MUSICAM and has a quality which is nearly equivalent to CD-quality audio. Its main advantage is that it allows the construction of simple encoders and decoders with medium performance and which will operate fairly well at 192 or 256 kbps.
- MPEG-Audio Level II – This is identical to the MUSICAM standard. It is also nearly equivalent to CD-quality audio and is optimized for a bit rate of 96 or 128 kbps per monophonic channel.
- MPEG-Audio Level III (MP-3) – This is a combination of the MUSICAM scheme and ASPEC, a sound compression scheme designed in Erlangen, Germany. Its main advantage is that it can produce reasonable quality audio at rates of 64 kbps per audio channel. At that speed, the quality is very close to CD quality and produces a sound quality which is better than MPEG Level-II operating at 64 kbps.

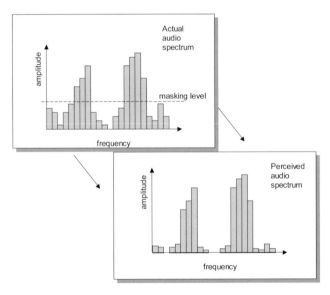

Figure B2.11   Difference between actual and perceived audio spectrum

The three levels are basically supersets of each other with Level III decoders being capable of decoding both Level I and Level II data. Level I is the simplest, while Level III gives the highest compression but is the most computational in coding.

The forward and backward compatible MPEG-2 system, following recommendations from SMPTE, EBU and others, has increased the audio capacity to five channels. Figure B2.12 shows an example of a 5-channel system; the key elements are:

- A centre channel.
- Left and right surround channels.
- Left and right channels (as hi-fi stereo).

MPEG-2 also includes a low-frequency effects channel (called LFE, essentially a sub-woofer). This has a much lower bandwidth than the other channels. This type of system is often called a 5.1-channel system (5 main channels and LFE channel).

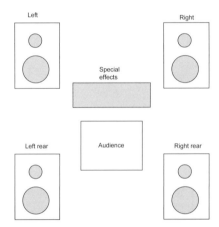

Figure B2.12 A 5.1 channel audio surround sound system

B2.8 Fax transmission

Facsimile (fax) transmission involves the transmission of images over a telephone line using a modem. A standalone fax consists of:

- An image scanner.
- A graphics printer (normally a thermal printer).
- A transmission/reception modem.

The fax scans an A4 image with 1142 scan lines (3.85 lines per millimeter) and 1728 pixels per line. The EIA and ITU originally produced the RS-328 standard for the transmission of analogue voltage levels to represent different brightness's. The ITU recommendations are known as Group I and Group II standards. The Group III standard defines the transmission of faxes using digital transmission with 1142×1728 pixels of black or white. Group IV is an extension to Group III but allows different gray scales and also color (unfortunately, it requires a high bit rate, such as ISDN).

An A4 scan would consist of 1 976 832 (1142×1728) scanned elements. If each element is scanned for black and white, then, at 9600 bps, it would take over 205 seconds (2 minutes and 25 seconds) to transmit. This transmission time can be drastically reduced by using RLE coding.

B2.8.1 Modified Huffman coding

Group III compression uses modified Huffman code to compress the transmitted bit stream. It uses a table of codes in which the most frequent run lengths are coded with a short code. Typically, documents contain long runs of white or black. A compression ratio of over 10:1 is easily achievable (thus a single-page document can be sent in under 20 seconds, for a 9600 bps transmission rate). Table B2.7 shows some code runs of white and Table B2.8 shows some codes for runs of black. The transmitted code always starts on white code. The codes range from 0 to 63. Values from 64 to 2560 use two codes. The first gives the multiple of 64 followed by the normally coded remainder.

For example, if the data to be encoded is:

16 white, 4 black, 16 white, 2 black, 63 white, 10 black, 63 white

it would be coded as:

```
101010   011 101010   11 00110100   0000100   00110100
```

This would take 40 bits to transmit the coding, whereas it would take 304 bits. (i.e. $16 + 4 + 16 + 2 + 128 + 10 + 128$). This results in a compression ratio of 7.6:1.

Table B2.7 White run-length coding

Run length	Coding	Run length	Coding	Run length	Coding
0	00110101	1	000111	2	0111
3	1000	4	1011	5	1100
6	1110	7	1111	8	10011
9	10100	10	00111	11	01000
12	001000	13	000011	14	110100
15	110101	16	101010	17	101011
18	0100111	19	0001100	61	00110010
62	00110011	63	00110100	EOL	00000000001

Table B2.8 Black run-length coding

Run length	Coding	Run length	Coding	Run length	Coding	Run length	Coding
0	0000110111	1	010	2	11	3	10
4	011	5	0011	6	0010	7	00011
8	000101	9	000100	10	0000100	11	0000101
12	0000111	13	00000100	14	00000111	15	000011000
16	0000010111	17	0000011000	18	0000001000	19	00001100111
61	000001011010	62	000000110011	63	000001100111	64	0000001111
					0		

B2.9 Video signals

This section discusses the main technologies using in TV signals and outlines the usage of digital TV. The Internet will, in the future, support many of the important video transmission standards. The five main classes of motion video are:

- High-definition television (HDTV).
- Studio-quality digital television (SQDV).
- Current broadcast-quality television.
- VCR-quality television.
- Low-speed video conferencing quality.

There are three main types of TV-type video signal:

- NTSC (American National Television Standards Committee).
- PAL (phase alternation line).
- SECAM (séquential couleur à mémoire).

These signals are based on composite color video which uses gaps in the black and white signal to transmit bursts of color information. In the UK this video signal is known as PAL (phase alternation line), whereas in the USA it is known as NTSC (named after the American National Television Standard Committee, who defined the original standard). Most of the countries of the world now use either PAL or NTSC. The only other standard format is SECAM, popular in French-speaking parts of the world.

B2.9.1 Color-difference signals

A motion video is basically single images scanned at a regular rate. If these images are displayed fast enough, the human eye sees the repetitive images in a smooth way. Video signals use three primary colors: red, green and blue.

An image is normally scanned only a row, one pixel at a time. When a signal row has been scanned, the scanner goes to the next row, and so on until it has scanned the last row, when it goes back to the start. The samples are then split into the three primary colors: red, green and blue, as illustrated in Figure B2.13.

The three main characteristics of a color signals are:

- Its brightness (luminance).
- Its colors (hues).
- Its color saturation (the amount of color).

Any hue can vary from very pale to very deep; the amount of the color is its saturation. When transmitting a TV signal it is important to isolate the luminance signal (the black and white element) so it can be sent to monochrome receivers. This is done by carefully adding a mixture of each of the RGB signals. PAL, NSTC and SECAM use the mixture:

$$Y = 0.3R + 0.59G + 0.11B$$

where the red, green and blue signals vary between 0 and 1. Thus the maximum level for luminance will be 1 (fully saturated, pure white color) and the minimum level will be 0 (black). It can be seen from this formula that the green signal has a much greater effect than the red, which in turn has a much higher influence than the blue. In terms of luminance, the green signal has almost six times the effect of the blue signal and twice the effect of the red.

Color information is then added to the luminance signal so that color receivers can obtain the additional color information for hue and saturation (often known as chroma signal). These signals are transmitted on a subcarrier which is suppressed at the transmitter and recreated at the receiver. The subcarrier is modulated with the three color-difference signals (but only two color-difference signals need to be transmitted).

The three color-difference signals are:

Red-luminance or $(R-Y)$
Green-luminance $(G-Y)$
Blue-luminance $(B-Y)$

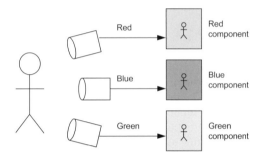

Figure B2.13   Conversion of an image into RGB components

There is no need to send all of the signals because if the $R-Y$ and $B-Y$ signals are sent then the $G-Y$ difference signal can be easily recovered. This is because the Y signal is sent in the luminance signal. Thus the red and blue signal are recovered by adding the luminance signal to red-luminance and blue-luminance signals, then using the correct RGB weighting given to give:

$$G = \frac{Y - 0.3R - 0.11B}{0.59}$$

The reason why the $R-Y$ and $B-Y$ signals are sent is that as the Y signal contains a great deal of green information, thus the $G-Y$ signal is likely to be smaller than the $R-Y$ and the $B-Y$ signals. The small $G-Y$ signal is then more likely to be affected by noise in the transmission system.

The receiver must be told when the signal is at its start, thus the transmitter sends a strong sync pulse to identify the start of the image. Figure B2.14 illustrates the transmitter with the baseband video signals, often known as composite video signals.

B2.9.2   Quadrature modulation

PAL and NSTC use an amplitude-modulated subcarrier wave. This subcarrier wave (4.433 618 7 MHz for PAL and 3.579 545 MHz for NSTC) is amplitude modulated using weighted $R-Y$ and by a weighted $B-Y$ signals shifted by 90° (quadrate modulation), as illustrated in Figure B2.15.

In PAL these difference components are called U and V, whereas in NSTC they are I and Q. SECAM uses frequency modulation, where the color-difference terms are D_R and D_B. These terms are defined by:

$$
\begin{aligned}
U &= 0.62R-0.52G-0.10B & \text{(PAL)} \\
V &= -0.15R-0.29G+0.44B & \text{(PAL)} \\
I &= 0.60R-0.28G-0.32B & \text{(NSTC)} \\
\\
Q &= 0.21R-0.52G+0.31B & \text{(NSTC)} \\
D_R &= -1.33R+1.11G+0.22B & \text{(SECAM)} \\
D_B &= -0.45R-0.88G+1.33B & \text{(SECAM)}
\end{aligned}
$$

It can be seen that if R, G and B are the same value, the color-difference terms will be zero (no color difference). PAL, NSTC and SECAM use:

$$Y=0.30R+0.59G+0.11B$$

Then, in PAL, these weighting values are:

$$V=0.877\,(R-Y)$$
$$U=0.493\,(B-Y)$$

In NSTC these are:

$$I=0.74\,(R-Y)-0.27\,(B-Y)$$
$$Q=0.48\,(R-Y)+0.41\,(B-Y)$$

The fundamental feature of this mode of signal addition is that by special detection at the receiver end it becomes possible to isolate the V/U or I/Q signals again and thus extract the original $R-Y$ and $B-Y$ modulation signals.

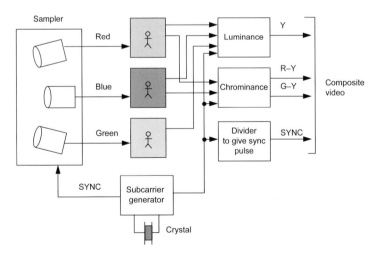

Figure B2.14   Conversion of an image into composite video components

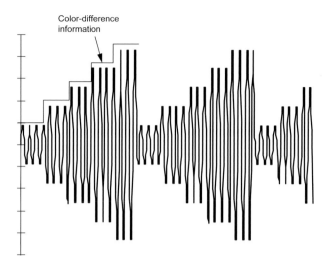

Figure B2.15 A PAL or NSTC waveform

Figure B2.16 shows examples of the color-difference signals in relation to various colors. In PAL, it can be seen that yellow has a strong Y component, a positive V component $(R - Y)$ and a negative U component $(B - Y)$. Whereas blue has a low Y component, a strong negative U component and a positive V component. Table B2.8 outlines the components for each color.

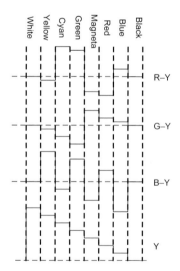

Figure B2.16 Color-difference signals for various colors

Figure B2.17 shows a phasor diagram with the V component at a phase difference of 90° from the U component. When the red signal is greater than the luminance, the V signal will be positive; and if the blue signal is greater than the luminance, the U signal will be positive. The signal vector will thus be in the first quadrant. The colors in this quadrant are likely to be lacking in green, but strong in reds and blues. Thus, the first quadrant contains purple-type colors. The example in Figure B2.17 shows how a U component of +0.5 and a V component of +0.5 give a color of magenta.

The colors in the second quadrant have a positive V component and a negative U component. For this to happen the red component must be greater than the luminance (for V to be positive) and the luminance must be greater than the blue component. This gives bright colors with a strong red component. An example of the color yellow is given in Figure B2.17.

The third quadrant has a negative value for the U and V component. This means that the luminance is greater than both the blue and red components. Thus, the colors have a strong green factor.

Table B2.9   Color examples with luminance and chrominance values

Color	Y	B - Y	R - Y	U	V	Amp.	Angle
Black	0	0	0	0	0	0	–
Blue	0.11	+0.89	−0.11	+0.439	−0.096	0.44	347
Red	0.3	-0.3	+0.7	−0.148	−0.614	0.63	103
Magenta	0.41	+0.59	+0.59	+0.291	+0.517	0.59	61
Green	0.59	−0.59	−0.59	−0.291	−0.517	0.59	241
Cyan	0.7	+0.3	−0.7	+0.148	−0.614	0.63	283
Yellow	0.89	−0.89	+0.11	−0.449	+0.096	0.44	167
White	1.0	0	0	0	0	0	–

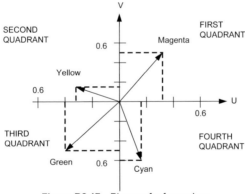

Figure B2.17   Phasors for four colors

In the fourth quadrant the U component is positive (the blue component is greater than the luminance) and the V component is negative (the luminance is greater than the red component). The colors in this quadrant will be strong in blues with a low luminance. An example of cyan is shown in Figure B2.17.

B2.9.3   Baseband video signals

Baseband video signals, or composite video, are signals in a form which is used in TV systems where the video is traced in interlacing lines. Initially, the top left-hand corner pixel is transmitted, followed by each pixel in turn on a single line. After the last pixel on the first line, the video traces back to the start of the next displayable line. This continues until it reaches the bottom of the screen. After this the video trace returns to the top left-hand pixel and starts again, as illustrated in Figure B2.18.

With PAL the screen refresh rate is based on the 50 Hz mains frequency while in NTSC it is based on the 60 Hz mains frequency. A 50 Hz refresh rate causes the screen to be updated 50 times every second. Each frame (or picture) is sent by sending the odd lines of the frame on the first update and then the even lines on the next screen update, and so on. This technique is known as interlaced scanning and is illustrated in Figure B2.19. For a 50 Hz system, the frame rate (or picture rate) is thus 25 Hz which means that one picture is drawn every 1/25 of a second (20 ms).

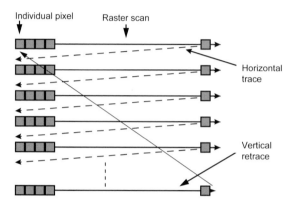

Figure B2.18 Video screen showing raster lines and retrace

A raster line is the smallest subdivision of this horizontal line. PAL systems have 625 video raster lines at a rate of 25 frames per second and NSTC uses 525 lines at a rate of 30 frames per second.

Thus, if the screen refresh rate is 50 Hz, the screen is updated once every 20 ms. Each update contains half a picture so one complete picture is sent every 40 ms. Thus 625 lines are sent every 40 ms, the time to transmit one raster line will thus be:

$$t_{raster} = \frac{40}{625} ms = 64 \, \mu s$$

With a black and white signal the voltage amplitude of the waveform at any instant gives the brightness of each part of the displayed picture. A negative voltage sync pulse of 4.7 μs indicates the start of the 625 lines. A blanking level indicates the start of each line, as illustrated in Figure B2.20. The largest voltage defines white while a zero voltage gives black.

Composite color video signals use gaps in the black and white signal to transmit bursts of color information. A composite video signal consists of a luminance (brightness) component and two chromatic (color) components. These chromatic components are transmitted simultaneously as the amplitude modulation sidebands of a pair of suppressed subcarriers which are identical in frequency but are in phase quadrature.

Figure B2.21 shows the frequency band for a composite video signal for PAL. The black and white (luminance) signal takes up the band from DC to 4.2 MHz, and a subcarrier is added in the higher-frequency portion of the band, at 4.43361875 MHz (3.58 MHz for NTSC); the modulated subcarrier can be thought of as superimposing itself on the luminance signal, as illustrated in Figure B2.22. The bandwidth for a PAL system is approximately 5.5 MHz.

Differences in color modulation between NSTC, PAL and SECAM

The start of the horizontal line is preceded by a sync pulse and then a color burst. This provides a reference for the phase information in the color signal. Figure B2.23 shows the horizontal blanking interval.

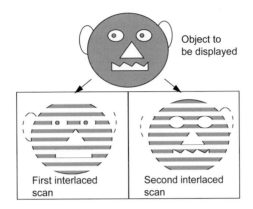

Figure B2.19 Interlaced scanning

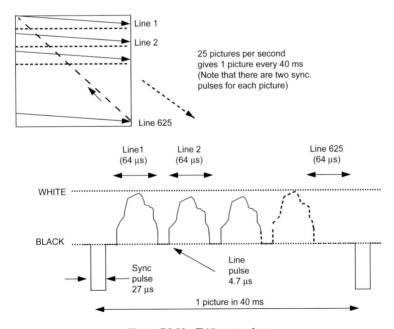

Figure B2.20 TV line waveform

In NSTC, the chrominance subcarrier is suppressed-carrier amplitude modulated on a

3.579 545 MHz. It is modulated by the I (for In-phase) and Q (for Quadrature) components, with the I component modulating the subcarrier at $0°$ and the Q component modulating at $90°$. The reference burst lasts 2.67 µs and is at an angle of $57°$ with respect to the I carrier. In NSTC, the Y bandwidth is 4.5 MHz while the I bandwidth is only 1.5 MHz and the Q bandwidth is 0.5 MHz (although many TV receivers allow a bandwidth of 0.5 MHz for I and Q and give perfectly acceptable results).

PAL is similar but has a carrier frequency of 4.433 6187 MHz. The modulating components are referred to as U ($0°$) and V ($90°$). The V component is alternated $180°$ on a line-by-line basis. The reference burst last 2.25 µs and also alternates on a line-by-line basis between an angle of $+135°$ and $-135°$ relative to the U component.

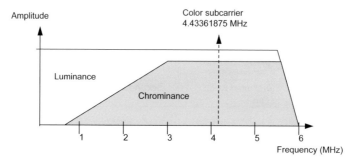

Figure B2.21 Composite video frequency spectrum

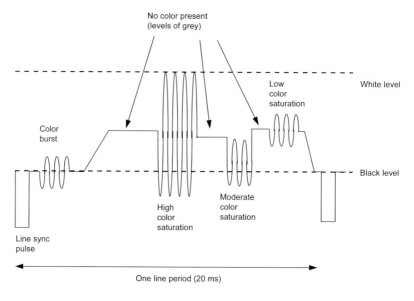

Figure B2.22 Composite video signal

SECAM uses a frequency-modulated (FM) color subcarrier for the chromatic signals, transmitting one of the color difference signals every other line, and the other color difference signal on the remaining lines.

Table B2.10 outlines the main parameters for the three technologies.

Table B2.10 The main differences between NSTC, PAL and SECAM

	NSTC	PAL	SECAM
Lines/frame	525	625	625
Frame/second	30	25	25
Interlace ratio	2:1	2:1	2:1
Color subcarrier	3.579 545 MHz	4.433 619 MHz	Two FM-modulated carriers at 4.40625 MHz and 4.25 MHz
Line period	63.55 µs	64.0 µs	64.0 µs
Horizontal sync pulse width	4.7 µs	4.7 µs	4.7 µs
Color burst width	2.67 µs	2.25 µs	
Vertical sync pulse width	27.1 µs	27.3 µs	27.3 µs

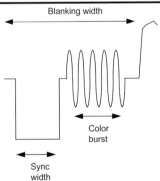

Blanking width

Color burst

Sync width

Figure B2.23 Color burst

B2.9.4 Digitizing TV signals

The composite video signal must be sampled at twice the highest frequency of the signal. To standardize this sampling, the ITU CCIR-601 (often known as ITU-R) has been devised. It defines three signal components: Y (for luminance), C_r (for $R - Y$) and C_b (for $B - Y$).

The biggest problem with sampling is that SECAM and PAL use 625 lines and NTSC use 525 lines. The ITU-R 601 standard defines that SECAM and PAL are sampled 858 times for each line and NTSC is sampled 864 times for each line. This produces the same scanning frequency in both cases:

$$\text{Scanning frequency (PAL, SECAM)} = 864 \times 625 \times 25 = 13.5 \, \text{MHz}$$

$$\text{Scanning frequency (NTSC)} = 858 \times 525 \times 30 = 13.5 \, \text{MHz}$$

With this technique, the luminance (the black and white level) is digitized at a rate for 13.5 MHz and color is sampled at an equivalent rate of 6.75 MHz. Each luminance and color sample is coded as 8 bits, thus the digitized rate is:

$$\text{Digitized video signal rate} = 13.5 \times 8 + 6.75 \times 8 = 162 \, \text{Mbps}$$

Thus the sample rate for all three systems will be:

$$\text{Sample rate} = \frac{1}{13.5 \times 10^6} = 74 \, \text{ns}$$

Normally the Y is sampled at 13.5 MHz and the chromatic components (such as U/V or C_b/C_r) are sampled at a quarter of this rate (that is, 3.375 MHz). The bits are then interleaved to give 12-bit YUV bundles, as illustrated in Figure B2.24. This shows that there are 12 bits transmitted every 74 ns, thus the bit rate is:

$$\text{Bit rate} = \frac{12}{74 \times 10^{-9}} = 162 \, \text{Mbps}$$

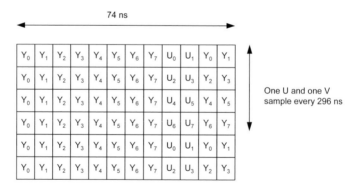

Figure B2.24   Interleaved luminance and chrominance data

Subsampling

Subsampling reduces the digitized bit rate by sampling the luminance and chrominance at different rates. The standard format uses integer values as a ratio, such as:

Y sampling frequency : C_{d1} sampling frequency : C_{d2} sampling frequency where C_d is the sampling frequency for the chominance. For example, standard studio-quality TV uses a 4:2:2 sampling ratio for the $Y:C_r:C_b$ ratio. This means that the number of samples for the color difference is half of the luminance. For example, if the image is:

R (720×486), G (720×486) and B (720×486) (NSTC)
R (720×576), G (720×576) and B (720×576) (PAL)

then using 4:2:2 gives the resultant YC_rC_b form:

Y (720×486), C_b (360×486) and C_r (360×486)   (NSTC)
Y (720×576), C_b (360×576) and C_r (360×576)   (PAL)

Thus, in NSTC, the number of terms has been reduced from 1 049 760 to 699 840 (a saving of 33%).

The H.261 standard, as used in video conferencing, uses a 4:1:1 ratio. Thus the color difference components are sampled at one-quarter of the luminance rate. For example, if the image is:

$\underline{R}$ (352×288), G (352×288) and B (352×288)

then using 4:1:1 gives the resultant YC_rC_b form:

Y (352×288), C_b (176×144) and C_r (176×144)

Thus, in NSTC, the number of terms has been reduced from 304 128 to 152 064 (a saving a 50%).

CCIR-601 active lines

CCIR defines a constant sampling rate of 13.5 MHz. Unfortunately, a delay is required to go from the end of one line to the start of the next (called horizontal retrace). A delay is also required when the scanning reaches the end of a frame and returns to the top of the frame (called vertical retrace). The time for active pixels has been defined as 720 per line, or 53 ns (in CCIR-601 the time of scan for a line is 64 µs). This is the same for NSTC (which samples at 858 per line) and PAL (which samples at 864 per line).

CCIR-601 quantization

Each of the samples for luminance and chrominance has 8 bits, which gives 256 levels. Only 220 values are used, the black level is coded as 16 and the peak white levels are coded as 235. Values from 0 to 16 and 235 to 255 are reserved for special code words. The color-difference signal can take on 225 different values; the zero corresponds to coded value 128 and the peak saturation to values 16 and 240. The values from 0 to 16 and 240 to 255 are reserved for special code words.

B2.9.5   100 Hz pictures

Digital transmission of video signals not only improves the transmission of the video signals, it can also be used to increase picture quality. Two typical problems with PAL, NSTC and SECAM systems are:

- Interline flicker – the flickering of sharp horizontal edges around the edges of objects.
- Large-area flicker – most noticeable on large screens.

Research indicates these problems disappear when the frame rate is 90 Hz eliminates all flickering. Thus as the video data is digitized it can be stored in a memory and recalled at any rate. A possible technique, for PAL/625, is to store the incoming video data in memory and then to read it out at a rate of 100 Hz. This will then be displayed to the speed at double-speed lines and field scan rates.

B2.9.6   Compressed TV

TV signals and motion video have a massive amount of redundant information. This is mainly because each image has redundant information and because there are very few changes from one image to the next. A typical standard is the MPEG standard which allows compression of about 130:1.

With MPEG-2 this transmission rate can be reduced to 4 Mbps for PAL and SECAM and 3 Mbps for NTSC, thus giving a compression ratio of 40:1 to high quality TV. MPEG-1 typically compresses TV signals to 1.2 Mbps, giving a compression ratio of 130:1. Unfortunately, the quality is reduced to near VCR-type quality. Table B2.11 outlines these parameters.

The base bit rate for a standard Ethernet network is 10 Mbps. This allows compressed video to be transmitted over the network when there is no other traffic on the network. The 4 Mbps rate will load the network by approximately 50%.

Table B2.11   Motion video compression

Type	Bit rate	Compression	Comment
Uncompressed TV	162 Mbps	1:1	
MPEG-1	4 Mbps	40:1	VCR quality
MPEG-2	1.2 Mbps	130:1	PAL, SECAM TV quality

B2.9.7   HDTV quality

HDTV (high-definition TV) has been supported by many companies for many years. Standards such as the European High-Definition MAC, a mainly analogue-based system, have been promoted then abandoned.

The main parameters in a TV system are the frame rate and the picture resolution; the main improvements are:

- HDTV-quality gives a higher picture resolution with a higher frame rate (1920×1080 at 60 frames per second). This gives excellent images of 1920 pixels per lines, 1080 lines per frame and 60 frames per second.
- HDTV-quality with a high resolution and a conventional frame rate (1920×1080 at 24 frames per second). The advantage with this system is that is gives much high resolution with a frame rate which is similar to the frame rate of current system (25 frames per second for PAL and 30 frames per second for NTSC).
- Improved resolution/conventional frame rate (1280×730 at 30 frames per second). The advantage of this system is that it gives an intermediate response between conventional

systems and the alternatives given above. This technology may allow the best intermediate migration between current TV and high-resolution technology. Its screen resolution is also similar to SVGA monitors.

Another important parameter in TV systems is the aspect ratio. Conventional TVs use an aspect ratio of 4:3 (which is defined as the width of the screen divided by its height). This aspect ratio does not really suit showing movies or sports events, and HDTV improves this to a 16:9 aspect ratio.

B2.10   GIF coding

The graphics interchange format (GIF) is the copyright of CompuServe Incorporated. Its popularity has increased mainly because of its wide usage on the Internet. CompuServe Incorporated, luckily, has granted a limited, non-exclusive, royalty-free license for the use of GIF (but any software using the GIF format must acknowledge the ownership of the GIF format).

Most graphics software supports the Version 87a or 89a format (the 89a format is an update the 87a format). Both have basic specification:

- A header with GIF identification.
- A logical screen descriptor block which defines the size, aspect ratio and color depth of the image place.
- A global color table.
- Data blocks with bitmapped images and the possibility of text overlay.
- Multiple images, with image sequencing or interlacing. This process is defined in a graphic-rendering block.
- LZW compressed bitmapped images.

A2.1.1 Color tables

Color tables store the color information of part of an image (a local color table) or they can be global (a global table).

A2.1.2 Blocks, extensions and scope

Blocks can be specified into three groups: control, graphic-rendering and special purpose. Control blocks contain information used to control the process of the data stream or information used in setting hardware parameters. They include:

- GIF Header – which contains basic information on the GIF file, such as the version number and the GIF file signature.
- Logical screen descriptor – which contains information about the active screen display, such as screen width and height, and the aspect ratio.
- Global color table – which contains up to 256 colors from a palette of 16.7M colors (i.e. 256 colors with 24-bit color information).
- Data subblocks – which contain the compressed image data.
- Image description – which contains, possibly, a local color table and defines the image width and height, and its top left coordinate.
- Local color table – an optional block which contains local color information for an image as with the global color table, it has a maximum of 256 colors from a palette of 16.7M.
- Table-based image data – which contains compressed image data.
- Graphic control extension – an optional block which has extra graphic-rendering infor-

mation, such as timing information and transparency.

- Comment extension – an optional block which contains comments ignored by the decoder.
- Plain text extension – an optional block which contains textual data.
- Application extension – which contains application-specific data. This block can be used by a software package to add extra information to the file.
- Trailer – which defines the end of a block of data.

A2.1.3 GIF header

The header is 6 bytes long and identifies the GIF signature and the version number of the chosen GIF specification. Its format is:

- 3 bytes with the characters 'G', 'I' and 'F'.
- 3 bytes with the version number (such as 87a or 89a). Version numbers are ordered with two digits for the year, followed by a letter ('a', 'b', and so on).

Program B2.1 is a C program for reading the 6-byte header. Sample run B2.1 shows a sample run with a GIF file. It can be seen that the file in the test run has the required signature and has been stored with Version 89a.

📄 **Program B2.1**

```c
#include    <stdio.h>

int    main(void)
{
FILE   *in;
char   fname[BUFSIZ], str[BUFSIZ];

    printf("Enter GIF file>>");
    gets(fname);

    if ((in=fopen(fname,"r"))==NULL)
    {
        printf("Can't find file %s\n",fname);
        return(1);
    }

    fread(str,3,1,in);
    str[3]=NULL; /* terminate string */
    printf("Signature: %s\n",str);
    fread(str,3,1,in);
    str[3]=NULL; /* terminate string */
    printf("Version: %s\n",str);
    fclose(in);
    return(0);
}
```

🖥 **Sample run B2.1**

```
Enter GIF file>> clouds.gif
Signature: GIF
Version: 89a
```

A2.1.4 Logical screen descriptor

The logical screen descriptor appears after the header. Its format is:

- 2 bytes with the logical screen width (unsigned integer).
- 2 bytes with the logical screen height (unsigned integer).
- 1 byte of a packed bit field, with 1 bit for global color table flag, 3 bits for color resolution, 1 bit for sort flag and 3 bits to give an indication of the number of colors in the global color table
- 1 byte for the background color index.
- 1 byte for the pixel aspect ratio.

Program B2.2 is a C program which reads the header and the logical descriptor field, and Sample run B2.2 shows a sample run. It can be seen, in this case, that the logic screen size is 640×480. The packed field, in this case, has a hexadecimal value of F7h, which is 1111 0111b in binary. Thus, all the bits of the packed bit field are set, apart from the sort flag. If this is set then the global color table is sorted in order of decreasing importance (the most frequent color appearing first and the least frequent color last). The total number of colors in the global color table is found by raising 2 to the power of 1 + the color value in the packed bit field:

$$\text{Number of colors} = 2^{\text{Color value in packed bit field}+1}$$

In this case, there is a bit field of seven colors, thus the total number of colors is 2^8, or 256.

It can be seen that the aspect ratio in Sample run B2.2 is zero. If it is zero then no aspect ratio is given. If it is not equal to zero then the aspect ratio of the image is computed by:

$$\text{Aspect ratio} = \frac{\text{Pixel aspect ratio}+15}{64}$$

where the pixel ratio is the pixel's width divided by its height.

Program B2.2

```c
#include     <stdio.h>

int    main(void)
{
FILE   *in;
char   fname[BUFSIZ], str[BUFSIZ];
int    x,y;
char   color_index, aspect, packed;

    printf("Enter GIF file>>");
    gets(fname);

    if  ((in=fopen(fname,"r"))==NULL)
    {
        printf("Can't find file %s\n",fname);
        return(1);
    }

    fread(str,3,1,in);    str[3]=NULL; /* terminate string */
    printf("Signature: %s\n",str);
    fread(str,3,1,in);    str[3]=NULL; /* terminate string */
    printf("Version: %s\n",str);

    fread(&x,2,1,in); str[3]=NULL; /* terminate string */
    printf("Screen width: %d\n",x);
    fread(&y,2,1,in); str[3]=NULL; /* terminate string */
```

```
    printf("Screen height: %d\n",y);

    fread(&packed,1,1,in);
    printf("Packed: %x\n",packed & 0xff); /* mask-off the bottom 8 bits */
    fread(&color_index,1,1,in);
    printf("Color index: %d\n",color_index);
    fread(&aspect,1,1,in);
    printf("Aspect ratio: %d\n",aspect);

    fclose(in);
    return(0);
}
```

Sample run B2.2
```
Enter GIF file>> clouds.gif
Signature: GIF
Version: 89a
Screen width: 640
Screen height: 480
Packed: f7
Color index: 0
Aspect ratio: 0
```

A2.1.5 Global color table

After the header and the logical display descriptor comes the global color table. It contains up to 256 colors from a palette of 16.7M colors. Each of the colors is defined as a 24-bit color of red (8 bits), green (8 bits) and blue (8 bits). The format in memory is:

RRRRRRRR

GGGGGGGG

BBBBBBBB

RRRRRRRR

GGGGGGGG

BBBBBBBB

  :   :

RRRRRRRR

GGGGGGGG

BBBBBBBB

Thus the number of bytes that the table will contain will be:

$$\text{Number of bytes} = 3 \times 2^{\text{Size of global color table}+1}$$

The 24-bit color scheme allows a total of 16 777 216 (2^{24}) different colors to be displayed. Table B2.12 defines some colors in the RGB (red/green/blue) strength. The format is rrggbbh, where rr is the hexadecimal equivalent for the red component, gg the hexadecimal equivalent for the green component and bb the hexadecimal equivalent for the blue component. For example, in binary:

00000000000000000000000000   represents black (000000h)
111111111111111111111111   represents white (FFFFFFh)
011101101110111011101110111   represents gray (777777h)

111110101110010100000011   represents yellow (FCE503h)
001110100000101101011001   represents purple (3A0B59h)

Table B2.12 Hexadecimal colors for 24-bit color representation

Color	Code	Color	Code
White	FFFFFFh	Dark red	C91F16h
Light red	DC640Dh	Orange	F1A60Ah
Yellow	FCE503h	Light green	BED20Fh
Dark green	088343h	Light blue	009DBEh
Dark blue	0D3981h	Purple	3A0B59h
Pink	F3D7E3h	Nearly black	434343h
Dark gray	777777h	Gray	A7A7A7h
Light gray	D4D4D4h	Black	000000h

Program B2.3 is a C program which reads the header, the image descriptor and the color table. Sample run B2.3 shows a truncated color table. The first three are:

0111 1011 1010 1101 1101 0110 (7BADD6h)
1000 0100 1011 0101 1101 1110 (84B5DEh)
0111 0011 1010 1101 1101 0110 (73ADD6h)

These colors have a strong blue component (D6h and DEh) and reduced strength red and green components. The image itself is a picture of clouds on a blue sky, thus the image is likely to have strong blue colors.

📄 **Program B2.3**

```
#include    <stdio.h>

int    main(void)
{
FILE   *in;
char   fname[BUFSIZ], str[BUFSIZ];
int    x,y,i;
char   color_index, aspect, packed,red,blue,green;

   printf("Enter GIF file>>");
   gets(fname);

   if ((in=fopen(fname,"r"))==NULL)
   {
      printf("Can't find file %s\n",fname);
      return(1);
   }

   fread(str,3,1,in);   str[3]=NULL; /* terminate string */
   printf("Signature: %s\n",str);
   fread(str,3,1,in);   str[3]=NULL; /* terminate string */
   printf("Version: %s\n",str);

   fread(&x,2,1,in); str[3]=NULL; /* terminate string */
   printf("Screen width: %d\n",x);
   fread(&y,2,1,in); str[3]=NULL; /* terminate string */
   printf("Screen height: %d\n",y);
```

```
    fread(&packed,1,1,in);
    printf("Packed: %x\n",packed & 0xff); /* mask-off the bottom 8 bits */
    fread(&color_index,1,1,in);
    printf("Color index: %d\n",color_index);
    fread(&aspect,1,1,in);
    printf("Aspect ratio: %d\n",aspect);

    for (i=0;i<64;i++)
    {
        fread(&red,1,1,in);
        printf("Red: %x ",red & 0xff);        /* display 8 bits */
        fread(&green,1,1,in);
        printf("Green: %x ",green & 0xff);   /* display 8 bits */
        fread(&blue,1,1,in);
        printf("Blue: %x\n",blue & 0xff);    /* display 8 bits */
    }

    fclose(in);

    return(0);

}
```

🖳 **Sample run B2.3**
```
Enter GIF file>> clouds.gif
Signature: GIF
Version: 89a
Screen width: 640
Screen height: 480
Packed: f7
Color index: 0
Aspect ratio: 0
Red: 7b Green: ad Blue: d6
Red: 84 Green: b5 Blue: de
Red: 73 Green: ad Blue: d6
Red: 7b Green: ad Blue: de
Red: 94 Green: bd Blue: de
Red: 7b Green: b5 Blue: de
Red: 8c Green: b5 Blue: de
Red: 8c Green: bd Blue: de
Red: 9c Green: c6 Blue: de
Red: ce Green: de Blue: ef
Red: de Green: e7 Blue: ef
Red: a5 Green: c6 Blue: e7
    ::::::
Red: 8c Green: bd Blue: e7
Red: ff Green: ff Blue: f7
Red: ad Green: d6 Blue: ef
Red: 8c Green: b5 Blue: e7
Red: 84 Green: b5 Blue: e7
```

A2.1.6 Image descriptor

After the global color table is the image descriptor. Its format is:

- 1 byte for the image separator (always 2Ch).
- 2 bytes for the image left position (unsigned integer).
- 2 bytes for the image top position (unsigned integer).
- 2 bytes for the image width (unsigned integer).
- 2 bytes for the image height (unsigned integer).
- 1 byte of a packed bit field, with 1 bit for local color table flag, 1 bit for interlace flag, 1 bit

for sort flag, 2 bits are reserved and 3 bits for the size of the local color table.

Program B2.4 is a C program which searches for the image separator (2Ch) and displays the image descriptor data that follows. Sample run B2.4 shows a sample run. It can be seen from this sample run that the image is to be displayed at $(0,0)$, its width is 640 pixels and its height is 480 pixels. The packed bit field contains all zeros, thus there is no local color table (and the global color table should be used).

📄 Program B2.4

```c
#include     <stdio.h>

int    main(void)
{
FILE   *in;
char   fname[BUFSIZ];
int    i,left,top,width,height;
char   ch,packed;
   printf("Enter GIF file>>");
   gets(fname);

   if ((in=fopen(fname,"r"))==NULL)
   {
      printf("Can't find file %s\n",fname);
      return(1);
   }
   do
   {
      fread(&ch,1,1,in);
   } while (ch!=0x2C); /* find image seperator */

   fread(&left,2,1,in);
   printf("Image left position: %d\n",left);
   fread(&top,2,1,in);
   printf("Image top position: %d\n",top);
   fread(&width,2,1,in);
   printf("Image width: %d\n",width);
   fread(&height,2,1,in);
   printf("Image height: %d\n",height);
   fread(&packed,1,1,in);
   printf("Packed: %x\n",packed & 0xff);
   fclose(in);
   return(0);
}
```

💻 Sample run B2.4

```
Enter GIF file>> clouds.gif
Image left position: 0
Image top position: 0
Image width: 640
Image height: 480
Packed: 0
```

A2.1.7 Local color table

The local color table is an optional block which defines the color map for the image that precedes it. The format is identical to the global color map, i.e. 3 bytes for each of the colors.

A2.1.8 Table-based image data

The table-based image data follows the local color table. This table contains compressed image data. It consists of a series of subblocks of up to 255 bytes. The data consists of an index to the color table (either global or local) for each pixel in the image. As the global (or local) color table has 256 entries, the data value (in its uncompressed form) will range from 0 to 255 (8 bits). The tables format is:

- 1 byte for the LZW minimum code size, which is the initial number of bits used in the LZW coding.
- N bytes for the LZW compressed image data. The first block is preceded by the data size.

GIF coding uses the variable-length-code LZW technique where a variable-length code replaces image data (pixel color references). These variable-length codes are specified in a Huffman code table. The encoder replaces the data from the input and builds a dictionary with the patterns in the data. Every new pattern is entered into the dictionary and the index value of the table is added to coded data. When a previously stored pattern is encountered, its dictionary index value is added to the coded data. The decoder takes the compressed data and builds the dictionary which is identical to the encoder. It then replaces indexed terms from the dictionary.

The VLC algorithm uses an initial code size to specify the initial number of bits used for the compression codes. When the number of patterns detected by the encoder exceeds the number of patterns encodable with the current number of bits then the number of bits per LZW is increased by 1.

Program B2.5 reads the LZW code size byte. The byte after this is the block size, followed by the number of bytes of data as defined in the block size byte. Sample run B2.5 gives a sample run. It can be seen that the initial LZW code size is 8 and that the block size of the first block is 254 bytes. The dictionary entries will thus start at entry 256 (2^8).

📄 Program B2.5

```c
#include     <stdio.h>

int    main(void)
{
FILE   *in;
char   fname[BUFSIZ];
int    i,left,top,width,height;
char   ch,packed,code,block;

    printf("Enter GIF file>>");
    gets(fname);

    if ((in=fopen(fname,"r"))==NULL)
    {
        printf("Can't find file %s\n",fname);
        return(1);
    }

    do
    {
        fread(&ch,1,1,in);
    } while (ch!=0x2C);
    fread(&left,2,1,in);
    printf("Image left position: %d\n",left);
    fread(&top,2,1,in);
    printf("Image top position: %d\n",top);
    fread(&width,2,1,in);
```

```
    printf("Image width: %d\n",width);
    fread(&height,2,1,in);
    printf("Image height: %d\n",height);
    fread(&packed,1,1,in);
    printf("Packed: %x\n",packed & 0xff);
    fread(&code,1,1,in);
    printf("LZW code size: %d\n",code & 0xff);
    fread(&block,1,1,in);
    printf("Block size: %d\n",block & 0xff);
    fclose(in);
    return(0);
}
```

🖳 **Sample run B2.5**
```
Enter GIF file>> clouds.gif
Image left position: 0
Image top position: 0
Image width: 640
Image height: 480
Packed: 0
LZW code size: 8
Block size: 254
```

A2.1.9 Graphic control extension

The graphic control extension is optional and contains information on the rendering of the image that follows. Its format is:

- 1 byte with the extension identifier (21h).
- 1 byte with the graphic control label (F9h).
- 1 byte with the block size following this field and up to but not including, the end terminator. It always has a fixed value of 4.
- 1 byte with a packed array of which the first 3 bits are reserved, 3 bits define the disposal method, 1 bit defines the user input flag and 1 bit defines the transparent color flag.
- 2 bytes with the delay time for the encode wait, in hundreds of a seconds, before encoding the image data.
- 1 byte with the transparent color index.
- 1 byte for the block terminator (00h).

A2.1.10 Comment extension

The comment extension is optional and contains information which is ignored by the encoder. Its format is:

- 1 byte with the extension identifier (21h).
- 1 byte with the comment extension label (FEh).
- N bytes, with comment data.
- 1 byte for the block terminator (00h).

A2.1.11 Plain text extension

The plain text extension is optional and contains text information. Its format is:

- 1 byte with the extension identifier (21h).
- 1 byte with the plain text label (01h).
- 1 byte with the block size. This is the number of bytes after the block size field up to but not including the beginning of the plain text data block. It always contains the value 12.

- 2 bytes for the text grid left position.
- 2 bytes for the text grid top position.
- 2 bytes for the text width.
- 2 bytes for the text height.
- 1 byte for the character cell width.
- 1 byte for the character cell height.
- 1 byte for the text foreground color.
- 1 byte for the text background color.
- N bytes for the plain text data.
- 1 byte for the block terminator (00h).

A2.1.12   Application extension

The application extension is optional and contains information for application programs. Its format is:

- 1 byte with the extension identifier (21h).
- 1 byte with the application extension label (FFh).
- 1 byte for the block size. This is the number of bytes after the block size field up to but not including the beginning of the application data. It always contains the value 11.
- 8 bytes for the application identifier.
- 3 bytes for the application authentication code.
- N bytes, for the application data.
- 1 byte for the block terminator (00h).

A2.1.13   Trailer

The trailer indicates the end of the GIF file. Its format is:

- 1 byte identifying the trailer (3Bh).

B2.11   TIFF coding

Tag image file format (TIFF) is an excellent method of transporting images between file systems and software packages. It is supported by most graphics import packages. It has a high resolution and thus is typically used when scanning images. There are two main types of TIFF coding, baseline TIFF and extended TIFF. It can also use different compression methods and different file formats, depending on the type of data stored.

In TIFF 6.0, defined in June 1992, the pixel data can be stored in several different compression formats, such as:

- Code number 1, no compression.
- Code number 2, CCITT Group 3 modified Huffman RLE encoding.
- Code number 3, Fax-compatible CCITT Group 3.
- Code number 4, Fax-compatible CCITT Group 4.
- Code number 5, LZW compression.

Codes 1 and 2 are baseline TIFF files whereas the others are extended.

A2.1.14   File structure

TIFF files have a three-level hierarchy:

- A file header.
- One or more IFDs (image file directories). These contain codes and their data (or pointers to the data).
- Data.

The file header contains 8 bytes: a byte order field (2 bytes), the version number field (2 bytes) and the pointer to the first IFD (4 bytes). Figure B2.25 shows the file header format. The byte order field defines whether Motorola architecture is used (the character sequence is 'MM', or 4D4Dh) or Intel architecture (the character sequence is 'II', or 4949h). The Motorola format defines that the bytes are ordered from the most significant to the least significant, the Intel format defines that the bytes are organized from least significant to the most significant.

The version number field always contains the decimal number 42 (maybe related to Douglas Adam's *Hitchhikers Guide to the Galaxy*, where 42 is described as the answer to the life, the universe and everything). It is used to identify that the file is TIFF format.

The first IFD offset pointer is a 4-byte pointer to the first IFD. If the format is Intel then the bytes are arranged from least significant to most significant else they are arranged from most significant to least significant.

Program B2.6 is a C program which reads the header of a TIFF file and Sample run B2.6 shows that, in this case, it uses the Intel format and the second byte field contains 2Ah (or 42 decimal).

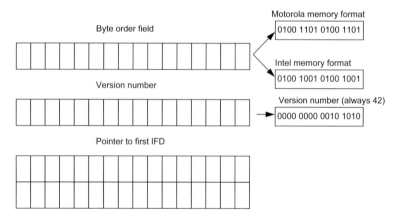

Figure B2.25   TIFF file header

📄 **Program B2.6**

```
#include    <stdio.h>

int    main(void)
{
FILE   *in;
char   ch1,ch2,fname[BUFSIZ];

    printf("Enter TIFF file>>");
    gets(fname);

    if ((in=fopen(fname,"r"))==NULL)
```

```
    {
        printf("Can't find file %s\n",fname);
        return(1);
    }

    ch1=fgetc(in); ch2=getc(in);
    printf("Memory model %c%c\n",ch1,ch2);
    ch1=fgetc(in); ch2=getc(in);
    printf("Version %x%x\n",ch2,ch1);

    fclose(in);
    return(0);
}
```

Sample run B2.6

```
Enter TIFF file>> image1.tif
Memory model II
Version 02a
```

A2.1.15   IFD

Typically the first IFD will be the only IFD, which is pointed to by the first IFD in the header field.

B3   Error coding

B3.1   Error coding principles

The data transmitted over communications channels, and the Internet must be protected against or detect errors. Error bits are added to data either to correct or to detect transmission errors. Normally, the more bits that are added, the better the correction or detection. Error detection allows the receiver to determine if there has been a transmission error. It cannot rebuild the correct data and must either request a retransmission or discard the data. With error correction, the receiver detects an error and tries to correct as many error bits as possible. Again, the more error coding bits are used, the more bits can be corrected. An error correction code is normally used when the receiver cannot request a retransmission.

In a digital communication system, a single transmission symbol can actually contain many bits. If a single symbol can represent M values then it is described as an M-ary digit. An example of this is in modem communication where 2 bits are sent as four different phase shifts, e.g. 0° for 00, 90° for 01, 180° for 10 and 270° for 11. To avoid confusion it is assumed in this chapter that the digits input to the digital coder and the digital decoder are binary digits and this chapter does not deal with M-ary digits.

B3.1.1   Modulo-2 arithmetic

Digital coding uses modulo-2 arithmetic where addition becomes the following operations:

$$0 + 0 = 0 \qquad\qquad 1 + 1 = 0$$
$$0 + 1 = 1 \qquad\qquad 1 + 0 = 1$$

It performs the equivalent operation to an exclusive-OR (XOR) function. For modulo-2 arithmetic, subtraction is the same operation as addition:

$$0 - 0 = 0 \qquad\qquad 1 - 1 = 0$$
$$0 - 1 = 1 \qquad\qquad 1 - 0 = 1$$

Multiplication is performed with the following:

$$0 \times 0 = 0 \qquad\qquad 0 \times 1 = 0$$
$$1 \times 0 = 0 \qquad\qquad 1 \times 1 = 1$$

which is an equivalent operation to a logical AND operation.

B3.1.2   Binary manipulation

Binary digit representation, such as 101110, is difficult to use when multiplying and dividing. A typical representation is to manipulate the binary value as a polynomial of bit powers. This technique represents each bit as an x to the power of the bit position and then adds each of the bits. For example:

10111	x^4+x^2+x+1
1000 0001	x^7+1
1111 1111 1111 1111	$x^{11}+x^{10}+x^9+x^8+x^7+x^6+x^5+x^4+x^3+x^2+x+1$
10101010	$x^6+x^4+x^2+x$

For example: 101×110
is represented as: $(x^2+1)\times(x^2+x)$
which equates to: $x^4+x^3+x^2+x$
which is thus: 11110

The addition of the bits is treated as a modulo-2 addition, that is, any two values which have the same powers are equal to zero. For example:

$$x^4+x^4+x^2+1+1$$

is equal to x^2 as x^4+x^4 is equal to zero and 1+1 is equal to 0 (in modulo-2). An example which shows this is the multiplication of 10101 by 01100.

Thus: 10101×01110
is represented as: $(x^4+x^2+1)\times(x^3+x^2+x)$
which equates to: $x^7+x^6+x^4+x^5+x^4+x^3+x^3+x^2+x$
which equates to: $x^7+x^6+x^5+x^4+x^4+x^3+x^3+x^2+x$
which equates to: $x^7+x^6+x^5+0+0+x^2+x$
which equates to: $x^7+x^6+x^5+x^2+x$
which is thus: 11100110

This type of multiplication is easy to implement as it just involves AND and XOR operations.

The division process uses exclusive-OR operation instead of subtraction and can be implemented with a shift register and a few XOR gates. For example, 101101 divided by 101 is implemented as follows:

```
           1011
     100 | 101101
           100
           110
           100
           101
           100
             1
```

Thus, the modulo-2 division of 101101 by 100 is 1011 remainder 1. As with multiplication this modulo-2 division can also be represented with polynomial values.

Normally, pure integer or floating-point multiplication and division require complex hardware and can cause a considerable delay in computing the result. Error coding multiplication and division circuits normally use a modified version of multiplication and division, which uses XOR operations and shift registers.

B3.1.3 Hamming distance

The Hamming distance, $d(C_1,C_2)$, between two code words C_1 and C_2 is defined as the number of places in which they differ. For example, the codes:

101101010 and 011101100

have a Hamming distance of 4 as they differ in 4 bit positions. Also $d(11111,00000)$ is equal to 5.

The Hamming distance can be used to determine how well the code will cope with errors. The minimum Hamming distance $\min\{d(C_1,C_2)\}$ defines by how many bits the code must change so that one code can become another code.

It can be shown that:

- A code C can detect up to N errors for any code word if $d(C)$ is greater than or equal to $N+1$ (that is, $d(C) \geq N+1$).
- A code C can correct up to M errors in any code word if $d(C)$ is greater than or equal to $2M+1$ (that is, $d(C) \geq 2M+1$).

For example the code:

{00000, 01101, 10110, 11011}

has a minimum Hamming distance of 3. Thus, the number of errors which can be detected is given by:

$$d(C) \geq N+1$$

since, in this case, $d(C)$ is 3 then N must be 2. This means that one or two errors in the code word will be detected as an error. For example, the following have 2 bits in error, and will thus be received as an error:

00011, 10101, 11010, 00011

The number of errors which can be corrected (M) is given by:

$$d(C) \geq 2M+1$$

thus M will be 1, which means that only one bit in error can be corrected. For example if the received code word was:

01111

then this code is measured against all the other codes and the Hamming distance calculated. Thus 00000 has a Hamming distance of 4, 01101 has a Hamming distance of 1, 10110 has a Hamming distance of 3, and 11011 has a Hamming distance of 2. Thus, the received code is nearest to 01101.

B3.1.4 General probability theory

Every digital system is susceptible to errors. These errors may happen once every few seconds or once every hundred years. The rate at which these occur is governed by the error probability.

If an event X has a probability of P(X) and event Y has a probability of P(Y) then the probability that either might occur is:

P(X or Y) = P(A) + P(B) − P(X and Y)

If one event prevents the other from happening, then they are mutually exclusive, thus P(X and Y) will be zero. This will give:

P(X or Y) = P(X) + P(Y)

If an event X has a probability of P(X) and event Y has a probability of P(Y) then the probability that both might occur is:

P(X and Y)=P(X)×P($Y\,|\,X$)
P(X and Y)=P(Y)×P($X\,|\,Y$)

where $P(Y\,|\,X)$ is the probability that event Y will occur, assuming that event X has already occurred, and $P(X\,|\,Y)$ is the probability that event X will occur, assuming that event Y has already occurred. If the two events are independent then $P(X\,|\,Y)$ will be $P(X)$ and $P(Y\,|\,X)$ will be $P(Y)$. This results with:

P(X and Y)=P(X)×P(Y)

For example, rolls of a die are independent of each other. If a die is rolled twice then the probability of a rolling two sixes will be:

$$P(6 \text{ and } 6) = P(6) \times P(6)$$
$$= \frac{1}{6} \times \frac{1}{6} = \frac{1}{36}$$

This formula is used as one roll of the die is mutually exclusive to the next throw.

The probability of throwing a three or a two in a single throw of the dice will be:

$$P(2 \text{ or } 3) = P(2) + P(3)$$
$$= \frac{1}{6} + \frac{1}{6} = \frac{1}{3}$$

B3.1.5 Error probability

Each digital system has its own characteristics and thus will have a different probability of error. Most calculations determine the 'worst-case' situation. The transmission channel normally assumes the following:

- That each bit has the same probability of being received in error.
- That there is an equal probability of a 0 and of a 1 (that is, the probability of a 0 is 0.5 and the probability of a 1 is a 1.0).

Thus if the probability of a binary digit being received incorrectly is p, then the probability of no error is $1 - p$. This is illustrated in Figure B3.1.

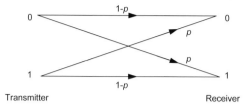

Figure B3.1   Probability or error model for a single bit

If the probability of no errors on a signal bit is $(1-p)$, then the probability of no errors of data with n bits will thus be:

Probability of no errors $= (1-p)^n$

The probability of an error will thus be:

Probability of an error $= 1-(1-p)^n$

The probability of a single error can be determined by assuming that all the other bits are received correctly, thus this will be:

$(1-p)^{n-1}$

Thus the probability of a single error at a given position will be this probability multiplied by the probability of an error on a single bit, thus:

$p(1-p)^{n-1}$

As there are n bit positions then the probability of a single bit error will be:

Probability of single error $= n.p(1-p)^{n-1}$

For example if the received data has 256 bits and the probability of an error in a single bit is 0.001 then:

Probability of no error $= (1-0.001)^{256}$
$= 0.774$

Thus the probability of an error is 0.226, and

Probability of single error $= 8 \times 0.001 \, (1-0.001)^{256-1}$
$= 0.0062$

B3.1.6 Combinations of errors

Combinational theory can be used in error calculation to determine the number of combinations of error bits that occur in some n-bit data. For example, in 8 bit data there are 8 combination of single-bit errors: (1), (2), (3), (4), (5), (6), (7) and (8). With 2 bits in error there are 28 combinations (1, 2), (1, 3), (1, 4), (1, 5), (1, 6), (1, 7), (1, 8), (2, 3), (2, 4), (2, 5), (2, 6), (2, 7), (2, 8), (3, 4), (3, 5)...(6, 6), (6, 7), (6, 8), (7, 8). In general the formula for the number of combinations of m-bit errors for n bits is:

$$\binom{n}{m} = \frac{n!}{m!(n-m)!}$$

Thus the number of double-bit errors that can occur in 8 bits is:

$$\binom{8}{2} = \frac{8!}{2!(8-2)!} = \frac{8!}{2!6!} = \frac{8 \times 7}{2} = 28$$

Table B3.1 shows the combinations for bit error with 8-bit data. It can thus be seen that there are 255 different error conditions (8 single-bit errors, 28 double-bit errors, 56 triple-bit errors, and so on).

Table B3.1 Combinations

No of bit errors	Combinations	No of bit errors	Combinations
1	8	5	56
2	28	6	28
3	56	7	8
4	70	8	1

To determine the probability with m bits at specific places, use the probability that $(n-m)$ bits will be received correctly:

$$(1-p)^{n-m}$$

Thus the probability that m bits, at specific places, will be received incorrectly is:

$$p^m(1-p)^{n-m}$$

The probability of an m-bit error in n bits is thus:

$$P_e(m) = \binom{n}{m} . p^m . (1-p)^{n-m}$$

Thus the probability of error in n n-bit data is:

$$P_e = \sum_{m=1}^{n} \binom{n}{m} . p^m . (1-p)^{n-m}$$

which is in the form of a binomial distribution.

Question

Determine the probability of error for a 4-bit data block using the formula:

$$P_e = \sum_{m=1}^{n} \binom{n}{m} . p^m . (1-p)^{n-m}$$

and prove this answer using $P_e = 1 - (1-p)^n$.

Answer

The probability of error will be:

$$P_e = \binom{4}{1} \cdot p \cdot (1-p)^3 + \binom{4}{2} \cdot p^2 \cdot (1-p)^2 + \binom{4}{3} \cdot p^3 \cdot (1-p)^1 + \binom{4}{4} \cdot p^4 \cdot (1-p)^0$$

$$= 4p(1-p)^3 + 6p^2 \left(1 - 2p - p^2\right) + 4p^3 - 4p^4 + p^4$$

$$= 4p(1-p)(1-p)^2 + 6p^2 - 12p^3 + 6p^4 + 4p^3 - 4p^4 + p^4$$

$$= 4p(1-p)\left(1 - 2p + p^2\right) + 6p^2 - 8p^3 + 3p^4$$

$$= 4p - 8p^2 + 4p^3 - 4p^2 + 8p^3 - 4p^4 + 6p^2 - 8p^3 + 3p^4$$

$$= 4p - 6p^2 + 4p^3 - p^4$$

To prove this result, the formula $P_e = 1 - (1-p)^n$ can be used to give:

$$P_e = 1 - (1-p)^4$$

$$= 1 - (1-p)^2 (1-p)^2$$

$$= 1 - \left(1 - 2p - p^2\right)\left(1 - 2p - p^2\right)$$

$$= 1 - \left(1 - 2p + p^2 - 2p + 4p^2 - 2p^3 + p^2 - 2p^3 + p^4\right)$$

$$= 1 - 1 + 2p - p^2 + 2p - 4p^2 + 2p^3 - p^2 + 2p^3 - p^4$$

$$= 4p - 6p^2 + 4p^3 - p^4$$

which is the same result as the previous derivation.

Question

For 4-bit data and a probability of error equal to 0.001, determine the actual probability of errors for 1, 2, 3 and 4 bit errors. Verify that the summation of the error probabilities is given by the formula derived in the previous question.

Answer

Table B3.2 shows the results using the formula:

$$P_e(m) = \binom{n}{m} . p^m . (1-p)^{n-m}$$

with $n = 4$ and $p = 0.001$.

It can be seen from the table that the probability of a single error is 3.988×10^{-3}. The probability of two errors is 5.99×10^{-6}, the probability of three errors is 4×10^{-9} and the probability of four errors is 1×10^{-12}. The summation of the probabilities is thus 3.994×10^{-3}. The formula derived earlier also gives this value for the probability.

$$P_e = 4p - 6p^2 + 4p^3 - p^4$$
$$= 4 \times 0.001 - 6 \times 0.001^2 - 4 \times 0.001^3 - 0.001^4$$
$$= 0.003\,994$$

Table B3.2 Probability of error

No of errors	Probability
1	3.988×10^{-3}
2	5.99×10^{-6}
3	4×10^{-9}
4	1×10^{-12}
Summation	3.994×10^{-3}

B3.1.7 Linear and cyclic codes

A linear binary code is one in which the sum of any two code words is also a code word. For example:

{00, 01, 10, 11}   and   {00000, 01101, 10110, 11011}

are linear codes, because any of the code words added (using modulo-2 addition) to another gives another valid code word. For example, in the second code, $01101 + 10110$ gives 11011, which is a valid code word.

Cyclic codes often involve complex mathematics but are extremely easy to implement with XOR gates and shift registers. A code is cyclic if:

- It is a linear code.
- When any cyclic shift of a code word is also a code word, i.e. whenever $a_0 a_1 \ldots a_{n-1}$ is a code word then so is $a_{n-1} a_0 a_1 \ldots a_{n-2}$.

For example, the code {0000, 0110, 0011, 1001, 1100, 0001, 0010, 0100, 1000} is cyclic because a shift in the bits, either left or right, produces a valid code word. Whereas the code {000, 010, 011, 100, 001} is not cyclic as a shift in the code word 011 to the left or right does not result in a valid code word. One of the most widely used codes, cyclic redundancy check (CRC) is an example of a cyclic code.

B3.1.8 Block and convolutional coding

The two main types of error coding are block codes and convolutional codes. A block code splits the data into k data bits and forms them into n blocks. This type of code is described as an (n, k) code. For example, an (12,8) code has 12 blocks of 8 bits, as illustrated in Figure B3.2. In a block code, the coder and decoder treat each block separately from all the other blocks.

Convolutional coding, on the other hand, treats the input and output bits as a continuous stream of binary digits. If the coder has an input of k bit(s) and outputs n bit(s), then the coder is described as k/n rate code. For example if the code takes 3 bits at a time and outputs 5 bits for each 3-bit input then it is described as a 3 / 5 rate code.

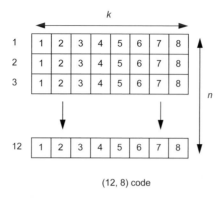

(12, 8) code

Figure B3.2   An (12,8) block code

B3.1.9   Systematic and unsystematic coding

Systematic code includes the input data bits in an unmodified form. Parity, or check bits, are then added to the unmodified bits. The main advantage of a systematic code is that the original data is still embedded in its original form within the coded data. Thus a receiver may ignore the extra error coding bits and simply read the uncoded data bits. Another decoder implementation could read the data and check the error bits for error detection, while a more powerful decoder might perform full error correction on the data. An unsystematic code modifies the input data bits and embeds the error coding into the coded bitstream. Thus, the decoder must normally decode the complete data stream.

B3.1.10 Feedforward and feedback error correction

An error code can give information on error detection or correction information. Normally error correcting codes require many more bits to be added to the data and they require more processing at the decoder. The error coding method used normally depends on many factors, including:

- The locality of the transmitter (which contains the encoder) and receiver (which contains the decoder). If the transmitter is located fairly near to the receiver and can respond quickly for a retransmission then it may be possible for the receiver simply to detect an error and ask for a retransmission. If this is not the case, the receiver must either discard the data or the system must use an error correction code. For example, a CD-ROM must contain powerful error correction codes because it is not possible for a CD player to ask for the data to be retransmitted, but two computers on the same network segment can easily ask for a retransmission.
- The characteristics of the transmission system. Normally the more errors that occur in the system, the greater the need for error correcting/detecting codes and the greater the need for a powerful coding scheme.

- The types of errors that can occur; for example, do the errors occur in bursts or in single bits at a time.
- The type of data. Normally computer-type data must be transmitted error-free whereas a few errors in an image or on audio data are unlikely to cause many problems. Thus with computer-type data, a correction code can correct the data as it is received (error correction) or there may be some method for contacting the transmitter to request a re-transmission (error detection).
- The power and speed of the encoder and decoder. For example, a powerful error correcting code it may not be possible to implement within a given time because of the need for low-cost decoder hardware. On the other hand, a powerful code may be inefficient for simple requirements.

With error detection the receiver must either discard the data or ask for a re-transmission. Many systems use an acknowledgment (ACK) from the receiver to acknowledge the receipt of data and a negative acknowledgment (NACK) to indicate an incorrect transmission. Typically, data is sent in data packets which contains the error code within them. Each packet also contains a value which identifies the packet number. The receiver then sends back an acknowledgment with the sequence number of the packet it is acknowledging. All previous packets before this value are automatically acknowledged. This method can be implemented in a number of modes, including:

- The transmitter transmits packets, up to a given number, and then waits for the receiver to acknowledge them. If it does not receive an acknowledgment it may resend them or reset the connection.
- The receiver sends back a NACK to inform the transmitter that it has received one or more frames in error, and would like the transmitter to retransmit them, starting with the packet number contained in the NACK.
- The receiver sends back a SREJ to selectively reject a single packet. The transmitter then retransmits this packet.

B3.1.11 Error types

Many errors can occur in a system. Normally, in a digital system, they are caused either when the noise level overcomes the signal level or when the digital pulses become distorted by the system (normally in the transmission systems). This causes a 0 to be interrupted as a 1, or a 1 as a 0.

Noise is any unwanted signal and has many causes, such as static pickup, poor electrical connections, electronic noise in components, crosstalk, and so on. It makes the reception of a signal more difficult and can also produce unwanted distortion on the unmodulated signal.

The main sources of noise on a communication system are:

- **Thermal noise** – thermal noise arises from the random movement of electrons in a conductor and is independent of frequency. The noise power can be predicted from the formula $N = kTB$ where N is the noise power in watts, k is Boltzmann's constant (1.38 × 10^{-23} J/K), T is the temperature (in K) and B is the bandwidth of the channel (Hz). Thermal noise is predictable and is spread across the bandwidth of the system. It is unavoidable but can be reduced by reducing the temperature of the components causing the thermal noise. Many receivers, which detect very small signals, require to be cooled to a very low temperature in order to reduce thermal noise. An example is in astronomy where the receiving sensor is reduced to almost absolute zero. Thermal noise is a fundamental limiting factor in the performance any communications system.

- **Crosstalk** – electrical signals propagate with an electric field and a magnetic field. If two conductors are laid beside each other then the magnetic field from one can couple into the other. This is known as crosstalk, where one signal interferes with another. Analogue systems tend to be more affected more by crosstalk than digital systems.
- **Impulse noise** – impulse noise is any unpredictable electromagnetic disturbance, such as from lightning or energy radiated from an electric motor. A relatively high-energy pulse of short duration normally characterizes it. It is of little importance to an analogue transmission system as it can usually be filtered at the receiver. However, impulse noise in a digital system can cause the corruption of a significant number of bits.

A signal can be distorted in many ways, by the electrical characteristics of the transmitter and receiver, and by the characteristics of the transmission media. An electrical cable possesses inductance, capacitance and resistance. The inductance and capacitance have the effect of distorting the shape of the signal whereas resistance causes the amplitude of the signal to reduce (and to lose power).

If, in a digital system, an error has the same probability of occurring at any time then the errors are random. If errors occur in several consecutive bits then they are called burst errors. A typical cause of burst errors is interference, often from lightning or electrical discharge.

If there is the same probability of error for both 1 and 0 then the channel is called a binary symmetric channel and the probability of error in binary digits is known as the bit error rate (BER).

B3.1.12 Coding gain

The effectiveness of an error correcting code is commonly measured with the coding gain and can therefore be used to compare codes. It can be defined as the saving in bits relative to an uncoded system delivering the same bit error rate.

B3.2   Error correction

The most important measure of error detection is the Hamming distance. This defines the number of changes in the transmitted bits that are required in order for a code word to be received as another code word. The more bits that are added, the greater the Hamming distance can be, and the objective of a good error detecting code is to be able to maximize the minimum Hamming distance between codes. For example, a code which has a minimum Hamming distance of 1 cannot be used to detect errors. This is because a single error in a specific bit in one or more code words causes the received code word to be received as a valid code word. A minimum Hamming distance of 2 will allow one error to be detected. In general, a code C can detect up to N errors for any code word if $d(C)$ is greater than or equal to $N+1$ (i.e. $d(C) \geq N+1$). For this it can be shown that:

The number of errors detected $= d-1$

where d is the minimum Hamming distance.

Error detection allows the receiver to determine if there has been a transmission error. It cannot rebuild the correct data and must either request a retransmission or discard the data.

B3.2.1 Parity

Simple parity adds a single parity bit to each block of transmitted symbols. This parity bit either makes them have an even number of 1's (even parity) or an odd number of 1's (odd parity). It is a simple method of error detection and requires only exclusive-OR (XOR) gates to generate the parity bit. This output can be easily added to the data using a shift register.

Parity bits can only detect an odd number of errors, i.e. 1, 3, 5, and so on. If an even number of bits is in error then the parity bit will be correct and no error will be detected. This type of coding is normally not used on its own or where there is the possibility of several bits being in error.

B3.2.2 Block parity

Block parity is a block code which adds a parity symbol to the end of a block of code. For example a typical method is to transmit the one's complement (or sometimes the two's complement) of the modulo-2 sum of the transmitted values. Using this coding, and a transmitted block code after every 8 characters, the data:

$$1, 4, 12, -1, -6, 17, 0, -10$$

would be arranged as:

1	0000 0001
4	0000 0100
12	0000 1100
−1	1111 1111
−6	1111 1010
17	0001 0001
0	0000 0000
−10	1111 0110
	1110 1011

It can be seen that modulo-2 addition is 1110 1011 (which is −21 in decimal). Thus the transmitted data would be:

0000 0001 0000 0100 0000 1100 1111 1111 1111
1010 0001 0001 0000 0000 1111 0110 1110 1011 ...

In this case, a single error will cause the checksum to be wrong. Unfortunately, as with simple parity, even errors in the same column will not show-up an error, but single errors in different columns will show up as an error. Normally when errors occur, they are either single-bit errors or large bursts of errors. With a single-bit error, the scheme will detect an error and it is also likely to detect a burst of errors, as the burst is likely to affect several columns and also several rows.

This error scheme is used in many systems as it is simple and can be implemented easily in hardware with XOR gates or simply calculated with appropriate software. The more symbols are used in the block, the more efficient the code will be. Unfortunately, when an error occurs the complete block must be retransmitted.

B3.2.3 Checksum

The checksum block code is similar to the block parity method but the actual total of the values is sent. Thus it is it very unlikely that an error will go undiscovered. It is typically used when ASCII characters are sent to represent numerical values. For example, the previous data was:

1, 4, 12, –1, –6, 17, 0, –10

which gives a total of 17. This could be sent in ASCII characters as:

'1' SPACE '4' SPACE '1' '2' SPACE '–' '1' SPACE '–' '6' SPACE '1' '7' SPACE '0' SPACE '–' '1' '0' SPACE '1' '7'

where the SPACE character is the delimiting character between each of the transmitted values. Typically, the transmitter and receiver will agree the amount of numbers that will be transmitted before the checksum is transmitted.

B3.2.4 Cyclic redundancy checking (CRC)

CRC is one of the most reliable error detection schemes and can detect up to 95.5% of all errors. The most commonly used code is the CRC-16 standard code which is defined by the CCITT.

The basic idea of a CRC can be illustrated using an example. Suppose the transmitter and receiver were both to agree that the numerical value sent by the transmitter would always be divisible by 9. Then should the receiver get a value which was not divisible by 9 would know it knows that there had been an error. For example, if a value of 32 were to be transmitted it could be changed to 320 so that the transmitter would be able to add to the least significant digit, making it divisible by 9. In this case the transmitter would add 4, making 324. If this transmitted value were to be corrupted in transmission then there would only be a 10% chance that an error would not be detected.

In CRC-CCITT, the error correction code is 16 bits long and is the remainder of the data message polynomial $G(x)$ divided by the generator polynomial $P(x)$ ($x^{16}+x^{12}+x^5+1$, i.e. 10001000000100001). The quotient is discarded and the remainder is truncated to 16 bits. This is then appended to the message as the coded word.

The division does not use standard arithmetic division. Instead of the subtraction operation an exclusive-OR operation is employed. This is a great advantage as the CRC only requires a shift register and a few XOR gates to perform the division.

The receiver and the transmitter both use the same generating function $P(x)$. If there are no transmission errors then the remainder will be zero.

The method used is as follows:

1. Let $P(x)$ be the generator polynomial and $M(x)$ the message polynomial.
2. Let n be the number of bits in $P(x)$.
3. Append n zero bits onto the right-hand side of the message so that it contains $m+n$ bits.

4. Using modulo-2 division, divide the modified bit pattern by $P(x)$. Modulo-2 arithmetic involves exclusive-OR operations, i.e. $0 - 1 = 1$, $1 - 1 = 0$, $1 - 0 = 1$ and $0 - 0 = 0$.
5. The final remainder is added to the modified bit pattern.

For a 7-bit data code 1001100 determine the encoded bit pattern using a CRC generating polynomial of $P(x) = x^3 + x^2 + x^0$. Show that the receiver will not detect an error if there are no bits in error.

$$P(x) = x^3 + x^2 + x^0 \qquad (1101)$$
$$G(x) = x^6 + x^3 + x^2 \qquad (1001100)$$

Multiply by the number of bits in the CRC polynomial.

$$x^3(x^6 + x^3 + x^2)$$
$$x^9 + x^6 + x^5 \qquad (1001100000)$$

Figure B3.3 shows the operations at the transmitter. The transmitted message is thus:

1001100001

and Figure B3.4 shows the operations at the receiver. It can be seen that the remainder is zero, so there have been no errors in the transmission. The CRC-CCITT is a standard polynomial for data communications systems and can detect:

- All single and double bit errors, and all errors with an odd number of bits.
- All burst errors of length 16 or less.
- 99.997% of 17-bit error bursts.
- 99.998% of 18-bit and longer bursts.

Table B3.3 lists some typical CRC codes. CRC-32 is used in Ethernet, Token Ring and FDDI networks, whereas ATM uses CRC-8 and CRC-10.

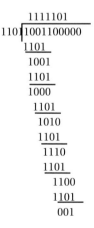

Figure B3.3   CRC coding example

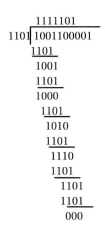

```
        1111101
1101 1001100001
     1101
     1001
     1101
     1000
     1101
      1010
      1101
      1110
      1101
       1101
       1101
        000
```

Figure B3.4   CRC decoding example

Table B3.3   Typical schemes

Type	Polynomial	Polynomial binary equivalent
CRC-8	$x^8+x^2+x^1+1$	100000111
CRC-10	$x^{10}+x^9+x^5+x^4+x^1+1$	11000110011
CRC-12	$x^{12}+x^{11}+x^3+x^2+1$	1100000001101
CRC-16	$x^{16}+x^{15}+x^2+1$	11000000000000101
CRC-CCITT	$x^{16}+x^{12}+x^5+1$	10001000000100001
CRC-32	$x^{32}+x^{26}+x^{23}+x^{16}+x^{12}+x^{11}$	100000100100000010001110110
	$+x^{10}+x^8+x^7+x^5+x^4+x^2+x+1$	110111

Mathematical representation of the CRC

The main steps to CRC implementation are:

1. Prescale the input polynomial of $M'(x)$ by the highest order of the generator polynomial $P(x)$. Thus:

$$M'(x) = x^n M(x)$$

2. Next divide $M'(x)$ by the generator polynomial to give:

$$\frac{M'(x)}{G(x)} = \frac{x^n M(x)}{G(x)} = Q(x) + \frac{R(x)}{G(x)}$$

which gives:

$$x^n M(x) = G(x)Q(x) + R(x)$$

and rearranging gives:

Error coding   241

$$x^n M(x) + R(x) = G(x)Q(x)$$

This means that the transmitted message $(x^n M(x) + R(x))$ is now exactly divisible by $G(x)$.

Quest: A CRC system uses a message of $1 + x^2 + x^4 + x^5$. Design a FSR cyclic encoder circuit with generator polynomial $G(x) = 1 + x^2 + x^3$ and having appropriate gating circuitry to enable/disable the shift out of the CRC remainder.

The generator polynomial is $G(x) = 1 + x^2 + x^3$, the circuit is given in Figure B3.5.

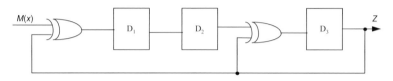

Figure B3.5 CRC coder

Now to prove that this circuit does generate the polynomial. The output $Z(x)$ will be:

$$Z(x) = Z(x)x^{-1} + \left[M(x)x^{-2} + Z(x)x^{-2} \right] x^{-1}$$
$$= Z(x)\left(x^{-3} + x^{-1} \right) + M(x)x^{-3}$$

Thus:

$$M(x) = \frac{Z(x)\left[1 + x^{-1} + x^{-3} \right]}{x^{-3}}$$

giving:

$$P(x) = \frac{M(x)}{Z(x)} = x^3 + x^2 + 1$$

Quest: If the previous CRC system uses a message of $1 + x^2 + x^4 + x^5$ then determine the sequence of events that occur and hence determine the encoded message as a polynomial $T(x)$. Synthesize the same code algebraically using modulo-2 division.

First prescale the input polynomial of $M(x)$ by x^3, the highest power of $G(x)$, thus:

$$M'(x) = x^3 . M(x) = x^3 + x^5 + x^7 + x^8$$

The input is thus $x^3 + x^5 + x^7 + x^8$ (000101011), and the generated states are:

Time	$M'(x)$	D_1	D_2	D_3	D_4	
1	000101011	0	0	0	0	
2	00010101	1	0	0	0	←MSD
3	0001010	1	1	0	0	
4	000101	0	1	1	1	
5	00010	0	0	0	0	
6	0001	0	0	0	0	
7	000	1	0	0	0	
8	00	0	1	0	0	
9	0	0	0	1	1	←LSD
10		1	0	1		

The remainder is thus 101, so $R(x)$ is $x^2 + 1$. The transmitted polynomial will be:

$$T(x) = x^3 M(x) + R(x) = x^8 + x^7 + x^5 + x^3 + x^2 + 1 \ (110101101)$$

To check this, use either modulo-2 division to give:

$$
\begin{array}{r}
x^5 \qquad\quad +1 \\
x^3+x^2+1 \,\overline{\big)\, x^8+x^7+x^5+x^3} \\
x^8+x^7+x^5 \\
\hline
x^3 \\
x^3+x^2+1 \\
\hline
\end{array}
$$

Remainder ⟶ $\boxed{x^2+1}$

This gives the same answer as the state table, i.e. x^2+1.

Quest: Prove that the transmitted message does not generate a remainder when divided by $P(x)$.

The transmitted polynomial, $T(x)$, is $x^8 + x^7 + x^5 + x^3 + x^2 + 1$ (110101101) and the generator polynomial, $G(x)$, is $1 + x^2 + x^3$. Thus:

$$
\begin{array}{r}
x^5 \qquad\quad +1 \\
x^3+x^2+1 \,\overline{\big)\, x^8+x^7+x^5+x^3+x^2+1} \\
x^8+x^7+x^5 \\
\hline
x^3+x^2+1 \\
x^3+x^2+1 \\
\hline
\end{array}
$$

Remainder ⟶ $\boxed{0}$

As there is a zero remainder, there is no error.

B3.3 Error (Detection)

Error bits are added to data either to correct or to detect transmission errors. Normally, the more bits that are added, the better the detection or correction. Error detection allows the receiver to determine if there has been a transmission error. It cannot rebuild the correct data and must either request a retransmission or discard the data. With error correction, the receiver detects an error and tries to correct as many error bits as possible. Again, the more error coding bits are used, the more bits can be corrected. An error correction code is normally used when the receiver cannot request a retransmission.

B3.3.1 Longitudinal/vertical redundancy checks (LRC/VRC)

RS-232 uses vertical redundancy checking (VRC) when it adds a parity bit to the transmitted character. Longitudinal (or horizontal) redundancy checking (LRC) adds a parity bit for all bits in the message at the same bit position. Vertical coding operates on a single character and is known as character error coding. Horizontal checks operate on groups of characters and described as message coding. LRC always uses even parity and the parity bit for the LRC character has the parity of the VRC code.

In the example given next, the character sent for LRC is thus `10101000` (28h) or a ' ('. The message sent is 'F', 'r', 'e', 'd', 'd', 'y' and ' ('.

Without VRC checking, LRC checking detects most errors but does not detect errors where an even number of characters have an error in the same bit position. In the previous example if bit 2 of the 'F' and 'r' were in error then LRC would be valid.

This problem is overcome if LRC and VRC are used together. With VRC/LRC the only time an error goes undetected is when an even number of bits, in an even number of characters, in the same bit positions of each character are in error. This is of course very unlikely.

On systems where only single-bit errors occur, the LRC/VRC method can be used to detect and correct the single-bit error. For systems where more than one error can occur it is not possible to locate the bits in error, so the receiver prompts the transmitter to retransmit the message.

Example

A communications channel uses ASCII character coding and LRC/VRC bits are added to each word sent. Encode the word 'Freddy' and, using odd parity for the VRC and even parity for the LRC; determine the LRC character.

	F	r	e	d	d	y	LRC
b0	0	0	1	0	0	1	0
b1	1	1	0	0	0	0	0
b2	1	0	1	1	1	0	0
b3	0	0	0	0	0	1	1
b4	0	1	0	0	0	1	0
b5	0	1	1	1	1	1	1
b6	1	1	1	1	1	1	0
VRC	0	1	1	0	0	0	1

B3.3.2 Hamming code

Hamming code is a forward error correction (FEC) scheme which can be used to detect and correct bit errors. The error correction bits are known as Hamming bits and the number that need to be added to a data symbol is determined by the expression:

$$2^n \geq m + n + 1$$

where m is number of bits in the data symbol
         n is number of Hamming bits

Hamming bits are inserted into the message character as desired. Typically, they are added at positions that are powers of 2, i.e. the 1st, 2nd, 4th, 8th, 16th bit positions, and so on. For example to code the character `011001` then, starting from the right-hand side, the Hamming bits would be inserted into the 1st, 2nd, 4th and 8th bit positions.

The character is   `011001`
The Hamming bits are   `HHHH`
The message format will be   `01H100H1HH`

10	9	8	7	6	5	4	3	2	1
0	1	H	1	0	0	H	1	H	H

Next each position where there is a 1 is represented as a binary value. Then each position value is exclusive-OR'ed with the others. The result is the Hamming code. In this example:

Position	Code
9	1001
7	0111
3	0011
XOR	1101

The Hamming code error bits are thus `1101` and the message transmitted will be `0111001101`.

10	9	8	7	6	5	4	3	2	1
0	1	1	1	0	0	1	1	0	1

At the receiver all bit positions where there is a 1 are exclusive-OR'ed. The result gives either the bit position error or no error. If the answer is zero there was no single-bit errors, it gives the bit error position.

Position	Code
Hamming	1101
9	1001
7	0111
3	0011
XOR	0000

If an error has occurred in bit 5 then the result is 5.

Position	Code
Hamming	1101
9	1001
7	0111
5	0101
3	0011
XOR	0101

B3.3.3 Representations of Hamming code

For a code with 4 data bits and 3 Hamming bits, the Hamming bits are normally inserted into the power-of-2 bit positions, thus code is known as (7, 4) code. The transmitted bit are $P_1P_2D_1P_3D_2D_3D_4$. In a mathematical form, the parity bits are generated by:

$$P_1 = D_1 \oplus D_2 \oplus D_4$$
$$P_2 = D_1 \oplus D_3 \oplus D_4$$
$$P_3 = D_2 \oplus D_3 \oplus D_4$$

111 110 101 100 011 010 001

D_4 D_3 D_2 P_3 D_1 P_2 P_1

At the receiver the check bits are generated by:

$$S_1 = P_1 \oplus D_1 \oplus D_2 \oplus D_4$$
$$S_2 = P_2 \oplus D_1 \oplus D_3 \oplus D_4$$
$$S_3 = P_3 \oplus D_2 \oplus D_3 \oplus D_4$$

Hamming coding can also be represented in a mathematical form. The steps are:

1. Calculate the number of Hamming bits using the formula $2^n \geq m + n + 1$, where m is number of bits in the data and n is number of Hamming bits. The code is known as an $(m + n, m)$ code. For example, (7, 4) code uses 4 data bits and 3 Hamming bits.
2. Determine the bit positions of the Hamming bits (typically they will be inserted in the power-of-2 bit positions, i.e. 1, 2, 4, 8, ...).
3. Generate the transmitted bit pattern with data bits and Hamming bits. For example if there are 4 data bits $(D_1D_2D_3D_4)$ and 3 Hamming bits $(P_1P_2P_3)$ then the transmitted bit pattern will be:

$$T = [P_1 \quad P_2 \quad D_1 \quad P_3 \quad D_2 \quad D_3 \quad D_4]$$

4. Transpose the **T** matrix to give $\mathbf{T}^T$; message bits $D_1D_2D_3D_4$ and Hamming bits $P_1P_2P_3$ would give:

$$\mathbf{T}^T = \begin{bmatrix} P_1 \\ P_2 \\ D_1 \\ P_3 \\ D_2 \\ D_3 \\ D_4 \end{bmatrix}$$

5. The Hamming matrix **H** is generated by an $[n, m + n]$ matrix, where n is the number of Hamming bits and m is the number of data bits. Each row identifies the Hamming bit and a 1 is placed in the row and column if that Hamming bit checks the transmitted bit. For example, in the case of a transmitted message of $P_1P_2D_1P_3D_2D_3D_4$ then if P_1 checks the D_1, D_2 and D_4, and P_2 checks the D_1, D_3 and D_4, and P_3 checks the D_2, D_3 and D_4, then the Hamming matrix will be:

$$H = \begin{bmatrix} 1 & 0 & 1 & 0 & 1 & 0 & 1 \\ 0 & 1 & 1 & 0 & 0 & 1 & 1 \\ 0 & 0 & 0 & 1 & 1 & 1 & 1 \end{bmatrix} \begin{matrix} \leftarrow \\ \leftarrow \\ \leftarrow \end{matrix} \begin{matrix} \text{Check of } P_1 \\ \text{Check of } P_2 \\ \text{Check of } P_3 \end{matrix}$$

The resulting matrix calculation of:

$$HT^T = \begin{bmatrix} 1 & 0 & 1 & 0 & 1 & 0 & 1 \\ 0 & 1 & 1 & 0 & 0 & 1 & 1 \\ 0 & 0 & 0 & 1 & 1 & 1 & 1 \end{bmatrix} \begin{bmatrix} P_1 \\ P_2 \\ D_1 \\ P_3 \\ D_2 \\ D_3 \\ D_4 \end{bmatrix}$$

gives the syndrome matrix **S** which is a $[1,3]$ matrix. The resulting terms for the syndrome will be:

$$S_1 = P_1 \oplus D_1 \oplus D_2 \oplus D_4$$
$$S_2 = P_2 \oplus D_1 \oplus D_3 \oplus D_4$$
$$S_3 = P_3 \oplus D_2 \oplus D_3 \oplus D_4$$

6. The parity bits are calculated to make all the terms of the syndrome zero. Using the current example:

$$S = HT^T = \begin{bmatrix} 0 \\ 0 \\ 0 \end{bmatrix}$$

At the receiver the steps are:

1. The Hamming matrix is multiplied by the received bits to give the syndrome matrix. Using the current example:

$$S = HR^T = \begin{bmatrix} 1 & 0 & 1 & 0 & 1 & 0 & 1 \\ 0 & 1 & 1 & 0 & 0 & 1 & 1 \\ 0 & 0 & 0 & 1 & 1 & 1 & 1 \end{bmatrix} \begin{bmatrix} P_1 \\ P_2 \\ D_1 \\ P_3 \\ D_2 \\ D_3 \\ D_4 \end{bmatrix} = \begin{bmatrix} S_1 \\ S_2 \\ S_3 \end{bmatrix}$$

2. A resulting syndrome of zero indicates no error, while any other values give an indication of the error position. If the Hamming bits are inserted into the bit positions in powers of 2 then the syndrome gives the actual position of the bit.

Question

(a)   A Hamming coded system uses 4 data bits and 3 Hamming bits. The Hamming bits are inserted in powers of 2 and they check the following bit positions:

$$1, 3, 5, 7 \quad 2, 3, 6, 7 \quad 4, 5, 6, 7$$

If the data bits are 1010 then find the coded message using matrix notation.

(b)   If the received message is 1011110 determine the syndrome to indicate the position of the error.

Answer

(a) The transmitted message is:

$$\mathbf{T} = \begin{bmatrix} P_1 & P_2 & D_1 & P_3 & D_2 & D_3 & D_4 \end{bmatrix}$$

and $D_1{=}1, D_2{=}0, D_3{=}1, D_4{=}0$

for even parity:

P_1 checks the 1st, 3rd, 5th and 7th, so $P_1 \oplus D_1 \oplus D_2 \oplus D_4 = 0$; thus $P_1 = 1$
P_2 checks the 2nd, 3rd, 6th and 7th, so $P_2 \oplus D_1 \oplus D_3 \oplus D_4 = 0$; thus $P_2 = 0$
P_3 checks the 4th, 5th, 6th and 7th, so $P_3 \oplus D_2 \oplus D_3 \oplus D_4 = 0$; thus $P_3 = 1$

$$\mathbf{H} = \begin{bmatrix} 1 & 0 & 1 & 0 & 1 & 0 & 1 \\ 0 & 1 & 1 & 0 & 0 & 1 & 1 \\ 0 & 0 & 0 & 1 & 1 & 1 & 1 \end{bmatrix} \quad \text{and} \quad \mathbf{T}^T = \begin{bmatrix} 1 \\ 0 \\ 1 \\ 1 \\ 0 \\ 1 \\ 0 \end{bmatrix} \begin{matrix} \\ \\ \leftarrow D_1 \\ \\ \leftarrow D_2 \\ \leftarrow D_3 \\ \leftarrow D_4 \end{matrix}$$

Thus $\mathbf{HT}^T$ should equal zero. To check:

$$\mathbf{HT}^T = \begin{bmatrix} 1 & 0 & 1 & 0 & 1 & 0 & 1 \\ 0 & 1 & 1 & 0 & 0 & 1 & 1 \\ 0 & 0 & 0 & 1 & 1 & 1 & 1 \end{bmatrix} \begin{bmatrix} 1 \\ 0 \\ 1 \\ 1 \\ 0 \\ 1 \\ 0 \end{bmatrix} = \begin{bmatrix} 1.1 \oplus 0.0 \oplus 1.1 \oplus 0.1 \oplus 1.0 \oplus 0.1 \oplus 1.0 \\ 0.1 \oplus 1.0 \oplus 1.1 \oplus 0.1 \oplus 0.0 \oplus 1.1 \oplus 1.0 \\ 0.1 \oplus 0.0 \oplus 0.1 \oplus 1.1 \oplus 1.0 \oplus 1.1 \oplus 1.0 \end{bmatrix} = \begin{bmatrix} 0 \\ 0 \\ 0 \end{bmatrix}$$

(b) The received message is:

$$\mathbf{R} = \begin{bmatrix} 1 & 0 & 1 & 1 & 1 & 1 & 0 \end{bmatrix}$$

Thus the syndrome is determine by:

$$\mathbf{HR}^T = \begin{bmatrix} 1 & 0 & 1 & 0 & 1 & 0 & 1 \\ 0 & 1 & 1 & 0 & 0 & 1 & 1 \\ 0 & 0 & 0 & 1 & 1 & 1 & 1 \end{bmatrix} \begin{bmatrix} 1 \\ 0 \\ 1 \\ 1 \\ 1 \\ 1 \\ 0 \end{bmatrix} = \begin{bmatrix} 1.1 \oplus 0.0 \oplus 1.1 \oplus 0.1 \oplus 1.1 \oplus 0.1 \oplus 1.0 \\ 0.1 \oplus 1.0 \oplus 1.1 \oplus 0.1 \oplus 0.1 \oplus 1.1 \oplus 1.0 \\ 0.1 \oplus 0.0 \oplus 0.1 \oplus 1.1 \oplus 1.1 \oplus 1.1 \oplus 1.0 \end{bmatrix} = \begin{bmatrix} 1 \\ 0 \\ 1 \end{bmatrix}$$

Thus, the resultant syndrome is not equal to zero, which means there is an error condition. Since $\mathbf{S} = 1\,0\,1$, the error must be in bit position 5, so inverting this bit gives the received message, 1011010.

B3.3.4 Single error correction/double error detection Hamming code

The Hamming code presented can only be used to correct a single error. To correct 2 bits, another parity bit is added to give an overall parity check. Thus for 4 data bits the transmitted code would be:

$$\mathbf{T} = \begin{bmatrix} P_1 & P_2 & D_1 & P_3 & D_2 & D_3 & D_4 & P_4 \end{bmatrix}$$

where P_4 gives an overall parity check. This can be removed at the decoder and Hamming code single error detection can be carried out as before. This then leads to four conditions:

- If the syndrome is zero and the added parity is the correct parity. There is no error (as before).
- If the syndrome is zero and the added parity is the incorrect parity. There is an error in the added parity bit.
- If the syndrome is non-zero and the added parity is the incorrect parity, there is a single error. The syndrome then gives an indication of the bit position of the error.
- If the syndrome is non-zero and the added parity is the correct parity, there is a double error.

Using the example of Section B3.3:

$$\mathbf{H} = \begin{bmatrix} 1 & 0 & 1 & 0 & 1 & 0 & 1 \\ 0 & 1 & 1 & 0 & 0 & 1 & 1 \\ 0 & 0 & 0 & 1 & 1 & 1 & 1 \end{bmatrix} \quad \text{and} \quad \mathbf{T}^T = \begin{bmatrix} 1 \\ 0 \\ 1 \\ 1 \\ 0 \\ 1 \\ 0 \end{bmatrix}$$

Then the parity bit would be a zero. Thus is if parity bit P_4 is a 1 and the syndrome is zero, it is the parity bit that is in error. If a single-bit is in error then the parity bit will be incorrect, so the syndrome will give the bit position in error. If there are two bits in error then the parity bit will be correct, thus if the syndrome is non-zero and the parity bit is correct then there are two errors (unfortunately the syndrome will be incorrect and the received message must be discarded).

B3.3.5 Reed-Solomon coding

In most cases, pure Hamming code can only correct a single-bit in error. A more powerful coding system is Reed-Solomon coding, which can correct multiple bits in error. It is a cyclic code and was devised in 1960 by Irvine Reed and Gustave Solomon at MIT. It is suitable for correcting bursts of errors.

B3.3.6 Convolution codes

The block codes, such as VRC/LRC and CRC have the disadvantage that many bits are sent before the message is actually checked. Convolution codes, on the other hand, embed the parity checks in the data stream. They feed the data bits into the coder one bit at a time through a shift register and the output bit(s) are generated with exclusive-OR operations. An example coder is shown in Figure B3.6. The total of the bits considered in the continuous data stream is called the constraint length. Figure B3.6 shows a coder with a constraint length of 3.

A convolution code takes groups of k bit digits at a time and produces groups of n output binary digits. As k is the input data rate and n is the output data time step then the code is known as a k/n code. For example if the coder takes one input bit at a time and outputs two then it is a 1/2 coder. The coder in Figure B3.6 has $k=1$, $n=2$ and has a constraint length, L, of 3.

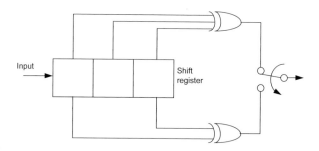

Figure B3.6   A Convolutional encoder

At any point in time, the digits in the shift register define the current state of the coder at that time step.

For example, let the input be 1101. Thus an extra two 0's are added to the input data so that the complete data can be clocked into the shift register. Table B3.4 gives the state table of the encoder. The output, from first to last, will thus be 11 01 01 00 10 11.

Table B3.4   State table of the encoder

Input	A	B	C	Output
001011	1	0	0	1,1
00101	1	1	0	0,1
0010	0	1	1	0,1
001	1	0	1	0,0
00	0	1	0	1,0
0	0	0	1	1,1

The system can also be analyzed for any input. First a coding tree is drawn up which defines the present and next state within the shift register. A 3-bit shift register will have a total of 8 states, and each of these states will have 2 next states, one for a 1 input and the other for a 0 input. Table B3.5 defines the coding tree in this case.

It can be seen that the next state when *ABC* is either 000 or 001 will always be 000 when a 0 is entered. These states can therefore be taken as the same, as can 010 and 011, 100 and 101, and 110 and 111. This also occurs with a 1 input, thus 4 of the states can be merged. This results in a coding tree with only 4 states, as given in Table B3.6.

Table B3.5 Coding tree

ABC	Next state 0 input	Output	Next state 1 input	Output
000	000	00	100	11
001	000	00	100	11
010	001	11	101	00
011	001	11	101	00
100	010	10	110	01
101	010	10	110	01
110	011	01	111	10
111	011	01	111	10

Next a state diagram can be produced to determine the change of the output state for a given input. This diagram represents the current state within a circle and the next state is linked by an arrow with an associated value x/yy denoting that the input is x and the output is yy. It is initially assumed that the circuit has been reset and that the initial state is $ABC=000$ (state *a*). An input of 0 causes the circuit to stay in that state and thus to output 00. If the input is a 1 then the next state is 10X (state *b*) and 11 is output. This produces the state diagram of Figure B3.7.

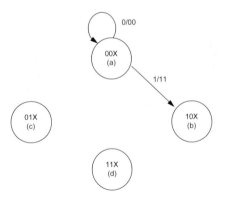

Figure B3.7 Intermediate state diagram

Next, from state *b*, a zero input causes ABC to become 01X (state *c*) and to output 10. If a 1 is input then the next state will be 11X (state *d*) and the output a 01. This is then continues until the state diagram is complete, as shown in Figure B3.8.

Next, from the state diagram a trellis diagram can be drawn. This has the number of states down the left-hand column; each time step is mapped with its mapping to the previous state and gives an indication of the generated output. The upper of the two lines represents a 0 input, and the lower represent a 1 input. For example the circuit starts in state *a*, then a 0 outputs 00 and stays in the same state, while a 1 puts the circuit into state *b* and outputs a 11. This is shown on the trellis diagram in Figure B3.9.

If the current state is *a* then a 0 input will make it stay in the same state and a 1 will take the next state to *b*. If the current state is *b* then a 0 will make the state change to *c*, else a 1 will change it to *d*. This is illustrated in Figure B3.10.

Table B3.6   Coding tree

ABC	Next state 0 input	Output	Next state 1 input	Output
00X	00X	00	10X	11
01X	00X	11	10X	00
10X	01X	10	11X	01
11X	01X	01	11X	10

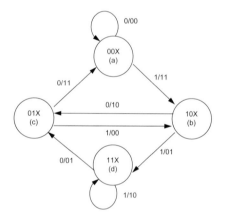

Figure B3.8   Final state diagram

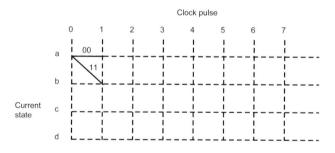

Figure B3.9   Initial trellis diagram

The rest of the states on the trellis diagram can now be mapped; the next state is given in Figure B3.11 and the final trellis diagram is shown in Figure B3.12. Note that the final two input states are both 0.

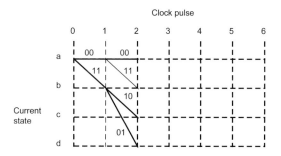

Figure B3.10 Intermediate trellis diagram

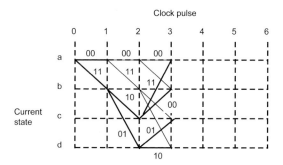

Figure B3.11 Intermediate trellis diagram

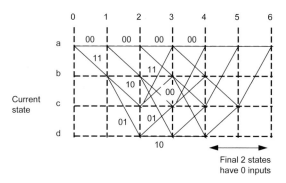

Figure B3.12 Final trellis diagram

Viterbi decoder

Convolution coding allows error correcting because only some of the possible sequences are valid outputs from the coder. These sequences correspond to the possible paths through the trellis. A Viterbi decoder tries to find the best match for the received bitstream with valid paths. The best path is called the maximum likelihood and discrepancies between the received bitstream and the possible transmitted stream are called path metrics.

The decoder stores the best single path to each of the time-step nodes (in the previous example this was 4: *a*, *b*, *c*, and *d*). Any other path to that node which has a greater number of discrepancies causes that path to be ignored. The number of remembered paths will thus be equal to the number of nodes and will remain constant. For each node, the decoder must store the best path to that node and the total metric corresponding to that path. By comparing the actual *n* received digits at time step $i+1$ with those corresponding to each possible path on the trellis from step *i* to step $i+1$, the decoder calculates the additional metric for each path. From these, it selects the best path to each node at time step $i+1$, and updates the stored records of the paths and metrics.

The best way to illustrate this process is with an example. For example if the input bit sequence is:

100110

this will give an output of:

11 10 11 11 01 01

with a tail of:

11 00 00

This gives an output of:

111011110101110000

Input: 1 0 0 1 1 0 0 0 0

Output: 11 10 11 11 01 01 11 00 00

State: b c a b d c a a a

Let's assume there are two errors in the bit stream and the receive stream is:

110011010101110000

First the difference in the number of bits is represented on the trellis diagram, as shown in Figure B3.13. Thus if the circuit stays in state *a* then the received input would require two changes to the transmitted data for it to be received as 11. There is no difference in the received bits when going from state *a* to state *b*. Thus the upper route scores a value of 2 and the lower route a value of 0.

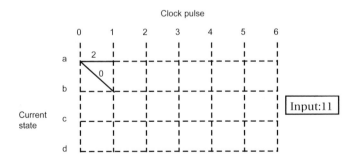

Figure B3.13 Representing the difference in the number of bits

Next 00 is received, if the circuit had been in state *a* and stayed in state *a* then 00 would have been transmitted. So this will have a discrepancy of 0 and the resulting metric for that route will be 2. If the circuit is in state *a* and moves to state *b* then 11 would have been transmitted, thus there would be a discrepancy of 2, giving the total path metrics as 4.

If the circuit is in state *b* and a 1 is received then the circuit goes into state *d*, else a 0 causes the circuit to go into state *c*. In going into state *c* the circuit will output a 10 (a discrepancy of 1, which gives a total path metric of 1) and going into state *d* will cause an output of 01 (a discrepancy of 1, which gives a total path metric of 1). Figure B3.14 shows the resulting trellis diagram. The resulting total metrics are:

Path	Metrics	Path	Metrics
a → a → a	2	a → a → b	4
a → b → c	1	a → b → d	1

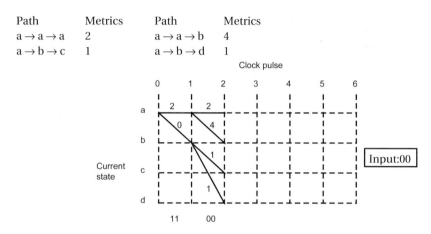

Figure B3.14 Calculating a path metric

Figure B3.15 shows the next state. This time two routes converge on the same state. The Viterbi decoder computes the metrics for each of the two paths then rejects the route with the greater metric. It can be seen that the top route (i.e. transmitted pattern 00, 00, 00) gives a metric of 4 but the other route to that state has a metric of 1. The route with a metric of 4 will be rejected. It can be seen that the lowest metric has a value of 1. Figure B3.16 shows the resulting preferred routes.

Figure B3.17 shows the next state and Figure B3.18 shows the resultant preferred routes. It can be seen that there are now three routes which have metric of 2 and one with a metric of 3.

Figure B3.19 shows the next state and Figure B3.20 shows the resulting preferred routes. Now the lowest metric is 2.

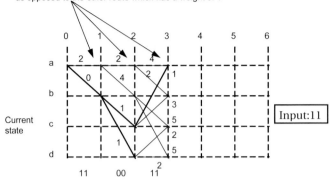

Input:11

Figure B3.15 In each pair the route with the greater metric is rejected.

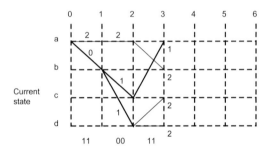

Figure B3.16 Trellis diagram up to state 3

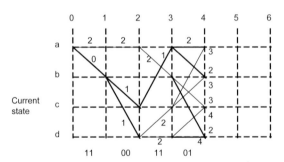

Figure B3.17 Trellis diagram up to state 4

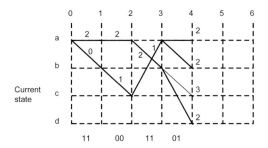

Figure B3.18 Preferred routes in Figure B3.17

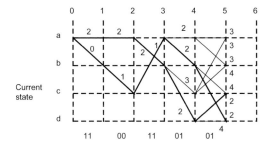

Figure B3.19 Trellis diagram up to state 5

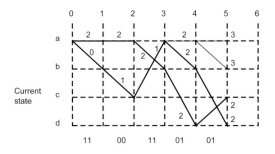

Figure B3.20 Preferred routes in Figure B3.19

Figure B3.21 shows the next state. It can be seen that there is now one preferred route with a metric of 2 (as expected as there are two errors in the received data). The highlighted route then continues to be the most favored route as there are no more errors in the received bit pattern. Thus all the other scores will gain and the favored route will stay constant (until another error comes along). Following this route gives the decoded output of 100110, which is the data pattern transmitted. The state transition is a-b (input is a 1), b-c (input is a 0), c-a (input is a 0), a-b (input is a 1), b-d (input is a 1) and d-c (input is a 0).

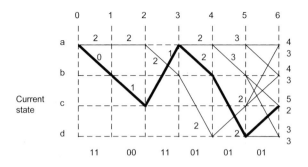

Figure B3.21   Trellis diagram up to state 6

Convolution coding analysis program

Program B3.1 gives a simple C program for analyzing the convolutional coder given in Figure B3.6. The operator ^ is the exclusive-OR function and the & operator is the bitwise AND function. In the program the input bitstream is specified with the array inseq[]. The circuit iterations for a given number of clock cycles (defined by NO_CLOCKS) and calculates the output for each clock tick. Note that the AND operator is used to mask off the least significant bit of the output values. Sample run B3.1 gives a sample output.

📄 **Program B3.1**

```
#include <stdio.h>

#define     NO_CLOCKS       6

int    main(void)
{
int    inseq[NO_CLOCKS]={1,0,1,1,0,0};
int    i,out1,out2,s1,s2,s3;

    puts("Bit 1 Bit 2");

    for (i=0;i<NO_CLOCKS;i++)
    {
        s1=inseq[i]; /* no shift */
        if (i>0) s2=inseq[i-1]; /* one bit shift */
        if (i>1) s3=inseq[i-2]; /* two bit shifts */
        out1=(s1^s2^s3) & 1; /* EX-OR and mask lsb */
        out2=(s1^s3) & 1; /* EX-OR and mask lsb */
        printf("  %d       %d\n",out1,out2);
    }
    return(0);
}
```

💻 **Sample run B3.1**

```
Bit 1 Bit 2
   1       1
   1       0
   0       0
   0       1
   0       1
   1       1
```

B4   RS-232

B4.1   Introduction

RS-232 is one of the most widely used techniques used to interface external equipment to computers. It uses serial communications where one bit is sent along a line, at a time. This differs from parallel communications which send one or more bytes, at a time. The main advantage that serial communications has over parallel communications is that a single wire is needed to transmit and another to receive. RS-232 is a de facto standard that most computer and instrumentation companies comply with. It was standardised in 1962 by the Electronics Industries Association (EIA). Unfortunately this standard only allows short cable runs with low bit rates. The standard RS-232 only allows a bit rate of 19 600 bps for a maximum distance of 20 m. New serial communications standards, such as RS-422 and RS-449, allow very long cable runs and high bit rates. For example, RS-422 allows a bit rate of up to 10 Mbps over distances up to 1 mile, using twisted-pair, coaxial cable or optical fibres. The new standards can also be used to create computer networks. This chapter introduces the RS-232 standard and gives simple programs which can be used to transmit and receive using RS-232.

B4.2   Electrical characteristics

B4.2.1   Line voltages

The electrical characteristics of RS-232 defines the minimum and maximum voltages of a logic '1' and '0'. A logic '1' ranges from –3 V to –25 V, but will typically be around –12 V. A logical '0' ranges from 3 V to 25 V, but will typically be around +12 V. Any voltage between –3 V and +3 V has an indeterminate logical state. If no pulses are present on the line the voltage level is equivalent to a high level, that is –12 V. A voltage level of 0 V at the receiver is interpreted as a line break or a short circuit. Figure B4.1 shows an example transmission.

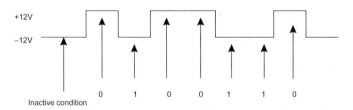

Figure B4.1   RS-232 voltage levels

B4.2.2   DB25S connector

The DB25S connector is a 25-pin D-type connector and gives full RS-232 functionality. Figure B4.2 shows the pin number assignment. A DCE (the terminating cable) connector has a male outer casing with female connection pins. The DTE (the computer) has a female outer casing with male connecting pins. There are three main signal types: control, data and ground. Table B4.1 lists the main connections. Control lines are active HIGH, that is, they are HIGH when the signal is active and LOW when inactive.

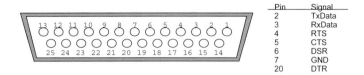

Pin	Signal
2	TxData
3	RxData
4	RTS
5	CTS
6	DSR
7	GND
20	DTR

Figure B4.2 RS-232 DB25S connector

B4.2.3   DB9S Connector

The 25-pin connector is the standard for RS-232 connections but as electronic equipment becomes smaller, there is a need for smaller connectors. For this purpose, most PCs now use a reduced function 9-pin D-type connector rather than the full function 25-way D-type. As with the 25-pin connector the DCE (the terminating cable) connector has a male outer casing with female connection pins. The DTE (the computer) has a female outer casing with male connecting pins. Figure B4.3 shows the main connections.

Pin	Signal
2	RxData
3	TxData
4	DTR
5	GND
6	DSR
7	RTS
8	CTS

Figure B4.3 RS-232 DB9S interface

B4.2.4   PC connectors

All PCs have at least one serial communications port. The primary port is named COM1: and the secondary is COM2:. There are two types of connectors used in RS-232 communications, these are the 25- and 9-way D-type. Most modern PCs use either a 9-pin connector for the primary (COM1:) serial port and a 25-pin for a secondary serial port (COM2:), or they use two 9-pin connectors for serial ports. The serial port can be differentiated from the parallel port in that the 25-pin parallel port (LPT1:) is a 25-pin female connector on the PC and a male connector on the cable. The 25-pin serial connector is a male on the PC and a female on the cable. The different connector types can cause problems in connecting devices. Thus a 25-to-9 pin adapter is a useful attachment, especially to connect a serial mouse to a 25-pin connector.

Table B4.1 Main pin connections used in 25-pin connector

Pin	Name	Abbreviation	Functionality
1	Frame ground	FG	This ground normally connects the outer sheath of the cable and to earth ground.
2	Transmit data	TD	Data is sent from the DTE (computer or terminal) to a DCE via TD.

3	Receive data	RD	Data is sent from the DCE to a DTE (computer or terminal) via RD.
4	Request to send	RTS	DTE sets this active when it is ready to transmit data.
5	Clear to send	CTS	DCE sets this active to inform the DTE that it is ready to receive data.
6	Data set ready	DSR	Similar functionality to CTS but activated by the DTE when it is ready to receive data.
7	Signal ground	SG	All signals are referenced to the signal ground (GND).
20	Data terminal ready	DTR	Similar functionality to RTS but activated by the DCE when it wishes to transmit data.

B4.2.5 Frame format

RS-232 uses asynchronous communication which has a start/stop data format (Figure B4.4). Each character is transmitted one at a time with a delay between them. This delay is called the inactive time and is set at a logic level high (–12 V) as shown in Figure B4.5. The transmitter sends a start bit to inform the receiver that a character is to be sent in the following bit transmission. This start bit is always a '0'. Next, 5, 6 or 7 data bits are sent as a 7-bit ASCII character, followed by a parity bit and finally either 1, 1.5 or 2 stop bits. Figure B4.5 shows a frame format and an example transmission of the character 'A', using odd parity. The timing of a single bit sets the rate of transmission. Both the transmitter and receiver need to be set to the same bit-time interval. An internal clock on both sets this interval. These only have to be roughly synchronised at approximately the same rate as data is transmitted in relatively short bursts.

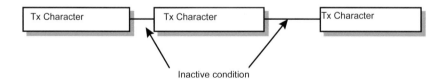

Figure B4.4 Asynchronous communications

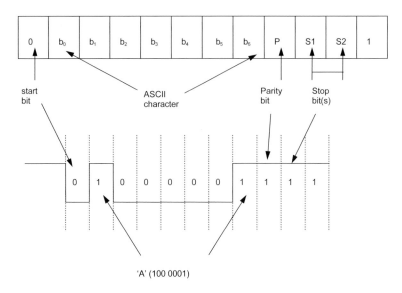

Figure B4.5   RS-232 frame format

Example

An RS-232 serial data link uses 1 start bit, 7 data bits, 1 parity bit, 2 stop bits, ASCII coding and even parity. Determine the message sent from the following bit stream.

First bit sent
⇓
1111101000001011000001111111111111110000011111111000110011110101 0
    0111111111111

Answer

The format of the data string sent is given next:

{idle} 11111 {start bit} 0 {'A'} 1000001 {parity bit} 0 {stop bits } 11 {start bit} 0 {'p'} 0000111 {parity bit} 1 {stop bits} 11 {idle} 11111111 {start bit} 0 {'p'} 0000111 {parity bit} 1 {stop bits} 11 {idle} 11 {start bit} 0 {'L'} 0011001 {parity bit} 1 {stop bits} 11

The message sent was thus 'AppL'.

Parity

Error control is data added to transmitted data in order to detect or correct an error in transmission. RS-232 uses a simple technique known as parity to provide a degree of error detection.

A parity bit is added to transmitted data to make the number of 1s sent either even (even parity) or odd (odd parity). It is a simple method of error coding and only requires exclusive-OR (XOR) gates to generate the parity bit. The parity bit is added to the transmitted data by inserting it into the shift register at the correct bit position.

A single parity bit can only detect an odd number of errors, that is, 1, 3, 5, and so on. If there is an even number of bits in error then the parity bit will be correct and no error will be detected. This type of error coding is not normally used on its own where there is the possibility of several bits being in error.

Baud rate

One of the main parameters, which specify RS-232 communications, is the rate of transmission at which data is transmitted and received. It is important that the transmitter and receiver operate at, roughly, the same speed.

For asynchronous transmission the start and stop bits are added in addition to the 7 ASCII character bits and the parity. Thus a total of 10 bits are required to transmit a single character. With 2 stop bits, a total of 11 bits are required. If 10 characters are sent every second and if 11 bits are used for each character, then the transmission rate is 110 bits per second (bps). Table B4.2 lists how the bit rate relates to the characters sent per second (assuming 10 transmitted bits per character). The bit rate is measured in bits per second (bps).

	Bits
ASCII character	7
Start bit	1
Stop bit	2
Total	10

Table B4.2 Bits per second related to characters sent per second

Speed (bps)	Characters per second
300	30
1200	120
2400	240

In addition to the bit rate, another term used to describe the transmission speed is the baud rate. The bit rate refers to the actual rate at which bits are transmitted, whereas the baud rate relates to the rate at which signalling elements, used to represent bits, are transmitted. As one signalling element encodes one bit, the two rates are then identical. Only in modems does the bit rate differ from the baud rate.

Bit stream timings

Asynchronous communications is a stop/start mode of communication and both the transmitter and receiver must be set up with the same bit timings. A start bit identifies the start of transmission and is always a low logic level. Next, the least significant bit is sent followed by the rest of the bits in the character. After this, the parity bit is sent followed by the stop bit(s). The actual timing of each bit relates to the baud rate and can be found using the following formula:

$$\text{Time period of each bit} = \frac{1}{\text{baud rate}} \text{ s}$$

For example, if the baud rate is 9600 baud (or bps) then the time period for each bit sent is $1/9600$ s or $104\,\mu$s. Table B4.3 shows some bit timings as related to baud rate. An example of the voltage levels and timings for the ASCII character 'V' is given in Figure B4.6.

Table B4.3 Bit timings related to baud rate

Baud rate	Time for each bit (μs)
1 200	833
2 400	417
9 600	104
19 200	52

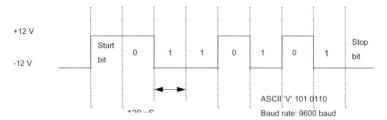

Figure B4.6 ASCII 'V' at RS-232 voltage levels

B4.3   Communications between two nodes

RS-232 is intended to be a standard but not all manufacturers abide by it. Some implement the full specification while others implement just a partial specification. This is mainly because not every device requires the full functionality of RS-232, for example, a modem requires many more control lines than a serial mouse.

The rate at which data is transmitted and the speed at which the transmitter and receiver can transmit/receive the data dictates whether data handshaking is required.

B4.3.1   Handshaking

In the transmission of data, there can be either no handshaking, hardware handshaking or software handshaking. If no handshaking is used then the receiver must be able to read the received characters before the transmitter sends another. The receiver may buffer the received character and store it in a special memory location before it is read. This memory location is named the receiver buffer. Typically, it may only hold a single character. If it is not emptied before another character is received then any character previously in the buffer will be overwritten. An example of this is illustrated in Figure B4.7. In this case, the receiver has read the first two characters successfully from the receiver buffer, but it did not read the third character as the fourth transmitted character has overwritten it in the receiver buffer. If this condition occurs then some form of handshaking must be used to stop the transmitter sending characters before the receiver has had time to service the received characters.

Hardware handshaking involves the transmitter asking the receiver if it is ready to receive data. If the receiver buffer is empty it will inform the transmitter that it is ready to receive data. Once the data is transmitted and loaded into the receiver buffer the transmitter is informed not to transmit any more characters until the character in the receiver buffer has been read. The main hardware handshaking lines used for this purpose are:

- CTS   –   Clear to send.
- RTS   –   Ready to send.
- DTR   –   Data terminal ready.
- DSR   –   Data set ready.

Software handshaking involves sending special control characters. These include the DC1 (Xon)-DC4 (Xoff) control characters.

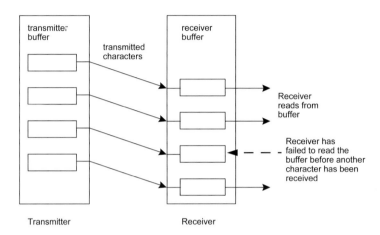

Figure B4.7   Transmission and reception of characters

B4.3.2   RS-232 set-up

Microsoft Windows allows the serial port setting to be set by selecting control panel → system → device manager → ports (COM and LPT) → port settings. The settings of the communications port (the IRQ and the port address) can be changed by selecting control panel → system → device manager → ports (COM and LPT) → resources for IRQ and addresses. Figure B4.8 shows example parameters and settings. The selectable baud rates are typically 110, 300, 600, 1200, 2400, 4800, 9600 and 19 200 baud for an 8250-based device. A 16650 UART also gives enhanced speeds of 38 400, 57 600, 115 200, 230 400, 460 800 and 921 600 baud. Notice that the flow control can either be set to software handshaking (Xon/Xoff), hardware handshaking or none. The parity bit can either be set to none, odd, even, mark or space. A mark in the parity option sets the parity bit to a '1' and a space sets it to a '0'.

In this case COM1: is set at 9600 baud, 8 data bits, no parity, 1 stop bit and no parity checking.

Figure B4.8 Changing port setting and parameters

B4.3.3 Simple no-handshaking communications

In this form of communication it is assumed that the receiver can read the received data from the receive buffer before another character is received. Data is sent from a TD pin connection of the transmitter and is received in the RD pin connection at the receiver. When a DTE (such as a computer) connects to another DTE, then the transmit line (TD) on one is connected to the receive (RD) of the other and vice versa. Figure B4.9 shows the connections between the nodes.

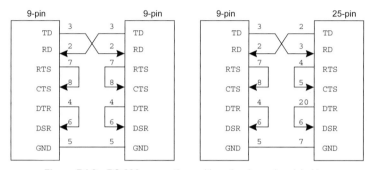

Figure B4.9   RS-232 connections with no hardware handshaking

B4.3.4 Software handshaking

There are two ASCII characters that start and stop communications. These are X-ON (^S , Cntrl-S or ASCII 11) and X-OFF (^Q, Cntrl-Q or ASCII 13). When the transmitter receives an X-OFF character it ceases communications until an X-ON character is sent. This type of handshaking is normally used when the transmitter and receiver can process data relatively quickly. Normally, the receiver will also have a large buffer for the incoming characters. When this buffer is full, it transmits an X-OFF. After it has read from the buffer the X-ON is transmitted, see Figure B4.10.

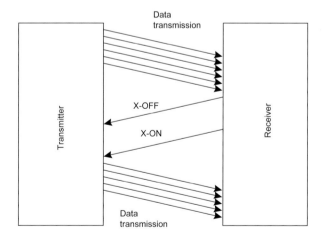

Figure B4.10   Software handshaking using X-ON and X-OFF

B4.3.5   Hardware handshaking

Hardware handshaking stops characters in the receiver buffer from being overwritten. The control lines used are all active HIGH. Figure B4.11 shows how the nodes communicate. When a node wishes to transmit data it asserts the RTS line active (that is, HIGH). It then monitors the CTS line until it goes active (that is, HIGH). If the CTS line at the transmitter stays inactive then the receiver is busy and cannot receive data, at the present. When the receiver reads from its buffer the RTS line will automatically go active indicating to the transmitter that it is now ready to receive a character.

Receiving data is similar to the transmission of data, but the lines DSR and DTR are used instead of RTS and CTS. When the DCE wishes to transmit to the DTE the DSR input to the receiver will become active. If the receiver cannot receive the character, it will set the DTR line inactive. When it is clear to receive it sets the DTR line active and the remote node then transmits the character. The DTR line will be set inactive until the character has been processed.

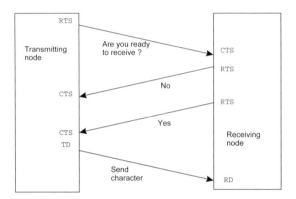

Figure B4.11   Handshaking lines used in transmitting data

B4.3.6   Two-way communications with handshaking

For full handshaking of the data between two nodes the RTS and CTS lines are crossed over (as are the DTR and DSR lines). This allows for full remote node feedback (see Figure B4.12).

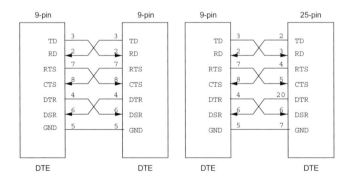

Figure B4.12   RS-232 communications with handshaking

B4.3.7 DTE-DCE connections (PC to modem)

A further problem occurs in connecting two nodes. A DTE/DTE connection requires crossovers on their signal lines, whereas DTE/DCE connections require straight-through lines. An example computer to modem connection is shown in Figure B4.13.

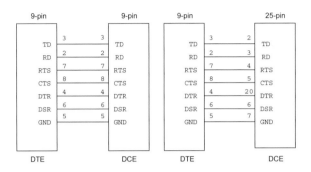

Figure B4.13 DTE to DCE connections

B4.4   Programming RS-232

Normally, serial transmission is achieved via the RS-232 standard. Although 25 lines are defined usually only a few are used. Data is sent along the TD line and received by the RD line with a common ground return. The other lines, used for handshaking, are RTS (ready to send) which is an output signal to indicate that data is ready to be transmitted and CTS (clear to send), which is an input indicating that the remote equipment is ready to receive data.

The 8250/NS16650 IC is commonly used in serial communications. It is typically integrated in the PC chip set, or can be mounted on an I/O card. This section discusses how it is programmed.

Programming the serial device

The main registers used in RS-232 communications are the line control register (LCR), the line status register (LSR) and the transmit and receive buffers (see Figure B4.14). The transmit and receive buffers share the same addresses.

The base address of the primary port (COM1:) is normally set at 3F8h and the secondary port (COM2:) at 2F8h. A standard PC can support up to four COM ports. These addresses are set in the BIOS memory and the address of each of the ports is stored at address locations 0040:0000 (COM1:), 0040:0002 (COM2:), 0040:0004 (COM3:) and 0040:0008 (COM4:). Program B4.1 can be used to identify these addresses. The statement:

```
ptr=(int far *)0x0400000;
```

initializes a far pointer to the start of the BIOS communications port addresses. Each address is 16 bits thus the pointer points to an integer value. A far pointer is used as this can access the full 1 MB of memory, a near pointer can only access a maximum of 64 kB.

📖 Program B4.1

```c
#include <stdio.h>
#include <conio.h>
int    main(void)
{
int    far *ptr; /* 20-bit pointer */
   ptr=(int far *)0x0400000; /* 0040:0000 */
   clrscr();
   printf("COM1: %04x\n",*ptr);
   printf("COM2: %04x\n",*(ptr+1));
   printf("COM3: %04x\n",*(ptr+2));
   printf("COM4: %04x\n",*(ptr+3));
   return(0);
}
```

Test run B4.1 shows a sample run. In this case, there are four COM ports installed on the PC. If any of the addresses is zero then that COM port is not installed on the system.

💻 Test run B4.1

```
COM1: 03f8
COM2: 02f8
COM3: 03e8
COM4: 02e8
```

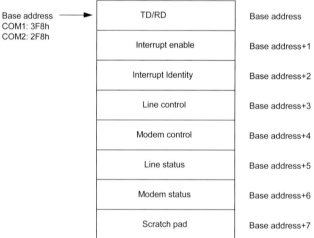

Figure B4.14 Serial communication registers

Line Status Register (LSR)

The LSR determines the status of the transmitter and receiver buffers. It can only be read from, and all the bits are automatically set by hardware. The bit definitions are given in Figure B4.15. When an error occurs in the transmission of a character one (or several) of the error bit is (are) set to a '1'.

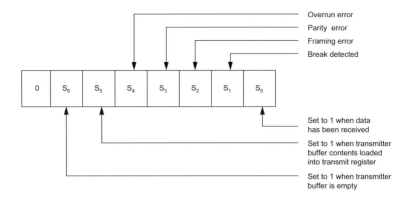

Figure B4.15 Line status register

One danger when transmitting data is that a new character can be written to the transmitter buffer before the previous character has been sent. This overwrites the contents of the character being transmitted. To avoid this, the status bit S_6 is tested to determine if there is still a character in the buffer. If there is then it is set to a '1', else, the transmitter buffer is empty.

To send a character

> *Test bit 6 until set;*
> *Send character;*

A typical Pascal routine is

```
repeat
   status := port[LSR] and $40;
until (status=$40);
```

When receiving data the S_0 bit is tested to determine if there is a bit in the receiver buffer. To receive a character

> *Test bit 0 until set;*
> *Read character;*

A typical Pascal routine is

```
repeat
      status := port[LSR] and $01;
until (status=$01);
```

Figure B4.16 shows how the LSR is tested for the transmission and reception of characters.

Line control register (LCR)

The LCR sets up the communications parameters. These include the number of bits per character, the parity and the number of stop bits. It can be written to or read from and has a similar function to that of the control registers used in the PPI (programmable parallel interface) and PTC (programmable timer/counter). The bit definitions are given in Figure B4.17.

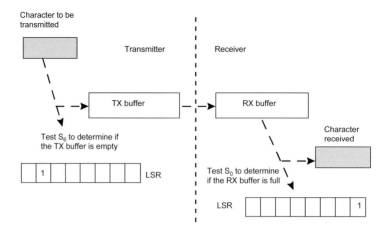

Figure B4.16 Testing of the LSR for the transmission and reception of characters

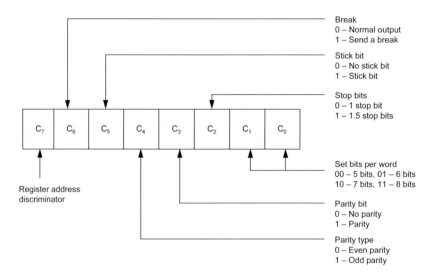

Figure B4.17 Line control register

The MSB, C_7, must to be set to a '0' in order to access the transmitter and receiver buffers, else if it is set to a '1' the baud rate divider is set up. The baud rate is set by loading an appropriate 16-bit divisor into the addresses of transmitter/receiver buffer address and the next address. The value loaded depends on the crystal frequency connected to the IC. Table B4.4 shows divisors for a crystal frequency of 1.8432 MHz. In general, the divisor, N, is related to the baud rate by:

$$\text{Baud rate} = \frac{\text{Clock frequency}}{16 \times N}$$

For example, for 1.8432 MHz and 9600 baud $N = 1.8432 \times 10^6 / (9600 \times 16) = 12$ (000Ch).

Table B4.4 Baud rate divisors

Baud rate	Divisor (value loaded into Tx/Rx buffer)
110	0417h
300	0180h
600	00C0h
1200	0060h
1800	0040h
2400	0030h
4800	0018h
9600	000Ch
19200	0006h

Register addresses

The addresses of the main registers are given in Table B4.5. To load the baud rate divisor, first the LCR bit 7 is set to a '1', then the LSB is loaded into divisor LSB and the MSB into the divisor MSB register. Finally, bit 7 is set back to a '0'. For example, for 9600 baud, COM1 and 1.8432 MHz clock then 0Ch is loaded in 3F8h and 00h into 3F9h.

When bit 7 is set at a '0' then a read from the base address reads from the RD buffer and a write operation writes to the TD buffer. An example of this is shown in Figure B4.18.

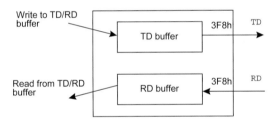

Figure B4.18 Read and write from TD/RD buffer

Table B4.5 Serial communications addresses

Primary	Secondary	Register	Bit 7 of LCR
3F8h	2F8h	TD buffer	'0'
3F8h	2F8h	RD buffer	'0'
3F8h	2F8h	Divisor LSB	'1'
3F9h	2F9h	Divisor MSB	'1'
3FBh	2FBh	Line Control Register	
3FDh	2FDh	Line Status Register	

B4.5   RS-232 programs

Figure B4.19 shows the main RS-232 connections for 9 and 25-pin connections without hardware handshaking. The loopback connections are used to test the RS-232 hardware and the software, while the null modem connections are used to transmit characters between two computers. Program B4.2 uses a loop back on the TD/RD lines so that a character sent by the computer will automatically be received into the receiver buffer. This set-up is useful in testing the transmit and receive routines. The character to be sent is entered via the keyboard. A CNTRL-D (^D) keystroke exits the program.

Program B4.3 can be used as a sender program (send.c) and Program B4.4 can be used as a receiver program (receive.c). With these programs, the null modem connections shown in Figure B4.19 are used.

Note that programs B4.2 to B4.4 are written for Microsoft Visual C++. For early versions of Borland C/C++ program change _inp for inportb and _outp for outportb.

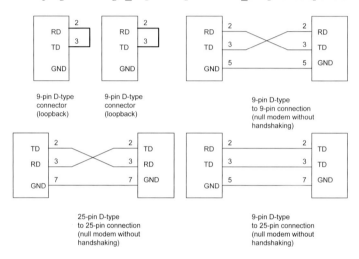

Figure B4.19   System connections

📖   Program B4.2

```
/* This program transmits a character from COM1: and receives */
/* it via this port. The TD is connected to RD.              */

#define   COM1BASE    0x3F8
#define   COM2BASE    0x2F8
#define   TXDATA      COM1BASE
#define   LCR         (COM1BASE+3)  /*   0x3FB line control   */
#define   LSR         (COM1BASE+5)  /*   0x3FD line status    */

#include <conio.h>   /* required for getch()                  */
#include <dos.h>     /*    */
#include <stdio.h>

/* Some ANSI C prototype definitions   */
void   setup_serial(void);
void   send_character(int ch);
int    get_character(void);

int       main(void)
{
int       inchar,outchar;

    setup_serial();
```

```
    do
    {
        puts("Enter char to be transmitted (Cntrl-D to end)");
        outchar=getch();
        send_character(outchar);
        inchar=get_character();
        printf("Character received was %c\n",inchar);
    } while (outchar!=4);
    return(0);
}

void    setup_serial(void)
{
    _outp( LCR, 0x80);
    /* set up bit 7 to a 1 to set Register address bit   */

    _outp(TXDATA,0x0C);
    _outp(TXDATA+1,0x00);
    /* load TxRegister with 12, crystal frequency is 1.8432MHz */

    _outp(LCR, 0x0A);
    /* Bit pattern loaded is 00001010b, from msb to lsb these are:*/
    /* 0 - access TD/RD buffer ,  0 - normal output          */
    /* 0 - no stick bit  , 0 - even parity                   */
    /* 1 - parity on,  0 - 1 stop bit                        */
    /* 10 - 7 data bits                                      */
}

void send_character(int ch)
{
char  status;
    do
    {
        status = _inp(LSR) & 0x40;
    } while (status!=0x40);
    /*repeat until Tx buffer empty ie bit 6 set*/

    _outp(TXDATA,(char) ch);
}

int  get_character(void)
{
int  status;
    do
    {
        status = _inp(LSR) & 0x01;
    } while (status!=0x01);
    /* Repeat until bit 1 in LSR is set */

    return( (int)_inp(TXDATA));
}
```

📖 **Program B4.3**
```
/*    send.c                                              */
#define  TXDATA    0x3F8
#define  LSR       0x3FD
#define  LCR       0x3FB

#include <stdio.h>
#include    <conio.h>   /* included for getch            */
#include    <dos.h>

void     setup_serial(void);
```

```c
void      send_character(int ch);

int       main(void)
{
int       ch;
    puts("Transmitter program. Please enter text (Cntl-D to end)");
    setup_serial();
    do
    {
        ch=getche();
        send_character(ch);
    } while (ch!=4);
    return(0);
}

void  setup_serial(void)
{
    _outp( LCR, 0x80);
    /* set up bit 7 to a 1 to set Register address bit    */
    _outp(TXDATA,0x0C);
    _outp(TXDATA+1,0x00);
    /* load TxRegister with 12, crystal frequency is 1.8432MHz */
    _outp(LCR, 0x0A);
    /* Bit pattern loaded is 00001010b, from msb to lsb these are:*/
    /* Access TD/RD buffer, normal output, no stick bit    */
    /* even parity, parity on, 1 stop bit, 7 data bits      */
}
void  send_character(int ch)
{
char  status;
    do
    {
        status = _inp(LSR) & 0x40;
    } while (status!=0x40);
    /*repeat until Tx buffer empty ie bit 6 set*/
    _outp(TXDATA,(char) ch);
}
```

📖   Program B4.4

```c
/*    receive.c                                           */
#define  TXDATA    0x3F8
#define  LSR       0x3FD
#define  LCR       0x3FB
#include    <stdio.h>
#include    <conio.h>   /* included for getch              */
#include    <dos.h>

void      setup_serial(void);
int       get_character(void);
int       main(void)
{
int       inchar;
    setup_serial();
    do
    {
        inchar=get_character();
        putchar(inchar);
    } while (inchar!=4);
    return(0);
}
void setup_serial(void)
{
    _outp( LCR, 0x80);
```

```
    /* set up bit 7 to a 1 to set Register address bit        */
    _outp(TXDATA,0x0C);
    _outp(TXDATA+1,0x00);
    /* load TxRegister with 12, crystal frequency is 1.8432MHz */
    _outp(LCR, 0x0A);
    /* Bit pattern loaded is 00001010b, from msb to lsb these are:*/
    /* Access TD/RD buffer, normal output, no stick bit        */
    /* even parity, parity on, 1 stop bit, 7 data bits         */
}
int    get_character(void)
{
int    status;
    do
    {
        status = _inp(LSR) & 0x01;
    } while (status!=0x01);    /* Repeat until bit 1 in LSR is set */
    return( (int)_inp(TXDATA));
}
```

B4.6   RS-232 for Windows

B4.6.1   Introduction

This chapter discusses how Visual Basic can be used to access serial communication functions. Windows hides much of the complexity of serial communications and automatically
puts any received characters in a receive buffer and characters sent into a transmission
buffer. The receive buffer can be read by the program whenever it has time and the transmit
buffer is emptied when it is free to send characters.

B4.6.2   Communications control

Visual Basic allows many additional components to be added to the toolbox. The Microsoft
Comm component is used to add a serial communication facility.

This is added to the toolbox with: Project → Components (Ctrl-T)

or in Visual Basic 4 with:Tools → Custom Controls (Ctrl-T)

Notice that both are selected by using the Ctrl-T keystroke. Figure B4.20 shows
how a component is added in Visual Basic . This then adds a Comms Component
into the toolbox, as shown in Figure B4.21.
    In order to use the Comms component the files MSCOMM16.OCX (for a 16-bit module)
or MSCOMM32.OCX (for a 32-bit module) must be present in the \WINDOWS\SYSTEM
directory. The class name is MSComm.

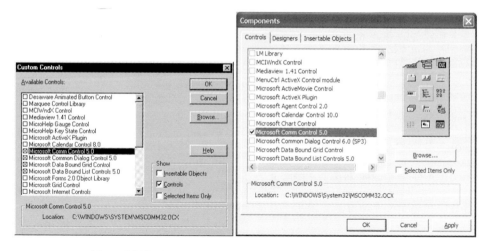

Figure B4.20 Adding Microsoft Comm component with Visual Basic

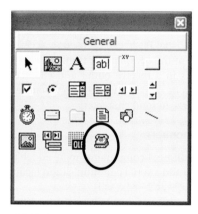

Figure B4.21 Toolbox showing Comms components.

The communications control provides the following two ways for handling communications:

- **Event-driven.** Event-driven communications is the best method of handling serial communication as it frees the computer to do other things. The event can be defined as the reception of a character, a change in CD (carrier detect) or a change in RTS (request to send). The OnComm event can be used to capture these events. and also to detect communications errors.

- **Polling.** CommEvent properties can be tested to determine if an event or an error has occurred. For example, the program can loop waiting for a character to be received. Once it is the character is read from the receive buffer. This method is normally used when the program has time to poll the communications receiver or that a known response is imminent.

Visual Basic uses the standard Windows drivers for the serial communication ports (such as serialui.dll and serial.vxd). The communication control is added to the application for each port. The parameters (such as the bit rate, parity, and so on) can be changed by selecting

Control Panel → System → Device Manager → Ports (COM and LPT) → Port Settings. The settings of the communications port (the IRQ and the port address) can be changed by selecting Control Panel → System → Device Manager → Ports (COM and LPT) → Resources for IRQ and Addresses.

B4.6.3 Properties

The Comm component is added to a form whenever serial communications are required (as shown in left-hand side of Figure B4.22). The right-hand side of Figure B4.22 shows its properties. By default, the first created object is named MSComm1 (the second is named MSComm2, and so on). It can be seen that the main properties of the object are: CommPort, DTREnable, EOFEnable, Handshaking, InBufferSize, Index, InputLen, InputMode, Left, Name, NullDiscard, OutBufferSize, ParityReplace, RThreshold, RTSEnable, Settings, SThreshold, Tag and Top. The main properties are defined in Table B4.6.

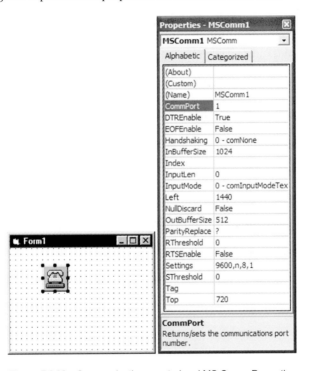

Figure B4.22 Communications control and MS Comm Properties

Table B4.6 The main communications control properties

Properties	Description
CommPort	Sets and returns the communications port number.
Input	Returns and removes characters from the receive buffer.
Output	Writes a string of characters to the transmit buffer.
PortOpen	Opens and closes a port, and gets port settings
Settings	Sets and returns port parameters, such as bit rate, parity, number of data bits and so on.

Settings

The Settings property sets and returns the RS-232 parameters, such as baud rate, parity, the number of data bit, and the number of stop bits. Its syntax is:

[*form.*]*MSComm.*Settings[= *setStr$*]

where the strStr is a string which contains the RS-232 settings. This string takes the form:

`"BBBB,P,D,S"`

where BBBB defines the baud rate, P the parity, D the number of data bits, and S the number of stop bits.
   The following lists the valid baud rates (default is 9600 Baud):

110, 300, 600, 1200, 2400, 9600, 14 400, 19 200, 38 400, 56 000, 128 000, 256 000.

The valid parity values are (default is N): E (Even), M (Mark), N (None), O (Odd), S (Space).

The valid data bit values are (default is 8): 4, 5, 6, 7 or 8.

The valid stop bit values are (default is 1). 1, 1.5 or 2.

An example of setting a control port to 4800 Baud, even parity, 7 data bits and 1 stop bit is:

`Com1.Settings = "4800,E,7,1"`

CommPort

The CommPort property sets and returns the communication port number. Its syntax is:

[*form.*]*MSComm.*CommPort[= *portNumber%*]

which defines the portNumber from a value between 1 and 99. A value of 68 is returned if the port does not exist.

PortOpen

The PortOpen property sets and returns the state of the communications port. Its syntax is:

[*form.*]*MSComm.*PortOpen[= {*True* | *False*}]

A True setting opens the port, while a False closes the port and clears the receive and transmit buffers (this automatically happens when an application is closed).
   The following example opens communications port number 1 (COM1:) at 4800 Baud with even parity, 7 data bits and 1 stop bit:

```
Com1.Settings = "4800,E,7,1"
Com1.CommPort = 1
Com1.PortOpen = True
```

Inputting data

The three main properties used to read data from the receive buffer are Input, InBuffer-Count and InBufferSize.

Input
The Input property returns and removes a string of characters from the receive buffer. Its syntax is:

[*form.*]*MSComm*.Input

To determine the number of characters in the buffer the InBufferCount property is tested (to be covered in the next section). Setting InputLen to 0 causes the Input property to read the entire contents of the receive buffer.

Program B4.5 shows an example of how to read data from the receiver buffer.

📖   **Program B4.5**

```
' Check for characters in the buffer
If Com1.InBufferCount Then
    ' Read data in the buffer
    InStr$ = Com1.Input
End If
```

InBufferSize
The InBufferSize property sets and returns the maximum number of characters that can be received in the receive buffer (by default it is 1024 bytes). Its syntax is:

[*form.*]*MSComm*.InBufferSize[= *numBytes%*]

The size of the buffer should be set so that it can store the maximum number of characters that will be received before the application program can read them from the buffer.

InBufferCount
The InBufferCount property returns the number of characters in the receive buffer. It can also be used to clear the buffer by setting the number of characters to 0. Its syntax is:

[*form.*]*MSComm*.InBufferCount[= *count%*]

Outputting data

The three main properties used to write data to the transmit buffer are Output, OutBuffer-Count and OutBufferSize.

Output
The Output property writes a string of characters to the transmit buffer. Its syntax is:

[*form.*]*MSComm*.Output[= *outString$*]

Program B4.6 uses the KeyPress event on a form to send the character to the serial port.

Program B4.6

```
Private Sub Form_KeyPress (KeyAscii As Integer)
   if (Com1.OutBufferCount < Com1.OutBufferSize)
      Com1.Output = Chr$(KeyAscii)
End Sub
```

OutBufferSize

The OutBufferSize property sets and returns the number of characters in the transmit buffer (default size is 512 characters). Its syntax is:

*[form.]MSComm.*OutBufferSize*[= NumBytes%]*

OutBufferCount

The OutBufferCount property returns the number of characters in the transmit buffer. The transmit buffer can also be cleared by setting it to 0. Its syntax is:

*[form.]MSComm.*OutBufferCount*[= 0]*

Other properties

Other properties are:

- **Break**. Sets or clears the break signal. A True sets the break signal, while a False clears the break signal. When True character transmission is suspended and a break level is set on the line. This continues until Break is set to False. Its syntax is:

  *[form.]MSComm.*Break*[= {True | False}]*

- **CDTimeout**. Sets and returns the maximum amount of time that the control waits for a carried detect (CD) signal, in milliseconds, before a timeout. Its syntax is:

  *[form.]MSComm.*CDTimeout*[= milliseconds&]*

- **CTSHolding**. Determines whether the CTS line should be detected. CTS is typically used for hardware handshaking. Its syntax is:

  *[form.]MSComm.*CTSHolding*[= {True | False}]*

- DSRHolding. Determines the DSR line state. DSR is typically used to indicate the presence of a modem. If is a True then the DSR line is high, else it is low. Its syntax is:

  *[form.]MSComm.*DSRHolding*[= setting]*

- **DSRTimeout**. Sets and returns the number of milliseconds to wait for the DSR signal before an OnComm event occurs. Its syntax is:

  *[form.]MSComm.*DSRTimeout*[= milliseconds&]*

- **DTEEnable.** Determines whether the DTR signal is enabled. It is typically send from the computer to the modem to indicate that it is ready to receive data. A True setting enables the DTR line (output level high). It syntax is:

  [form.]MSComm.DTREnable[= {*True* | *False*}]

- **RTSEnable.** Determines whether the RTS signal is enabled. Normally used to handshake incoming data and is controlled by the computer. Its syntax is:

  [form.]MSComm.RTSEnable[= {*True* | *False*}]

- **NullDiscard.** Determines whether null characters are read into the receive buffer. A True setting does not transfer the characters. Its syntax is:

  [form.]MSComm.NullDiscard[= {*True* | *False*}]

- **SThreshold.** Sets and returns the minimum number of characters allowable in the transmit buffer before the OnComm event. A 0 value disables generating the OnComm event for all transmission events, while a value of 1 causes the OnComm event to be called when the transmit buffer is empty. Its syntax is:

  [form.]MSComm.SThreshold[= *numChars%*]

- **Handshaking.** Sets and returns the handshaking protocol. It can be set to no handshaking, hardware handshaking (using RTS/CTS) or software handshaking (XON/XOFF). Valid settings are given in Table B4.7. Its syntax is:

  [form.]MSComm.Handshaking[= *protocol%*]

- **CommEvent.** Returns the most recent error message. Its syntax is:

  [form.]MSComm.CommEvent

Table B4.7 Settings for handshaking

Setting	*Value*	*Description*
comNone	0	No handshaking (Default).
comXOnXOff	1	XON/XOFF handshaking.
comRTS	2	RTS/CTS handshaking.
comRTSXOnXOff	3	RTS/CTS and XON/XOFF handshaking.

When a serial communication event (OnComm) occurs then the event (error or change) can be determined by testing the CommEvent property. Table B4.8 lists the error values and Table B4.9 lists the communications events.

Table B4.8 CommEvent property

Setting	Value	Description
comBreak	1001	Break signal received.
comCTSTO	1002	CTSTimeout. Occurs when transmitting a character and CTS was low for CTSTimeout milliseconds.
comDSRTO	1003	DSRTimeout. Occurs when transmitting a character and DTR was low for DTRTimeout milliseconds.
comFrame	1004	Framing Error.
comOverrun	1006	Port Overrun. The receive buffer is full and another character was written into the buffer, overwriting the previously received character.
comCDTO	1007	CD Timeout. Occurs CD was low for CDTimeout milliseconds, when transmitting a character.
comRxOver	1008	Receive buffer overflow.
comRxParity	1009	Parity error.
comTxFull	1010	Transmit buffer full.

Table B4.9 Communications events

Setting	Value	Description
comEvSend	1	Character has been sent.
comEvReceive	2	Character has been received.
comEvCTS	3	Change in CTS line.
comEvDSR	4	Change in DSR line from a high to a low.
comEvCD	5	Change in CD line.
comEvRing	6	Ring detected.
comEvEOF	7	EOF character received.

B4.6.4 Events

The Communication control generates an event (OnComm) when the value CommEvent property changes its value. Figure B4.23 shows the event subroutine and Program B4.7 shows an example event routine which tests the CommEvent property. It also shows the property window which is shown with a right click on the comms component.

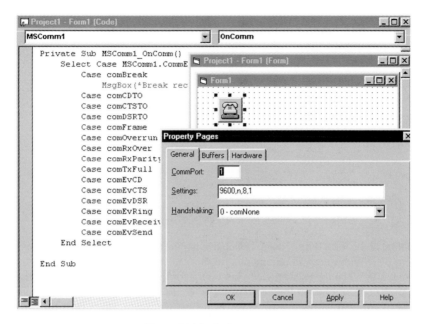

Figure B4.23 OnComm event

📖 **Program B4.7**

```
Private Sub MSComm_OnComm ()
   Select Case MSComm1.CommEvent
      Case comBreak          ' A Break was received.
      MsgBox("Break received")
      Case comCDTO           ' CD (RLSD) Timeout.
      Case comCTSTO          ' CTS Timeout.
      Case comDSRTO          ' DSR Timeout.
      Case comFrame          ' Framing Error
      Case comOverrun        ' Data Lost.
      Case comRxOver         ' Receive buffer overflow.
      Case comRxParity       ' Parity Error.
      Case comTxFull         ' Transmit buffer full.
      Case comEvCD           ' Change in the CD.
      Case comEvCTS          ' Change in the CTS.
      Case comEvDSR          ' Change in the DSR.
      Case comEvRing         ' Change in the RI.
      Case comEvReceive
      Case comEvSend
   End Select
End Sub
```

B4.6.5 Example program

Program B4.8 shows a simple transmit/receive program which uses COM1: to transmit and receive. A loopback connection which connects the transmit line to the receive line can be used to test the communications port. All the characters that are transmitted should be automatically received. A sample form is given in Figure B4.24.

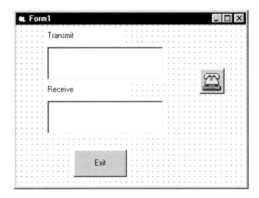

Figure B4.24 Simple serial communications transmit/receive form.

The loading of the form (Form_Load) is called when the program is initially run. This is used to set-up the communication parameters (in this case to 9600 Baud, no parity, 8 data bits and 1 stop bit). When the user presses a key on the form, the Form_Keypress event is called. This is then used to transmit the entered character and display it to the Transmit text window (Text1). When a character is received the OnComm event is called and the MSComm1.CommEvent is set to 2 (comEvReceive) which identifies that a character has been received. This character is then displayed to the Receive text window (Text2). Figure B4.25 shows a sample run.

📖 Program B4.8

```
Private Sub Form_Load()

  MSComm1.CommPort = 1        ' Use COM1.
  MSComm1.Settings = "9600,N,8,1" ' 9600 baud, no parity, 8 data,
                              '  and 1 stop bit.
  MSComm1.InputLen = 0        ' Read entire buffer when Input
                              ' is used
  MSComm1.PortOpen = True     ' Open port
End Sub

Private Sub Form_KeyPress(KeyAscii As Integer)
    MSComm1.Output = KeyAscii
    Text1.Text = KeyAscii
End Sub

Private Sub MSComm1_OnComm()
    If (MSComm1.CommEvent = comEvReceive) Then
        Text2.Text = MSComm1.Input
    End If
End Sub

Private Sub Command1_Click()
    End
End Sub
```

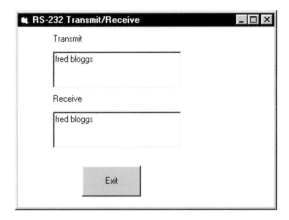

Figure B4.25 Sample run

B4.6.6 Error messages

Table B4.10 identifies the run-time errors that can occur with the Communications control.

Table B4.10 Error messages

Error number	Message explanation	Error number	Message explanation
8000	Invalid operation on an opened port	8010	Hardware is not available
8001	Timeout value must be greater than zero	8011	Cannot allocate the queues
8002	Invalid port number	8012	Device is not open
8003	Property available only at run-time	8013	Device is already open
8004	Property is read-only at run-time	8014	Could not enable Comm notification
8005	Port already open	8015	Could not set Comm state
8006	Device identifier is invalid	8016	Could not set Comm event mask
8006	Device identifier is invalid	8018	Operation valid only when the port is open
8007	Unsupported Baud rate	8019	Device busy
8008	Invalid Byte size is invalid	8020	Error reading Comm device
8009	Error in default parameters		

B4.6.7 RS-232 polling

The previous program used interrupt-driven RS-232. It is also possible to use polling to communicate over RS-232. Program B4.9 uses COM2 to send the message 'Hello' and then waits for a received string. It determines that there has been a response by continually testing the number of received characters in the receive buffer (InBufferCount). When there is more than one character in the input buffer, it is read into the program.

📖 **Program B4.9**

```
Private Sub Form_Load()
  Dim Str As String                    ' String to hold input

  MSComm1.CommPort = 2                 ' Use COM2
  MSComm1.Settings = "9600,N,8,1"      ' 9600 baud, no parity, 8 data,
                                       ' and 1 stop bit
  MSComm1.InputLen = 0                 ' Read entire buffer when Input
                                       ' is used
  MSComm1.PortOpen = True              ' Open port

  Text1.Text = "Sending: Hello"
  MSComm1.Output = "Hello"       ' Send message

  Do  ' Wait for response from port
      DoEvents
  Loop Until MSComm1.InBufferCount >= 2
  Str = MSComm1.Input                  ' Read input buffer
  Text1.Text = "Received: " + Str
  MSComm1.PortOpen = False  ' Close serial port.
End Sub
```

B4.7   RS-232 in Delphi

B4.7.1   Introduction

RS-232 is one of the most widely used communications port and can be used to send data from one device to another. It is common that computer systems, and interface devices have serial ports. The standard RS-232 ports on a PC are COM1:, COM2:, COM3: and COM4:. These ports are normally configured by the operating system from Control Panel→Modems (or from BIOS).

Delphi can interface to the RS-232 ports using a Win32 API call. This call is named CreateFile, which allow the serial port to be treated as a normal file. The format of CreateFile is:

```
HANDLE      CreateFile(LPCTSTC Name, DWORD Access,
            DWORD ShareMode, LPSECURITY_ATTRIBUTES Attr,
            DWORD Create, DWORD AttrAndFlags,
            HANDLE Template);
```

Where:

- **Name**. This is the name of the file.
- **Access**. This is the access mode. Valid types are GENERIC_READ and GENERIC_WRITE.
- **ShareMode**. This is the shared mode. 0 – Prevents sharing, FILE_SHARE_READ – read-only, FILE_SHARE_WRITE – any operations.
- **Create**. This is the create mode. CREATE_NEW – create new file, CREATE_ALWAYS – always create, OPEN_EXISTING – open existing file, OPEN_ALWAYS and TRUNCATE_EXISTING.
- **AttrAndFlags**. The attributes include: FILE_ATTRIBUTE_ARCHIVE (archive attribute), FILE_ATTRIBUTE_NORMAL (normal file attribute), FILE_ATTRIBUTE_HIDDEN (hidden file attribute), FILE_ATTRIBUTE_READONLY (read only file attribute, FILE_ATTRIBUTE_SYSTEM (system file attribute).
- **Template**. This defines a template.

The communication port can be defined by its name (such as COM1, COM2, and so on). Sample code which creates the file handle for the serial port (COM3) is:

```
const
CommPort = 'COM3';
var
ComFile: THandle;
NumberWritten: cardinal;

begin
  ComFile := CreateFile(PChar(CommPort),  GENERIC_WRITE,
             0,  nil, OPEN_EXISTING,
             FILE_ATTRIBUTE_NORMAL,0);
```

The ReadFile and WriteFile routines can then be used to read and write data to and from the serial port, respectively. The format of WriteFile is:

```
BOOL        WriteFile(HANDLE File, LPCVOID Buffer,
                 DWORD NumberOfBytesToWrite,
                 LPDWORD NumberOfBytesWritten,
                 LPOVERLAPPED Overlap);
```

Where:

- **File**. File handle.
- **Buffer**. Pointer to data to be written.
- **NumberOfBytesToWrite**. Bytes to write.
- **NumberOfByesWritten**. Returns the number of bytes written.
- **Overlap**. Defines an overlapping structure.

The overall return from the function is a True or a False (which determines the success or failure of the write). For example, after the file has been created, the following will send the string 'HELLO' to the COM3 serial port:

```
Str:='Hello';
rtn:=WriteFile(ComFile, PChar(Str),
         Length(Str), NumberWritten, nil)
```

Data can be read from the serial port using the ReadFile routine. Its format is:

```
BOOL        ReadFile(HANDLE File, LPVOID Buffer,
                 DWORD NumberOfBytesToRead,
                 LPDWORD NumberOfBytesRead,
                 LPOVERLAPPED Overlap);
```

Where:

- **File**. File handle.
- **Buffer**. Pointer to data to be read into.
- **NumberOfBytesToRead**. Bytes to read.
- **NumberOfByesRead**. Returns the number of bytes read.

- **Overlap**. Defines an overlapping structure.

```
if ReadFile(ComFile, PChar(InputBuffer)^,
                MaxBytesToRead,NumberOfBytesRead, nil) = false then
begin
   ShowMessage('Error');
   exit;
end;
// Show InputBuffer
```

It is important to set timeouts for the RS-232. This can be achieved with:

```
        var
        TimeoutBuffer: PCOMMTIMEOUTS;

        begin
          GetMem(TimeoutBuffer, sizeof(COMMTIMEOUTS));
          GetCommTimeouts (ComFile, TimeoutBuffer^);
          TimeoutBuffer.ReadIntervalTimeout         := 300;
          TimeoutBuffer.ReadTotalTimeoutMultiplier  := 300;
          TimeoutBuffer.ReadTotalTimeoutConstant    := 300;
          SetCommTimeouts (ComFile, TimeoutBuffer^);

          FreeMem(TimeoutBuffer, sizeof(COMMTIMEOUTS));
```

The following program reads and writes from a serial port.

📖 Program B4.10

```
unit rs2;

interface

uses
  Windows, Messages, SysUtils, Variants, Classes, Graphics, Controls, Forms,
  Dialogs, StdCtrls;

type
  TForm1 = class(TForm)
    Button1: TButton;
    send: TMemo;
    Button2: TButton;
    Button3: TButton;
    receive: TMemo;
    procedure FormCreate(Sender: TObject);
    procedure Button1Click(Sender: TObject);
    procedure Button3Click(Sender: TObject);
    procedure Button2Click(Sender: TObject);
  private
    { Private declarations }
  public
    { Public declarations }
  end;

var
  Form1: TForm1;
  ComFile: THandle;

implementation

{$R *.dfm}
```

```
procedure TForm1.FormCreate(Sender: TObject);
const
CommPort = 'COM1';
var      TimeoutBuffer: PCOMMTIMEOUTS;

begin
  ComFile := CreateFile(PChar(CommPort),  GENERIC_WRITE + GENERIC_READ,
                0,  nil, OPEN_EXISTING,
                FILE_ATTRIBUTE_NORMAL,0);

  GetMem(TimeoutBuffer, sizeof(COMMTIMEOUTS));
  GetCommTimeouts (ComFile, TimeoutBuffer^);
  TimeoutBuffer.ReadIntervalTimeout         := 300;
  TimeoutBuffer.ReadTotalTimeoutMultiplier  := 300;
  TimeoutBuffer.ReadTotalTimeoutConstant    := 300;
  SetCommTimeouts (ComFile, TimeoutBuffer^);

  FreeMem(TimeoutBuffer, sizeof(COMMTIMEOUTS));

end;


procedure TForm1.Button1Click(Sender: TObject);
var NumberWritten: cardinal;
        rtn:Boolean;
        s: string;
begin

s:=send.Lines.Text +  #13 + #10;
rtn:=WriteFile(ComFile, PChar(s)^,Length(s), NumberWritten, nil);

end;


procedure TForm1.Button3Click(Sender: TObject);
begin
        close;
end;

procedure TForm1.Button2Click(Sender: TObject);
var InputBuffer:string;
        MaxBytesToRead, NumberOfBytesRead: cardinal;
begin
if ReadFile(ComFile, PChar(InputBuffer)^,
Length(InputBuffer),NumberOfBytesRead, nil) = false then
begin
   ShowMessage('Error');
        closehandle(ComFile);
   exit;
end
else
        receive.lines.text:=inttostr(NumberOfBytesRead) + inputbuffer;
end;

end.
```

Modem control

Most modems are Hayes compatible. Hayes was the company that pioneered modems and defined the standard method of programming the mode of the modem, which is the AT command language. A computer gets the attention of the modem by sending an 'AT' command. For example, 'ATDT' is the touch-tone dial command. Initially, a modem is in the command mode and accepts commands from the computer. These commands are sent at either 300 bps or 1200 bps (the modem automatically detects which of the speeds is being used).

Most commands are sent with the AT prefix. Each command is followed by a carriage return character (ASCII character 13 decimal); a command without a carriage return character is ignored (after a given time delay). More than one command can be placed on a single line and, if necessary, spaces can be entered to improve readability. Commands can be sent in either upper or lower case. Table B4.11 lists some AT commands.

Table B4.11   Example AT modem commands

Command	Description
ATDT54321	Automatically phones number 54321 using touch-tone dialling. Within the number definition, a comma (,) represents a pause and a W waits for a second dial tone and an @ waits for a 5 second silence.
ATPT12345	Automatically phones number 12345 using pulse dialling.
AT S0=2	Automatically answers a call. The S0 register contains the number of rings the modem uses before it answers the call. In this case there will be two rings before it is answered. If S0 is zero, the modem will not answer a call.
ATH	Hang up telephone line connection.
+++	Disconnect line and return to on-line command mode.
AT A	Manually answer call.
AT E0	Commands are not echoed (AT E1 causes commands to be echoed). See Table C11.2.
AT L0	Low speaker volume (AT L1 gives medium volume and AT L2 gives high speaker volume).
AT M0	Internal speaker off (ATM1 gives internal speaker on until carrier detected, ATM2 gives the speaker always on, AT M3 gives speaker on until carrier detect and while dialing).
AT Q0	Modem sends responses (AT Q1 does not send responses). See Table C11.2.
AT V0	Modem sends numeric responses (AT V1 sends word responses). See Table C11.2.

The modem can enter one of two states: the normal state and the command state. In the normal state, the modem transmits and/or receives characters from the computer. In the command state, characters sent to the modem are interpreted as commands. Once a command is interpreted, the modem goes into the normal mode. Any characters sent to the modem are then sent along the line. To interrupt the modem so that it goes back into command mode, three consecutive '+' characters are sent, i.e. '+++'.

Figure B4.26 shows a sample design for calling another modem, and disconnecting a connection. Program B4.11 shows the associated code.

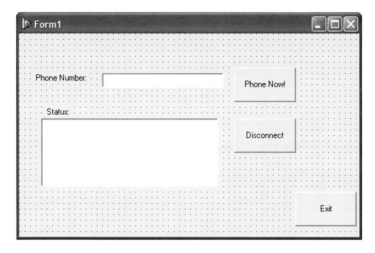

Figure B4.26 Sample design

The CommPort setting must be set to the currently connected modem port (as shown in Figure B4.27). In this case, the connected port is COM3.

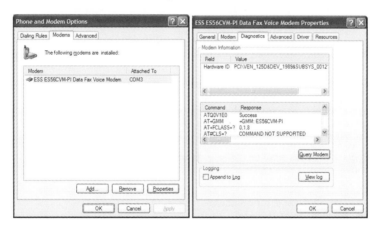

Figure B4.27 Sample design

📖 **Program B4.11**

```
unit rs;

interface

uses
  Windows, Messages, SysUtils, Variants, Classes, Graphics, Controls,
    Forms,  Dialogs, StdCtrls;

type
  TForm1 = class(TForm)
    Phone: TEdit;
```

```
    Label1: TLabel;
    Button1: TButton;
    Status: TMemo;
    Label2: TLabel;
    Button2: TButton;
    procedure FormCreate(Sender: TObject);
    procedure Button1Click(Sender: TObject);
    procedure Button2Click(Sender: TObject);
  private
    { Private declarations }
  public
    { Public declarations }
  end;

var
  Form1: TForm1;
  ComFile: THandle;

implementation

{$R *.dfm}

procedure TForm1.FormCreate(Sender: TObject);
const
   CommPort = 'COM3';  // Change as required!

begin
  ComFile := CreateFile(PChar(CommPort),  GENERIC_WRITE,
               0,  nil, OPEN_EXISTING, FILE_ATTRIBUTE_NORMAL,0);
end;

procedure TForm1.Button1Click(Sender: TObject);
var   NumberWritten: cardinal;
      rtn:Boolean;
      phone_no: string;
begin

   phone_no:='ATDT ' + phone.text + #13 + #10;
   rtn:=WriteFile(ComFile, PChar(phone_no)^,
            Length(phone_no), NumberWritten, nil);

   if (rtn=false) then status.Text:='Error making connection'
   else status.Text:='Success';
end;

procedure TForm1.Button2Click(Sender: TObject);
var   NumberWritten: cardinal;
      rtn:Boolean;
      phone_no: string;
begin
   phone_no:='+++ ATH ' + #13 + #10;
   rtn:=WriteFile(ComFile, PChar(phone_no)^,
            Length(phone_no), NumberWritten, nil);

   if (rtn=false) then status.Text:='Error disconnecting'
   else status.Text:='Disconnected';

end;
end.
```

B5 Modems

B5.1 Introduction

Modems (MOdulator/DEModulator) connect digital equipment to a telephone line. It connects digital equipment to a speech bandwidth-limited communications channel. Typically, modems are used on telephone lines, which have a bandwidth of between 400 Hz and 3.4 kHz. If digital pulses were applied directly to these lines, they would end up severely distorted.

Modem speeds range from 300 bps to 56 kbps. A modem normally transmits about 10 bits per character (each character has 8 bits). Thus, the maximum rate of characters for a high-speed modem is 2880 characters per second. This chapter contains approximately 15 000 characters and thus to transmit the text in this chapter would take approximately 5 seconds. Text, itself, is relatively fast transfer; unfortunately, even compressed graphics can take some time to be transmitted. A compressed image of 20 KB (equivalent to 20 000 characters) will take nearly 6 seconds to load on the fastest modem.

The document that was used to store this chapter occupies, in an uncompressed form, 360 KB. Thus to download this document over a modem, on the fastest modem, would take

$$\text{Time taken} = \frac{\text{Total file size}}{\text{Characters per second}} = \frac{360\,000}{2\,800} = 125\,\text{s}$$

A 14.4 kbps modem would take 250 seconds. Typically, home users connect to the Internet and WWW through a modem (although increasingly ISDN and ADSL are being used). The example above shows the need to compress files when transferring them over a modem. On the WWW, documents and large files are normally compressed into a ZIP file and images and video compressed in GIF and JPG.

Most modems are able to do the following:

- Automatically dial (known as auto-dial) another modem using either touch-tone or pulse dialling.
- Automatically answer (known as auto-answer) calls and make a connection with another modem.
- Disconnect a telephone connection when data transfer has completed or if an error occurs.
- Automatic speed negotiation between the two modems.
- Convert bits into a form suitable for the line (modulator).
- Convert received signals back into bits (demodulator).
- Transfer data reliably with the correct type of handshaking.

Figure B5.1 shows how two computers connect to each other using RS-232 converters and modems. The RS-232 converter is normally an integral part of the computer, while the modem can either be external or internal to the computer. If it is externally connected then it is normally connected by a cable with a 25-pin male D-type connector on either end.

Modems are either synchronous or asynchronous. A synchronous modem recovers the clock at the receiver. There is no need for start and stop bits in a synchronous modem.

Asynchronous modems are, by far, the most popular types. Synchronous modems have a typical speed of 56 Kbps whereas for asynchronous modems it is 33 Kbps. A measure of the speed of the modem is the baud rate or bps (bits per second).

There are two types of circuits available from the public telephone network: either direct dial or a permanent connection. The direct dial type is a dial-up network where the link is established in the same manner as normal voice calls with a standard telephone or some kind of an automatic dial/answer machine. They can use either touch-tones or pulses to make the connection. With private line circuits, the subscriber has a permanent dedicated communication link.

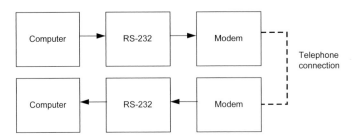

Figure B5.1   Data transfer using modems

B5.2   RS-232 communications

The communication between the modem and the computer is via RS-232. RS-232 uses asynchronous communication which has a start–stop data format. Each character is transmitted one at a time with a delay between characters. This delay is called the inactive time and is set at a logic level high as shown in Figure B5.2. The transmitter sends a start bit to inform the receiver that a character is to be sent in the following bit transmission. This start bit is always a '0'. The following data bits are sent as a 7-bit ASCII character, followed by a parity bit and finally either 1, 1.5 or 2 stop bits. The rate of transmission is set by the timing of a single bit. Both the transmitter and receiver need to be set to the same bit-time interval. An internal clock on both of them sets this interval. They only have to be roughly synchronised and approximately at the same rate as data is transmitted in relatively short bursts.

B5.2.1   Bit rate and the baud rate

One of the main parameters for specifying RS-232 communications is the rate at which data is transmitted and received. It is important that the transmitter and receiver operate at roughly the same speed.

For asynchronous transmission the start and stop bits are added in addition to the seven ASCII character bits and the parity. Thus, a total of 10 bits are required to transmit a single character. With 2 stop bits, a total of 11 bits are required. If 10 characters are sent every second and if 11 bits are used for each character, then the transmission rate is 110 bits per second (bps). The fastest modem thus has a character transmission rate of 2880 characters per second.

In addition to the bit rate, another term used to describe the transmission speed is the baud rate. The bit rate refers to the actual rate at which bits are transmitted, whereas the baud rate is the rate at which signalling elements, used to represent bits, are transmitted. As one signalling element encodes 1 bit, the two rates are then identical. Only in modems does the bit rate differ from the baud rate.

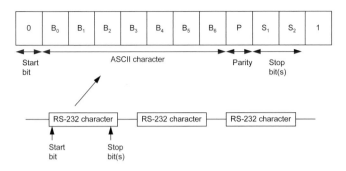

Figure B5.2 RS-232 frame format

B5.3   Modem standards

The CCITT (now known as the ITU) has defined standards which relate to RS-232 and modem communications. Each uses a V number to define their type. Modems tend to state all the standards they comply with. An example FAX/modem has the following compatibility:

•	V.32bis	(14.4 Kbps).	V.32	(9.6 Kbps).
•	V.22bis	(2.4 Kbps).	V.22	(1.2 Kbps).
•	Bell 212A	(1.2 Kbps).	Bell 103	(300 bps).
•	V.17	(14.4 bps FAX).	V.29	(9.6 Kbps FAX).
•	V.27ter	(4.8 Kbps FAX).	V.21	(300 bps FAX – secondary channel).
•	V.42bis	(data compression).	V.42	(error correction).
•	MNP5	(data compression).	MNP2–4	(error correction).

A 28.8 Kbps modem also supports the V.34 standard.

B5.4   Modem commands

Most modems are Hayes compatible. Hayes was the company that pioneered modems and defined the standard method of programming the mode of the modem, which is the AT command language. A computer gets the attention of the modem by sending an 'AT' command. For example, 'ATDT' is the touch-tone dial command. Initially, a modem is in the command mode and accepts commands from the computer. These commands are sent at either 300 bps or 1200 bps (the modem automatically detects which of the speeds is being used).

Most commands are sent with the AT prefix. Each command is followed by a carriage return character (ASCII character 13 decimal); a command without a carriage return character is ignored (after a given time delay). More than one command can be placed on a single line and, if necessary, spaces can be entered to improve readability. Commands can be sent in either upper or lower case. Table B5.1 lists some AT commands. The complete set is defined in Appendix 1.

Table B5.1 Example AT modem commands

Command	Description
ATDT54321	Automatically phones number 54321 using touch-tone dialling. Within the number definition, a comma (,) represents a pause and a W waits for a second dial tone and an @ waits for a 5 second silence.
ATPT12345	Automatically phones number 12345 using pulse dialling.
AT S0=2	Automatically answers a call. The S0 register contains the number of rings the modem uses before it answers the call. In this case, there will be two rings before it is answered. If S0 is zero, the modem will not answer a call.
ATH	Hang up telephone line connection.
+++	Disconnect line and return to on-line command mode.
AT A	Manually answer call.
AT E0	Commands are not echoed (AT E1 causes commands to be echoed). See Table B5.2.
AT L0	Low speaker volume (AT L1 gives medium volume and AT L2 gives high speaker volume).
AT M0	Internal speaker off (ATM1 gives internal speaker on until carrier detected, ATM2 gives the speaker always on, AT M3 gives speaker on until carrier detect and while dialing).
AT Q0	Modem sends responses (AT Q1 does not send responses). See Table B5.2.
AT V0	Modem sends numeric responses (AT V1 sends word responses). See Table B5.2.

The modem can enter one of two states: the normal state and the command state. In the normal state, the modem transmits and/or receives characters from the computer. In the command state, characters sent to the modem are interpreted as commands. Once a command is interpreted, the modem goes into the normal mode. Any characters sent to the modem are then sent along the line. To interrupt the modem so that it goes back into command mode, three consecutive '+' characters are sent, i.e. '+++'.

After the modem has received an AT command it responds with a return code. Some return codes are given in Table B5.2 (a complete set is defined in Appendix 1). For example, if a modem calls another which is busy then the return code is 7. A modem dialling another modem returns the codes for OK (when the ATDT command is received), CONNECT (when it connects to the remote modem) and CONNECT 1200 (when it detects the speed of the remote modem). Note that the return code from the modem can be suppressed by sending the AT command 'ATQ1'. The AT code for it to return the code is 'ATQ0'; normally this is the default condition.

Figure B5.3 shows an example session when connecting one modem to another. Initially the modem is set up to receive commands from the computer. When the computer is ready to make a connection, it sends the command 'ATDH 54321' which makes a connection with telephone number 54321 using tone dialling. The modem then replies with an OK response (a 0 value) and the modem tries to make a connection with the remote modem. If it cannot make the connection it returns back a response of NO CARRIER (3), BUSY (7), NO DIALTONE (6) or NO ANSWER (8). If it does connect to the remote modem then it returns a connect response, such as CONNECT 9600 (13). The data can then be transmitted between the modem at the assigned rate (in this case 9600 bps). When the modem wants to end the connection it gets the modem's attention by sending it three '+' characters ('+++'). The modem will then wait for a command from the host computer. In this case the command is hang-up the connection (ATH). The modem will then return an OK response when it has successfully cleared the connection.

The modem contains various status registers called the S-registers which store modem settings. Table B5.3 lists some of these registers (Appendix 1 gives a complete listing). The S0 register sets the number of rings that must occur before the modem answers an incoming call. If it is set to zero (0) then the modem will not answer incoming calls. The S1 register stores the number of incoming rings when the modem is rung. S2 stores the escape character, normally this is set to the '+' character and the S3 register stores the character which defines the end of a command, normally the CR character (13 decimal).

Table B5.2 Example return codes

Message	Digit	Description
OK	0	Command executed without errors
CONNECT	1	A connection has been made
RING	2	An incoming call has been detected
NO CARRIER	3	No carrier detected
ERROR	4	Invalid command
CONNECT 1200	5	Connected to a 1200 bps modem
NO DIALTONE	6	Dial-tone not detected
BUSY	7	Remote line is busy
NO ANSWER	8	No answer from remote line
CONNECT 600	9	Connected to a 600 bps modem
CONNECT 2400	10	Connected to a 2400 bps modem
CONNECT 4800	11	Connected to a 4800 bps modem
CONNECT 9600	13	Connected to a 9600 bps modem
CONNECT 14400	15	Connected to a 14 400 bps modem
CONNECT 19200	61	Connected to a 19 200 bps modem
CONNECT 28800	65	Connected to a 28 800 bps modem
CONNECT 1200/75	48	Connected to a 1200/75 bps modem

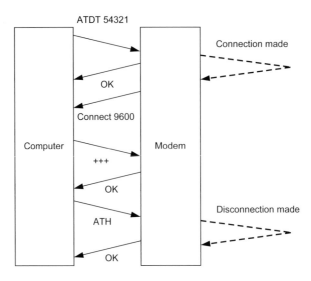

ATDT 54321

Connection made

OK

Connect 9600

Computer   Modem

+++

OK

Disconnection made

ATH

OK

Figure B5.3 Commands and responses when making a connection

Table B5.3 Modem registers

Register	Function	Range (typical default)
S0	Rings to auto-answer	0–255 rings (0 rings)
S1	Ring counter	0–255 rings (0 rings)
S2	Escape character	(43)
S3	Carriage return character	(13)
S6	Wait time for dial tone	2–255 s (2 s)
S7	Wait time for carrier	1–255 s (50 s)
S8	Pause time for automatic dialling	0–255 (2 s)

B5.5   Modem set-ups

Figure B5.4 shows a sample window from the Microsoft Windows Terminal program (in both Microsoft Windows 3.*x* and Windows 95/98 - the equivalent of this in Windows 2000/XP is HyperTerminal). It shows the modem commands window. In this case, it can be seen that when the modem dials a number the prefix to the number dialled is 'ATDT'. The hang-up command sequence is '+++ ATH'. A sample dialling window is shown in Figure B5.5. In this case, the number dialled is 9,123456789. A ',' character represents a delay. The actual delay is determined by the value in the S8 register (see Table B5.3). Typically, this value is about 2 seconds.

On many private switched telephone exchanges in the UK a '9' must prefix the number if an outside line is required (in Australia it is a '0', by contrast). A delay is normally required after the 9 prefix before dialling the actual number. To modify the delay to 5 seconds, dial the number 9 0112432 and wait 30 seconds for the carrier, then the following command line can be used:

```
ATDT 9,0112432 S8=5 S7=30
```

It can be seen in Figure B5.4 that a prefix and a suffix are sent to the modem. This is to ensure there is a time delay between the transmission prefix and the suffix string. For example, when the modem is to hang-up the connection, the '+++' is sent followed by a delay then the 'ATH'.

In Figure B5.4 there is an option called Originate. This string is sent initially to the modem to set it up. In this case the string is 'ATQ0V1E1S0=0'. The Q0 part informs the modem to return a send status code. The V1 part informs the modem that the return code message is to be displayed rather than just the value of the return code; for example, it displays CONNECT 1200 rather than the code 5 (V0 displays the status code). The E1 part enables the command message echo (E0 disables it).

Figure B5.6 shows the modem set-up windows for CompuServe access. The string in this case is:

```
ATS0=0 Q0 V1 &C1&D2^M
```

as previously seen, S0 stops the modem from auto-answering. V1 causes the modem to respond with word responses. &C1 and &D2 set up the hardware signals for the modem. Finally ^M represents Cntrl-M which defines the carriage return character.

The modem reset command in this case is AT &F. This resets the modem and restores the factor default settings.

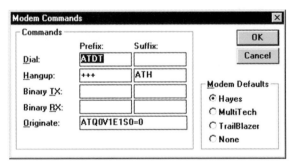

Figure B5.4   Modem commands

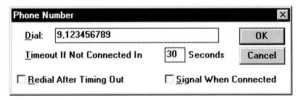

Figure B5.5   Dialling a remote modem

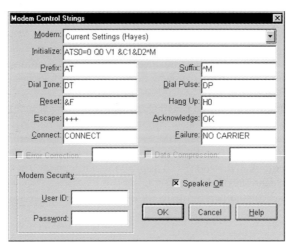

Figure B5.6 Example modem settings

B5.6　Modem indicator

Most external modems have status indicators to inform the user of the current status of a connection. Typically, the indicator lights are:

- AA – is ON when the modem is ready to receive calls automatically. It flashes when a call is incoming. If it is OFF then it will not receive incoming calls. Note that if the S0 register is loaded with any other value than 0 then the modem goes into auto-answer mode. The value stored in the S0 register determines the number of rings before the modem answers.
- CD – is ON when the modem detects the remote modem's carrier, else it is OFF.
- OH – is ON when the modem is on-hook, else it is OFF.
- RD – flashes when the modem is receiving data or is getting a command from the computer.
- SD – flashes when the modem is sending data.
- TR – shows that the DTR line is active (i.e. the computer is ready to transmit or receive data).
- MR – shows that the modem is powered up.

B5.7　Profile viewing

The settings of the modem can be determined by using the AT command with &V. An example is shown next (which uses a program from Chapter B4). In this, it can be seen that the settings include: B0 (CCITT 300 or 1200 bps for call establishment), E1 (enable command echo), L2 (medium volume), M1 (speaker is off when receiving), Q1 (prohibits modem from sending result codes to the DTE) T (set tone dial) and V1 (display result codes in a verbose form). It can be seen that the S0 register is set to 3 which means that the modem waits for three rings before it will automatically answer the call.

```
+++
AT &V
ACTIVE PROFILE:
B0 E1 L2 M1 Q1 T V1 X4 Y0 &C1 &D0 &E0 &G2 &L0 &M0 &O0 &P1 &R0 &S0 &X0 &Y1
%A000 %C1 %D1 %E1 %P0 %S0 \A3 \C0 \E0 \G0 \J0 \K5 \N6 \Q0 \T000 \V1 \X0
S00:003 S01:000 S06:004 S07:045 S08:002 S09:006 S10:014 S11:085 S12:050
S16:1FH S18:000 S21:20H S22:F6H S23:B2H S25:005 S26:001 S27:60H S28:00H
STORED PROFILE 0:
B0 E1 L2 M1 Q0 T V1 X4 Y0 &C1 &D2 &E0 &G2 &L0 &M0 &O0 &P1 &R0 &S0 &X0
%A000 %C1 %D1 %E1 %P0 %S0 \A3 \C0 \E0 \G0 \J0 \K5 \N6 \Q3 \T000 \V1 \X0
S00:000 S16:1FH S21:30H S22:F6H S23:89H S25:005 S26:001 S27:000 S28:000
STORED PROFILE 1:
B0 E0 L2 M1 Q1 T V1 X4 Y0 &C1 &D0 &E0 &G2 &L0 &M0 &O0 &P1 &R0 &S0 &X0
%A000 %C1 %D1 %E1 %P0 %S0 \A3 \C0 \E0 \G0 \J0 \K5 \N6 \Q0 \T000 \V1 \X0
S00:003 S16:1FH S21:20H S22:F6H S23:95H S25:005 S26:001 S27:096 S28:000
TELEPHONE NUMBERS:
&Z0=
&Z1=
&Z2=
&Z3=
```

B5.8   Test modes

There are several modes associated with the modems.

B5.8.1   Local analogue loopback (&T1)

In the analogue loopback test the modem connects the transmit and receive lines on its output, as illustrated in Figure B5.7. This causes all transmitted characters to be received. It is initiated with the &T1 mode. For example:

```
AT &Q0          <Enter>
AT S18=0 &T1  <Enter>
CONNECT 9600
Help the bridge is on fire <Enter>
+++
OK
AT &T0
OK
```

The initial command AT &Q0 sets the modem into an asynchronous mode (stop–start). Next the AT S18=0 &T1 command sets the timer test time to zero (which disables any limit to the time of the test) and &T1 sets an analogue test. The modem responds with the message CONNECT 9600. Then the user enters the text Help .... on fire followed by an <Enter>. Next the user enters three + characters which puts the modem back into command mode. Finally, the user enters AT &T0 which disables the current test.

If a time-limited test is required then the S18 register is loaded with the number of seconds that the test should last. For example, a test that last 2 minutes will be set up with:

```
AT S18=120 &T1
```

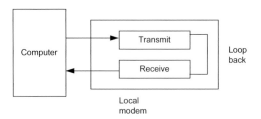

Figure B5.7 Analogue loopback with self-test

B5.8.2 Local analogue loopback with self-test (&T8)

In the analogue loopback test with self-test the modem connects the transmit and receive lines on its output and then automatically sends a test message which is then automatically received, as illustrated in Figure B5.8. The local error checker then counts the number of errors and displays a value when the test is complete. For example, the following test has found two errors:

```
AT &Q0       <Enter>
AT S18=0 &T8 <Enter>
+++
AT &T0
002
OK
```

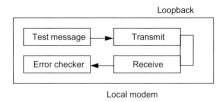

Figure B5.8 Analogue loopback with self-test

B5.8.3 Remote digital loopback (&T6)

The remote digital loopback checks the local computer to modem connection, the local modem, the telephone line and the remote modem. The remote modem performs a loop-back at the connection from the remote modem to its attached computer. Figure B5.9 illustrates the test set-up. An example session is:

```
AT &Q0         <Enter>
AT S18=0 &T6 <Enter>
CONNECT 9600
Help the bridge is on fire <Enter>
+++
OK
AT &T0
OK
```

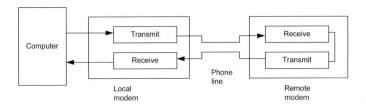

Figure B5.9   Remote digital loopback test

B5.8.4   Remote digital loopback with self-test (&T7)

The remote digital loopback with self-test checks the local computer to modem connection, the local modem, the telephone line and the remote modem. The remote modem performs a loopback at the connection from the remote modem to its attached computer. The local modem sends a test message and checks the received messages for errors. On completion of the test, the local modem transmits the number of errors. Figure B5.10 illustrates the test setup. An example session is:

```
AT &Q0        <Enter>
AT S18=0 &T7 <Enter>
+++
AT &T0
004
OK
```

or with a test of 60 seconds then the user does not have to send the break sequence:

```
AT &Q0          <Enter>
AT S18=60 &T7 <Enter>
004
OK
```

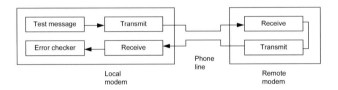

Figure B5.10   Remote digital loopback test with self-test

B5.8.5   Windows diagnostics

Microsoft Windows NT/2000/XP has a diagnostic facility which can be used to determine the operation of the modem. Figure B5.11 shows a sample run, and the results from the diagnostic tests are:

```
ATQ0V1E0 - OK
AT+GMM - +GMM: ES56CVM-PI
AT+FCLASS=? - 0,1,8
```

```
AT#CLS=? - COMMAND NOT SUPPORTED
AT+GCI? - B5
AT+GCI=? - +GCI:
(B5,00,04,B4,3D,0A,59,09,A5,31,7E,61,26,9C,6C,9F,8A,2E,51,50,AE,A0,B3,0F,3C,46,
52,7B,69,82,B5,8B,B5,A4,A9,88,58,1B,07,73,B5,20,16,57,B5,62,98,36,AD,77,0C,53,5
4,25,6A,1A,89,2D,68,70,B5,27,49,8C,BB,14,35,84,85,BC,37,4F,33,87,B7,4E)
ATI1 - ES2828/ES1988
ATI2 - RXF2-V90A
ATI3 - V4.43.049-CVM-PI
ATI4 - ESS Technology, Inc.
ATI5 - ES56CVM-PI
ATI6 - OK
ATI7 - OK
```

Figure B5.11   Diagnostics for Microsoft Windows

It can be seen that the In request returns a product code. In this case the results are:

```
ATI1 - ES2828/ES1988
ATI2 - RXF2-V90A
ATI3 - V4.43.049-CVM-PI
ATI4 - ESS Technology, Inc.
ATI5 - ES56CVM-PI
ATI6 - OK
ATI7 - OK
```

In this case, I3 returns the product the product revision code and I4 returns the OEM (ESS Technology, Inc).

C1   Introduction to networks

C1.1   Introduction

Networking involves the interconnection of workstations, terminals and other networked devices. In most cases a network allows computers of different types to intercommunicate using a network protocol. The protocol that the computers use is thus more important to communication, than their actual make. Thus, in order for them to intercommunicate, computers on a network must have a common protocol.

Many of the first computers were standalone devices, and thus worked independently from other computers. This caused many problems, including:

- The difficulty in intercommunicating between computers.
- The difficulty in managing the configuration of the computers.
- The requirement for duplication of resources, as each computer required its own resource, such as a dedicated printer, a dedicated modem, and so on.

These problems were solved with local area networks (LANs), which connect computers and other devices within a single building. One of the great advantages of LANs was that they allowed the sharing of files and printers. They are also efficient in transferring files within an organization, but it was still difficult to transmit data over a large geographical area. This led to the development of WANs (wide area networks), and MANs (metropolitan area networks).

The order of size for networks are:

- **Local area networks** (LANs), which connect over a relatively small geographical area, typically connecting computers within a single office or building. In most cases they connect to a common electronic connection – commonly known as a network backbone. LANs can connect to other networks either directly or through a WAN or MAN.
- **Metropolitan area networks** (MANs), which normally connect networks around a town or city. They are smaller than a WAN, but larger than a LAN. An example of a MAN is the EaStMAN (Edinburgh and Stirling MAN) network that connects universities and colleges in Edinburgh and Stirling, UK, as illustrated in Figure C1.1.
- **Wide area networks** (WANs), which connect networks over a large geographical area, such as between different buildings, towns or even countries.

The four main methods of connecting a network (or an independently connected computer) to another network are:

- Through a **modem** connection. A modem converts digital data into an analogue form that can be transmitted over a standard telephone line.
- Through an **ISDN** connection. An ISDN (integrated services digital network) connection uses the public telephone service and differs from a modem connection in that it sends data in a digital form.
- Through a **gateway**. A gateway connects one type of network to another type.
- Through a **bridge** or **router**. Bridges and routers normally connect one type of network to one of the same type. Normally, these days, gateways are routers.

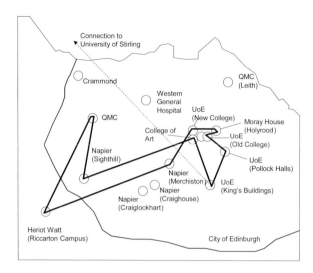

Figure C1.1   Layout of the EaStMAN network

The 1980s saw a growth in networks, but in many cases they became difficult to configure as new networking technologies used different types of hardware and software implementations, which caused incompatibilities with other types of networking equipment. Soon a number of specifications started to appear, each of which had difficulty in communicating with other types. To overcome this, in 1984, the International Organization for Standardization (ISO) developed a new model called the OSI Reference Model, which was based on research into network technologies such as:

- **SNA** (Systems Network Architecture). Developed by IBM in the 1970s. It is large and complex, and is similar in its approach to the developed OSI reference model, especially, as it also has seven layers.
- **DECNET.** Developed by DEC, and has been recently developed into DECnet/OSI which supports both OSI protocols and proprietary DEC protocols.
- **TCP/IP** (Transmission Control Protocol/Internet Protocol). Developed by US Department of Defense in the 1970s. Its main function was to allow the intercommunication of computers over a global network (the Internet). It is now used by all of the computers which connect to the Internet.

The developed model has since allowed:

- Compatibility – allows manufacturers to create networks which are compatible with each other.
- Interoperability – allows the transfer of data between different types of computers, no matter their architecture, their operating system, or their network connection type.

Along with the developed model, a number of standards have been defined, which are basically a set of rules or procedures that are either widely used or officially specified.

C1.2 Advantages and disadvantages of networks

Networks allow the orderly flow of information between connected nodes. Their main advantages are that:

- It is easier to set up new users and equipment.
- It allows the sharing of resources (see Figure C1.2).
- It is easier to administer users.
- It is easier to administer software licenses.
- It allows electronic mail to be sent between users.
- It allows simple electronic access to remote computers and sites.
- It allows the connection of different types of computers which can communicate with each other.

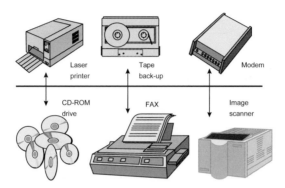

Figure C1.2   Local network with a range of facilities

C1.2.1   Sharing information

A major advantage of LANs is their ability to share information over a network. Normally, it is easier to store application programs at a single location and make them available to users rather than having copies individually installed on each computer (unless the application program requires special configurations or there are special licensing agreements). This saves on expensive disk space and increases the availability of common data and configurations. The disadvantage of this is that it increases the traffic on a network.

Most networks have a network manager, or network group, who manage the users and peripherals on a network. On a well-maintained network the network manager will:

- Control the users on the network, that is, who can and cannot login.
- Control which of the users are allowed to use which facilities.
- Control which of the users are allowed to run which application programs.
- Control the usage of software packages by limiting users to license agreements.
- Standardize the set up of application programs to a single source.
- Back-up important files on a regular basis onto a mass back-up system.
- Set up simple-to-use procedures to access programs, such as icons, menus, and so on.
- Possibly control PC (personal computer) viruses by running automatic scanning programs.
- Update application programs by modifying them at a single source.

C1.2.2 Sharing disk resources (network file servers)

Many computer systems require access to a great deal of information and to run many application programs such as word processors, spreadsheets, compilers, presentation packages, computer-aided design (CAD) packages, and so on. Most local hard disks could not store all the required data and application programs, thus a network allows users to access files and application programs on remote disks.

Some distributed, multitasking operating systems such as UNIX and VMS allow all the hard disks on a network to be electronically linked as a single file system. Most PCs normally are networked to file servers, which provide networked file systems. A network file server thus allows users to access a central file system (for PCs) or a distributed file system (for UNIX/VMS). This is illustrated in Figure C1.3.

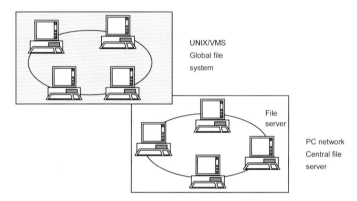

Figure C1.3   Sharing disk space with UNIX/VMS and PC network

C1.2.3 Sharing resources

Computers not connected to a network may require extra peripherals such as printers, fax machines, modems, plotters, and so on. This may be resource inefficient, as other users cannot get access to them unless they are physically disconnected and connected to their own computer. Normally, it is more efficient to share resources over a network.

Access to networked peripherals is also likely to be simpler as the system manager can standardize configurations. Peripherals that are relatively difficult to set up such as plotters, fax machines and modems can be set up once and their configuration stored. The network manager can also bar certain users from using certain peripherals.

There is normally a trade-off between the usage of a peripheral and the number required. For example a single laser printer in a busy office may not be able to cope with the demand. A good network copes with this by segmentation, so that printers are assigned to different areas or users. The network may also allow for re-direction of printer data if a printer was to fail, or become busy.

C1.2.4 Electronic mail

Electronic mail (e-mail) is one use of the Internet, which, according to most businesses, improves productivity. Traditional methods of sending mail within an office environment are inefficient, as it normally requires an individual requesting a secretary to type the letter. This must then be proofread and sent through the internal mail system, which is relatively slow and can be open to security breaches.

A faster, and more secure method of sending information is to use electronic mail, where messages are sent almost in an instant. For example, a memo with 100 words can be sent within a fraction of a second. It is also simple to send to specific groups, various individuals, company-wide, and so on. Other types of data can also be sent with the mail message such as images, sound, and so on. It may also be possible to determine if a user has read the mail. The main advantages can be summarized as:

- It is normally much cheaper than using the telephone (although, as time equates to money for most companies, this relates any savings or costs to a user's typing speed).
- Many different types of data can be transmitted, such as images, documents, speech, and so on.
- It is much faster than the postal service.
- Users can filter incoming e-mail easier than incoming telephone calls.
- It normally cuts out the need for work to be typed, edited and printed by a secretary.
- It reduces the burden on the mailroom.
- It is normally more secure than traditional methods.
- It is relatively easy to send to groups of people (traditionally, either a circulation list was required or a copy to everyone in the group was required).
- It is usually possible to determine whether the recipient has actually read the message (the electronic mail system sends back an acknowledgement).

The main disadvantages are:

- It stops people using the telephone.
- It cannot be used as a legal document.
- Electronic mail messages can be sent impulsively and may be later regretted (sending by traditional methods normally allows for a rethink). In extreme cases, messages can be sent to the wrong person (typically when replying to an e-mail message, where a message is sent to the entire mailing list [Reply to All] rather than the originator).
- It may be difficult to send to some remote sites. Some organizations have either no electronic mail or merely an intranet. Large companies are particularly wary of Internet connections and limit the amount of external traffic.
- Not everyone reads his or her electronic mail on a regular basis (although this is changing as more organizations adopt e-mail as the standard communications medium).

C1.2.5 Peer-to-peer communication

A major problem with computers is to make them communicate with a different computer type or with another that possibly uses a different operating system. A local network allows different types of computers running different operating systems to share information over the network. This is named peer-to-peer exchange and is illustrated in Figure C1.4.

C1.2.6 Remote login

A major advantage of networks is that they allow users to remotely log into other computers. The computer being logged into must be running a multitasking operating system, such as UNIX. Figure C1.5 shows an example of three devices (a workstation, an X-windows terminal and a PC) logging into a powerful workstation. This method allows many less powerful computers to be linked to a few powerful machines.

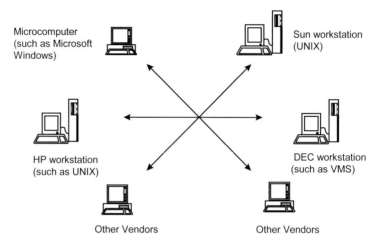

Figure C1.4 Peer-to-peer exchange over a network

C1.2.7 Protecting information

Most computers have information which must not be read or modified by certain users. It is difficult to protect information on a stand-alone computer, as typically all that is required is to wait until the user is not using the computer. On a network, each user can be granted certain rights and privileges to stored information, which can be protected by a password.

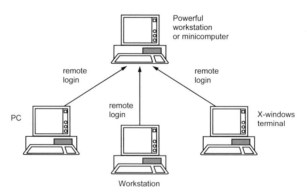

Figure C1.5 Remote login into other nodes

C1.2.8 Centralized storage and backup of information

A particular problem with stand-alone computers is that when they crash the user can lose a lot of information, especially if they have not made regular backups. As file sizes have increased it has also become more difficult for users to perform these backups as it normally involves spanning several floppy disks. Thus, a better solution is to have a networked central storage and backup device. The network manager can then schedule backups at regular intervals (typically each day). If a network crash occurs on the central storage, the manager can recover the previous backup, thus only losing a small amount of newly created data.

C1.2.9 Disadvantages and potential pitfalls of networks

The main disadvantage of networks is that users become dependent upon them. For example, if a network file server develops a fault then many users may not be able to run application programs and get access to shared data. To overcome this a back-up server can be switched into action when the main server fails. A fault on a network may also stop users from being able to access peripherals such as printers and plotters. To minimize this, a network is normally segmented so that a failure in one part of it does not affect other parts.

Another major problem with networks is that their efficiency is very dependent on the skill of the system manager. A badly managed network may operate less efficiently than non-networked computers. Also, a badly run network may allow external users into it with little protection against them causing damage. Damage could also be caused by novices causing problems, such as deleting important files.

The main disadvantages are summarized:

- If a network file server develops a fault then users may not be able to run application programs.
- A fault on the network can cause users to lose data (especially if they have not saved the files they have recently been working with).
- If the network stops operating then it may not be possible to access various resources.
- Users' work-throughput becomes dependent upon the network and the skill of the system manager.
- It is difficult to make the system secure from hackers, novices or industrial espionage (again this depends on the skill of the system manager).
- Decisions on resource planning tend to become centralized, for example, what word processor is used, what printers are bought, and so on.
- Networks that have grown with little thought can be inefficient in the long term.
- As traffic increases on a network, the performance degrades unless it is designed properly.
- Resources may be located too far away from some users.
- The larger the network becomes the more difficult it is to manage.

C1.3   OSI model

The OSI reference model makes networks more manageable and then eases the problem of moving information between computers by dividing the problem into seven smaller and more manageable tasks. A layer of the model solves each of the seven problem areas, these are: the physical layer, the data link layer, the network layer, the transport layer, the session layer, the presentation layer, and the application layer.

A major problem in the electronics industry is the interconnection of equipment and software compatibility. Other problems can occur in the connection of electronic equipment in one part of the world to another, in another part. For these reasons, the International Standards Organization (ISO) developed a model known as the OSI (open systems interconnection) model. Its main objects were to:

- Allow manufacturers of different systems to interconnect their equipment through standard interfaces.
- Allow software and hardware to integrate well and be portable on differing systems.

- Create a model which all the countries of the world would use.

Figure C1.6 shows the OSI model. Data passes from the top layer of the sender to the bottom and then up from the bottom layer to the top to the recipient. Each layer on the sender, though, communicates directly to the recipient's corresponding layer, which creates a virtual data flow between layers.

The top layer (the application layer) initially gets data from an application and appends it with data that the recipient's application layer reads. This appended data passes to the next layer (the presentation layer). Again, it appends it with its own data, and so on, down to the physical layer. The physical layer is then responsible for transmitting the data to the recipient. The data sent can be termed as a data frame, whereas data sent by the network and the transport layers are typically referred to as a data packet and a data segment, respectively.

The basic function of each of the layers are:

1. **Physical.** TRANSMISSION OF BINARY DATA. Defines the electrical characteristics of the communications channel and the transmitted signals, such as voltage levels, connector types, cabling, and so on.
2. **Data link.** MEDIA ACCESS. Ensures that the transmitted bits are received in a reliable way, such as adding extra bits to define the start and end of the data frame, adding extra error detection/correction bits and ensuring that multiple nodes do not try to access a common communication channel at the same time.
3. **Network.** ADDRESSING AND DETERMINING THE BEST PATH. Routes data packets through a network. If data packets need to go out of a network then the transport layer routes them through interconnected networks. Its task may involve, for example, splitting data for transmission and re-assembling it upon reception. The IP part of TCP/IP is involved with the network layer (or IPX in Novell NetWare).
4. **Transport.** END-TO-END CON-NECTION RELIABILITY. Network transparent data transfer and transmission protocol, which supports the transmission of multiple streams from a single computer. The TCP part of TCP/IP is involved with the transport layer (or SPX in Novell NetWare).
5. **Session.** INTERHOST COM-MUNICATION. Provides an open communications path with the other system. It involves the setting up, maintaining and closing down of a session. The communication channel and the internetworking of the data should be transparent to the session layer. A typical session protocol is telnet, which allows for remote login over a network.
6. **Presentation.** DATA REPRE-SENTATION and INTERPRETING. Uses a set of translations that allows the data to be interpreted properly. For example it may have to translate between two systems if they use different presentation standards, such as different character sets or differing character codes. The presentation layer can also add data encryption for security purposes.
7. **Application.** NETWORK SERVICES TO APPLICATION PROGRAMS. Provides network services to application programs, such as file transfer and electronic mail.

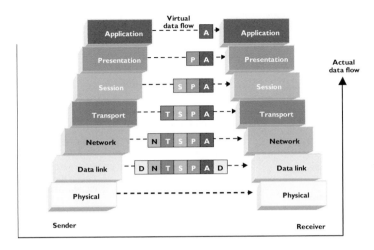

Figure C1.6 Seven-layer OSI model

Figure C1.7 shows how typical networking systems fit into the OSI model. The data link and physical layers are covered by networking technologies such as Ethernet, Token Ring and FDDI. The networking layer is covered by IP (internet protocol) and transport by TCP (transport control protocol).

The layers can be grouped as follows:

- **Media layers.** This covers the physical and data link layers, as they control the physical delivery of messages over the network.
- **Host layers.** This covers the application, presentation, session and transport layers, as they provide for accurate delivery of data between computers on the network.

In general the OSI model has:

- **Increased evolution.** Systems are allowed to quickly change, as they still integrate well with existing systems. This speeds evolution.
- **Allows modular engineering.** This allows for systems to be designed in a modular way so that each of the components, whether they be hardware or software, can interface well with each other.
- **Guarantees interoperable technology.** This allows the transfer of data between computers of different types, either in their software, operating system, network hardware or computer hardware.
- **Reduced complexity.** The task of transmitting data from one application to another over a network is reduced in complexity as it is reduced to seven smaller tasks.
- **Simplifies teaching and learning.** The OSI model has been used as a standard method for teaching networking, and, as it is built up of layers, allows for easier learning of networking. Students can easily visualize the network in a given layer of abstraction.
- **Standardizes interfaces.** This allows for designers to design their products so that they can be easily plugged into one or more of the layers of the model. The actual implementation of the layer can be invisible to other layers.

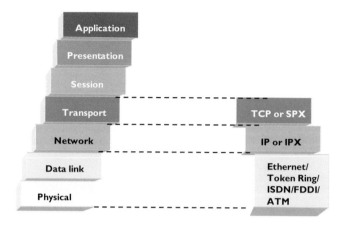

Figure C1.7 Typical technologies used in network communications

C1.4   Foundations of the OSI model

The OSI reference model is purely an abstract model, and provides a conceptual framework which defines the network functions at each layer. It thus defines how data from the source (the network device that is sending data) is transmitted to the destination (the network device that is receiving data). This data is transmitted in the form of data packets. At the source the data is passed through all of the layers of the OSI model, with each layer adding its own information. The process of adding the extra information is known as encapsulation. The data packet is thus wrapped in a particular protocol header. For example, Ethernet networks require an Ethernet protocol header before transmitting onto the Ethernet network.

Figure C1.8 shows how the data link, network and transport layers are responsible for transporting data between applications (which basically covers the session, presentation and application layers). The data link layer delivers data between devices on a network segment, and the network layer is responsible for passing it between network segments and delivers the data at the destination (using routers). The transport layer concentrates (multiplexes) the data into a single data stream for transmission, and demultiplexes it at the destination.

C1.4.1   Physical layer – cables, voltages and connectors

Computers store information using digital digits (or bits), which have a level of a '0' or a '1'. The foundation level of the OSI model is the physical layer, and provides for the actual transmission of the binary digits. In most cases, this is converted to an electrical voltage and sent over a copper cable, or converted in pulses of light and transmitted over a fiber-optic cable. The physical layer is thus responsible for the electrical, mechanical, procedural, and functional specifications for activating, maintaining, and deactivating the physical link between end systems (the end-user device on a network) and covers:

- **Cable.** Typically, these are coaxial cable, twisted-pair cable or fiber-optic cable. Fiber-optic cable gives the best specification, and can be run for longer lengths than the other two types. Twisted-pair cable has the advantage over the other two in that it is relatively inexpensive to install, but does not have as good a specification as the others. The main decision for choosing a cable type relates to how much data can be transmitted over it (the required bandwidth), its location (for example copper cables can cause electrical sparks, so they tend not to be used in flammable situations), its expense and its long-term usage. Typically cabling should have a lifetime of over 10 years (which is much longer than most of the computers that connect to the network), thus they must have the potential to support future growth.

- **Electrical voltages, electrical currents, and intensities of light pulses.** Defines the levels of the voltages or light levels for transmission of the binary digits over the cable. Electrical impulses representing data are known as signals.
- **Connectors.** Defines the physical specifications of the connector, and the connections that are made.
- **Encoding.** Defines how the bits are represented by electrical or light signals. This normally involves matching the transmission of binary digits to the required transmission specification. Important considerations are to embed the clock signal into the transmitted signals (which is important to properly recover the received data), or to try and reduce the average transmitted value to zero (as the average value does not contain any embedded information). A typical encoding scheme is Manchester encoding which encodes the 0 and 1 as either a positive edge or a negative edge.

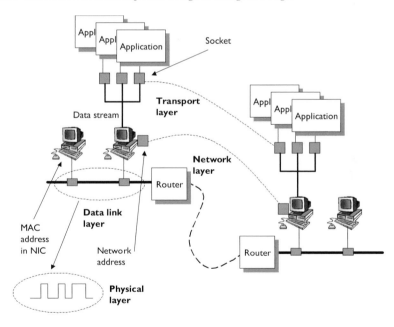

Figure C1.8 Networking showing lower-level layers

C1.4.2 Data link layer – MAC addresses and NICs

Computers connect to the physical media using an NIC (network interface card). The data link layer provides for the access to the network media and thus builds on the physical layer.

It takes data packets from the upper levels and frames them so that they can be transmitted from one node to another. The data link layer provides for:

- **Error control.** This provides for the addition of binary digits that can be used to identify if there has been an error in the transmission of one of more bits. If possible, there should be some mechanism for the destination to tell the source that it has received bits in error, and to request a retransmission.
- **Flow control.** This is where there is an orderly flow of transmitted data between the source and the destination, so that the source does not swamp the destination with data. Typically the destination sends back messages that indicate whether the destination can receive data, or not.
- **Line discipline.** This provides for the orderly access to the network media. If there was no orderly access, many nodes could try to get access to the network, at the same time, thus swamping the network. Typically, only one node is allowed access to the network at a time. Techniques which allow an orderly access are collision detection (which detects when other nodes are trying to transmit at the same time) and token passing (which involves nodes passing an electronic token from one node to the next, nodes can only transmit when they capture the token).
- **Network topology.** Physical arrangement of network nodes and media within an enterprise networking structure.
- **Ordered delivery of frames.** This provides for sequencing of the data frames in the correct order, and allows the recipient to determine if there are any gaps in the sequence of the received data frames.
- **Physical addressing.** Each node on a network has a unique physical address (or hardware address), this is normally known as a MAC (Media Access Control) address. This address must be used if a node is to receive the transmitted data frame. The only other data frame that a node can receive is when the destination address is a broadcast (which is also received by all the nodes on the network). On Ethernet networks, the MAC address has six bytes, which is allocated by the IEEE.

Physical addresses and network addresses

The MAC address identifies the physical address of the NIC, and differs from the network address (which is also known as a protocol address) which is used by the network layer. An Ethernet address takes the form of a hexadecimal number, such as:

```
0000.0E64.5432        or      00-00-0E-64-54-32
```

and the network address, for IP, takes the form of a dot address, such as:

```
146.176.151.130
```

All computers that connect onto the Internet must have a unique IP address.

IPX addresses (for Novell NetWare) use an eight-digit hexadecimal address for the network address and the node portion is the 12-digit MAC address. From example:

> **Network addresses:**
>
> ```
> 146.176.151.130 (IP)
> F5332B10:00000E645432  (IPX)
> ```
>
> **MAC address:**
>
> ```
> 00-00-0E-64-54-32
> ```

```
| F5332B10 : 00000E645432 |
```
Network address Node address

AppleTalk uses alphabet characters, such as:

```
NewPrinter
```

The physical address is physically setup in the NIC when it is manufactured and cannot be changed. It gives no information on the physical location of the NIC. The network address, on the other hand, is a software address, and gives some information on where a computer is logically located. The only way that a MAC address can be changed is to change the NIC card, whereas the network address is changed when the computer is moved from one network to another.

In Ethernet networks the following occurs:

- A data frame is transmitted onto the network with the destination MAC address.
- All the devices on the network read the destination MAC address to see if it matches their address.
- If it does not match the physical address, the device ignores the rest of the data frame, otherwise, the NIC card copies the data frame into its buffer, which is then read when the device is ready.

C1.4.3 Network layer – protocols for reliable delivery

The network layer defines the protocols that are responsible for data delivery at the required destination, and requires:

- **Network addresses.** This identifies the actual logical location of the node (the network address), and the actual node (the node address). The form of the network address depends on the actual protocol. IP uses a dot address, such as 146.176.151.130 that identifies the network and the host. IPX address (for Novell NetWare) uses an eight-digit hexadecimal address to identify the network address and the node portion with a 12-digit MAC address, such as F5332B10: 00000E645432. Network addresses are setup in software and are loaded into the computer when it starts (assuming that it has some storage device to store its network address). This differs from the MAC address which is setup in the hardware. Like MAC addresses, no two computers on a network can have the same network address.
- **Routing.** This is passing of the data packets from one network segment to another, and involves routers. A router reads the network address and decides on which of its connections it should pass the data packet on to. Routing information is not static and must change as the conditions on the network change. Thus, each route must maintain a routing table which is used to determine the route that the data packet takes. These routing tables are updated by each of the routers talking to each other using a routing protocol. Two typical routing protocols are Routing Information Protocol (RIP) and Open Shortest Path First (OSPF). RIP uses the least number of hops (which relates to the number of routers between the destination and the current router), whereas OSPF uses other metrics to determine the best route (such as latency and bandwidth capacity).

C1.4.4 Transport layer – validates transmission and structures messages

The transport layer provides for reliable end-to-end error and flow control. This is required as the network layer does not validate that any data packets have been successfully received, thus it is up to the transport layer to provide for error and flow control. It involves:

- **Connection type.** This defines the method of handshaking of data between the source and the destination, and can be connection-oriented or connectionless. In a connectionless connection there are no acknowledgements and responses when the data is transmitted from the source to the destination. In a connection-oriented system, a virtual connection is set up, and data is acknowledged by the destination, by sending acknowledgement data from the destination to the source. The source will thus know if the data has been received correctly. In order to detect if data segments have been lost or are in error, each data segment has a sequence number. The destination sends back the acknowledgement with the data packet segment that it expects to receive from the source (thus acknowledging all previously transmitted data segment to the acknowledged data segment number). Figure C1.9 shows an example flow of information. Initially, for a connection-oriented connection, the transport layer creates a connection by negotiation, where both the source and destination pass the details of their connection, such as details of their socket (which is a unique number that defines the connection) and the data segment number that they will start to send on.
- **Name resolution.** This allows for the resolution of logical names to logical network addresses. It is often easier to access networked devices using a logical name, rather than their logical address, as these are easier to remember. A typical implementation on TCP/IP networks is the Domain Name Service (DNS) which resolves domain names to IP addresses. For example, a domain name of www.fredandco.com could be resolved to the network address of 11.22.33.44.

C1.4.5 Session layer

The session layer involves the setting up, maintaining and closing down of a session. This builds on the transport layer which provides the foundation for the connection over the network. The session provides a higher-level connection, such as a login procedure, or a remote connection. It is important that the session layer does not depend on any specific transport or network layer, and should be able to communicate as if the session was created on a stand-alone computer (that is, the network is transparent to the session layer). A typical session protocol is telnet, which allows for the remote login over a network.

C1.4.6 Presentation layer

The presentation layer transforms the data into a form which the session layer and the application layer expect. It can perform encryption, translate character sets (such as converting binary values into text for transmitting a binary program over a text-based system), data compression and network redirections. An example protocol for the presentation layer is XDR.

C1.4.7 Application layer

The application layer provides application programs, such as file transfer, print access and electronic mail.

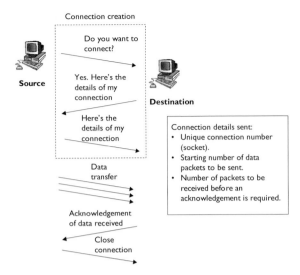

Figure C1.9 Basic transport layer connection-oriented protocol

C1.5 Internetworking

Networks can be constructed using a common connection for all the nodes that connect to the network. Unfortunately, the more devices that connect, the slower the network becomes. Thus there is a need for devices that split networks into segments, each of which contain locally attached nodes. Internetworking devices have many advantages, such as:

- They increase the number of nodes that can connect to the network than would be normally possible. Limitations on the number of nodes that connect to a network relate to the cable lengths and traffic constraints.
- They extend the physical distance of the network (the range of the network).
- They localize traffic within a network. Typically computers, which are geographically located close to each other, need to communicate with each other. Thus local communications should not have an effect on communications outside a given network segment.
- Merge existing networks. This allows connected networks to intercommunicate.
- Isolate network faults. This allows faults on one network to be contained within a given network, so that they do not affect other connected networks.

Typical internetworking devices are:

- **Repeater.** These operate at Layer 1 of the OSI model, and extend the physical length of a connection that would normally be possible with the cable type. They basically boost the electrical or light signals.
- **Bridges.** These pass data frames between networks using the MAC address (Layer 2 address).
- **Hubs.** These allow the interconnection of nodes and create a physically attached network.

- **Switches.** These allow simultaneous communication between two or more nodes, at a time.
- **Routers.** These pass data packets between connected networks, and operate on network addresses (Layer 3 address).

Networks connect to other networks through repeaters, bridges or routers. A repeater corresponds to the physical layer of the OSI model and routes data from one network segment to another. Bridges, on the other hand, route data using the data link layer (with the MAC address), whereas routers route data using the network layer (that is, using a network address, such as an IP address). Normally, at the data link layer, the transmitted data is known as a data frame, while at the network layer it is referred to as a data packet. Figure C1.10 illustrates the three interconnection types.

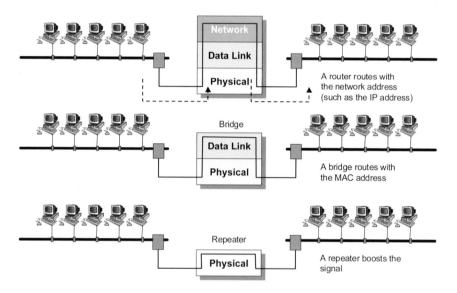

Figure C1.10   Repeaters, bridges and routers

C1.5.1   Repeaters
All network connections suffer from a reduction in signal strength (attenuation) and digital pulse distortion. Thus, for a given cable specification and bit rate, each connection will have a maximum cable length that can be used to transmit the data reliably. Repeaters can be used to increase the maximum interconnection length, and may do the following:

- Reshape signal pulses.
- Pass all signals between attached segments.
- Boost signal power.
- Possibly translate between two different media types (such as between fiber-optic and twisted-pair cable).

Transmit to more than one network. These are multiport repeaters and send data frames from any received segment to all the others. Multiport repeaters do not filter the traffic, as they blindly send received data frames to all the physically connected network segments.

C1.5.2 Bridges

Bridges filter input and output traffic so that only data frames distended for another network segment are actually routed into that segment and only data frames destined for the outside are allowed out of the network segment.

The performance of a bridge is governed by two main factors:

- **The filtering rate.** A bridge reads the MAC address of the Ethernet/Token ring/FDDI node and then decides if it should forward the frames into the network. Filter rates for bridges range from around 5000 to 70,000 pps (packets per second).
- **The forward rate.** Once the bridge has decided to route the frame into the internetwork, the bridge must forward the frame onto the destination network. Forwarding rates range from 500 to 140,000 pps and a typical forwarding rate is 90,000 pps.

An example Ethernet bridge has the following specifications:

Bit rate:	10 Mbps	**Filtering rate:**	1,7 500 pps
Forwarding rate:	11,000 pps		
Connectors:	Two DB15 AUI (female), one DB9 male console port, two BNC (for 10BASE2) or two RJ-45 (for 10BASE-T).		
Algorithm:	Spanning tree protocol. This automatically learns the addresses of all devices on both interconnected networks and builds a separate table for each network.		

Spanning tree architecture (STA) bridges

The IEEE 802.1 standard has defined the spanning tree algorithm, and is normally implemented as software on STA-compliant bridges. On power-up they automatically learn the addresses of all the nodes on both interconnected networks and build up a separate table for each network.

They can also support two connections between two LANs so that when the primary path becomes disabled, the spanning tree algorithm re-enables the previously disabled redundant link, as illustrated in Figure C1.11.

Source route bridging

With source route bridging, a source device, not the bridge, is used to send special explorer packets. These are then used to determine the best path to the destination. Explorer packets are sent out from the source routing bridges until they reach their destination workstation.

Each source routing bridge along the route enters its address in the routing information field (RIF) of the explorer packet. The destination node then sends back the completed RIF field to the source node. When the source device has determined the best path to the destination, it sends the data message along with the path instructions to the local bridge, which then forwards the data message according to the received path instructions.

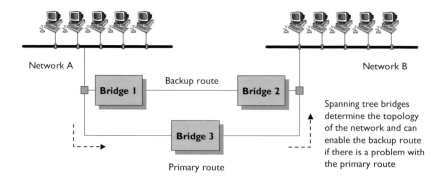

Network A

Network B

Backup route

Bridge 1

Bridge 2

Spanning tree bridges
determine the topology
of the network and can
enable the backup route
if there is a problem with
the primary route

Bridge 3

Primary route

Figure C1.11   Spanning tree bridges

C1.5.3   Routers

Routers examine the network address field and determine the best route for a data packet. They have the great advantage in that they normally support several different types of network layer protocols.

Routers need to communicate with other routers so that they can exchange routing information. Most network operating systems have associated routing protocols which support the transfer of routing information. Typical routing protocols for Internet communications are:

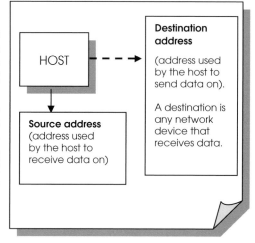

HOST

Destination address

(address used by the host to send data on).

A destination is any network device that receives data.

Source address
(address used by the host to receive data on)

- BGP (border gateway protocol).
- EGP (exterior gateway protocol).
- OSPF (open shortest path first).
- RIP (routing information protocol).

Most routers support RIP and EGP. In the past, RIP was the most popular router protocol standard, and its widespread use is due, in no small part, to the fact that it was distributed along with the Berkeley Software Distribution (BSD) of UNIX (from which most commercial versions of UNIX are derived). It suffers from several disadvantages and has been largely replaced by OSFP and EGB. These newer protocols have the advantage over RIP in that they can handle large internetworks, as well as reducing routing table update traffic.

RIP uses a distance-vector algorithm, which measures the number of network jumps (known as

Bridges:
- Forward broadcasts.
- Forward traffic to unknown addresses.
- Do not modify data frame.
- Build tables of MAC addresses.
- Use the same network address for all of its ports.

Routers:
- Do not forward broadcasts.
- Do not forward traffic to unknown addresses.
- Modify data packet header.
- Build tables of network addresses.
- Use a different network address for each of its ports.

hops), up to a maximum of 16, to the destination router (a value of 16 identifies that the destination is not reachable). This has the disadvantage that the smallest number of hops may not be the best route from a source to a destination. The OSPF and EGB protocol uses a link state algorithm that can decide between multiple paths to the destination router. These are based, not only on hops, but also on other parameters such as delay (latency), capacity, reliability and throughput.

With distance-vector routing, each router maintains routing tables by communicating with neighboring routers. The number of hops in its own table is then computed as it knows the number of hops to local routers. Unfortunately, their routing tables can take some time to be updated when changes occur, because it takes time for all the routers to communicate with each other (known as slow convergence).

C1.6 Broadcasts

A puzzling question that most people ask is how the host knows what the network address of the computer it is communicating with is, and how it knows the MAC address of the host that it communicates with. In order to determine these, a host must send out a broadcast to all of the hosts on its network segment. There are two main types of broadcasts:

- **Requests for a destination MAC address.** If a host does not know what the destination MAC address is, it sends out a broadcast request to all the hosts on the network segment. The host, which has a matching network address, responds back with its MAC address in the source MAC address field. The MAC and network addresses are then stored in the memory of the host, so that they can be used in future communications. This process is known as ARP (Address Resolution Protocol), and is illustrated in Figure C1.12.
- **Requests for a network address.** If a host does not know the network address for a given MAC address, it sends out a request with the MAC address. A server on the network normally then responds back with the network address, for the given MAC address. This process is known as RARP (Reverse Address Resolution Protocol), as it is only really used when a node needs to know what its own network address is (as it has no local storage to store it).

Most networking technologies have a special MAC address for a broadcast. Ethernet uses the address:

FF-FF-FF-FF-FF-FF

for a broadcast. There are also network broadcast addresses using the network address (known as multicast), where all the nodes on the network listen to the communication (such as transmitting a video conference to many nodes on a network, at the same time), but they are used for different purposes than broadcast MAC addresses, which are used to get network information.

Bridges always forward broadcast addresses, but routers do not. Another advantage of routers over bridges is that a router will not forward to an unknown address, whereas a bridge will. The blocking of broadcasts is a great advantage in routers as it stops the broadcasts being sent to hosts on other networks, thus limiting the traffic on other networks.

C1.7   Bits, frames, packets and segments

As has been seen, each of the OSI layers communicates directly with the equivalent layer on the receiving host. The data that is transmitted in each of the lower layers is referred to in a different way. Data that passes from layer to layer is called protocol data units (PDUs). These PDUs are referred to in different ways in each of the layers. At the physical level they are referred to as bits, at the data link layer they are referred to as frames, at the network layer they are referred to as packets, and at the transport layer they are referred to as segments. This is illustrated in Figure C1.13.

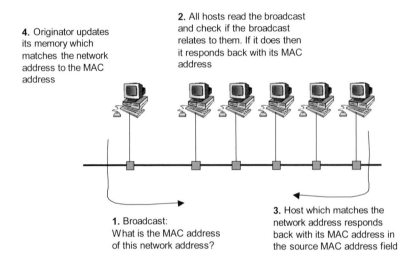

4. Originator updates its memory which matches the network address to the MAC address

2. All hosts read the broadcast and check if the broadcast relates to them. If it does then it responds back with its MAC address

1. Broadcast: What is the MAC address of this network address?

3. Host which matches the network address responds back with its MAC address in the source MAC address field

Figure C1.12   Broadcasts for MAC address

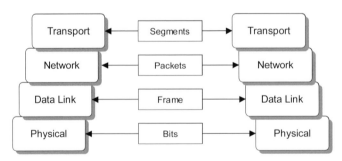

Figure C1.13   Bits, frames, packets and segments

C2 Networking types

C2.1 Introduction

Most computers in organizations connect to a network using a LAN (local area network). These networks normally consist of a backbone, which is the common link to all the other networks within the organization. This backbone allows users on different network segments to communicate and allows data into and out of the local network. Figure C2.1 shows a local area network which contains various segments: LAN A, LAN B, LAN C, LAN D, LAN E and LAN F. These are connected to the local network via the BACKBONE 1. Thus, if LAN A communicates with LAN E then the data must travel out of LAN A, onto BACKBONE1, then into LAN D and through onto LAN E.

Networks are partitioned from other networks using either a bridge, a gateway or a router. A bridge links a network of one type to an identical type, such as Ethernet to Ethernet, or Token Ring to Token Ring. A gateway connects two dissimilar types of networks and routers operate in a similar way to gateways and can either connect similar or dissimilar networks. The essential operation of a gateway, bridge or router is that they only allow data traffic through that is intended for another network, which is outside the connected network. This filters traffic and stops traffic, not intended for the network, from clogging-up the backbone. Most modern bridges, gateways and routers are intelligent and can automatically determine the topology of the network. They do this by intercommunicating with each other.

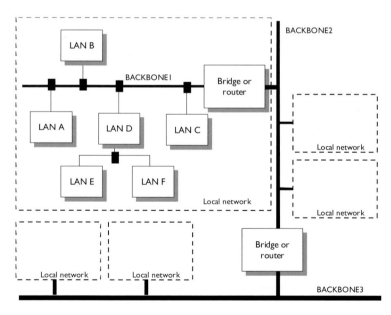

Figure C2.1 Interconnection of local networks

C2.2 Network topologies

There are three basic topologies for LANs, which are shown in Figure C2.2. These are:

- A **star** network. This type of network uses a central server to route data between clients.
- A **ring** network. This type of network uses a ring in which data is passed from node to node, either in a clockwise or an anti-clockwise direction. Normally a token is passed from node to node, and a node can only transmit when it gets the token.
- A **bus** network. In this type of network all the nodes on a network segment connect to the same physical cable. They must thus contend to get access to the network.

There are other topologies which are a combination of either two or more of the basic topologies or are derivatives of the main types. A typical topology is a **tree** topology, that is essentially a combined star and a bus network, as illustrated in Figure C2.3. A concentrator (or hub) is used to connect the nodes to the network.

C2.2.1 Star network

In a star topology, a central server (or switching hub) switches data around the network (Figure C2.4). Data traffic between nodes and the server will thus be relatively low. Its main advantages are:

- Since the data rate is relatively low between central server and the node, a low-specification twisted-pair cable can be used to connect the nodes to the server.
- A fault on one of the nodes will not affect the rest of the network. Typically, mainframe computers use a central server with terminals connected to it.

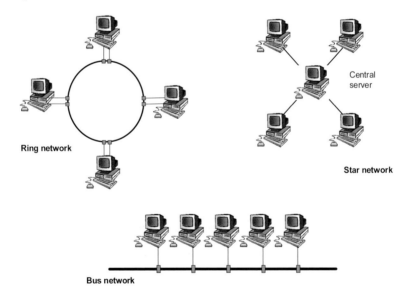

Figure C2.2 Network topologies

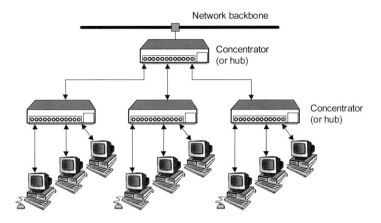

Figure C2.3 Tree topology

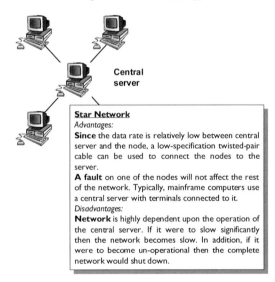

Central server

Star Network
Advantages:
Since the data rate is relatively low between central server and the node, a low-specification twisted-pair cable can be used to connect the nodes to the server.
A fault on one of the nodes will not affect the rest of the network. Typically, mainframe computers use a central server with terminals connected to it.
Disadvantages:
Network is highly dependent upon the operation of the central server. If it were to slow significantly then the network becomes slow. In addition, if it were to become un-operational then the complete network would shut down.

Figure C2.4 Star topology

The main disadvantage of this type of topology is that the network is highly dependent upon the operation of the central server. If it were to slow significantly then the network becomes slow. In addition, if it were to become un-operational then the complete network would be shut down.

An Ethernet hub acts as multiport repeaters (a concentrator). They can be either active or passive. An active hub connects to the network media, and regenerates the signal, whereas a passive hub simply connects devices onto the networking media.

C2.2.2 Ring network

In a ring network, computers link together to form a ring. To allow an orderly access to the ring, a single electronic token passes from one computer to the next around the ring, as illustrated in Figure C2.5. A computer can only transmit data when it captures the token. In a manner similar to the star network, each link between nodes is a point-to-point link and allows the usage of almost any type of transmission medium. Typically, twisted-pair cables allow a bit rate of up to 16 Mbps, but coaxial and fiber-optic cables are normally used for extra reliability and higher data rates.

A typical ring network is IBM Token Ring. The main advantage of token ring networks is that all nodes on the network have an equal chance of transmitting data. Unfortunately, it suffers from several problems; the most severe is that if one of the nodes goes down then the whole network may go down (as it is not able to pass the token onto the next node).

C2.2.3 Bus network

A bus network uses a multi-drop transmission medium, as shown in Figure C2.6, where all nodes on the network share a common bus and thus share communications. This allows only one device to communicate at a time. A distributed medium access protocol determines which station is to transmit. As with the ring network, data frames contain source and destination addresses, where each station monitors the bus and copies frames addressed to itself.

Twisted-pair cables give data rates up to 100 Mbps, whereas, coaxial and fiber-optic cables give higher bit rates and longer transmission distances. A bus network is a good compromise over the other two topologies as it allows relatively high data rates. In addition, if a node goes down, it does not normally affect the rest of the network. The main disadvantage of this topology is that it requires a network protocol to detect when two nodes are transmitting at the same time. It also does not cope well with heavy traffic rates. A typical bus network is Ethernet 2.0.

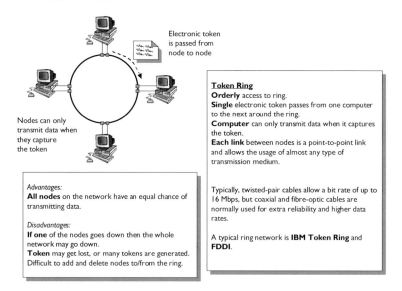

Figure C2.5   Token passing ring network

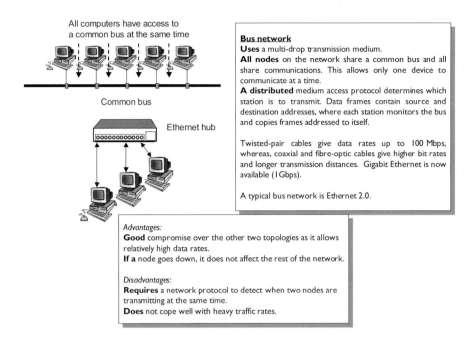

All computers have access to
a common bus at the same time

Common bus

Ethernet hub

Bus network
Uses a multi-drop transmission medium.
All nodes on the network share a common bus and all
share communications. This allows only one device to
communicate at a time.
A distributed medium access protocol determines which
station is to transmit. Data frames contain source and
destination addresses, where each station monitors the bus
and copies frames addressed to itself.

Twisted-pair cables give data rates up to 100 Mbps,
whereas, coaxial and fibre-optic cables give higher bit rates
and longer transmission distances. Gigabit Ethernet is now
available (1 Gbps).

A typical bus network is Ethernet 2.0.

Advantages:
Good compromise over the other two topologies as it allows
relatively high data rates.
If a node goes down, it does not affect the rest of the network.

Disadvantages:
Requires a network protocol to detect when two nodes are
transmitting at the same time.
Does not cope well with heavy traffic rates.

Figure C2.6 Bus topology

Bus networks require a termination at either end of the bus, as the signal needs to be absorbed at the end of the bus (else it would bounce off the end of the open-circuited bus).
This prevents signals from bouncing back and being received again by workstations attached to the bus. Ring and star networks do not require termination as they are
automatically terminated. With a star network the connected nodes automatically terminate
the end of the connection.

C2.3   Token ring

Token Ring networks were developed by several manufacturers, the most prevalent being
the IBM Token Ring. Unlike Ethernet, they cope well with high network traffic loadings, and
were at one time extremely popular but Ethernet has since overtaken their popularity. Token Ring networks have, in the past, suffered from network management problems and
poor network fault tolerance.

C2.3.1 Operation

A Token Ring network circulates an electronic token (named a control token) around a
closed electronic loop. Each node on the network reads the token and repeats it to the next
node. The control token circulates around the ring even when there is no data being
transmitted.

Nodes on a Token Ring network wishing to transmit must await a token. When they get
it, they fill a frame with data and add the source and destination addresses then send it to
the next node. The data frame then circulates around the ring until it reaches the destination node. It then reads the data into its local memory area (or buffer) and marks an

acknowledgement on the data frame. This then circulates back to the source (or originating) node. When it receives the frame, it tests it to determine whether it contains an acknowledgement. If it does then the source node knows that the data frame was received correctly, else the node is not responding. If the source node has finished transmitting data then it transmits a new token, which can be used by other nodes on the ring.

Figure C2.7(a)–(d) shows a typical interchange between node B and node A. Initially, in (a), the control token circulates between all the nodes. This token does not contain any data and is only a few bytes long. When node B finally receives the token, it then transmits a data frame, as illustrated in (b). This data frame is passed to node C, then to node D and finally onto A. Node A then reads the data in the data frame and returns an acknowledgement to node B, as illustrated in (c). After node B receives the acknowledgement, it passes a control token onto node C and this then circulates until a node wishes to transmit a data frame. No nodes are allowed to transmit data unless they have received a valid control token. A distributed control protocol determines the sequence in which nodes transmit. This gives each node equal access to the ring, as each node is only allowed to send one data frame (although some Token Ring systems, such as FDDI, allow for a time limit on transmitting data, before the token is released). It must then give up the token to the next node, and wait for the token to return before it can transmit another data frame.

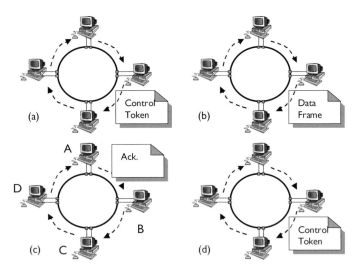

Figure C2.7 Example data exchange

C2.3.2 Token Ring maintenance

A Token Ring system requires considerable maintenance; it must perform the following functions:

- Ring initialization – when the network is started, or after the ring has been broken, it must be reinitialized. A co-operative decentralized algorithm sorts out which node starts a new token, which goes next, and so on.
- Deletion from the ring – a node can disconnect itself from the ring by joining its predecessor and its successor. Again, the network may have to be shut down and reinitialized.

- Adding to the ring – if a new node is to be physically connected to the ring then the network must be shut down and reinitialized.
- Fault management – typical Token Ring errors occur when two nodes think it is their turn to transmit, or when the ring is broken as no node thinks that it is their turn.

C2.3.3 Token Ring multistation access units (MAUs)

The problems of adding and deleting nodes to or from a ring network are significantly reduced with a multistation access unit (MAU). Normally, a MAU allows nodes to be switched in and out of a network using a changeover switch or by automatic electronic switching (known as auto-loopback). This has the advantage of not shutting down the network when nodes are added and deleted or when they develop faults.

C2.4   Ethernet

Most of the computers in business now connect through a LAN and the most commonly used LAN is Ethernet. DEC, Intel and the Xerox Corporation initially developed Ethernet and the IEEE 802 committee has since defined standards for it, the most common of which are Ethernet 2.0 and IEEE 802.3.

In itself, Ethernet cannot make a network and needs some other protocol such as TCP/IP to allow nodes to communicate. Unfortunately, Ethernet in its standard form does not cope well with heavy traffic, but the following offset this:

- Ethernet networks are easy to plan and cheap to install.
- Ethernet network components, such as network cards and connectors, are cheap and well supported.
- It is a well-proven technology, which is fairly robust and reliable.
- It is simple to add and delete computers on the network.
- It is supported by most software and hardware systems.

A major problem with Ethernet is that, because computers must contend to get access to the network, there is no guarantee that they will get access within a given time. This contention also causes problems when two computers try to communicate at the same time, they must both back off and no data can be transmitted. In its standard form Ethernet allows a bit rate of 10 Mbps, but new standards for fast Ethernet systems minimize the problems of contention and also increase the bit rate to 100 Mbps (and even 1Gbps). Ethernet uses coaxial, fiber-optic or twisted-pair cable.

Ethernet uses a shared-media, bus-type network topology where all nodes share a common bus. These nodes must then contend for access to the network as only one node can communicate at a time. Data is then transmitted in frames which contain the MAC (media access control) source and destination addresses of the sending and receiving node, respectively. The local shared media is known as a segment. Each node on the network monitors the segment and copies any frames addressed to it.

Ethernet uses carrier sense, multiple access with collision detection (CSMA/CD). On a CSMA/CD network, nodes monitor the bus (or Ether) to determine if it is busy. A node wishing to transmit data waits for an idle condition then transmits its message. Unfortunately, collisions can occur when two nodes transmit at the same time, thus nodes must monitor the cable when they transmit. When a collision occurs, both nodes stop transmitting frames and transmit a jamming signal. This informs all nodes on the network that a collision has occurred. Each of the nodes involved in the collision then waits a random period of time before attempting a re-transmission. As each node waits for a random delay time then there can be a prioritization of the nodes on the network, as illustrated in Figure C2.8.

Each node on the network must be able to detect collisions and be capable of transmitting and receiving simultaneously. These nodes either connect onto a common Ethernet connection or can connect to an Ethernet hub, as illustrated in Figure C2.8. Nodes thus contend for the network and are not guaranteed access to it. Collisions generally slow the network.

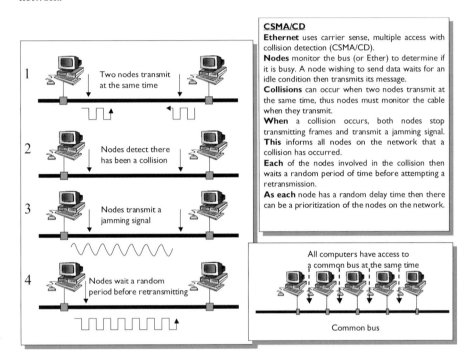

CSMA/CD

Ethernet uses carrier sense, multiple access with collision detection (CSMA/CD).

Nodes monitor the bus (or Ether) to determine if it is busy. A node wishing to send data waits for an idle condition then transmits its message.

Collisions can occur when two nodes transmit at the same time, thus nodes must monitor the cable when they transmit.

When a collision occurs, both nodes stop transmitting frames and transmit a jamming signal. **This** informs all nodes on the network that a collision has occurred.

Each of the nodes involved in the collision then waits a random period of time before attempting a retransmission.

As each node has a random delay time then there can be a prioritization of the nodes on the network.

1 Two nodes transmit at the same time

2 Nodes detect there has been a collision

3 Nodes transmit a jamming signal

4 Nodes wait a random period before retransmitting

All computers have access to a common bus at the same time

Common bus

Figure C2.8   CSMA/CD

C2.4.1 Hubs, bridges and routers

Repeaters operate at layer 1 of the OSI model, and are used to increase the number of nodes that can connect to a network segment, and the distance that it can cover. They do this by amplifying, retiming and reshaping the digital signals. A hub is a repeater with multiple ports, and can be thought of as being the centre point of a star topology network. It is often known as a multiport repeater (or as a concentrator in Ethernet). Hubs generally:

- Amplify signals.
- Propagate the signal through the network.
- Do not filter traffic. This is a major disadvantage with hubs and repeaters as data arriving at any of the ports is automatically transmitted to all the other ports connected to the hub.
- Do not determine the path.

- Centralize the connection to the network. This is normally a major problem when using a star connected network, but hubs are normally reliable and can be easily interchanged if they do not operate properly.

Hubs do not filter traffic, so that collisions affect all the connected nodes within the collision domain. The more collisions there are the slower the network segment becomes. There are two main ways to overcome this:

- **Bridges.** These examine the destination MAC address (or station address) of the transmitted data frame, and will not retransmit data frames which are not destined for another network segment. They maintain a table with connected MAC addresses, and do not forward any data frames if the MAC address is on the network segment that originated it, else it forwards to all connected segments.
- **Router.** These examine the network (typically the IP or IPX address) of the transmitted data packet, and will only transmit it out of a network segment if it is destined for a node on another network.

Bridges and routers bound a network segment, whereas a repeater extends it, as illustrated in Figure C2.9. As they are outside the network segment, bridges and routers thus do not forward collisions. Broadcast data frames are sent out by a node if it does not know the MAC address of the destination. Bridges forward these broadcasts to all the connected network segments, and every device on the connected network segments must listen to these data frames. Broadcast storms result when too many broadcasts are sent out over the network, which can cause network time-outs, where the network slows down. Routers do not forward broadcasts and thus cope better with broadcast storms.

Routers are the key components of the Internet. They communicate with each other and try and determine the best way to get to a remote network. As every computer which connects to the Internet must have an IP address, they use these addresses to route data around the Internet. Without routers we would not have an Internet. Routers are generally the best devices to isolate traffic from one network and another, as they will only forward data packets if the destination is not on the current network.

Advantages of routers:
- Intelligently route data to find the best path using the network address. A bridge will route if the MAC address is not on the originating segment, whereas a router will intelligently decide whether to forward, or not.
- They do not forward broadcasts, thus they reduce the effect of broadcast storms.

Disadvantages of routers:
- Slower than bridges, as they must process the data packet at a higher level. The data frame is then forwarded in a modified form.
- They are network protocol dependent, whereas bridges will forward any high-level protocol as it is operating on the level 2 (as long as it connects two networks of the same types, such as Ethernet-to-Ethernet). Routers interpret the network level data using the required protocol, such as IP or IPX.

The advantage of bridges are:

- Segment networks.
- Reduce collision domains.
- Filter network traffic.
- Bridges work best in connecting network segments which do not require a great amount of internetwork traffic.
- They forward any high-level protocol (TCP/IP, SPX/IPX, and so on).

And their disadvantages are:

- If the internetwork traffic is large, the bridge can become a bottleneck for traffic.
- Bridges forward broadcast data frames to all connected networks.

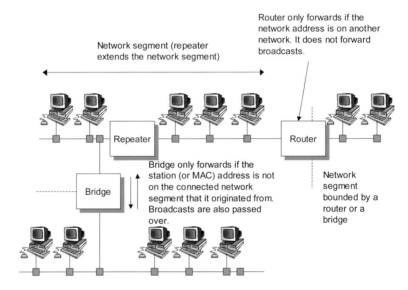

Figure C2.9   Repeaters, bridges and routers

C2.5   LAN components

LANs are high-speed, low-error data networks that span a relatively small geographic area. They connect workstations, peripherals, terminals, and other devices in a single building or other geographically limited area. The required hardware is:

- **Workstations.** These are the devices that users use to gain access to the network. Typically they are PCs, and they run the application programs, thus important decisions in purchasing a computer are: whether they run the required application software packages; whether they run the required network operating system; and whether they can run as a stand-alone computer (when the network fails).
- **Networking media.** This is the media that connects the parts of the network. There are four main types of media: unshielded twisted-pair cable, shielded twisted-pair cable, coaxial cable, and fiber-optic cable. Network media is fundamentally important, as the rest of the network will not work without it. It is often said that a network is as reliable

as its cabling, and that the networking media is the most important part of the whole network. It is the most limiting factor in the network, and sets the maximum limit for network traffic. In most cases, it has a life of more than ten years, and thus must be chosen to support expansion over that time.

- **NIC cards.** This is the device that connects the workstation or file server to the network, and is where the physical or MAC address is located. Every workstation and file server has a NIC card, which typically plugs into one of the expansion slots on the motherboard. Its three main functions are:

  o   To form data frames and send them out onto the networking media.
  o   To receive data frames coming from the networking media and transform them into information that the workstation can understand.
  o   To provide an orderly access to the shared networking media.

- **Hub or wiring centre.** In networks with a file server, it is not possible to connect every workstation to it, each with a separate NIC card within the server. Thus, most LANs use a hub, which is a network device that serves as the center of a star-topology network, each of the connections being independent. On Ethernet networks, hubs are multiport repeaters and are used to provide for multiple connections.

Additionally a network may have one or more file servers, which are used to store important network information, and are a central storage facility for the network. Typically they contain networked application programs and have several general features:

- **Highly optimized.** As many users have access to them they must operate quickly and are thus generally built to a high specification with an optimized architecture. Normally they contain a large amount of memory and storage facilities.
- **Located in a convenient place** for the workstations that connect to it. This is important as most of the workstations which connect to the network require the file server to provide application software, and other networking facilities, such as being a print server, login validation, and so on. Thus the file server must be located in an optimum place so that each workstation can have fast access to it.
- **Reliable connection**. The file server is typically the most important computer on the network, and if it were to fail to communicate with the rest of the network it may cause a significant loss of service. Thus the file server is typically connected using reliable cabling with a robust network connection.

C2.5.1   Cables

Cabling is one of the most important elements in a network, and is typically the limiting factor on the speed of the network. The four main types of networking media are:

- Shielded twisted-pair cable (STP).
- Unshielded twisted-pair cable (UTP).
- Coaxial cable.
- Fiber-optic cable.

The type of network media determines how fast the data travels along the media, and also the maximum data rate that can be carried. Twisted-pair and coaxial cable use copper wires to carry electrical signals, while fiber-optic cable carries light pulses. Fiber-optic cables generally support the fast data transfer rate.

All signals are affected by degradation when they are applied onto networking media. These are either internal or external, such as:

- **Internal.** In copper cables electrical parameters such as resistance (opposition to the flow of electrons), capacitance (the opposition to changes in voltage) and inductance (the opposition to changes in current) can cause signals to degrade. Resistance causes a loss of power (or signal attenuation), whereas capacitance and inductance cause the signals to lose their shape.
- **External.** These are external sources of electrical impulses that cause the electrical signals to change their shape. They are caused either by electromagnetic interference (EMI) radio frequency interference (RFI), and are typically generated from lighting, electrical motors, and radio systems. In copper cables, each wire of the cable acts as an antenna, and absorbs electrical signals from other wires in the cable (know as crosstalk) and from EMI and RFI sources outside the cable. These sources are known as noise and can distort the electrical signals so that it is difficult to determine the original data.

Methods used to reduce signal attenuation, and coupled noise are:

- **Cancellation.** Electrical conductors produce a small circular magnetic field around themselves when an electrical current flows in them. If two wires are placed beside each other, and there is an opposite current flowing, then the magnetic fields will tend to cancel. This magnetic field can be reduced to almost zero by twisting the two opposite wires together. This technique is called twisted-pairs. The same goes for external magnetic fields coupling into the twisted-pairs; again, they will cancel each other out. Thus, twisted-pairs (or self-shielding) are useful for reducing external coupling of electromagnetic noise and crosstalk. The direction of these magnetic lines of force is determined by the direction in which current flows along the wire. If two wires are part of the same electrical circuit, electrons flow from the negative voltage source to the destination along one wire and from the destination to the positive voltage source along the other wire.
- **Shielding.** This combats EMI and RFI by wrapping a metal braid or foil around each wire pair or group of wire pairs, which acts as a barrier from external noise. This increases the size and cost of the cable, and is typically only used when there are large sources of external radiation, such as when placed near electrical motors. However, as with increasing the size of the conductors, using braid or foil covering increases the diameter of the cable, and it will increase the cost as well. Therefore, cancellation is the more commonly used technique to protect the wire from undesirable interference.
- **Match cables.** The characteristic impedance of a cable is important, and cables and connectors must always be chosen so that they have the same characteristic impedance. If they are not matched there can be a significant power loss or pulse reflections from the junction between the cable and the connection. For twisted-pair cables, this characteristic impedance is typically $100\,\Omega$, and for coaxial cable, it is $50\,\Omega$ (for networking) and $75\,\Omega$ (for TV applications).
- **Improve the cable.** Increasing the thickness of the conductors reduces the electrical resistance, and increasing the thickness of the insulating material reduces the amount of crosstalk. These changes tend to be expensive and increase the size of the cable.

An important consideration when selecting a cable, especially in hazardous areas, is its jacket. Typically it is made from plastic, Teflon, or composite material. Problem areas are:

- **Carrying fire.** This is where the cable can carry fire from one part of a building to another. Typically it is where cables are installed between walls, in an elevator shaft or pass through an air-handling unit.
- **Producing toxic smoke when lit.** When burnt, plastic cable jackets can create toxic smoke.

To protect against these problems, network cables must always comply with fire codes, building codes, and safety standards. These are more important than other factors, such as cable size, speed, cost, and difficulty of installation.

C2.5.2   Unshielded twisted-pair cable

The most popular type of cabling is unshielded twisted-pair, which comprises four-wire pair. Unshielded twisted-pair cable does not have a shield around each of the pairs. It thus relies on:

- **Cancellation effect.** The twists of each pair produces a cancellation effect which limits degradation caused by EMI and RFI.
- **Variation of twists.** With this, the number of twists in the wire pairs varies from one to the other, which reduces the amount of crosstalk between the pairs. There are strict limits on the maximum number twists or braids per foot of cable.
- **Accurate characteristic impedance.** For this, the characteristic impedance is around $100\,\Omega$ in order to produce a good match between the cable and any connection.

Advantages of UTP:

- The cable is thin and easy to work with. This makes it easy to install.
- Less expensive than other types of networking media.
- When used with an RJ connector (RJ-45 or RJ-11), it provides a reliable connection.
- Data rates can be as fast as coaxial cables (as UTP cables now have an excellent specification).

Disadvantages of UTP:

- More prone to electrical noise and interference than other types of networking media (as there is no shield between the pairs).
- Can carry electrical surges.

C2.5.3   Shielded twisted-pair cable

STP cable is similar to UTP but has shielding on each of the pairs, thus reducing the effect of crosstalk, EMI and RFI. Unlike coaxial cable, the shielding does not act as part of the circuit, but it must be properly grounded at each end to enhance the shielding effect (as a non-ground shield will act like an antenna and pick up electrical noise). Its only disadvantage is that it is more expensive than UTP, although it can suffer from the same problems of coaxial cable if either end of the shield is not grounded.

C2.5.4   Coaxial cable

Coaxial cable is typically available in two main flavors:

- **Thicknet.** Thick and rigid cable which is difficult to bend and often difficult to install. It typically has a distinctive yellow outer cover.
- **Thinnet.** Thinner cable which is easier to work with (0.18 inch).

Advantages of coaxial cable:

- Outer copper braid or metallic foil provides a shield to reduce the amount of interference.
- They can be run unboosted for longer distances than either shielded or unshielded twisted-pair cable.
- Less expensive than fiber-optic.
- Well-known technology. Coaxial cable has been used extensively in the past, especially in radio, TV and microwave applications.

Disadvantages of coaxial cable:

- The cable is relatively thick, and the thicker the cable the more difficult it is to work with.
- More expensive than twisted-pair cable.
- In thinnet, the outer copper or metallic braid of the cable comprises half the electrical circuit. Thus, special care must be taken to ensure that it is properly grounded, at both ends of the cable. If it is not properly grounded, it can result in electrical noise that interferes with transmittal of the signal on the networking media.

C2.5.5   Fiber-optic cables

One of the greatest revolutions in data communications is the usage of light waves to transmit digital pulses through fiber-optic cables. A light carrying system has an almost unlimited information capacity, and theoretically, it has more than 200,000 times the capacity of a satellite TV system.

Advantages of fiber optic cables:

- Excellent reliability, and are extensively used as network backbones.
- Immune from crosstalk, EMI and RFI.
- Can be run for longer distances than copper cables.
- They do not create grounding problems, thus they can be used to connect between two sites with a different ground potential.
- Very thin flat cable that can be easily run within confined spaces.
- Can be used in hazardous conditions, as it does not create electrical sparks.
- Immune from lightning strikes.

Disadvantages of fiber optic cables:

- More expensive and more difficult to install than any other networking media.
- Requires a trained installer to create a good cable connection.
- Too expensive in most situations to provide fibre connections to every workstation.

Optoelectronics is the branch of electronics which deals with light, and uses electronic devices that use light which operate within the optical part of the electromagnetic frequency spectrum, as shown in Figure C2.10. There are three main bands in the optical frequency spectrum, these are:

- Infrared – the band of light wavelengths that are too long to been seen by the human eye.
- Visible – the band of light wavelengths that the human eye responds to.
- Ultraviolet – band of light wavelengths that are too short for the human eye to see.

Wavelength and color

Wavelength is defined as the physical distance between two successive points of the same electrical phase. Figure C2.11 (a) shows a wave and its wavelength. The wavelength is dependent upon the frequency of the wave f, and the velocity of light, c (3×10^8 m/s) and is given by:

$$\lambda = \frac{c}{f}$$

The optical spectrum ranges from wavelengths of 0.005 mm to 4000 mm. In frequency terms these are extremely large values from 6×10^{16} Hz to 7.5×10^{10} Hz. It is thus much simpler to talk in terms of wavelengths rather than frequencies.

The human eye sees violet at one end of the color spectrum and red on the other. In-between, the eye sees blue, indigo, green, yellow and orange. Two beams of light that have the same wavelength are seen as the same color and the same colors usually have the same wavelength. Figure C2.11 (b) shows the color spectrum.

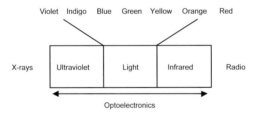

Figure C2.10   EM optoelectronics spectrum

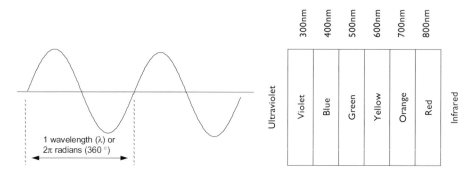

Figure C2.11 Wavelength of wave and color spectrum

Velocity of propagation and refractive index

In free space electromagnetic waves travel at approximately $300,000000$ m/sec ($186,000$ miles/sec). However, their velocity is lower when they travel through denser materials. When traveling from one material to another which is less dense the light ray is refracted (or bent) away from the normal, as illustrated in Figure C2.12.

The amount of bending or refraction at the interface between two materials of different densities depends on the refractive index of the two materials. This index is the ratio of the velocity of propagation of a light ray in free space to the velocity of propagation of a light ray in the material, as given by:

$$n = \frac{c}{v}$$

where c is speed of light in free space and v is the speed of light in a given medium. Typical refractive indexes are given in Table C2.1.

Optical fibers

Optical fibers are transparent, dielectric cylinders surrounded by a second transparent dielectric cylinder. Light is transported by a series of reflections from wall to wall from the interface between a core (inner cylinder) and its cladding (outer cylinder). A cross-section of a fiber is given in Figure C2.13.

Reflections occur because the core has a higher reflective index than the cladding (it thus has a higher density). Abrupt differences in the refractive index causes the light wave to bounce from the core/cladding interface back through the core to its opposite wall. Thus, the light is transported from a light source to a light detector at the other end of the fiber.

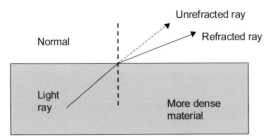

Figure C2.12   Refracted ray

Table C2.1 Refractive index of sample materials

Medium	Refractive index
Air	1.0003
Water	1.33
Glass fiber	1.5–1.9
Diamond	2.0–2.42
Gallium arsenide	3.6
Silicon	3.4

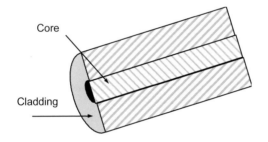

Figure C2.13   Cross-section of an optical fiber

Optical fibers transmit light by total internal reflection (TIR), where light rays passing between the boundaries of two optically transparent media of different densities experience refraction, as shown in Figure C2.14. This changed direction can be determined according to Snell's law:

$$n_1 \sin \theta_1 = n_2 \sin \theta_2$$

Thus
$$\theta_2 = \sin^{-1}\left[\frac{n_1}{n_2}\sin \theta_1\right]$$

The angle at which the ray travels along the interface between the two materials is called the critical angle (θ_c). If the incident ray is greater than this angle, the ray will be totally reflected from the outer cladding. It then propagates along the fiber being reflected by the cladding on the way, as shown in Figure C2.15. The angle at which the reflection occurs is called the acceptance angle, and if the initial ray is entered at an angle of at least the acceptance angle, then the ray will bounce along the inner core.

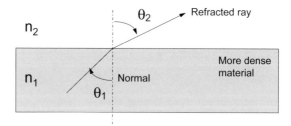

Figure C2.14   Refraction

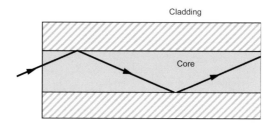

Figure C2.15   Light propagating in an optical fiber

Fiber-optic losses result in a lower transmitted light power, which reduces the system bandwidth, information transmission rate, efficiency and overall system capacity. The main losses are:

- **Absorption losses.** Impurities in the glass fiber cause the transmitted wave to be absorbed and converted into heat.
- **Material scattering.** Extremely small irregularities in the structure of the cable cause light to be diffracted. This causes the light to disperse or spread out in many directions. A greater loss occurs at visible wavelengths than at infrared.
- **Chromatic distortion.** Caused by each wavelength of light traveling at differing speeds. They thus arrive at the receiver at different times causing a distorted pulse shape. Monochromatic light reduces this type of distortion.
- **Radiation losses.** Caused by small bends and kinks in the fiber that scatters the wave.
- **Modal dispersion.** Caused by light taking different paths through the fiber. This will each have a different propagation time to travel along the fiber. These different paths are described as modes. Figure C2.16 shows two rays taking different paths. Ray 2 will take a longer time to get to the receiver than ray 1.
- **Coupling losses.** Caused by light being lost at mismatches at terminations between fiber/fiber, light source/fiber, and so on.

Optical fiber cables are either glass-based or plastic-based, and typically carry infrared signals (it is thus important to never look directly into a fiber optic cable which is transmitting infrared signals, as it can damage your eyes). Table C2.2 shows the characteristics of two typical fiber-optic cables, one using glass, and the other plastic. It can be seen that the inside core and the cladding diameters are relatively small, i.e. fractions of a millimeter.

Normally the cladding is covered in a coating which is then covered in a jacket. These give the cable mechanical strength and also make it easier to work with. In the case of the 50/125 μm glass cable in Table C2.2 the outer diameter of the cable is 3.2 mm but the inner core diameter is just 50 μm. Normally glass fiber cables have better electrical characteristic over plastic equivalents, but are more prone to breakage and damage. It can be seen that the glass cable has improved bandwidth and lower attenuation over the plastic equivalent.

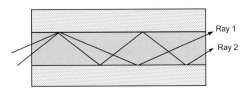

Figure C2.16 Light propagating in different modes

There are many advantages in using fiber optics, including:

- Fiber systems have a greater capacity due to the inherently larger bandwidths available with optical frequencies. Metallic cables contain capacitance and inductance along their conductors, which cause them to act like low-pass filters. This limits bandwidth and also the speed of propagation of the electrical pulse.
- Fiber systems are immune from cross-talk between cables caused by magnetic induction. Glass fibers are non-conductors of electricity and therefore do not have a magnetic field associated with them. In metallic cables, the primary cause of cross-talk is magnetic induction between conductors located near each other.
- Fiber cables do not suffer from static interference caused by lightning, electric motors, fluorescent lights, and other electrical noise sources. This immunity is because fibers are non-conductors of electricity.
- Fiber systems have greater electrical isolation thus allowing equipment greater protection from damage due to external sources. For example if a part of a network was hit by a lightning pulse then it may damage one of the optical receivers but a high voltage pulse cannot travel along the optical cable and damage sensitive equipment on other parts of the network. They also prevent electrical noise traveling from one part of a network to another, as illustrated in Figure C2.17.
- Fiber cables do not radiate energy and therefore cannot cause interference with other communications systems. This characteristic makes fiber systems ideal for military applications, where the effect of nuclear weapons (EMP-electromagnetic pulse interference) has a devastating effect on conventional communications systems.
- Fiber cables are more resistant to environmental extremes. They operate over a larger temperature variation than copper cables and are affected less by corrosive liquids and gases.
- Fiber cables are safer to install and maintain, as glass and plastic have no electrical currents or voltages associated with them. Optical fibers can be used around volatile liquids and gases without worrying about the risk of explosions or fires. They are also smaller and more lightweight than copper cables.
- Fiber cables are more secure than copper cables and are virtually impossible to tap into without users knowing about it.

Table C2.2 Typical fiber-optic cable characteristics

	50/125 μm glass	*200 μm PCS*
Construction	Glass	Plastic coated silica (PCS)
Core diameter	50 μm	200 μm
Cladding diameter	125 μm	389 μm
Coating diameter	250 μm	600 μm
Jacket material	Polyethylene	PVC
Overall diameter	3.2 mm	4.8 mm
Connector	9 mm SMA	9 mm SMA
Bandwidth	400 MHz/km	25 MHz/km
Minimum bend radius	30 mm	50 mm
Temperature range	–15 °C to +60 °C	–10 °C to +50 °C
Attenuation @820 nm	3 dB/km	7 dB/km

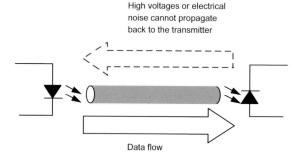

High voltages or electrical
noise cannot propagate
back to the transmitter

Data flow

Figure C2.17 Fiber-optic isolation

C2.6   Cabling standards

The main standards agencies for network cabling are:

- Institute of Electrical and Electronic Engineers (IEEE). The IEEE defined cabling standards for Ethernet and Token Ring in their 802.3 and 802.5 standards, respectively.
- Underwriters Laboratories (UL). An independent agency in the United States that tests product safety. In networking it rates twisted-pair cables. The UL has also defined a cable marking system which identifies the cable and whether it is shielded or not. An example marking is 'IEEE 802.3 Coaxial Trunk (**UL**) Type CL2'. This is known as the UL marking system.
- Electrical Industries Association (EIA)/Telecommunications Industry Association (TIA). These organizations have developed many of the networking media standards, especially:

  o   EIA/TIA-568. This standard defines UTP cabling, such as Category 1 (Cat-1), Category 2 (Cat-2), Category 3 (Cat-3), Category 4 (Cat-4) and Category 5 (Cat-5) cables. Cat-5 cables offer the best specification of the five types of cables, and are the most often used (although Cat-6 cabling is now become popular). Networking does not use Cat-1 or Cat-2 cable as these are used for voice circuits.

  o   EIA/TIA-568A. Updated standard to EIA/TIA-568 which includes fiber-optic cable and link performance.

- o   EIA/TIA-569. This standard defines cable interconnections and pathways, such as telecommunications closets, backbones, and so on.

The EIA/TIA has defined most of the important standards relating to networking media, and provide a foundation for multi-product and multi-vendor networks. The EIA/TIA-568A standard defines six main elements of cabling in a LAN (as illustrated in Figure C2.18):

- **Horizontal cabling.** This is defined as the cabling that runs from the telecommunications outlet to a horizontal cross-connect, and is basically the cable which runs from a wiring closet (a central point for cabling) to a workstation, and consists of:

  - o   *Horizontal cabling*: It may be up to 90m of 4- or 25-pair of Cat- 5 UTP cable.
  - o   *Telecommunications outlet*: The device in which the horizontal cable terminates at the work area.
  - o   *Cable terminations.*
  - o   *Cross-connections*: The device for interconnecting cable runs
  - o   *Patch Cords*: These are used in points were the network configuration will change frequently.
  - o   *Transition or consolidation point*: It connects standard horizontal cable to special flat cable designed to run under carpets.

- **Wiring closets.** This is where the horizontal distribution cables are terminated. All recognized types of horizontal cabling are terminated on compatible connecting hardware. Cross connection occurs with jumpers or patch cords to provide flexible connectivity for extending various services to users at the telecommunications outlets.
- **Backbone cabling.** This is defined as the interconnections between wiring closets, entrance facilities and between buildings that are part of the same LAN. It is also known as vertical cabling, and consists of the backbone cables, main and intermediate cross-connects, mechanical terminations, and patch cords or jumpers used for backbone-to-backbone cross-connection. This includes:

  - Vertical connections between floors (risers)
  - Cables between an equipment room and building entrance facilities.
  - Cables between buildings (inter-building).

- **Equipment rooms.** This is a centralized space for telecommunications equipment that serves users in the building. Equipment rooms usually house equipment of higher complexity than telecommunication closets. Any or all of a telecommunications closet may be provided by an equipment room.
- **Work areas.**
- **Entrance facilities.** This is the point where the outside cables and associated hardware are brought into the building interfacing and interfaces with the backbone cabling. The Entrance facility is typically in the basement (where access can be carefully controlled).

The EIA/TIA-568A specification defines for horizontal cabling:

- Four-pair unshielded $100\,\Omega$ cable.
- Two-pair shielded $150\,\Omega$ cable.
- Two fibers of $62.5/125\,\mu$m multimode cable. One cable for sending and the other for receiving.
- $50\,\Omega$ coaxial cable. This cable is not recommended for new installations, and is unlikely to be supported in future specifications.

The maximum lengths of horizontal cabling for unshielded twisted-pair cable are given in Figure C2.18. They are 90 m (295 feet) for a horizontal cable run, 3 m (9.8 feet) for a workstation cable and 6 m (20 feet) for a patch cord.

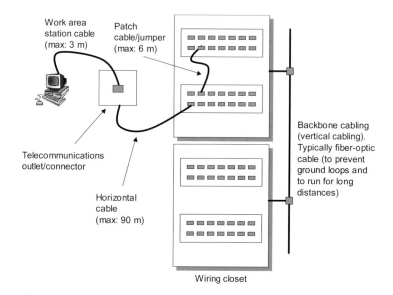

Figure C2.18 Cabling classifications

Most modern Ethernet and Token Ring networks connect onto a hub, which is basically a physically star connected network. As has been seen the maximum length of horizontal cabling is 90 m, along with a 6m patch cord and a workstation connect cable of 3 m, giving the maximum length of cabling from the hub to the workstations of 100 m, as illustrated in Figure C2.19. This gives a maximum coverage area of approximately 200 m by 200 m. It can be seen that workstations outside this area could not be connected using EIA/TIA-568A cabling. This is because attenuation and interference may cause unreliable reception of the data. One solution to this is to add a repeater if the connection is greater than 100 m. This leads to an extended star topology.

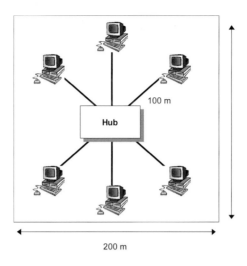

100 m

Hub

200 m

Figure C2.19 Maximum cabling area for a LAN for horizontal cabling runs

C2.6.1 RJ-45 jacks

The RJ-45 connector is the standard connector used with the EIA/TIA-568A standard for connecting Cat-5 UTP at the telecommunications outlet. It has eight pins into which the four pairs connect into, each of which are color coded (a telephone-type connector only contains four pins), with blue, green, orange and brown terminals, which correspond to the wires found in each of the twisted-pairs used in Cat-5 UTP. The blue wire with a white strip and the white wire with the blue strip (the blue twisted-pair) are connected to the blue terminals, and so on. The wires are connected into the terminals, using a punch tool to force the wires into the terminals and also to strip the sheath away from each of the wires.

Normally the socket is mounted onto the wall so that the RJ-45 plug can connect to it. The two main types of socket are surface mounted and flush mounted. The surface mount technique is the easiest and fastest method of mounting an RJ-45 jack and does not involve cutting into the wall. They are permanently mounted onto the wall with an adhesive-backed box. Once mounted it cannot be moved. If it is required to be moved, the surface mounted RJ-45 jack can use a screw-mounted instead of an adhesive box. Surface-mounted jacks must be used where it is not possible to cut the wall, such as with concrete block walls. A flush mounted unit involves cutting into the wall.

The cable can either be mounted behind a wall (such as in plasterboard walls) or can be mounted to the wall, typically with a raceway, which is a wall-mounted channel with a removable cover. Raceways are made out of plastic or metal and are available in two forms:

- **Decorative.** These have a good-looking finish and are typically used within rooms, but are limited in the number of cables they can enclose (typically a maximum of two cables).
- **Gutter.** Not as good-looking as decorative raceways, but they can be used to hold many more cables. They are typically used in attics.

An important factor is never to run power cables alongside UTP cables, as power cables emit EMI which can corrupt data signals. If possible, cables should never be loose run along ceilings, but should be supported by ladder racks. Cable, which is laid through spaces where air is circulated, must be fire-rated in order to ensure that the cable does not carry the fire from one place to another. In addition, whenever someone is working within an attic, ceiling or wall, the electrical power must be isolated to prevent electrical shock.

C2.6.2 Rules for installing cable

Once the cable is run, it is important for future reference to make a cut sheet, which is a diagram which shows the location of cable runs, and all the rooms and hallways within a building. The EIA/TIA-606 standard defines terminations, media, pathways, spaces, grounding of communications equipment in commercial buildings. It also defines the labels for the end of the cables and their termination (and compliance with the UL969 specification for legibility and adhesion). Labels should be long lasting, and should, if possible, reflect the actual location of the destination connection and be color coded to identify the usage of each of the cables. For example, all the cables that go into Production will be labeled with green labels, while all the cables that go to Sales would be labeled with blue labels. Figure C2.20 shows an example of a cut sheet diagram. In this case the rooms are 100, 101, 102, 103 and 104. Different cables which run to RJ-45 jacks in a single room are labeled with an A, B, C, and so on. In room 100 there are three cables, these are labeled 100A, 100B and 100C. These would be labeled on the hub, on either end of the cables, and on the faceplate of the RJ-45 jack.

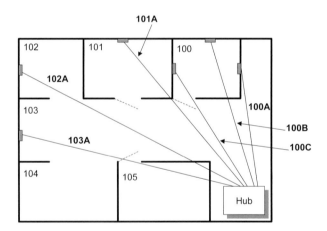

Figure C2.20   Cut sheets example

C2.6.3 Patch panels and wiring closets

Wiring closets provide a convenient place where cables can be terminated, and is the center of the topology. Along with cables, it is typically the location for routers, bridges, patch panels and hubs. A patch panel is an interconnecting device which connects workstations to hubs and repeaters together using horizontal cabling. It is basically a switchboard with a collection of pin locations (the terminals at the back of the patch connector) and ports (the RJ-45 jack connections on the front of the patch panel). They are typically mounted into a 19 in rack, as illustrated in Figure C2.21. Some larger networks have more than one wiring closet, and have a main distribution facility (MDF) and other intermediate distribution facilities (IDFs), which connect to the MDF.

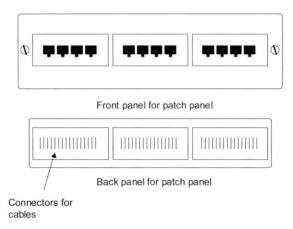

Front panel for patch panel

Back panel for patch panel

Connectors for cables

Figure C2.21 Patch panel front and back

C2.6.4 Cable testing

Testing of network cables is important not only in detecting faults but also in determining if the cabling is conforming to the required specification. Both the IEEE and the EIA/TIA have tests for cabling after installation. These tests provide the baseline for the network. Along with a wire map (which shows the location of all the cable connections), an important device in testing the network is a cable tester, which determines:

- **Cable distance.** This is an important measure to verify that the connected cables are not too long for the given specification. Time domain reflectometers (TDRs) can measure distance, as they send a pulse down the cable which is then reflected from an open- or short-circuit connection at the far end of the cable. The TDR measures the time that the pulse takes to come back and as it can approximate the speed of propagation, it can determine the cable distance (speed of propagation multiplied by time). This device is typically accurate to within a meter. TDRs can also be used to determine the distance to a cable break (an open circuit) or a cable short (a short circuit).
- **Signal attenuation**. To measure attenuation a signal inject is applied at the far end of the cable, and the signal level is measured at the near end. From this, attenuation is calculated. Typically, this is measured at various frequencies, such as 100 MHz for Cat-5 cable (as it must support up to 100 Mbps). The EIA/TIA-568A specification defines the maximum amount of attenuation on the cable.
- **Near-end crosstalk**. A typical problem which causes near-end crosstalk is when the pairs have become untwisted (such as when they have been pulled too tightly or have been untwisted too far where they are terminated), and the cable tester measures the crosstalk. On detecting large amounts of near-end crosstalk, the wires should be visually inspected for any problems. A typical source of near-end crosstalk is split pairs. This is because the twisted-pairs do not carry opposite signals and thus the cancellation effect does not occur. The signal will thus interact with other pairs. Figure C2.22 shows an example of split pairs.

- **Crossed-pairs.** As illustrated in Figure C2.23.
- **External noise.** To detect external noise, all cables should be disconnected from the computer equipment and the noise level measured. If high levels are detected the source can be found by disconnecting each potential source, one by one, and then measuring the new level.

There are basically three main types of patch cable connection:

- **RJ-45 straight-through patch cable** (as shown on the left-hand side of Figure C2.24). This is the normal connection, where the cables connect directly from Pin 1 of the RJ-45 connector to Pin 1 of the other RJ-45 connector, and so on. In 10BASE-T only the orange and green pairs are used). The crossover between the transmit (TxData) and receive (RxData) occurs within the hub.
- **RJ-45 crossover patch cable** (as shown on the right-hand side of Figure C2.24). This is used when connecting between two workstations without the use of a hub or when connecting between hubs. It has a crossover between the orange (TxData) and the green (RxData).
- **RJ-11 connection.** An RJ-11 connector has six connectors, but only the middle four are used, and is typically used in telephone applications. In telephone applications, the colors which connect to these are BRGY (black-red-green-yellow) on one end, and YGRB on the other (the colors are reversed on one end of the cable). In networking applications the connections are: White/Orange (W/O), Blue (B), White/Blue (W/B) and Orange (O) and on the other side it is reversed. The blue pair make pair 1 and the orange pair make pair 2. White/Blue is a replacement for Green, Blue (/White) is a replacement for Red, White/Orange is a replacement for Black, and Orange (/White) is a replacement for Yellow.

The color codes for the RJ-45 connectors are defined in T-568A and T-568B standards (which are both part of the TIA/EIA-568A standard). A straight-through connection will work for either type (as Ethernet is color-blind), but the **T-568A** standard is recommended for new installations. The T-568A standard is an older standard (which was defined by AT&T and was previously known as 258A). Of course, a crossover cable can be made by wiring one end with T-568A and the other with T-568B.

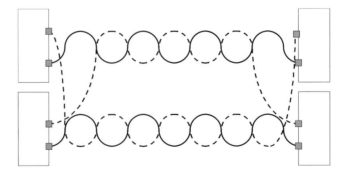

Figure C2.22 Split pairs

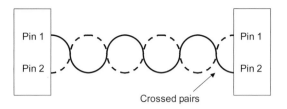

Figure C2.23 Crossed pairs

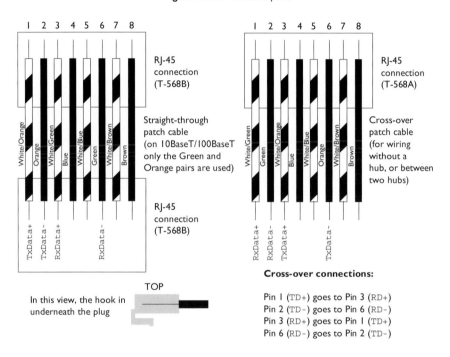

Figure C2.24 T-568A and T-568B connections

C2.7 Important networking definitions

Collision: The result of two nodes transmitting at the same time. This causes frames from each of the nodes to be damaged when they meet each other on the physical media.

Collision domain: On an Ethernet network, when two or more nodes try to transmit at the same time the data frame is damaged, and the nodes must back off from the network. The network area within which data packets originate and collide is called a collision domain.

Backoff: The retransmission delay enforced when a collision occurs.

Broadcasts: Data frames that are sent to all the nodes within a network segment, and is identified by a broadcast address.

Network architecture: Defines the rules that the network complies with, and the protocols that nodes use to intercommunicate.

C3   Ethernet

C3.1   Introduction

The two main winners in networking technologies are likely to be Ethernet and ATM. Ethernet will be a winner because of its **popularity, reliability, compatibility, simplicity, ease-of-use** and **upgradeability**. These six simple words can overcome any great technological advancement, as Microsoft and Intel have found, in operating systems and in processors, respectively. Ethernet successfully beat off networking technologies, such as Token Ring, but its major weakness is that it does not cope well when the required bandwidth approaches the maximum bandwidth. This is due to the contentious nature of Ethernet, where nodes must contend to get access to the network. ATM and FDDI looked to be the solution for large-scale backbone-based networks, but Ethernet has a final trump card to play. Every time it looks like losing the battle, it improves itself ten-fold.

Another problem with Ethernet is that it cannot guarantee bandwidth, and thus does not cope well with real-time traffic, such as video and audio. These disadvantages have generally been overcome by simply increasing the bandwidth each time there is an increased requirement. It has thus gone from 10 Mbps to 100 Mbps, and now to 1 Gbps. The other trump card that Ethernet has is its popularity. It is estimated that Ethernet accounts for more than 85% of all installed network connections, which is well over 120 million computers. The other main types are: Token Ring, Fiber Distributed Data Interface (FDDI) and Asynchronous Transfer Mode (ATM). To make a network, a network protocol must sit above the networking technology. The most popular of these protocols are TCP/IP (for most Internet-based traffic, and on UNIX networks), SPX/IPX (on Novell NetWare networks) and NetBEUI (on Microsoft networks).

Several factors have contributed to making Ethernet the most popular network technology, these include:

- **Simplicity.** Easy to plan and cheap to install. The introduction of network hubs and twisted-pair cables has made Ethernet networks easy to connect to. It also has cheap and well-supported network components, such as network interface cards (NICs) and connectors (BNC and RJ-45).
- **Reliability.** Well-proven technology, which is fairly robust and reliable.
- **Ease-of-use.** It is simple to add and remove computers to/from the network.
- **Upgradeability and compatibility.** Ethernet has evolved from 10 Mbps, to 100 Mbps (Fast Ethernet, in 1985) and now to 1 Gbps (Gigabit Ethernet, in 1998). All three Ethernet speeds use the same basic data frame format (IEEE 802.3), have full-duplex operation and have the same flow control methods.
- **Popularity.** Supported by most software and hardware systems.

Ethernet was initially developed by DEC, Intel and the Xerox Corporation and has since been standardized by the IEEE 802 committee (as IEEE 802.3)

A major problem with Ethernet is that, computers must contend to get access to the network; there is no guarantee that they will get access within a given time. This contention also causes problems when two computers try to communicate at the same time, they must both back off and no data can be transmitted. In its standard form Ethernet allows a bit rate of 10 Mbps, but new standards for fast Ethernet systems minimize the problems of contention and also increase the bit rate to 100 Mbps (and even 1 Gbps). Ethernet uses coaxial, fiber-optic or twisted-pair cable.

Ethernet uses a shared-media, bus-type network topology where all nodes share a common bus. These nodes must then contend for access to the network as only one node can communicate at a time. Data is then transmitted in frames which contain the MAC (media access control) source and destination addresses of the sending and receiving node, respectively. The local shared media is known as a segment, and each node on the network must monitor the segment and copy any frames addressed to it.

Ethernet uses carrier sense, multiple access with collision detection (CSMA/CD). On a CSMA/CD network, nodes monitor the bus (or Ether) to determine if it is busy. A node wishing to send data waits for an idle condition and then transmits its data frame. Unfortunately, collisions can occur when two nodes transmit at the same time, thus nodes must monitor the cable when they transmit. When a collision occurs, the nodes that caused the collision stop transmitting data frames and transmit a jamming signal. This informs all nodes on the network that a collision has occurred. Each of the nodes involved in the collision then wait a random period of time before attempting a re-transmission. As each node has a random delay time then there can be a prioritization of the nodes on the network.

Each node on the network must be able to detect collisions and be capable of transmitting and receiving simultaneously. These nodes either connect onto a common Ethernet connection or can connect to an Ethernet hub. Nodes thus contend for the network and are not guaranteed access to it, as illustrated in Figure C3.1. Collisions generally slow the network.

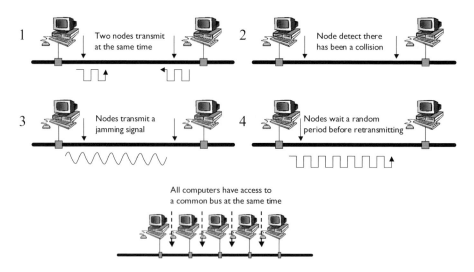

Figure C3.1 Connections to an Ethernet network

C3.2   IEEE standards

The IEEE is the main standards organization for LANs and it refers to the standard for Ethernet as CSMA/CD. Figure C3.2 shows how the IEEE standards for CSMA/CD fit into the OSI model. The two layers of the IEEE standards correspond to the physical and data link layers of the OSI model. On Ethernet networks, most hardware complies with IEEE 802.3 standard. The MAC layer allows many nodes to share a single communication channel. It also adds the start and end frame delimiters, error detection bits, access control information, and source and destination addresses. Each frame also has an error detection scheme known as cyclic redundancy check (CRC).

C3.2.1 Ethernet II

Most currently available systems implement either Ethernet II or IEEE 802.3 (although most networks are now defined as being IEEE 802.3 compliant). An Ethernet II frame is similar to the IEEE 802.3 frame; it consists of 8 bytes of preamble, 6 bytes of destination address, 6 bytes of source address, 2 bytes of frame type, between 46 and 1500 bytes of data, and 4 bytes of the frame check sequence field.

When the protocol is IPX/SPX the type field contains the bit pattern 1000 0001 0011 0111, but when the protocol is TCP/IP the type field contains 0000 1000 0000 0000.

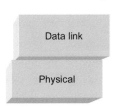

Figure C3.2
Standards for IEEE 802 LANs

C3.3 Ethernet – media access control (MAC) layer

When sending data the MAC layer takes the information from the LLC link layer. Figure C3.3 shows the IEEE 802.3 frame format. It contains 2 or 6 bytes for the source and destination addresses (16 or 48 bits each), 4 bytes for the CRC (32 bits) and 2 bytes for the LLC length (16 bits). The LLC part may be up to 1500 bytes long. The preamble and delay components define the start and end of the frame. The initial preamble and start delimiter are, in total, 8 bytes long and the delay component is a minimum of 96 bytes long.

A 7-byte preamble precedes the Ethernet 802.3 frame. Each byte of the preamble has a fixed binary pattern of 10101010 and each node on the network uses it to synchronize their clock and transmission timings. It also informs nodes that a frame is to be sent and for them to check the destination address in the frame.

At the end of the frame there is a 96-bit delay period, which provides the minimum delay between two frames. This slot time delay allows for the worst-case network propagation delay. The start delimiter field (SDF) is a single byte (or octet) of 10101011, and follows the preamble and identifies that there is a valid frame being transmitted. Most Ethernet systems use a 48-bit MAC address for the sending and receiving node. Each Ethernet node has a unique MAC address, which is normally defined as hexadecimal digits, such as:

> 4C - 31 - 22 - 10 - F1 - 32
> or   4C31 : 2210: F132.

A 48-bit address field allows 2^{48} different addresses (or approximately 281 474 976 710 000 different addresses). The LLC length field defines whether the frame contains information or it can be used to define the number of bytes in the logical link field. The logical link field can contain up to 1500 bytes of information and has a minimum of 46 bytes. If the information is greater than this upper limit then multiple frames are sent. In addition, if the field is less than the lower limit then it is padded with extra redundant bits.

The 32-bit frame check sequence (or FCS) is an error detection scheme. It is used to determine transmission errors and is often referred to as a cyclic redundancy check (CRC) or simply as a checksum.

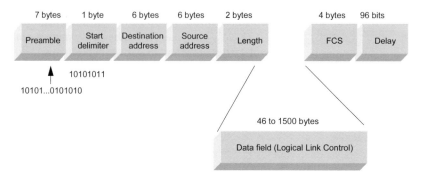

Figure C3.3   IEEE 802.3 frame format

If the transmission rate is 10 Mbps, the time for one bit to be transmitted will be:

$$T = \frac{1}{\text{bit rate}} = \frac{1}{10 \times 10^6} s = 100 \, \text{ns}$$

Thus the maximum and minimum times to transmit a frame will be:

$$T_{\text{max}} = (7+1+6+6+2+1500+4+12) \times 8 \times 100 \, \text{ns} = 1.2 \, \text{ms}$$
$$T_{\text{min}} = (7+1+6+6+2+46+4+12) \times 8 \times 100 \, \text{ns} = 67 \, \mu\text{s}$$

It may be assumed that an electrical signal propagates at about half the speed of light ($c = 3 \times 10^8 \, \text{m/s}$). Thus, the time for a bit to propagate a distance of 500 m is:

$$T_{500m} = \frac{\text{dist}}{\text{speed}} = \frac{500}{1.5 \times 10^8} = 3.33 \mu\text{s}$$

by which time, the number of bits transmitted will be:

$$\text{Number of bits transmitted} = \frac{T_{500m}}{T_{bit}} = \frac{3.33 \mu\text{s}}{100 \, \text{ns}} = 33.33$$

Thus, if two nodes are separated by 500 m then it will take more than 33 bits to be transmitted before a node can determine if there has been a collision on the line, as illustrated in Figure C3.4 (it will also take twice as long before a collision is detected by the transmitting node). If the propagation speed is less that this, it will take even longer. This shows the need for the preamble and the requirement for specifying a maximum segment length.

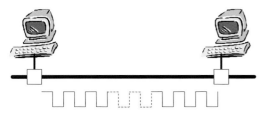

Figure C3.4
Bits transmitted before a collision is detected

For a distance of 500m, there are approximately 33.33 bits transmitted before the sender can sense a collision

C3.3.1   MAC address format

The MAC address is split into two parts. The first 24 bits identifies the manufacturer of the network card, and the second 24 bits identifies the serial number of the NIC. Example manufacturer codes are:

```
00000C  Cisco
00000E  Fujitsu
02608C  3Com
```

An example of an Ethernet card connected to a notebook (via the PCMCIA slot) is given next. It can be seen that the MAC address is 00-60-B3-68-B1-10, and the IP address is 192.168.0.12. In Microsoft Windows, the command used to determine these settings is IPCONFIG (or WINIPCFG can be used, as given in Figure C3.16). The definition of the default gateway is important as this allows the node to communicate with nodes outside the current network segment.

```
C> ipconfig /all
Description . . . . . . . . . . . : IEEE 802.11 Wireless LAN/PC Card(5V)
Physical Address. . . . . . . . . : 00-60-B3-68-B1-10
Dhcp Enabled. . . . . . . . . . . : No
IP Address. . . . . . . . . . . . : 192.168.0.12
Subnet Mask . . . . . . . . . . . : 255.255.255.0
Default Gateway . . . . . . . . . : 192.168.0.254
```

C3.4   IEEE 802.2 and Ethernet SNAP

The LLC is embedded in the Ethernet frame and is defined by the IEEE 802.2 standard. Figure C3.5 illustrates how the LLC fields are inserted into the IEEE 802.3 frame. The DSAP and SSAP fields define the types of network protocol used. A SAP code of 1110 0000 identifies the network operating system layer as NetWare, whereas 0000 0110 identifies the TCP/IP protocol. The IEEE issues these SAP numbers. The control field is, among other things, for the sequencing of frames.

In some cases, it was difficult to modify networks to be IEEE 802-compliant. Thus, an alternative method was to identify the network protocol, known as Ethernet SNAP (Subnetwork Access Protocol). This was defined to ease the transition to the IEEE 802.2 standard and is illustrated in Figure C3.6. It simply adds an extra two fields to the LLC field to define an organization ID and a network layer identifier. NetWare allows for either Ethernet SNAP or Ethernet 802.2 (as Novell used Ethernet SNAP to translate to Ethernet 802.2).

Non-compliant protocols are identified with the DSAP and SSAP code of 1010 1010, and a control code of 0000 0011. After these fields:

- Organization ID which indicates where the company that developed the embedded protocol belongs. If this field contains all zeros it indicates a non-company-specific generic Ethernet frame.
- EtherType field which defines the networking protocol. A TCP/IP protocol uses 0000 1000 0000 0000 for TCP/IP, while NetWare uses 1000 0001 0011 0111. NetWare frames adhering to this specification are known as NetWare 802.2 SNAP.

C3.4.1 LLC protocol

The 802.3 frame provides some of the data link layer functions, such as node addressing (source and destination MAC addresses), the addition of framing bits (the preamble) and error control (the FCS). The rest of the functions of the data link layer are performed with the control field of the LLC field; these functions are:

- **Flow and error control.** Each data frame sent has a frame number. A control frame is sent from the destination to a source node informing it that it has or has not received the frames correctly.
- **Sequencing of data.** Large amounts of data are sliced and sent with frame numbers. The spliced data is then reassembled at the destination node.

Figure C3.7 shows the basic format of the LLC frame. There are three principal types of frame: information, supervisory and unnumbered. An information frame contains data, a supervisory frame is used for acknowledgment and flow control, and an unnumbered frame is used for control purposes. The first two bits of the control field determine which type of frame it is. If they are 0X (where X is a don't care) then it is an information frame, 10 specifies a supervisory frame and 11 specifies an unnumbered frame.

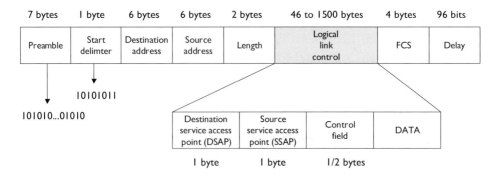

Figure C3.5 Ethernet IEEE 802.3 frame with LLC

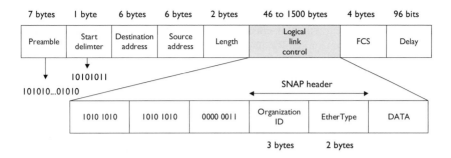

Figure C3.6 Ethernet IEEE 802.3 frame with LLC containing SNAP header

An information frame contains a send sequence number in the control field which ranges from 0 to 127. Each information frame has a consecutive number, N(S) (note that there is a roll-over from frame 127 to frame 0). The destination node acknowledges that it has received the frames by sending a supervisory frame. The 2-bit S-bit field specifies the function of the supervisory frame. This can either be set to Receiver Ready (RR), Receiver Not Ready (RNR) or Reject (REJ). If an RNR function is set then the destination node acknowledges that all frames up to the number stored in the receive sequence number N(R) field were received correctly. An RNR function also acknowledges the frames up to the number N(R), but informs the source node that the destination node wishes to stop communicating. The REJ function specifies that frame N(R) has been rejected and all other frames up to N(R) are acknowledged.

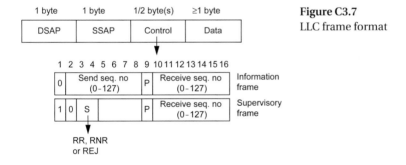

Figure C3.7

LLC frame format

C3.5 OSI and the IEEE 802.3 standard

Ethernet fits into the data link and the physical layer of the OSI model. These two layers only deal with the hardware of the network. The data link layer splits into two parts: the LLC and the MAC layer.

The IEEE 802.3 standard splits into three sub-layers:

- MAC (media access control).
- Physical signaling (PLS).
- Physical media attachment (PMA).

The interface between PLS and PMA is called the attachment unit interface (AUI) and the interface between PMA and the transmission media is called the media dependent interface (MDI). This grouping into modules allows Ethernet to be very flexible and to support a number of bit rates, signaling methods and media types. Figure C3.8 illustrates how the layers interconnect.

C3.5.1 Media access control (MAC)

CSMA/CD is implemented in the MAC layer. The functions of the MAC layer are:

- **When sending frames:** receive frames from LLC; control whether the data fills the LLC data field, if not add redundant bits; make the number of bytes an integer, and calculate the FCS; add the preamble, SFD and address fields to the frame; send the frame to the PLS in a serial bit stream.
- **When receiving frames:** receive one frame at a time from the PLS in a serial bit stream; check whether the destination address is the same as the local node; ensure the frame contains an integer number of bytes and the FCS is correct; remove the preamble, SFD, address fields, FCS and remove redundant bits from the LLC data field; send the data to the LLC.
- **Avoid collisions** when transmitting frames and keep the right distance between frames by not sending when another node is sending; when the medium is free, wait a specified period before starting to transmit.
- **Handle any collision** that appears by sending a jam signal; generate a random number and back off from sending during that random time.

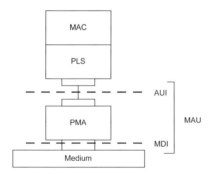

Figure C3.8
Organization of the IEEE 802.3 standard

C3.5.2 Physical signaling (PLS) and physical medium attachment (PMA)

PLS defines transmission rates, types of encoding/decoding and signaling methods. In PMA a further definition of the transmission media is accomplished, such as coaxial, fiber or twisted-pair. PMA and MDI together form the media attachment unit (MAU), often known as the transceiver.

C3.6   Novell NetWare and Ethernet

Ethernet is available in several different encapsulation (or frame types), which are supported by most networking components. Ethernet 1, as developed by Xerox, Intel, and Digital, was released in Ethernet in 1980. This was followed, two years later, by the Ethernet

II standard, which is the standard encapsulation type for TCP/IP. Around the same time, the Institute of Electrical and Electronic Engineers (IEEE) began work on an improved Ethernet frame. Unfortunately Novell required to release a networking system, and could not wait for the final standard, so in 1983, they released its frame specifications based on the incomplete work of the 802.3 committee. This frame type was named frame type 802.3 (Ethernet 802.3). In 1985, the IEEE released the final 802.3 specification, which included the logical link control (LLC) header. The LLC contains identify service access points, which make the IEEE's specification (now called 802.2) incompatible with Novell's 802.3. The encapsulations are typically known as:

- **Ethernet 802.3**. This is the raw Ethernet format, and is used with Novell NetWare Version 2 to Version 3.11.
- **Ethernet SAP/ Ethernet_802.2/ Novell Ethernet_802.2 or 802.3**. This type refers the IEEE 802.2 frame format (where SAP stands for service access points), and includes the 802.2 LLC header. This was supported by Novell NetWare 3.12 onwards.
- **Ethernet II/ ARPA/ Novell Ethernet_II or Ethernet Version II**. This type uses the standard Ethernet Version II header and is used with TCP/IP.
- **Ethernet SNAP/ snap or Novell Ethernet_SNAP**. This type extends the IEEE 802.2 header with a Subnetwork Access Protocol (SNAP) header. A SNAP encapsulation the type of encapsulation in the header, which defines the Layer 3/4 type, such as TCP/IP or AppleTalk.

C3.7   Ethernet transceivers

Ethernet requires a minimal amount of hardware. The cables used to connect it are typically either unshielded twisted-pair cable (UTP) or coaxial cables. These cables must be terminated with their characteristic impedance, which is $50\,\Omega$ for coaxial cables and $100\,\Omega$ for UTP cables.

Each node has transmission and reception hardware to control access to the cable and also to monitor network traffic. The transmission/reception hardware is called a transceiver (short for *trans*mitter/re*ceiver*) and a controller builds up and strips down the frame. For 10 Mbps Ethernet, the transceiver builds the transmitted bits at a rate of 10 Mbps – thus the time for one bit is $1/10 \times 10^6$, which is $0.1\,\mu s$ (100 ns).

The Ethernet transceiver transmits onto a single ether. When there are no nodes transmitting, the voltage on the line is $+0.7\,V$. This provides a carrier sense signal for all nodes on the network, it is also known as the heartbeat. If a node detects this voltage then it knows that the network is active and there are no nodes currently transmitting.

Thus, when a node wishes to transmit a message it listens for a quiet period. Then, if two or more transmitters transmit at the same time, a collision results. When they detect a collision, each node transmits a 'jam' signal. The nodes involved in the collision then wait for a random period of time (ranging from 10 to 90 ms) before attempting to transmit again. Each node on the network also awaits a retransmission. Thus, collisions are inefficient in networks as they stop nodes from transmitting. Transceivers normally detect collisions by monitoring the DC (or average) voltage on the line.

When transmitting, a transceiver unit transmits the preamble of consecutive 1s and 0s. The coding used is a Manchester coding, which represents a 0 as a high to a low voltage transition and a 1 as a low to high voltage transition. A low voltage is $-0.7\,V$ and a high is $+0.7\,V$. Thus, when the preamble is transmitted the voltage changes between $+0.7\,V$ and

−0.7 V; as illustrated in Figure C3.9. If, after the transmission of the preamble, no collisions are detected then the rest of the frame is sent.

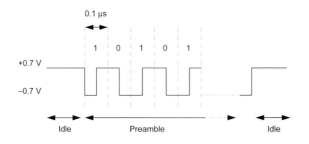

Figure C3.9 Ethernet digital signal

C3.8   Ethernet types

The six main types of standard Ethernet are:

- Standard, or thick-wire, Ethernet (**10BASE5**).
- Thinnet, or thin-wire Ethernet, or Cheapernet (**10BASE2**).
- Twisted-pair Ethernet (**10BASE-T**).
- Optical fiber Ethernet (**10BASE-FL**).
- Fast Ethernet (**100BASE-TX** and 100VG-Any LAN).
- Gigabit Ethernet (1000BASE-SX, **1000BASE-T**, 1000BASE-LX and 1000BASE-CX).
- 10 Mbps broadband Ethernet using broadband coaxial cable (**10Broad36**). This has a distance limit of 3600 meters per segment.

The thin- and thick-wire types connect directly to an Ethernet segment; these are shown in Figure C3.10 and Figure C3.11. Standard Ethernet, 10BASE5, uses a high specification cable (RG-50) and N-type plugs to connect the transceiver to the Ethernet segment. A node connects to the transceiver using a 9-pin D-type connector and a vampire (or bee-sting) connector can be used to clamp the transceiver to the backbone cable.

Thin-wire, or Cheapernet, uses a lower specification cable (it has a lower inner conductor diameter). The cable connector required is also of a lower specification, that is, BNC rather than N-type connectors. In standard Ethernet the transceiver unit is connected directly onto the backbone tap. On a Cheapernet network the transceiver is integrated into the node.

Most modern Ethernet connections are to a 10BASE-T hub, which connects UTP cables to the Ethernet segment. An RJ-45 connector is used for 10BASE-T. The fiber-optic type, 10BASE-FL, allows long lengths of interconnected lines, typically up to 2 km. They use either SMA connectors or ST connectors. SMA connectors are screw-on types while ST connectors are push-on. Table C3.1 shows the basic specifications for the different types.

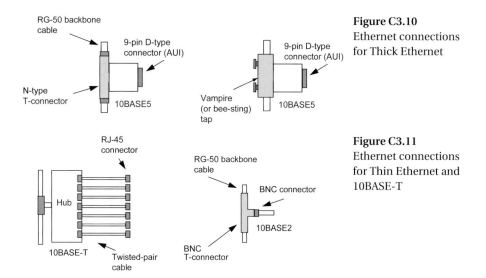

Figure C3.10
Ethernet connections for Thick Ethernet

Figure C3.11
Ethernet connections for Thin Ethernet and 10BASE-T

Table C3.1   Comparison of different Ethernet types

Parameter	10BASE5	10BASE2	10BASE-T
Common name	Standard or thick-wire	Thinnet or thin-wire	Twisted-pair
Data rate	10 Mbps	10 Mbps	10 Mbps
Maximum segment length	500 m	200 m	100 m
Maximum nodes on a segment	100	30	30
Maximum number of repeaters/nodes	2/1024	4/1024	4
Minimum node spacing	2.5 m	0.5 m	No limit
Location of transceiver electronics	Cable connection	In the node	In the node
Typical cable type	RG-50 (0.5 in diameter)	RG-6 (0.25 in diameter)	UTP cables
Connectors	N-type	BNC	RJ-45/Telco
Cable impedance	50 Ω	50 Ω	100 Ω

C3.9   Twisted-pair hubs

Twisted-pair Ethernet (10BASE-T) nodes normally connect to the backbone using a hub, as illustrated in Figure C3.12. Connection to the twisted-pair cable is via an RJ-45 connector. The connection to the backbone can either be to thin- or thick-Ethernet. Hubs are also stackable, with one hub connected to another. This leads to concentrated area networks (CANs) and can be used to reduce the amount of traffic on the backbone. Twisted-pair hubs normally improve network performance.

10BASE-T uses two twisted-pair cables, one for transmit and one for receive. A collision occurs when the node (or hub) detects that it is receiving data when it is currently transmitting data.

C3.10   100Mbps Ethernet

Standard 10 Mbps Ethernet does not perform well when many users are running multimedia applications. Two improvements to the standard are Fast Ethernet and 100VG-AnyLAN. The IEEE has defined standards for both of them, IEEE 802.3u for Fast Ethernet and 802.12 for 100VG-AnyLAN. They are supported by many manufacturers and use bit rates of 100 Mbps, which gives at least 10 times the performance of standard Ethernet.

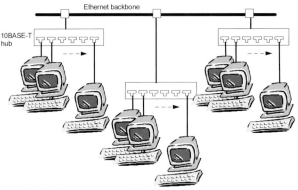

Figure C3.12
10BASE-T connection

Standards relating to 100 Mbps Ethernet are:

- 100BASE-TX (twisted-pair) – which uses 100 Mbps over two pairs of Cat-5 UTP cable or two pairs of Type 1 STP cable. 100BASE-TX has become the most popular in 100BASE-T Physical layers and was based on the FDDI/CDDI Physical layer using a coding technique known as 4B/5B.
- 100BASE-T4 (twisted-pair) – which is the physical layer standard for 100 Mbps over Cat-3, Cat-4 or Cat-5 UTP, and uses four pairs of UTP cable.
- 100VG-AnyLAN (twisted-pair) – which uses 100 Mbps over two pairs of Cat-5 UTP cable or two pairs of Type 1 STP cable.
- 100BASE-FX (fiber-optic cable) – which is the physical layer standard for 100 Mbps over fiber-optic cables.
- 100BASE-T2 (802.3y) physical standard came which uses only 2 pairs of Category 3 cable.

The following table gives a summary of the different 100BASE-T Physical layers and the 10BASE-T Physical layer.

Physical Parameter	10BASE-T	100BASE-TX	100BASE-T4	100BASE-T2
IEEE Standard	802.3i – 1990	802.3u – 1995	802.3u – 1995	802.3y - 1996
Encoding	Manchester	4B/5B	8B/6T	PAM 5x5
Cabling required	UTP Cat 3/4/5	UTP Cat 5	UTP Cat 3/4/5	UTP Cat 3/4/5
Number of pairs	2	2	4	2
Number of transmit pairs	1	1	3	2
Signal Frequency	20 MHz	125 MHz	25 MHz	25 MHz
Full-duplex	Yes	Yes	No	Yes

C3.10.1 100BASE-TX

Fast Ethernet, or 100BASE-TX, is simply 10BASE-T running at 10 times the bit rate. It is a natural progression from standard Ethernet and thus allows existing Ethernet networks to be easily upgraded. Unfortunately, as with standard Ethernet, nodes contend for the network, reducing the network efficiency when there are high traffic rates. Also, as it uses collision detect, the maximum segment length is limited by the amount of time for the farthest nodes on a network to properly detect collisions. On a Fast Ethernet network with twisted-pair copper cables this distance is 100 m, and for a fiber-optic link, it is 400 m. Table C3.2 outlines the main network parameters for Fast Ethernet.

Since 100BASE-TX standards are compatible with 10BASE-TX networks then the network allows both 10 Mbps and 100 Mbps bit rates on the line. This makes upgrading simple, as the only additions to the network are dual-speed interface adapters. Nodes with the 100 Mbps capabilities can communicate at 100 Mbps, but they can also communicate with slower nodes, at 10 Mbps (initially a 10/100 Mbps NIC negotiates with the hub on the communicate speed).

The basic rules of a 100BASE-TX network are:

* The network topology is a star network and there must be no loops. The internals of the bus still connect the network as a bus network, but the hub can be seen as the central point of a star network, as when it becomes inoperative then the connected devices on the hub will not be able to communicate. This is illustrated in Figure C3.13.
* Cat-5 cable is used.
* Up to two hubs can be cascaded in a network.
* Each hub is the equivalent of 5 meters in latency.
* Segment length is limited to 100 meters.
* Network diameter must not exceed 200 meters. This is illustrated in Figure C2.19.

Table C3.2   Fast Ethernet network parameters

	100BASE-TX	100VG-AnyLAN
Standard	IEEE 802.3	IEEE 802.12
Bit rate	100 Mbps	100 Mbps
Actual throughput	Up to 50 Mbps	Up to 96 Mbps
Maximum distance (hub to node)	100 m (twisted-pair, CAT-5) 400 m (fiber)	100 m (twisted-pair, CAT-3) 200 m (twisted-pair, CAT-5) 2 km (fiber)
Scaleability	None	Up to 400 Mbps
Advantages	Easy migration from 10BASE-T	Greater throughput, greater distance

Line code

100BASE-TX uses two pairs of UTP cable with a maximum length of 100m as defined by the TIA/EIA-568A wiring Standard. One pair receives and the other one transmits. The electrical signaling frequency for 10BASE-T is 20MHz allowing transmission over Cat 3 cable. But, 100BASE-TX on the other hand requires a much better quality cable due to its higher frequency. It uses a 4B/5B conversion, followed by a stream scrambler and MLT-3 encoding (multi-line transmission). 4B/5B block coding makes sure that all symbols corresponding to numerical data include at least two changes of state, and never more than three bits with the same value are transmitted successively. Converting four bits for transmission to five has as an effect that the signal's frequency is increased by 25%. However, a Category 5 cable has a bandwidth of 100MHz. For that reason, the data is then scrambled so that the signal energy is spread across the whole spectrum and then an encoding scheme is used, called Multi-level Threshold 3 (MLT-3). MLT uses three physical levels to reduce the main signal frequency to 31.25 MHz (one fourth of the original one).

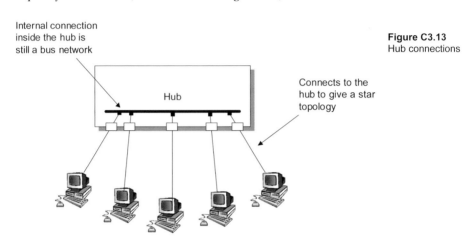

Internal connection
inside the hub is
still a bus network

Hub

Connects to the
hub to give a star
topology

Figure C3.13
Hub connections

MLT-3 uses three different voltage levels : –1, 0, +1. The level stays the same for consecutive logical ones or zeros. A change in a bit means a change in the voltage level. The change occurs in a circular, pattern 0V, +1, 0, –1, 0, +1. This circular, sinusoidal pattern change means that MLT-3 encoded data sine wave of a much lower frequency that the original, making it ideally suited for high-speed data transmission over UTP. MLT-3 has a bandwidth efficiency of two thirds, meaning that the transmitted signal requires a bandwidth of only a quarter of the original transmission rate.

C3.10.2 100BASE-T4

100BASE-T4 allows the use of standard Cat-3 cables, with eight wires made up of four twisted-pairs. 100BASE-T4 uses all of the pairs to transmit at 100 Mbps. This differs from 10BASE-T in that 10BASE-T uses only two pairs, one to transmit and one to receive. 100BASE-T allows compatibility with 10BASE-T in that the first two pairs (Pair 1 and Pair 2) are used in the same way as 10BASE-T connections. 100BASE-T4 then uses the other two pairs (Pair 3 and Pair 4) with half-duplex links between the hub and the node. The connections are illustrated in Figure C3.14.

Line code

100BASE-4T uses four separate Cat-3 twisted-pair wires. The maximum clock rate that can be applied to Cat-3 cable is 30 Mbps. Thus, some mechanism must be devised which reduces the line bit rate to under 30 Mbps but gives a symbol rate of 100 Mbps. This is achieved with a three-level code (+, – and 0) and is known as 8B6T. This code converts eight binary digits into six ternary symbols.

The first six codes are:

Data byte	Code	Data byte	Code	Data byte	Code
00000000	−+0 0−+	00000001	0−+ −+0	00000010	0−+ 0−+
00000011	0−+ +0−	00000100	−+0 +0−	00001001	+0− −+0

Thus, the bit sequence 00000000 will be coded as a negative voltage, a positive voltage, a zero voltage, a zero voltage, a negative voltage and a positive voltage.

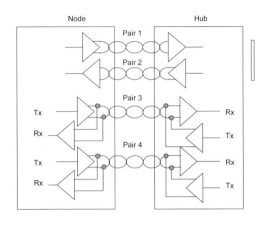

Figure C3.14 100BASE-T4 connections

The maximum base frequency for a 100 Mbps signal will be produced when the input bit stream is 010101010...01010. As each bit lasts 10 ns then the period between consecutive levels is 20 ns. Thus, the minimum frequency contained will be 50 MHz. This is greater than the bandwidth of Cat-3 cable, so it would not pass through the cable.

Apart from reducing the frequencies with the digital signal, the 8B6T code has the advantage of reducing the DC content of the signal. Most of the codes contain the same number of positive and negative voltages. This is because only 256 of the possible 729 (3^6) codes are actually used. The codes are also chosen to have at least two transitions in every code word, thus the clock information is embedded into the signal.

Unfortunately, it is not possible to have all codes with the same number of negative voltages as positive voltages. Thus, there are some codes that have a different number of negatives and positives, these include:

0100 0001   + 0 − 0 0 +
0111 1001   + + + − 0 −

Most transceiver circuits use a transformer to isolate the external equipment from the computer equipment. These transformers do not allow the passage of DC current. Thus if the line code has a sequence which consecutively has more positives than negatives, the DC current will move away from its zero value. As this does not pass across the transformer, the receive bit stream on the output of the transformer can reduce the amplitude of the received signal (and may thus cause errors). This phenomenon is known as DC wander. A code that has one more positive level than the negative levels is defined as having a weighing of +1.

The technique used to overcome this is to invert consecutive codes that have a weighing of +1. For example, suppose the line code were

Ethernet 369

$$+0++-- \qquad ++0+-- \qquad +++--0 \qquad +++--0$$

it would actually be coded as

$$+0++-- \qquad --0-++ \qquad +++--0 \qquad ---++0$$

The receiver detects the –1 weighted codes as an inverted pattern.

C3.10.3 100VG-AnyLAN

The 100VG-AnyLAN standard (IEEE 802.12) was developed mainly by Hewlett Packard and overcomes the contention problem by using a priority-based round-robin arbitration method, known as the demand priority access method (DPAM). Unlike Ethernet, nodes always connect to a hub, which regularly scans its input ports to determine whether any nodes have requests pending. It has the great advantage that it supports both IEEE 802.3 (Ethernet) and IEEE 802.5 (Token Ring) frames and can thus integrate well with existing 10BaseT and Token Ring networks (allowing for gradual migration).

100VG-AnyLAN also has an in-built priority mechanism with two priority levels: a high-priority request and a normal-priority request. A normal-priority request is used for non-real-time data, such as data files, and so on. High-priority requests are used for real-time data, such as speech or video data. At present, there is limited usage of this feature and there is no support mechanism for this facility after the data has left the hub.

100VG-AnyLAN allows up to seven levels of hubs (i.e. one root and six cascaded hubs) with a maximum distance of 150 m between nodes. Unlike other forms of Ethernet, it allows any number of nodes to be connected to a segment (it is only limited to the speed of the hub).

Connections

100BASE-TX, 100BASE-T4 and 100VG-AnyLAN use the RJ-45 connector, which has eight connections. 100BASE-TX uses pairs 2 and 3, whereas 100BASE-T4 and 100VG-AnyLAN use pairs 1, 2, 3 and 4. The connections for the cables are defined in Table C3.3. The white/orange color identifies the cable which is white with an orange stripe, whereas orange/white identifies an orange cable with a white stripe.

Table C3.3 Cable connections for 100BASE-TX

Pin	Cable color	Cable color	Pair
1	white/orange	white/orange	Pair 4
2	orange/white	orange/white	Pair 4
3	white/green	white/green	Pair 3
4	blue/white	blue/white	Pair 3
5	white/blue	white/blue	Pair 1
6	green/white	green/white	Pair 1
7	white/brown	white/brown	Pair 2
8	brown/white	brown/white	Pair 2

C3.10.4 Migration to Fast Ethernet

If an existing network is based on standard Ethernet then, in most cases, the best network upgrade is either to Fast Ethernet or 100VG-AnyLAN. Since the protocols and access methods are the same, there is no need to change any of the network management software or application programs. The upgrade path for Fast Ethernet is simple and could be:

- Upgrade high data rate nodes, such as servers or high-powered workstations to Fast Ethernet.
- Gradually upgrade NICs (network interface cards) on Ethernet segments to cards which support both 10BASE-T and 100BASE-T. These cards automatically detect the transmission rate to give either 10 or 100 Mbps.

The upgrade path to 100VG-AnyLAN is less easy as it relies on hubs and, unlike Fast Ethernet, most NICs have different network connectors, one for 10BASE-T and the other for 100VG-AnyLAN (although it is likely that more NICs will have automatic detection). A possible path could be:

- Upgrade high data rate nodes, such as servers or high-powered workstations to 100VG-AnyLAN.
- Install 100VG-AnyLAN hubs.
- Connect nodes to 100VG-AnyLAN hubs and change over connectors.

It is difficult to assess the performance differences between Fast Ethernet and 100VG-AnyLAN. Fast Ethernet uses a well-proven technology, but suffers from network contention. 100VG-AnyLAN is a relatively new technology and the handshaking with the hub increases delay time. The maximum data throughput of a 100BASE-TX network is limited to around 50 Mbps, whereas 100VG-AnyLAN allows rates up to 96 Mbps. 100VG-AnyLAN allows possible upgrades to 400 Mbps.

C3.11   Gigabit Ethernet

The IEEE 802.3 working group initiated the 802.3z Gigabit Ethernet task force to create the Gigabit Ethernet standard (which was finally defined in 1998). The Gigabit Ethernet Alliance (GEA) was founded in May 1996 and promotes Gigabit Ethernet collaboration between organizations. Companies, which were initially involved in the GEA, include: 3Com, Bay Networks, Cisco Systems, Compaq, Intel, LSI Logic, Sun and VLSI.

With Gigabit Ethernet, the amount of available bandwidth for a single segment is massive. For example, almost 125 million characters (125 MB) can be sent in a single second. A large reference book with over 1000 pages could be send over a network segment, ten times in a single second. Compare it also with a ×24, CD-ROM drive which transmits at a maximum rate of 3.6 MB/s (24×150 kB/sec). Gigabit Ethernet operates almost 35 times faster than this drive. With network switches, this bandwidth can be multiplied by a given factor, as they allow multiple simultaneous connections.

Gigabit Ethernet is an excellent challenger for network backbones as it interconnects 10/100BASE-T switches, and also provides a high-bandwidth to high-performance servers. Initial aims were:

- Half/full-duplex operation at 1000 Mbps.
- Standard 802.3 Ethernet frame format. Gigabit Ethernet uses the same variable-length frame (64- to 1514-byte packets), and thus allows for easy upgrades.
- Standard CSMA/CD access method.
- Compatibility with existing 10BASE-T and 100BASE-T technologies.
- Development of an optional Gigabit Media Independent Interface (GMII).

The compatibility with existing 10/100BASE standards makes the upgrading to Gigabit Ethernet much easier, and considerably less risky than changing to other networking types, such as FDDI and ATM. It will happily interconnect with, and autosense, existing slower rated Ethernet devices. Figure C3.15 illustrates the functional elements of Gigabit Ethernet. Its main characteristics are:

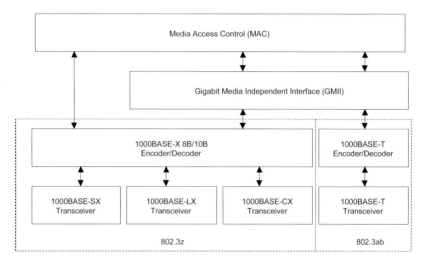

Figure C3.15   Gigabit Ethernet functional elements

- **Full-duplex communication.** As defined by the IEEE 802.3x specification, two nodes connected via a full-duplex, switched path can simultaneously send and receive frames (thus doubling the bandwidth). Gigabit Ethernet supports new full-duplex operating modes for switch-to-switch and switch-to-end-station connections, and half-duplex operating modes for shared connections using repeaters and the CSMA/CD access method.

- **Standard flow control.** Gigabit Ethernet uses standard Ethernet flow control to avoid congestion and overloading. When operating in half-duplex mode, Gigabit Ethernet adopts the same fundamental CSMA/CD access method to resolve contention for the shared media.

- **Enhanced CSMA/CD method.** This maintains a 200 m-collision diameter at gigabit speeds. Without this, small Ethernet packets could complete their transmission before the transmitting node could sense a collision, thereby violating the CSMA/CD method. To resolve this issue, both the minimum CSMA/CD carrier time and the Ethernet slot time (the time, measured in bits, required for a node to detect a collision) have been extended from 64 bytes (which is 51.2 μs for 10BASE and 5.12 μs for 100BASE) to 512 bytes (which is 4.1 μs for 1000BASE). The minimum frame length is still 64 bytes. Thus, frames smaller than 512 bytes have a new carrier extension field following the CRC field. Packets larger than 512 bytes are not extended.

- **Packet bursting.** The slot time changes affect the small-packet performance, but this has been offset by a new enhancement to the CSMA/CD algorithm, called packet bursting. This allows servers, switches and other devices to send bursts of small packets in order to fully utilize the bandwidth.

Devices operating in full-duplex mode (such as switches and buffered distributors) are not subject to the carrier extension, slot time extension or packet bursting changes. Full-duplex devices use the regular Ethernet 96-bit interframe gap (IFG) and 64-byte minimum frame size.

C3.11.1 Ethernet transceiver

The IEEE 802.3z task force spent much of their time defining the Gigabit Ethernet standard for the transceiver (physical layer), which is responsible for the mechanical, electrical and procedural characteristics for establishing, maintaining and deactivating the physical link between network devices. The physical layers are:

- **1000BASE-SX** (Low cost, multi-mode fiber cables). These can be used for short inter-connections and short backbone networks. The IEEE 802.3z task force has tried to integrate the new standard with existing cabling, whether it is twisted-pair cable, coaxial cable or fiber-optic cable. These tests involved firing lasers in long lengths of multi-mode fiber cables. From these tests it was found that a jitter component results which is caused by a phenomenon known as differential mode delay (DMD). The 1000BASE-SX standard has resolved this by carefully defining the shape of the laser signal, and enhanced conformance tests. Typical maximum lengths are: 62.5 μm, multi-mode fiber (up to 220 m) and 50 μm, multi-mode fiber (550 m).
- **1000BASE-LX** (Multi-mode/single mode-mode fiber cables). These can be used for longer runs, such as on backbones and campus networks. Single-mode fibers are covered by the long-wavelength standard, and provide for greater distances. External patch cords are used to reduce DMD. Typical lengths are: 62.5 μm, multi-mode fiber (up to 550 m), 50 μm, multi-mode fiber (up to 550 m) and 50 μm, single-mode fiber (up to 5 km).
- **1000BASE-CX** (Shielded Balanced Copper). This standard supports interconnection of equipment using a copper-based cable, typically up to 25 m. As with the 1000BASE-LX/SX standards, it uses the Fiber Channel-based 8B/10B coding to give a serial line rate of 1.25 Gbps. The 1000BASE-T is likely to supersede this standard, but it has been relatively easy to define, and to implement.
- **1000BASE-T** (UTP). This is a useful standard for connecting directly to workstations. The 802.3ab Task Force has been assigned the task of defining the 1000BASE-T physical layer standard for Gigabit Ethernet over four pairs of Cat-5 UTP cable, for cable distances of up to 100 m, or networks with a diameter of 200 m. As it can be used with existing cabling, and allows easy upgrades. Unfortunately, it requires new technology and new coding schemes in order to meet the potentially difficult and demanding parameters set by the previous Ethernet and Fast Ethernet standards.

C3.11.2 Fiber Channel components

The IEEE 802.3 committee based much of the physical layer technology on the ANSI-backed X3.230 Fiber Channel project. This allowed many manufacturers to re-use physical-layer Fiber Channel components for new Gigabit Ethernet designs, and has allowed a faster development time than is normal, and increased the volume production of the components. These include optical components and high-speed 8B/10B encoders.

The 1000BASE-T standard uses enhanced DSP (Digital Signal Processing) and enhanced silicon technology to enable Gigabit Ethernet over UTP cabling. As Figure C3.15 shows, it does not use the 8B/10B encoding.

C3.11.3 Buffered distributors

Along with repeaters, bridges and switches, a new device called a buffered distributor (or full-duplex repeater) has been developed for Gigabit Ethernet. It is a full-duplex, multiport, hub-like device that connects two or more Gigabit Ethernet segments. Unlike a bridge, and like a repeater, it forwards all the Ethernet frames from one segment to the others, but unlike a standard repeater, a buffered distributor buffers one, or more, incoming frames on each link before forwarding them. This reduces collisions on connected segments. The maximum bandwidth for a buffered distributor will still only be 1 Gbps, as opposed to Gigabit switches which allow multi-Gigabit bandwidths (but it reduces the number of collisions on a segment, as it buffers frames and waits until the segment is clear).

C3.11.4 Quality of Service

Many, real-time, networked applications require a given Quality of Server (QoS), which might relate to bandwidth requirements, latency (network delays) and/or jitter. Unfortunately, there is nothing built into Ethernet that allows for a QoS, thus new techniques have been developed to overcome this. These include:

- **RSVP.** Allows nodes to request and guarantee a QoS, and works at a higher-level to Ethernet. For this, each network component in the chain must support RSVP and communicate appropriately. Unfortunately, this may require an extensive investment to totally support RSVP, thus many vendors have responded in implementing proprietary schemes, which may make parts of the network vendor-specific.
- **IEEE 802.1p and IEEE 802.1Q.** Allow a QoS over Ethernet by 'tagging' packets with an indication of the priority or class of service desired for the frames. These tags allow applications to communicate the priority of frames to internetworking devices. RSVP support can be achieved by mapping RSVP sessions into 802.1p service classes.
- **Routing.** Implemented at a higher layer.

C3.11.5 Gigabit Ethernet migration

The greatest advantage of Gigabit Ethernet is that it is easy to upgrade existing Ethernet-based networks to higher bit rates. A typical migration might be:

- Switch-to-switch links. Involves upgrading the connections between switches to 1 Gbps. As 1000BASE switches support both 100BASE and 1000BASE then not all the switches require to be upgraded at the same time; this allows for gradual migration.
- Switch-to-Server links. Involves upgrading the connection between a switch and the server to 1 Gbps. The server requires an upgraded Gigabit Ethernet interface card.
- Switched Fast Ethernet Backbone. Involves upgrading a Fast Ethernet backbone switch to a 100/1000BASE switch. It thus supports 100BASE and 1000BASE switching, using existing cabling.
- Shared FDDI Backbone. Involves replacing FDDI attachments on the ring with Gigabit Ethernet switches or repeaters. Gigabit Ethernet uses the existing fiber-optic cable, and provides a greatly increased segment bandwidth.
- Upgrade NICs on nodes to 1 Gbps. It is unlikely that users will require 1 Gbps connections, but this facility is possible.

C3.11.6 1000BASE-T

One of the greatest challenges of Gigabit Ethernet is to use existing Cat-5 cables, as this will allow fast upgrades. Two critical parameters, which are negligible at 10BASE speeds, are:

- Return loss. Defines the amount of signal energy that is reflected back towards the transmitter due to impedance mismatches in the link (typically from connector and cable bends).
- Far-End Crosstalk. Noise that is leaked from another cable pair. The higher the bit rate, the more crosstalk that is generated.

The 1000BASE-T Task Force estimates that less than 10% of the existing Cat-5 cables were improperly installed (as defined in ANSI/TIA/EIA568-A in 1995) and might not support 1000BASE-T (or even, 100BASE-TX). 100BASE-T uses two pairs, one for transmit and one for receive, and transmits at a symbol rate of 125Mbaud with a 3-level code. 1000BASE-T uses:

- All four pairs with a symbol rate of 125 MBaud (symbols/sec). One symbol contains two bits of information.
- Each transmitted pulse uses a 5-level PAM (Pulse Amplitude Modulation) line code, which allows two bits to be transmitted at a time.
- Simultaneous send and receive on each pair. Each connection uses a hybrid circuit to split the send and receive signals.
- Pulse shaping. Matches the characteristics of the transmitted signal to the channel so that the signal-to-noise ratio is minimized. It effectively reduces low frequency terms (which contain little data information, can cause distortion and cannot be passed over the transformer-coupled hybrid circuit), reduces high frequency terms (which increase crosstalk) and rejects any external high-frequency noise. It is thought that the transmitted signal spectrum for 1000BASE will be similar to 100BASE.
- Forward Error Correction (FEC). This provides a second level of coding that helps to recover the transmitted symbols in the presence of high noise and crosstalk. The FEC bit uses the fifth level of the 5-level PAM.

A 5-level code (−2, −1, 0, +1, +2) allows two bits to be sent at a time, if all four pairs are used then eight bits are sent at a time. If each pair transmits at a rate of 125 Mbaud (symbols/sec, giving 250 Mbps), the resulting bit rate will be 1 Gbps.

C3.12 Bridges

Bridges are an excellent method of reducing traffic on network segments. A particular problem is when there is too much traffic on a network segment, as this can result in a great deal of collisions, and resultant back off periods. The distance in which a collision can travel is called the collision domain. Collisions do not travel across a bridge and they thus reduce the impact of a collision on other network segments. Hubs, on the other hand, operate at the physical level and transmit the data to all the connected ports.

A bridge operates at the data link layer and uses the MAC address to forward data frames from one network segment to another. For this maintains a table which maps the MAC addresses of all the nodes on the network that it connects to. Ethernet networks normally use transparent bridges which automatically build up an address table from the nodes that connect to each of their ports, as illustrated in Figure C3.16. Token ring networks typically use source route bridges, where the entire route to a destination is predetermined, in real time, before sending of data to the destination.

A bridge determines if it should forward a data frame onto a network by examining the destination MAC address in the data frame. If the destination MAC address is not on the segment that originated the data frame, then the bridge forwards it to all the other connected segments. Thus, a bridge does not actually determine on which segment the destination is on, and blindly forwards data frames onto all other connected segments.

The two major problems with bridges are:

- They work well when there is not too much intersegment traffic, but when the intersegment traffic becomes too heavy the bridge can actually become a bottleneck for traffic, and actually slow down communications.
- They spread and multiply broadcasts. A bridge forwards all broadcasts (which is identified with the FF-FF-FF-FF-FF-FF MAC address) to all other connected segments. If there are too many broadcasts, it can result in a broadcast storm, where broadcasts swamp transmitted data. The best way to overcome these storms is to use routers which do not forward broadcasts.

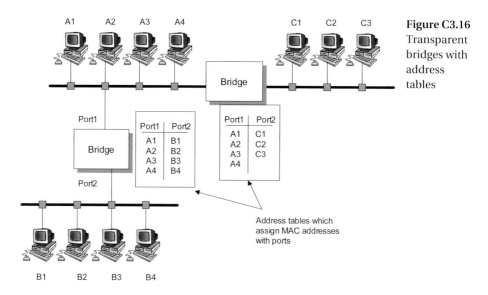

Figure C3.16 Transparent bridges with address tables

C3.13 ARP

In order for data to be received by a node, the station address (typically the MAC address) and the network address (typically the IP address) must match. Thus, how does a computer know the MAC address of the computer that it wants to communicate with? This is achieved with ARP (Address Resolution Protocol) which translates IP addresses to Ethernet addresses, and is used when IP packets are sent from a computer, and the Ethernet address is added to the Ethernet frame. A table look-up, called the ARP table, is used to translate the addresses. One column has the IP address and the other has the Ethernet address. The following insert is an example ARP table.

The sequence of determining the Ethernet address is as follows:

1. An ARP request packet with a broadcast Ethernet address (FF-FF-FF-FF-FF-FF) is sent out on the network segment to every computer on the segment.
2. All the computers on the network segment read the broadcast Ethernet frame, and examine the Type field to determine if it is an ARP packet. If it is, then it is passed to the ARP module.
3. If the IP address of a receiving station matches the IP address in the IP data packet then it sends a response directly to the source Ethernet address.
4. The originator then receives the Ethernet frame and checks the Type field to determine if it is an ARP packet. If it is, then it adds the sender's IP address and Ethernet address to its ARP table. The IP packet can now be sent with the correct Ethernet address.

Each computer has a separate ARP table for each of its Ethernet interfaces, which is stored in the local memory (cache memory). The table is thus not static and is updated as the network changes. Figure C3.17 shows an example of an ARP request and an ARP reply. In this case the node with the IP address of 146.176.151.100 wants to communicate with a node with an IP address of 146.176.151.130, but does not know its MAC address. To determine it, it sends out an ARP request which is broadcast to all the nodes on the segment. All the nodes read the ARP request, and examine the destination IP address in the IP header. When the node whose IP address matches the destination IP address read the data frame, it sends back a data frame with its own IP address in the source IP address field and its MAC address in the data frame source MAC address. The destination addresses will be the same as the source address of the initial ARP request. Once the node that sent the request receives the reply it will update its local ARP table so that it can use the correct MAC address for the address node. Storing the ARP table thus reduces network traffic, as nodes only require to communicate with a destination node once in order to determine its MAC address. If this was not stored then each time a node wished to communicate with another node on the segment it would have to send an ARP request. All the nodes on the network listen to the ARP request and reply, even if they are not involved in passing their MAC address. When they hear the ARP reply they can all update their ARP tables.

ARP tables only remain current for a given amount of time, and must be updated in order to remain current. This is important as nodes can be added and deleted from the network. The process of deleting an ARP entry from the table is known as *ageing out*. With this, after a certain time period, nodes delete ARP entries.

C3.13.1 Routers and ARP

It has been shown how ARP allows a node to determine the MAC address of a node on the same network segment, but what happens when the destination is on a different network segment. This is done through routers, and shows the reason why a computer must know the IP address of the gateway node (normally a router).

Each router has a port (or interface) that connects to each of the network segments that it connects to. Each of these ports has an IP address, and each of them build-up ARP tables for each of its ports. The overall table maps IP addresses, MAC addresses and ports. For example:

Protocol	Address	MAC address	Port
IP	146.176.151.100	65-F1-21-10-05-01	Port_1
IP	146.176.151.100	23-EA-21-B8-F5-71	Port_1
IP	146.176.153.100	4F-DD-21-EE-05-22	Port_2
IP	146.176.153.100	21-F2-21-32-11-00	Port_2

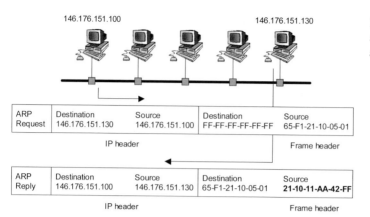

Figure C3.17 Example ARP request and reply

ARP Request	Destination 146.176.151.130	Source 146.176.151.100	Destination FF-FF-FF-FF-FF-FF	Source 65-F1-21-10-05-01
		IP header		Frame header

ARP Reply	Destination 146.176.151.100	Source 146.176.151.130	Destination 65-F1-21-10-05-01	Source **21-10-11-AA-42-FF**
		IP header		Frame header

In addition to IP addresses and MAC addresses of devices located on networks it is connected to, a router also possesses IP addresses and MAC addresses of other routers. It uses these addresses to direct data towards its final destination. If a router receives a data packet whose destination addresses are not in its routing table, it forwards the packet to the addresses of other routers which presumably do contain information about the destination host in their routing tables.

A node on a network cannot send an ARP request to a device on another network, as ARP requests are sent in broadcast mode and these are not forwarded by routers to other networks. If the node is on another network and it does not know its MAC address, it must seek out the services of a router. In this case, the router is known as the default gateway, and the source node transmits a data frame with the MAC address of the router (the default gateway) and the IP address of the destination device (and not of the router). When the router reads the data frame it examines the destination IP address to determine if it requires to forward the data packet. For this, it uses its routing tables. If it knows that the destination node is connected to one of its network segments it constructs a data frame and data packet with the required destination IP address and MAC address, and sends it onto the required network segment.

If the router does not detect that the destination node is not on one of its connected segments, it locates the MAC address of another router that is likely to know where it may be located and forwards the data to that router. This type of routing is known as indirect routing.

So what happens if the router does not know the MAC address of the addressed router (as ARP requests are confined to the one network segment)? For this, the router sends out an ARP request on the local network segment. Another router, which is connected to the local network segment, then sends back an ARP reply which will contain the MAC address to the destination router.

Figure C3.18 shows an example of communication between two nodes on different network segments. In this case Node_A is communicating with Node_B. The sequence of operations will be:

- Node_A sends out a data frame with the MAC address of the gateway (00-80-55-43-FE-FF) and the destination node's IP address (146.176.120.2). The source MAC address of the data frame will be the MAC address of Node_A, and the source IP address will be the

IP address of Node_A.

- Router_1 then sends a data frame with the MAC address of Router_2 (00-65-21-44-33-A1) and the destination node's IP address (146.176.120.2). The source MAC address will be the MAC address of Port_2 of Router_1 (which is 00-60-DD-E0-12-34), and the source IP address will be the IP address of Node_A.
- Router_2 then sends a data frame with the MAC address of Node_B (00-90-10-33-DE-EE) and the destination node's IP address (146.176.120.2). The data is thus received by Node_B. The source MAC address will be the MAC address of Port_1 of Router_2 (which is 00-10-32-11-BC-B1), and the source IP address will be the IP address of Node_A.

It should be noted that each port (or interface) of a router has a unique network address, and a unique MAC address.

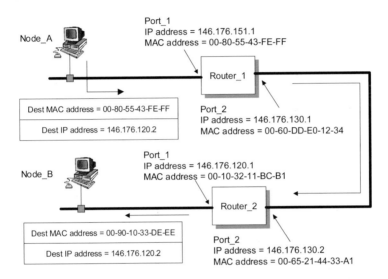

Figure C3.18 Example address over network segments

C3.13.2 ARP definition

The RFC826 document defines the specification for ARP. The Ethernet frame allows for the definition of a 16-bit Ethernet Type field. This is set to ADDRESS_RESOLUTION for ARP and reverse ARP (RARP). Figure C3.19 shows the format of the ARP (and RARP) data packet format. The first two bytes define the hardware address space (ar$hrd). For Ethernet, this is set to ETHERNET (a value of 1). The next field defines the protocol address space (ar$pro). For IP, this is set to IP (a value of 2048). After this there are two fields (ar$hln and ar$pln) which define the length of the hardware (MAC address) and the protocol address (IP address). Typically this is six for MAC addresses, and four for IP addresses. After these two fields the opcode (ar$op) defines whether the packet is an ARP request or an ARP reply (a value of 1 for REQUEST, and 2 for REPLY). After these fields come the source MAC address and the source IP address (ar$sha and ar$spa), next the target MAC address and the target IP address (ar$tha and ar$tpa). If the data packet is an ARP request the target IP address will be unknown, as the source does not know what the target's MAC address is. Thus typical settings are:

ar$hrd = 1 [for Ethernet]   ar$pro = 2048 [for IP]
ar$hln = 6 [for 48-bit MAC address]   ar$pln = 4 [for 32-bit IP address]
ar$op = 1 | 2 [for REQUEST or REPLY]

Where the opcode is set to REQUEST, the hardware address of the source (ar$sha) and the target (ar$tha), and the source protocol address (ar$spa) will be defined, but the target protocol address (ar$tpa) will be undefined. If the opcode is a REPLY, then all the fields will be defined.

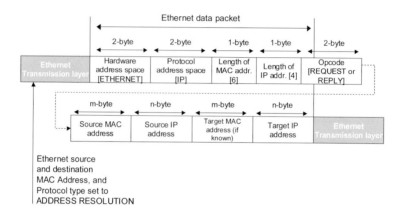

Figure C3.19   ARP data packet format

C3.14   RARP

Reverse ARP (RARP) is much less common than ARP, and is the reverse of ARP. With RARP a node knows its MAC address but does not know what its IP address is. Most computers know what their IP address is as they have a hard disk to store it. Some computers, such as terminals or a diskless workstation, do not have local storage and thus must determine their IP address. To run a RARP service there must be a server which responds to RARP requests. These servers have a table of IP and MAC addresses. In the transmission of RARP the network IP broadcast is used, which is the host part of the IP address set to all 1's (this will be covered in more detail in Chapter D1). Figure C3.20 shows an example RARP request and reply. Initially the RARP requester sends out a RARP request with an IP broadcast address (in this case 146.176.151.255), which is read by the RARP server. It then looks in its RARP table for the MAC address in the source MAC address field (in this case it is 65-F1-21-10-05-01). It then determines the IP address which corresponds to this MAC address (in this case it is 146.176.151.100), and sends back a RARP reply with the corresponding IP address, with the destination MAC address (in this case it is 65-F1-21-10-05-01).

The RFC903 document defines the specification for RARP. It defines that ARP treats all hosts (nodes on the network) as being equal, whether they be a client or a server, whereas RARP requires a server to maintain a database to map hardware addresses to IP addresses. It uses the same data packet as ARP (see Figure C3.20), but different opcode definitions:

ar$op = 3 | 4 [for REVERSE_REQUEST or REPLY_REVERSE]

Where the Opcode is set to REVERSE_REQUEST, the hardware address of the source (ar$sha) and the target (ar$tha) will be defined, whereas, the source protocol address (ar$spa) and the target protocol address (ar$tpa) will be undefined. If the source wishes to determine its protocol address then the target hardware address (ar$sha) will be set to the hardware address of the source.

Where the opcode is set to REPLY_REVERSE, the responder's hardware address (ar$sha) will be set to the hardware address of the responder, the responder's protocol address (ar$spa) will be set to the protocol address of the responder. The hardware address (ar$tha) will be set to the hardware address of the target (which is the same as the address in the request), and the target protocol address (ar$tpa) is set to the protocol address of the target (which is the main result of the reply).

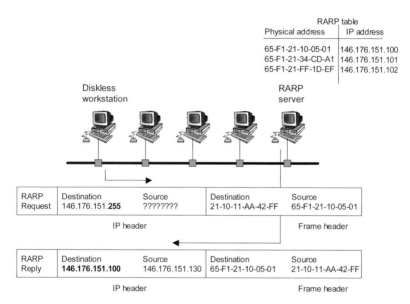

Figure C3.20 Example RARP request and reply

C3.15   Spanning-Tree Protocol

The spanning-tree protocol (STP) allows for redundant switched and bridge connections. Unicast frames have a specific destination MAC address, on which bridges and switches make their forwarding decisions. If they know that the MAC address is not on the source network segment, the bridge/switch floods the data frame onto all ports. The same thing will happen with frames with a broadcast address (FF-FF-FF-FF-FF-FF).

The best known STP is the Spanning Tree Algorithm (STA), which prevents loops by determining a stable spanning-tree network topology. Typically, fault-tolerance networks are created with redundant paths. The STA is used to calculate a loop-free path using spanning-tree frames called bridge protocol data units (BPDUs). These are sent out by all STA-enabled bridges and switches are regular intervals, and are used to determine the spanning tree topology.

STP can quickly detect faults on a network connection and activates the stand-by network. The STP states are:

- Blocking. No frames forwarded, BPDUs heard.
- Listening. No frames forwarded, listening for frames.
- Learning. No frames forwarded, learning addresses.
- Forwarding. Frames forwarded, learning addresses.
- Disabled. No frames forwarded, no BPDUs heard.

C3.16 Additional

The standard connections for 10BASE and 100BASE given are given in Figure C3.21. Here RD is the receive signals (this is known as RECEIVE in 100BASE) and TD the transmit signals (TRANSMIT). These cable connections are difficult to setup and most connections use a straight through connection. Ports which have the crossover connection internal in the port are marked with an 'X'.

The standard connections for 100BASE-T4 is also given, where BI represents the bi-directional transmission signals, TX the transmit signals and RX the receive signals. These cable connections are difficult to set-up and most connections use a straight through connection. Ports which have the cross-over connection internal in the port are marked with an 'X'.

Winipcfg is a useful program for determining networking settings. An example run is given in Figure C3.22. It can be seen that this program shows the MAC address, IP address, Host Name, and so on.

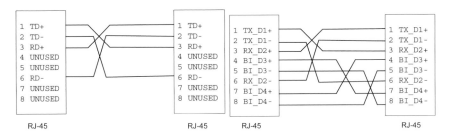

Figure C3.21   Ethernet connections

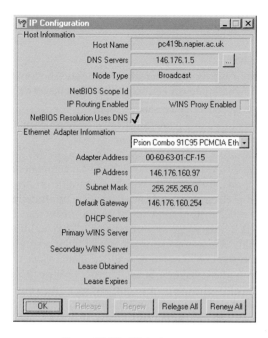

Figure C3.22 Winipcfg program

C3.17 Network interface card design

When receiving data, the network interface card (NIC) copies all data transmitted on the network, decodes it and transfers it to the computer. An Ethernet NIC contains three parts:

- Physical medium interface – the physical medium interface corresponds to the PLS and PMA in the standard and is responsible for the electrical transmission and reception of data. It consists of two parts: the transceiver, which receives and transmits data from or onto the transmission media; and a code converter that encodes/decodes the data. It also recognizes a collision on the media.
- Data link controller – the controller corresponds to the MAC layer.
- Computer interface.

It can be split into four main functional blocks:

- Network interface.
- Manchester decoder.
- Memory buffer.
- Computer interface.

C3.17.1 Network interface

The network interface must listen, recreate the waveform transmitted on the cable into a digital signal and transfer the digital signal to the Manchester decoder. The network interface consists of three parts:

- BNC/RJ-45 connector.
- Reception hardware – the reception hardware translates the waveforms transmitted on the cable to digital signals then copies them to the Manchester decoder.
- Isolator – the isolator is connected directly between the reception hardware and the rest of the Manchester decoder; it guarantees that no noise from the network affects the computer, and vice versa (as it isolates ground levels).

The reception hardware is called a receiver and is the main component in the network interface. It acts as an earphone, listening and copying the traffic on the cable. Unfortunately, the Ether and transceiver electronics are not perfect. The transmission line contains resistance and capacitance which distort the shape of the bit stream transmitted onto the Ether. Distortion in the system causes pulse spreading, which leads to intersymbol interference. There is also a possibility of noise affecting the digital pulse as it propagates through the cable. Therefore, the receiver also needs to recreate the digital signal and filter noise.

Figure C3.23 shows a block diagram of an Ethernet receiver. The received signal goes through a buffer with high input impedance and low capacitance to reduce the effects of loading on the coaxial cable. An equalizer passes high frequencies and attenuates low frequencies from the network, flattening the network passband. A 4-pole Bessel low-pass filter provides the average dc level from the received signal. The quench circuit activates the line driver only when it detects a true signal. This prevents noise activating the receiver.

C3.17.2 Manchester decoder

Manchester coding has the advantage of embedding timing (clock) information within the transmitted bits. A positively edged pulse (low to high) represents a 1 and a negatively edged pulse (high to low) a 0, as shown in Figure C3.24. Another advantage of this coding method is that the average voltage is always zero when used with equal positive and negative voltage levels.

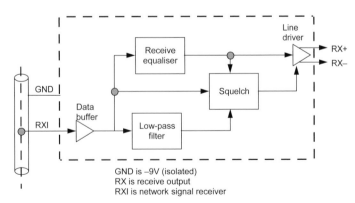

GND is –9V (isolated)
RX is receive output
RXI is network signal receiver

Figure C3.23 Ethernet receiver block diagram

Figure C3.24 is an example of transmitted bits using Manchester encoding. The receiver passes the received Manchester-encoded bits through a low-pass filter. This extracts the lowest frequency in the received bit stream, i.e. the clock frequency. With this clock the receiver can then determine the transmitted bit pattern.

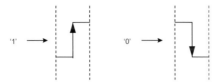

Figure C3.24 Manchester encoding

For Manchester decoding, the Manchester-encoded signal is first synchronized to the receiver (called bit synchronization). A transition in the middle of each bit cell is used by a clock recovery circuit to produce a clock pulse in the center of the second half of the bit cell. In Ethernet, the bit synchronization is achieved by deriving the clock from the preamble field of the frame using a clock and data recovery circuit. Many Ethernet decoders use the SEEQ 8020 Manchester code converter, which uses a phase-locked loop (PLL) to recover the clock. The PLL is designed to lock onto the preamble of the incoming signal within 12-bit cells. Figure C3.25 shows a circuit schematic of bit synchronization using Manchester decoding and a PLL.

The PLL is a feedback circuit which is commonly used for the synchronization of digital signals. It consists of a phase detector (such as an EXOR gate) and a voltage-controlled oscillator (VCO) which uses a crystal oscillator as a clock source.

The frequency of the crystal is twice the frequency of the received signal. It is so constant that it only needs irregular and small adjustments to be synchronized to the received signal. The function of the phase detector is to find irregularities between the two signals and adjust the VCO to minimize the error. This is accomplished by comparing the received signals and the output from the VCO. When the signals have the same frequency and phase the PLL is locked. Figure C3.27 shows the PLL components and the function of the EXOR.

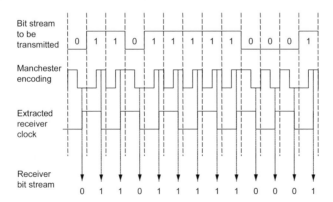

Figure C3.25 Example of Manchester coding

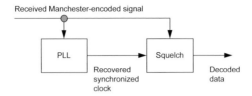

Figure C3.26 Manchester decoding with bit synchronization

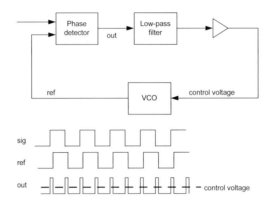

Figure C3.27 PLL and example waveform for the phase detector

C3.17.3 Memory buffer

The rate at which data is transmitted on the cable differs from the data rate used by the receiving computer, and the data appears in bursts. To compensate for the difference between the data rate, a first-in first-out (FIFO) memory buffer is used to produce a constant data rate. An important condition is that the average data input rate should not exceed the frequency of the output clock; if this is not the case the buffer will be filled up regardless of its size.

A FIFO is a RAM that uses a queuing technique where the output data appears in the same order that it went in. The input and output are controlled by separate clocks, and the FIFO keeps track of the data that has been written and the data that has been read and can thus be overwritten. This is achieved with a pointer. Figure C3.28 shows a block diagram of the FIFO configuration. The FIFO status is indicated by flags, the empty flag (EF) and the full flag (FF), which show whether the FIFO is either empty or full.

C3.17.4 Ethernet implementation

The completed circuit for the Ethernet receiver is given in Appendix 8 and is outlined in Figure C3.29. It uses the SEEQ Technologies 82C93A Ethernet transceiver as the receiver and the SEEQ 8020 Manchester code converter which decodes the Manchester code. A transformer and a dc-to-dc converter isolate the SEEQ 82C92A and the network cable from the rest of the circuit (and the computer). The isolated dc-to-dc converter converts a 5 V supply to the -9 V needed by the transceiver.

The memory buffer used is the AMD AM7204 FIFO which has 4096 data words with 9-bit words (but only eight bits are actually used). The output of the circuit is eight data lines, the control lines $\overline{FF}$, $\overline{EF}$, $\overline{RS}$, $\overline{R}$ and $\overline{W}$, and the +5 V and GND supply rails.

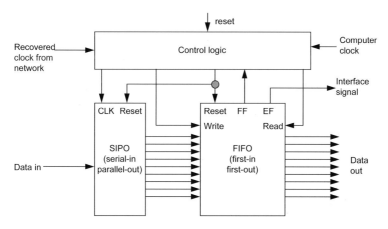

Figure C3.28 Memory buffering

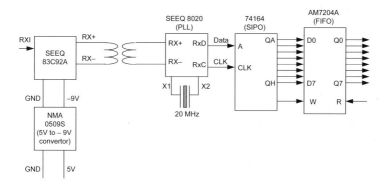

Figure C3.29 Ethernet receiver

C3.18 82559-based Ethernet

The Intel 82559 supports both 10 and 100 Mbps (using IEEE 802.3u auto-negotiation) and integrates with PCI-based systems. It is typically used for PC LAN On Motherboard (LOM) designs, embedded systems and networking system products. A major advantage of this device is that it supports ACPI (Advanced Configuration and Power Interface), which allows the device to shutdown and wake-up on an interesting data packet. It also allows the device to be powered-down and then remotely awoken.

Figure 3.30 shows how the 82559 integrates into a modern hub-based system. The processor (SC242) interfaces directly to the memory hub controller, which then interfaces with a PCI interface controller (in this case it is the PC164H, but it can equally interface to an I/O controller hub, such as 82801A device), which converts the memory hub controller interface to 32-bit and 64-bit PCI busses. The LOM interfaces directly onto the 32-bit PCI bus.

The main network connections are:

- **TDP/TDN**. Analogue twisted-pair transmit differential pairs. These connect directly to an isolating transformer.
- **RDP/RDN**. Analogue twisted-pair transmit receive pairs. These connect directly to an isolating transformer.
- **ACTIVELED#** - Activity LED (active low). This shows that there is activity on the link, and can be directly connected to an LED (as it can sink up to 10mA of current).
- **LILED#** - Link integrity (active low). This shows that the link is still connected, and can be directly connected to an LED (as it can sink up to 10mA of current).
- **SPEEDLED#** - Speed LED (active low). This shows the connected speed (either 10Mbps or 100Mbps).
- **RBIAS100** – Reference bias resistor for 100Mbps. Typically set to 619Ω.
- **RBIAS10** – Reference bias resistor for 10Mbps. Typically set to 549Ω.
- **VREF** – 1.5V reference voltage.

The 82559 can derive its timings from an internal 25MHz clock, or an external clock can be applied to the X1/X2 inputs. Figure C3.31 outlines how it interfaces to an RJ-45 connector. Notice that the transmit and receive lines must be isolated through a 1:1 transformer before they connect to the network interface.

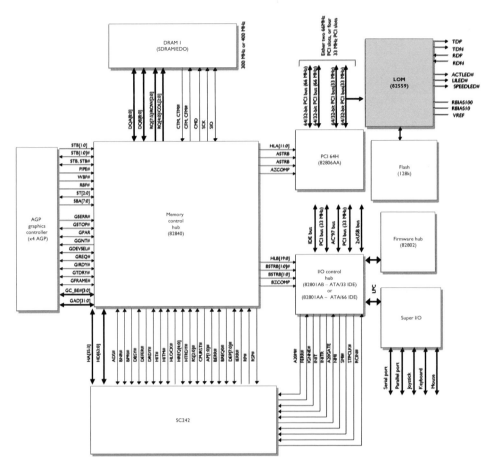

Figure C3.30 82559-based Ethernet

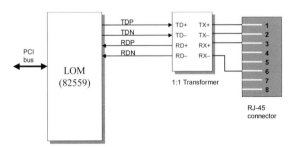

Figure C3.31 82559 interface to an RJ-45 connector

C3.19   Comparison of fast Ethernet with other technologies

Table C3.4 compares fast Ethernet with other types of networking technologies.

Table C3.4 Comparison of fast Ethernet with other networking technologies

Feature	100VG-AnyLAN (Cat 3, 4, or 5)	100BASE-T (TX/FX/T4)	FDDI	ATM	Gigabit Ethernet (802.3z)
Maximum segment length	100 m	100 m (Cat-5) 412 m (Fiber)	2000 m	200 m (Cat-5) 2000 m (Fiber)	100 m (Cat 5) 1k m (Fiber)
Maximum network diameter with repeater(s)	6000 m	320 m	100 km	N/A	To be determined by the standard
Bit rate	100 Mbps	100 Mbps	100 Mbps	155 Mbps	1 Gbps
Media access method	Demand priority	CSMA/CD	Token passing	PVC/SVC	CSMA/CD
Maximum nodes on each domain	1024	Limited by hub	500	N/A	To be determined
Frame type	Ethernet and Token Ring	Ethernet	802.5	53-byte cell	Ethernet
Multimedia support	✓	×	FDDI-I (×) FDDI-II (✓)	✓	YES (with 802.1p)
Integration with 10BASE2	Yes with bridges, switches and routers	Yes with switches	Yes with routers and switches	Yes with routers or switches	Yes with 10/100 Mbps switching
Relative cost	Low	Low	Medium	High	Medium
Relative complexity	Low	Low	Medium	High	Low

C4 Network design, switches and vLANs

C4.1 Introduction

This chapter discusses methods that can be used to design a network, in its local connection, and in its connection to wider networks (including the Internet). A major problem in the past has been security and contention on Ethernet network. Switching overcomes both these problems as it can create vLANs (Virtual LANs) which allow nodes to be isolated from each other, even though they connect to the same device. Switches avoid the problem of contention on a network, as they take frames from one interface, and forward it to another. This can take place at either Layer 2 (Data Link layer) or Layer 3 (Network Layer). Routers implement Layer 3 switching to route data packets and switches (Layer 2 switches) use Layer 2 switching to forward frames. In Layer 3 switching the router examines the network address, and decides on whether it should forward it to another port, whereas with Layer 2 the switch examines the MAC address of the data frame (it thus ignores any network layer information). A Layer 2 switch must build and maintain a switching table that keeps track of the MAC addresses that belong to each port or interface. As with the ARP protocol, the Layer 2 switch sends out a broadcast on all of its ports if it does not know where to send a data frame. When the addressed node detects its address, it sends back an ARP reply, and the switch adds the new address to its switching table. The MAC address itself is a 48-bit address, made up of the manufacturing (MFG) code and the unique identifier. Organizations have no control over MAC addresses, and they have a flat addressing structure, whereas Layer 3 address are typically organized in a hierarchical way, typically using IP, IPX or AppleTalk addresses.

C4.2 Network design

In the past networks have grown with little thought of their long-term structure. As they are now a key part of most organizations it is important to properly design the network, as incorrect planning can cause problems in the future. The basic steps are:

- **Analyze requirements.** This involves understanding and specifying the requirements of the network, especially its major uses. If possible, future plans should be incorporated. One of the key features is the bandwidth requirements and the size of the network.
- **Develop LAN structure.** This step involves developing a LAN structure for these requirements. Typically, in organizational networks this will be based on a star topology using Ethernet hubs/switches.
- **Set up addressing and routing.** The final step involves setting up IP addresses and subnets to add structure.

The most important information that is required is the structure of the organization and how information flows between the units, as the designed network is likely to reflect this structure. The information will include:

- **Strengths and weaknesses.** Understand the current network (if one exists) especially its strengths and weaknesses.

- **Geographical layout**. Gather information on geographical locations.
- **Applications**. Determine current applications, and future plans for each site and for the organization.
- **Organizational contacts**. These will be the important people who will be involved in the development of the network. A mixture of technical and business skills always helps. Technical people tend to be driven by technology ('it should transfer files faster', 'it's easier to install', and so on), whereas business people tend to be driven by applications ('I just want access to a good spreadsheet', 'I want to be able to send e-mails to anyone in the company', and so on). It is also important to get someone involved who has experience of legal matters, and/or someone involved in Personnel matters.
- **Requirements for external network connections**. This is an important decision as the security of the whole network may depend on the choices made on the external connections. Many large companies have a single point of connection to the external Internet as this allows organizations to manage internal and external connections to the Internet.
- **Key objectives of the organization**. This is especially related to mission-critical data and mission-critical operations. These should have top priority over other parts of the network. For example a hospital would declare its ambulance service as a mission-critical unit, whereas the cuts and bruises unit (if there was one) would not be.
- **Control of information services**. This may be distributed over the organization or over centralized in an MIS (Management Information Service) unit.

The main requirements can then be split into three main areas:

- **Business requirements.**
- **Technical requirements.** The main issues are media contention, reducing excessive broadcasts (routing tables, ARP requests, and so on), backbone requirements, support for real-time traffic and addressing issues.
- **Performance requirements.** This is likely to involve a network load requirement analysis for the typical loading on the network, and also for the worst-case traffic loading. This will determine the requirement for client/server architectures. An analysis should also be made for the impact of new workstations being added to the network. It should also involve an analysis of the requirements for application software, especially in its bandwidth requirements. Multimedia applications tend to have a large bandwidth requirement, along with centralized database applications and file servers.
- **New application requirements.**
- **Availability requirements.** This defines the usefulness of the network, such as response time, resource availability, and so on.

The OSI model can be used to design the network, but splitting it into identifiable areas:

- **Physical layer.** Network media (typically Cat-5 cable or fiber-optic cable), hubs and repeaters. Cables are normally run conforming to the EIA/TIA-568A standard. This layer should allow for future expansion.
- **Data link layer.** Switches and bridges. These devices will define the size of the collision and broadcast domains.
- **Network layer.** Routers and addressing. This layer filters data packets between network segments.

A weakness in many Ethernet-based networks is that there are too many **collisions** when the traffic on the network segment approaches its capacity. Ethernet collisions occur when two nodes try and transmit onto a network segment at the same time. When the transmitting nodes detect this, they transmit a jamming signal to the rest of the network. All the other nodes on the network detect this, and wait for one of the two colliding nodes to get access onto the network segment. These collisions reduce the overall bandwidth of the network segment. An important concept is the collision domain, which defines the physical distance by which a collision is propagated. Repeaters and hubs propagate collisions, but switches, bridges and routers do not. Thus if you want to reduce the amount of collision insert either a switch, a router or a bridge in a network segment.

Broadcasts are sent out when a node wants help from other nodes. Typically, this happens when a node requires the MAC address for a known network address. The broadcast domain defines the physical distance by which a broadcast will be propagated. Hub, bridges and switches all propagate broadcasts, but routers do not. Thus, if you want to reduce the number of broadcasts on a network segment, insert a router, and it will intelligently route data packets into and out of a network segment without too many broadcasts (as the router handles external data routing).

C4.3   Hierarchical network design

The complexity of a system can be reduced by organizing it into a hierarchy of connected components. As much as possible broadcasts should be limited within local domains, and collisions should be minimized. Routers do not broadcast broadcasts, and switches can be used to reduce collisions.

C4.3.1   One-layer design

In a one-layer design, the nodes connect to create workgroups, which each have a local server to provide local services (as illustrated in Figure C4.1). Each workgroup connects to a local switch and thus create a broadcast domain. These are isolated from each other using routers, which provide interconnectivity between workgroups. The local of the servers within workgroups has the advantage that each of the workgroups can work independently from the other workgroups. This type of design is useful when there are only a few remote locations in the company (Site A and Site B, in this case), and where applications are delivered from a local file server.

C4.3.2   Two-layer model

In a two-layer design, WAN links provide connections between different sites, as illustrated in Figure C4.2. In this case, Router_A provides interconnectivity between the two sites, and Router_B and Router_C provide interconnectivity between local workgroups. The advantage of Router_B is that it will route traffic between Site A and Site B, which will not be routed out to other sites, unless it is destined for them.

C4.3.3   Three-layer model

Figure C4.3 outlines the three-layer model. If possible, the model should mirror the requirements of the network at different levels, such as connectivity (gaining access to the network), creating workgroups, security, policy and distribution. Figure C4.1 shows a three-layer model for designing networks. Routers are used at each layer to limit the broadcasts to within that layer. The layers can be defined as:

- **Core**. Provides optimal transport between sites, which provides fast wide-area connections between geographically remote sites within an organization. Normally these are point-to-point links between routers. Typically connections are T1/T3, ATM, Frame Relay and SMDS), and are often provided by telecommunications provider. The core layer provides **low latency** connections between remote sites, and does not generally implement any filtering of the traffic (such as with firewalls and ACLs). If possible, there should be **redundant paths** which can be switched-in when a route becomes unavailable, or slows down. The redundant paths can also be used to share **traffic loads**. There should also be **rapid convergence** of the network (*see* Routing Protocols).
- **Distribution**. Provides policy-based connectivity, which connects multiple LANs into a larger network infrastructure, such as an organizational backbone. It will typically connect between buildings. Typically, connections to the LANs are with Fast Ethernet, or even Gigabit Ethernet, and to the core layer with ATM, FDDI and SMDS. This layer also provides the demarcation point between the access and core layers and thus helps to define the operation of the core, and isolate it from the access layer. At this layer packets can be filtered using a policy-based system (typically using a firewall). At this level campus-wide networks would be implemented, with the possibility of campus-wide servers. It is unlikely that nodes would connect directly onto the distribution layer. In a non-campus-based network, this would be the layer at which remote sites would connect to each other. Typical functions include: concentration of LANs, access to core layer, VLAN routing, and media translations (such as between Frame Relay and Ethernet) and security.
- **Access**. Provides workgroup and user access to the network, which creates LANs, and workgroups. At this level, most of the hosts connect to a network. There can be some policy-based filtering of network traffic at this layer, which will refine the access control implemented at the distribution level. At this layer, the filter will typically be based on user access (such as whether certain individuals are allowed access to certain services). The main functions at this layer are: shared bandwidth (using hubs), switched bandwidth (using switches); MAC-layer filtering (routing based on MAC address, such as using in a switch or a bridge), isolating broadcast traffic, creating workgroups, and microsegmentation.

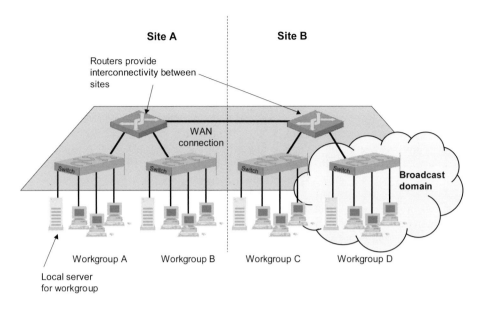

Figure C4.1   One-layer component model

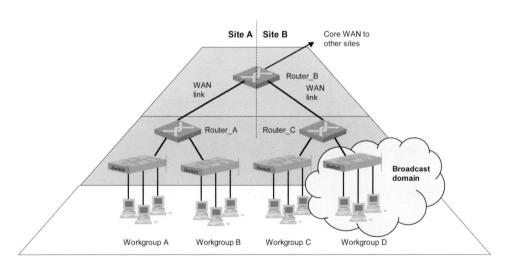

Figure C4.2   Two-layer component model

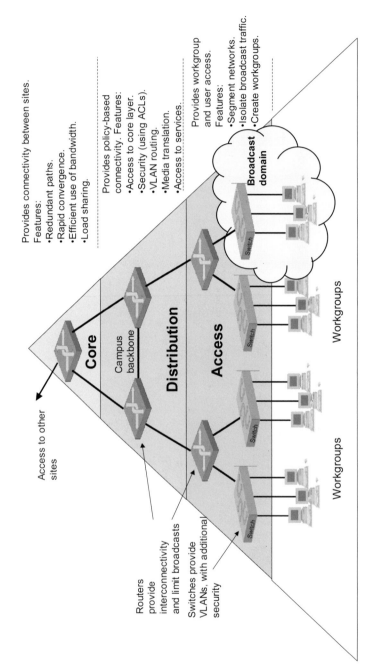

Provides connectivity between sites.
Features:
•Redundant paths.
•Rapid convergence.
•Efficient use of bandwidth.
•Load sharing.

Provides policy-based
connectivity. Features:
•Access to core layer.
•Security (using ACLs).
•VLAN routing.
•Media translation.
•Access to services.

Provides workgroup
and user access.
Features:
•Segment networks.
•Isolate broadcast traffic.
•Create workgroups.

Broadcast
domain

Access to other
sites

Core

Campus
backbone

Distribution

Access

Switch

Workgroups

Workgroups

Routers
provide
interconnectivity
and limit broadcasts

Switches provide
VLANs, with additional
security

Figure C4.3 Three-layered component model

C4.3.4 Server placement

Servers provide services for clients, such as file servers, application servers, email servers, and so on. The placement of these servers on the network is important as a great deal of bandwidth can be wasted if they are not placed in the correct place on the topology. Generally, servers can be classified as:

- **Enterprise servers**. These are typically used when all the users within an organization require access to a single resource, such as with electronic mail. As all the users typically require to access them, it is inefficient to place them at the access layer, as traffic to and from the server will generally reduce the amount of additional traffic which can travel to and from workgroups which connect to the network which the server is connected to. For example if the enterprise server was to connect to the switch which connects to Workgroup A, then the additional traffic from the other workgroups which connect to the enterprise server may reduce the available capacity on the routes into and out of Workgroup A. Thus, if possible, enterprise servers should be placed at the **distribution layer**, as illustrated in Figure C4.4.
- **Workgroup servers**. Workgroup servers provide local access to data and application programs, and isolate traffic around these severs. Workgroup servers should be physically located where they are most required. Typically enterprise servers require to be more centralized in their location (at the **distribution layer**), and are more robust than workgroup servers, as the whole organization depend on them. Mirror servers (servers which have exact copies of the main enterprise server) can be used with an enterprise in order to reduce data traffic to the main server.

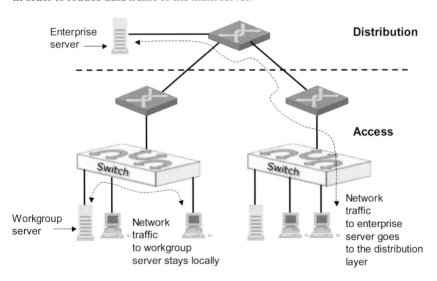

Figure C4.4 Connection of servers

C4.4   Switches and switching hubs

A switch is a very fast, low-latency, multiport bridge that is used to segment LANs. They are typically also used to increase communication rates between segments with multiple parallel conversations and also communication between differing networking technologies (such as between ATM and 100BASE-TX).

A 4-port switching hub is a repeater that contains four distinct network segments (as if there were four hubs in one device). Through software, any of the ports on the hub can connect directly to any of the four segments at any time. This allows for a maximum capacity of 40 Mbps in a single hub (using 10 Mbps for each network segment).

Ethernet switches overcome the contention problem on normal CSMA/CD networks, as they segment traffic by giving each connect a guaranteed bandwidth allocation. Figure C4.5 and Figure C4.6 show the two types of switches; their main features are:

- **Desktop switch** (or workgroup switch). These connect directly to nodes. They are economical with fixed configurations for end-node connections and are designed for standalone networks or distributed workgroups in a larger network.
- **Segment switch.** These connect both 10 Mbps workgroup switches and 100 Mbps interconnect (backbone) switches that are used to interconnect hubs and desktop switches. They are modular, high-performance switches for interconnecting workgroups in mid- to large-size networks.

C4.4.1 Segment switch

A segment switch allows simultaneous communication between any two nodes, and can simply replace existing Ethernet hubs. Figure C4.6 shows a switch with five ports each transmitting at 10 Mbps; this allows up to five simultaneous connections giving a maximum aggregated bandwidth of 50 Mbps. If the nodes support 100 Mbps communication then the maximum aggregated bandwidth will be 500 Mbps. To optimize the network, nodes should be connected to the switch that connects to the server with which it most often communicates. This allows for a direct connection with that server.

C4.4.2 Desktop switch

A desktop switch can simply replace an existing 10BASE-T/100BASE-T hub. It has the advantage that any of the ports can connect directly to any other. In the network in Figure C4.5, any of the computers in the local workgroup can connect directly to any other, or to the printer, or a local server. This type of switch works well if there is a lot of local traffic, typically between a local server and local peripherals.

C4.4.3 Asymmetric and symmetric switches

Switches can either be symmetric or asymmetric. A symmetric switch provides switched connections between ports with the same bandwidth, such as all 10 Mbps or all 100 Mbps ports. This gives an even distribution of network traffic across the switch. For example an 8-port, 10 Mbps switch will give a maximum throughput of 80 Mbps, as each of the ports can communicate at 10 Mbps.

Asymmetric switches provide differing bandwidths on each of the ports, typically either 10/100 Mbps (known as 10/100 switching) to 100 Mbps/1 Gbps. This type of switch is typically used in client/server applications, where the server requires a higher bandwidth than the client connections. Memory buffering is then used to store the faster bit rate port (such as 100 Mbps), and send it over the slower rate port (such as 10 Mbps). Figure C4.7 illustrates this.

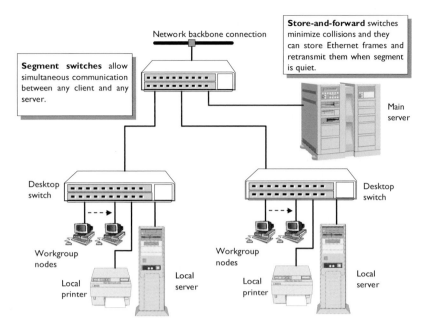

Network backbone connection

Store-and-forward switches minimize collisions and they can store Ethernet frames and retransmit them when segment is quiet.

Segment switches allow simultaneous communication between any client and any server.

Main server

Desktop switch

Desktop switch

Workgroup nodes

Workgroup nodes

Local printer

Local server

Local printer

Local server

Figure C4.5   Desktop switch

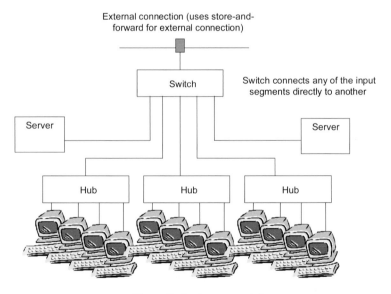

External connection (uses store-and-forward for external connection)

Switch

Switch connects any of the input segments directly to another

Server

Server

Hub

Hub

Hub

Figure C4.6   Segment switch

C4.4.4   Memory buffering

Memory buffers are important devices in a switch as they allow incoming data packets to be stored, before they are transmitted to the destination. The switch can use port based memory buffering or shared memory buffering. In a port-based system, data frames are stored in an area of memory that is associated with the incoming port. The data packet is then transmitted to the outgoing port only when all the packets ahead of it in the queue have been successfully transmitted. It is possible for a single packet to delay the transmission of all the packets in memory because of a busy destination port. This can stop other data packets which are destined for other unbusy ports from being delivered, as the packet at the top of the queue must be transmitted before they can.

With a shared memory technique, all the incoming packets are buffered in a common memory buffer, which is shared with all the switch ports. The packets in the buffer are then dynamically linked to the transmit port. This allows the packet to be received on one port and transmitted on another port without moving it into a different queue.

Cut-through switching

With cut-through switching, the switch reads the destination address before receiving the entire frame. The data frame is then forwarded before the entire frame arrives. This method has the advantage that there is less delay (latency) between the reception and transmission of a data packet, but has poor error detection, because it does not have a chance to detect any errors, before it has started to transmit the received data frame.

Cut-though switching is a packet switching in which data streams leave a destination before the end of the data stream has been fully received. This technique is also known as on-the-fly packet switching.

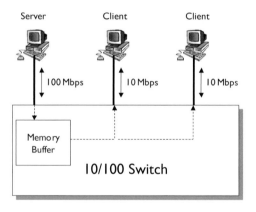

Figure C4.7   Asymmetric switching

Store-and-forward switching

Store-and-forwarding techniques have been used extensively in bridges and routers, and are now used with switches. It involves reading the entire Ethernet frame, before forwarding it, with the required protocol and at the correct speed, to the destination port. This has the advantages of:

- Improved error checking. Bad frames are blocked from entering a network segment.
- Protocol filtering. Allows the switch to convert from one protocol to another.
- Speed matching. Typically, for Ethernet, reading at 10 Mbps or 100 Mbps and transmit-

ting at 100 Mbps or 10 Mbps. Also, it can be used for matching between ATM (155 Mbps), FDDI (100 Mbps), Token Ring (4/16 Mbps) and Ethernet (10/100 Mbps).

The main disadvantage is system delay, as the frame must be totally read before it is transmitted thus there is a delay in the transmission. The improvement in error checking normally overcomes this disadvantage.

Figure C4.8 illustrates the two switching methods. With cut-though the data frame is forwarded to the destination before it is fully received. This technique operates on data frames, thus it is normally only used to transmit between networks of the same type (such as Ethernet), the same speed, and the same protocol. Store-and-forward techniques obviously have a greater latency but can be used to improve error detection, and interfacing between different network types (for example Ethernet to ATM), and different speeds.

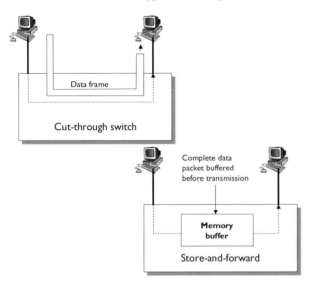

Figure C4.8
Cut-through and store-and-forward switches

C4.4.5 Ethernet connections

Standard Ethernet (10BASE) uses a half-duplex connection, where the TX connects to the RX, and the RX to the TX, as illustrated in Figure C4.9. In full-duplex, Ethernet uses switching to create a virtual circuit between two nodes (known as a FDES – full-duplex Ethernet switch). As there is a virtual point-to-point connection, nodes can transmit and receive at the same time. A wire is used to transmit and another to receive, thus the maximum total bandwidth for a single port operating at 10 Mbps is 20 Mbps. As it is a point-to-point connection there should be no collisions. This increases the actual bandwidth of a full-duplex Ethernet to nearly 100% of its capacity (while standard, half-duplex can only achieve a maximum of around 50% capacity).

Switches learn the MAC address of devices by reading the source address of each data packet that they receive, and noting at which port the frame came from. This information is then added to its forwarding database (dynamic learning), which stores addresses in content addressable memory (CAM). Each address has a time stamp associated with it, and new references to the address cause the time stamp to be updated. Addresses which are not used for a given time, are aged-out.

Ethernet Transceiver   Ethernet Transceiver

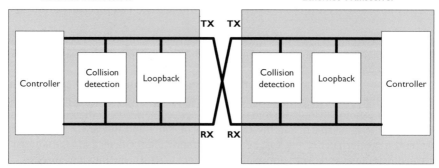

Figure C4.9   Ethernet transceiver

C4.5   vLANs

vLANs are a new technology, which uses software to define a broadcast domain, rather than any physical connections. In a vLAN a message transmitted by one node is only received by other nodes with a certain criteria to be in the domain. It is made by logically grouping two or more nodes and a vLAN-initialized switching device, such as intelligent switches (which use the MAC address to forward data frames) or routers (which use the network address to route data packets). The important concept with vLANs is that the domain is defined by software, and not by physical connections.

There are two methods that can define the logical grouping of nodes within a vLAN:

- **Implicit tagging.** This uses a special tagging field which is inserted into the data frames or within data packets. It can be based upon the MAC address, a switch port number, protocol, or another parameter by which nodes can be logically grouped. The main problem with implicit tagging is that different vendors create different tags which make vendor interoperability difficult. This is known as frame filtering.
- **Explicit tagging.** This uses an additional field in the data frame or packet header. This can also lead to incompatibility problems, as different vendor equipment may not be able to read or process the additional field. This is known as frame identification.

It is thus difficult to create truly compatible vLANs until standards for implicit and explicit tags are standardized. One example of creating a vLAN is to map ports of a switch to create two or more virtual LANs. For example, a switch could connect to two servers and 16 clients. The switch could be configured so that eight of the clients connected to one server through a vLAN, and the other eight onto the other server. This setup is configured in software, and not by the physical connection of the network. Figure C4.10 shows a possible implementation where nodes 1 to 8 create a vLAN through the switch with SERVER1, and nodes 9 to 16 create a vLAN with SERVER2. The switch would map ports to create the vLANs, where the two networks are now independent broadcast domains (network segments), and will only receive the broadcasts from each of their virtual LANs. Normally a switch would connect any one of its ports to another port, and allow simultaneous connection. In this case, the switch allows for multiple connections onto a segment. Now, with the vLAN, data frames transmitted on one network segment will stay within that segment and are not transmitted to the other vLAN.

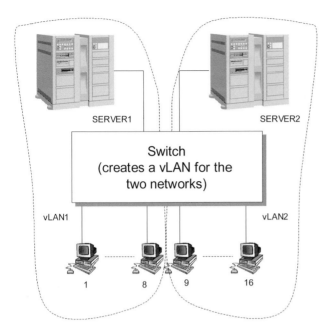

Figure C4.10
Creating a vLAN by mapping ports of a switch

The main advantages of using vLAN are:

- **Creation of virtual networks.** Just as many organizations build open-plan offices which can be changed when required, vLANs can be used to reconfigure the logical connections to a network without actually having to physically move any of the resources. This is especially useful in creating workgroups where users share the same resources, such as databases and disk storage.
- **Ease of administration.** vLANs allow networks to be easily configured, possibly at a distance from the configured networks. In the past reconfiguration has meant recabling and the movement of networked resources. With vLANs the resources can be configured with software to setup the required network connections.
- **Improved bandwidth usage.** Normally users who work in a similar area share resources. This is typically known as a workgroup. If workgroups can be isolated from other workgroups then traffic which stays within each of the workgroups does not affect other workgroups. A vLAN utilizes this concept by grouping users who share information and configuring the networked resources around them. This makes much better usage of bandwidth than workgroup users who span network segments. The amount of broadcast traffic on the whole network is also reduced, as broadcasts can be isolated within each of the workgroups. A typical drain on network bandwidth is when network servers broadcast their services at regular intervals (in Novell NetWare this can be once every minute, and is known as the Service Advertising Protocol). With vLANs these broadcasts would be contained within each of the vLANs that the server is connected to.
- **Microsegmentation.** This involves dividing a network into smaller segments, which will increase the overall bandwidth available to networked devices.
- **Enhanced security.** vLANs help to isolate network traffic so that traffic which stays

within a vLAN will not be transmitted outside it. Thus it is difficult for an external user to 'listen' to any of the data that is transmitted across the vLAN, unless they can get access to one of the ports of the vLAN device. This can be difficult as this would require a physical connection, and increases the chances of the external user being caught 'spying' on the network.

- **Relocate servers into secured locations.** vLANs allows for servers to be put in a physical location in which they cannot be tampered with. This will typically be in a secure room, which is under lock and key. The vLAN can be used to map hosts to servers.
- **Easy creation of IP subnets.** vLANs allow the creation of IP subnets, which are not dependent on the physical location of a node. Users can also remain part of a subnet, even if they move their computer.

There are also a number of key issues which need to be considered when installing a vLAN:

- **Multivendor compatibility.** This is an important issue as each vendor may try to implement a vLAN is a different way which may be incompatible with other equipment. Typically they differ in their tagging method, which is either implicit (such as tagging ports or MAC addresses) or explicit.
- **Interdomain communications.** In a vLAN frames or packets stay within the domain in which they are assigned (the broadcast domain). A problem occurs, though, when a host on one domain wants to communicate with another on another domain. One of the main objectives of a vLAN is to constrain traffic within a domain, and interdomain communications go against this objective.
- **Support upgradeability.** A major objective in any network is to allow an upgrade path for all the network components, as it is difficult to upgrade a network in a single stroke. Thus an important issue to install vLAN-aware equipment is the need to communicate with non-vLAN-aware (vLAN-unaware) equipment.
- **IP multicast address support.** The IP multicast address allows a single data packet to be received by many hosts. Thus an issue is how the vLAN deals with interdomain communications with IP multicast addresses.

A vLAN can be created by connecting workgroups by a common backbone, where broadcast frames are switched only between ports within the same vLAN. This requires port-mapping to establish the broadcast domain, which is based on a port ID, MAC address, protocol or application. Each frame is tagged with a VLAN ID. Figure C4.11 illustrates that switches are one of the core components of a VLAN. Each switch is intelligent enough to decide whether to forward data frame, based on VLAN metrics (such as port ID, MAC address or network address), and to communicate this information to other switches and routers within the network. The switching is based on frame filtering or frame identification.

Most early vLANs were based on frame filters, but the IEEE 802.1q vLAN standard is based on frame tagging, as this allows for scaleable networks. With frame tagging, each frame has a uniquely assigned user-defined ID. A unique identifier in the header of each frame is forwarded throughout the network backbone (vertical cabling), as illustrated in Figure C4.12. Each switch then reads the identifier, and if the frame is part of a network which it controls, the switch removes the identifier before the frame is transmitted to the target node (horizontal cabling). As the switching occurs at the data link layer, there is not a great processing time overhead.

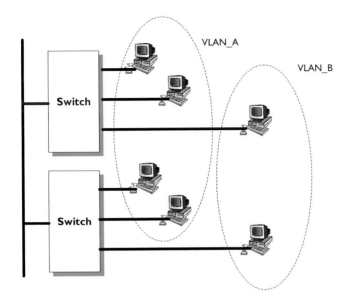

vLANs rely on broadcasts to the virtual network, but they are constrained within the virtual network, and thus are not transmitted to other virtual networks. This should reduce the amount of overall network broadcasts (especially from broadcast storms). The broadcast domain can be reduced by limiting the number of switched ports which connect to a specific vLAN. The smaller the grouping, the lower the broadcast effect.

vLANs increase security of data as transmitted data is confined to the vLAN in which it is transmitted. These provide natural firewalls, in which external users cannot gain access to the data within a vLAN. This security occurs, as switch ports can be grouped based on the application type and access privileges. Restricted applications and resources can be placed in a secured VLAN group.

The two types of vLANs are:

- **Static vLANs.** These are ports on a switch that are statically assigned to a VLAN. These remain permanently assigned, until they are changed by the administrator. Static vLANs are secure and easy to configure, and are useful where vLANs are fairly well defined.
- **Dynamic VLANs.** These are ports on a switch which automatically determine their VLAN assignments. This is achieved with intelligent management software, using MAC addresses, logical addressing, or the protocol type of the data packets. Initially, where a node connects to the switch, the switch detects its MAC address entry in the VLAN management database and dynamically configures the port with the corresponding VLAN configuration. The advantage of dynamic vLANs is that they require less setup from the administrator (but the database must be initially created).

The broadcast domain in a vLAN is defined by each vLAN, as illustrated in Figure C4.13. A node broadcasting into the vLAN will only be transmitted to nodes within its vLAN. Nodes not connected to the same vLAN, even although they connect to the same switch as the broadcasting node, will not receive the broadcast. The only way for nodes to intercommunicate across differing vLANs is to be routed through a router (as illustrated in Figure C4.14).

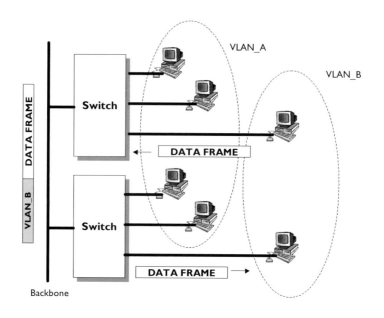

Figure C4.12 vLANs using frame tagging

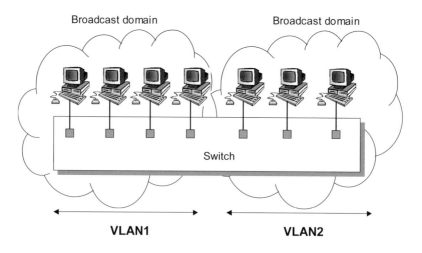

Figure C4.13 Broadcast domains for vLANs

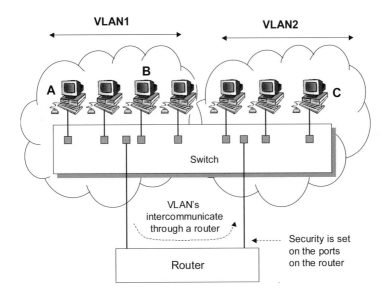

Figure C4.14   Broadcast domains for vLANs

Note that a broadcast domain extends the full length of the vLAN, and not onto other vLANs. A router does not forward broadcasts, thus the vLAN is isolated from other networks. The router provides intercommunicate between vLANs, and security is enhanced by implement security restrictions on the ports of the router.

As previously mentioned the broadcast domain is important, as nodes use it to determine the MAC addresses of nodes within their vLAN. In Figure C4.14, a node on VLAN1 could only communicate with a node on VLAN2 if would use the network address of the node on VLAN2. For example if Node A communicates with Node B, it would broadcast an ARP request into its vLAN for the MAC address of Node B, which would return it back to the vLAN. Node A can then communicate with Node B, as it uses the MAC address of Node B, and its network layer address. If Node A wishes to communicate with Node C, it will send out an ARP request to the port on the router to which it connects to (its gateway). This port will respond back with its MAC address. Node A will then send out a data frame with the MAC address of the gateway, and the destination address of Node C. The router will then forward it onto the port which has Node C connected to it, and changes the destination MAC address to the MAC address of Node C (if it already knows it, else it would initially send out an ARP request for it). The router will generally test the incoming data frame for security purposes, and will only forward it if Node A is allowed to communicate with Node C (allowing for certain conditions).

C5 Token Ring

C5.1 Introduction

Token Ring networks were developed by several manufacturers, the most prevalent being the IBM Token Ring. Token Ring networks cope well with high network traffic loadings. They were at one time extremely popular but their popularity has since been overtaken by Ethernet. Token Ring networks have, in the past, suffered from network management problems and poor network fault tolerance.

Token Ring networks are well suited to situations which have large amounts of traffic and also work well with most traffic loadings. They are not suited to large networks or networks with physically remote stations. The main advantage of Token Ring is that it copes better with high traffic rates than Ethernet, but requires a great deal of maintenance, especially when faults occur or when new equipment is added to or removed from the network. Many of these problems have now been overcome by MAUs (multistation access units), which are similar to the hubs using in Ethernet.

The IEEE 802.5 standard specifies the MAC layer for a Token Ring network with a bit rate of either 4 Mbps or 16 Mbps. There are two main types of Token Ring networks. Type 1 Token Ring uses Type 1 Token Ring cable (shielded twisted-pair) with IBM style universal connectors. Type 3 Token Ring use either Cat-3, Cat-4 or Cat-5 unshielded twisted-pair cables with modular connectors. Cat-3 has the advantage of being cheap to install and is typically used in telephone connections. Unfortunately, the interconnection distance is much less than for Cat-4 and Cat-5 cables.

C5.2 Operation

A Token Ring network circulates an electronic token (named a control token) around a closed electronic loop. Each node on the network reads the token and repeats it to the next node. The control token circulates around the ring even when there is no data being transmitted.

Nodes on a Token Ring network wishing to transmit must await a token. When they get it, they fill a frame with data and add the source and destination addresses then send it to the next node. The data frame then circulates around the ring until it reaches the destination node. It then reads the data into its local memory area (or buffer) and marks an acknowledgment on the data frame. This then circulates back to the source (or originating) node. When it receives the frame, it tests it to determine whether it contains an acknowledgment. If it does then the source nodes knows that the data frame was received correctly, else the node is not responding. If the source node has finished transmitting data then it transmits a new token, which can be used by other nodes on the ring.

Figure C5.1(a)–(d) shows a typical interchange between node B and node A. Initially, in (a), the control token circulates between all the nodes. This token does not contain any data and is only 3 bytes long. When node B finally receives the control token, it then transmits a data frame, as illustrated in (b). This data frame is passed to node C, then to node D and finally onto A. Node A will then read the data in the data frame and return an acknowledgment to node B, as illustrated in (c). After node B receives the acknowledgment, it passes a control token onto node C and this then circulates until a node wishes to transmit a data frame. Nodes are not allowed to transmit data unless they have received a valid control token. A distributed control protocol determines the sequence in which nodes transmit. This gives each node equal access to the ring.

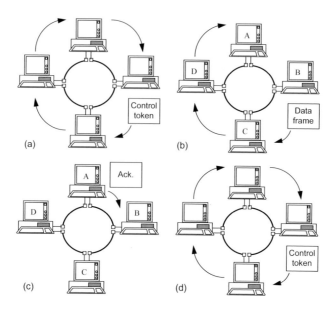

Figure C5.1 Example data exchange.

C5.3   Token Ring - media access control (MAC)

Token passing allows nodes controlled access to the ring. Figure C5.2 shows the token format for the IEEE 802.5 specification. There are two main types of frame: a control token and a data frame. A control token contains only a start and end delimiter, and an access control (AC) field. A data frame has start and end delimiters (SD/ED), an access control field, a frame control field (CF), a destination address (DA), a source address (SA), frame check sequence (FCS), data and a frame status field (FS).

The access control and frame control fields contain information necessary for managing access to the ring. This includes priority reservation, priority information and information on whether the data is user data or control information. It also contains an express indicator which informs networked nodes that an individual node requires immediate action from the network management node.

The destination and source addresses are 6 bytes in length. Logical link control information has variable length and is shown in Figure C5.2. It can either contain user data or network control information. The frame check sequence (FCS) is a 32-bit cyclic redundancy check (CRC) and the frame control field is used to indicate whether a destination node has read the data in the token.

The start and end delimiters are special bit sequences which define the start and end of the frame and thus cannot occur anywhere within the frame. As with Ethernet the bits are sent using Manchester coding. The start and end delimiters violate the standard coding scheme. The standard Manchester coding codes a 1 as a low-to-high transition and a 0 as a high-to-low transition. In the start and end delimiters, two of the bits within the delimiters are set to either a high level (H) or a low level (L). These bits disobey the standard coding as there is no change in level, i.e. from a high to a low or a low to a high. When the receiver detects this violation and the other standard coded bits in the received bit pattern, it knows that the accompanying bits are a valid frame. The coding is as follows:

- If the preceding bit is a 1 then the start delimiter is HL0HL000, else
- If the preceding bit is a 0 then the start delimiter is LH0LH000.

They are shown in Figure C5.3. The end delimiter is similar to the start delimiter, but 0's are replaced by 1's. An error detection bit (E) and a last packet indicator bit (I) are added.

    If the bit preceding the end delimiter is a 1 then the end delimiter is HL1HL1IE. If it is a 0 then it is LH1LH1IE. The E bit is used for error detection and is initially set by the originator to a 0. If any of the nodes on the ring detects an error the E bit is set to a 1. This indicates to the originator that the frame has developed an error as it was sent. The I bit determines whether the data being sent in a frame is the last in a series of data frames. If the I bit is a 0 then it is the last, else it is an intermediate frame.

    The access control field controls the access of nodes on the ring. It takes the form of PPPTMRRR, where:

PPP   –   indicates the priority of the token; this indicates which type of token the destination node can transmit.

T   –   is the token bit and is used to discriminate between a control token and a data token.

M   –   is the monitor bit and is used by an active ring monitor node to stop tokens from circulating around a network continuously.

RRR   –   are the reservation bits and allow nodes with a high priority to request the next token.

The frame control field contains control information for the MAC layer. It takes the form FFDDDDDD, where:

FF   –   indicates whether the frame is a data frame; if it is not then the DDDDDD bits control the operation of the Token Ring MAC protocol.

DDDDDD   –   controls the operation of the Token Ring MAC protocol.

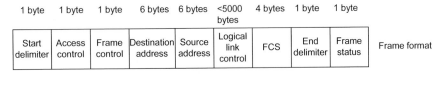

1 byte	1 byte	1 byte	6 bytes	6 bytes	<5000 bytes	4 bytes	1 byte	1 byte	
Start delimiter	Access control	Frame control	Destination address	Source address	Logical link control	FCS	End delimiter	Frame status	Frame format

1 byte	1 byte	1 byte	
Start delimiter	Access control	End delimiter	Control token

Figure C5.2   IEEE 802.5 frame format

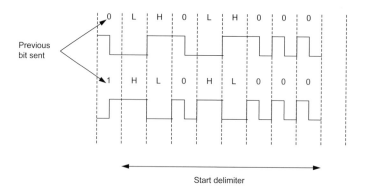

Figure C5.3 Start delimiter

The source and destination addresses can either be 2 or 6 bytes (that is, 16 or 48 bits) in length. This size must be the same for all nodes on a ring. The first bit specifies the type of address. If it is a 0 then the address is an individual node address, else it is a group address. An individual node address is used to transmit to a single node, whereas a group address transmits to all nodes with the same group address. The source address will always by an individual address as it indicates the node which originated the token. A special destination address of all 1's is used to transmit to all nodes on a ring.

The frame status field contains information on how a frame has been operated upon as it circulates round the ring. It takes the form ACXXACXX, where:

A – indicates if the destination address has been recognized. It is initially set to a 0 by the source node and is set to a 1 when the destination reads the data. If the source node detects that this bit has not been set then it knows the destination is either not present on the network or is not responding.

C – indicates that a destination node has copied a frame into its memory. This bit is also initially set to a 0 by the source node. When the destination node reads the data from the frame it is set to a 1. By testing this bit and the A bit, the source node can determine whether the destination node is active but not reading data from the frame.

C5.4   Token Ring maintenance

A Token Ring system requires considerable maintenance; it must perform the following function:

- **Ring initialization** – when the network is started, or after the ring has been broken, it must be reinitialized. A cooperative decentralized algorithm sorts out which nodes start a new token, which goes next, and so on.
- **Adding to the ring** – if a new node is to be physically connected to the ring then the network must be shut down and reinitialized.
- **Deletion from the ring** – a node can disconnect itself from the ring by joining together its predecessor and its successor. Again, the network may have to be shut down and re-initialized.

- **Fault management** – typical Token Ring errors occur when two nodes think it is their turn to transmit or when the ring is broken as no node thinks that it is their turn.

C5.5　Token Ring multistation access units (MAUs)

The problems of connecting and deleting nodes to or from a ring network are significantly reduced with a multistation access unit (MAU). Figure C5.4 shows two 3-way MAUs connected to produce a 6-node network. Normally, an MAU allows nodes to be switched in and out of a network using a changeover switch or by automatic electronic switching (known as auto-loopback). This has the advantage of not shutting down the network when nodes are added and deleted or when they develop faults.

If the changeover switches in Figure C5.4 are in the down position then the node is bypassed; if they are in the up position then the node connects to the ring.

A single coaxial (or twisted-pair) cable connects one MAU to another and two coaxial (or twisted-pair) cables connect a node to the MAU (for the in ports and the out ports). Most modern application use STP cables.

The IBM 8228 is a typical passive MAU. It can operate at 4 Mbps or 16 Mbps and has 10 connection ports, i.e. 8 passive node ports along with ring in (RI) and ring out (RO) connections. The maximum distance between MAUs is typically 650 m (at 4 Mbps) and 325 m (at 16 Mbps).

Most MAUs either have 2, 4 or 8 ports and can automatically detect the speed of the node (i.e. either 4 or 16 Mbps). Figure C5.4 shows a 32-node Token Ring network using four 8-port MAUs. Typical connectors are RJ-45 and IBM Type A connectors. The ring cable is normally either twisted-pair (Type 3), fiber-optic or coaxial cable (Type 1). MAU are intelligent devices and can detect faults on the cables supplying nodes then isolate them from the rest of the ring. Most MAUs are passive devices in that they do not require a power supply. If there are large distances between nodes then an active unit is normally used.

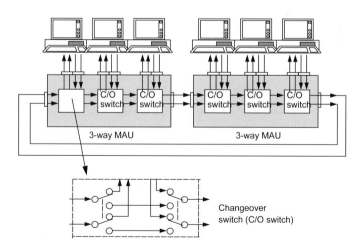

Figure C5.4　Six-node Token Ring network with two MAUs

Modern Token Ring networks normally use twisted-pair cables instead of coaxial cables. These twisted-pair cables can either be high-specification shielded twisted-pair (STP) or lower-specification unshielded twisted-pair (UTP). Cabling is discussed in the next section.

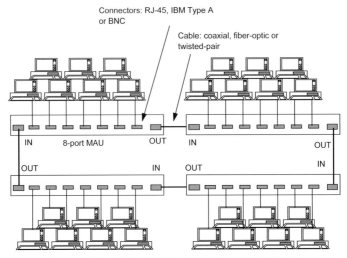

Figure C5.5 A 32-node Token Ring network with 4 MAUs

C5.6   Cabling and connectors

There are two main types of cabling used in Token Ring networks: Type 1 and Type 3. Type 1 uses STP (shielded twisted-pair) cables with IBM style male-female connectors. Type 3 networks uses Cat-3 or Cat-5 UTP (unshielded twisted-pair) cables with RJ-45 connectors. Unfortunately, Cat-3 cables are unshielded which reduces the maximum length of the connection. Type 1 networks can connect up to 260 nodes, whereas Type 3 networks can only connect up to 72 nodes.

A further source of confusion comes from the two different types of modern STP cables used in Token Ring networks. IBM type 1 cable has four cores with a screen tinned copper braid around them. Each twisted-pair is screened from each other with aluminized polyester tape. The characteristic impedance of the twisted-pairs is 150 Ω. The IBM type 6 cable is a lightweight cable which is preferred in office environments. It has a similar construction but, because it has a thinner core, signal loss is higher.

C5.7   Repeaters

A repeater is used to increase either main-ring or lobe lengths in a Token Ring LAN. The main-ring length is the distance between MAUs. The lobe length is the distance from an MAU to a node. Table C5.1 shows some typical maximum cable lengths for different bit rates and cable types. Fiber-optic cables provide the longest distances with a range of 1 km. The next best are STP cables, followed by Cat-5 and finally the lowest specification Cat-3 cables. Figure C5.6 shows the connection of two MAUs with repeaters. In this case, four repeaters are required as each repeater has only two ports (IN and OUT). The token will circulate clockwise around the network.

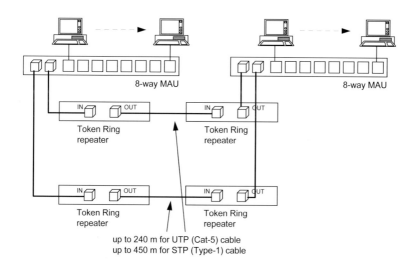

Figure C5.6 16-node Token Ring network with repeaters.

Table C5.1 Typical maximum cable lengths for different cables and bit rates.

Type	Bit rate	Cable type	Maximum distance
Type 1	4 Mbps	STP	730 m
Type 3	4 Mbps	UTP (Cat-3 cable)	275 m
Type 3	16 Mbps	UTP (Cat-5 cable)	240 m
Type 1	16 Mbps	STP	450 m
Type 1	16 Mbps	Fiber	1000 m

C5.8   Jitter suppression

Jitter can be a major problem with Token Ring networks. It is caused when the nodes on the network operate with different clock rates. It can lead to network slowdown, data corruption and station loss. Jitter is the reason that the number of nodes on a Token Ring is limited to 72 at 16 Mbps. With a jitter suppressor, the number of nodes can be increased to 256 nodes. It also allows Cat-3 cable to be used at 16 Mbps. Normally, a Token Ring Jitter Suppresser is connected to a group of MAUs. Thus, the network in Figure C5.6 could have one jitter suppresser unit connected to two of the MAUs (this would obviously limit to 7 the number of nodes connected to these MAUs).

C6 FDDI

C6.1 Introduction

A token-passing mechanism allows orderly access to a network. Apart from Token Ring, the most commonly used token-passing network is the Fiber Distributed Data Interchange (FDDI) standard. This operates at 100 Mbps and, to overcome the problems of line breaks, has two concentric Token Rings, as illustrated in Figure C6.1. Fiber optic cables have a much high-specification than copper cables and allow extremely long connections. The maximum circumference of the ring is 100 km (62 miles), with a maximum 2 km between stations (FDDI nodes are also known as stations). It is thus an excellent mechanism for connecting networks across a city or over a campus. Up to 500 stations can connect to each ring with a maximum of 1000 stations for the complete network. Each station connected to the FDDI highway can be a normal station or a bridge to a conventional local area network, such as Ethernet or Token Ring.

The two rings are useful for fault conditions but are also used for separate data streams. This effectively doubles the data-carrying capacity of FDDI (to 200 Mbps). However, if the normal traffic is more than the stated carrying capacity, or if one ring fails, then its performance degrades.

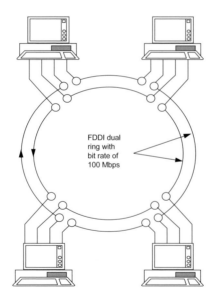

FDDI dual ring with bit rate of 100 Mbps

Figure C6.1 FDDI network

The main features of FDDI are:

- Point-to-point Token Ring topology.
- A secondary ring for redundancy.
- Dual counter rotating ring topology.
- Distributed clock for the support of large numbers of stations on the ring.

- Distributed FDDI management – equal rights and duties for all stations.
- Data integrity ensured through sophisticated encoding techniques.

C6.2 Operation

As with Token Ring, FDDI uses a token passing medium access method. Unlike Token Ring there are two types of (control) token:

- **A restricted token** – which is the normal token. The restricted token circulates around the network. A station wishing to transmit data captures the unrestricted token. It then transmits frames for a period of time made up of a fixed part (T_f) and a variable part (T_v). The variable time depends on the traffic on the ring. When the traffic is light, a station may keep the token much longer than when it is heavy.
- **An unrestricted token** – which is used for extended data interchange between two stations. To enter into an extended data interchange a station must capture the unrestricted token and change it to a restricted token. This token circulates round the network until the exchange is complete, or the extended time is over. Other stations on the network may use the ring only for the fixed period of time T_f. Once complete the token is changed back to an unrestricted type.

FDDI uses a timed token-passing protocol to transmit data because a station can hold the token no longer than a specified amount of time. Therefore, there is a limit to the amount of data that a station can transmit on any given opportunity.

The sending station must always generate a new token once it has transmitted its data frames. The station directly downstream from a sending station has the next opportunity to capture the token. This feature and the timed token ensures that the ring's capacity is divided almost equally among the stations on the ring.

C6.3 FDDI layers

The ANSI-defined FDDI standard defines four key layers:

- Media access control (MAC) layer.
- Physical layer (PHY).
- Physical media dependent (PMD).
- Station management (SMT) protocol.

FDDI covers the first two layers of the OSI model; Figure C6.2 shows how these layers fit into the model.

The MAC layer defines addressing, scheduling and data routing. Data is formed into data packets with a PHY layer. It encodes and decodes the packets into symbol streams for transmission. Each symbol has 4 bits and FDDI then uses the 4B/5B encoding to encode them into a group of 5 bits. The 5 bits are chosen to contain, at most, two successive zeros. Table C6.1 shows the coding for the bits. This type of coding ensures that there will never be more than four consecutive zeros. FDDI uses NRZI (non-return to zero with inversion) to transmit the bits. With NRZI, a 1 is coded with an alternative light (or voltage) level transition for each 1, and a zero does not change the light (or voltage) level. Figure C6.3 shows an example.

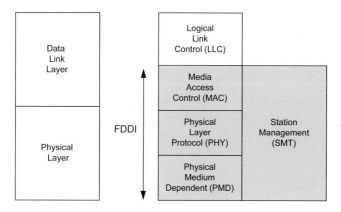

Figure C6.2 FDDI network

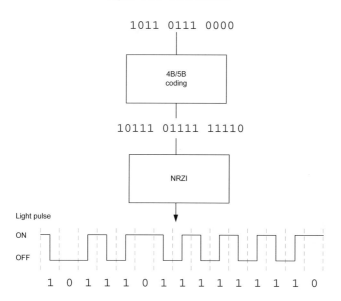

Figure C6.3 Example of bit encoding

In this case, the input bitsteam is 1011, 0111 and 0000. This is encoded, as in Table C6.1, as 10111, 01111 and 11110. This is then transmitted in NRZI. The first bit sent is a 1 and is represented as a high-to-low transition. The next bit is a zero and thus has no transition. After this a 1 is encoded, this will be transmitted as a low-to-high transition, and so on. The main advantage of NRZI coding is that the timing information is inherent within the transmitted signal and can be easily filtered out.

Apart from the 16 encoded bit patterns given Table C6.1 there are also eight control and eight violation patterns. Table C6.2 shows the eight other control symbols (QUIET, HALT, IDLE, J, K, T, R and S) and eight other violation symbols (the encoded bitstream binary values are 00001, 00010, 00011, 00101, 00110, 01000, 01100 and 10000).

The coding of the data symbols is chosen so that there are no more than three consecutive zeros in a row. This is necessary to ensure that all the stations on the ring have their clocks synchronized with all the others. Each station on an FDDI has its own independent clock. The control and violation symbols allow the reception of four or more zero bits in a row.

Table C6.1 4B/5B coding

Symbol	Binary	Bit stream	Symbol	Binary	Bit stream
0	0000	11110	8	1000	10010
1	0001	01001	9	1001	10011
2	0010	10100	A	1010	10110
3	0011	10101	B	1011	10111
4	0100	01010	C	1100	11010
5	0101	01011	D	1101	11011
6	0110	01110	E	1110	11100
7	0111	01111	F	1111	11101

Table C6.2 4B/5B coding

Symbol	Bit stream	Symbol	Bit stream
QUIET	00000	K	10001
HALT	00100	T	01101
IDLE	11111	R	00111
J	11000	S	11001

C6.4   SMT protocol

The SMT protocol handles the management of the FDDI ring, which includes:

- Adjacent neighbor indication.
- Fault detection and reconfiguration.
- Insertion and deletion from the ring.
- Traffic statistics monitoring.

C6.5   Physical connection management

Within each FDDI station there are SMT entities called PCM (physical connection management). The number of PCM entities with a station is exactly equal to the number of ports the station has. This is because each PCM is responsible for one port. The PCM entities are the parts of the SMT, which control the ports. In order to make a connection, two ports must be physically connected to each other by means of a fiber or copper cable.

C6.6   Fault tolerance method

When a station on a ring malfunctions or there is a break in one of the rings then the rest of the stations can still use the other ring. When a station on the network malfunctions then both of the rings may become inoperative. FDDI allows other stations on the network to detect this and to implement a single rotating ring. Figure C6.4 shows an FDDI network with four connected stations. In this case, the link between the upper stations have developed a fault. These stations will quickly determine that there is a fault in both cables and will inform the other stations on the network to implement a single rotating ring with the outer ring transmitting in the clockwise direction and the inner ring in the counterclockwise direction. This fault tolerance method also makes it easier to insert and delete stations from the ring.

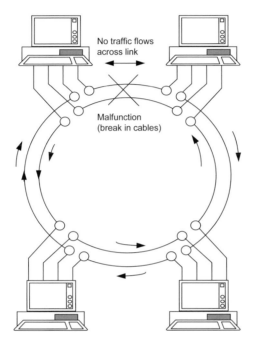

Figure C6.4   Fault tolerant network

C6.7   FDDI token format

A token circulates around the ring until a station captures it and then transmits its data in a data frame (see next section). Figure C6.5 shows the basic token format. The preamble (PA) field has four or more symbols of idle (bit stream of 11111). This is followed by the start delimiter (SD) which has a fixed pattern of 'J' (bit stream of 11000) and 'K' (bit stream of 10001). The end delimiter (ED) is two 'T' symbols (01101). The start and end delimiter bit patterns cannot occur anywhere else in the frame as they violate the standard 4B/5B coding (i.e. they may contain three or more consecutive zeros).

C6.8   FDDI Frame format

Figure C6.6 shows the FDDI data frame format, which is similar to the IEEE 802.6 frame. The PA, SD and ED fields are identical to the token fields. The frame control field (FC) contains information on the kind of frame that is to follow in the INFO field.

FDDI   421

The fields are:

- Preamble. The preamble field contains 16 idle symbols which allow stations to synchronize their clocks.
- Start delimiter. This contains a fixed field of the 'J' and 'K' symbols.
- Control field. The format of the control field is SAFFxxxx where S indicates whether it is synchronous or asynchronous. A indicates whether it is a 16-bit or 48-bit address; FF indicates whether this is an LLC (01), MAC control (00) or reserved frame. For a control frame, the remaining 4 bits (xxxx) are reserved for control types. Typical (decoded) codes are:

0100 0000 – void frame   0101 0101 – station management frame
1100 0010 – MAC frame   0101 0000 – LLC frame

When the frame is a token the control field contains either 10000000 or 11000000.

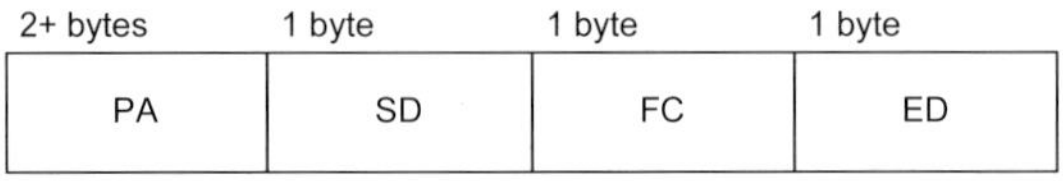

2+ bytes	1 byte	1 byte	1 byte
PA	SD	FC	ED

PA – preamble (4 or more symbols of idle)
SD – start delimiter ('J' and 'K')
FC – frame control (2 symbols)
ED – end delimiter (two 'T' symbols)

Figure C6.5 FDDI token format

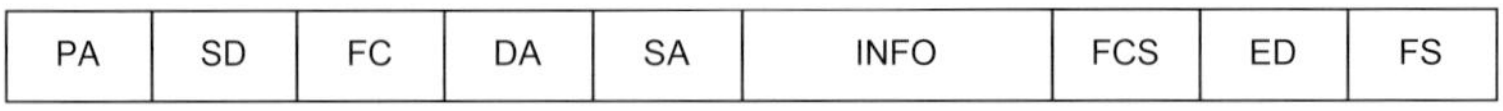

PA	SD	FC	DA	SA	INFO	FCS	ED	FS

PA – preamble (2+ bytes)   INFO – information (N bytes)
SD – starting delimiter (1 byte)   FCS – frame check sequence (4 bytes)
FC – frame control (1 byte)   ED – end delimiter (1/2 symbols)
DA – destination address (6 bytes)   FS – frame status (3 symbols)
SA – source address (6 bytes)

Figure C6.6 FDDI data frame format

- The destination address (DA) and source address (SA) are 12-symbol (6-byte) codes which identify the address of the station from where the frame has come or to where the frame is heading. Each station has a unique address and each station on the ring compares it with its own address. If the frame is destined for a particular station, that station copies the frame's contents into its buffer.

    A frame may also be destined for a group of stations. Group addresses are identified by the start bit 1. If the start bit is 0 then the frame is destined for an individual station. A broadcast address of all 1's is used to send information to all the stations on the ring.

    Station addresses can be either locally or globally administered. For global addresses the first six symbols are the manufacturer's OUI; each manufacturer has a unique OUI for all its products. The last six symbols of the address differentiate between stations of the same manufacturer.

The second bit in the address field identifies whether the address is local or global. If it is set (a 1) then it is a locally administered address, if it is unset then it is a globally administered address. In a locally administered network, the system manager sets the addresses of all network stations.

- The information field (INFO) can contain from 0 to 4 478 bytes of data. Thus the maximum frame size will be as follows:

Field	Number of bytes
Start delimiter	1
Frame control	1
Destination address	6
Source address	6
DATA (maximum)	4 478
Frame check sequence	4
End delimiter	2
End of frame sequence	2
TOTAL	4 500

- The frame check sequence contains a 32-bit CRC which is calculated from the FC, DA, SA and information fields.
- The ending delimiter contains two 'T' symbols.
- The frame status contains extra bits which identify the current status, such as frame copied indicators (F), errors detected (E) and address recognized (A).

FDDI supports either synchronous or asynchronous traffic, but the terms are actually confusing. Frames that are transmitted during their capacity allocation are known as synchronous.

C6.9　MAC protocol

The MAC protocol of FDDI MAC is similar to IEEE 802.5. It can be thought of as train, filled with passengers, traveling around a track. The train travels around the ring continuously. When a passenger wishes to get on the train, they get in front of the train, which then pushes them round the ring. The passenger then travels around the ring, and delivers their message to the destination station. The passenger stays on the train until the train reaches the source again, where they will get off. Other passengers can get on the train and deliver their own messages while there are others on the train. These passengers go in between the train and the existing passengers.

The actual operational parts work like this:

- A node cannot transmit until it captures a token (the train).
- When a node captures the token, it transmits its frame then the token.
- The frame travels around the ring from source back to source station.
- If another station wishes to transmit a frame it waits for the end of the frames currently on the ring, adds its frame after these frames then appends the token onto the end.
- The station, which initiates a frame, is responsible for taking it off the ring.
- Each station reads the frame as it circulates around the ring.

- Each station can modify the status bits as the frame passes. If a station detects an error then it sets the E bit; if it has copied the frame into its buffer then it sets the C bit; if it detects its own address it sets the A bit.
- Thus a correctly received frame will be received back at the source node with the C and A bits set.
- A frame which is received back at the source with the E bit is not automatically retransmitted. A message is sent to higher layer in the protocol (such as the LLC layer).

C6.10   Applications of FDDI networks

As was seen in Chapter C3, Ethernet is an excellent method of attaching stations to a network cheaply but is not a good transport mechanism for a backbone network or with high traffic levels. It also suffers, in its standard form, from a lack of speed. FDDI networks overcome these problems as they offer a much higher bit rate, higher reliability and longer interconnections. Thus typical applications of FDDI networks are:

- As a backbone network in an internetwork connection.
- Any applications which requires high security and/or a high degree of fault tolerance. Fiber-optic cables are generally more reliable and are difficult to tap into without it being detected.
- As a subnetwork connecting high-speed computers and their peripheral devices (such as storage units).
- As a network connecting stations where an application program requires high-speed transfers of large amounts of data (such as computer-aided design – CAD). Maximum data traffic for an FDDI network is at least 10 times greater than for standard Ethernet and Token Ring networks. As it is a token-passing network, it is less susceptible to heavy traffic loads than Ethernet.

C6.11   FDDI backbone network

The performance of the network backbone is extremely important as many users on the network depend on it. If the traffic is too heavy, or if it develops a fault, then it affects the performance of the whole network. An FDDI backbone helps with these problems because it has a high bit rate and normally increases the reliability of the backbone.

Figure C6.7 shows an FDDI backbone between four campuses. In this case, the FDDI backbone only carries traffic which is transmitted between campuses. This is because the router only routes traffic out of the campus network when it is intended for another campus. As tokens circulate round both rings, two data frames can be transmitted round the rings at the same time.

C6.12   FDDI media

FDDI networks can use two types of fiber-optic cable, either single-mode or multimode. The mode refers to the angle at which light rays are reflected and propagated through the fiber core. Single-mode fibers have a narrow core, such as 10 µm for the core and 125 µm for the cladding (known as 10/125 micron cable). This type allows light to enter only at a single angle. Multimode fiber has a relatively thick core, such as 62.5 μm for the core and 125 μm for the cladding (known as 62.5/125 micron cable). Multi-mode cable reflects light rays at many angles. The disadvantage of these multiple propagation paths is that it can cause the light pulses to spread out and thus limit the rate at which data is accurately received. Thus, single-mode fibers have a higher bandwidth than multimode fibers and allow longer interconnection distances. The fibers most commonly used in FDDI are 62.5/125, and this type of cable is defined in the ANSI X3T9.5 standard.

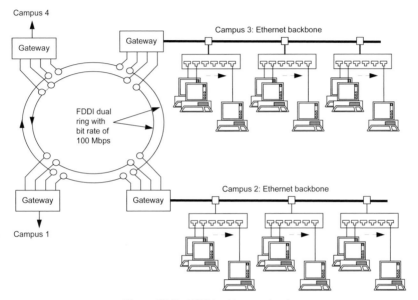

Figure C6.7   FDDI backbone network

C6.13   FDDI attachments

There are four types of station which can attach to an FDDI network:

- Dual attachment stations (DAS).
- Single attachment stations (SAS).
- Dual attachment concentrators (DAC).
- Single attachment concentrators (SAC).

Figure C6.8 shows an FDDI network configuration that includes all these types of station. An SAS connects to the FDDI rings through a concentrator, so it is easy to add, delete or change its location. The concentrator automatically bypasses disconnected stations.

Each DAS and DAC requires four fibers to connect it to the network: Primary In, Primary Out, Secondary In and Secondary Out. The connection of an SAS only requires two fibers. Normally Slave In and Slave Out on the SAS are connected to the Master Out and Master In on the concentrator unit, as shown in Figure C6.9.

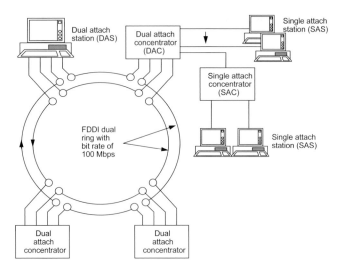

Figure C6.8 FDDI network configuration

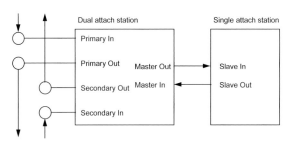

Figure C6.9 Connection of a DAS and a SAS

FDDI stations attach to the ring using a media interface connector (MIC). An MIC receptacle connects to the stations and an MIC plug on the network end of the connection. A dual attachment station has two MIC receptacles. One provides Primary Ring In and Secondary Ring Out, the other has Primary Ring Out and Secondary Ring In, as illustrated in Figure C6.10.

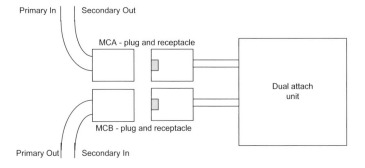

Figure C6.10 Connection of dual attach units

C6.14 FDDI specification

Table C6.3 describes the basic FDDI specification. Notice that the maximum interconnection distance for multimode cable is 2 km as compared with 20 km for single-mode cable.

Table C6.3 Basic FDDI specification

Parameter	Description
Topology	Token Ring
Access method	Time token passing
Transport media	Optical fiber, shield twisted pair, unshielded twisted pair
Maximum number of stations	500 each ring (1000 total)
Data rate	100 Mbps
Maximum data packet size	4 500 bytes
Maximum total ring length	100 km
Maximum distance between stations	2 km (for multimode fiber cable), 20 km (for single-mode fiber cable)
Attenuation budget	11 dB (between stations), 1.5 dB/km at 1300 nm for 62.5/125 fiber
Link budget	< 11 dB

C6.15 FDDI-II

FDDI-II is an upward-compatible extension to FDDI that adds the ability to support circuit-switched traffic in addition to the data frames supported by the original FDDI. With FDDI-II, it is possible to set up and maintain a constant data rate connection between two stations.

The circuit-switched connection consists of regularly repeating time slots in the frame, often called an isochronous frame. This type of data is common when real-time signals, such as speech and video, are sampled. For example, speech is sampled 8000 times per second, whereas high-quality audio is sampled at 44 000 times per second.

Figure C6.11 shows a layer diagram of an FDDI-II station. The physical layer and the station management are the same as the original FDDI. Two new layers have been added to the MAC layer; known as hybrid ring control, they consist of:

- Hybrid multiplexer (HMUX).
- Isochronous MAC (IMAC).

The IMAC module provides an interface between FDDI and the isochronous service, represented by the circuit-switched multiplexer (CS-MUX). The HMUX multiplexes the packet data from the MAC and the isochronous data from the IMAC.

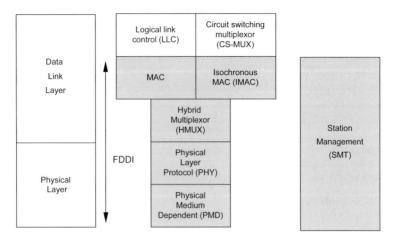

Figure C6.11   FDDI-II layered model

An FDDI-II network operates in a basic mode or a hybrid mode. In the basic mode the FDDI ring operates as the original FDDI specification where tokens rotate around the network. In the hybrid mode a connection can either be circuit-switched or packet-switched. It uses a continuously repeating protocol data unit known as a cycle. A cycle is a data frame that is similar to synchronous transmission systems. The content of the cycle is visible to all stations as it circulates around the ring. A station called the cycle master generates a new cycle 8 000 times a second. At 100 Mbps, this gives a cycle size of 12 500 bits. As each cycle completes its circuit of the ring, the cycle master strips it. Figure C6.12 shows the two different types of transmission.

Figure C6.12   Circuit-switched and packet-switched data

C6.16   Standards

The FDDI standard was defined by the ANSI committee X3T9.5. This has since been adopted by the ISO as ISO 9314 which defines FDDI using five main layers:

- ISO 9314-1: Physical Layer Protocol (PHY).
- ISO 9314-2: Media Access Control (MAC).
- ISO 9314-3: Physical Media Dependent (PMD).
- ISO 9314-4: Station Management (SMT).
- ISO 9314-5: Hybrid Ring Control (HRC), FDDI-II.

C6.17 Practical FDDI network – EaStMAN

The EaStMAN (Edinburgh and Stirling Metropolitan Area Network) consortium comprises seven institutions of Higher Education in the Edinburgh and Stirling area of Scotland. The main institutions are: the University of Edinburgh, the University of Stirling, Napier University, Heriot-Watt University, Edinburgh College of Art, Moray House Institute of Education and Queen Margaret College. FDDI and ATM networks have been installed around Edinburgh with an optical link to Stirling.

Figure C6.13 shows the connections of Phase 1 of the project and Figure C6.14 shows the rings. The total circumference of the rings is 58 km (which is less than the maximum limit of 100 km). The FDDI ring provides intercampus communications and also a link to the Super-JANET (Joint Academic NETwork) and the ATM ring is for future development.

C6.17.1 Fiber optic cables

The FDDI ring is 58 km and, for the purpose of FDDI standardization across the MAN, the outer FDDI ring is driven anticlockwise and the inner ring clockwise. Figure C6.15 shows the attenuation rates and distance between each site (in dBs). Note that an extra 0.4 dB should be added onto each fiber connection to take into account the attenuation at the fiber termination. Thus, the total attenuation between the New College and Moray House will be approximately 2.4 dB.

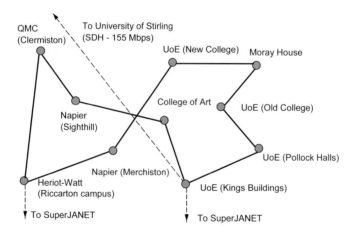

Figure C6.13   EaStMAN Phase 1 connections.

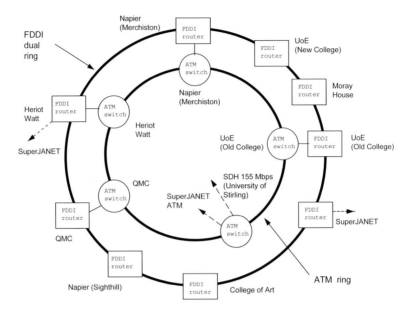

Figure C6.14 EaStMAN ring connections

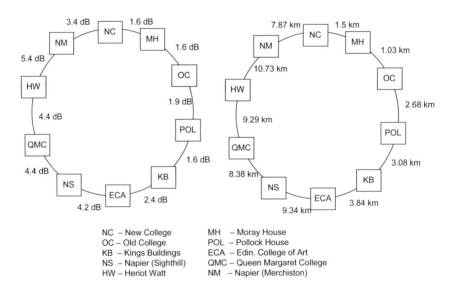

NC – New College MH – Moray House
OC – Old College POL – Pollock House
KB – Kings Buildings ECA – Edin. College of Art
NS – Napier (Sighthill) QMC – Queen Margaret College
HW – Heriot Watt NM – Napier (Merchiston)

Figure C6.15 Attenuation and distances of EaStMAN Phase I

C7 ATM

C7.1 Introduction

Most of the networking technologies discussed so far are good at carrying computer-type data and they provide a reliable connection between two nodes. Unfortunately, they are not as good at carrying real-time sampled data, such as digitized video or speech. Real-time data from speech and video requires constant sampling and these digitized samples must propagate through the network with the minimum of delay (latency). Any significant delay in transmission can cause the recovered signal to be severely distorted or for the connection to be lost. Ethernet, Token Ring and FDDI simply send the data into the network without first determining whether there is a communication channel for the data to be transported (and rely on the Transport layer to create a reliable connection).

Figure C7.1 shows some traffic profiles for sampled speech and computer-type data (a loading of 1 is the maximum loading). It can be seen that computer-type data tends to burst in periods of time. These bursts have a relatively heavy loading on the network. On the other hand, sampled speech has a relatively low loading on the network but requires a constant traffic throughput. It can be seen that if these traffic profiles were to be mixed onto the same network then the computer-type data would swamp the sampled speech data at various times.

Asynchronous transfer mode (ATM) overcomes the problems of transporting computer-type data and sampled real-time data by:

- Analyzing the type of connection to be made. The type of data dictates the type of connection; for example, computer data requires a reliable connection, whereas real-time sampled data requires a connection with a low propagation delay.
- Analyzing the type of data to be transmitted and knowing its traffic profile. Computer data tends to create bursts of traffic whereas real-time data will be constant traffic.
- Reserving a virtual path for the data to allow the data profile to be transmitted within the required quality of service.
- Splitting the data into small packets which have the minimum overhead in the number of extra bits. These 'fast-packets' traverse the network using channels which have been reserved for them.

ATM has been developed mainly by the telecommunications companies. Unfortunately two standards currently exist. In the USA the ANSI T1S1 subcommittee have supported and investigated ATM and in Europe it has been investigated by ETSI. There are small differences between the two proposed standards, but they may converge into one common standard. The ITU-T has also dedicated study group XVIII to ATM-type systems with the objective of merging differences and creating one global standard for high-speed networks throughout the world. The main advantages are:

- Defined QoS (Quality of Service). This quality of service may relate to bandwidth, error rates, delays, peak bandwidth support, guaranteed path, and so on.
- Scaleable bandwidths. ATM integrates well with existing PCM-TDM systems and can fit into any layer of the existing telecommunication service.

- Connection-oriented. This involves the setup of a virtual circuit prior to data transfer. The sender of the data can thus be sure that the receiver is willing to accept the data, and that the required path has been setup.

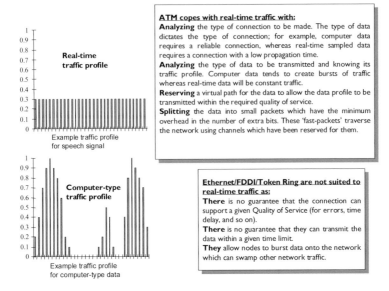

ATM copes with real-time traffic with:
Analyzing the type of connection to be made. The type of data dictates the type of connection; for example, computer data requires a reliable connection, whereas real-time sampled data requires a connection with a low propagation time.
Analyzing the type of data to be transmitted and knowing its traffic profile. Computer data tends to create bursts of traffic whereas real-time data will be constant traffic.
Reserving a virtual path for the data to allow the data profile to be transmitted within the required quality of service.
Splitting the data into small packets which have the minimum overhead in the number of extra bits. These 'fast-packets' traverse the network using channels which have been reserved for them.

Ethernet/FDDI/Token Ring are not suited to real-time traffic as:
There is no guarantee that the connection can support a given Quality of Service (for errors, time delay, and so on).
There is no guarantee that they can transmit the data within a given time limit.
They allow nodes to burst data onto the network which can swamp other network traffic.

Figure C7.1
Traffic profiles for sampled speech and computer-type data

Its disadvantages are that it:

- Is a complex networking technology. ATM is an extremely complex networking technology that requires a great deal of software processing.
- Requires an overlaying of existing protocols. ATM, itself, can provide the network layer of the OSI model, and does not required protocols such as IP. Unfortunately it would be too expensive to setup an infrastructure of ATM address servers, thus, IP addressing is typically used to route data between interconnected networks. This means that the network layer is implemented twice.

Note that ATM does not have any mechanisms for guaranteeing delivery of a cell, as it is assumed that higher-level protocols, such as TCP will be used to provide for acknowledgements.

C7.2   Objectives of ATM

The major objective of ATM is to integrate real-time data (such as voice and video signals) and non-real-time data (such as computer data and file transfer). Computer-type data can typically be transferred in non-real-time but it is important that the connection is error free. In many application programs, a single bit error can cause serious damage. On the other hand, voice and video data require a constant sampling rate and low propagation delays, but are more tolerant to errors and any losses of small parts of the data.

An ATM network relies on user-supplied information to profile traffic flows so that the connection has the desired quality of service. Figure C7.2 gives four basic data types. These are further complicated by differing data types either sending data in a continually repeating fashion (such as telephone data) or with a variable frequency (such as interactive video). For example a high-resolution video image may need to be sent as several megabytes of data in a short time burst, but then nothing for a few seconds. For speech the signal must be sampled constantly at approximately 8 000 times per second.

Computer data will typically be sent in bursts, with either a high transfer rate (perhaps when running a computer package remotely over a network) or with a relatively slow transfer (such as when reading textural information). Conventional circuit-switched technology (such as ISDN and PCM-TDM) are thus wasteful in their connection because they either allocate a switched circuit (ISDN) or reserve a fixed time slot (PCM-TDM), no matter whether any data is being transmitted at that time. With circuit-switched technologies it may not be possible to service high burst rates by allocating either time slots or switched circuits when all of the other time slots are full, or because other switched circuits are being used.

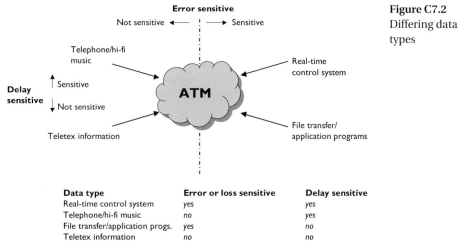

Figure C7.2 Differing data types

Data type	Error or loss sensitive	Delay sensitive
Real-time control system	yes	yes
Telephone/hi-fi music	no	yes
File transfer/application progs.	yes	no
Teletex information	no	no

C7.3   ATM versus ISDN and PCM-TDM

ISDN and PCM-TDM use a synchronous transfer mode (STM) technique where a connection is made between two devices by circuit switching. For this the transmitting device is assigned a given time slot to transmit the data, which is fixed for the period of the transmission. The main problems with this type of transmission are:

- Not all the time slots are filled by data when there is light data traffic; this is wasteful in data transfer.
- When a connection is made between two endpoints a fixed time slot is assigned and data from that connection is always carried in that time slot. This is also wasteful because there may be no data being transmitted in certain time periods.

ATM overcomes these problems by splitting the data up into small fixed-length packets, known as cells. Each data cell is sent with its routing address and follows a fixed route through the network. The packets are small enough so that, if they are lost, possibly due to congestion, they can either be requested (for high reliability) or cause little signal degradation (typically in voice and video traffic).

The address of devices on an ATM network are identified by a virtual circuit identifier (VCI), instead of by a time slot as in an STM network. The VCI is carried in the header portion of the fast packet.

C7.4 ATM cells

The ATM cell, as specified by the ANSI T1S1 subcommittee, has 53 bytes, as shown in Figure C7.3. The first five bytes are the header and the remaining bytes are the information field which can hold up to 48 bytes of data. Optionally the data can contain a 4-byte ATM adaptation layer and 44 bytes of actual data. A bit in the control field of the header sets the data to either 44 or 48 bytes. The ATM adaptation layer field allows for fragmentation and reassembly of cells into larger packets at the source and destination, respectively. The control field also contains bits which specify whether it is a flow control cell or an ordinary data cell, and a bit to indicate whether this packet can be deleted in a congested network, and so on.

The ETSI definition of an ATM cell also contains 53 bytes with a 5-byte header and 48 bytes of data. The main differences are the number of bits in the VCI field, the number of bits in the header checksum, and the definitions and position of the control bits.

The IEEE 802.6 standard for the MAC layer of the metropolitan area network (MAN) DQDB (distributed queue dual bus) protocol is similar to the ATM cell.

Figure C7.3
ATM cell

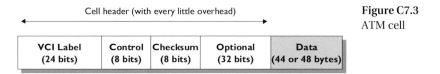

VCI Label (24 bits)	Control (8 bits)	Checksum (8 bits)	Optional (32 bits)	Data (44 or 48 bytes)

Cell header (with every little overhead)

C7.5 Routing cells within an ATM network

A user network interface (UNI) allows users to gain access to an ATM network. The UNI transmits data into the network with a set of agreed specifications and the network must then try to ensure the connection stays within those requirements. These requirements define the required quality of service for the entire duration of the connection.

In STM networks, data can change its position in each time slot in the interchanges over the global network. This can occur in ATM where the VCI label changes between intermediate nodes in the route. When a transmitting node wishes to communicate through the network it makes contact with the UNI and negotiates parameters such as destination, traffic type, peak and traffic requirements, delay and cell loss requirement, and so on. The UNI forwards this request to the network, from which the network computes a route based on the specified parameters and determines which links on each leg of the route can best support the requested quality of service and data traffic. It sends a connection set-up request to all the nodes in the path en route to the destination node.

Figure C7.4 shows an example of ATM routing. In this case, User 1 connects to Users 2 and 3. The virtual path set up between User 1 and User 2 is through the ATM switches 2, 3 and 4, whereas User 1 and User 3 connect through ATM switches 1, 5 and 6. A VCI number of 12 is assigned to the path between ATM switches 1 and 2, in the connection between User 1 and User 2. When ATM switch 2 receives a cell with a VCI number of 12 then it sends the cell to ATM switch 3 and gives it a new VCI number of 6. When it gets to ATM switch 3 it is routed to ATM switch 4 and given the VCI number of 22. The virtual circuit for User 1 to User 3 is through ATM switches 1, 5 and 6, and the VCI numbers used are 10 and 15. Once a connection is terminated the VCI labels assigned to the communications are used for other connections.

Certain users, or applications, can be assigned reserved VCI labels for special services that may be provided by the network. However, as the address field only has 24 bits it is unlikely that many of these requests would be granted. ATM does not provide for acknowledgements when the cells arrive at the destination (as it relies on the Transport layer for these services).

Note that as there is a virtual circuit set up between the transmitting and receiving node then cells are always delivered in the same order as they are transmitted. This is because cells cannot take alternative routes to the destination. Even if the cells are buffered at a node, they will still be transmitted in the correct sequence.

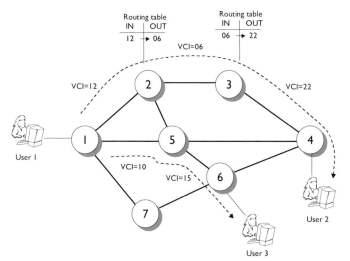

Figure C7.4

A virtual ATM virtual connection

C7.5.1 VCI header

The 5-byte ATM user network cell header splits into six main fields:

- GFC (4 bits), which is the generic control bit, and is used only for local significance and is not transmitted from the sender to the receiver.
- VPI (8 bits), which is the path connection identifier (VPI). See next section for an explanation of virtual paths.
- VCI (16 bits) which is the virtual path/channel identifier (VCI). Its usage was described in the previous section. Each part of the route is allocated a VCI number.
- PT (3 bits), which is the payload type field. This is used to identify the higher-layer application or data type.
- CLP (1 bit), which is the cell loss priority, bit and indicates if a cell is expendable. When the network is busy an expendable cell may be deleted. If CLP = 1, cells are dropped before any CLP = 0 cells are dropped.
- HEC (8 bits), which is the header error control field. This is an 8-bit checksum for the

header. It uses a cyclic code with a generating polynomial of $x^8 + x^2 + x + 1$. The first 4 bytes, written as a polynomial, are multiplied by x^8 and divided by the generating polynomial. Next 01010101 is added. The remainder is the HEC field, and transmitted to the receiver. At the receiver, 01010101 is first subtracted before further interpretation.

Note that the user-to-network cell differs from the network-to-network cell. A network-to-network cell, for a network-network interface (NNI), uses a 12-bit VPI field and does not have a GFC field. Otherwise, it is identical. Figure C7.5 shows the format of the UNI (User-network interface) cell, and the NNI cell.

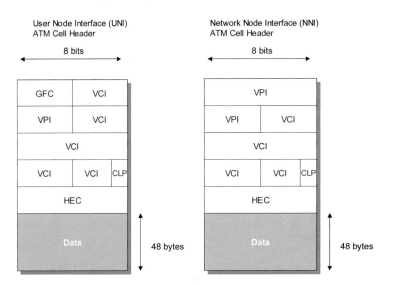

Figure C7.5 ATM cells for UNI and NNI

C7.6   Virtual channels and virtual paths

Virtual circuits are set up between two users when a connection is made. Cells then travel over this fixed path through a reserved route. Often several virtual circuits take the same path, which can be grouped together to form a virtual path.

A virtual path is defined as a collection of virtual channels which have the same start and end points, as illustrated in Figure C7.6. These channels will take the same route. This makes the network administration easier and allows new virtual circuits, with the same route, to be easily set up.

Some of the advantages of virtual paths are:

- Network user groups or interconnected networks can be mapped to virtual paths and are thus easily administered.
- Simpler network architecture that consists of groups (virtual paths) with individual connections (virtual circuits).
- Less network administration and shorter connection times arise from fewer set-up connections.

Virtual circuits and virtual paths allow two levels of cell routing through the network. A VC switch routes virtual circuits and a VP switch routes virtual paths. Figure C7.7 shows a VP switch and a VC switch. In this case, the VP switch contains the routing table which maps VP1 to VP2, VP2 to VP3 and VP3 to VP1. This switch does not change the VCI number of the incoming virtual circuits (for example VC1 goes in as VC1 and exits as VC1).

The diagram shows the concepts between both types of switches. The VP switch on the left-hand side redirects the contents of a virtual path to a different virtual path. The virtual connections it contains are unchanged. This is similar to switching an input cable to a different physical cable. In a VC switch the virtual circuits are switched. In the case of Figure C7.7 the routing table will contain VC7 mapped to VC5, VC8 to VC6, and so on. The VC switch thus ignores the VP number and only routes the VC number. Thus the input and output VP number can change.

A connection is made by initially sending routing information cells through the network. When the connection is made, each switch in the route adds a link address for either a virtual path and or a virtual connection. The combination of VP and VC addressing allows for the support of any addressing scheme, including subscriber telephone numbering or IP addresses. Each of these address can be broken down in a chain of VPI/VCI addresses.

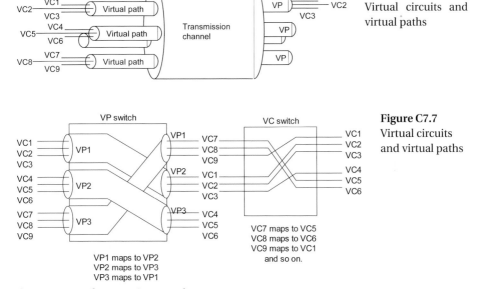

Figure C7.6
Virtual circuits and virtual paths

Figure C7.7
Virtual circuits and virtual paths

The two types of connections are thus:

- Permanent Virtual Connections (PVC). These are connections which are set up by some external mechanism, such as with network management software. Each of the switches on the route from the ATM source and destination ATM system are set up with the appropriate VPI/VCI values. Normally these are setup manually.
- Switched Virtual Connections (SVC). These are connections which are automatically set up using the signaling protocol. They are set up automatically, and require no manual interaction.

C7.7 Statistical multiplexing, ATM signalling and call set-up

Fast packet switching attempts to solve the problem of unused time slots of STM. This is achieved by statistically multiplexing several connections on the same link based on their traffic characteristics. Applications, such as voice traffic, which requires a constant data transfer, are allowed safe routes through the network. Whereas several applications, which have bursts of traffic, may be assigned to the same link in the hope that statistically they will not all generate bursts of data at the same time. Even if some of them were to burst simultaneously, their data could be buffered and sent later. This technique is called statistical multiplexing and allows the average traffic on the network to be evened out over a relatively short time period. This is impossible on an STM network.

ATM, as with most telecommunications systems, uses a single-pass approach to setting up a connection. Initially, the source connection (the source end-system) communicates a connection request to the destination connection (the destination end-point). The routing protocol manages the routing of the connection request and all subsequent data flow. The call is established with:

- A set-up message. This is initially sent, across the UNI, to the first ATM switch. It contains:
  - Destination end-system address.
  - Desired traffic.
  - Quality of service.
  - Information Elements (IE) defining particular desired higher-layer protocol bindings and so on.

- The initial ATM switch sends back a local call proceeding acknowledgement to the source end-system.
- The initial ATM switch invokes an ATM routing protocol, and propagates a signaling request across the network; it finally reaches the ATM switch connected to the destination end-system.
- The destination ATM switch connected to the destination end-system forwards the set-up message to the end-system, across its UNI.
- The destination end-system either accepts or rejects the connection. If necessary, the destination can negotiate the connection parameters. If the destination end-system rejects the connection request, it returns a release message. This is also sent back to the source end-system and clears the connection, such as clearing any allocated VCI labels. A release message can also be used by any of the end-systems, or by the network, to clear an established connection.
- If the destination end-system accepts the call then the ATM switch, which connects to it, returns a connect message through the network, along the same path.
- When the source end-system receives and acknowledges the connection message, either node can then start transmitting data on the connection (the chain of allocated VCI labels defines the route).

The connections in an ATM network are:

- UNI (user-network interface). The UNI connects to ATM end-systems.

- NNI (network-node interface). The NNI is any physical or logical link across which two ATM switches exchange the NNI protocol.

C7.7.1 Signaling packets

A connection is set up using signal information, which are sent using signaling packets. It uses a one-pass approach to setting up the virtual path, Along this path, each of the ATM switches are also preconfigured to receive any signaling packets sent across a connection, they pass them to the signaling process which will service them. In general, VCI labels from 0 to 31 for each VPI are reserved for control purposes. Thus, all allocated VCI labels will be above 32. The signaling packet has the VCI label of **five**, and a VPI label of **zero**, and is passed from switch to switch. As it passes each switch, they will set up a connection identifier (VCI/VPI labels) for the connection. Two labels are used for each connection to identify the traffic flowing in one either of the two directions (such as from Switch X to Switch Y, and from Switch Y to Switch X). Figure C7.8 shows an example of a call set up from End system A to End system B. The phases of the connection will be:

- **Signaling request.** Initially a signal packet is initiated from End system A which requests to Switch 1 that it wants to connect with End system B, this is then passed onto Switch 2, then to Switch 3, and so on, until it reaches End system B. This is achieved with a Connect message.
- **Connection routed.** Each of the switches along the route will reserve VCI/VPI labels for data traveling in one of the two directions.
- **Connection accept/reject.** End system B will decide if it wishes to accept or reject the connection. If it accepts it sends back an Okay signal to all the switches along the route.
- **Data flow.** After the virtual circuit has been setup, the two end systems can transmit data using the VCI/VPI labels that have been allocated for the connection. If the end system rejects the connection, all the switches along the reserved route will delete the reserved VCI/VPI labels from their routing tables (using a Release message).
- **Connection teardown.** After the data has been transmitted a signaling packet is sent along the route, and all the switches delete the allocated VCI/VPI labels from their routing tables. This is achieved with a Release message.

The routing of the connection request, and the resultant virtual data path is defined by an ATM routing protocol, such as the P-NNI (Private-NNI) protocol. These protocols route the connection request using:

- Destination address.
- Traffic information. The ATM routing protocols can pass information on traffic flows, so that connections can be setup so that they can avoid heavily used traffic routes. The ATM routing protocol will thus allow the network to made better use of the available bandwidth.
- QoS parameters. These are the parameters requested by the source end-system.

The two fundamental types of ATM connections are:

- **Point-to-point connections.** This is a connection which connects two ATM end-systems, and data flow can either be unidirectional or bidirectional.
- **Point-to-multipoint connections.** This is a connection which connects a single source

end-system (*the root node*) to many destination end-systems (*the leaves*). In this, an ATM switch replicates the cells for the multiply connected branches. This type of connection is unidirectional, and allows the root to transmit to the leaves, but not the leaves to transmit to the root, or to each other, on the same connection. This technique is similar to multicasting and/or broadcasting, which is typically used in Ethernet systems. The reason that these are unidirectional, is that if leaf nodes were to transmit cells they would be received by both the root node and all other leaf nodes.

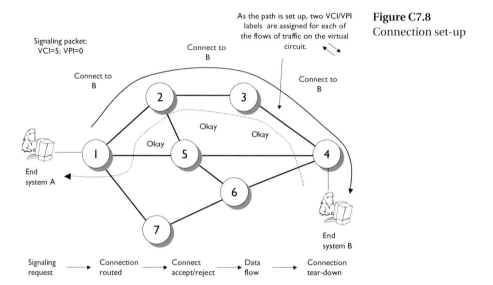

Figure C7.8
Connection set-up

C7.8   ATM and the OSI model

The basic ATM cell fits roughly into the data link layer of the OSI model, but contains some network functions, such as end-to-end connection, flow control, and routing. It thus fits into layers 2 and 3 of the model, as shown in Figure C7.9. The layer 4 software layer, such as TCP, can communicate directly with ATM.

The ATM network provides a virtual connection between two gateways and the IP protocol fragments IP packets into ATM cells at the transmitting UNI which are then reassembled into the IP packet at the destination UNI.

With TCP/IP each host is assigned an IP address as is the ATM gateway. Once the connection has been made then the cells are fragmented into the ATM network and follow a predetermined route through the network. At the receiver the cells are reassembled using the ATM adaptation layer. This reforms the original IP packet which is then passed to the next layer.

The functions of the three ATM layers are:

- ATM adaptation layer (AAL) – segmentation and reassembly of data into cells and vice-versa, such as convergence (CS) and segmentation (SAR). It is also involved with quality of service (QOS).
- ATM data link (ADL) – maintenance of cells and their routing through the network, such as generic flow control, cell VPI/VCI translation, cell multiplex and demultiplex.

- ATM physical layer (PHY) – transmission and physical characteristics, such as cell rate decoupling, HEC header sequence generation/verification, cell delineation, transmission frame adaptation, transmission frame generation/recovery.

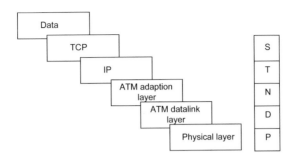

Figure C7.9　ATM and the OSI model

C7.9　ATM physical layer

The physical layer is not an explicit part of the ATM definition, but is currently being considered by the standards organizations. T1S1 has standardized on SONET (Synchronous Optical NETwork) as the preferred physical layer, with STS-3c at 155.5 Mbps, STS-12 at 622 Mbps and STS-48 at 2.4 Gbps.

The SONET physical layer specification provides a standard worldwide digital telecommunications network hierarchy, known internationally as the Synchronous Digital Hierarchy (SDH). The base transmission rate, STS-1, is 51.84 Mbps. This is then multiplexed to make up higher bit rate streams, such as STS-3 which is 3 times STS-1, STS-12 which is 12 times STS-1, and so on. The 155 Mbps stream is the lowest bit rate for ATM traffic and is also called STM-1 (synchronous transport module - level 1).

The SDH specifies a standard method on how data is framed and transported synchronously across fiber-optic transmission links without requiring that all links and nodes have the same synchronized clock for data transmission and recovery.

C7.10　AAL service levels

The AAL layer uses cells to process data into a cell-based format and to provide information to configure the level of service required.

C7.10.1 Processing data

The AAL performs two essential functions for processing data as shown: the higher-level protocols present a data unit with a specific format. This data frame is then converted using a convergence sublayer with the addition of a header and trailer that give information on how the data unit should be segmented into cells and reassembled at the destination. The data is then segmented into cells, together with the convergence subsystem information and other management data, and sent through the network.

C7.10.2 AAL functionality

The AAL layer, as part of the process, also defines the level of service that the user wants from the connection. The following shows the four classes supported. For each class there is an associated AAL.

Timing information between source and destination
CLASS A: Required   CLASS B: Required
CLASS C: Not required   CLASS D: Not required

Bit rate characteristics
CLASS A: Constant   CLASS B: Variable
CLASS C: Variable   CLASS D: Variable

Connection mode
CLASS A: Connection-oriented   CLASS B: Connection-oriented
CLASS C: Connection-oriented   CLASS D: Connectionless

C7.10.3 AAL services

Thus, class A supports a constant bit rate with a connection and preserves timing information. This is typically used for voice transmission. Class B is similar to A but has a variable bit rate. Typically, it is used for video/audio data. Class C also has a variable bit rate and is connection-oriented, although there is no timing information. This is typically used for non-real-time data, such as computer data. Class D is the same as class C but is connectionless. This means there is no connection between the sender and the receiver before the data is transmitted.

There are four AAL services: AAL1 (for class A), AAL2 (for class B), AAL3/4 or AAL5 (for class C) and AAL3/4 (for class D).

AAL1

The AAL1 supports class A and is intended for real-time voice traffic; it provides a constant bit rate and preserves timing information over a connection. The format of the 48 bytes of the data cell consists of 47 bytes of data, such as PCM or ADPCM code and a 1-byte header. Figure C7.10 shows the format of the cell, including the cell header. The 47-byte data field is described as the SAR-PDU (segmentation and reassembly protocol data units). The header consists of:

- SN (4 bits) which is a sequence number.
- SNP (4 bits) which is the sequence number protection.

5 bytes	4 bits	4 bits	47 bytes
Cell header	SNP	SNP	SAR-PDU data

Figure C7.10   ATM and the OSI model

AAL type 2

AAL type 2 is under further study.

AAL type 3/4

Type 3/4 is connection-oriented where the bit rate is variable and there is no need for timing information (Figure C7.11). It uses two main formats:

- SAR (segment and reassemble) which is segments of CPCS PDU with a SAR header and trailer. The extra SAR fields allow the data to be reassembled at the receiver. When the CPCS PDU data has been reassembled the header and trailer are discarded. The fields in the SAR are:
    - Segment type (ST) identifies has the SAR has been segmented. Figure C7.11 show how the CPCS PDU data has been segmented into five segments: one beginning segment, three continuation segments and one end segment. The ST field has 2 bits and can therefore contain one of four possible types:

        - SSM (single sequence message) identifies that the SAR contains the complete data.
        - BOM (beginning of message) identifies that it is the first SAR PDU in a sequence.
        - COM (continuation of message) identifies that it is an intermediate SAR PDU.
        - EOM (end of message) identifies that it is the last SAR PDU.

    - Sequence number (SN) which is used to reassemble a SAR SDU and thus verify that all of the SAR PDUs have been received.
    - Message identifier (MI) which is a unique identifier associated with the set of SAR PDUs that carry a single SAR SDU.
    - Length indication (LI) which defines the number of bytes in the SAR PDU. It can have a value between 4 and 44. The COM and BOM types will always have a value of 44. If the EOM field contains fewer than 44 bytes, it is padded to fill the remaining bytes. The LI then indicates the number of value bytes. For example if the LI is 20; there are only 20 value bytes in the SAR PDU the other 24 are padding bytes.
    - CRC which is a 10-bit CRC for the entire SAR PDU.

- CPCS (convergence protocol sublayer) takes data from the PDU. As this can be any length, the data is padded so it can be divided by 4. A header and trailer are then added and the completed data stream is converted into one or more SAR PDU format cells. Figure C7.12 shows the format of the CPCS-PDU for AAL type 3/4.

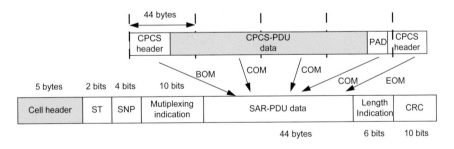

Figure C7.11   AAL type 3/4 cell format

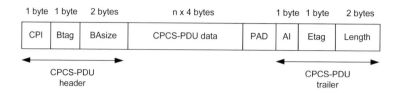

Figure C7.12   CPCS-PDU type 3/4 frame format

The fields in the CPCS-PDU are:

- CPI (common part indicator) which indicates how the remaining fields are interpreted (currently one version exists).
- Btag (beginning tag) which is a value associated with the CPCS-PDU data. The Etag has the same value as the Btag.
- BASize (buffer allocation size) which indicates the size of the buffer that must be reserved so that the completed message can be stored.
- AI (alignment) a single byte which is added to make the trailer equal to 32 bits.
- Etag (end tag) which is the same as the Btag value.
- Length which gives the length of the CPCS PDU data field.

AAL type 5

AAL type 5 is a connectionless service; it has no timing information and can have a variable bit rate. It assumes that one of the levels above the AAL can establish and maintain a connection. Type 5 provides stronger error checking with a 32-bit CRC for the entire CPCS PDU, whereas type 3/4 only allows a 10-bit CRC which is error checking for each SAR PDU. The type 5 format is given in Figure C7.13. The fields are:

- CPCS-UU (CPCS user-to-user) indication.
- CPI (common part indicator) which indicates how the remaining fields are interpreted (currently one version exists).
- Length which gives the length of the CPCS-PDU data.
- CRC which is a 32-bit CRC field.

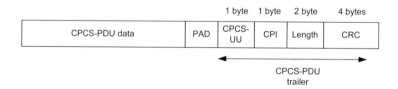

Figure C7.13   CPCS-PDU type 5 frame format.

The type 5 CPCS-PDU is then segmented into groups of 44 bytes and the ATM cell header is added. Thus type 5 does not have the overhead of the SAR-PDU header and trailer (i.e. it does not have ST, SN, MID, LI or CRC). This means it does not contain any sequence numbers. It is thus assumed that the cells will always be received in the correct order and none of the cells will be lost. Types 3/4 and 5 can be summarized as follows:

Type 3/4: SAR-PDU overhead is 4 bytes, CPCS-PDU overhead is 8 bytes.
Type 5: SAR-PDU overhead is 0 bytes, CPCS-PDU overhead is 8 bytes.

Type 5 can be characterized as:

- Strong error checking.
- Lack of sequence numbers.
- Reduced overhead of the SAR-PDU header and trailer.

C7.11   ATM flow control

ATM cannot provide for a reactive end-to-end flow control because by the time a message is returned from the destination to the source, large amounts of data could have been sent along the ATM pipe, possibly making the congestion worse. The opposite can occur when the congestion on the network has cleared by the time the flow control message reaches the transmitter. The transmitter will thus reduce the data flow when there is little need. ATM tries to react to network congestion quickly, and it slowly reduces the input data flow to reduce congestion.

This rate-based scheme of flow control involves controlling the amount of data to a specified rate, agreed when the connection is made. It then automatically changes the rate based on the history of the connection as well as the present congestion state of the network.

Data input is thus controlled by early detection of traffic congestion through closely monitoring the internal queues inside the ATM switches, as shown in Figure C7.14. The network then reacts gradually as the queues lengthen and reduces the traffic into the network from the transmitting UNI. This is an improvement over imposing a complete restriction on the data input when the route is totally congested. In summary, anticipation is better than desperation. A major objective of the flow control scheme is to try to affect only the streams which are causing the congestion, not the well-behaved streams.

The great advantage of ATM is that it guarantees a QoS, which involves setting up a suitable connection for the given QoS. It is thus important to understand how network traffic will vary over the time of the connection. The source node must inform the network about the traffic parameters and desired QoS for each direction of the requested connection upon initial set-up, such as bandwidth or delay (latency).

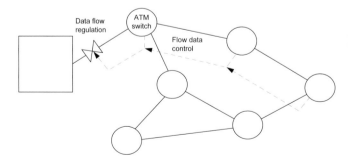

Figure C7.14
Flow control feedback from ATM switches

Current and proposed QoS levels are:

- **CBR** (Continuous Bit Rate). This is used to support constant bit rate traffic with a fixed timing relationship between data samples (such as with real-time speech).
- **VBR-RT** (Variable Bit Rate – Real Time). This is used to carry variable bit rate traffic that has a fixed time between samples. A typical application is variable bit rate video compression.
- **VBR-NRT** (Variable Bit Rate – Non-Real Time). This is used to carry variable bit rate traffic that has no timing relationship between data samples, but still requires a guaranteed QoS on bandwidth or latency. An example of this is in the interconnection of frame relay devices, where a guaranteed bandwidth is required for the connection.
- **ABR** (Available Bit Rate). This is used when the source and destination do not need to support a given bit rate, or any timing information. It is similar to VBR-NRT, but ABR service does not guarantee any bandwidth to the user, and the network will try to achieve the best service possible using feedback (flow control mechanisms, as shown in Figure C7.14) to increase the bandwidth available to the user, which is the Allowed Cell Rate (ACR). There may also be a Minimum Cell Rate (MCR), which will be the lowest value that the ACR can reach. It is likely this ABR will be supported with a rate-based system for ABR congestion control. With this Resource Management Cells (RMCs) or the explicit forward congestion indication (EFCI) bit within the ATM cell will be used to indicate to the source system that there is congestion in the network. The ACR is then controlled by a traffic-pacing algorithm, which will determine the traffic entering the network. The pacing will be either based on the number of received RM cells with a congestion indication or an explicit rate indication from the network. ABR is excellent at carrying LAN-type traffic, as the protocols that are used in LANs typically expect the maximum bandwidth that is available on the network, but will back-off or buffer data when the network becomes busy.
- **UBR** (Unspecified Bit Rate). This is used when there is no guarantee of QoS. Users can transmit as much data into the network as they want, but there is no guarantee on cell lost rate, delay, or delay variation. As UBR does not support any flow control mechanisms, it is important that there is cell buffering.

As has been seen there is no explicit priority field for an ATM connection. The only priority indicator in the cell is Cell Loss Priority (CLP) bit, which defines whether the cell can be dropped, or not. Cells with a CLP of 1 are dropped before cells with a CLP of 0. This bit can either be set by the end user, but is more likely to be set by the network. The basic parameters for defining traffic are:

- Burst Tolerance (BT). In VBR, the BT defines the maximum burst of transmitted contiguous cells.
- Cell Delay Variation Tolerance (CDVT).
- Minimum Cell Rate (MCR), if supported.
- Peak Cell Rate (PCR). In ABR, this defines the maximum value of ACR. The ACR will thus vary between MCR and PCR.
- Sustainable Cell Rate (SCR). In VBR, the SCR defines the long-term average cell rate.

These define the limits of a connection, but only some of these will be used for a given QoS.

C7.12   Practical ATM networks

As mentioned in Chapter C6 a metropolitan area network has been set-up around Edinburgh, UK. It consists of two rings on ATM and FDDI. The two rings of FDDI and ATM have been run around the Edinburgh sites. This also connects to the University of Stirling through a 155 Mbps SDH connection. Two connections on the ring are made to the SuperJANET network, connections at Heriot-Watt University and the University of Edinburgh.

The 100 Mbps FDDI dual rings link 10 Edinburgh city sites. This ring provides for IP traffic on SuperJANET and also for high-speed metropolitan connections. Initially a 155 Mbps SDH/STM-1 ATM network connects five Edinburgh sites and the University of Stirling. This also connects to the SuperJANET ATM pilot network. Figure C7.15 shows the FDDI and ATM connections.

The two different network technologies allow the universities to operate a two-speed network. For computer-type data the well-established FDDI technology provides good reliable communications and the ATM network allows for future exploitation of mixed voice, data and video transmissions.

The JANET and SuperJANET networks provide connections to all UK universities. A gateway out of the network to the rest of the world is located at University College London (UCL), as illustrated in Figure C7.16. Most of the connections on SuperJANET are with ATM, running at speeds from 155Mbps, upwards. ATM is a scaleable technology, and allows the base speed to be increased, as bandwidth requirements increase. SuperJANET gives a good model of the future of WAN's, which are based around MAN's, which connect to create WANs. The advantage of this topology is that a fault on any one of the MANs will not affect the other connected MANs. Also if the core develops a fault, then the MANs can still operate successfully, but, of course, they will not be able to communicate with other MANs, or the Internet. The core, though, can be made from robust devices, which have a low failure rate. The core thus provides inconnectivity between MAN's, and a gateway provides access to the external Internet, as illustrated in Figure C7.17. This type of setup of creates an autonomous domain, which defines a complete network, with a single reference gateway point.

The gateway creates a point of connection to the Internet, which allows for the security of the internal network to be controlled from a single point. The gateway can thus be monitored for incoming and outgoing traffic. If there are any problems with this traffic, such as from an internal or external attack, it can be easily controlled. The gateway can also be monitored for inappropriate user accesses. This normally involves the usage of an audit log which monitors network traffic, for its source, its destination, and its content.

The AS concept can be expanded further onto the wider Internet, where AS's connect to a core provider. This make the structure of the Internet simpler, and allows for easier routing of data between domains. This is illustrated in Figure C7.18. The core is typically provided by Internet connectivity providers such as: BBNPlanet [www.bbnplanet.com]; AT&T [www.ipservices.att.com]; WORLDCOM [www1.worldcom.com]; and Level 3 [www.level3.com].

The gateway also allows for different types of networking technology to be connected to either side. In this case ATM connects to one side of the gateway, and other networking technologies, such as Gigabit Ethernet or FDDI could connect on the other side. As covered later, the gateway allows routing information to be contained within the AS.

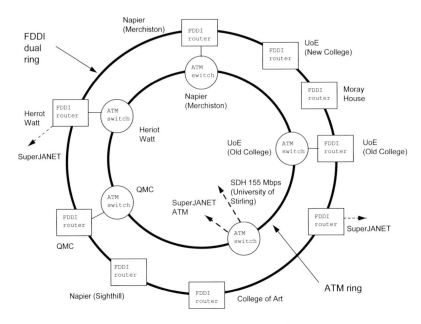

Figure C7.15 EaStMAN ring connections

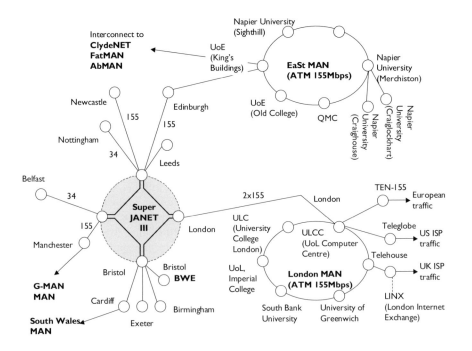

Figure C7.16 SuperJANET connections

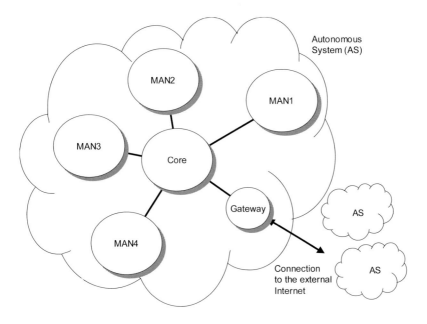

Figure C7.17 AS connections

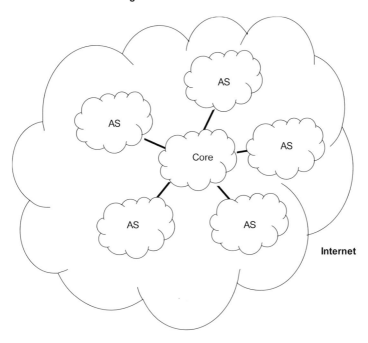

Figure C7.18 AS connections to the Internet

C8　HDLC

C8.1　Introduction

The data link layer is the second layer in the OSI seven-layer model and its protocols define rules for the orderly exchange of data information between two adjacent nodes connected by a data link. Final framing, flow control between nodes, and error detection and correction are added at this layer. In previous chapters the data link layer was discussed in a practical manner. It is a use protocol as it provides a model for interfacing to a serial bus.

The two types of protocol are:

- Asynchronous protocol.
- Synchronous protocol.

Asynchronous communications uses start-stop method of communication where characters are sent between nodes, as illustrated in Figure C8.1. Special characters are used to control the data flow. Typical flow control characters are End of Transmission (EOT), Acknowledgement (ACK), Start of Transmission (STX) and Negative Acknowledgement (NACK).

Synchronous communications involves the transmission of frames of bits with start and end bit characters to delimit the frame. The two of the most popular are IBM's synchronous data link communication (SDLC) and high-level data link control (HDLC). Many network data link layers are based upon these standards, examples include the LLC layer in IEE 802.*x* LAN standards and LAPB in the X.25 packet switching standard.

Synchronous communications normally uses a bit-oriented protocol (BOP), where data is sent one bit at a time. The data link control information is interpreted on a bit-by-bit basis rather than with unique data link control characters.

HDLC is a standard developed by the ISO to provide a basis for the data link layer for point-to-point and multi-drop connections. It can transfer data either in a simplex, half-duplex, or full-duplex mode. Frames are generally limited to 256 bytes in length and a single control field performs most data link control functions.

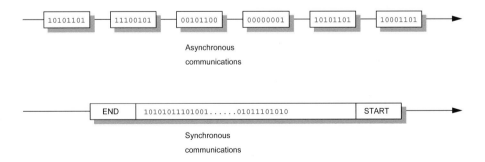

Figure C8.1　Asynchronous and synchronous communications

C8.2 HDLC protocol

In HDLC, a node is either defined as a primary station or a secondary station. A primary station controls the flow of information and issues commands to secondary stations. The secondary station then sends back responses to the primary. A primary station with one or more secondary stations is known as unbalanced configuration.

HDLC allows for point-to-point and multi-drop. In point-to-point communications a primary station communicates with a single secondary station. For multi-drop, one primary station communications with many secondary stations.

In point-to-point communications it is possible for a station be operate as a primary and a secondary station. At any time, one of the stations can be a primary and the other the secondary. Thus, commands and responses flow back and forth over the transmission link. This is known as a balanced configuration, or combined stations.

C8.2.1 HDLC modes of operation

HDLC has three modes of operation. Unbalanced configurations can use the normal response mode (NRM). Secondary stations can only transmit when specifically instructed by the primary station. When used as a point-to-point or multi-drop configuration only one primary station is used. Figure C8.2 shows a multi-drop NRM configuration.

Unbalanced configurations can also use the asynchronous response mode (ARM). It differs from NRM in that the secondary is allowed to communicate with the primary without receiving permission from the primary.

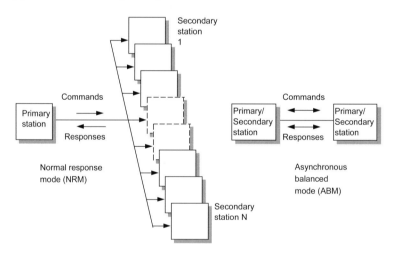

Figure C8.2 NRM and ABM mode

In asynchronous balanced mode (ABM) all stations have the same priority and can perform the functions of a primary and secondary station.

C8.2.2 HDLC frame format

HDLC frames are delimited by the bit sequence 01111110. Figure C8.3 shows the standard format of the HDLC frame, the 5 fields are the:

- Flag field.
- Address field.
- Control field.
- Information field.
- Frame check sequence (FCS) field.

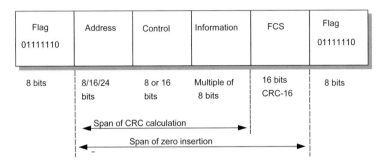

Figure C8.3 HDLC frame structure

C8.2.3 Information field

The information fields contain data, such as OSI level 3, and above, information. It contains an integer number of bytes and thus the number of bits contained is always a multiple of eight. The receiver determines the number of bytes in the data because it can detect the start and end flag. By this method, it also finds the FCS field. Note that the number of characters in the information can be zero as not all frames contain data.

C8.2.4 Flag field

A unique flag sequence, 01111110 (or 7Eh), delimits the start and end of the frame. As this sequence could occur anywhere within the frame a technique called bit-insertion is used to stop this happening except at the start and end of the frame.

C8.2.5 Address field

The address field is used to address connected stations an, in basic addressing, it contains an 8-bit address. It can also be extended, using extended addressing, to give any multiple of 8 bits.

When it is 8 bits wide it can address up to 254 different nodes, as illustrated in Figure C8.4. Two special addresses are 00000000 and 11111111. The 00000000 address defines the null or void address and the 11111111 broadcasts a message to all secondaries. The other 254 addresses are used to address secondary nodes individually.

If there are a large number of secondary stations then extended address can be used to extend the address field indefinitely. A 0 in the first bit of the address field allows a continuation of the address, or a 1 ends it. For example:

```
XXXXXXX1 XXXXXXX0 XXXXXXX0 XXXXXXX0
```

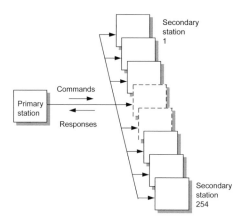

Figure C8.4 HDLC addressing range

C8.2.6 Control field

The control field can either be 8 or 16 bits wide. It is used to identify the frame type and can also contain flow control information. The first two bits of the control field define the frame type, as shown in Figure C8.5. There are three types of frames, these are:

- Information frames.
- Supervisory frames.
- Unnumbered frames.

When sent from the primary the P/F bit indicates that it is polling the secondary station. In an unbalanced mode, a secondary station cannot transmit frames unless the primary sets the poll bit.

When sending frames from the secondary, the P/F bit indicates whether the frame is the last of the message, or not. Thus if the P/F bit is set by the primary it is a poll bit (P), if it is set by the secondary it is a final bit (F).

The following sections describe 8-bit control fields. Sixteen-bit control fields are similar but reserve a 7-bit field for the frame counter variables N(R) and N(S).

Information frame

An information frame contains sequenced data and is identified by a 0 in the first bit position of the control field. The 3-bit variable N(R) is used to confirm the number of transmitted frames received correctly and N(S) is used to number an information frame. The first frame transmitted is numbered 0 as (000), the next as 1 (001), until the eighth which is numbered 111. The sequence then starts back at 0 again and this gives a sliding window of eight frames.

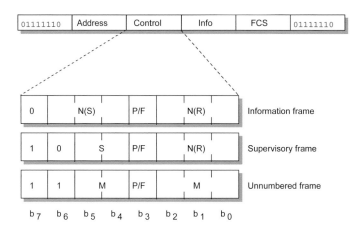

Figure C8.5 Format of an 8-bit control field

Supervisory frame

Supervisory frames contain flow control data. They confirm or reject previously received information frames and also can indicate whether a station is ready to receive frames.

The N(S) field is used with the S bits to acknowledge, or reject, previously transmitted frames. Responses from the receiver are set in the S field, these are receiver ready (RR), ready not to receive (RNR), reject (REJ) and selectively reject (SREJ). Table C8.1 gives the format of these bits.

RR informs the receiver that it acknowledges the frames sent up to N(R). RNR tells the transmitter that the receiver cannot receive any more frames at the present time (RR will cancel this). It also acknowledges frames up to N(R). The REJ control rejects all frames after N(R). The transmitter must then send frames starting at N(R).

Table C8.1 Supervisory bits

b_5	b_4	Receiver status
0	0	Receiver ready (RR)
1	0	Receiver not ready (RNR)
0	1	Reject (REJ)
1	1	Selectively reject (SREJ)

Unnumbered frame

If the first two bits of the control field are 1's then it is an unnumbered frame. Apart from the P/F flag the other bits are used to send unnumbered commands. When sending commands, the P/F flag is a poll bit (asking for a response), and for responses it is a flag bit (end of response).

The available commands are SARM (set asynchronous response mode), SNRM (set normal response mode), SABM (set asynchronous balance mode), RSET (reset), FRMR (frame reject) and Disconnect (DISC). The available responses are UA (unnumbered acknowledge), CMDR (command reject), FRMR (frame reject) and DM (disconnect mode). Bit definitions for some of these are:

| SABM | 1111P110 | DM | 1111F000 | DISC | 1100P010 |
| UA | 1100F110 | FRMR | 1110F001 | | |

C8.2.7 Frame check sequence field

The frame check sequence (FCS) field contains an error detection code based on cyclic redundancy check (CRC) polynomials. It is used to check the address, control and information fields, as previously illustrated in Figure C8.2. HDLC uses a polynomial specified by CCITT V.41, which is $G(x) = x^{16} + x^{12} + x^5 + x^1$. This is also known as CRC-16 or CRC-CCITT.

C8.3 Transparency

The flag sequence 01111110 can occur anywhere in the frame. To prevent this, a transparency mechanism called zero-bit insertion or zero stuffing is used. There are two main rules that are applied, these are:

- In the transmitter, a 0 is automatically inserted after five consecutive 1's, except when the flag occurs.
- At the receiver, when five consecutive 1's are received and the next bit is a 0 then the 0 is deleted and removed. If it is a 1 then it must be a valid flag.

In the following example a flag sequence appears in the data stream where it is not supposed to (spaces have been inserted around it). Notice that the transmitter detects five 1's in a row and inserts a 0 to break them up.

| Message: | 00111000101000 01111110 01011111 1111010101 |
| Sent: | 00111000101000 011111010 0101111101111010101 |

C8.4 Flow control

Supervisory frames (S[]) send flow control information to acknowledge the reception of data frames or to reject frames. Unnumbered frames (U[]) set up the link between a primary and a secondary, by the primary sending commands and the secondary replying with responses. Information frames (I[]) contain data.

C8.4.1 Link connection

Figure C8.6 shows how a primary station (node A) sets up a connection with a secondary station (node B) in NRM (normal response mode). In this mode one or many secondary stations can exist. First the primary station requests a link by sending an unnumbered frame with: node B's address (ADDR_B), the set normal response mode (SNRM) command and with poll flag set (P=1), that is, U[SNRM,ABBR_B,P=1]. If the addressed secondary wishes to make a connection then it replies back with an unnumbered frame containing: its own address (ADDR_B), the unnumbered acknowledge (UA) response and the final bit set (F=1), i.e. U[UA,ABBR_B,F=1]. The secondary sends back its own address because many secondaries can exist and it thus identifies which station has responded. There is no need to send the primary station address as only one primary exists.

Once the link is set up data can flow between the nodes. To disconnect the link, the primary station sends an unnumbered frame with: node B's address (ADDR_B), the disconnect (DISC) command and the poll flag set (P=1), that is, U[DISC,ABBR_B,P=1]. If the addressed secondary accepts the disconnection then it replies back with an unnumbered frame containing: its own address (ADDR_B), the unnumbered acknowledge (UA) response and the final bit set (F=1), i.e. U[UA,ABBR_B,F=1].

When two stations act as both primaries and secondaries then they use the asynchronous balanced mode (ABM). Each station has the same priority and can perform the functions of a primary and secondary station. Figure C8.7 shows a typical connection. The ABM mode is set up initially using the SABM command (U[SABM,ABBR_B,P=1]). The connection between node A and node B is then similar to the NRM but, as node B operates as a primary station, it can send a disconnect command to node A (U[DISC,ABBR_B,P=1]).

The SABM, SARM and SNRM modes set up communications using an 8-bit control field. Three other commands exist which set up a 16-bit control field, these are SABME (set asynchronous balanced mode extended), SARME and SNRME. The format of the 16-bit control field is given in Figure C8.8.

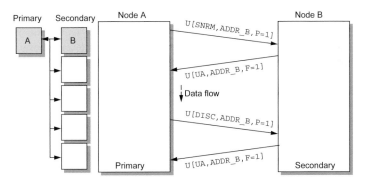

Figure C8.6   Connection between a primary and secondary in NRM

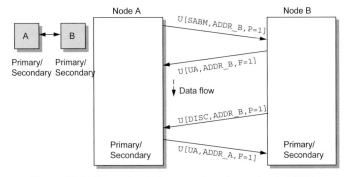

Figure C8.7   Connection between a primary/secondary in SABM

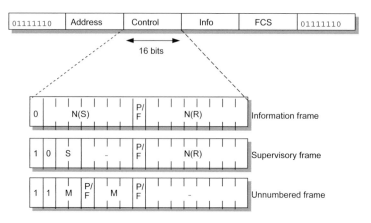

Figure C8.8 Extended control field

Figure C8.9 shows an example conversation between a sending station (node A) and a receiving station (node B). Initially three information frames are sent numbered 2, 3 and 4 (`I[N(S)=2]`, `I[N(S)=3]` and `I[N(S)=4, P=1]`). The last of these frames has the poll bit set, which indicates to node B that node A wishes it to respond, either to acknowledge or reject previously unacknowledged frames. Node B does this by sending back a supervisory frame (`S[RR, N(R)=5]`) with the receiver ready (RR) acknowledgement. This informs node A that node B expects to receive frame number 5 next. Thus, it has acknowledged all frames up to and including frame 4.

In the example in Figure C8.9, an error has occurred in the reception of frame 5. The recipient informs the sender by sending a supervisory frame with a reject flow command (`S[REJ, N(R)=5]`). After the sender receives this it resends each frame after and including frame 5.

If the receiver does not want to communicate, at the present, it sends a receiver not ready flow command. For example `S[RNR, N(R)=5]` tells the transmitter to stop sending data, at the present. It also informs the sender that all frames up to frame 5 have been accepted. The sender will transmit frames once it has received a receiver ready frame from the receiver.

Figure C8.9 shows an example of data flow in only the one direction. With ABM, both stations can transmit and receive data. Thus each frame sent contains receive and send counter values. When stations send information frames the previously received frames can be acknowledged, or rejected, by piggybacking the receive counter value. In Figure C8.10, node A sends three information frames with `I[N(S)=0,N(R)=0]`, `I[N(S)=1, N(R)=0]`, and `I[N(S)=2,N(R)=0]`. The last frame informs node B that node A expects to receive frame 0 next. Node B then sends frame 0 and acknowledges the reception of all frames up to, and including frame 2 with `I[N(S)=0,N(R)=3]`, and so on.

C8.5 Derivatives of HDLC

There are many derivatives of HDLC, including:

- LAPB (link access procedure balanced) is used in X.25 packet switched networks;
- LAPM (link access procedure for modems) is used in error correction modems;

- LLC (logical link control) is used in Ethernet and Token Ring networks;
- LAPD (link access procedure D-channel) is used in Integrated Services Digital Networks (ISDNs).

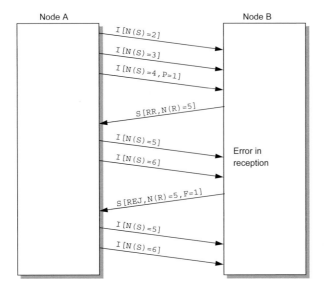

Figure C8.9   Example flow

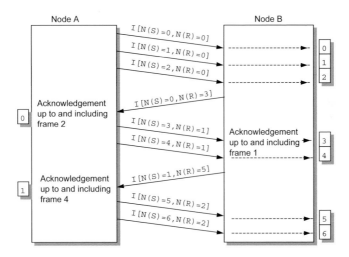

Figure C8.10   Example flow with piggybacked acknowledgement

C9 ISDN

C9.1 Introduction

A major problem in data communications and networks is the integration of real-time sampled data with non-real-time (normal) computer data. Sampled data tends to create a constant traffic flow whereas computer-type data has bursts of traffic. In addition, sampled data normally needs to be delivered at a given time but computer-type data needs a reliable path where delays are relatively unimportant.

The basic rate for real-time data is speech. It is normally sampled at a rate of 8 kHz and each sample is coded with eight bits. This leads to a transmission bit rate of 64 kbps. ISDN uses this transmission rate for its base transmission rate. Computer-type data can then be transmitted using this rate or can be split to transmit over several 64 kbps channels. The basic rate ISDN service uses two 64 kbps data lines and a 16 kbps control line, as illustrated in Figure C9.1. Table C9.1 summarizes the I series CCITT standards.

Typically, modems are used in the home for the transmission of computer-type data. Unfortunately, modems have a maximum bit rate of 56 kbps. With ISDN, this is automatically increased, on a single channel, to 64 kbps. The connections made by a modem and by ISDN are circuit switched.

The great advantage of an ISDN connection is that the type of data transmitted is irrelevant to the transmission and switching circuitry. Thus, it can carry other types of digital data, such as facsimile, teletex, videotex and computer data. This reduces the need for modems, which convert digital data into an analogue form, only for the public telephone network to convert the analogue signal back into a digital form for transmission over a digital link. It is also possible to multiplex the basic rate of 64 kbps to give even higher data rates. This multiplexing is known as N × 64 kbps or broadband ISDN (B-ISDN).

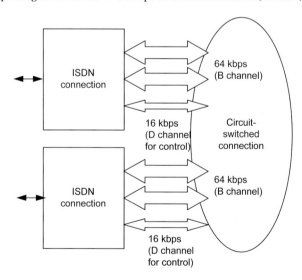

Figure C9.1 Basic rate ISDN services

Table C9.1 CCITT standards on ISDN

CCITT standard number	Description
I.1XX	ISDN terms and technology
I.2XX	ISDN services
I.3XX	ISDN addressing
I.430 and I.431	ISDN physical layer interface
I.440 and I.441	ISDN data layer interface
I.450 and I.451	ISDN network layer interface
I.5XX	ISDN internetworking
I.6XX	ISDN maintenance

Another advantage of ISDN is that it is a circuit-switched connection where a permanent connection is established between two nodes. This connection is guaranteed for the length of the connection. It also has a dependable delay time and is thus suited to real-time data.

C9.2 ISDN channels

ISDN uses channels to identify the data rate, each based on the 64 kbps provision. Typical channels are B, D, H0, H11 and H12. The B-channel has a data rate of 64 kbps and provides a circuit-switched connection between endpoints. A D-channel operates at 16 kbps and it controls the data transfers over the B channels. The other channels provide B-ISDN for much higher data rates. Table C9.2 outlines the basic data rates for these channels.

The two main types of interface are the basic rate access and the primary rate access. Both are based around groupings of B- and D-channels. The basic rate access allows two B-channels and one 16 kbps D-channel.

Primary rate provides B-ISDN, such as H12 which gives 30 B-channels and a 64 kbps D-channel. For basic and primary rates, all channels multiplex onto a single line by combining channels into frames and adding extra synchronisation bits. Figure C9.2 gives examples of the basic rate and primary rate.

The basic rate ISDN gives two B-channels at 64 kbps and a signalling channel at 16 kbps. These multiplex into a frame and, after adding extra framing bits, the total output data rate is 192 kbps. The total data rate for the basic rate service is thus 128 kbps. One or many devices may multiplex their data, such as two devices transmitting at 64 kbps, a single device multiplexing its 128 kbps data over two channels (giving 128 kbps), or by several devices transmitting a sub-64 kbps data rate over the two channels. For example, four 32 kbps devices could simultaneously transmit their data, eight 16 kbps devices, and so on.

Table C9.2 ISDN channels

Channel	Description
B	64 kbps
D	16 kbps signaling for channel B (ISDN)
	64 kbps signaling for channel B (B-ISDN)
H0	384 kbps (6×64 kbps) for B-ISDN
H11	1.536 Mbps (24×64 kbps) for B-ISDN
H12	1.920 Mbps (30×64 kbps) for B-ISDN

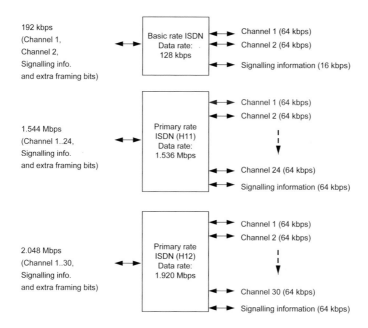

Figure C9.2 Basic rate, H11 and H12 ISDN services

For H12, 30×64 kbps channels multiplex with a 64 kbps-signalling channel, and with extra framing bits, the resulting data rate is 2.048 Mbps (compatible with European PCM-TDM systems). This means the actual data rate is 1.920 Mbps. As with the basic service this could contain a number of devices with a data rate of less than or greater than a multiple of 64 kbps.

For H11, 24×64 kbps channels multiplex with a 64 kbps-signalling channel, and with extra framing bits, it produces a data rate of 1.544 Mbps (compatible with USA PCM-TDM systems). The actual data rate is 1.536 Mbps.

C9.3　ISDN physical layer interfacing

The physical layer corresponds to layer 1 of the OSI seven-layer model and is defined in CCITT specifications I.430 and I.431. Pulses on the line are not coded as pure binary, they use a technique called alternate mark inversion (AMI).

C9.3.1　Alternative mark inversion (AMI) line code

AMI line codes use three voltage levels. In pure AMI, 0 V represents a '0', and the voltage amplitude for each '1' is the inverse of the previous '1' bit. ISDN uses the inverse of this, i.e. 0 V for a '1' and an inverse in voltage for a '0', as shown in Figure C9.3. Normally the pulse amplitude is 0.75 V.

Inversion of the AMI signal (i.e. inverting a '0' rather than a '1') allows for timing information to be recovered when there are long runs of zeros, which is typical in the idle state. AMI line code also automatically balances the signal voltage, and the average voltage will be approximately zero even when there are long runs of zeros (this is a requirement as the connection to the network is transformer coupled).

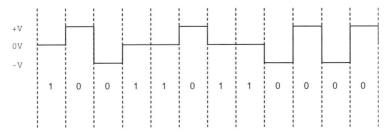

Figure C9.3 AMI used in ISDN

C9.3.2 System connections

In basic rate connections, up to eight devices, or items of termination equipment (TE), can connect to the network termination (NT). They connect over a common four-wire bus using two sets of twisted-pair cables. The transmit output (T_X) on each TE connects to the transmit output on the other TEs, and the receive input (R_X) on each TE connects to all other TEs. On the NT the receive input connects to the transmit of the TEs, and the transmit output of the NT connects to the receive input of the TEs. A contention protocol allows only one TE to communicate at a time.

An 8-pin ISO 8877 connector connects a TE to the NT; this is similar to the RJ-45 connector. Figure C9.4 shows the pin connections. Pins 3 and 6 carry the T_X signal from the TE, pins 4 and 5 provide the R_X to the TEs. Pins 7 and 8 are the secondary power supply from the NT and pins 1 and 2 the power supply from the TE (if used). The T_X/R_X lines connect via transformers, thus only the AC part of the bitstream transfers into the PCM circuitry of the TE and the NT. This produces a need for a balanced DC line code such as AMI, as the DC component in the bitstream will not pass through the transformers.

C9.3.3 Frame format

Figures C9.5 and C9.6 show the ISDN frame formats. Each frame is 250 μs long and contains 48 bits; this give a total bit rate of 192 kbps ($48/250 \times 10^{-6}$) made up of two 64 kbps B channels, one 16 kbps D-channel and extra framing, DC balancing and synchronisation bits.

The F/L pair of bits identify the start of each transmitted frame. When transmitting from a TE to an NT there is a 10-bit offset in the return of the frame back to the TE. The E bits echo the D-channel bits back to the TE.

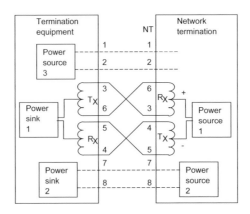

Figure C9.4 Power supplies between NT and TE

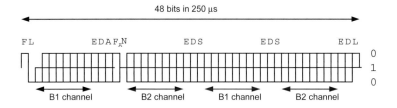

Figure C9.5 ISDN frame format for NT to TE

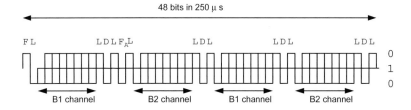

Figure C9.6 ISDN frame format for TE to NT

where

F	–	framing bit	N	–	set to a 1
L	–	DC balancing bit	D	–	D-channel bit
E	–	D-echo channel bit	F_A	–	auxiliary framing bit ($= 0$)
S	–	reserved for future use	A	–	activation bit
M	–	multiframing bit	B1	–	bits for channel 1
B2	–	bits for channel 2			

When transmitting from the NT to the TE, the bits after the F/L bits, in the B-channel, have a volition in the first 0. If any of these bits is a 0 then a volition will occur, but if they are 1s then no volition can occur. To overcome this the F_A bit forces a volition. As it is followed by 0 (the N bit) it will not be confused with the F/L pair. The start of the frame can thus be traced backwards to find the F/L pair.

There are 16 bits for each B-channel, giving a basic data rate of 64 kbps ($16/250 \times 10^{-6}$) and there are 4 bits in the frame for the D-channel, giving a bit rate of 16 kbps ($4/250 \times 10^{-6}$).

The L bit balances the DC level on the line. If the number of zeros following the last balancing bit is odd then the balancing bit is a 0, else it is a 1. When synchronised the NT informs the TEs by setting the A bit.

C9.4 ISDN data link layer

The data link layer uses a protocol known as the link access procedure for the D-channel (LAPD). Figure C9.7 shows the frame format. The unique bit sequence 01111110 identifies the start and end of the frame. This bit pattern cannot occur in the rest of the frame due to zero bit-stuffing.

The address field contains information on the type of data contained in the frame (the service access point identifier) and the physical address of the ISDN device (the terminal endpoint identifier). The control field contains a supervisory, an unnumbered or an information frame. The frame check sequence provides error detection information.

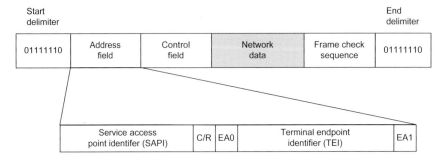

Figure C9.7   D-channel frame structure

C9.4.1   Address field

The data link address only contains addressing information to connect the TE to the NT and does not have network addresses. Figure C9.7 shows the address field format. The SAPI identifies the type of ISDN service. For example, a frame from a telephone would be identified as such, and only telephones would read the frame.

All TEs connect to a single multiplexed bus, thus each has a unique data link address, known as a terminal endpoint identifier (TEI). The user or the network sets this; the ranges of available addresses are:

0–63	non-automatic assignment TEIs
64–126	automatic assignment TEIs
127	global TEI

The non-automatic assignment involves the user setting the address of each of the devices connected to the network. When a device transmits data it inserts its own TEI address and only receives data which has its TEI address. In most cases devices should not have the same TEI address, as this would cause all devices with the same TEI address, and the SAPI, to receive the same data (although, in some cases, this may be a requirement).

The network allocates addresses to devices requiring automatic assignment before they can communicate with any other devices. The global TEI address is used to broadcast messages to all connected devices. A typical example is when a telephone call is incoming to a group on a shared line where all the telephones would ring until one was answered.

The C/R bit is the command/response bit and EA0/EA1 are extended address field bits.

C9.4.2   Bit stuffing

With zero bit stuffing the transmitter inserts a zero into the bitstream when transmitting five consecutive 1s. When the receiver receives five consecutive 1s it deletes the next bit if it is a zero. This stops the unique 01111110 sequence occurring within the frame. For example if the bits to be transmitted are

```
10100010101111110000101000101000011111110101010
```

then with the start and end delimiter this would be

0111111010100010101111110000101000101000011111010101001111110

It can be seen from this bitstream that the stream to be transmitted contains the delimiter within the frame. This zero bit insertion is applied to give

011111101010001010*01111101*0000101000101000011111**0**010101001111110

Notice that the transmitter has inserted a zero when five consecutive 1s occur. Thus the bit pattern 01111110 cannot occur anywhere in the bitstream. When the receiver receives five consecutive 1s it deletes the next bit if it is a zero. If it is a 1 then it is a valid delimiter. In the example the received stream will be

011111101010001010101111110000101000101000011111010101001111110

C9.4.3 Control field

ISDN uses a 16-bit control field for information and supervisory frames and an 8-bit field for unnumbered frames, as illustrated in Figure C9.8. Information frames contain sequenced data. The format is 0SSSSSSSXRRRRRRR, where SSSSSSS is the send sequence number and RRRRRRR is the frame sequence number that the sender expects to receive next (X is the poll/final bit). As the extended mode uses a 7-bit sequence field then information frames are numbered from 0 to 127.

Supervisory frames contain flow control data. Table C9.3 lists the supervisory frame types and the control field bit settings. The RRRRRRR value represent the 7-bit receive sequence number.

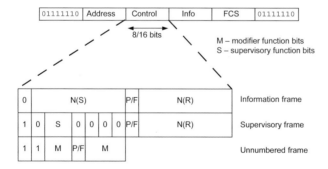

Figure C9.8 ISDN control field

Table C9.3 Supervisory frame types and control field settings

Type	Control field setting
Receiver ready (RR)	10000000PRRRRRRR
Receiver not ready (RNR)	10100000PRRRRRRR
Reject (REJ)	10010000PRRRRRRR

Unnumbered frames set up and clear connections between a node and the network. Table C9.4 lists the unnumbered frame commands and Table C9.5 lists the unnumbered frame responses.

Table C9.4 Unnumbered frame commands and control field settings

Type	Control field setting
Set asynchronous balance mode extended (SABME)	1111P110
Unnumbered information (UI)	1100F000
Disconnect mode (DISC)	1100P010

Table C9.5 Unnumbered frame responses and control field settings

Type	Control field setting
Disconnect mode (DM)	1111P110
Unnumbered acknowledgment (UA)	1100F000
Frame reject (FRMR)	1110P001

In ISDN all connected nodes and the network connection can send commands and receive responses. Figure C9.9 shows a sample connection of an incoming call to an ISDN node (address TEI_1). The SABME mode is set up initially using the SABME command (U[SABME,TEI_1,P=1]), followed by an acknowledgement from the ISDN node (U[UA,TEI_1,F=1]). At any time, either the network or the node can disconnect the connection. In this case the ISDN node disconnects the connection with the command U[DISC,TEI_1,P=1]. The network connection acknowledges this with an unnumbered acknowledgement (U[UA,TEI_1,F=1]).

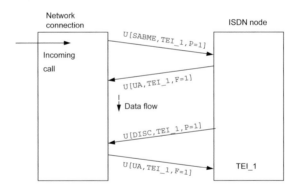

Figure C9.9 Example connection between a primary/secondary

C9.4.4 D-channel contention

The D-channel contention protocol ensures that only one terminal can transmit its data at a time. This happens because the start and the end of the D-channel bits have the bit stream 01111110, as shown below:

    1111101111110XXXXXXXXX...XXXXXXXX011111101111

When idle, each TE floats to a high-impedance state, which is taken as a binary 1. To transmit, a TE counts the number of 1s in the D-channel. A 0 resets this count. After a predetermined number, greater than a predetermined number of consecutive 1s, the TE transmits its data and monitors the return from the NT. If it does not receive the correct D-channel bitstream returned through the E bits then a collision has occurred. When a TE detects a collision it immediately stops transmitting and monitors the line.

When a TE has finished transmitting data it increases its count value for the number of consecutive 1s by 1. This gives other TEs an opportunity to transmit their data.

C9.4.5 Frame check sequence

The frame check sequence (FCS) field contains an error detection code based on cyclic redundancy check (CRC) polynomials. It uses the CCITT V.41 polynomial, which is $G(x) = x^{16} + x^{12} + x^5 + x^1$.

C9.5 ISDN network layer

The D-channel carriers network layer information within the LAPD frame. This information establishes and controls a connection. The LAPD frames contain no true data as this is carried in the B-channel. Its function is to set up and manage calls and to provide flow control between connections over the network.

Figure C9.10 shows the format of the layer-three signalling message frame. The first byte is the protocol discriminator. In the future, this byte will define different communications protocols. At present it is normally set to 0001000. After the second byte the call reference length value is defined. This is used to identify particular calls with a reference number. The length of the call reference value is defined within the second byte. As it contains a 4-bit value, up to 16 bytes can be contained in the call reference value field. The next byte gives the message type and this type defines the information contained in the proceeding field.

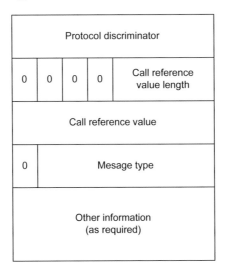

Figure C9.10 Signalling message structure

There are four main types of message: call establish, call information, call clearing and miscellaneous messages. Table C9.6 outlines the main messages. Figure C9.11 shows an example connection procedure. The initial message sent is the setup. This may contain some of the following:

- Channel identification – identifies a channel with an ISDN interface.
- Calling party number.
- Calling party subaddress.
- Called party number.
- Called party subnumber.
- Extra data (2–131 bytes).

After the calling TE has sent the setup message, the network then returns the setup ACK message. If there is insufficient information in the setup message then other information needs to flow between the called TE and the network. After this the network sends back a call proceeding message and it also sends a setup message to the called TE. When the called TE detects its TEI address and SAPI, it sends back an alerting message. This informs the network that the node is alerting the user to answer the call. When it is answered, the called TE sends a connect message to the network. The network then acknowledges this with a connect ACK message, at the same time it sends a connect message to the calling TE. The calling TE then acknowledges this with a connect ACK. The connection is then established between the two nodes and data can be transferred.

To disconnect the connection the disconnect, release and release complete messages are used.

Table C9.6   ISDN network messages

Call establish	Information messages	Call clearing
ALERTING	RESUME	DISCONNECT
CALL PROCEEDING	RESUME ACKNOWLEDGE	RELEASE
CONNECT	RESUME REJECT	RELEASE COMPLETE
CONNECT ACKNOWLEDGE	SUSPEND	RESTART
PROGRESS	SUSPEND ACKNOWLEDGE	RESTART ACKNOWLEDGE
SETUP	SUSPEND REJECT	
SETUP ACKNOWLEDGE	USER INFORMATION	

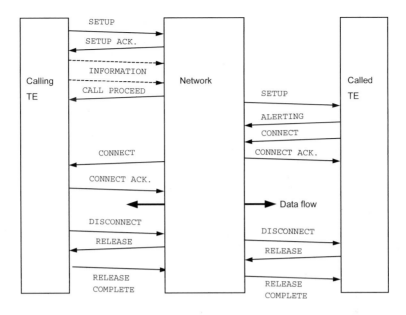

Figure C9.11 Call establishment and clearing

C9.6 Speech sampling

With telephone-quality speech the signal bandwidth is normally limited to 4 kHz, thus it is sampled at 8 kHz. If each sample is coded with eight bits then the basic bit rate will be:

Digitised speech signal rate = 8×8 kbps = 64 kbps

Table C9.7 outlines the main compression techniques for speech. The G.722 standard allows the best-quality signal, as the maximum speech frequency is 7 kHz rather than 4 kHz in normal coding systems; and has the equivalent of 14 coding bits. The G.728 allows extremely low bit rates (16 kbps).

Table C9.7 Speech compression standards

ITU standard	Technology	Bit rate	Description
G.711	PCM	64 kbps	Standard PCM
G.721	ADPCM	32 kbps	Adaptive delta PCM where each value is coded with four bits
G.722	SB-ADPCM	48, 56 and 64 kbps	Subband ADPCM allows for higher-quality audio signals with a sampling rate of 16 kHz
G.728	LD-CELP	16 kbps	Low-delay code excited linear prediction for low bit rates

C9.7 ISDN router programming

ISDN connections are typically used for point-to-point connections. On a Cisco router with a TE1 interface (native BRI), the ISDN port is identified with a BRI label, and is accessed with the `interface` command. For example for an ISDN connection (BRI0):

```
Router > enable
Router # config t
Router(config)# int bri0
Router(config-if)# encapsulation ppp
Router(config-if)# ppp chap password mypass
Router(config-if)# exit
```

which encapsulates PPP within the ISDN interface. This allows many different networking protocols to be embedded into the ISDN transmission (see Chapter D5 for more information on PPP).

If the interface is a TE2 device (that is, it does not have a native BRI connection), then it can interface to an external ISDN terminal adapter. It can then be interfaced through the serial interface. For example:

```
Router > enable
Router # config t
Router(config)# int s0
Router(config-if)# encapsulation ppp
Router(config-if)# ppp chap password mypass
Router(config-if)# exit
```

Encapsulating with PPP also allows for multiple dial-up connections.

C9.8 HDLC encapsulation

The default encapsulation for a serial interface is HDLC (as covered in the previous chapter). This is programmed for a Cisco router as follows (for Serial 1):

```
Router > enable
Router # config t
Router (config) # interface Serial 1
Router (config-if) # no shutdown
Router (config-if) # ip address 201.100.11.2 255.255.255.0
Router (config-if) #  encapsulation hdlc
Router(config-if)# exit
```

C10 X.25

C10.1 Introduction

A wide area network (WAN) connects one node to another over relatively large distances via an arbitrary graph of switching nodes. For the transmission of digital data, then data is either sent through a public data network (PDN) or through dedicated company connections.

As shown in Figure C10.1, there are two main types of connection over the public telephone network, circuit-switching and packet-switching. With circuit switched, a physical, or a reserved multiplexed, connection exists between two nodes, a typical example is the public-switched telephone network (PSTN). The connection must be made before transferring any data. In the past this connection took a relatively long time to set-up (typically over 10 seconds), but with the increase in digital exchanges it has reduced to less than a second. The usage of digital exchanges has also allowed the transmission of digital data, over PSTNs, at rates of 64 kbps and greater. This type of network is known as a circuit-switched digital network (CSDN). Its main disadvantage is that a permanent connection is set-up between the nodes. This is wasteful in time and can be costly. Another disadvantage is that the transmitting and receiving nodes must be operating at the same speed. A CSDN, also, does not perform any error detection or flow control.

Packet-switching involves segmenting data into packets that propagate within a digital network. They either follow a pre-determined route or are routed individually to the receiving node via packet-switched exchanges (PSE) or routers. These examine the destination addresses and based on an internal routing directory pass it to the next PSE on the route. As with circuit-switching, data can propagate over a fixed route. This differs from circuit-switching in that the path is not an actual physical circuit (or a reserved multiplexed channel). As it is not a physical circuit it is normally defined as a virtual circuit. This virtual circuit is less wasteful on channel resources as other data can be sent when there are gaps in the data flow.

Table C10.1 gives a comparison of the two types.

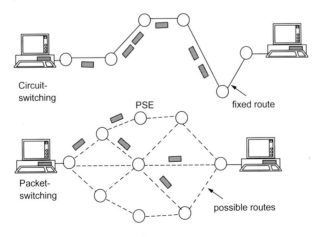

Figure C10.1 Circuit- and packet-switching

	Circuit-switching	*Packet-switching*
Investment in equipment	Minimal as it uses existing connections	Expensive for initial investment
Error and flow control	None, this must be supplied by the end users	Yes, using the FCS in the data link layer
Simultaneous transmissions and connections	No	Yes, nodes can communicate with many nodes at the same time and over many different routes
Allows for data to be sent without first setting up a connection	No	Yes, using datagrams
Response time	Once the link is set-up it provides a good reliable connection with little propagation delay	Response time depends on the size of the data packets and the traffic within the network

C10.2   Packet-switching and the OSI model

The CCITT developed the X.25 standard for packet switching and it fits-in well with the OSI model. In a packet-switched network the physical layer is normally defined by the X.21 standard and the data link layer by a derivative HDLC, known as LAPB. The network, or packet, level is defined by X.25.

C10.2.1 The physical layer (X.21)

The CCITT recommendation X.21 defines the physical interface between a node (the DTE) and the network connection (the DCE). Figure C10.2 shows the connections between the node and the network connection.

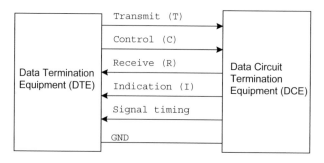

Figure C10.2   X.21 connections

A second standard, known as X.21 (bis), has also been defined and is similar to the RS-232/V.24 standards. This allows RS-232 equipment to directly connect to the network.

The Transmit (T) line sends data from the DTE to the DCE and the Receive (R) sends data from the DCE to the DTE. A DCE controls the Indicate (I) line to indicate that it is ready to receive data. The DTE controls the Control (C) line to request to the DCE that it is ready to send data.

Figure C10.3 shows a simplified flow control between a sending DTE and a receiving DCE. With reference to the state numbers in the diagram the sequence of operations is as follows:

1	Initially, the Transmit (T) and Receive (R) lines are high to indicate that the DTE and the DCE are active and ready to communicate, respectively.
2	When the DTE wishes to transmit data it first sets the Control (C) line low (ON). At the same time it sets the Transmit (T) line low.
3	When the DCE accepts the data transfer it sets the Indicate (I) line low.
4-12	Data is transmitted on the Transmit (T) line and, in some modes, it is echoed back on the Receive (R) line.
12	When the DTE finishes transmitting data it sets the Control (C) line high (OFF).
13	The DCE responds to the Control (C) line going high by setting the Indication (I) line high.
14	The DCE sets the Receive (R) line high to indicate that it is active and ready to communicate.
15	The DTE sets the Transmit (T) line high to indicate that it is active and ready to communicate.

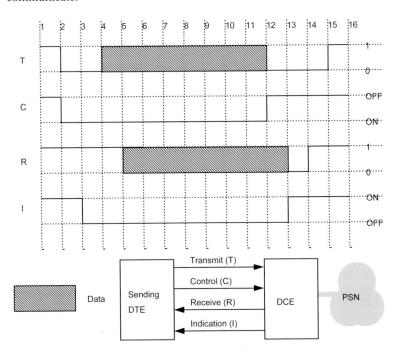

Figure C10.3 Example X.21 signals

C10.2.2 Data link layer (LAPB)

The data link layer provides a reliable method of transferring packets between the DTE and the local PSE. Frames sent contain no information on the addressing of the remote node, this information is contained within the packet. The standard, known as the Link Access Procedure Version B is based on HDLC. It uses ABM (asynchronous balance mode) where both the DTE and the PSE can initiate commands and responses at any time.

C10.2.3 Network (packet) layer

The packet layer is equivalent to the network layer in the OSI model. Its main purpose is to route data over a network.

C10.3   X.25 packets

X.25 packets contain a header and either control information and/or data. The LAPB frame envelops the packet and physical layer transmits it. Figure C10.4 shows the format of the transmitted frame.

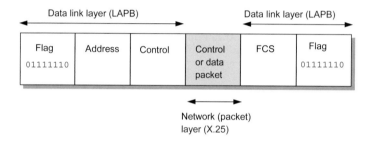

Figure C10.4   Transmitted frame

C10.3.1 Packet headers

Packet headers are 3 bytes long. Figure C10.5 shows a packet represented both as a bit stream and arranged in groups of 8 bits. The first two bytes of the header contain the group format identifier (GFI), the logical group number (LGN) and the logical channel number (LCN). The third byte identifies the packet type.

The GFI number is a 4-bit binary value of QdYY, where the Q bit is the qualifier bit and the D bit is the delivery confirmation bit. The d bit requests an acknowledgement from the remote node, this is discussed in more detail in section 7.4.3. The YY bits indicate the range of packet sequence numbers. If they are 01 then packets are numbered from 0 to 7 (modulo-8), or if they are 10 then packets are numbered from 0 to 127 (modulo-128). This packet sequencing is similar to the method that HDLC uses to provide confirmation of received frames. As LAPB (the HDLC-derivative) provides reliable data link error control, the sequencing of packets is mainly used as flow control rather than for error control.

The LGN and LCN together define a 12-bit virtual circuit identifier (VCI). This allows packets to find logical routes though the packet switched network. For example, all packets could take the same route or each group of packets could find different routes.

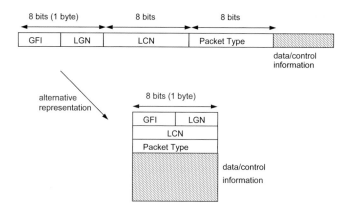

Figure C10.5 Packet header

C10.3.2 Packet types

The third byte of the packet header defines the packet type, Table C10.2 lists some of these. A 0 in the eighth bit position identifies that it is a data packet while a 1 marks it as a flow control or a call set-up packet.

The call set-up and clearing packets have differing definitions depending on whether they are sent or received. For example if the calling node sends a packet type of 00001011 then it is a Call Request packet, if it is received it is interpreted as an Incoming Call packet.

Table C10.2 The main packet types

Packet type	Identifier	Description
Data Packet	RRRMSSS0	The Data packet is sent with a send sequence number (SSS) and a receive sequence number (RRR).
Call Request/ Incoming Call	00001011	If a node sends this packet to the network it is a Call Request packet, if the node receives it, it is an Incoming Call packet.
Call Accepted/ Call Confirma- tion	00001111	If a node sends this packet to the network it is a Call Accepted packet, if a node receives it, it is a Call Confirmation.
Receive Ready	RRR00001	The Receive Ready packet is sent from a node to inform the other node that it is ready to receive data. It also informs the other node that the next data packet it expects to receive should have sequence number RRR.
Receive Not Ready	RRR00101	The Receive Not Ready packet is sent from a node to inform the other node that it is not ready to receive data. It also informs the other node that the next data packet it expects to receive should have sequence number RRR.

Reject	RRR01001	The Reject packet is sent from a node to inform the other node that it rejects packet number RRR. All other packets before this are acknowledged.
Clear Request/ Clear Indication	00010011	If the calling node sends this packet to the network it is a Clear Request packet, if the called node receives it is a Clear Indication packet.
Clear Confirm/ Clear Confirm	00010111	If the called node sends this packet to the network it is a Clear Confirm packet, if the calling node receives it is a Clear Confirm.

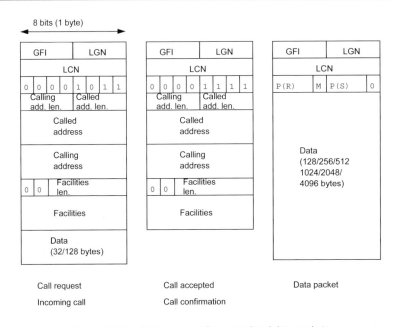

Figure C10.6 Call request, call accepted and data packets

Figure C10.6 shows the format of the Call Request/ Incoming Call, Call Accepted/ Call Confirmation and the Data packets. With the Call Request/ Incoming Call and the Call Accepted/ Call Confirmation packets the fourth byte of the packet contains two 4-bit numbers which define the number of bytes in the calling and called address. After this byte, the called and the calling addresses are sent. Following this, the next byte defines the number of bytes in the facilities field. The facilities field enables selected operational parameters to be negotiated when a call is being set up, these include:

- The data packet size (typically, 128 bytes).
- Number of packets to be received before an acknowledgement is required (typically, two).
- Data throughput, in bytes per second.
- Reverse charging.
- Usage of extended sequence numbers.

A data packet contains the standard packet header followed by a byte that contains the send and receive sequence number. The M bit identifies that there is more data to be sent to complete the message. Notice that the data packet does not contain either the calling or the called addresses. This is because once the connection is made then the VCI label identifies the path between the called and the calling node.

The P(R) variable is the sequence number of the packet that the sending node expects to receive next, and P(S) is the sequence number of the current packet. With modulo-8 sequencing, the packets are numbered from 0 to 7. The first packet sent is 0, the next is 1 and so on until the eighth packet that is numbered 7. The next is then numbered as 0 and so on. With modulo-128 sequencing, the packets are numbered 0 to 127.

The data size can be 128, 256, 512, 1024, 2048 or 4096 bytes, although its size is normally limited, by the public-carrier packet-switched network, to 128. This achieves a reasonable response time.

Figure C10.7 shows the format of the Receive Ready (RR), Receive Not Ready (RNR), Reject (REJ), Clear Confirmation and Clear Request packets. The RR, RNR and REJ packets contain a receive sequence number. This is the sequence number of the packet that the receiving node expects to receive next.

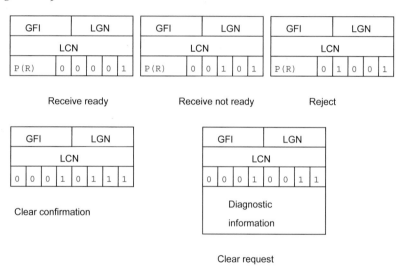

Figure C10.7   RR, RNR, REJ and Clear Confirm and Request packets

C10.4   X.25 packet flow

The three types of packets are:

- Call set-up and clearing - Call Request, Incoming Call, Clear Request, Clear Indication and Clear Confirmation.
- Data packets.
- Flow control - Receive Ready (RR), Receive Not Ready (RNR) and Reject (REJ).

C10.4.1 Call set-up and clearing

Figure C10.8 shows a typical data transfer. Initially the calling node (Node A) sends a Call Request packet (P[Call_request]) to the network. When this propagates through the packet-switched network the receiving node (Node B) receives it as an Incoming Call packet (P[Incoming_call]). When Node B accepts the call it sends a Call Accepted packet (P[Incoming_call]), which propagates through the network and Node A receives it as a Call Confirmation (P[Call_confirmation]).

The call initialization sets up a virtual circuit between the nodes and sequenced data packets and flow control information can now flow between the nodes.

To clear the connection Node A sends a Clear Request packet (P[Clear_request]) to the network. When this propagates through the network, Node B receives it as a Clear Indication packet (P[Clear_indication). When Node B accepts that the call is to be cleared then it sends a Clear Confirmation packet (P[Clear_confirm]). This propagates through the network and Node A receives it as a Clear Confirm (P[Call_confirmation]).

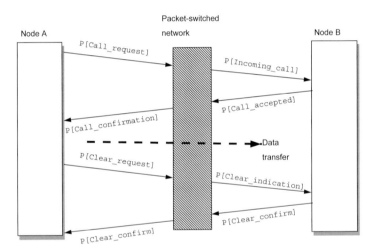

Figure C10.8   Call set-up and clearing

C10.4.2 Data transmission and flow control

After a virtual circuit has been set-up then sequenced data packets and flow control information can flow between the nodes.

A data packet contains sends two sequence numbers P[D, N(R), N(S)]. For 3-bit sequence numbers, N(S) and N(R) range from 0 to 7. N(S) is the sequence number of the data packet and N(R) is the sequence number of the packet that the sending node expects to receive next.

Figure C10.9 shows an example conversation between a sending node (Node A) and a receiving node (Node B). The flow control window has been set at 3. This window defines the number of packets that can be sent before the receiver must send an acknowledgement. Initially, in the example, three information frames are sent, numbered 2, 3 and 4 (P[D, N(R)=0, N(S)=2], P[D, N(R)=0, N(S)=3] and P[D, N(R)=0, N(S)=4]). The window is set to 3 thus Node B must send an acknowledgement for the packets it has received. It does this by sending a Receive Ready packet (P[RR, N(R)=5]). This informs node A that Node B expects to receive packet number 5 next. This acknowledges all frames before, and including, frame 4.

In the example in Figure C10.9 an error has occurred in the reception of frame 5. The recipient informs the sender by sending a Reject packet (P[REJ, N(R)=5]). After the sender receives this it re-sends each frame after, and including, frame 5.

If a node does not wish to communicate, at the present, it sends a Receive Not Ready packet. For example P[RNR, N(R)=5] tells the transmitter to stop sending data, at the present. It also informs the sender that all frames up to frame 5 have been accepted. The sender will transmitting frames only once it has received a Receive Ready packet from the receiver.

Figure C10.8 shows an example of data flow in only the one direction. With X.25 both stations can transmit and receive data. Thus each packet sent contains receive and send counter values. When nodes send data packets the previously received frames can be acknowledged, or rejected, by piggybacking the receive counter value. In Figure C10.9, node A sends 3 data packets with P[D, N(R)=0, N(S)=0], P[D, N(R)=0, N(S)=1], and P[D, N(R)=0, N(S)=2]. The last data packet informs Node B that Node A expects to receive data packet 0 next. Node B then sends data packet 0 and acknowledges the reception of all frames up to, and including frame 2 with P[D, N(R)=3, N(S)=0], and so on.

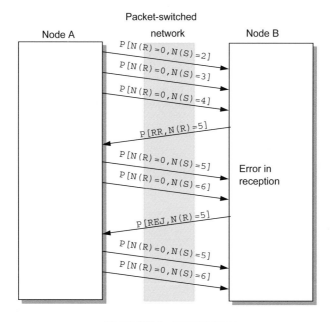

Figure C10.9 Example flow

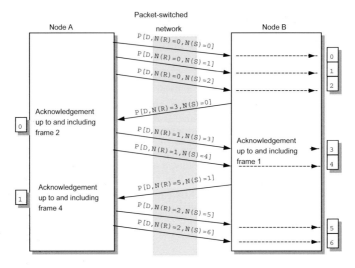

Figure C10.10 Example flow with piggybacked acknowledgement

C10.4.3 The delivery bit

The delivery bit (d) identifies which connection should respond with an acknowledgement. If it is not set then the local network connection sends an acknowledgement for data packets. If it is set then the remote nodes sends the acknowledgement. The latter was the case in the example given in Figure C10.9. An example is given in Figure C10.11. The number of packets before an acknowledgement is set by the window. When the d-bit is not set then the window does not have any significance as the network connection returns back all packets sent.

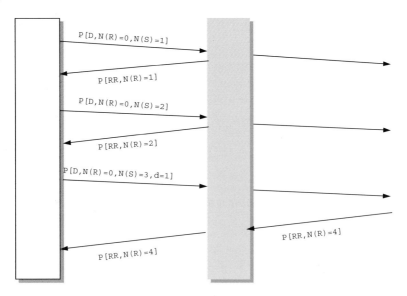

Figure C10.11 Usage of the D-bit

C10.5   Packet switching routing

There are three main types of routing used in X.25, these are:

- Permanent virtual call.
- Virtual call.
- Datagram.

A virtual call sets up a route for the two-way flow of packets between two specific nodes, whereas a datagram is sent into the network without first establishing a route. A datagram is analogous to a letter sent by the post, where a letter is addressed and sent without first finding out if the letter will be received. The virtual call is analogous to a telephone call where a direct connection is made before the call is initiated.

A datagram is normally only used where there is a small amount of data in a few packets, whereas a virtual call is set-up where there are relatively large amounts of data to be sent in many packets. With a datagram there is no need to initiate the call set-up procedures, as previously shown in Figure C10.8. The call set-up and clearing packets (Call Request, Call Indication, and so on) are only used when a virtual circuit is used. An example of a datagram might be to transmit an electronic mail message, as there is no need to establish a virtual circuit before the message is sent.

Once a virtual circuit is set-up then it is used until all the data has been transferred. A new conversation establishes a new virtual circuit. In some applications, though, a reliable permanent circuit is required, this is described as a permanent virtual call where two nodes have a permanent virtual connection. There is no need, in this case, to set-up a connection as the virtual circuit between the two nodes is dedicated to them.

When a calling node wishes to communicate through the network it makes contact with the called node and negotiates such things as the packet size, reverse charging and maximum data throughput. The window size is the number of packets that are sent before an acknowledgement must be sent back. Maximum data throughput is the maximum number of bytes that can be sent per second. These flow control parameters are contained in the facilities field of the Call Request packet. If the called node accepts them then a connection is made.

The network computes a route based on the specified parameters and determines which links on each part of the route best supports the requested flow control parameters. It sets up request to all the packet routing nodes on the path en-route to the destination node. Figure C10.12 shows an example route between packet-switched routers (PSR) from a calling node to a destination node. The route selected is PSR1 → PSR2 → PSR3 → PSR4. Each of the router selects an unused VCI label on their respective links and reserves it for the virtual circuit in their connection lookup tables.

For example PSR1 could use VC_2 (for example the VCI could have a value of 17), this can be sent to PSR2. PSR2 in turn picks VC_3 and associates it with VC_2 in its connection table. It then forwards VC_3 to PSR3. PSR3 selects VC_4 and associates it with VC_3. It then forwards VC_4 to PSR4. PSR4 selects VC_5 and associates it with VC_4. If the called node accepts the call then it sends back a Call Accepted packet back over the virtual circuit. Each of the nodes on way back to the calling node assigns a new VCI number. Thus, the acknowledgement passes back from PSR4 to PSR3, PSR3 to PSR2 and so on to the calling node to confirm that the connection has been established. Data packets can then be transmitted between the two nodes. As has been previously discussed, there is no need to transmit the calling or called addresses with the packet as the source and destination is identified using the VCI label. When the connection is terminated the VCI labels assigned to the communications can be used for other connections.

If a single virtual circuit is set-up then packets are always delivered in the order these were transmitted. This is because packets cannot take alternative routes to the destination. Even if the packets are buffered within a node they will still be transmitted in the correct sequence.

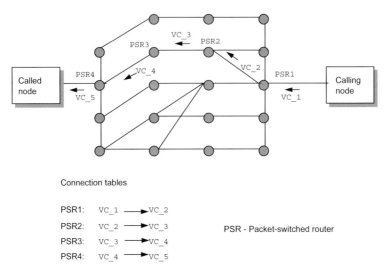

Connection tables

PSR1:   VC_1 ⟶ VC_2
PSR2:   VC_2 ⟶ VC_3   PSR - Packet-switched router
PSR3:   VC_3 ⟶ VC_4
PSR4:   VC_4 ⟶ VC_5

Figure C10.12   Virtual call set-up

C10.6 Logical channels

The VCI label contains a 4-bit logical group number (LGN) and a 16-bit logical channel number (LCN) to define the VCI. There can be 16 groups and within each group there can be 256 different channels. This allows for a node to communicate with several nodes simultaneously. Figure C10.13 shows an example of a node communicating with four nodes over four channels. Node A is communicating with Node B, C, D and E. The route for Node A to Node E is through routers A, B, C, G, and I. For Node A to Node D it is through routers A, F, G and H.

C10.7 X.25 node addressing

Nodes on an X.25 network have an individual NSAP (network service access point) address. Since these nodes operate globally over international networks the addresses must be assigned a globally unique network address. The network on which the node is connected is usually a countrywide network. Each of these packet-switched public digital networks are known as a subnet.

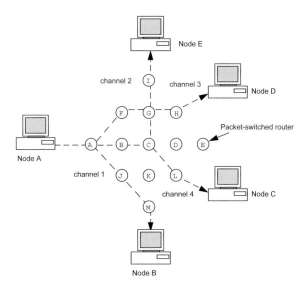

Figure C10.13 Multiple channels

The definition of the addresses is defined either in pure binary or a binary-coded decimal (BCD) digits. For example, if the network address is defined in BCD then the binary address `0011 0110 0001 0111 1001 0011` corresponds to `361792`. The NSAP address is made up of up-to 40 decimal digits or 20 bytes (as one BCD digit is represented by 4 bits). The calling and called address length are defined within the X.25 packet.

The NSAP address is made up of parts, the initial domain part (IDP) and the domain specific part (DSP), as illustrated in Figure C10.14. An IDP is made up of two sub-parts, the authority and format identifier (AFI), and the initial domain identifier (IDI). As several authorities can grant NSAP addresses, the AFI field contains two BCD digits which identify the granting authority and the format of the rest of the address field.

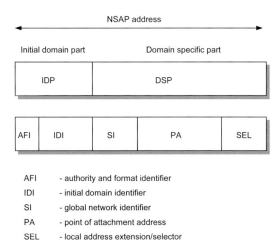

Figure C10.14 NSAP address

For example, if the AFI value is 36 then the granting authority is the CCITT and the format is defined in the X.121 recommendation. The resulting address is:

36XXXXXXXXXXXXXXXXXYYYYYYYYYYYYYYYYYYYYYYYY

where XX..XXX is the IDI part (14 digits) and YY...YYY is the DSP part (24 digits). This gives a total of 40 digits.

If the AFI value is 38 then the granting authority is the ISO and the format is defined by the ISO-assigned country codes, or ISO DCC. The resulting address is:

38XXXYYYYYYYYYYYYYYYYYYYYYYYYYYYYYYYYYYYY

where XX..XXX is the IDI part (3 digits) and YY...YYY is the DSP part (35 digits). With ISO address the IDI portion is assigned by the country the network is resident.

After the initial domain is defined then the DSP part defines a smaller and smaller sub-network within the domain. Figure C10.15 shows an example addressing structure. The SEL part defines the local node with at the point of attachment of the packet switched network.

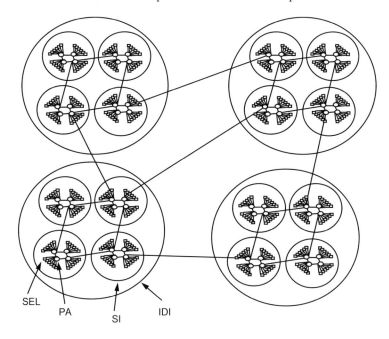

Figure C10.15   NSAP addressing structure

C11 Wireless Networks (IEEE 802.11b)

C11.1 Introduction

Wireless networks use high-frequency radio waves to transmit from node to node. The 11Mbps IEEE 802.11b standard has been designed so that nodes can connect using a peer-to-peer connection (known as an ad-hoc connection) or connect to a wireless hub (known as an infrastructure connection). The bit rate is equivalent to a base-rate Ethernet connection, and is thus able to easily integrate with existing Ethernet networks. The advantages of IEEE 802.11b include:

- Integrates well with existing Ethernet networks.
- Is supported by most network operating systems.
- Provides a range of up to 800 feet, in an open environment.
- Provides increased mobility.
- Reduces the cost of wiring.
- Supports 1, 2, 5.5 and 11 Mbps bit rates.
- Supports either a point-to-point (ad-hoc) and point-to-multipoint (infrastructure) access.
- Supports Plug and Play, and is easy to install.
- Used strong encryption using WEP encryption (64-bit and 128-bit)
- Uses Direct Sequence Spread Spectrum (DSSS) which is a robust, interference-resistant and secure wireless connection.

The applications of wireless technology is likely to increase over the forthcoming year, especially with the increasing processing power of mobile devices, but typical applications include:

- Environments which have frequently change, such as in a retail environment, or in workplaces which are continually rearranged.
- High security networks. Ethernet has suffered from security problems, thus wireless networks with encryption can overcome this.
- Providing remote access for a corporate network.
- Providing temporary LANs which could be used for special projects.
- Remote access to databases in mobile applications, such as for medical practitioners, or office staff.
- Supporting networks in environments where cable runs are difficult, such as in old buildings, hazardous areas, and in open spaces.
- Support for users who use SOHO (Small Office and Home Office), as it provides a quick access to networks.

C11.2 Basic specification

IEEE 802.11b uses a number of channels in frequency range around 2.4 GHz to 2.45 GHz. This high frequency allows the radio wave to propagate fairly well through building and air. At 11Mbps, the maximum range is around 140 meters, but this reduces when there are obstacles in the way. At 1Mbps, the range increases to 400 meters. The frequencies are split into a number of channels. In Northern America, there are 11 channels, in Japan, there are 14, and in Europe, there are 13 channels (as shown in Figure C11.1).

Operating Channels:	11 for N. America, 14 Japan, 13 Europe (ETSI), 2 Spain, 4 France
Operating Frequency:	2.412-2.462 GHz (North America), 2.412-2.484 GHz (Japan), 2.412-2.472 GHz (Europe ETSI), 2.457-2.462 GHz (Spain), 2.457-2.472 GHz (France)
Data Rate:	1, 2, 5.5 or 11Mbps
Media Access Protocol:	CSMA/CA, 802.11 Compliant
Range:	11Mbps: 140m (460 feet)
	5.5Mbps: 200m (656 feet)
	2Mbps: 270m (885 feet)
	1Mbps: 400m (1311 feet)
RF Technology:	Direct Sequence Spread Spectrum
Modulation:	CCK (11Mps, 5.5Mbps), DQPSK (2Mbps), DBPSK (1Mbps)
Output Power:	13 dBm
Sensitivity:	11Mbps < -83 dBm
	5.5Mbps < -86dBm
	2Mbps < -89dBm
	1Mbps < -91dBm

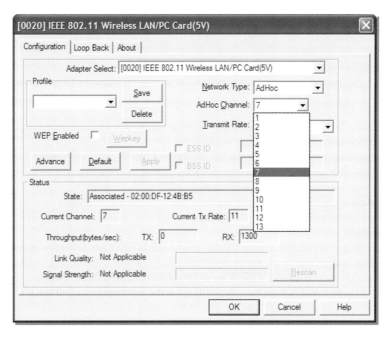

Figure C11.1   IEEE802.11 channel setting for Europe

The wireless adapter will typically connect to a node using one of a number of ways, such as through the USB port, PCI card, PCMCIA card, and so on. The wireless protocol corresponds to a network adapter, and can thus support most higher layer protocols, such as TCP/IP, NetBEUI, and IPX/SPX, as shown in Figure C11.2.

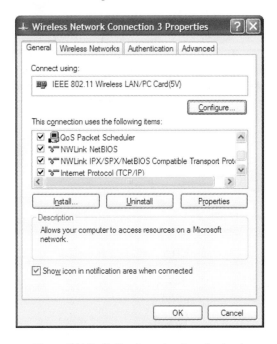

Figure C11.2   Setting for protocols and network

C11.3   Wireless network connections

IEEE 802.11b can be either connected as an infrastructure network or as an ad-hoc network. Figure C11.3 shows an infrastructure network where the wireless nodes connect to an access point. The access point defines the domain of the wireless network. These domains can then interconnect through an Ethernet backbone. Figure C11.4 shows the usage of SSID, which is a unique ID given to the access point. All the clients which connect to a certain access point must define the correct name (otherwise they may connect to another access point). If the access point ID is not known then ANY can be used (although this is not recommended for security reasons).

An ad-hoc network uses channels to define different networks, as illustrated in Figure C11.5. In this example, LAN 1 uses channel 3, and LAN 2 uses channel 7. In Europe, for example, it would be possible to create up to 13 different ad-hoc networks, within a certain range (between 100 and 400 meters, depending on the environment, and the bit rate). If an ad-hoc network has a range of L meters, then an infrastructure network will have a diameter range of 2L, as illustrated in Figure C11.6.

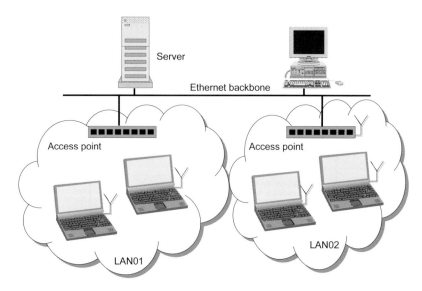

Figure C11.3   Infrastructure network

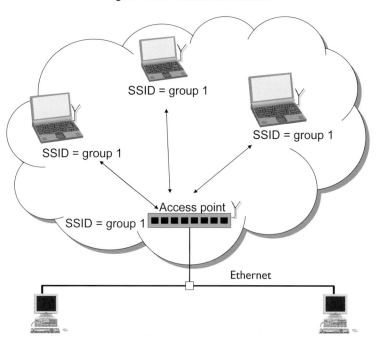

Figure C11.4   SSID for a wireless network

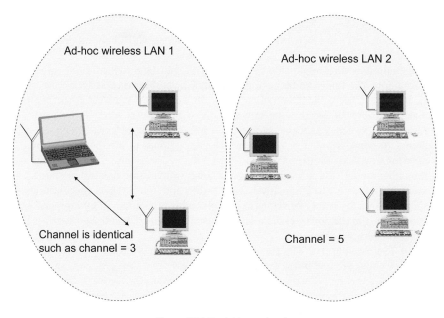

Figure C11.5 Ad-hoc networks

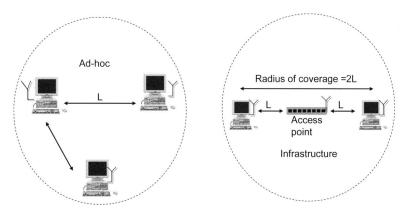

Figure C11.6 Span of networks

C11.4   IEEE 802.11b settings

The IEEE 802.11b device **must** be set up properly as the communications can be picked-up by other users, who, if the connection is not setup properly, could read all the communications sent and received. They may allow be able to connect to the resources of the node connected to the wireless adapter. Figure C11.7 shows some of the setting which must be set-up on the adapter. The settings are:

- **Authentication algorithm**. This sets whether the adapter uses an open system (where other nodes can listen to the communications), or uses encryption (using either a WEP key, or a shared key).

- **Channel**. If an ad-hoc network is used, then the nodes which communicate must use the same channel.
- **Fragmentation threshold**. This can be used to split large data frames into smaller fragements. The value can range from 64 to 1500 bytes. This is used to improve the efficiency when there is a high amount of traffic on the wireless network, as smaller frames make more efficient usage of the network.
- **Network type**. This can either be set to an infrastructure network (which use access points, or wireless hubs) or Ad-hoc, which allows nodes to interconnect without the need for an access point.
- **Preamble mode**. This can either be set to Long (which is the default) or short. A long preamble allows for interoperatively with 1Mbps and 2Mbps DSSS specifications. The shorter allows for faster operations (as the preamble is kept to a minimum) and can be used where the transmission parameters must be maximized, and that there are no interoperatablity problems.
- **RTS/CTS threshold**. The RTS Threshold prevents the *Hidden Node* problem, where two wireless nodes are within range of the same access point, but are not within range of each other. As they do not know that they both exist on the network, they may try to communicate with the access point at the same time. When they do, their data frames may collide when arriving simultaneously at the Access Point, which causes a loss of data frames from the nodes. The RTS threshold tries to overcome this by enabling the handshaking signals of Ready To Send (RTS) and Clear To Send (CTS). When a node wishes to communicate with the access point it sends a RTS signal to the access point. Once the access point defines that it can then communicate, the access point sends a CTS message. The node can then send its data.

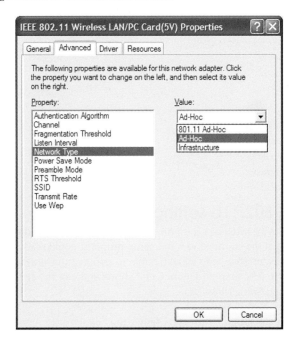

Figure C11.7   Setting for IEEE 802.11b adaptor

C11.5 Encryption

Figure C11.8 shows that IEEE 802.11b has three encryption operations. These are:

- **Disable**. No encryption used.
- **64-bit WEP**. Data encryption with an access point using a 64-bit key.
- **128-bit WEP**. Data encryption with an access point using a 128-bit key.

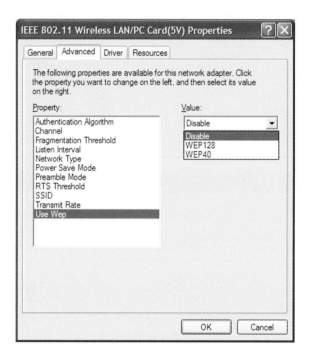

Figure C11.8   Setting encryption mode

Figure C11.9 shows that that it is possible to set the encryption key as a pass phase or manually. For 64-bit encryption, 5 alphanumeric characters or 10 hexadecimal values is used to define the encryption key, or for 128-bits encryption, the key is specified with 13 alphanumeric values or a 26 hexadecimal characters. The system will only use one of the four keys for its encryption. All the stations and connected access point, if connected, must use the same encryption key. For example a 64-bit key could be:

```
Edin1
```

Whereas 128-bit encryption could use:

```
Edinburgh Network 11
```

This encryption can be optional (only use, if necessary) or mandatory (where it will only ever use encryption).

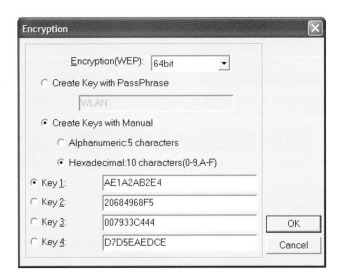

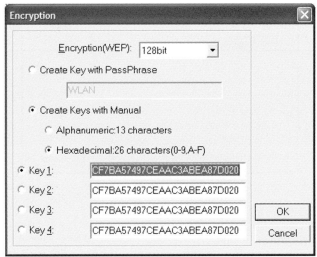

Figure C11.9 Setting encryption key

D1   IP

D1.1   Introduction

Networking technologies such as Ethernet, Token Ring and FDDI provide a data link layer function, that is, they allow a reliable connection between one node and another on the same network. They do not provide internetworking where data can be transferred from one network to another or from one network segment to another. For data to be transmitted across a network requires an addressing structure which is read by a gateway or a router. The interconnection of networks is known as internetworking (or an internet). Each part of an internet is a subnetwork (or subnet), and Transmission Control Protocol (TCP) and Internet Protocol (IP) are a pair of protocols that allow one subnet to communicate with another.

A protocol is a set of rules that allows the orderly exchange of information. The IP part corresponds to the network layer of the OSI model and the TCP part to the transport layer. Their operation is transparent to the physical and data link layers and can thus be used on Ethernet, FDDI or Token Ring networks. This is illustrated in Figure D1.1. The address of the data link layer corresponds to the physical address of the node, such as the MAC address (in Ethernet and Token Ring) or the telephone number (for a modem connection). The IP address is assigned to each node on the internet, and is used to identify the location of the network and any subnets.

TCP/IP was originally developed by the US Defense Advanced Research Projects Agency (DARPA), and its objective was to connect a number of universities and other research establishments to DARPA. The resultant internet is now known as the Internet. It has since outgrown this application and many commercial organizations now connect to the Internet. The Internet uses TCP/IP to transfer data, where each node on the Internet is assigned a unique network address, called an IP address. Note that any organization can have its own internets, but if it is to connect to the Internet then the addresses must conform to the Internet addressing format. Common applications that use TCP/IP communications are remote login and file transfer. Typical programs used in file transfer and login over TCP communication are `ftp` for file transfer program and `telnet` which allows remote log into another computer. The `ping` program determines if a node is responding to TCP/IP communications.

The ISO has adopted TCP/IP as the basis for the standards relating to the network and transport layers of the OSI model, and is known as ISO-IP. Most currently available systems conform to the IP addressing standard.

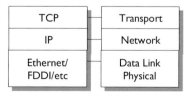

Figure D1.1   TCP/IP and the OSI model

D1.2 Data encapsulation

The OSI model provides a clear model in understanding how data is transferred from one system to another. Each layer of the OSI model depends on the layers above and/or below it to provide a certain function. To achieve this data is encapsulated when passing from one layer to the next. Encapsulation happens when a lower layer gets a PDU (Protocol Data Unit) from an upper layer and uses this as a data field. It then adds to its own headers and trailers so that it can perform the required function. For example, as illustrated in Figure D1.2, if a user was sending an e-mail to another user the host computer would go through the following:

- **Step 1.** The application program makes contact with a network application program for electronic mail transfer [Application].
- **Step 2.** The computer converts the data into a form that can be transmitted over the network [Presentation].
- **Step 3.** The computer sets up a connection with the remote system and asks if it is willing to make a connection with it. Once accepted it will ask the remote system as to whether the user for whom the e-mail message is destined for actually exists on that system [Session].
- **Step 4.** The transport layer negotiates with the remote system about how it wants to receive the data, it then splits the data into a number of segments, each of which are numbered. Any problems with lost segments will be dealt with at this step [Transport]. DATA SEGMENT.
- **Step 5.** The network address of the destination and source are added to all the data segments [Network]. DATA PACKET.
- **Step 6.** The data packet is then framed in a format so that it can be transmitted over the local connection [Data link]. DATA FRAME.
- **Step 7.** The data frame is then taken and converted into a binary form and transmitted over a physical connection. BITS.

D1.3 TCP/IP gateways and hosts

TCP/IP hosts are nodes which communicate over interconnected networks using TCP/IP communications. A TCP/IP gateway node connects one type of network to another. It contains hardware to provide the physical link between the different networks and the hardware and software to convert frames from one network to the other. Typically, it converts a Token Ring MAC layer to an equivalent Ethernet MAC layer, and vice versa.

A router connects a network of a similar type to another of the same kind through a point-to-point link. The main operational difference between a gateway, a router, and a bridge is that for a Token Ring and Ethernet network, the bridge uses the 48-bit MAC address to route frames, whereas the gateway and router use the IP network address. As an analogy to the public telephone system, the MAC address would be equivalent to a randomly assigned telephone number, whereas the IP address would contain the information on where the telephone is logically located, such as which country, area code, and so on.

Figure D1.3 shows how a gateway (or router) routes information. It reads the data frame from the computer on network A, and reads the IP address contained in the frame and makes a decision whether it is routed out of network A to network B. If it does then it relays the frame to network B.

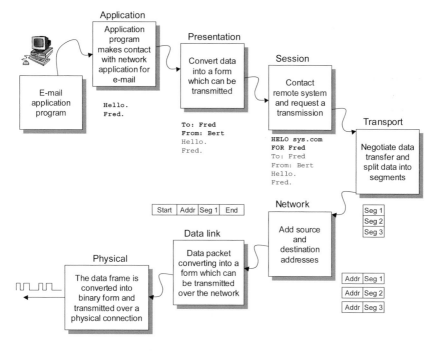

Figure D1.2   Data encapsulation

D1.4   Functions of the IP protocol

The main functions of the IP protocol are to:

- Route IP data packets – which are called internet datagrams – around an internet. The IP protocol program running on each node knows the location of the gateway on the network. The gateway must then be able to locate the interconnected network. Data then passes from node to gateway through the internet.
- Fragment the data into smaller units, if it is greater than a given amount (64 kB). Most data packets will be much smaller than 64kB. For example the maximum size of a data packet that can be contained in an Ethernet frame is 1500 bytes.
- Report errors. When a datagram is being routed or is being reassembled an error can occur. If this happens then the node that detects the error reports back to the source node. Datagrams are deleted from the network if they travel through the network for more than a set time. Again, an error message is returned to the source node to inform it that the Internet routing could not find a route for the datagram or that the destination node, or network, does not exist.

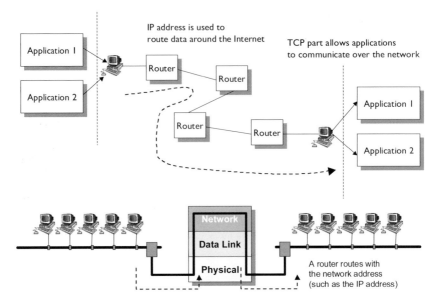

Figure D1.3 Internet gateway layers

D1.5   Internet datagram

The IP protocol is an implementation of the network layer of the OSI model. It adds a data header onto the information passed from the transport layer, the resultant data packet is known as an internet datagram. The header contains information such as the destination and source IP addresses, the version number of the IP protocol and so on. Figure D1.4 shows its format.

The datagram can contain up to 65,536 bytes (64 KB) of data. If the data to be transmitted is less than, or equal to 64 KB, then it is sent as one datagram. If it is more than this then the sender splits the data into fragments and sends multiple datagrams. When transmitted from the source each datagram is routed separately through the internet and the received fragments are finally reassembled at the destination.

The fields in the IP datagram are:

- **Version.** The TCP/IP `version number` helps gateways and nodes interpret the data unit correctly. Differing versions may have a different format. Most current implementations will have a version number of four (IPv4).
- **Type of service.** The `type of service` bit field is an 8-bit bit pattern in the form `PPPDTRXX`, where `PPP` defines the priority of the datagram (from 0 to 7). The precedence levels are:

111 (Network control)
110 (Internetwork control)
001 (Priority)

`D` sets a low delay service (0 – normal delay, 1 – low delay).

T sets high throughput (0 – normal throughput, 1 – high throughput).

R sets high reliability (0 – normal reliability, 1 – high reliability).

- **Header length** (4 bits). The header length defines the size of the data unit in multiples of four bytes (32 bits). The minimum length is five bytes and the maximum is 65,536 bytes. Padding bytes fill any unused spaces.
- **Identification** (16 bits). A value which is assigned by the sender to aid the assembly of the frames of a datagram.
- **D** and **M** bits. A gateway may route a datagram and split it into smaller fragments. The D bit informs the gateway that it should not fragment the data and thus it signifies that a receiving node should receive the data as a   single unit or not at all. The M bit is the 'more fragments' bit and is used when data is split into fragments. The fragment offset contains the fragment number. The bit settings are:

  D – Don't fragment.   0 – may fragment,
  1 – don't fragment.
  M – Last fragment.   0 – last fragment,
  1 – more fragments.

- **Fragment offset** (13 bits). Indicates which datagram this fragment belongs to. The fragment offset is measured in units of 8 bytes (64 bits). The first fragment has an offset of zero.
- **Time-to-live** (8 bits). A datagram could propagate through the internet indefinitely. To prevent this, the 8-bit time-to-live value is set to the maximum transit time in seconds and is set   initially by the source IP. Each gateway then decrements this value by a defined amount. When it becomes zero the datagram is discarded. It can also be used to define the maximum amount of time that a destination IP node should wait for the next datagram fragment.
- **Protocol** (8 bits). Different IP protocols can be used on the datagram. The 8-bit protocol field defines the type to be used. Typical values are: 1 – ICMP and 6 – TCP.
- **Header checksum** (16 bits). The header checksum contains a 16-bit pattern for error detection. Since values within the header change from gateway to gateway (such as the time-to-live field), it must be recomputed every time the IP header is processed. The algorithm is:

  The 16-bit 1's complement of the 1's complement sum of all the 16-bit words in the header. When calculating the checksum the header checksum field is assumed to be set to a zero.

- **Source and destination IP addresses** (32 bits). The source and destination IP addresses are stored in the 32-bit source and destination IP address fields.
- **Options**. The options field contains information such as debugging, error control and routing information.

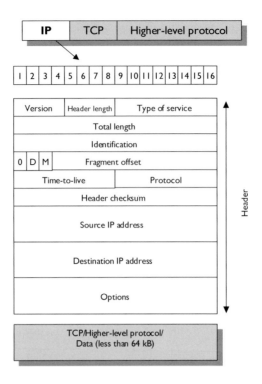

IP	TCP	Higher-level protocol

| 1 | 2 | 3 | 4 | 5 | 6 | 7 | 8 | 9 | 10 | 11 | 12 | 13 | 14 | 15 | 16 |

Version	Header length	Type of service

Total length

Identification

| 0 | D | M | Fragment offset |

| Time-to-live | Protocol |

Header checksum

Source IP address

Destination IP address

Options

TCP/Higher-level protocol/
Data (less than 64 kB)

Figure D1.4 Internet datagram format and contents

D1.6   TCP/IP internets

Figure D1.5 illustrates a sample TCP/IP implementation. A gateway MERCURY provides a link between a Token Ring network (NETWORK A) and the Ethernet network (ETHER C). Another gateway PLUTO connects NETWORK B to ETHER C. The TCP/IP protocol allows a host on NETWORK A to communicate with VAX01.

D1.6.1   Selecting internet addresses

Each node using TCP/IP communications requires an IP address which is then matched to its Token Ring or Ethernet MAC address. The MAC address allows nodes on the same segment to communicate with each other. In order for nodes on a different network to communicate, each must be configured with an IP address.

Nodes on a TCP/IP network are either hosts or gateways. Any node that runs application software or are terminals are hosts. Any node that routes TCP/IP packets between networks is called a TCP/IP gateway node. This node must have the necessary network controller boards to physically interface to other networks it connects with.

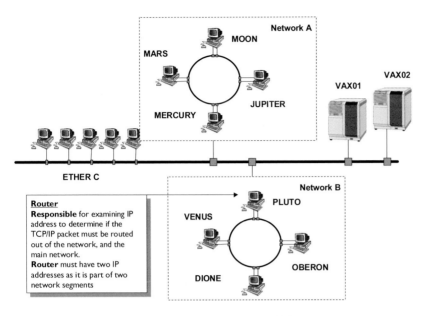

Figure D1.5 Example internet

D1.6.2 Format of the IP address

A typical IP address consists of two fields: the left field (or the network number) identifies the network, and the right number (or the host number) identifies the particular host within that network. Figure D1.6 illustrates this. The IP address is 32 bits long and can address over four billion physical addresses (2^{32} or $4,294,967,296$ hosts). There are three main address formats and these are shown in Figure D1.7.

Each of these types is applicable to certain types of networks. Class A allows up to 128 (2^7) different networks and up to $16,777,216$ (2^{24}) hosts on each network. Class B allows up to $16,384$ (2^{14}) networks and up to $65,536$ (2^{16}) hosts on each network. Class C allows up to $2,097,152$ (2^{21}) networks each with up to 256 (2^8) hosts.

The class A address is thus useful where there are a small number of networks with a large number of hosts connected to them. Class C is useful where there are many networks with a relatively small number of hosts connected to each network. Class B addressing gives a good compromise of networks and connected hosts.

When selecting internet addresses for the network, the address can be specified simply with decimal numbers within a specific range. The standard DARPA IP addressing format is of the form:

```
W.X.Y.Z
```

where W, X, Y and Z represent 1 byte of the IP address. As decimal numbers, they range from 0 to 255. The 4 bytes together represent both the network and host address.

Table D1.1 Ranges of addresses for type A, B and C internet address

Type	Network portion	Host portion
A	1 – 126	0.0.1 – 255.255.254
B	128.1 – 191.254	0.1 – 255.254
C	192.0.1 – 223.255.254	1 – 254

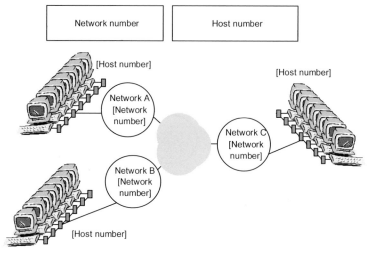

Figure D1.6 IP addressing over networks

The valid range of the different IP addresses given in Table D1.1 defines the valid IP addresses. Thus for a class A type address there can be 127 networks and 16,711,680 ($256\times256\times255$) hosts. Class B can have 16,320 (64×255) networks and class C can have 2,088,960 ($32\times256\times255$) networks and 255 hosts. Addresses above `223.255.254` are reserved, as are addresses with groups of zeros.

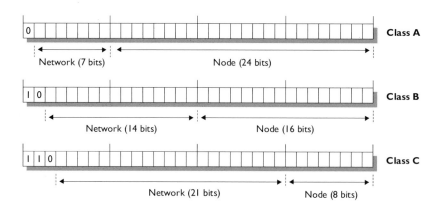

Figure D1.7 Type A, B and C IP address classes

D1.6.3 Range of IP addresses

The IP address splits into two main parts: the network part (which is assigned by InterNIC), and the host part (which is assigned by the local system administrator). The type of address that is allocated depends on the size of the organization and the number of hosts that it has on its network. Figure D1.8 shows how the binary notation can be represented in dotted notation, of which there are three commercial address classifications, these are:

- **Class A.** Large organizations with many nodes. MIT has a Class A address (18.0.0.0).
- **Class B.** Medium sized organizations with an average number of hosts. For example, Napier University has a Class B address (146.176.0.0).
- **Class C.** Small organizations or setups, with only a few hosts on each network.

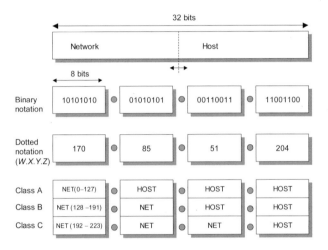

Figure D1.8 IP address format

The other two address classifications are used for multicast and research purposes. These are:

- **Class D.** Multicast. Single packets copied by the network and sent to a specific subset of network addresses. These addresses are specified in the destination address field.
- **Class E.** Research purposes.

Not all the IP addresses in the host part can be used to assign to a host. The two exceptions are:

- **All 0's in the host part** are reserved for the entire network. For example:

  32.0.0.0 (Class A network address).
  146.176.0.0 (Class B network address).
  199.20.30.0 (Class C network address).

- **All 1's in the host part** are reserved for the broadcast address, which is used to send a data packet to all the hosts on the network. For example:

32.255.255.255 (Class A broadcast address for the network 32.0.0.0).
146.176.255.255 (Class B broadcast address for the network 146.176.0.0).
199.20.30.255 (Class C broadcast address for the network 199.20.30.0).

The other broadcast address is 255.255.255.255. Routers will not transmit broadcast addresses from one network segment to another.

D1.6.4 Creating IP addresses with subnet numbers

Besides selecting IP addresses of internets and host numbers, it is also possible to designate an intermediate number called a subnet number. Subnets extend the network field of the IP address beyond the limit defined by the type A, B, C scheme. They thus allow for a hierarchy of internets within a network. For example, it is possible to have one network number for a network attached to the internet, and various subnet numbers for each subnet within the network. This is illustrated in Figure D1.9. For an address W.X.Y.Z and type for a type A address, typically W specifies the network and X the subnet. For type B the Y field typically specifies the subnet, as illustrated in Figure D1.10.

To connect to a global network a number is normally assigned by a central authority. For the Internet network it is assigned by the Network Information Center (NIC). Typically, on the Internet an organization is assigned a type B network address. The first two fields of the address specify the organization network, the third specifies the subnet within the organization and the final value specifies the host.

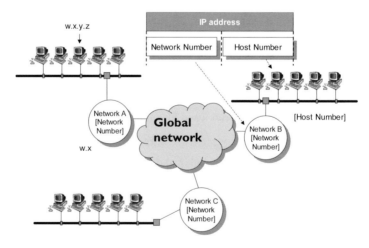

Figure D1.9 IP addresses with subnets

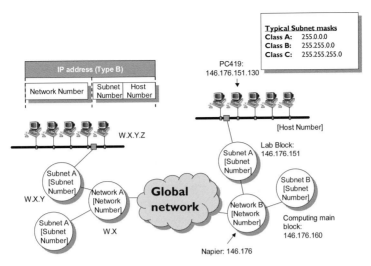

Figure D1.10 Internet addresses with subnets

D1.6.5 Specifying subnet masks

If a subnet is used then a bit mask, or subnet mask, must be specified to show which part of the address is the network part and which is the host. The subnet mask is a 32-bit number that has 1's for bit positions specifying the network and subnet parts and 0's for the host part. A text file called *hosts* is normally used to set up the subnet mask. Table D1.2 shows example subnet masks. To set up the default mask the following line is added to the *hosts* file.

```
 Hosts file
255.255.255.0  defaultmask
```

Table D1.2 Default subnet mask for type A, B and C IP addresses

Address type	Default mask
Class A	255.0.0.0
Class B	255.255.0.0
Class C and Class B with a subnet	255.255.255.0

The subnet can use any number of bits from the host portion of the address. Table D1.3 outlines the subnet masks for Class B addresses, and Table D1.4 outlines the subnet masks for Class C addresses, and Table D1.8 outlines Class A subnets. The number of bits borrowed from the host address defines the maximum number of subnetworks. For example, four bits borrowed from the host field will allow 14 different subnetworks ($2^4 - 2$, as 0000 is reserved for the whole network and 1111 is reserved for the broadcast address). The subnets will thus be defined by 0001, 0010, 0011 … 1101 and 1110. The maximum number of hosts will be the number of bits left in the host part, after the bits have been borrowed for the subnet, to the power of two, less two. The reason that the value is reduced by two is that the 0.0 address is reserved for the network, and the all 1's address is reserved for a broadcast address to that subnet.

Table D1.3 Subnet masks for a Class B address

Binary subnet address	Dotted notation	Maximum number of subnets	Maximum number of hosts on each subnet
11111111.11111111.11000000.00000000	255.255.192.0	2	16,382
11111111.11111111.11100000.00000000	255.255.224.0	6	8,190
11111111.11111111.11110000.00000000	255.255.240.0	14	4,094
11111111.11111111.11111000.00000000	255.255.248.0	30	2,046
11111111.11111111.11111100.00000000	255.255.252.0	62	1,022
11111111.11111111.11111110.00000000	255.255.254.0	126	510
11111111.11111111.11111111.00000000	255.255.255.0	254	254
11111111.11111111.11111111.10000000	255.255.255.128	510	126
11111111.11111111.11111111.11000000	255.255.255.192	1,022	62
11111111.11111111.11111111.11100000	255.255.255.224	2,046	30
11111111.11111111.11111111.11110000	255.255.255.240	4,094	14
11111111.11111111.11111111.11111000	255.255.255.248	8,190	6
11111111.11111111.11111111.11111100	255.255.255.252	16,382	2

Table D1.4 Subnet masks for a Class C address

Binary subnet address	Dotted notation	Max. subnets	Max. hosts on each subnet
11111111.11111111. 11111111.11000000	255.255.255.192	2	62
11111111.11111111. 11111111.11100000	255.255.255.224	6	30
11111111.11111111. 11111111.11110000	255.255.255.240	14	14
11111111.11111111. 11111111.11111000	255.255.255.248	30	6
11111111.11111111. 11111111.11111100	255.255.255.252	62	2

For example for a subnet with a subnet mask of 255.255.248.0, which has been given a Class B address of 144.32.Y.Z. Then the first usable subnet address will be (the brackets signify the binary address, and the bold text identifies the subnet address):

144.32.[**00001** 000].[0000 0000]
    which is 144.32.8.0 (this starts from **00001** as 00000 is reserved for the whole network)

The addresses that can be allocated to the computers will then be:

First address: 144.32.8.1.
Second address: 144.32.8.2.
...
Last address: 144.32.15.254 (143.32.[00001 111].[1111 1110]).

The second subnet of the network will be:

144.32.[**00010** 000].[0000 0000]
    which is 144.32.16.0 (this will be the network address of the subnet)

The addresses that can be allocated to the computers will then be:

First address: 144.32.16.1. (144.32.16.0 cannot be used as it is the address for all the subnets)

Second address: 144.32.16.2.

...

Last address: 144.32.23.254 (143.32.[00010 111].[1111 1110]).

The last subnet of the network will be:

144.32.[**11110** 000].[0000 0000]

which is 144.32.240.0 (this will be the network address of the subnet)

The addresses that can be allocated to the computers will then be:

First address: 144.32.240.1.

Second address: 144.32.240.2.

...

Last address: 144.32.247.254 (143.32.[11110 111].[1111 1110]).

D1.6.6 Subnet calculator

A basic subnet calculator program is available on the CD-ROM (and from the WWW site). An outline of the code is given next.

```
Dim mask(21) As String
Dim net_address(42) As String

Private Sub bits_for_subnet_Change()
    subnets.Text = (2 ^ Val(bits_for_subnet.Text)) - 2
    host.Text = "-"
    netadd1st.Text = "-"
    netadd2nd.Text = "-"

    If (ipclass.ListIndex = 0) Then
        Select Case Val(bits_for_subnet.Text)
        Case 2 To 22:
            subnet_mask.Text = mask(bits_for_subnet.Text - 1)
            host.Text = (2 ^ (24 - Val(bits_for_subnet.Text))) - 2
            netadd1st.Text = net_address(Val(bits_for_subnet.Text))
            netadd2nd.Text = net_address(Val(bits_for_subnet.Text) - 1)
        Case Else
            subnet_mask.Text = "INVALID"
            subnets.Text = "-"
        End Select
    End If

     If (ipclass.ListIndex = 1) Then
        Select Case Val(bits_for_subnet.Text)
        Case 2 To 14:
            subnet_mask.Text = mask(bits_for_subnet.Text + 7)
            host.Text = (2 ^ (16 - Val(bits_for_subnet.Text))) - 2
            netadd1st.Text = net_address(Val(bits_for_subnet.Text) + 22)
            netadd2nd.Text = net_address(Val(bits_for_subnet.Text) + 21)
        Case Else:  subnet_mask.Text = "INVALID"
                    subnets.Text = "-"
        End Select
    End If
```

```
      If (ipclass.ListIndex = 2) Then
          Select Case Val(bits_for_subnet.Text)
          Case 2 To 6:
              subnet_mask.Text = mask(bits_for_subnet.Text + 15)
              host.Text = (2 ^ (8 - Val(bits_for_subnet.Text))) - 2
              netadd1st.Text = net_address(Val(bits_for_subnet.Text) + 36)
              netadd2nd.Text = net_address(Val(bits_for_subnet.Text) + 35)
          Case Else:  subnet_mask.Text = "INVALID"
                      subnets.Text = "-"
          End Select
      End If
End Sub

Private Sub class_Change()
    Call bits_for_subnet_Change
End Sub

Private Sub Exitbutton_Click()
    End
End Sub

Private Sub Form_Load()
    mask(0) = "INVALID"
    mask(1)  = "255.192.0.0"
    mask(2)  = "255.224.0.0"
    mask(3)  = "255.240.0.0"
    mask(4)  = "255.248.0.0"
    mask(5)  = "255.252.0.0"
    mask(6)  = "255.254.0.0"
    mask(7)  = "255.255.0.0"
    mask(8)  = "255.255.128.0"
    mask(9)  = "255.255.192.0"
    mask(10) = "255.255.224.0"
    mask(11) = "255.255.240.0"
    mask(12) = "255.255.248.0"
    mask(13) = "255.255.252.0"
    mask(14) = "255.255.254.0"
    mask(15) = "255.255.255.0"
    mask(16) = "255.255.255.128.0"
    mask(17) = "255.255.255.192.0"
    mask(18) = "255.255.255.224.0"
    mask(19) = "255.255.255.240.0"
    mask(20) = "255.255.255.248.0"
    mask(21) = "255.255.255.252.0"
    net_address(1)  = "w.128.0.0"
    net_address(2)  = "w.64.0.0"
    net_address(3)  = "w.32.0.0"
    net_address(4)  = "w.16.0.0"
    net_address(5)  = "w.8.0.0"
    net_address(6)  = "w.4.0.0"
    net_address(7)  = "w.2.0.0"
    net_address(8)  = "w.1.0.0"
    net_address(9)  = "w.0.128.0"
    net_address(10) = "w.0.64.0"
    net_address(11) = "w.0.32.0"
    net_address(12) = "w.0.16.0"
    net_address(13) = "w.0.8.0"
    net_address(14) = "w.0.4.0"
    net_address(15) = "w.0.2.0"
    net_address(16) = "w.0.1.0"
    net_address(17) = "w.0.0.128"
    net_address(18) = "w.0.0.64"
    net_address(19) = "w.0.0.32"
```

```
      net_address(20)  = "w.0.0.16"
      net_address(21)  = "w.0.0.8"
      net_address(22)  = "w.0.0.4"
      net_address(23)  = "w.x.128.0"
      net_address(24)  = "w.x.64.0"
      net_address(25)  = "w.x.32.0"
      net_address(26)  = "w.x.16.0"
      net_address(27)  = "w.x.8.0"
      net_address(28)  = "w.x.4.0"
      net_address(29)  = "w.x.2.0"
      net_address(30)  = "w.x.1.0"
      net_address(31)  = "w.x.0.128"
      net_address(32)  = "w.x.0.64"
      net_address(33)  = "w.x.0.32"
      net_address(34)  = "w.x.0.16"
      net_address(35)  = "w.x.0.8"
      net_address(36)  = "w.x.0.4"
      net_address(37)  = "w.x.y.128"
      net_address(38)  = "w.x.y.64"
      net_address(39)  = "w.x.y.32"
      net_address(40)  = "w.x.y.16"
      net_address(41)  = "w.x.y.8"
      net_address(42)  = "w.x.y.4"
End Sub
```

Figure D1.11 gives an example of a Class A subnet with 4 bits borrowed from the host portion of the address. There will thus be 14 usable subnets, as two of the subnet addresses (0000 and 1111) cannot be used as they are reserved. The subnet mask will thus be:

255.1111 0000b.00000000b.00000000b [255.240.0.0]

The first usable subnet address (in the form w.x.y.z) will thus be:

w.0001 0000b.00000000b.00000000b [w.16.0.0]

and the second usable subnet address will be:

w.0010 0000b.00000000b.00000000b [w.32.0.0]

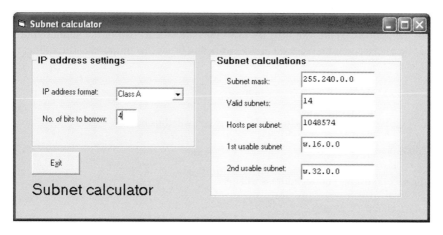

Figure D1.11   Class A subnetting example

Figure D1.12 gives an example of a Class B subnet with 12 bits borrowed from the host portion of the address. There will thus be 4096 usable subnets, as two of the subnet addresses cannot be used as they are reserved (for network and broadcast purposes). The subnet mask will thus be:

255.255.11111111b.11110000b [255.255.255.240]

The first usable subnet address (in the form w.x.y.z) will thus be:

w.x.00000000b.0001 0000b [w.x.0.16]

and the second usable subnet address will be:

w.x.00000000b.0010 0000b [w.x.0.32]

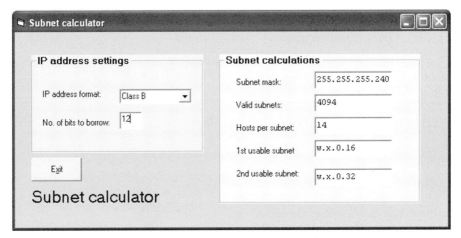

Figure D1.12 Class B subnetting example

Figure D1.13 gives an example of a Class C subnet with 4 bits borrowed from the host portion of the address. There will thus be 14 usable subnets, as two of the subnet addresses cannot be used as they are reserved (for network and broadcast purposes). The subnet mask will thus be:

255.255.255.11110000b [255.255.255.240]

The first usable subnet address (in the form w.x.y.z) will thus be:

w.x.y.0001 0000b [w.x.y.16]

and the second usable subnet address will be:

w.x.y.0010 0000b [w.x.y.32]

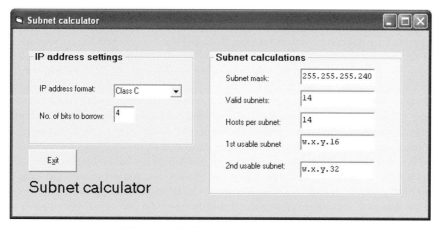

Figure D1.13 Class C subnetting example

D1.7 Internet naming structure

The Internet naming structure uses labels separated by periods; an example is dcs.napier.ac.uk. It uses a hierarchical structure where organizations are grouped into primary domain names, such as com (for commercial organizations), edu (for educational organizations), gov (for government organizations), mil (for military organizations), net (Internet network support centers) or org (other organizations). The primary domain name may also define the country in which the host is located, such as uk (United Kingdom), fr (France), and so on. All hosts on the Internet must be registered to one of these primary domain names.

The labels after the primary field describe the subnets within the network. For example in the address eece.napier.ac.uk, the ac label relates to an academic institution within the uk, napier to the name of the institution and eece the subnet within that organization. An example structure is illustrated in Figure D1.14.

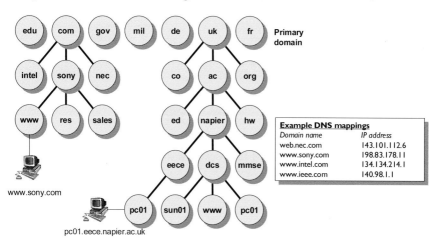

Figure D1.14 Example of domain naming

D1.8   Domain name system

IP addresses are difficult to remember, thus Domain Name Services (DNS) are used to allow users to use symbolic names rather than IP addresses. DNS computers on the Internet determine the IP address of the named destination resource or application program. This dynamic mapping has the advantage that users and application programs can move around the Internet and are not fixed to an IP address. An analogy relates to the public telephone service. A telephone directory contains a list of subscribers and their associated telephone number. If someone looks for a telephone number, first the user name is looked up and their associated telephone number found. The telephone directory listing thus maps a user name (symbolic name) to an actual telephone number (the actual address). When a user enters a domain name (such as `www.fred.co.uk`) into the WWW browser, the local DNS server must try and   resolve the domain name to an IP address, which can then be used to send the data to it. If it cannot resolve the IP address then the DNS server interrogates other servers to see if they know the required IP address, as illustrated in Figure D1.15. If it cannot be resolved then the WWW browser displays an error message.

Table D1.5 lists some Internet domain assignments for WWW servers. Note that domain assignments are not fixed and can change their corresponding IP addresses, if required. The binding between the symbolic name and its address can thus change at any time.

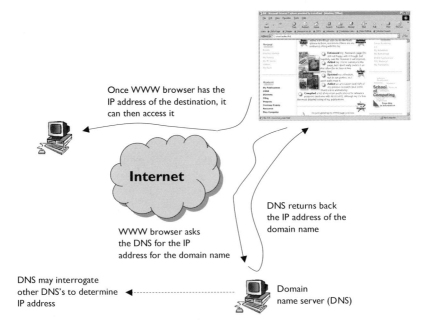

Once WWW browser has the IP address of the destination, it can then access it

Internet

DNS returns back the IP address of the domain name

WWW browser asks the DNS for the IP address for the domain name

DNS may interrogate other DNS's to determine IP address

Domain name server (DNS)

Figure D1.15   Domain name server

Table D1.5 Internet domain assignments for web servers

Web server	Internet domain name	Internet IP address
NEC	web.nec.com	143.101.112.6
Sony	www.sony.com	198.83.178.11
Intel	www.intel.com	134.134.214.1
IEEE	www.ieee.com	140.98.1.1
University of Bath	www.bath.ac.uk	136.38.32.1
University of Edinburgh	www.ed.ac.uk	129.218.128.43
IEE	www.iee.org.uk	193.130.181.10
University of Manchester	www.man.ac.uk	130.88.203.16

D1.9 Example network

A university network is shown in Figure D1.16. The connection to the outside global Internet is via the Janet gateway node and its IP address is 146.176.1.3. Three subnets, 146.176.160, 146.176.129 and 146.176.151, connect the gateway to departmental bridges. The Computer Studies router address is 146.176.160.1 and the Electrical Department router has an address 146.176.151.254.

The Electrical Department router links, through other routers, to the subnets 146.176.144, 146.176.145, 146.176.147, 146.176.150 and 146.176.151. The main bridge into the department connects to two Ethernet networks of PCs (subnets 146.176.150 and 146.176.151) and to another router (Router 1). Router 1 connects to the subnet 146.176.144. Subnet 146.176.144 connects to workstations and X-terminals. It also connects to the gateway Moon that links the Token Ring subnet 146.176.145 with the Ethernet subnet 146.176.144. The gateway Oberon, on the 146.176.145 subnet, connects to an Ethernet link 146.176.146. This then connects to the gateway Dione that is also connected to the Token Ring subnet 146.176.147.

The topology of the Electrical Department network is shown in Figure D1.17. Each node on the network is assigned an IP address. The *hosts* file for the set up in Figure D1.17 is shown next. For example the IP address of Mimas is 146.176.145.21 and for miranda it is 146.176.144.14. Notice that the gateway nodes, Oberon, Moon and Dione, all have two IP addresses.

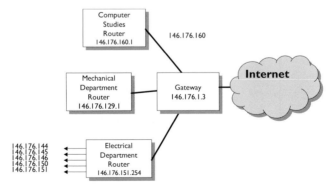

Figure D1.16 A university network

Contents of host file

```
146.176.1.3          janet
146.176.144.10       hp
146.176.145.21       mimas
146.176.144.11       mwave
146.176.144.13       vax
146.176.144.14       miranda
146.176.144.20       triton
146.176.146.23       oberon
146.176.145.23       oberon
146.176.145.24       moon
146.176.144.24       moon
146.176.147.25       uranus
146.176.146.30       dione
146.176.147.30       dione
146.176.147.31       saturn
146.176.147.32       mercury
146.176.147.36       neptune
146.176.147.42       pluto
 ::   ::
146.176.144.58       spica
146.176.151.254      cubridge
146.176.151.99       bridge_1
146.176.151.98       pc2
146.176.151.97       pc3
          : : : : :
146.176.151.70       pc30
146.176.151.99       ees99
146.176.150.61       eepc01
255.255.255.0        defaultmask
```

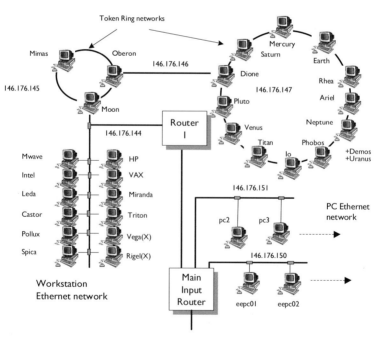

Figure D1.17   Network topology for the Department network

D1.10   IP addresses for routers

Routers require an IP address for each of their ports, but they cannot use the zero host address as this is used to identify the whole network. For example, if there were five nodes on the 177.132.1 network (NETA), and six nodes on the 177.131.2 network (NETB), which are interconnected by a router (AB). Then the IP address could be assigned as:

Node NETA_1	177.131.1.2	Node NETA_2	177.131.1.3
Node NETA_3	177.131.1.4	Node NETA_4	177.131.1.5
Node NETA_5	177.131.1.6		

Node NETB_1	177.131.2.2	Node NETB_2	177.131.2.3
Node NETB_3	177.131.2.4	Node NETB_4	177.131.2.5
Node NETB_5	177.131.2.6	Node NETA_6	177.131.2.7

Router AB_E0	177.131.1.1	Router AB_E1	177.131.2.1

The router, in this case, has two ports. These have been defined with the IP address 177.131.1.1 (which connects to the 177.131.1 network), and 177.131.2.1 (which connects to the 177.131.2 network).

D1.11   IP multicasting

Many applications of modern communications require the transmission of IP datagrams to multiple hosts. Typical applications are video conferencing, remote teaching, and so on. This is supported by IP multicasting, where a host group is identified by a single IP address. The main parameters of IP multicasting are:

> **ICMP messages**
>
> - Destination unreachable.
> - Time-to-live exceeded.
> - Parameter problem.
> - Source quench.
> - Redirect.
> - Echo.
> - Echo reply.
> - Timestamp.
> - Timestamp reply.
> - Information request.
> - Information reply.
> - Address request.
> - Address reply.
>
> ICMP is used to send error and control messages.

- The group membership is dynamic.
- Hosts may join and leave the group at any time.
- There is also no limit to the location or number of members in a host group.
- A host may be a member of more than one group at a time.
- A host group may be permanent or transient. Permanent groups are well known and are administratively assigned a permanent IP address. The group is then dynamically associated with this IP address. IP multicast addresses that are not reserved to permanent groups are available for dynamic assignment to transient groups.
- Multicast routers forward IP multicast datagrams into the Internet.

D1.11.1 Group addresses

A special group of addresses are assigned to multicasting. These are known as Class D addresses, and they begin with 1110 as their starting 4 bits (Class E addresses with the upper bits of 1111 are reserved for future uses). The Class D addresses thus range from:

224.0.0.0
   (11100000 00000000 00000000 00000000)
239.255.255.255
   (11101111 11111111 11111111 11111111)

The address 224.0.0.0 is reserved. 224.0.0.1 is also assigned to the permanent group of all IP hosts (including gateways), and is used to address all multicast hosts on the directly connected network.

D1.12   IP Version labels

There are various assigned values for the IP version label. These are:

Value	Keyword	Description
0		Reserved
4	IP	Internet Protocol (RFC791)
5	ST	ST Datagram Mode (RFC1190)
6	SIP	Simple Internet Protocol
7	TP/IX	TP/IX: The Next Internet
8	PIP	The P Internet Protocol
9	TUBA	TUBA
10–14		Unassigned
15		Reserved

D1.13   IPv6

The IP header (IP Ver4) is added to higher-level data (as defined in RFC791). This header contains a 32-bit IP address of the destination node. Unfortunately, the standard 32-bit IP address is not large enough to support the growth in nodes connecting to the Internet. Thus a new standard, IP Version 6 (IP Ver6, aka, IP, The Next Generation, or IPng), has been developed to support a 128-bit address, as well as additional enhancements, such as authentication and data encryption.

The main techniques being investigated are:

- **TUBA** (TCP and UDP with bigger addresses).
- **CATNIP** (common architecture for the Internet). The main idea was to define a common packet format which was compatible with IP, CLNP (Connectionless Network Protocol) and IPX. CLNP was proposed by the OSI as a new protocol to replace IP, but it has never really been adopted (mainly because it was too inefficient).
- **SIPP** (Simple Internet protocol plus). This scheme increases the number of address bits from 32 to 64, and gets rid of unused fields in the IP header.

It is likely that none of these will provide the complete standard and the resulting standard will be a mixture of the three. The RFC1883 specification outlines the main changes as:

- **Expanded addressing capabilities.** The size of the IP address will be increased to 128 bits, rather than 32 bits. This will allow for more levels of addressing hierarchy, an increased number of addressable nodes and a simpler auto-configuration of addresses. With multicast routing, the scalability is improved by adding a scope field to the multicast addresses. As well as this, an anycast address has been added so that packets can be sent to any one of a group of nodes.

- **Improved IP header format.** This tidies the IPv4 header fields by dropping the least used options, or making them optional.
- **Improved support for extensions and options.** These allow for different encodings of the IP header options, and thus allow for variable lengths and increased flexibility for new options.
- **Flow labeling capability.** A new capability is added to enable the labeling of packet belonging to particular traffic *flows* for which the sender requests special handling, such as non-default quality of service or *real-time* service.
- **Authentication and privacy capabilities**. Extensions to support authentication, data integrity, and (optional) data confidentiality are specified for IPv6.

D1.13.1 Autoconfiguration and multiple IP addresses

IPv4 requires a significant amount of human intervention to set up the address of each of the nodes. IPv6 improves this by supplying autoconfiguration renumbering facilities, which allows hosts to renumber without significant human intervention.

IPv4 has a stateful address structure, which either requires the user to manually set up the IP address of the computer or to use DHCP servers to provide IP addresses for a given MAC address. If a node moves from one subnet to another, the user must reconfigure the IP address, or request a new IP address from the DHCP. IPv6 supports a stateless autoconfiguration, where a host constructs its own IPv6. This occurs by adding its MAC address to a subnet prefix. The host automatically learns which subnet it is on by communicating from the router which is connected to the network that the host is connected to.

IPv6 supports multiple IP addresses for each host. These addresses can be either *valid*, *deprecated* or *invalid*. A valid address would be used for new and existing communications. A deprecated address could be used only for the existing communications (as they perhaps migrated to the new address). An invalid address would not be used for any communications. When renumbering, a host would deprecate the existing IP address, and set the new IP address as valid. All new communications would use the new IP address, but connections to the previous address would still operate. This allows a node to gradually migrate from one IP address to another.

D1.13.2 IPv6 header format

Figure D1.18 shows the basic format of the IPv6 header. The main fields are:

- Version number (4 bits) – contains the version number, such as 6 for IP Ver6. It is used to differentiate between IPv4 and IPv6.
- Priority (4 bits) – indicates the priority of the datagram, and gives 16 levels of priority (0 to 15). The first eight values (0 to 7) are used where the source is providing congestion control (which is traffic that backs-off when congestion occurs), these are:

  - 0 defines no priority.
  - 1 defines background traffic (such as netnews).
  - 2 defines unattended transfer (such as e-mail), 3 (reserved).
  - 4 defines attended bulk transfer (FTP, NFS), 5 (reserved).

- 6 defines interactive traffic (such as telnet, X-windows).
- 7 defines control traffic (such as routing protocols, SNMP).

  The other values are used for traffic that will not back off in response to congestion (such as real-time traffic). The lowest priority for this is 8 (traffic which is the most willing to be discarded) and the highest is 15 (traffic which is the least willing to be discarded).

- Flow label (24 bits) – still experimental, but will be used to identify different data flow characteristics. It is assigned by the source and can be used to label data packets which require special handling by IPv6 routers, such as defined QoS (Quality of Service) or real-time services.
- Payload length (16 bits) – defines the total size of the IP datagram (and includes the IP header attached data).
- Next header – this field indicates which header follows the IP header (it uses the same IPv4). For example: 0 defines IP information; 1 defines ICMP information; 6 defines TCP information and 80 defines ISO-IP.
- Hop limit – defines the maximum number of hops that the datagram takes as it traverses the network. Each router decrements the hop limit by 1; when it reaches 0 it is deleted. This has been renamed from IPv4, where it was called time-to-live, as it better describes the parameter.
- IP addresses (128 bits) – defines IP address. There will be three main groups of IP addresses: unicast, multicast and anycast. A unicast address identifies a particular host, a multicast address enables the hosts within a particular group to receive the same packet, and the anycast address will be addressed to a number of interfaces on a single multicast address.

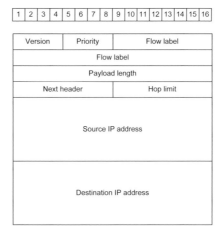

Figure D1.18 IP Ver6 header format

IPv6 has a simple header, which can be extended if required. These are:

- Routing header.
- Fragment header.

- Authentication header.
- Destinations options header.
- Encrypted security payload.

IPv6 addresses do not use the dotted notion and are written in a hexadecimal format, such as:

114F: 0000: 0000: 0000: 0006: 0600: 4411: CB1D

Often the leading zero's are omitted to give:

114F: 0: 0: 0: 6: 600: 4411: CB1D

This address can be shorted further by converting all zero values to a double colon, to give:

114F::6:600:4411:CB1D

The unicast address contains 128 bits, and has the following fields:

- **Field Prefix (FP) field (3 bits)**. This identifies when the address is unicast, multicast, and so on). A value of 001 identifies aggregatable global unicasts.
- **Top-Level Aggregation Identifier (TLA ID field) (13 bits)**. This is used to identify the authority responsible for the address at the highest level of the routing hierarchy.
- **Res field (8 bits)**. This is reserved so that the TLA or NLA IDs can be expanded for future use.
- **NLA ID field (24 bits)**. This is used to identify ISPs, and can be organized to reflect a hierarchy, or multitiered relationship, among providers.
- **SLA ID field (16 bits)**. This is used by individual organizations in order to defined a local addressing hierarchy and to identify subnets.
- **Interface ID field (64 bits)** – This uses an IEEE EUI-64 format and is a unique ID for the network interface. In Ethernet-type networks, it uses the 16 bits from the MAC address of the network port.

D1.14 Allocating IP addresses

IP addresses can either be allocated statically or dynamically. A static address is permanently assigned to a node, whereas a dynamically allocated address is assigned to a host when it requires connecting to the Internet. Dynamically assigned addresses have the following advantages over static addresses:

- **Limiting access to the Internet.** IP addresses can be mapped to MAC addresses. A node which requires an IP address will ask the IP granting server for an IP address. The server then checks the host's MAC address to determine if it is allowed to access the Internet. If it is not, the server does not return an IP address. The system administrator can thus set up a table which only includes the hosts which are required to connect to the Internet.

- **Authenticating nodes.** A typical hacking method is to steal an IP address and use it for the time of a connection. This can be overcome by making all of the nodes on the network ask the IP granting server for their IP address. It is thus not possible to steal an address, as the IP granting server will check the MAC address of the host.
- **Allocating from a pool of IP addresses.** An organization may be granted a limited range of IP addresses which is not enough to allocate to all the nodes in the organization. The IP granting server can thus be set up to allocate IP addresses to nodes as they require them. When all the IP addresses have been allocated, no more IP addresses can be given out. When a node is finished with its IP address, the IP address that was granted to it can be put back in the pool when it is finished with it.
- **Centralized configuration of IP addresses.** The system manager can easily setup IP addresses to nodes from the central IP granting server.
- **Barring computers from connecting to a network.** Some networks are set up so that they must get a valid IP address before they can connect to the network (typically in UNIX-type networks). The IP granting server will check the MAC address of the requester, if it is not allowed the server will not grant it an IP address.

The two main protocols which are used to dynamically allocate IP addresses are DHCP (Dynamic Host Configuration Program) and bootp (Bootstrap Protocol). DHCP is typically used by Microsoft Windows to get IP addresses, while bootp is sometimes used in UNIX environments. The main disadvantage of dynamically assigned IP addresses is that the network is centralized on the single DHCP server. If this were to crash, no IP addresses can be assigned.

D1.15 Domain name server and DHCP

Each institution on the Internet has a host that runs a process called the domain name server (DNS). The DNS maintains a database called the directory information base (DIB) which contains directory information for that institution. When a new host is added, the system manager adds its name and its IP address. It can then access the Internet.

Dynamic Host Configuration Protocol (DHCP) allows for the transmission of configuration information over a TCP/IP network. Microsoft implemented DHCP on its Microsoft Windows operating system and many other vendors are incorporating it into their systems. It is based on the Bootstrap Protocol (bootp) and adds additional services, such as:

- Automatic allocation of reusable IP network addresses.
- Additional TCP/IP configuration options.

It has two components:

- A protocol for delivering host-specific configuration parameters from a DHCP server to a host.
- A mechanism for allocation of network addresses to hosts.

DHCP uses a client-server architecture, where the designated DHCP server hosts (servers) allocate network addresses and deliver configuration parameters to dynamically configured hosts (clients).

The three techniques that DHCP uses to assign IP addresses are:

- **Automatic allocation**. DHCP assigns a permanent IP address to a client.
- **Dynamic allocation**. DHCP assigns an IP address to a client for a limited period of time or when the client releases the address. It allows for automatic reuse of IP addresses that are no longer used by clients. It is typically used when there is a limited pool of IP addresses (which is less than the number of hosts) so that a host can only connect when it can get one of the IP addresses from the pool.
- **Manual allocation**. DHCP is used to convey an IP address which has been assigned by the network administrator. This allows DHCP to be used to eliminate assigning an IP address to a host through its operating system.

Networks can use several of these techniques.

DHCP messages are based on bootp messages, which allows DHCP to listen to a bootp relay agent and to allow integration of bootp clients and DHCP servers. A bootp relay agent is an Internet host or router that passes DHCP messages between DHCP clients and DHCP servers. DHCP uses the same relay agent behaviour as the bootp protocol specification. bootp relay agents are useful because they eliminate the need for having a DHCP server on each physical network segment.

Some of the objectives of DHCP are:

- DHCP should be a mechanism rather than a policy. DHCP must allow local system administrators control over configuration parameters where desired.
- No requirements for manual configuration of clients.
- DHCP does not require a server on each subnet and should communicate with routers and bootp relay agents and clients.
- Ensure that the same IP address cannot be used by more than one DHCP client at a time.
- Restore DHCP client configuration when the client is rebooted.
- Provide automatic configuration for new clients.
- Support fixed or permanent allocation of configuration parameters.

D1.16 ICMP

Messages, such as control data, information data and error recovery data, are carried between Internet hosts using the Internet Control Message Protocol (ICMP). These messages are sent with a standard IP header. Typical messages are:

- Destination unreachable (message type 3) – which is sent by a host on the network to say that a host is unreachable. The message can also include the reason the host cannot be reached.
- Echo request/echo reply (message type 8 or 0) – which is used to check the connectivity between two hosts. The `ping` command uses this message, where it sends an ICMP 'echo request' message to the target host and waits for the destination host to reply with an 'echo reply' message.
- Redirection (message type 5) – which is sent by a router to a host that is requesting its routing services. This helps to find the shortest path to a desired host.
- Source quelch (message type 4) – which is used when a host cannot receive anymore IP packets at the present (or reduce the flow).

An ICMP message is sent within an IP header, with the Version field, Source and Destination IP Addresses, and so on. The Type of Service field is set to a 0 and the Protocol field is set to a 1 (which identifies ICMP). After the IP header, follows the ICMP message, which starts with three fields, as shown in Figure D1.19. The message type has eight bits and identifies the type of message; as Table D1.6. The code fields are also eight bits long and a checksum field is 16 bits long. The checksum is the 1's complement of the 1's complement sum of all 16-bit words in the header (the checksum field is assumed to be zero in the addition).

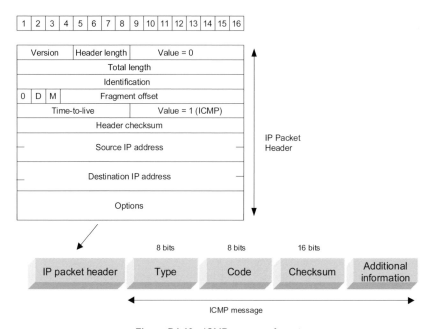

Figure D1.19 ICMP message format

The information after this field depends on the type of message, such as:

- For echo request and reply, the message header is followed by an 8-bit identifier, then an 8-bit sequence number followed by the original IP header.
- For destination unreachable, source quelch and time, the message header is followed by 32 bits which are unused and then the original IP header.
- For timestamp request, the message header is followed by a 16-bit identifier, then by a 16-bit sequence number, followed by a 32-bit originating timestamp.

Where:

- Pointer (8-bit). Identifies the byte location of the parameter error in the original IP header. For example, a value of 9 would identify the Protocol field, and 12 would identify the Source IP address field.
- Identifier (16-bit). Helps the matching of requests and replies (possibly set to zero). It can be used to identify a unique connection.
- Sequence Number (16-bit). Helps in matching request and replies (possibly set to zero).
- Timestamps (32-bit) – This is the time in milliseconds since midnight UT (Universal

Time). If this is not possible then it is anytime, as long as the high-order bit of the time-stamp is set to a 1 to indicate that it is non-standard time.

- Gateway address (32-bit). The address of the gateway to which network traffic specified in the original datagram should be sent to.
- Internet Header + 64 bits of Data Datagram. This is the original IP header and the first 64 byte of the data part. It is used by the host to match the match to the required high-level application (such as TCP port values).

Table D1.6 Message type field value

Value	Description	Code field	Additional information
0	Echo reply message	0	16-bit identifier 16-bit sequence number
3	Destination Unreachable	0 = net unreachable 1 = host unreachable 2 = protocol unreachable 3 = port unreachable 4 = fragmentation needed and D bit set 5 = source route failed	32 bits unused. Internet header + 64 bits of original data datagram
4	Source quench message	0	32 bits unused. Internet header + 64 bits of original data datagram
5	Redirect message	0 = redirect datagram for the network 1 = redirect datagram for the host 2 = redirect datagram for the type of service and network 3 = redirect datagram for the type of service and host	32 bits gateway address. Internet header + 64 bits of original data datagram
8	Echo request	0	
11	Time-to-live exceeded	0 = time-to-live exceeded in transit 1 = fragment reassembly time exceeded	32 bits unused. Internet header + 64 bits of original data datagram
12	Parameter problem	0 = pointer indicates the error	8-bit pointer. 24 bits unused. Internet header + 64 bits of original data datagram
13	Timestamp request	0	16-bit identifier 16-bit sequence number 32-bit originate timestamp 32-bit receive timestamp 32-bit transmit timestamp
14	Timestamp reply	0	As above
15	Information request	0	16-bit identifier 16-bit sequence number
16	Information reply	0	As above

The descriptions of the messages and replies are:

- Source quench message (4) – sent by a gateway or a destination host when it discards a datagram (possibly through lack of buffer memory), and identifies that the sender should reduce the flow of traffic transmission. The host should then reduce the flow, and gradually increase it, as long as it does not receive any more source quench messages.
- Time exceeded message (11) – this is sent either by a gateway when a datagram has a Time-to-Live field which is zero and has been deleted, or when a host cannot reassemble a fragmented datagram due to missing fragments, within a certain time limit.
- Parameter problem message (12) – sent by a gateway or a host when they encounter a problem with one of the parameters in an IP header.
- Destination unreachable message (3) – sent by a gateway to identify that a host cannot be reached or a TCP port process does not exist.
- Redirected message (5) – sent by a gateway to inform other gateways that there is a better route to a given network destination address.
- Information reply message (15)– sent in reply to an information request.(see information request (16) for a typical usage).
- Information request (16) – this request can be sent with a fully specified source IP address, and a zero destination IP address. The replying IP gateway then replies with an information reply message with its fully specified IP address. In this way the host can determine the network address that it is connected to.
- Echo message (8) – requests an echo. (see echo reply message (0)).
- Echo reply message (0) – the data received in the echo message (8) must be returned in this message.

D1.17 Additional material

D1.17.1 Assigned Internet protocol numbers

Table D1.7 outlines the values that are used in the protocol field of the IP header.

Table D1.7   Assigned Internet protocol numbers

Value	Protocol	Value	Protocol
0	Reserved	18	Multiplexing
1	ICMP	19	DCN
2	IGMP (Internet group management)	20	TAC monitoring
3	Gateway-to-gateway	21–62	
4	CMCC gateway monitoring message	63	Any local network
5	ST	64	SATNET and backroom EXPAK
6	TCP	65	MIT subnet support
7	UCL	66–68	Unassigned
8	EGP (exterior gateway protocol)	69	SATNET monitoring
9	Secure	70	Unassigned
10	BBN RCC monitoring	71	Internet Packet core utility

11	NVP	72–75	Unassigned
12	PUP	76	Backroom SATNET monitoring
13	Pluribus	77	Unassigned
14	Telenet	78	WIDEBAND monitoring
15	XNET	79	WIDEBAND EXPAK
16	Chaos	80–254	Unassigned
17	User datagram	255	Reserved

D1.17.2 Options field in an IP header

The options field in an IP header is an optional field which may or may not appear in the header, and is also variable in length. It is a field which must be implemented by all hosts and gateways. There are two classes of option:

- An option-type byte.
- An option-type byte, followed by an option-length byte, and then the actual option-data bytes. The option-length byte counts all the bytes in the options field.

The option-type byte is the first byte and has three fields, as illustrated in Figure D1.20. The copied flag indicates that this option is (or is not) copied into all fragments on fragmentation.

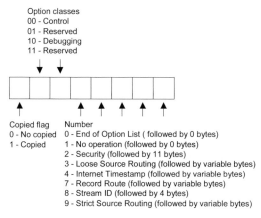

Figure D1.20 Options-type byte

D1.17.2.1 End of option list (Type = 0)

This option indicates the end of the option list, but does not necessarily need to coincide with the end of the IP header according to the internet header length. It is used at the end of all options, but not the end of each option. It may be copied, introduced, or deleted on fragmentation, or for any other reason.

D1.17.2.2 No operation (type = 1)

This option may be used between options, and can be used to align the beginning of a subsequent option on a 32-bit boundary. It may be copied, introduced, or deleted on fragmentation, or for any other reason.

D1.17.2.3 Security (type = 130)

This option allows hosts to send security, compartmentation, handling restrictions, and TCC (closed user group) parameters. In this option, the Type field is a 2, and the Class field is also a 2. Thus the option-type byte has a value of 130 (0100 0010), and has 11 bytes in total. Its format is

```
+--------+--------+---...---+---...---+---...---+---...---+
|10000010|00001011|SSS   SSS|CCC   CCC|HHH   HHH|   TCC   |
+--------+--------+---...---+---...---+---...---+---...---+
```

The fields are

- SSS...SSS, security (16 bits) – These specify one of 16 levels of security, such as

00000000 00000000 – Unclassified	11110001 00110101 – Confidential
01111000 10011010 – EFTO	10111100 01001101 – MMMM
01011110 00100110 – PROG	10101111 00010011 – Restricted
11010111 10001000 – Secret	01101011 11000101 – Top Secret
00110101 11100010 – Reserved	10011010 11110001 – Reserved
01001101 01111000 – Reserved	00100100 10111101 – Reserved
00010011 01011110 – Reserved	10001001 10101111 – Reserved
11000100 11010110 – Reserved	11100010 01101011 – Reserved

- CCC...CCC, compartments (16 bits) – When this field contains all zero values then the transmitted information is not compartmented, other values can be obtained from the Defense Intelligence Agency.

- HHH...HHH, handling restrictions (16 bits) – This field is defined in the Defense Intelligence Agency Manual DIAM 65-19.

- TCC, transmission control code (24 bits) – This field allows the segregation of traffic and to define controlled communities of interest among subscribers (available from HQ DCA Code 530). Must be copied on fragmentation.

D1.17.2.4 Loose source and record route (Type = 131)

Loose source and record route (LSRR) allows for the source of an internet datagram to supply routing information to be used by the gateways in forwarding the datagram to the destination. It can also be used to record routing information.

When routing the source host adds the IP addresses of the route to the route data, and each gateway routes the datagram using the recorded route, and not with its own internal routing table. This allows datagrams to take alternative routes through the Internet. Its format is

```
+--------+--------+--------+---------...--------+
|10000011| Length | Pointer|     Route data     |
+--------+--------+--------+---------...--------+
```

where
- Length – this is a single byte which contains the number of bytes in the option field.
- Pointer – this is a pointer, which is relative to this option, into the route data which indicates the byte which begins the next source address to be processed. The smallest value is 4.
- Route data – this is constructed with a number of internet addresses, each of 4 bytes in length. If the pointer is greater than the length, the source route is empty (and the recorded route full) and the routing is to be based on the destination address field.

When reaching the address in the destination address field, and when the pointer is not greater than the length in the route data, then the next address in the source route data replaces the address in the destination field. The pointer is also incremented by 4, to point to the next address. It is loose as the gateways are allowed to use any route to get to the next specified address in the routing table.

It must be copied on fragmentation and occurs, at the most, once in a datagram.

D1.17.2.5 Strict source and record route (Type = 137)

The SSRR is similar to the LSRR, but the routing must follow, exactly, the addresses in the routing table. It thus cannot use any intermediate routes to get to these addresses. Its format is

```
+--------+--------+--------+---------...--------+
|10001001| Length | Pointer|     Route data     |
+--------+--------+--------+---------...--------+
```

D1.17.2.6 Record route (type = 7)

The record route option records the route of an internet datagram. It can thus be used by such utilities as Traceroute. Its format is

```
+--------+--------+--------+---------...--------+
|00000111| Length | Pointer|     Route data     |
+--------+--------+--------+---------...--------+
```

where
- Length – this is a single byte which contains the number of bytes in the option field.
- Pointer – this is a pointer, which is relative to this option, into the route data which indicates the byte at which the next address should be added to. The smallest value is 4.
- Route data – contains a list of the route which a datagram has taken. Each entry has 4 bytes. The originating host must reserve enough area for the total number of addresses in the routing table, as the size of this option does not change as it transverses over the Internet. If there is a problem adding the address then an ICMP Parameter Problem can be sent back to the source host.

It is not copied on fragmentation, and goes in the first fragment only. In addition, it occurs, at the most, once in a datagram.

D1.17.2.7 Internet timestamp (type = 68)

The Internet timestamp option records a timestamp for each gateway along the route of a datagram. It allows the source host to trace the time that each part of the route takes. Its format is

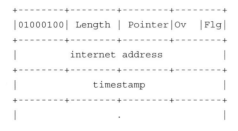

```
+--------+--------+--------+--------+
|01000100| Length | Pointer|Ov  |Flg|
+--------+--------+--------+--------+
|            internet address      |
+--------+--------+--------+--------+
|              timestamp           |
+--------+--------+--------+--------+
|                  .               |
                   .
```

where

- Length. – is a single byte which contains the number of bytes in the option field (maximum is 40).
- Pointer – this is a pointer, which is relative to this option, into the route data which indicates the byte at which the next timestamp should be added to. The smallest value is 5.
- Overflow (Ov) – this has four bits and holds the number of IP modules that cannot register timestamps due to lack of space.
- Flag (Flg) – this has four bits and defines the format of the timestamp. Valid values are:

  0 – Store only the time stamps as 32-bit words.
  1 – Store IP address followed by a time stamp.
  3 – In this mode the IP addresses are specified in a table. A gateway only adds its timestamp if its IP address is in this table.

- Timestamp – this is a 32-bit value for the number of milliseconds since midnight UT (universal time). If this is not possible then it is any time, as long as the high-order bit of the timestamp is set to a 1 to indicate that it is non-standard time.

The originating host must reserve enough area for the total number of timestamps, as the size of this option does not change as it transverses over the Internet. If there is a problem adding the address then an ICMP parameter problem can be sent back to the source host. Initially the contents of the timestamp data area is either zero, or has IP addresses with zero time stamps. The timestamp area is full when the pointer is greater than the length.

It is not copied on fragmentation, and goes in the first fragment only. Also, it occurs, at the most once in a datagram.

D1.17.2.8 Stream identifier (type =136)

This option allows for a 16-bit SATNET stream identifier to be carried through networks that do not support the stream concept. Its format is

```
+--------+--------+--------+--------+
|10001000|00000010|   Stream ID    |
+--------+--------+--------+--------+
```

D1.17.3 Ethernet multicast/broadcast addresses

The following is a list of typical Ethernet multicast addresses:

Ethernet address	Type field	Usage
01-00-5E-00-00-00	0800	Internet multicast (RFC-1112)
01-80-C2-00-00-00	0802	Spanning tree (for bridges)
09-00-09-00-00-01	8005	HP probe
09-00-09-00-00-04	8005	HP DTC
09-00-1E-00-00-00	8019	Apollo DOMAIN
09-00-2B-00-00-03	8038	DEC lanbridge traffic monitor (LTM)
09-00-4E-00-00-02	8137	Novell IPX
CF-00-00-00-00-00	9000	Ethernet configuration test protocol

The following is a list of typical Ethernet broadcast addresses:

Ethernet address	Type field	Usage
FF-FF-FF-FF-FF-FF	0600	XNS packets, hello or gateway search.
FF-FF-FF-FF-FF-FF	0800	IP (such as RWHOD with UDP)
FF-FF-FF-FF-FF-FF	0804	CHAOS
FF-FF-FF-FF-FF-FF	0806	ARP (for IP and CHAOS) as needed
FF-FF-FF-FF-FF-FF	0BAD	Banyan
FF-FF-FF-FF-FF-FF	1600	VALID packets, hello or gateway search.
FF-FF-FF-FF-FF-FF	8035	Reverse ARP
FF-FF-FF-FF-FF-FF	807C	Merit Internodal (INP)
FF-FF-FF-FF-FF-FF	809B	EtherTalk

D1.18　Class A subnet masks

Table D1.8　Subnet masks for a Class A address

Binary subnet address	Dotted notation	Maximum number of subnets	Maximum number of hosts on each subnet
11111111.11000000.00000000.00000000	255.192.0.0	2	4,194,302
11111111.11100000.00000000.00000000	255.224.0.0	6	2,097,150
11111111.11110000.00000000.00000000	255.240.0.0	14	1,048,574
11111111.11111000.00000000.00000000	255.248.0.0	30	524,286
11111111.11111100.00000000.00000000	255.252.0.0	62	262,142
11111111.11111110.00000000.00000000	255.254.0.0	126	131,070
11111111.11111111.00000000.00000000	255.255.0.0	254	65,534
11111111.11111111.10000000.00000000	255.255.128.0	510	32,766
11111111.11111111.11000000.00000000	255.255.192.0	1,022	16,382
11111111.11111111.11100000.00000000	255.255.224.0	2,046	8,190
11111111.11111111.11110000.00000000	255.255.240.0	4,094	4,094
11111111.11111111.11111000.00000000	255.255.248.0	8,190	2,046
11111111.11111111.11111100.00000000	255.255.252.0	16,382	1,022
11111111.11111111.11111110.00000000	255.255.254.0	32,766	510
11111111.11111111. 11111111.00000000	255.255.255.0	65,534	254
11111111.11111111. 11111111.10000000	255.255.255.128	131,070	126
11111111.11111111. 11111111.11000000	255.255.255.192	262,142	62
11111111.11111111. 11111111.11100000	255.255.255.224	524,286	30
11111111.11111111. 11111111.11110000	255.255.255.240	1,048,574	14
11111111.11111111. 11111111.11111000	255.255.255.248	2,097,150	6
11111111.11111111. 11111111.11111100	255.255.255.252	4,194,302	2

D2   TCP/UDP

D2.1   Introduction

The transport layer is important as it segments the data from the upper layers, and passes these onto the network layer, which adds the network address to the segments (these are then called packets). The network layer allows for delivery of these segments at the receiver. Once delivered the transport layer then takes over and reassembles the data segments back into a form that can be delivered to the layer above. These services are often known as end-to-end services, as the transport layer provides a logical connection between two end points on a network.

The network layer cannot be considered reliable, as the transmitter has no idea that the data packets have been received correctly. It is thus up to the transport layer to provide this, using:

- **Synchronization and acknowledgement.** Initially, when the transmitter makes contact with the receiver it makes a unique connection. The transmitter thus knows that the receiver is on-line, and willing to receive data.
- **Acknowledgements and retransmissions.** This allows the receiver to send back acknowledgements which tell the transmitter that the data segments have been received correctly. If no acknowledgements have been received, the transmitter can either resend the data, or can assume that the receiver has crashed and that the connection is to be terminated.
- **Flow control.** This allows the receiver to tell the transmitter that it cannot receive any more data at present. This typically happens when the receiver has filled-up its receiving buffer.
- **Windowing.** This is where the transmitter and the receiver agree on a window size when the connection is initially made. The window then defines the number of data segments that can be sent before the transmitter must wait for an acknowledgement from the receiver.
- **Multiple connections onto a single data stream.** The transport layer takes data from one or more applications; it then marks them with a unique connection number and segment number. At the receiver these can be demultiplexed to the correct application program.
- **Reordering of data segments.** All the data segments that are transmitted are marked with a sequence number. Thus if any are delivered in the incorrect order, or if any of them are missing, the receiver can easily reorder them or discard segments if one or more are missing.

The most important transport protocol is TCP, which is typically uses IP as an addressing scheme. TCP and IP (TCP/IP) are the standard protocols that are used on the Internet and also on UNIX networks (where TCP/IP grew up, but have since dwarfed their parent). TCP works well because it is simple, but reliable, and it is an open system where no single vendor has control over its specification and its development.

An important concept of TCP/IP communications is the usage of ports and sockets. A port identifies a process type (such as FTP, TELNET, and so on) and the socket identifies a unique connection number. In this way, TCP/IP can support multiple simultaneous connections of applications over a network, as illustrated in Figure D2.1.

The IP header is added to higher-level data, and contains the 32-bit IP address of the destination node. Unfortunately, the standard 32-bit IP address is not large enough to support the growth in nodes connecting to the Internet. Thus a new standard, IP Version 6, has been developed to support 128-bit addresses, as well as additional enhancements.

The transport layer really provides a foundation for the application program to create a data stream were from one application program to another, just as if the two programs were running on the same computer, thus the data transfer operation should be transparent to the application program. It is thus important that the network protocol and the network type are invisible to the layers about the transport layer, as illustrated in Figure D2.2. This is important as application programmers can write programs which will run on any type of network protocol (such as SPX/IPX or TCP/IP) or any network type (such as, over ISDN, ATM or Ethernet). The protocol stack is the software that is used to provide the transport and network layers.

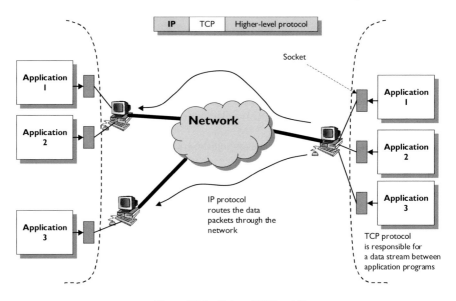

Figure D2.1   Roles of TCP and IP

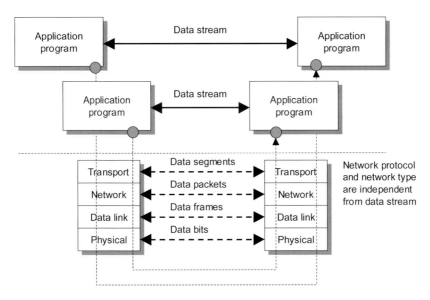

Figure D2.2   Data streams

D2.2   Functions of the transport layer

The great trick of the transport level is to allow multiple applications to communicate over a network, at the same time. This is achieved by identifying each connection with a unique value (a socket number) and adding sequence numbers on each of the segments. Segments can also be sent to many different destinations (using the network layer to identify the destination).

D2.2.1   Establishing connections

An important concept in the transport layer is to make a reliable connection with a destination node. This requires that the transport layer on one host makes contact with the transport layer on the destination host, and create a connection-oriented session with the peer system. Before data can be transmitted the sender and the receiver negotiate the connection and agree the parameters for the data to be sent, such as how many data segments that can be sent before an acknowledgement, the unique connection number, and so on. This process is called synchronization. Once the connection has been agreed, the data can pass between the transmitter and receiver on a data stream.

Figure D2.3 shows an example of the negotiation between a transmitter and a receiver. Initially the transmitter requests synchronization, after which the transmitter and the receiver negotiate the connection parameters. If acceptable, the receiver sends a synchronization signal, after which the transmitter acknowledges this with an acknowledgement. The connection is now made, and a data stream can flow between the two systems.

D2.2.2   Flow control

Data that is received is typically buffered in memory, as the processor cannot deal with it immediately. If there is too much data arriving to be processed, the data buffer can often overflow, and all newly arriving data will be discarded (as there is no place to store it). Another problem can occur when several hosts are transmitting to a single host. There is thus a need for a mechanism which can tell hosts to stop sending data segments, and to wait until the data has been properly processed.

The transport layer copes with these problems by issuing a Not Ready indicator, which tells a transmitter not to send any more data, until the host sends a Ready indicator. After this the transmitter can send data. This process is illustrated in Figure D2.4.

D2.2.3 Acknowledgement and windowing

The transport layer uses a technique called positive acknowledgement which only acknowledges correctly received data segments. The transmitter thus assumes that, after a certain period of time, if no acknowledgement has been received then the data has not been received correctly, and will thus retransmit the unacknowledged data segments. These will be sent with the same segment numbers as the original data segments so that the receiver does not end up with identical data segments. Thus two or more received data segments with the same sequence number will be deleted so that only a single copy is left.

Windowing provides for a method where the transmitter is forced to wait for an acknowledgement for the data segments that it has sent. The number of data segments that it is allowed to be sent before an acknowledgement, is set up when the connection is made. If the transmitter does not receive an acknowledgement within a given time limit, it will assume that the data did not arrive at the destination, and will then retransmit the data segments which were sent after the last acknowledged data segment.

If the window were set to unity, every data segment would have to be acknowledged. This, of course, would be inefficient and slow, as the transmitter would have to wait for every segment to be acknowledged. Thus the window allows for a number of segments to be transmitted before the requiring acknowledgements.

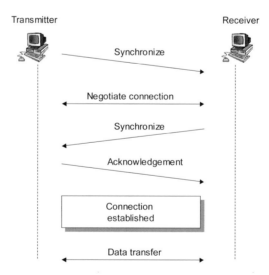

Figure D2.3 Synchronization and acknowledgement

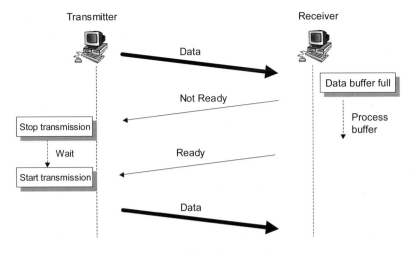

Figure D2.4 Flow control

Figure D2.5 shows the transmission of data segments with a window size of three. Initially the transmitter sends data segments with a send sequence number (S) of 1–3. It then waits for the receiver to send an acknowledgement, which it does by informing the transmitter that it expects to receive a data segment with a value of 4, next (R=4). If no acknowledgement was received from the receiver, the transmitter would resend the data segments 1 to 3. Note that the sequence numbers can either relate to the packet number (such as 1, 2, 3, ...) or to the byte number of the data being transmitted (this is the case in TCP communications). The reason that there is a different send (S) and receive (R) number is that both nodes may be transmitting and receiving data, thus they must both keep track of the data segments that are being sent and received.

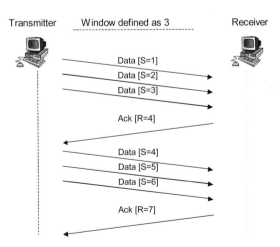

Figure D2.5 Windowing with a window of three

Often the start sequence number does not start at zero or one, as previous connections could be confused with new connections, thus a time-based initial value is used to define the start sequence number. Both the transmitter and the receiver agree on the start sequence number when the connection is negotiated.

D2.3   TCP/IP model

No networking technology fits into the OSI model, as many of the existing networking standards were developed before the model was developed. In addition, the OSI model was meant to be an abstract method of viewing a network from its physical connection, through its hardware/software interface, right up to the application program. The key element that allows computers over the world to intercommunicate, no matter their operating system, their hardware, their network connection, or their application program is the networking protocol. At one time networking protocols were tied to specific systems, such as DECNET (for DEC-based network), DLC (for IBM-based networks), NetBEUI (for Microsoft networks) and SPX/IPX (for Novell NetWare networks). While most of these networking protocols are still used for local area networks, the most common protocol for worldwide communications is TCP/IP.

TCP/IP does not quite fit into the OSI model, as illustrated in Figure D2.6. The OSI model uses seven layers where the TCP/IP model uses four layers, which are:

- **Network access layer.** Specifies the procedures for transmitting data across the network, including how to access the physical medium, such as Ethernet and FDDI.
- **Internet layer.** Responsible for data addressing, transmission, and packet fragmentation and reassembly (IP protocol).
- **Transport layer.** Manages all aspects of data routing and delivery including session initiation, error control and sequence checking (TCP/UDP protocols). This includes part of the session layer of the OSI model.
- **Application layer.** Responsible for everything else. Applications must be responsible for all the presentation and part of the session layer.

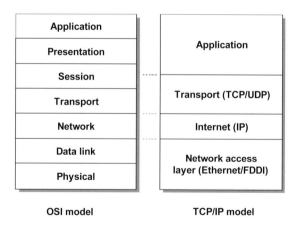

OSI model   TCP/IP model

Figure D2.6   OSI and TCP/IP model

D2.4　Transmission control protocol

In the OSI model, TCP fits into the transport layer and IP fits into the network layer. TCP thus sits above IP, which means that the IP header is added onto the higher-level information (such as transport, session, presentation and application). The main function of TCP is to provide a robust and reliable transport protocol. It is characterized as a reliable, connection-oriented, acknowledged and data stream-oriented server service. IP, itself, does not support the connection of two nodes, whereas TCP does. With TCP, a connection is initially established and is then maintained for the length of the transmission.

The main aspects of TCP are:

- **Data transfer.** Data is transmitted between two applications by packaging the data within TCP segments. This data is buffered and forwarded whenever necessary. A push function can be used when the data is required to be sent immediately.
- **Reliability.** TCP uses sequence numbers and positive acknowledgements (ACK) to keep track of transmitted segments. Thus, it can recover from data that is damaged, lost, duplicated, or delivered out of order, such as:

  - **Time-outs.** The transmitter waits for a given time (the timeout interval), and if it does not receive an ACK, the data is retransmitted.
  - **Sequence numbers.** The sequence numbers are used at the receiver to correctly order the packets and to delete duplicates.
  - **Error detection and recovery.** Each packet has a checksum, which is checked by the receiver. If it is incorrect the receiver discards it, and can use the acknowledgements to indicate the retransmission of the packets.

- **Flow control.** TCP returns a window with every ACK. This window indicates a range of acceptable sequence numbers beyond the last segment successfully received. It also indicates the number of bytes that the sender can transmit before receiving further acknowledgements.
- **Multiplexing.** To support multiple connections to a single host, TCP provides a set of ports within each host. This, along with the IP addresses of the source and destination, makes a socket, and a pair of sockets uniquely identifies each connection. Ports are normally associated with various services and allow server programs to listen for defined port numbers.
- **Connections.** A connection is defined by the sockets, sequence numbers and window sizes. Each host must maintain this information for the length of the connection. When the connection is closed, all associated resources are freed. As TCP connections can be made with unreliable hosts and over unreliable communication channels, TCP uses a handshake mechanism with clock-based sequence numbers to avoid inaccurate connection initialization.
- **Precedence and security.** TCP allows for different security and precedence levels.

TCP information contains simple acknowledgement messages and a set of sequential numbers. It also supports multiple simultaneous connections using destination and source port numbers, and manages them for both transmission and reception. As with IP, it supports data fragmentation and reassembly, and data multiplexing/ demultiplexing.

The set-up and operation of TCP is as follows:

- When a host wishes to make a connection, TCP sends out a request message to the destination machine that contains unique numbers called a socket number, and a port number. The port number has a value which is associated with the application (for example a TELNET connection has the port number 23 and an FTP connection has the port number 21). The message is then passed to the IP layer, which assembles a datagram for transmission to the destination.
- When the destination host receives the connection request, it returns a message containing its own unique socket number and a port number. The socket number and port number thus identify the virtual connection between the two hosts.
- After the connection has been made, the data can flow between the two hosts (called a data stream).

After TCP receives the stream of data, it assembles the data into packets, called TCP segments. After the segment has been constructed, TCP adds a header (called the protocol data unit) to the front of the segment. This header contains information such as a checksum, the port number, the destination and source socket numbers, the socket number of both machines and segment sequence numbers. The TCP layer then sends the packaged segment down to the IP layer, which encapsulates it and sends it over the network as a datagram.

D2.4.1 Ports and sockets

As previously mentioned, TCP adds a port number and socket number for each host. The port number identifies the required service, whereas the socket number is a unique number for that connection. Thus, a node can have several TELNET connections with the same port number but each connection will have a different socket number. A port number can be any value but there is a standard convention that most systems adopt. Table D2.1 defines some of the most common values. Standard applications normally use port values are:

- **0–255**. Public applications.
- **255–1023**. Assigned to companies for commercial products.
- **Above 1023**. Unregulated, and can be used by application programmers, or dynamically assigned by an application.

Table D2.1   Typical TCP port numbers

Port	Process name	Notes
20	FTP-DATA	File Transfer Protocol – data
21	FTP	File Transfer Protocol – control
23	TELNET	Telnet
25	SMTP	Simple Mail Transfer Protocol
49	LOGIN	Login Protocol
53	DOMAIN	Domain Name Server
79	FINGER	Finger
161	SNMP	SNMP

D2.4.2 TCP header format

The sender's TCP layer communicates with the receiver's TCP layer using the TCP protocol data unit. It defines parameters such as the source port, destination port, and so on, and is illustrated in Figure D2.7.

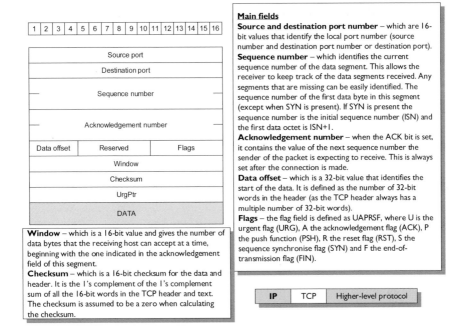

Main fields
Source and destination port number – which are 16-bit values that identify the local port number (source number and destination port number or destination port).
Sequence number – which identifies the current sequence number of the data segment. This allows the receiver to keep track of the data segments received. Any segments that are missing can be easily identified. The sequence number of the first data byte in this segment (except when SYN is present). If SYN is present the sequence number is the initial sequence number (ISN) and the first data octet is ISN+1.
Acknowledgement number – when the ACK bit is set, it contains the value of the next sequence number the sender of the packet is expecting to receive. This is always set after the connection is made.
Data offset – which is a 32-bit value that identifies the start of the data. It is defined as the number of 32-bit words in the header (as the TCP header always has a multiple number of 32-bit words).
Flags – the flag field is defined as UAPRSF, where U is the urgent flag (URG), A the acknowledgement flag (ACK), P the push function (PSH), R the reset flag (RST), S the sequence synchronise flag (SYN) and F the end-of-transmission flag (FIN).

Window – which is a 16-bit value and gives the number of data bytes that the receiving host can accept at a time, beginning with the one indicated in the acknowledgement field of this segment.
Checksum – which is a 16-bit checksum for the data and header. It is the 1's complement of the 1's complement sum of all the 16-bit words in the TCP header and text. The checksum is assumed to be a zero when calculating the checksum.

| IP | TCP | Higher-level protocol |

Figure D2.7   TCP header format

The fields are:

- **Source and destination port number** – which are 16-bit values that identify the local port number (source number and destination port number or destination port).
- **Sequence number** – which identifies the current sequence number of the data segment. This allows the receiver to keep track of the data segments received. Any segments that are missing can be easily identified. The sequence number is the first data byte of the DATA segment (except when SYN is present). If SYN is present the sequence number is the initial sequence number (ISN) and the first data octet is ISN + 1.
- **Acknowledgement number** – when the ACK bit is set, it contains the value of the next sequence number the sender of the packet is expecting to receive. This is always set after the connection is made.
- **Data offset** – which is a 32-bit value that identifies the start of the data. It is defined as the number of 32-bit words in the header (as the TCP header always has a multiple number of 32-bit words).
- **Flags** – the flag field is defined as UAPRSF, where U is the urgent flag (URG), A the acknowledgement flag (ACK), P the push function (PSH), R the reset flag (RST), S the sequence synchronize flag (SYN) and F the end-of-transmission flag (FIN).
- **Window** – which is a 16-bit value and gives the number of data bytes that the receiving host can accept at a time, beginning with the one indicated in the acknowledgement field of this segment.
- **Checksum** – which is a 16-bit checksum for the data and header. It is the 1's complement of the 1's complement sum of all the 16-bit words in the TCP header and data. The checksum is assumed to be a zero when calculating the checksum.

- **UrgPtr** – which is the urgent pointer and is used to identify an important area of data (most systems do not support this facility). It is only used when the URG bit is set. This field communicates the current value of the urgent pointer as a positive offset from the sequence number in this segment.
- **Padding** (variable) – the TCP header padding is used to ensure that the TCP header ends and data begins on a 32-bit boundary. The padding is composed of zeros.
- **Options** – possibly added to segment header.

In TCP, a packet is termed as the complete TCP unit; that is, the header and the data. A segment is a logical unit of data, which is transferred between two TCP hosts. Thus a packet is made up of a header and a segment.

D2.5   UDP

TCP allows for a reliable connection-based transfer of data. The User Datagram Protocol (UDP) is an unreliable connection-less approach, where datagrams are sent into the network without any acknowledgements or connections (and thus relies on high-level protocols to provide for these). It is defined in RFC768 and uses IP as its underlying protocol. Its main advantage over TCP is that it has a minimal protocol mechanism, but does not guarantee delivery of any of the data. Figure D2.8 shows its format, which shows that the Protocol field in the IP header is set to 17 to identify UDP.

The fields are:

- **Source port.** This is an optional field and is set to a zero if not used. It identifies the local port number which should be used when the destination host requires to contact the originator.
- **Destination.** Port to connect to on the destination.
- **Length.** Number of bytes in the datagram, including the UDP header and the data.
- **Checksum.** The 16-bit 1's complement of the 1's complement sum of the IP header, the UDP header, the data (which, if necessary, is padded with zero bytes at the end, to make an even number of bytes).

UDP is used when hosts do not require to make a connection with the other side, and where reliability is built into a high-layer protocol. It is also used when there is no segmentation of data (as there are no segment values). Some applications are solely TCP or solely UDP, whereas the rest can use either. For example:

- **TCP applications.** FTP, TELNET, SMTP, FINGER, DNS and LOGIN.
- **UDP applications.** RIP, TFTP, NFS and SNMP.
- **TCP or UDP applications.** HTTP, POP-3 and ECHO.

Applications of UDP include:

- **DNS.** Supports domain name mapping to IP addresses.
- **NFS.** Supports a distributed file system.
- **SNMP.** Supports network management for network devices.
- **TFTP** (Trivial FTP). A simplified version of FTP (typically used to update computers/routers with firmware updates).

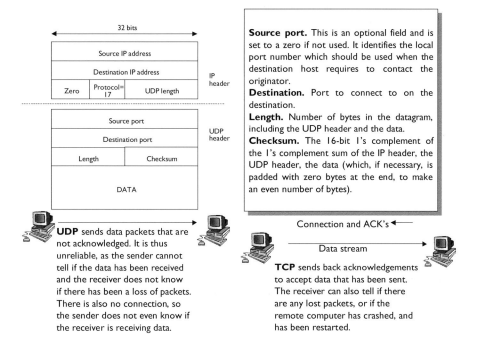

Source port. This is an optional field and is set to a zero if not used. It identifies the local port number which should be used when the destination host requires to contact the originator.

Destination. Port to connect to on the destination.

Length. Number of bytes in the datagram, including the UDP header and the data.

Checksum. The 16-bit 1's complement of the 1's complement sum of the IP header, the UDP header, the data (which, if necessary, is padded with zero bytes at the end, to make an even number of bytes).

UDP sends data packets that are not acknowledged. It is thus unreliable, as the sender cannot tell if the data has been received and the receiver does not know if there has been a loss of packets. There is also no connection, so the sender does not even know if the receiver is receiving data.

Connection and ACK's ◄──

Data stream ──►

TCP sends back acknowledgements to accept data that has been sent. The receiver can also tell if there are any lost packets, or if the remote computer has crashed, and has been restarted.

Figure D2.8   UDP header format

D2.6   TCP specification

TCP is made reliable with the following:

- **Sequence numbers.** Each TCP packet is sent with a sequence number (which identifies byte numbers). Theoretically, each data byte is assigned a sequence number. The sequence number of the first data byte in the segment is transmitted with that segment and is called the segment sequence number (SSN).
- **Acknowledgements.** Packets contain an acknowledgement number, which is the sequence number of the next expected transmitted data byte in the reverse direction. On sending, a host stores the transmitted data in a storage buffer, and starts a timer. If the packet is acknowledged then this data is deleted, else, if no acknowledgement is received before the timer runs out, the packet is retransmitted.
- **Window.** With this, a host sends a window value which specifies the number of bytes, starting with the acknowledgement number, that the host can receive.

D2.6.1   Connection establishment, clearing and data transmission

The main interfaces in TCP are shown in Figure D2.9. The calls from the application program to TCP include:

- OPEN and CLOSE. To open and close a connection.
- SEND and RECEIVE. To send and receive.

- STATUS. To receive status information.

The OPEN call initiates a connection with a local port and foreign socket arguments. A Transmission Control Block (TCB) stores the information on the connection. After a successful connection, TCP adds a local connection name by which the application program refers to the connection in subsequent calls.

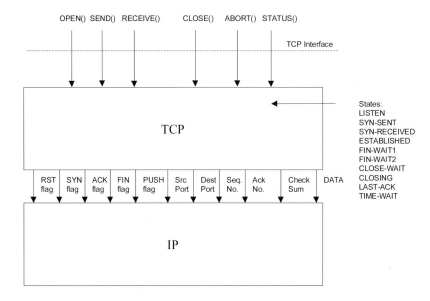

Figure D2.9 TCP interface

The OPEN call supports two different types of call, as illustrated in Figure D2.10. These are:

- **Passive OPEN.** TCP waits for a connection from a foreign host, such as from an active OPEN. In this case, the foreign socket is defined by a zero. This is typically used by servers, such as TELNET and FTP servers. The connection can either be from a fully specified or an unspecified socket.
- **Active OPEN.** TCP actively connects to a foreign host, typically a server (which is opened with a passive OPEN) or with a peer-to-peer connection (with two active OPEN calls, at the same time, on each computer).

A connect is established with the transmission of TCP packets with the SYN control flag set and uses a three-way handshake (see Section D2.8). A connection is cleared by the exchange of packets with the FIN control flag set. Data flows in a stream using the SEND call to send data and RECEIVE to receive data.

The PUSH flag is used to send data in the SEND immediately to the recipient. This is required as a sending TCP is allowed to collect data from the sending application program and sends the data in segments when convenient. Thus, the PUSH flag forces it to be sent. When the receiving TCP sees the PUSH flag, it does not wait for any more data from the sending TCP before passing the data to the receiving process.

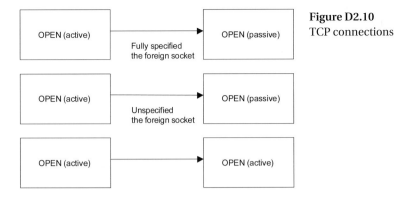

Figure D2.10
TCP connections

D2.7 Connection states

Figure D2.11 outlines the states which the connection goes into, and the events which cause them. The events from applications programs are: OPEN, SEND, RECEIVE, CLOSE, ABORT, and STATUS, and the events from the incoming TCP packets include the SYN, ACK, RST and FIN flags. The definition of each of the connection states are:

- **LISTEN.** This is the state in which TCP is waiting for a remote connection on a given port.
- **SYN-SENT.** This is the state where TCP is waiting for a matching connection request after it has sent a connection request.
- **SYN-RECEIVED.** This is the state where TCP is waiting for a confirming connection request acknowledgement after having both received and sent a connection request.
- **ESTABLISHED.** This is the state that represents an open connection. Any data received can be delivered to the application program. This is the normal state for data to be transmitted.
- **FIN-WAIT-1.** This is the state in which TCP is waiting for a connection termination request, or an acknowledgement of a connection termination, from the remote TCP.
- **FIN-WAIT-2.** This is the state in which TCP is waiting for a connection termination request from the remote TCP.
- **CLOSE-WAIT.** This is the state where TCP is waiting for a connection termination request from the local application.
- **CLOSING.** This is the state where TCP is waiting for a connection termination request acknowledgement from the remote TCP.
- **LAST-ACK.** This is the state where TCP is waiting for an acknowledgement of the connection termination request previously sent to the remote TCP.
- **TIME-WAIT.** This is the state in which TCP is waiting for enough time to pass to be sure the remote TCP received the acknowledgement of its connection termination request.
- **CLOSED.** This is the notational state, which occurs after the connection has been closed.

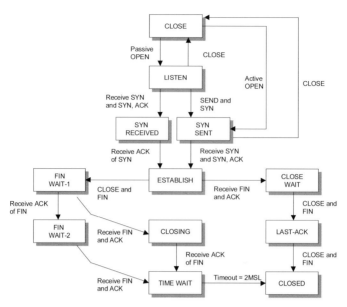

Figure D2.11 TCP connection states

The following shows a sample session (using the `netstat` command). The local address is defined with the node address followed by the port number (for example for the first entry, artemis is the local address and the local port is 1023). Ports that are known (such as login, shell and imap) are given names, while non-assigned ports are just defined with a port number. It can be seen that the local host has three current logins with the hosts aphrodite and leto. These connect to the remote ports of 1018, 1023 and 1019. The send and receive windows do not vary on each of the connections, and are set at 8760. An important field is Send-Q, for which a nonzero value indicates that the network for that particular host is severely congested, as it defines the number of unacknowledged segments.

```
Local Address        Remote Address        Swind Send-Q Rwind  Recv-Q  State
-------------------  -------------------   ----- ------ -----  ------  -------
artemis.1023         poseidon.shell        8760       0 8760        0 FIN_WAIT_2
artemis.1022         poseidon.1022         8760       0 8760        0 ESTABLISHED
artemis.1021         poseidon.shell        8760       0 8760        0 FIN_WAIT_2
artemis.1020         poseidon.1021         8760       0 8760        0 ESTABLISHED
artemis.43939        hades.701             8760       0 8760        0 CLOSE_WAIT
artemis.login        aphrodite.1018        8760       0 8760        0 ESTABLISHED
artemis.login        leto.1023             8760       0 8760        0 ESTABLISHED
artemis.login        aphrodite.1019        8760       0 8760        0 ESTABLISHED
artemis.50925        poseidon.imap         8760       0 8760        0 CLOSE_WAIT
```

D2.7.1 Sequence numbers

TCP packets contain a 32-bit sequence number (0 to 4 294 967 295), which relates to every byte sent. It uses a cumulative acknowledgement scheme, where an acknowledgement with a value of VAL, validates all bytes up to, but not including, byte VAL. Each byte at which the packet starts is numbered consecutively, after the first byte.

When sending data, TCP should receive acknowledgements for the transmitted data. The required TCB parameters will be:

SND.UNA	Oldest unacknowledged sequence number.
SND.NXT	Next sequence number to send.
SEG.ACK	Acknowledgement from the receiving TCP (next sequence number expected by the receiving TCP).
SEG.SEQ	First sequence number of a segment.
SEG.LEN	Number of bytes in the TCP packet.
SEG.SEQ+SEG.LEN–1	Last sequence number of a segment.

On receiving data, the following TCB parameters are required:

RCV.NXT	Next sequence number expected on an incoming segment, and is the left or lower edge of the receive window.
RCV.NXT+RCV.WND–1	Last sequence number expected on an incoming segment, and is the right or upper edge of the receive window.
SEG.SEQ	First sequence number occupied by the incoming segment.
SEG.SEQ+SEG.LEN–1	Last sequence number occupied by the incoming segment.

D2.7.2 ISN selection

The initial sequence number (ISN) is selected so that previous sockets are not confused with new sockets. Typically, this can happen when a host application crashes and then quickly re-establishes the connection before the other side time-outs the connection. To avoid this a 32-bit initial sequence number (ISN) generator is created when the connection is made, which is a number generated by a 32-bit clock, and is incremented approximately every $4\,\mu s$ (giving an ISN cycle of 4.55 hours). Thus, within 4.55 hours, each ISN will be unique.

As each connection has a send and receive sequence number, these are an initial send sequence number (ISS) and an initial receive sequence number (IRS). When establishing a connection, the two TCPs synchronize their initial sequence numbers. This is done by exchanging connection establishing packets, with the SYN bit set and with the initial sequence numbers (these packets are typically called SYNs). Thus, four packets must be initially exchanged:

A sends to B. SYN with A_{SEQ}.
B sends to A. ACK of the sequence number (A_{SEQ}).   ⎤ Can be merged into a
B sends to A. SYN with B_{SEQ}.   ⎦ single state.
A sends to B. ACK of the sequence number (B_{SEQ}).

Note that the two intermediate steps can be combined into a single message, which is sometimes known as a three-way handshake. This handshake is necessary as the sequence numbers are not tied to a global clock, only to local clocks, and has many advantages, including the fact that old packets will be discarded as they occurred in a previous time.

To make sure that a sequence number is not duplicated, a host must wait for a maximum segment lifetime (MSL) before starting to retransmit packets (segments) after start-up or when recovering from a crash. An example MSL is 2 minutes. However, if it is recovering, and it has a memory of the previous sequence numbers, it may not need to wait for the MSL, as it can use sequence numbers which are much greater than the previously used sequence numbers.

D2.8   Opening and closing a connection

Figure D2.12 shows a basic three-way handshake. The steps are:

- The initial state on the initiator is CLOSED and, on the recipient, it is LISTEN (the recipient is waiting for a connection).
- The initiator goes into the SYN-SENT state and sends a packet with the SYN bit set and then indicates that the starting sequence number will be 999 (the current sequence number, thus the next number sent will be 1000). When this is received the recipient goes into the SYN-RECEIVED state.
- The recipient sends back a TCP packet with the SYN and ACK bits set (which identifies that it is a SYN packet and also that it is acknowledging the previous SYN packet). In this case, the recipient tells the originator that it will start transmitting at a sequence number of 100. The acknowledgement number is 1000, which is the sequence number that the recipient expects to receive next. When this is received, the originator goes into the ESTABLISHED state.
- The originator sends back a TCP packet with the SYN and ACK bits set and the   acknowledgement number is 101, which is the sequence number it expects to see next.
- The originator transmits data with the sequence number of 1000.

Originator		Recipient
1. CLOSED		LISTEN
2. SYN-SENT	$\rightarrow$ <SEQ = 999><CTL=SYN>	SYN-RECEIVED
3. ESTABLISHED	<SEQ = 100><ACK = 1000><CTL = SYN,ACK> $\leftarrow$	SYN-RECEIVED
4. ESTABLISHED	$\rightarrow$ <SEQ = 1000><ACK = 101> <CTL = ACK>	ESTABLISHED
5. ESTABLISHED	$\rightarrow$ <SEQ = 1000><ACK = 101> <CTL = ACK><DATA>	ESTABLISHED

Figure D2.12   TCP connection

Note that the acknowledgement number acknowledges every sequence number up to but not including the acknowledgement number.

Figure D2.13 shows how the three-way handshake prevents old duplicate connection initiations from causing confusion. In state 3, a duplicate SYN has been received, which is from a previous connection. The recipient sends back an acknowledgement for this (4), but when this is received by the originator, the originator sends back a RST (reset) packet. This causes the recipient to go back into a LISTEN state. It will then receive the SYN packet sent in 2, and after acknowledging it, a connection is made.

TCP connections are half-open if one of the TCPs has closed or aborted, and the other end is still connected. Half-open connections can also occur if the two connections have become desynchronized because of a system crash. This connection is automatically reset if data is sent in either direction. This is because the sequence numbers will be incorrect, otherwise the connection will time-out.

A connection is normally closed with the CLOSE call. A host who has closed cannot continue to send, but can continue to RECEIVE until it is told to close by the other side. Figure D2.14 shows a typical sequence for closing a connection. Normally the application program sends a CLOSE call for the given connection. Next, a TCP packet is sent with the FIN bit set, the originator enters into the FIN-WAIT-1 state. When the other TCP has acknowledged the FIN and sent a FIN of its own, the first TCP can ACK this FIN.

Originator			Recipient
1. CLOSED			LISTEN
2. SYN-SENT	→	<SEQ=999><CTL=SYN>	
3. (duplicate)	→	<SEQ=900><CTL=SYN>	
4. SYN-SENT		<SEQ=100><ACK=901> <CTL=SYN,ACK> ←	SYN-RECEIVED
5. SYN-SENT	→	<SEQ=901><CTL=RST>	LISTEN
		(packet 2 received) →	
7. SYN-SENT		<SEQ=1 00><ACK=1000><CTL=SYN,ACK> ←	SYN-RECEIVED
8. ESTABLISHED	→	<SEQ=1 000><ACK=101><CTL=ACK><DATA>	ESTABLISHED

Figure D2.13 TCP connection with duplicate connections

Originator			Recipient
1. ESTABLISHED			ESTABLISHED
(*CLOSE call*)			
2. FIN-WAIT-1	→ <SEQ=1000><ACK=99> <CTL=SFIN,ACK>		CLOSE-WAIT
3. FIN-WAIT-2	<SEQ=99><ACK=1001> <CTL=ACK>	←	CLOSE-WAIT
4. TIME-WAIT	<SEQ=99><ACK=101><CTL=FIN,ACK>	←	LAST-ACK
5. TIME-WAIT	→ <SEQ=1001><ACK=102><CTL=ACK>		CLOSED

Figure D2.14 TCP close connection

D2.9 TCP user commands

The commands in this section characterize the interface between TCP and the application program. Their actual implementation depends on the operating system. Section 12.10 discusses practical WinSock implementations.

D2.9.1 OPEN

The OPEN call initiates an active or a passive TCP connection. The basic parameters passed and returned from the call are given next. Parameters in brackets are optional.

Parameters passed: local port, foreign socket, active/ passive [, timeout] [, prece-dence] [, security/compartment] [, options]

Parameters returned: local connection name

These parameters are defined as:

- Local port. The local port to be used.
- Foreign socket. The definition of the foreign socket.
- Active/passive. A passive flag causes TCP to LISTEN, else it will actively seek a connection.
- Timeout. If present, this parameter allows the caller to set up a timeout for all data submitted to TCP. If the data is not transmitted successfully within the timeout period

the connection is aborted.

- Security/compartment. Specifies the security of the connection.
- Local connection name. A unique connection name is returned which identifies the socket.

D2.9.2   SEND

The SEND call causes the data in the output buffer to be sent to the indicated connection. Most implementations return immediately from the SEND call, even if the data has not been sent, although some implementation will not return until either there is a timeout or the data has been sent. The basic parameters passed and returned from the call are given next. Parameters in brackets are optional.

Parameters passed: local connection name, buffer address, byte count, PUSH flag, URGENT flag [, timeout]

These parameters are defined as:

- Local connection name. A unique connection name which identifies the socket.
- Buffer address. Address of data buffer.
- Byte count. Number of bytes in the buffer.
- PUSH flag. If this flag is set then the data will be transmitted immediately, else the TCP may wait until it has enough data.
- URGENT flag. Sets the urgent pointer.
- Timeout. Sets a new timeout for the connection.

D2.9.3   RECEIVE

The RECEIVE call allocates a receiving buffer for the specified connection. Most implementations return immediately from the RECEIVE call, even if the data has not been received, although some implementation will not return until either there is a timeout or the data has been received. The basic parameters passed and returned from the call are given next.

Parameters passed: local connection name, buffer address, byte count
Parameters returned: byte count, URGENT flag, PUSH flag

These parameters are defined as:

- Local connection name. A unique connection name which identifies the socket.
- Buffer address. Address of the receive data buffer.
- Byte count. Number of bytes received in the buffer.
- PUSH flag. If this flag is set then the PUSH flag has been set on the received data.
- URGENT flag. If this flag is set then the URGENT flag has been set on the received data.

D2.9.4   CLOSE

The CLOSE call closes the connections and releases associated resources. All pending SENDs will be transmitted, but after the CLOSE call has been implemented, no further SENDs can occur. RECEIVEs can occur until the other host has also closed the connection. The basic parameters passed and returned from the call are given next.

Parameters passed: local connection name

D2.9.5   STATUS

The STATUS call determines the current status of a connection, typically listing the TCBs. The basic parameters passed and returned from the call are given next.

Parameters passed: local connection name
Parameters returned: status data

The returned information should include status information on the following:

- local socket, foreign socket, local connection name
- receive window, send window, connection state
- number of buffers awaiting acknowledgement, number of buffers pending receipt
- urgent state, precedence, security/compartment
- transmission timeout.

D2.9.6   ABORT

The ABORT call causes all pending SENDs and RECEIVEs to be aborted. All TCBs are also removed and a RESET message sent to the other TCP. The basic parameters passed and returned from the call are given next.

Parameters passed: local connection name

D2.10   TCP/IP services reference

Port	Service	Comment	Port	Service	Comment
1	TCPmux		7	echo	
9	discard	Null	11	systat	Users
13	daytime		15	netstat	
17	qotd	Quote	18	msp	Message send protocol
19	chargen	ttytst source	21	ftp	
23	telnet		25	smtp	Mail
37	time	Timserver	39	rlp	Resource location
42	nameserver	IEN 116	43	whois	Nicname
53	domain	DNS	57	mtp	Deprecated
67	bootps	BOOTP server	67	bootps	
68	bootpc	BOOTP client	69	tftp	
70	gopher	Internet Gopher	77	rje	Netrjs
79	finger		80	www	WWW HTTP
87	link	Ttylink	88	kerberos	Kerberos v5
95	supdup		101	hostnames	
102	iso-tsap	ISODE	105	csnet-ns	CSO name server
107	rtelnet	Remote Telnet	109	pop2	POP version 2
110	pop3	POP version 3	111	sunrpc	
113	auth	Rap ID	115	sftp	

117	uucp-path		119	nntp	USENET
123	ntp	Network Time	137	netbios-ns	NETBIOS Name Service
138	netbios-dgm	NETBIOS	139	netbios-ssn	NETBIOS session
143	imap2		161	snmp	SNMP
162	snmp-trap	SNMP trap	163	cmip-man	ISO management over IP
164	cmip-agent		177	xdmcp	X Display Manager
178	nextstep	NeXTStep	179	bgp	BGP

RFC (Request For Comment) documents are published by the IAB (Internet Advisor Board) and are a quick way to quickly define new standards, in which anyone can comment on. They are continually updated, but various documents define the main standards used on the Internet, these are:

RFC768   UDP
RFC791   IP
RFC792   ICMP
RFC793   TCP
RFC821   SMTP
RFC822   Format of email messages
RFC854   Telnet
RFC959   FTP
RFC1034 Domain names
RFC1058 RIP
RFC1157 SNMP
RFC1521 MIME Pt. 1
RFC1522 MIME Pt. 2
RFC1939 POP Version 3

D3   SPX/IPX

D3.1   Introduction

IBM introduced the PC in 1981 and ever since there has been a great battle for dominance in the operating system market, which splits into providing the basic client operating system, and the server operating system. As sales of the PC grew, IBM soon realized that they had also lost the market leadership for hardware development, as there were many companies cloning the PC, and selling their systems at a reduced price. IBM then decided to try to turn the market for operating system software: OS/2. With the success of DOS and Microsoft Windows, it was becoming obvious that the operating system held the key to the hardware architectures and application software. In a perfect world, an operating system can hide the hardware from the application software, so the hardware becomes less important. Thus, if the software runs fast enough, the hardware can be of any type and of any architecture, allowing application programmers to write their software for the operating system and not for the specific hardware. Whichever company developed the standards for the operating system would hold the key to hardware architecture, and also the range of other packages, such as office tools, networking applications, and so on.

Unfortunately, for IBM, OS/2 was a compromised operating system that was developed for all their computers, whether they be mainframes or low-level PCs. Unlike the development of the PC, many of the organizational units within IBM, including the powerful mainframe divisions, had a say about what went into OS/2 and what was left out. For the IBM PC, the PC team at Boca Raton was given almost total independence from the rest of the organization, but the development of OS/2 was riddled with compromises, reviews and specification changes. At the time, mainframes differed from PCs in many different ways, such as:

- **Boot times**. One of the most noticeable ways was the way that they were booted, and the regularity of system crashes. Most users of PCs demanded fast boot times (less than a minute if possible), but had no great problems when it crashed a few times a day, which were typically due to incorrectly functioning and configured hardware, and incorrectly installed software. In the mainframe market, an operating system performs a great deal of system checks and tries to properly configure the hardware. This causes long boot-up times, which is not a problem with a mainframe that typically runs for many weeks, months or years without requiring a re-boot. However, for the PC, a boot time of anything more than a few minutes is a big problem. In the end, OS/2 had too long a boot time, and was too slow (possibly due to its complexity) to compete in the marketplace.
- **User interface**. At the time, mainframes tended to be oriented around standard text interfaces, and had little requirements for a graphical user interface, especially in its usage of fonts. Thus

IBM released OS/2 in 1987, but it was never really adopted. In the end they spent over $2 billion on OS/2 with very little in return.

Initially DOS controlled the operating system market, and it was in 1981 that Novell Data Systems created a simple networking operating system that allowed two computers to share a single hard disk drive. In 1983 Novell, (as they were now known) developed their Novell NetWare operating system, which allowed computers to share resources over a network, especially disk and printer resources. Their approach created an innovate solution where commands entered at the DOS prompt would be first interpreted by the Novell program which would decide if it should direct the command to the DOS operating system, or to the Novell server. Thus a call to the C: drive would be sent to the DOS, and a call to a network drive would be sent to the file server. By 1985, Novell NetWare had evolved in Version 2.0 and by 1989 they were releasing the first copies of their NetWare Version 3.0 operating system. Novell seemed unstoppable as they released the class NetWare Version 3.11 in 1991. No computer could come near Novell in the PC market, and they even moved, in 1992, to buy the rights for AT&T UNIX.

1993 would be a key year for the future of networking operating systems as NetWare released their NetWare 4.0 produce. Unfortunately, for Novell, Microsoft had been busy spinning-off work from their OS/2 work with IBM, and released a totally re-engineered operating system: Windows NT. As many predicted the end of DOS, and the eventual dominance of UNIX, a new operating system was released alongside NT and NetWare: Linux. Within two years NetWare still had over 50% of the server market, whereas Microsoft had less than 10%, but in 1996 Microsoft successfully integrated their work on the graphical user interface used by Windows 95, into NT, and released one of the great network operating systems of all time: Windows NT 4.0. Within a year of its release it was the market leader with over 36% of the market, pushing NetWare into second place with 26%, and Unix into third place with 21% (the new coming, Linux, even managed to push OS/2 into fifth place with nearly 7% of the market, while OS/2 could only manage 6%). Ever since NetWare has struggled against the might of Windows, and Unix, by 1998 NetWare played a trump card with their NetWare 5.0 operating system which included the innovative NDS file structure, followed by NetWare 5.1 in 2000, and NetWare 6.0 in 2001.

Novell NetWare is still one of the most popular network operating systems for PC LANs and provides file and print server facilities. Its default network protocol is normally **SPX/IPX**, which can also be used with Microsoft Windows to communicate with other Windows nodes and with NetWare networks. The Internet Packet Exchange (**IPX**) protocol is a network layer protocol for transportation of data between computers on a NetWare network. IPX is very fast and has a small connectionless datagram protocol. The Sequenced Packet Interchange (**SPX**) provides a communications protocol which supervises the transmission of the packet and ensures its successful delivery.

NetWare is typically used in organizations and works well on a local network. Network traffic which travels out on the Internet or that communicates with UNIX networks must be in TCP/IP form. IP tunneling encapsulates the IPX packet within the IP packet. This can then be transmitted into the Internet network. When the IP packet is received by the destination NetWare gateway, the IP encapsulation is stripped off. IP tunneling thus relies on a gateway into each IPX-based network that also runs IP. The NetWare gateway is often called an IP tunnel peer.

Novell NetWare servers, unlike Windows severs, can only run as servers and cannot be used as clients. They advertise their services in broadcasts around the network. A Novell NetWare client can also request a service from the nearest server. Routers can now be setup so that they can listen to advertisements, and build up tables of these services, which can be passed onto clients when they require specific services. These routers can also route IPX traffic from one network to another over the local network.

D3.2   NetWare architecture

NetWare provides many services, such as file sharing, printer sharing, security, user administration and network management. The interface between the network interface card (NIC) and the SPX/IPX stack is ODI (Open Data-link Interface). NetWare clients run software which connects them to the server; the supported client operating systems are DOS, Windows, Windows NT, UNIX, OS/2 and Macintosh.

With NetWare Version 3, DOS and Windows 3.*x* clients use a NetWare shell called NETx.COM. This shell is executed when the user wants to log into the network and stay resident. It acts as a command redirector and processes requests which are either generated by application programs or from the keyboard. It then decides whether they should be handled by the NetWare network operating system or passed to the client's local DOS operating system. NETx builds its own tables to keep track of the location of network-attached resources rather than using DOS tables. Figure D3.1 illustrates the relationship between the NetWare shell and DOS, in a DOS-based client. Note that Windows 3.*x* uses the DOS operating system, but Windows NT/2000 and 95 have their own operating systems and only emulate DOS. Thus, Windows NT/2000 and 95 do not need to use the NETx program.

The ODI allows NICs to support multiple transport protocols, such as TCP/IP and IPX/SPX, simultaneously. In addition, in an Ethernet interface card, the ODI allows simultaneous support of multiple Ethernet frame types such as Ethernet 802.3, Ethernet 802.2, Ethernet II, and Ethernet SNAP.

To install NetWare, the server must have a native operating system, such as DOS or Windows NT, and it must be installed on its own disk partition. NetWare then adds a partition in which the NetWare partition is added. This partition is the only area of the disk the NetWare kernel can access.

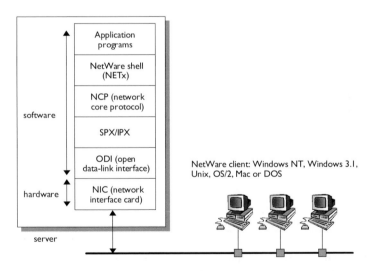

Figure D3.1   NetWare architecture

D3.2.1   NetWare loadable modules (NLMs)

NetWare allows enhancements from third-party suppliers using NLMs. The two main categories are:

- **Operating systems enhancements** – these allow extra operating system functions, such as a virus checker and also client hardware specific modules, such as network interface drivers.
- **Application programs** – these programs actually run on the NetWare server rather than on the client machine.

D3.2.2 Bindery services

NetWare allows enhancements from third-party suppliers using NLMs. The two main categories are:

- **Operating systems enhancements** – these allow extra operating system functions, such as a virus checker and also client hardware specific modules, such as network interface drivers.
- **Application programs** – these programs actually run on the NetWare server rather than on the client machine.

NetWare must keep track of users and their details. Typically, NetWare must keep track of:

- User names and passwords.
- Groups and group rights.
- File and directory rights.
- Print queues and printers.
- User restrictions (such as allowable login times, the number of times a user can simultaneously login to the network).
- User/group administration and charging (such as charging for user login).
- Connection to networked peripherals.

This information is kept in the bindery files. Whenever a user logs into the network their login details are verified against the information in the bindery files.

The bindery is organized with objects, properties and values. Objects are entities that are controlled or managed, such as users, groups, printers (servers and queues), disk drives, and so on. Each object has a set of properties, such as file rights, login restrictions, restrictions to printers, and so on. Each property has a value associated with it. Here are some examples:

Object	Property	Value
User	Login restriction	Wednesday 9 am till 5pm
User	Simultaneous login	2
Group	Access to printer	No

Objects, properties and values are stored in three separate files which are linked by pointers on every NetWare server:

1. NET$OBJ.SYS (contains object information).
2. NET$PROP.SYS (contains property information).
3. NET$VAL.SYS (contains value information).

If multiple NetWare servers exist on a network then bindery information must be exchanged manually between the servers so that the information is the same on each server. In a multiserver NetWare 3.*x* environment, the servers send SAP (service advertising protocol) information between themselves to advertise available services. Then the bindery services on a particular server update their bindery files with the latest information regarding available services on other reachable servers. This synchronization is difficult when just a few servers exist but is extremely difficult when there are many servers. Luckily, NetWare 4.1 has addressed this problem with NetWare directory services; this will be discussed later.

D3.3   NetWare protocols

NetWare uses IPX (Internet Packet Exchange) for the network layer and either SPX (Sequenced Packet Exchange) or NCP (NetWare Core Protocols) for the transport layer. The routing information protocol (RIP) is also used to transmit information between NetWare gateways. These protocols are illustrated in Figure D3.2.

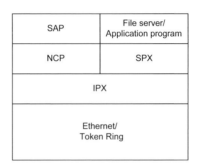

Figure D3.2   NetWare reference model

D3.3.1   IPX

IPX performs a network function that is similar to IP. The higher information is passed to the IPX layer which then encapsulates it into IPX envelopes. It is characterized by:

- A connectionless connection – each packet is sent into the network and must find its own way through the network to the final destination (connections are established with SPX).
- It is unreliable – as with IP it only basic error checking and no acknowledgement   (acknowledgements are achieved with SPX).

IPX uses a 12-byte station address (whereas IP uses a 4-byte address), which is made up of an 80-bit IPX address and a socket number. The format of the 80-bit address is:

- **Network part**. This uses the 32 bits of the network address. This is assigned by the network administrator.
- **Node part**. This typically uses the 48-bit MAC address of the node, and is automatically assigned.

The IPX fields are:

- **Checksum** (2 bytes) – this field is rarely used in IPX, as error checking is achieved in the SPX layer. The lower-level data link layer also provides an error detection scheme (both Ethernet and Token Ring support a frame check sequence).
- **Length** (2 bytes) – this gives the total length of the packet in bytes (i.e. header + DATA). The maximum number of bytes in the DATA field is 546, thus the maximum length will be 576 bytes (2 + 2 + 1 + 1 + 12 + 12 + 546).
- **Transport control** (1 byte) – this field is incremented every time the frame is processed by a router. When it reaches a value of 16 it is deleted. This stops packets from traversing the network for an infinite time. It is also typically known as the time-to-live field or hop counter.
- **Packet type** (1 byte) – this field identifies the upper layer protocol so that the DATA field can be properly processed.
- **Addressing** (12 bytes) – this field identifies the address of the source and destination station. It is made up of three fields: a network address (4 bytes), a host address (6 bytes) and a socket address (2 bytes). The 48-bit host address is the 802 MAC LAN address. NetWare supports a hierarchical addressing structure where the network and host addresses identify the host station and the socket address identifies a process or application and thus supports multiple connections (up to 50 per node).

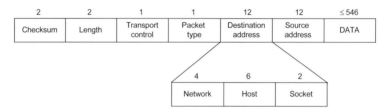

Figure D3.3 IPX packet format

Sometimes the IP network address is converted into a hexadecimal format and is used for the IPX network number. For example, the subnet 154.181.66.128/27 (where the /27 identifies that 27 bits are used for the network part of the address) would become 9AB54280.

Figure D3.4 illustrate the connection of two IPX networks: 2B10 and 2F30. Unlike in an IP network, there is no need for ARP, as the nodes can determine their IPX address once they have been assigned a network address. For example the node on the 2B10 with a MAC address of 0000.00CC.0125 has an IPX address of 2B10.0000.00CC.0125. A serial interface on the network will use the MAC address of the Ethernet interface for their IPX node address.

To enable IPX routing on a port the `ipx routing [address]` command is used.

```
MyRouter# config t
MyRouter (config)# ipx routing
MyRouter (config)# ipx maximum-paths
```

The *address* parameter is a 48-bit address which defines the node address of the interface. If no address is given and the interface is Ethernet, then the router uses the MAC address. Also if no address is given, and the interface is a serial interface, then a node address must be given. The `ipx maximum-paths` command can be used to enable load sharing on parallel paths. The default is set to 1, but can support up to 512 parallel routes. The value after the command defines the number of maximum parallel paths.

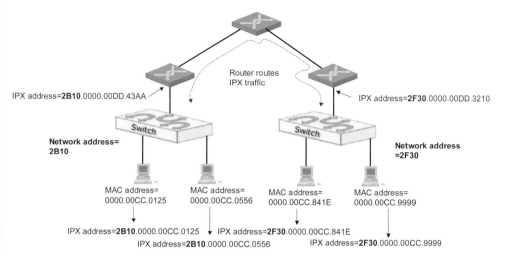

Figure D3.4 IPX address allocation and IPX routing

The `ipx maximum-paths` command allows throughput to be increased by supporting several equal-cost, parallel paths. If a route has a lower cost, it will be used instead of other high-cost routes. In load sharing the packets are distributed equally to each of the equal cost routes on a round-robin basis. If the number of equal-cost paths is limited, it can save on the memory requirements of the router.

Each interface is then setup with network numbers and encapsulation types. For example to program Ethernet0 for Novell-Ether, and for network 2B10, and Ethernet1 for SAP and for network 2F30:

```
MyRouter# config t
MyRouter (config)# ipx routing
MyRouter (config)# ipx maximum-paths
MyRouter (config)# interface ethernet0
MyRouter (config-int)# ipx encapsulation novell-ether
MyRouter (config-int)# ipx network 2B10
MyRouter (config-int)# exit
MyRouter (config)# interface ethernet1
MyRouter (config-int)# ipx encapsulation sap
MyRouter (config-int)# ipx network 2F30
MyRouter (config-int)# exit
```

The IPX interface can be interrogated using the `show ipx interface [interface]` command, such as:

```
MyRouter# show ipx interface ethernet 0
Ethernet0 is up, line protocol is up
        IPX address is 2B10.0000.00DD.43AA, NOVELL-ETHER [up] line-up,
                   RIPPQ:0,SAPPQ :0
        Delay of this Novell network, in ticks is 5
        IPXWAN processing not enabled on this interface.
        IPX SAP update interval is 1 minute(s)
```

This shows that the IPX interface on Ethernet0 is up, and that there is a connection with the other end (as the protocol is up). There is a five tick delay on the interface, and that its address is 2B10.0000.00DD.43AA. The encapsulation is NOVELL-ETHER (which is standard encapsulation used in NetWare 3.12, onwards. The RIPPQ and SAPPQ show the number of packets in the RIP and SAP queues, respectively. In addition, the SAP update time is set to 60 seconds.

Typical Ethernet encapsulations include:

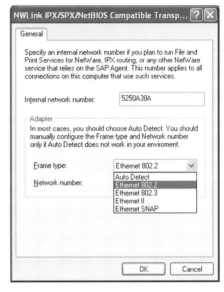

- Ethernet_802.3, novell-ether. Contains an 802.3 header, followed by IPX. NetWare up to NetWare 3.11.
- Ethernet_802_3, sap. Contains 802.3 header, with an 802.2 LLC, followed by IPX. NetWare up to NetWare 3.12, onwards.
- Ethernet_II, arpa. Contains the Ethernet II header, followed by IPX.
- Ethernet_SNAP, snap. Contains the 802.3 header, with an 802.2 LLC and a Subnetwork Access Protocol (SNAP) field, followed by IPX.

The interface can be tested using the `ping ipx` command. For example

```
Myrouter #> ping ipx 2B10.0000.00DD.43AA
Sending 5 100-byte Novell echoes to 2B10.0000.00DD.43AA, timeout is 2 seconds.
!!!!!
Success rate is 100%, round trip min/avg/max = 2/10/5 ms.
```

An exclamation mark (!) identifies a successful ping, a period (.) represents a time-out, and a U identifies that the destination is unreachable.

D3.3.2 SPX

On a NetWare network the level above IPX is either NCP or SPX. The SPX protocol sets up a virtual circuit between the source and the destination (just like TCP). Then all SPX packets follow the same path and will thus always arrive in the correct order. This type of connection is described as connection-oriented.

SPX also allows for error checking and an acknowledgement to ensure that packets are received correctly. Each SPX packet has flow control and also sequence numbers. Figure D3.5 illustrates the SPX packet.

The fields in the SPX header are:

- **Connection control** (1 byte) – this is a set of flags which assist the flow of data. These flags include an acknowledgement flag and an end-of-message flag.
- **Datastream type** (1 byte) – this byte contains information which can be used to determine the protocol or information contained within the SPX data field.
- **Destination connection ID** (2 bytes) – the destination connection ID allows the routing of the packet through the virtual circuit.
- **Source connection ID** (2 bytes) – the source connection ID identifies the source station when it is transmitted through the virtual circuit.

- **Sequence number** (2 bytes) – this field contains the sequence number of the packet sent. When the receiver receives the packet, the destination error checks the packet and sends back an acknowledgement with the previously received packet number in it.
- **Acknowledgement number** (2 bytes) – this acknowledgement number is incremented by the destination when it receives a packet. It is in this field that the destination station puts the last correctly received packet sequence number.
- **Allocation number** (2 bytes) – this field informs the source station of the number of buffers the destination station can allocate to SPX connections.
- **Data** (up to 534 bytes).

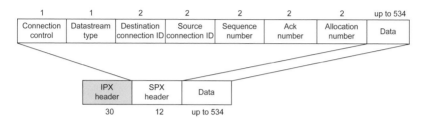

Figure D3.5 SPX packet format

D3.3.3 RIP

The NetWare Routing Information Protocol (RIP) is used to keep routers updated on the best routes through the network. RIP information is delivered to routers via IPX packets. Figure D3.6 illustrates the information fields in an RIP packet. The RIP packet is contained in the field which would normally be occupied by the SPX packet.

Routers are used within networks to pass packets from one network to another in an optimal way (and error-free with a minimal time delay). A router reads IPX packets and examines the destination address of the node. If the node is on another network then it routes the packet in the required direction. This routing tends not to be fixed as the best route will depend on network traffic at given times. Thus, the router needs to keep the routing tables up to date; RIP allows routers to exchange their current routing tables with other routers.

The RIP packet allows routers to request or report on multiple reachable networks within a single RIP packet. These routes are listed one after another (Figure D3.6 shows two routing entries). Thus each RIP packet has only one operation field, but has multiple entries of the network number, the number of router hops, and the number of tick fields, up to the length limit of the IPX packet.

The fields are:

- **Operation** (2 bytes) – this field indicates that the RIP packet is either a request or a response.
- **Network number** (4 bytes) – this field defines the assigned network address number to which the routing information applies.
- **Number of router hops** (2 bytes) – this field indicates the number of routers that a packet must go through in order to reach the required destination. Each router adds a single hop.
- **Number of ticks** (2 bytes) – this field indicates the amount of time (in 1/18 second) that it takes a packet to reach the given destination. Note that a route which has the fewest hops may not necessarily be the fastest.

RIP packets add to the general network traffic as each router broadcasts its entire routing table every 60 seconds. This shortcoming has been addressed by NetWare 4/5.

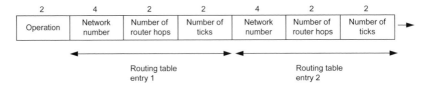

Figure D3.6 RIP packet format

D3.3.4 SAP

Every 60 seconds each server transmits a **SAP** (Service Advertising Protocol) packet which gives its address and tells other servers which services it offers. These packets are read by special agent processes running on the routers which then construct a database that defines which servers are operational and where they are located.

When the client node is first booted it transmits a request in the network asking for the location of the nearest server. The agent on the router then reads this request and matches it up to the best server. This choice is then sent back to the client. The client then establishes an **NCP** (NetWare Core Protocol) connection with the server, from which the client and server negotiate the maximum packet size. After this, the client can access the networked file system and other NetWare services.

Figure D3.7 illustrates the contents of a SAP packet. It can be seen that each SAP packet contains a single operation field and data on up to seven servers. The fields are:

- **Operation type** (2 bytes) – defines whether the SAP packet is server information request or a broadcast of server information.
- **Server type** (2 bytes) – defines the type of service offered by a server. These services are identified by a binary pattern, such as:

File server	0000 1000	Job server	0000 1001
Gateway	0000 1010	Print server	0000 0111
Archive server	0000 1001	SNA gateway	0010 0001
Remote bridge server	0010 0100	TCP/IP gateway	0010 0111
NetWare access server	1001 1000		

- **Server name** (48 bytes) – which identifies the actual name of the server or host offering the service defined in the service type field.
- **Network address** (4 bytes) – which defines the address of the network to which the server is attached.
- **Node address** (6 bytes) – which defines the actual MAC address of the server.
- **Socket address** (6 bytes) – which defines the socket address on the server assigned to this particular type of service.
- **Hops to server** (2 bytes) – which indicates the number of hops to reach the particular service.

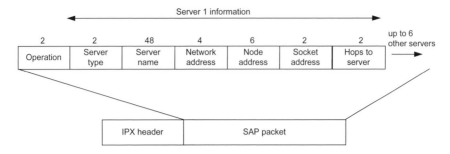

Figure D3.7 SAP packet format

The SAP protocol allows network resources to advertise their services, every 60 seconds (by default, but this can be changed if the SAP advertisements cause too much network traffic). For example a print server would advertise with a SAP server of 7. Devices which route data across networks, such as routers, listen to the SAP updates and build a table of all known services and associated network addresses. When a Novell client requires a particular network server, the client sends out a GNS (Get Nearest Server) request. If a Novell server is on the current network segment it will respond to the GNS request, otherwise the router responds with a server address from its own SAP table. The client is then able to communicate with the service directly. The SAP protocol is thus creates a dynamic system, where new services can be quickly advertised, and existing services can be deleted from the network. For example a printer server can be easily added to the network, as it will advertise itself using SAP. Connected routers will build up their own SAP table, in order that they may respond to GNS requests from Novell clients. An aging technique is used by the routers to age-out SAP table entries if they have not advertised their services for a while (as they have probably gone off-line, or are too busy). Note that routers do not forward SAP broadcasts, but use them to build up their own SAP table, which they then pass to neighboring routers. The router can setup, with ACLs, whether SAP tables are accepted or forwarded.

The Cisco IOS command to display the connected Novell servers is as follows:

```
Myrouter > show ipx servers
Codes: P - Periodic, I - Incremental, H - Holddown, S - Static
1 Total IPX Servers         ◄──────────────  Number of servers


Table ordered is based on router and server info
    Type  Name          Net Address Port        Route   Hops  Itf
P   7     Nap_server    CC00.0043.1123.3DDE:0451  200/1   2     Eth0
```

where Type identifies the SAP service number, Name identifies the server name, the Net Address and Port identifies the IPX address and the port.

To show the IPX routing table:

```
Myrouter > show ipx route
Codes: C - Connected primary network, c - connected secondary network, R - RIP,
E - EIGRP, S - Static, W - IPXWAN connected
5 total IPX routes     ◄──────────────  Number of routes in the IPX table

Up to 2 parallel paths allowed. Novell routing protocol variant in use
```

```
R Net 2B10 [8/1] via 2B20.0000.0c03.13d3,  40 sec,  Serial1
   via 2B30.0000.0000.D101.aa11,  40 sec,  Serial 0
C Net 2B30 (X25),   Serial0
C Net 2B20 (HDLC),  Serial1
C Net 2B40 (NOVELL-ETHER),  Ethernet0
C Net 2B50 (NOVELL-ETHER),  Ethernet1
```

[R] Route learnt through an RIP update.
Net 2B10 – Destination network address is 2B10.
[8/1] identifies that the network is eight clock ticks away or one hop. The general format is [*delay/ metric*], where *delay* defines the number of ticks of the IBM clock to the destination, and *metric* is the number of hops to the network.
Via. The *via* defines the next hop on the route. The address follows it.
2B20.*etc.* Defines the next hop on the path.
40 sec. This defines the time that information was last received about the network (age).
Serial1. Next port is reachable from this port.

The first line shows that there are two possible routes to the destination (2B10), and that there is a possibility to load share as both Serial1 (2B20 network) and Serial0 (2B30 network) have an equal hop metric. In this case, the destination is one hop away (or 8 IBM clock ticks). The next four lines show the directly connected networks (2B20, 2B30, 2B40 and 2B5). It can be seen, for example, that the network number is 2B40, and the encapsulation is NOVELL-ETHER. The C shows that the information was learned from a directly connected primary network.

Other IPX commands include:

- `show ipx interface`   IPX status and parameters
- `show ipx route`   Routing table contents
- `show ipx traffic`   Number and types of packets

and debug parameters with:

- `debug ipx routing activity`   Information on routing updates
- `debug ipx sap`   Information on SAP update packets

D3.3.5   SAP debugging

Cisco routers can uses the:

```
debug ipx sap [events|activity]
```

command to display information on SAP packets that are transmitted or received. The events option provides simple information, while activity gives more detail. SAP responses can be:

0x1   General query
0x2   General response
0x3   GNS request
0x4   GNS response

The following gives a sample run:

```
Novel SAP: at 00278978
I SAP Response type 0x2 len 180  arc:  180.0000.1c20.470e
                                 dest: 180.ffff.ffff.ffff (452)
type 0x4, "HELLO" 111.1002.1004.0F05 (451), 2 hops
```

D3.3.6 Defining maximum paths

When there are two or more routes with an equal cost, the router can uses load sharing on these routes. To set the maximum number of equal-cost paths the router uses:

```
Router # config t
Router(config)# ipx maximum-paths paths
```

command, where paths defines the maximum number of equal-cost paths (from 1 to 512). It is unset using the following command:

```
Router # config t
Router(config)# no ipx maximum-paths paths
```

The sharing is a global configuration, and will thus apply to all the ports on a router. In addition, the sharing occurs on a packet-by-packet basis, in a round-robin approach. For example if there are three equal cost routes, the router sends the first packet on the first path, the next packet on the second route, and the next packet on the third route. Next, it sends the next packet on the first route again, and so on.

A reduction in the number of equal-cost paths reduces the amount of memory used within the router if the network has a large configuration.

D3.3.7 NCP

The clients and servers communicate using the NetWare Core Protocols (NCPs). They have the following operation:

- The NETx shell reads the application program request and decides whether it should direct it to the server.
- If it does redirect, then it sends a message within an NCP packet, which is then encapsulated within an IPX packet and transmitted to the server.

Figure D3.8 illustrates the packet layout and encapsulation of an NCP packet. The fields are:

- **Request type** (2 bytes) – which gives the category of NCP communications. Among the possible types are:

Busy message	1001 1001 1001 1001
Create a service	0001 0001 0001 0001
Service request from workstation	0010 0010 0010 0010
Service response from server	0011 0011 0011 0011
Terminate a service connection	0101 0101 0101 0101

For example, the create-a-service request is initiated at login time and a terminate-a-connection request is sent at logout.

- **Sequence number** (1 byte) – which contains a request sequence number. The client reads the sequence number so that it knows the request to which the server is responding.
- **Connection number** (1 byte) – a unique number which is assigned when the user logs into the server.
- **Task number** (1 byte) – which identifies the application program on the client which issued the service request.
- **Function code** (1 byte) – which defines the NCP message or commands. Example codes are:

Close a file	0100 0010	Create a file	0100 1101
Delete a file	0100 0100	Get a directory entry	0001 1111
Get file size	0100 0000	Open a file	0100 1100
Rename a file	0100 0101	Extended functions	0001 0110

Extended functions can be defined after the 0001 0110 field.
- **NCP message** (up to 539 bytes) – the NCP message field contains additional information which is passed between the clients and servers. If the function code contains 0001 0110 then this field will contain subfunction codes.

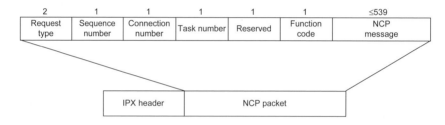

Figure D3.8 NCP packet format

D3.4   Novel NetWare set-up

NetWare 3.x and 4/5 use the Open Data-Link Interface (**ODI**) to interface NetWare to the NIC. Figure D3.9 shows how the NetWare fits into the OSI model. ODI is similar to NDIS in Windows NT and was developed jointly between Apple and Novell. It provides a standard vendor-independent method to interface the software and the hardware.

A typical login procedure for a NetWare 3.x network is:

```
LSL.COM
NE2000
IPXODI
NETx /PS=EECE_1
F:
LOGIN
```

The program LSL (link support layer) provides a foundation for the MAC layer to communicate with multiple protocols. An interface adapter driver (in this case NE2000) provides a MAC layer driver and is used to communicate with the interface card. This driver is known as a multilink interface driver (**MLID**). After this driver is installed, the program IPXODI is then installed. This program normally communicates with LSL and applications.

The NETx program communicates with the server and sets up a connection with the server EECE_1. This then sets up a local disk partition of F: (onto which the user's network directory will be mounted). Next the user logs into the network with the command LOGIN.

D3.4.1 ODI

ODI allows users to load several protocol stacks (such as TCP/IP and SPX/IPX) simultaneously for operation with a single NIC. It also allows support to link protocol drivers to adapter drivers. Figure D3.9 shows the architecture of the ODI interface. The **LSL** layer supports multiple protocols and it reads from a file NET.CFG, which contains information on the network adapter and the protocol driver, such as the interface adapter, frame type and protocol.

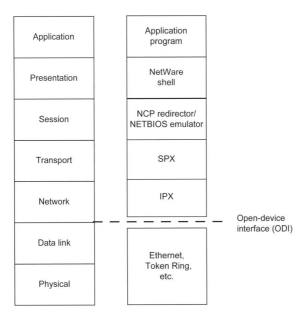

Figure D3.9 OSI model and NetWare 3.x

A sample NET.CFG file is:

```
Link Driver NE2000
    Int #1 11
    Port #1 320
    Frame Ethernet_II
    Frame Ethernet_802.3
    Protocol IPX 0 Ethernet_802.3
        Protocol Ethdev 0 Ethernet_II
```

This configuration file defines the interface adapter as using interrupt line 11, having a base address of 320h, operating IPX, Ethernet 802.3 frame type and following the Ethernet II protocol. Network interface card drivers (such as NE2000, from the previous set-up) are referred to as a multilink interface driver (MLID).

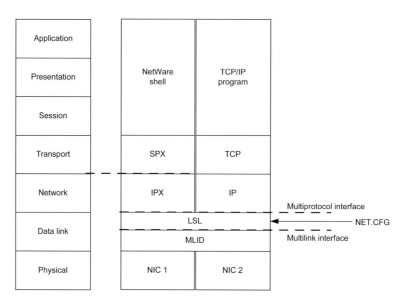

Figure D3.10   ODI architecture

D4   NetBEUI and NetBIOS

D4.1   Introduction

NetBEUI (NetBIOS Extended User Interface) has been used with network operating systems, such as Microsoft LAN manager and OS/2 LAN server. It is the Microsoft implementation of the NetBIOS standard. In Microsoft Windows, the NetBEUI frame (NBF) protocol stack gives backward compatibility with existing NetBEUI implementations and also provides for enhanced implementations. NetBEUI is the standard technique that NT clients and servers use to intercommunicate.

NBF is similar to TCP/IP and SPX/IPX. It is used to establish a session between a client and a server, and also to provide the reliable transport of the data across the connection-oriented session. Thus, NetBEUI tries to provide reliable data transfer through error checking and acknowledgement of each successfully received data packet. In the standard form of NetBEUI each packet must be acknowledged after its delivery. This is wasteful in time. Windows NT uses NBF which improves NetBEUI as it allows several packets to be sent before requiring an acknowledgement (called an adaptive sliding window protocol).

Each NetBEUI is assigned a 1-byte session number and thus allows a maximum of 254 simultaneously active sessions (as two of the connection numbers are reserved). NBF enhances this by allowing 254 connections to computers with 254 sessions for each connection (thus there is a maximum of 254×254 sessions).

The basic NetBIOS specification does not allow data to be routed over interconnected networks, but two RFC's exist for the integration NetBIOS to be used over routers:

- **RFC1001**. Protocol Standard for a NetBIOS Service on a TCP/UDP Transport: Concepts and Methods
- **RFC1002**. Protocol Standard for a NetBIOS Service on a TCP/UDP Transport: Detailed Specifications

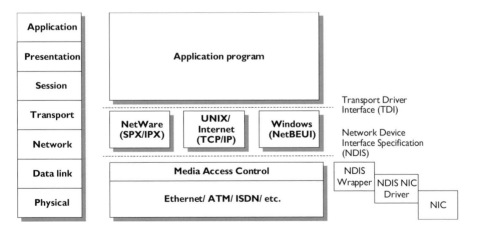

Figure D4.1   Microsoft Windows network interfaces

D4.2   NetBIOS

When the PC was first introduced it had limited power, and typically did not connect to other computers. Mainframe computers typically used fairly complex networking protocols to allow them to communicate in a robust fashion. NetBIOS was designed for groups of PCs to be part of a shared broadcast system. It has following features:

- Connection-oriented or connectionless. It can be connection oriented (using sessions) and connectionless (using datagrams).
- Permits broadcasts and multicasts.
- Dynamic and distributed allocation of names.
- Dynamic mechanisms for the location of resources, establish connections, send and receive data with an application peer, and the terminate connections. These are typically named NetBIOS Service.

D4.2.1   Interface to application programs

NetBIOS uses a flat naming structure with 16 alphanumeric characters (which cannot start with a *). All resources are referenced by name, and an application, representing a resource, registers one or more names that it wishes to use. The registration is achieved through a bidding system (that is, a contentious system), where a bid is made for an exclusive (unique) or shared (group) ownership. Each application then contends with the other applications in real time. There is a period of time where stations must contend for a name, if no objectives are received then implicit permission is granted to the station. A unique name can only be held by one station at a time. In a Microsoft network, computers identify themselves with their NetBIOS name. Each is 16 characters long, and the 16th character represents the purpose of the name. An example list of a WINS database is:

```
Name            Type      Status
FRED            <00>      UNIQUE   Registered
BERT            <00>      UNIQUE   Registered
STAFF           <1C>      GROUP    Registered
STUDENT         <1E>      GROUP    Registered
```

The values for the 16th byte are:

00	Workstation	03	Message service
06	RAS server service	1B	Domain master browser
1C	Domain group name	1D	Master brower's name
1E	Normal group name (workgroup)	1F	NetDDE service
20	Server service	21	RAS client
BE	Network Monitor Agent	BF	Network Monitor Utility

On Windows, the names in the WINS database can be shown with the `nbstat` command. The Lmhosts file can be setup to hold NetBIOS names (commonly used for computer names) to IP addresses for hosts that are not located on the local subnet. This file is typically contained in *systemroot*\System32\Drivers\Etc folder. An example format is:

```
#IP-address        host-name
146.176.1.3        bills_pc
```

```
146.176.144.10    fred_pc    #DOM:STAFF

#BEGIN_ALTERNATE
#INCLUDE \\myserver\public\lmhosts
#INCLUDE \\remoteserver\public\lmhosts
#END_ALTERNATE
```

where comments have a preceding '#' symbol. To preserve compatibility with previous version of Microsoft LAN Manager, special commands have been included after the comment symbol. These include:

```
#PRE
#DOM:domain
#INCLUDE fname
#BEGIN_ALTERNATE
#END_ALTERNATE
```

where

#PRE	specifies the name is preloaded into the memory of the computer and no further references to the LMHOSTS file will be made.
#DOM:domain	specifies the name of the domain that the node belongs to.
#BEGIN_ALTERNATE and #END_ALTERNATE	are used to group multiple #include's
#include fname	specifies other LMHOST files to include.

The HOSTS file format is IP address followed by the fully qualified name (FQDN) and then any aliases. Comments have a preceding '#' symbol. For example:

```
#IP Address      FQDN         Aliases
146.176.1.3      superjanet   janet
146.176.144.10   hp
146.176.145.21   mimas
146.176.144.11   mwave
146.176.144.13   vax
146.176.146.23   oberon
146.176.145.23   oberon
```

The basic primitives for the Name Service are:

- **Add Name.** Used when a requesting application wants exclusive use of a name.
- **Add Group Name.** Used when the requesting application wants to share a name with other applications.
- **Delete Name.** Provides for an explicit name deletion function which allows applications to remove a registered name. This can occur when a computer goes off-line, and must release the name. The application no longer requires use of the name.

In Windows, an error 642 is generated when a node tries to use a NetBIOS name that has already been registered.

D4.2.2 Session service

The session server is important is it provides for a robust mechanism for two NetBIOS applications to communicate. These are sent as sequenced messages, where each message can use up to 131,071 bytes. There can also be multiple sessions between any two named applications.

The basic Session Service primitives are:

- **Call**. This initiates a session with a process that listens under the specified name. A calling entity indicates its calling name (which has been previously registered to the caller) and a called name.
- **Listen**. This is used to accept an incoming call from any caller, or from a specific caller.
- **Hang Up**. This is used to hang-up a session. Any session data in involved in the session is sent before the session is terminated.
- **Send**. This is used to transmit a single message. If the message cannot be sent, the session is terminated.
- **Receive data**. This is used to receive messages.
- **Session Status**. This is used to gain information on the current sessions, under the specified name.

D4.2.3 Datagram service

The NetBIOS datagram service is similar to UDP, which is an unreliable, non-sequenced, connectionless service. These datagrams are send using a previously registered name, which can either be a specific name or a broadcast (to all the holders of a name). The datagram receiver is informed of the sending and receiving names.

The primitives for the Datagram Service are:

- **Send Datagram**. This is used to send a datagram to an application that is associated with the specified name (either unique or a group). If it is sent to a group then every member of the group will receive the datagram.
- **Send Broadcast Datagram**. This is used to broadcast a datagram to any application with a Receive Broadcast Datagram set.
- **Receive Datagram**. This is used to receive a datagram sent by a specified originating name to the specified name.
- **Receive Broadcast Datagram**. This is used to receive a datagram which has been sent as a broadcast.

D4.3   NetBIOS over TCP/IP (NetBT)

NetBIOS over TCP/IP is important as it may not be possible to connect to computers running the Microsoft Windows operating system from other operating systems, typically ones running TCP/IP or AppleTalk. If it is disabled on a Windows computer, the node cannot use broadcast-based NetBIOS name resolution to resolve computer names to IP addresses for computers on a network segment (known as a subnet). When disabled there must be a DNS server and the nodes must be registered with the DNS server, or configure the entries in the local Hosts file for each computer.

The outline specification is defined in RFC1001 and RFC1002, and supports many of the important Internet specifications, such as:

- TCP [RFC793] and UDP [RFC768].
- IP [RFC791].
- Assigned Numbers [RFC 990],

- Subnets [RFC922, RFC950, RFC919],
- DNS [RFC882, RFC883, RFC973, RFC974].
- Internet Multicast [RFC966, RFC988].

As previously mentioned NetBIOS uses registered names. The range of which the name is known is the NetBIOS *scope*. All broadcast and multicast datagram will reach the full extent to the NetBIOS scope. Each NetBIOS scope has a *scope identifier*, which is an identifier defining the requirements of the domain name system for domain names.

As each of the nodes must run over an internet (thus can either be a private internet, or connection to the Internet), they must have an IP address associated with them. Each end-node then has a defined functionality:

- **Broadcast nodes** (B nodes). These nodes communicate using a mixture of UDP datagrams and TCP connections. They can freely interoperate with each other in the broadcast area.
- **Point-to-point nodes** (P nodes). These nodes communicate using only directed UDP datagrams and TCP sessions. They do not listen for broadcast UDP packets, and rely on rely on NetBIOS name and datagram distribution servers.
- **Mixed mode** (M nodes). These nodes operate as P nodes, but have certain B node characteristics, and can thus use broadcast and unicast. They can use both broadcast and unicast. In a broadcast mode, the nodes are most likely to exist on the local network, rather than on the wider internet.

If the NetBIOS nodes to not have a preloaded name-to-address table, they must dynamically resolve names. This can either be achieved with a broadcast or a mediated point-to-point method.

D4.4 NWLink IPX/SPX/NetBIOS Compatible Transport Protocol

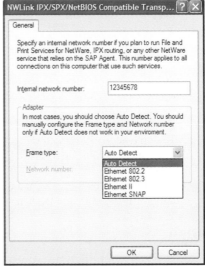

The NWLink IPX/SPX/NetBIOS protocol is a useful protocol in running applications over a network, as it does not use TCP/IP (which is open to users reading the contents of the data packets). The external network number is a 4-byte hexadecimal number that is used for addressing and routing. It corresponds to the physical network adapters and networks. For the network to operation, all computers must have the same external network number, and all external network numbers must be **unique** to the IPX internetwork. The external network number can be determined using the IPXROUTE command. For example:

```
C:\>ipxroute config
```

NWLink IPX Routing and Source Routing

```
Control Program v2.00

Num  Name                        Network    Node            Frame
===================================================================
0.   Internal                    12345678   000000000001    [None ]
1.   IpxLoopbackAdapter          12345678   000000000002    [802.2]
2.   Network Bridge (Network B   00000000   02038a000011    [802.2]
3.   Wireless Network Connecti   00000000   0060b368b110    [802.2]
4.   NDISWANIPX                  00000000   509c20524153    [EthII] -
```

This shows that the network number is 12345678. Notice that the MAC address of the network card is taken as part of the node address, such as:

```
Ethernet adapter Wireless Network Connection 3:

        Connection-specific DNS Suffix  . :
        Description . . . . . . . . . .: IEEE 802.11 Wireless LAN/PC Card(5V)
        Physical Address. . . . . . .: 00-60-B3-68-B1-10
        Dhcp Enabled. . . . . . . . .: No
        IP Address. . . . . . . . . .: 192.168.0.12
        Subnet Mask . . . . . . . . .: 255.255.255.0
```

The internal network number is a 4-byte hexadecimal number which is used for addressing and routing purposes. It identifies a **virtual network** inside a computer, and does not have to be unique, as it is a local network. This type of network address is useful for setting up a local network, which does not connect to a unique network address. It is thus useful in running games over a home network.

A listing help option for the IPXROUTE command gives:

```
NWLink IPX Routing and Source Routing Control Program v2.00
Display and modify information about the routing tables used by IPX.

IPX Routing Options
-------------------
IPXROUTE servers [/type=xxxx]
   servers       Displays the SAP table for the specified
                 server type. Server type is a 16-bit integer value.
                 For example use IPXROUTE servers /type=4 to display
                 all file servers. If no type is specified,
                 servers of all types are shown. The displayed
                 list is sorted by server name.

IPXROUTE ripout network
   ripout        Discovers the reachability of "network" (specified
                 in host order) by consulting the IPX Stack's
                 route table and sending out a rip request if
                 neccessary.

IPXROUTE resolve guid|name adapter-name
   resolve       Resolves the name of the given adapter to its
                 guid or friendly version.

Source Routing Options
----------------------
IPXROUTE board=n clear def gbr mbr remove=xxxxxxxxxxx
IPXROUTE config

   board=n       Specify the board number to check.
   clear         Clear the source routing table
   def           Send packets that are destined for an
```

	unknown address to the ALL ROUTES broadcast (Default is SINGLE ROUTE broadcast).
gbr	Send packets that are destined for the broadcast address (FFFF FFFF FFFF) to the ALL ROUTES broadcast (Default is SINGLE ROUTE broadcast).
mbr	Send packets that are destined for a multicast address (C000 xxxx xxxx) to the ALL ROUTES broadcast (Default is SINGLE ROUTE broadcast).
remove=xxxx	Remove the given mac address from the source routing table.
config	Displays information on all the bindings that IPX is configured for.

All parameters should be separated by spaces.

D5 PPP, SLIP and VPN's

D5.1 Introduction

The Serial Line Internet Protocol (SLIP) was one of the first standard protocols which allows access to remote servers. It is typically used with UNIX remote access servers. The standards which relate to SLIP include:

RFC1144   Compressing TCP/IP Headers for Low-Speed Serial Links
RFC1055   A Nonstandard for Transmission of IP Datagrams Over Serial Lines: SLIP

The Point-to Point Protocol (PPP) has many enhancements over SLIP, and has been defined as a set of protocols which allow remote access to different types of computer systems, and operating systems (Figure D5.1). It is typically used in dial-up connections, and also allows a remote access server to receive calls from users. PPP permits several different types of authentication, and data compression and encryption. As the complete login service can be automated, it can be used in applications where remote data requires to be sent, without the requirement for user intervention.

PPP is now one of the most widely used WAN protocols, as it supports:

- Data link setup.
- Dynamic assignment of IP addresses.
- Error detection.
- Link configuration and link quality testing.
- Negotiation options for capabilities such as network-layer address negotiation and data compression negotiations
- Network protocol multiplexing.

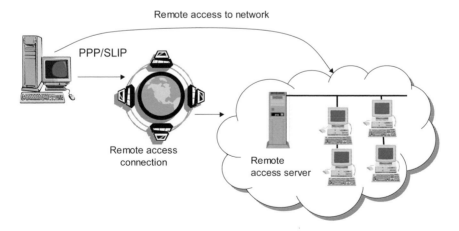

Figure D5.1   PPP/SLIP

PPP provides router-to-router and host-to-network connections over both synchronous and asynchronous circuits. It also supports multiple networking protocols, including TCP/IP, NetBEUI and IPX. Along with PPP, Point-to-Point Tunneling Protocol (PPTP) and Layer 2 Tunneling Protocol (L2TP) can be used to set up Virtual Private Networks (VPN). A VPN is a logical extension to private networks and involves encapsulating, encrypting, and authenticated connections over shared or public networks. VPN connections can provide remote access and routed connections to private networks over the Internet.

PPTP enables remote users to access corporate networks in a secure way over the Internet or from a dial-up connection provided through an Internet service provider (ISP). It tunnels, or encapsulates, IP, IPX, AppleTalk, DECNet or NetBEUI traffic into IP packets (Figure D5.2). Thus, users can run remote applications using the required network protocol. The L2TP differs from PPTP in that it does not require IP connectivity between the client and the server. In L2TP, only the tunnel mechanism provide packet-oriented point-to-point connectivity. It can thus be used over main different types of networks, such as ATM, Frame Relay, and X.25.

The main PPP specifications are defined in the following RFC's:

RFC1331   PPP
RFC1332   PPP Internet Protocol Control Protocol (IPCP)
RFC1334   PPP Authentication Protocols
RFC1549   PPP in HDLC Framing
RFC1552   PPP Internetwork Packet Exchange Control Protocol (IPXCP)
RFC1570   PPP LCP Extensions
RFC1661   Link Control Protocol (LCP)
RFC1962   The PPP Compression Control Protocol (CCP)

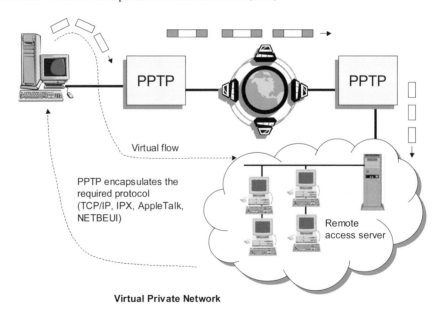

Figure D5.2   PPTP

RFC1990 PPP Multilink Protocol
RFC2097 PPP NetBIOS Frames Control Protocol (NBFCP)
RFC2125 PPP Bandwidth Allocation Protocol (BAP), The PPP Bandwidth Allocation Control Protocol (BACP)
RFC2284 PPP Extensible Authentication Protocol (EAP)

PPP uses a layered architecture, as shown in the Figure. With its lower-level functions, PPP can use:

- Synchronous physical media. This would include services such as in ISDN networks.
- Asynchronous physical media. This includes dialup connections for modems.

PPP has been designed to encapsulate many of the widely available network layer protocols, such as IP, IPX and AppleTalk. These are supported with NCPs, as illustrated in Figure D5.3. Examples include:

- ACP   AppleTalk Control Protocol
- IPCP   Internet Protocol Control Protocol
- IPXCP   Internetwork Packet Exchange Control Protocol

These are functional fields containing standardized codes to indicate the network-layer protocol type that PPP encapsulates.

Figure 5.4 shows an example window from a Dial-up connection on a Windows-based computer. It can be seen that this connection can support both PPP and SLIP. PPP is normally supported by more remote access systems, and allows for advanced authentication and for the support of more network protocols.

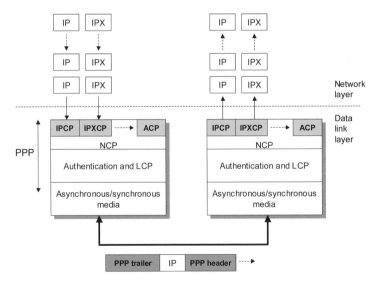

Figure D5.3   PPP protocol stack

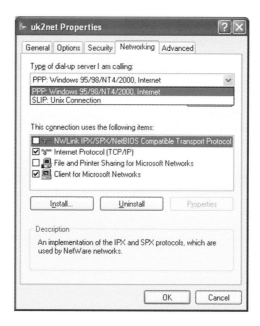

Figure D5.4 PPP or SLIP protocol selection for a dial-up connection

D5.2   Frame format

The PPP frame format is based on HDLC (as defined in Chapter C8). The fields are illustrated in Figure D5.5, and are defined as:

- **Flag**. This indicates the start or end of a frame, and uses the 01111110b sequence. Bit stuffing is used in the rest of the frame to avoid the same sequence occurring in any other part of the frame.
- **Address**. In PPP this is set to the standard broadcast address of 11111111b. PPP does not assign any individual station addresses.
- Control. [1 byte]. This is set to 00000011b (Unnumbered Information (UI) command with the P/F bit set to zero), which defines that the transmission of data in an unsequenced frame format.
- **Protocol**. [2 bytes] This identifies the protocol encapsulated in the data field of the frame.
- **Data**. [0 or more bytes]. This contains the encapsulated data protocol. The maximum length is typically set to 1500 bytes, but its size is dynamically determined as the end flag defines the end, thus the end of the data field is two bytes away from the end flag (as the FCS is 2 bytes long).
- **FCS**. Typically 2 bytes]. This is used to provide error control.

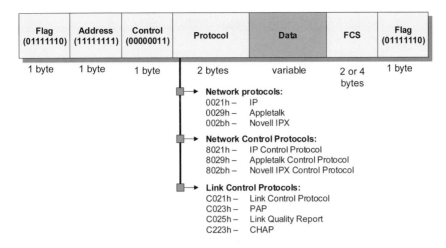

Figure D5.5 PPP frame format

The protocol values are grouped:

0xxx – 3xxx – Network Layer Protocols
0021	Internet Protocol (IP)
0023	OSI Network Layer
0025	Xerox NS IDP
0027	DECnet Phase IV
0029	Appletalk
002b	Novell IPX
002d	Van Jacobson Compressed TCP/IP
002f	Van Jacobson Uncompressed TCP/IP
0031	Bridging PDU
0033	Stream Protocol (ST-II)
0035	Banyan Vines
0201	802.1d Hello Packets
0231	Luxcom
0233	Sigma Network Systems

8xxx – Bxxx – Network Control Protocols (NCPs)
8021	Internet Protocol Control Protocol (IPCP)
8023	OSI Network Layer Control Protocol
8025	Xerox NS IDP Control Protocol
8027	DECnet Phase IV Control Protocol
8029	Appletalk Control Protocol (ACP)
802b	Novell IPX Control Protocol (IPXCP)
8031	Bridging NCP
8033	Stream Protocol Control Protocol
8035	Banyan Vines Control Protocol

Cxxx- Fxxxx – Link Layer Protocols (LLPs)
c021	Link Control Protocol (LCP)

c023	Password Authentication Protocol (PAP)
c025	Link Quality Report
c223	Challenge Handshake Authentication Protocol (CHAP)

D5.3   Point-to-Point Protocol over Ethernet (PPPoE)

The PPPoE protocols allow remote users to connect to an Ethernet network over a point-to-point connection. It has been defined by the Internet Engineering Task Force (IETF) in:

RFC2516   A Method for Transmitting PPP over Ethernet (PPPoE)

D5.4   PPP operation

After an initial connection to a remote PPP server (see Figure D5.1 for the setting up the initial connection), PPP goes though several negotiation states, these are:

- **Link Control Protocols (LCP)**. This state is used to establish and configure link and framing settings, such as maximum frame size.
- **Authentication protocols**. This state is used to determine the level of security required, which can range from a plaintext (unencrypted) password-based authentication, to encrypted, highly secure smart card authentication.
- **Network control protocols (NCP)**. This state is used to establish and configure different network protocol settings for IP and IPX. This might also include the negotiated protocol header compression and the compression control protocol (CCP).

If successful, the peer (client) can be authenticated to the server. Finally, NCP packets are sent to select and configure one or more network-layer protocols. If successful, the PPP encapsulated packets can be sent. The link remains configured until explicit LCP or NCP packets close the link down, or until either the user or the administrator hangs up the line, or the connection breaks. Figure 5.6 shows the main states of the connection, and Figure 5.6 illustrates the exchange of LCP and NCP frames. In the Link Dead state, the connection is inactive. For a connection LCP configure packets are used to set the connection up (Link Establishment Phase). The UP event indicates that the lower layer can carry packets, while the Down event indicates that the link cannot carry packets.

D5.4.1   Link Control Protocols

Once the two devices to be connected have made a connection, they must first send LCP packets to configure and test the data link (Figure D5.7). For the LCP packets, the protocol field is set to **c021**. There are three classes of LCP packets:

- **Link Configuration packets**. These are used to establish and configure a link (Configure-Request, Configure-Ack, Configure-Nak and Configure-Reject).
- **Link Termination packets**. These are used to terminate a link (Terminate-Request and Terminate-Ack).
- **Link Maintenance packets**. These are used to manage and debug a link (Code-Reject, Protocol-Reject, Echo-Request, Echo-Reply, and Discard-Request).

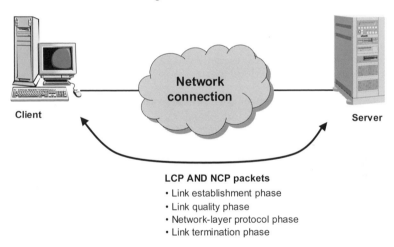

LCP configuration
packets

Figure D5.6 PPP states

LCP AND NCP packets
- Link establishment phase
- Link quality phase
- Network-layer protocol phase
- Link termination phase

Figure D5.7 LCP and NCP frames

The format of the LCP is given in Figure 5.8. The values for the Code field define the LCP packet type; the Identifier field helps in matching requests with replies, and the Length field is two octets and indicates the length of the LCP packet including the Code, Identifier, Length and Data fields.

The Code values are:

1	Configure-Request	2	Configure-Ack
3	Configure-Nak	4	Configure-Reject
5	Terminate-Request	6	Terminate-Ack
7	Code-Reject	8	Protocol-Reject

9   Echo-Request   10   Echo-Reply
11 Discard-Request   12   RESERVED

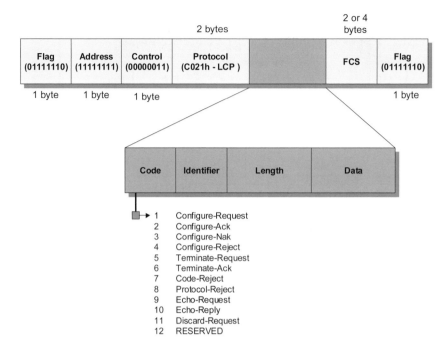

Figure D5.8   LCP frames format

Initially a connection starts with an exchange of Configure-Request packets, and the LCP Opened State is entered with the successful exchange of Configure-Ack packets. The Configure-Request packet contains an Options field in which the link parameters can be negotiate, such as the maximum receive unit, asynchronous control character mappings, the authentication method, quality protocol, and so on. The first 8 bits of the Format field defines the parameter, these are:

1   Maximum-Receive-Unit. Defines the maximum frame size. This is typical set to a maximum of 1500 bytes.
2   Async-Control-Character-Map.
3   Authentication-Protocol. The settings are either C023h (Password Authentication Protocol) or C223h (Challenge Handshake Authentication Protocol).
4   Quality-Protocol.
5   Magic-Number.
6   RESERVED
7   Protocol-Field-Compression.
8   Address-and-Control-Field-Compression.

D5.4.2   Authentication protocols

The authentication phase allows the peer connection to be authenticated before the network protocol is negotiated. By default, no authentication is required. The two main authentication protocols are PAP and CHAP. Figure 5.9 shows some of the authentication available for a PPP connection. These include PAP, CHAP, SHAP and MS-CHAP.

Figure D5.9 LCP frames format

D5.4.3 Network Control Protocols

After the authentication phase, each network-layer protocol must be configured separately using the required NCP. After the NCP has reached the Open state then the link carries the corresponding protocol packets, but it can also carry LCP and NCP packets.

D5.4.4 Link termination phase

The link is terminated when there is a loss of the carrier, an authentication failure, link quality failure, or when the link has been inactive for a given amount of time (defined by the idle-period timer). The link can also be closed with an LCP packet (such as with Terminate-Request).

D5.4.5 FCS

The code to produce the FCS is given next, where u16 is an unsigned 16-bit value. It is calculated over the Address, Control, Protocol and Information fields, but not including any bits inserted for bit stuffing.

```
typedef unsigned short u16;
```

```c
static u16 fcstab[256] = {
    0x0000, 0x1189, 0x2312, 0x329b, 0x4624, 0x57ad, 0x6536, 0x74bf,
    0x8c48, 0x9dc1, 0xaf5a, 0xbed3, 0xca6c, 0xdbe5, 0xe97e, 0xf8f7,
    0x1081, 0x0108, 0x3393, 0x221a, 0x56a5, 0x472c, 0x75b7, 0x643e,
    0x9cc9, 0x8d40, 0xbfdb, 0xae52, 0xdaed, 0xcb64, 0xf9ff, 0xe876,
    0x2102, 0x308b, 0x0210, 0x1399, 0x6726, 0x76af, 0x4434, 0x55bd,
    0xad4a, 0xbcc3, 0x8e58, 0x9fd1, 0xeb6e, 0xfae7, 0xc87c, 0xd9f5,
    0x3183, 0x200a, 0x1291, 0x0318, 0x77a7, 0x662e, 0x54b5, 0x453c,
    0xbdcb, 0xac42, 0x9ed9, 0x8f50, 0xfbef, 0xea66, 0xd8fd, 0xc974,
    0x4204, 0x538d, 0x6116, 0x709f, 0x0420, 0x15a9, 0x2732, 0x36bb,
    0xce4c, 0xdfc5, 0xed5e, 0xfcd7, 0x8868, 0x99e1, 0xab7a, 0xbaf3,
    0x5285, 0x430c, 0x7197, 0x601e, 0x14a1, 0x0528, 0x37b3, 0x263a,
    0xdecd, 0xcf44, 0xfddf, 0xec56, 0x98e9, 0x8960, 0xbbfb, 0xaa72,
    0x6306, 0x728f, 0x4014, 0x519d, 0x2522, 0x34ab, 0x0630, 0x17b9,
    0xef4e, 0xfec7, 0xcc5c, 0xddd5, 0xa96a, 0xb8e3, 0x8a78, 0x9bf1,
    0x7387, 0x620e, 0x5095, 0x411c, 0x35a3, 0x242a, 0x16b1, 0x0738,
    0xffcf, 0xee46, 0xdcdd, 0xcd54, 0xb9eb, 0xa862, 0x9af9, 0x8b70,
    0x8408, 0x9581, 0xa71a, 0xb693, 0xc22c, 0xd3a5, 0xe13e, 0xf0b7,
    0x0840, 0x19c9, 0x2b52, 0x3adb, 0x4e64, 0x5fed, 0x6d76, 0x7cff,
    0x9489, 0x8500, 0xb79b, 0xa612, 0xd2ad, 0xc324, 0xf1bf, 0xe036,
    0x18c1, 0x0948, 0x3bd3, 0x2a5a, 0x5ee5, 0x4f6c, 0x7df7, 0x6c7e,
    0xa50a, 0xb483, 0x8618, 0x9791, 0xe32e, 0xf2a7, 0xc03c, 0xd1b5,
    0x2942, 0x38cb, 0x0a50, 0x1bd9, 0x6f66, 0x7eef, 0x4c74, 0x5dfd,
    0xb58b, 0xa402, 0x9699, 0x8710, 0xf3af, 0xe226, 0xd0bd, 0xc134,
    0x39c3, 0x284a, 0x1ad1, 0x0b58, 0x7fe7, 0x6e6e, 0x5cf5, 0x4d7c,
    0xc60c, 0xd785, 0xe51e, 0xf497, 0x8028, 0x91a1, 0xa33a, 0xb2b3,
    0x4a44, 0x5bcd, 0x6956, 0x78df, 0x0c60, 0x1de9, 0x2f72, 0x3efb,
    0xd68d, 0xc704, 0xf59f, 0xe416, 0x90a9, 0x8120, 0xb3bb, 0xa232,
    0x5ac5, 0x4b4c, 0x79d7, 0x685e, 0x1ce1, 0x0d68, 0x3ff3, 0x2e7a,
    0xe70e, 0xf687, 0xc41c, 0xd595, 0xa12a, 0xb0a3, 0x8238, 0x93b1,
    0x6b46, 0x7acf, 0x4854, 0x59dd, 0x2d62, 0x3ceb, 0x0e70, 0x1ff9,
    0xf78f, 0xe606, 0xd49d, 0xc514, 0xb1ab, 0xa022, 0x92b9, 0x8330,
    0x7bc7, 0x6a4e, 0x58d5, 0x495c, 0x3de3, 0x2c6a, 0x1ef1, 0x0f78
};

#define PPPINITFCS      0xffff   /* Initial FCS value */
#define PPPGOODFCS      0xf0b8   /* Good final FCS value */

/*
 * Calculate a new fcs given the current fcs and the new data.
 */
u16 pppfcs(register u16 fcs, register unsigned char *cp,
    register int len)
{
    ASSERT(sizeof (u16) == 2);
    ASSERT(((u16) -1) > 0);
    while (len--)
        fcs = (fcs >> 8) ^ fcstab[(fcs ^ *cp++) & 0xff];
    return (fcs);
}
```

D5.5   Remote scripts

Many systems require to mount resources automatically within the user having any interaction with the systems. PPP supports this with remote scripts which allow the login process to be automated. This script is a simple text files which contains a number of commands, parameters, and expressions that are required for the connection. Typically, a generic template is used, and edited for the required purpose.

The basic format of the script is:

```
;
; Comments
;
proc main
; Variables and commands follow
    variable declarations
    command block
endproc
```

The script contains a main procedure between the proc and endproc keywords, with variables declared before the commands. Variables are case insensitive and are defined with the integer, string (a sequence of characters defined in single quotation marks, such as "Enter user name") or Boolean (TRUE or FALSE). There are also certain system variables, which are read-only, and cannot be c hanged. These include:

Name	Type	Description
$USERID	String	This is set to the user identification of the current connection, and is the value of the user name specified in the Connect To dialog box.
$PASSWORD	String	This is set to the password of the current connection, and is the value of the password specified in the Connect To dialog box.
$SUCCESS	Boolean	This is set on a successful execution of a command
$FAILURE	Boolean	This is set on a unsuccessful execution of a command

For example the user ID can be transmitted with:

```
transmit $USERID
```

The reserved words include:

```
and        boolean      databits   delay      do
endif      endproc      endwhile   even       FALSE
getip      goto         halt       if         integer
ipaddr     keyboardmark matchcase  none       odd
off        on           or         parity     port
proc       raw          screen     set        space
stopbits   string       then       transmit   TRUE
until      waitfor      while
```

Along with this scripting supports certain escape sequences and caret translations, such as:

String literal	Description
^char	If char is a value between '@' and '_', the character sequence is translated into a single-byte value from 0 through 31. A common sequence is ^M which is converted to a carriage return.
<cr>	Carriage return.
<lf>	Line feed.
\"	Quotation mark.
\^	Single caret.
\<	Single angle bracket.
\\	Backslash.

For example:

```
transmit "<cr><lf>"
waitfor "<cr><lf>"
transmit "^M"
transmit "User01^M"
```

Expression can be used to evaluate certain conditions, the typical operators are:

Unary

- Unary minus
! One's complement

The binary operators are:

Operators	Type of operation	Type restrictions
* /	Multiplicative	Integers
+ -	Additive integers	Strings (+ only)
<> <= >=	Relational	Integers
== !=	Equality	Integers, strings, booleans
and	Logical AND	Booleans
or	Logical OR	Booleans

The basic commands include:

delay nsecs   Pause for a number of seconds (such as delay 2, which waits for 2 seconds).

getip value	Wait for an IP address to be returned (such as getip newipadd).
goto value	Go to a label
halt	Halts the script

if condition then
commands
endif
	If condition

label:	Label
set port databits 5 | 6 | 7 | 8	Sets the number of data port bits
set screen keyboard on | off	Enables or disables keyboard input
set ipaddr string	Set the IP address (such as set ipaddress "192.168.0.10")
waitfor string	Waits for a given string to be returned (such as waitfor "ACK")
waitfor string time	Waits for a given amount of time (such as waitfor "Login:" 10, which waits for 10 seconds)

while condition do
commands
endwhile
	While loop

An example SCP is:

```
; This is a script file that demonstrates how
; to establish a PPP connection with a host
; that uses a menu system.
;
; A script file must have a 'main' procedure.
; All script execution starts with this 'main'
; procedure.
;

; Main entry point to script
;
proc main

    ; Change these variables to customize for your
    ; specific Internet service provider

    integer nTries = 3

    ; This is the login prompt and timeout values

    string szLogin = "username:"
    integer nLoginTimeout = 3
```

```
; This is the password prompt and timeout values

string szPW = "password:"
integer nPWTimeout = 3

; This is the prompt once your password is verified

string szPrompt = "annex:"

; This is the command to send to establish the
; connection.  This script assumes you only need
; to issue one command to continue.


; This provider has a menu list like this:
;
;   1                  : Our special GUI
;   2                  : Establish slip connection
;   3                  : Establish PPP connection
;   4                  : Establish shell access
;   5                  : Download our software
;   6                  : Exit
;
;   annex:
;

string szConnect = "3^M"

; Set this to FALSE if you don't want to get an IP
; address

boolean bUseSlip = FALSE

    ; --------------------------------------------------

; Delay for 2 seconds first to make sure the
; host doesn't get confused when we send the
; two carriage-returns.

delay 2
transmit "^M^M"

; Attempt to login at most 'nTries' times

while 0 < nTries do

    ; Wait for the login prompt before entering
    ; the user ID, timeout after x seconds

    waitfor szLogin then DoLogin
      until nLoginTimeout

TryAgain:
    transmit "^M"          ; ping
    nTries = nTries - 1

endwhile

goto BailOut

DoLogin:
  ; Enter user ID

  transmit $USERID, raw
```

```
    transmit "^M"

    ; Wait for the password prompt

    waitfor szPW until nPWTimeout
    if FALSE == $SUCCESS then
        goto TryAgain
    endif

    ; Send the password

    transmit $PASSWORD, raw
    transmit "^M"

    ; Wait for the prompt

    waitfor szPrompt

    transmit szConnect

    if bUseSlip then
        ; An alternative to the following line is
        ;
        ;       waitfor "Your address is "
        ;       set ipaddr getip
        ;
        ; if we don't know the order of the IP addresses.

        set ipaddr getip 2
    endif
    goto Done

BailOut:
    ; Something isn't responding.  Halt the script
    ; and let the user handle it manually.

    set screen keyboard on
    halt

Done:

endproc
```

A specific version to connect to Compuserve is:

```
;
; This is a script file that demonstrates how
; to establish a PPP connection with Compuserve,
; which requires changing the port settings to
; log in.
;

; Main entry point to script
;
proc main

    ; Set the port settings so we can wait for
    ; non-gibberish text.

    set port databits 7
    set port parity even

    transmit "^M"
```

```
    waitfor "Host Name:"
    transmit "CIS^M"

    waitfor "User ID:"
    transmit $USERID, raw
    transmit "/go:pppconnect^M"

    waitfor "Password: "
    transmit $PASSWORD, raw
    transmit "^M"

    waitfor "One moment please..."

    ; Set the port settings back to allow successful
    ; negotiation.

    set port databits 8
    set port parity none

endproc
```

The SLIP template is similar:

```
;
; This is a script file that demonstrates how
; to establish a slip connection with a host.
;
; A script file must have a 'main' procedure.
; All script execution starts with this 'main'
; procedure.
;


; Main entry point to script
;
proc main

    ; Change these variables to customize for your
    ; specific Internet service provider.

    integer nTries = 3

    ; This is the login prompt and timeout values

    string szLogin = "Userid:"
    integer nLoginTimeout = 3

    ; This is the password prompt and timeout values

    string szPW = "Password?"
    integer nPWTimeout = 3

    ; This is the prompt once your password is verified

    string szPrompt = "InternetLR/E>"

    ; This is the command to send to establish the
    ; connection.  This script assumes you only need
    ; to issue one command to continue.  Feel free
    ; to add more commands if your provider requires
    ; it.
```

```
    string szConnect = "slip^M"

    ; Set this to FALSE if you don't want to get an IP
    ; address

    boolean bUseSlip = TRUE


    ; Delay for 2 seconds first to make sure the
    ; host doesn't get confused when we send the
    ; two carriage-returns.

    delay 2
    transmit "^M^M"

    ; Attempt to login at most 'nTries' times

    while 0 < nTries do

        ; Wait for the login prompt before entering
        ; the user ID, timeout after x seconds

        waitfor szLogin then DoLogin
          until nLoginTimeout
TryAgain:
        transmit "^M"          ; ping
        nTries = nTries - 1

    endwhile

    goto BailOut

DoLogin:
    ; Enter user ID

    transmit $USERID, raw
    transmit "^M"

    ; Wait for the password prompt
    waitfor szPW until nPWTimeout
    if FALSE == $SUCCESS then
        goto TryAgain
    endif

    ; Send the password
    transmit $PASSWORD, raw
    transmit "^M"

    ; Wait for the prompt

    waitfor szPrompt

    transmit szConnect

    if bUseSlip then
        ; An alternative to the following line is
        ;
        ;       waitfor "Your address is "
        ;       set ipaddr getip
        ;
        ; if we don't know the order of the IP addresses.

        set ipaddr getip 2
```

```
    endif

    goto Done

BailOut:
    ; Something isn't responding.  Halt the script
    ; and let the user handle it manually.

    set screen keyboard on
    halt

Done:

endproc
```

D5.6   PPP programming for routers

PPP is encapsulated on an interface using the encapsulate ppp command, such as:

```
Router > enable
Router # config t
Router (config) # int s0
Router (config-if) # ip address 192.168.0.10 255.255.255.0
Router (config-if) # encapsulate ppp
Router (config-if) # exit
Router (config) # exit
Router #
```

By default there is no authentication. If it is required one of the following can be used after the encapsulate command:

```
ppp authentication chap
ppp authentication chap pap
ppp authentication pap chap
ppp authentication pap
```

If authentication is enabled, then the user must have a username and password on the router which the user is connecting to. For example, this is achieved using the username command for a user named fred, with a password of mypass:

```
Router > enable
Router # config t
Router (config) # username fred password mypass
Router (config) # exit
Router #
```

For example for a serial interface (SO), and an ISDN connection (BRI0):

```
Router > enable
Router # config t
Router(config)# int s0
Router(config-if)# encapsulation ppp
Router(config-if)# ppp chap password mypass
```

```
Router(config-if)# exit
Router(config)# int bri0
Router(config-if)# encapsulation ppp
Router(config-if)# ppp chap password mypass
Router(config-if)# exit
```

The show interfaces command can be used to check the LCP and NCP states. PAP authentication provides a simple method for a remote node to identify itself, using a two-way handshake. After the successful completion of the link establishment phase, a username/password pair is sent repeatedly by the calling node to the called node. Unfortunately, passwords are sent over the link in clear text, thus, there is no protection against external parties listening to the communications.

   With CHAP, after successful completion of link establishment phase, it periodically verifies the identity of the remote node, using a three-way handshake. With CHAP, the called party sends a challenge to the calling node; the calling node must then encrypt the message, and send it back. The called node will thus check the result and verify the other node.

D5.7   Securing a PPP connection

Microsoft Windows XP, and on, provide network security on a dial-up connection using an Internet Connection Firewall. Figure D5.10 shows that the user can change the options on ICMP, such as not allowing incoming requests for echoes, for router, and so on, and for outgoing requests for redirect, and so on. It can also restrict the servers that Internet users can access, including email (SMTP, POP3 and IMAP), FTP and WWW servers (HTTP).

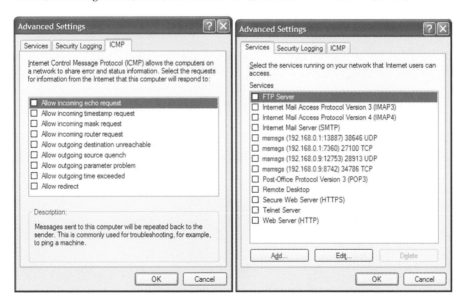

Figure D5.10   Internet firewall settings

D6   TCP/IP Commands

D6.1   Introduction

There are several standard programs and protocols available over TCP/IP connections, these include:

- FTP (File Transfer Protocol) – transfers file between computers.
- PING – determines if a node is responding to TCP/IP communications. The PING command is probably the easiest way to determine if a node is alive, and responding to communications.
- TRACEROUTE (or tracert) – determines the route to a remote host.
- NSLOOKUP – determines the IP address of a remote host for a given host name.
- TELNET – allows remote login using TCP/IP.
- HTTP (Hypertext Transfer Protocol) – which is the protocol used in the World Wide Web (WWW) and can be used for client-server applications involving hypertext.
- MIME (Multipurpose Internet Mail Extension) – gives enhanced electronic mail facilities over TCP/IP.
- SMTP (Simple Mail Management Protocol) – gives simple electronic mail facilities.

An interface to a host has two components: the physical (the hardware) and the logical (the software). The hardware is the actual connection between devices, and the software controls the messages that are passed between adjacent devices. When a fault develops on a network, the administrator will use a number of methods to test the link, normally using the PING, TRACEROUTE and TELNET programs. The first steps might be as given in Figure D6.1. These are:

- **PING.** This is the simplest method in determining if a node is reachable by TCP/IP communications. It also gives a measure of the delay in reaching the remote host. If the host is reachable by PING it is likely that it has not crashed and that the network connection to it is reliable. With ping, the host sends out a packet to the destination host and then waits for a reply packet from that host. The results give path-to-host reliability, delays over the path, and whether the host can be reached or is functioning. If possible the user should test the ping command with both the domain name and the IP address of the host, as this will test to see if the domain name server is operating correctly (or reachable). If the ping command works with the IP address, and not with the domain name, then either the domain name has been specified wrongly or the domain name server is not operating correctly.
- **TELNET.** If the remote host is a server, and the user needs to test if the server is responding to server applications, a TELNET session is typically initiated (or often an FTP session is also used). Another method of testing a server is to determine if it is responding to the HTTP protocol (if it has been setup to run a WWW server). The Telnet connection has the advantage of testing the application layer of the OSI model.
- **TRACEROUTE.** The traceroute command can be used to determine the route that data takes to reach a remote host. This will show if the data is being dropped at any point in the connection. It is similar to the ping command, except that instead of testing end-to-

end connectivity, traceroute tests each step along the way. The traceroute command takes advantage of the error messages generated by routers when a packet exceeds its Time-To-Live (TTL) value. It sends several packets and displays the round-trip time for each. The main advantage of the traceroute command is that it shows which router in the path was the last one to be reached (fault isolation). An administrator can then determine the parts of the network that are operating properly.

If the administrator determines that there is a local software problem with a host, it is likely that the computer would be given a hardware reboot. If there is a local problem with a router, bridge or hub, the administrator would check the equipment by asking the following questions:

- Is the carrier detect signal active? Most transmission lines transmit a signal even when there are no data frames being transmitted at a time. This is called carrier detect, and many devices will either give a software indication on whether a link is active, or activate an LED to show an active link.
- Are the keepalive messages being received? Many devices send keepalive signals between each other to show that they are still responding to communications (normally a good network connection will be identified with an active green LED).
- Can data packets be sent across the physical link?
- Is there a good physical link between devices? This involves inspecting the cable that connects to a device. A typical problem is when a user disconnects a cable to connect another device.

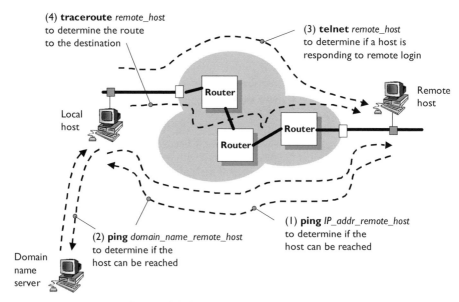

Figure D6.1 Methods used to test a connection

D6.2   ping

The `ping` program (Packet Internet Gopher) determines whether a node is responding to TCP/IP communication. It is typically used to trace problems in networks and uses the Internet Control Message Protocol (ICMP) to send a response request from the target node. Sample run D6.1 shows that `miranda` is active and `ariel` isn't.

🖥   Sample run D6.1: Using PING command

```
C:\WINDOWS>ping miranda
miranda (146.176.144.14) is alive
C:\WINDOWS>ping ariel
no reply from ariel (146.176.147.35)
```

The `ping` program can also be used to determine the delay between one host and another, and also if there are any IP packet losses. In Sample run D6.2 the local host is `pc419.eece.napier.ac.uk` (which is on the `146.176.151` segment); the host `miranda` is tested (which is on the `146.176.144` segment). It can be seen that, on average, the delay is only 1 ms and there is no loss of packets.

In Sample run D6.3 the destination node (`www.napier.ac.uk`) is located within the same building but is on a different IP segment (`147.176.2`). It is also routed through a router. It can be seen that the packet delay has increased to between 9 and 10 ms. Again, there is no packet loss.

🖥   Sample run D6.2: Using PING command

```
225 % ping miranda
PING miranda.eece.napier.ac.uk: 64 byte packets
64 bytes from 146.176.144.14: icmp_seq=0. time=1. ms
64 bytes from 146.176.144.14: icmp_seq=1. time=1. ms
64 bytes from 146.176.144.14: icmp_seq=2. time=1. ms
3 packets transmitted, 3 packets received, 0% packet loss
round-trip (ms)  min/avg/max = 1/1/1
```

🖥   Sample run D6.3: Using PING command

```
226 % ping www.napier.ac.uk
PING central.napier.ac.uk: 64 byte packets
64 bytes from 146.176.2.3: icmp_seq=0. time=9. ms
64 bytes from 146.176.2.3: icmp_seq=1. time=9. ms
64 bytes from 146.176.2.3: icmp_seq=2. time=10. ms
3 packets transmitted, 3 packets received, 0% packet loss
round-trip (ms)  min/avg/max = 9/9/10
```

Sample run D6.4 shows a connection between Edinburgh and Bath in the UK (`www.bath.ac.uk` has an IP address of `138.38.32.5`). This is a distance of approximately 500 miles and it can be seen that the delay is now between 30 and 49 ms. This time there is 25% packet loss.

Finally, in Sample run D6.5 the `ping` program tests a link between Edinburgh, UK, and a WWW server in the USA (`home.microsoft.com`, which has the IP address of `207.68.137.51`). It can be seen that in this case, the delay is between 447 and 468 ms, and the loss is 60%.

⌨ Sample run D6.4: Using PING command

```
222 % ping www.bath.ac.uk
PING jess.bath.ac.uk: 64 byte packets
64 bytes from 138.38.32.5: icmp_seq=0. time=49. ms
64 bytes from 138.38.32.5: icmp_seq=2. time=35. ms
64 bytes from 138.38.32.5: icmp_seq=3. time=30. ms
4 packets transmitted, 3 packets received, 25% packet loss
round-trip (ms)  min/avg/max = 30/38/49
```

A similar utility program to `ping` is `spray` which uses Remote Procedure Call (RPC) to send a continuous stream of ICMP messages. It is useful when testing a network connection for its burst characteristics. This differs from `ping`, which waits for a predetermined amount of time between messages.

⌨ Sample run D6.5: Ping command with packet loss

```
224 % ping home.microsoft.com
PING home.microsoft.com: 64 byte packets
64 bytes from 207.68.137.51: icmp_seq=2. time=447. ms
64 bytes from 207.68.137.51: icmp_seq=3. time=468. ms
5 packets transmitted, 2 packets received, 60% packet loss
```

D6.3 ftp (file transfer protocol)

The `ftp` program uses the TCP/IP protocol to transfer files to and from remote nodes. If necessary, it reads the *hosts* file to determine the IP address. Once the user has logged into the remote node, the commands that can be used are similar to DOS commands such as `cd` (change directory), `dir` (list directory), `open` (open node), `close` (close node), `pwd` (present working directory). The `get` command copies a file from the remote node and the `put` command copies it to the remote node.

The type of file to be transferred must also be specified. This file can be ASCII text (the command `ascii`) or binary (the command `binary`). The FTP protocol is defined in RFC959, and a full set of commands and responses are detailed in Appendix 10.

Another typical file transfer protocol is Trivial File Transfer Protocol, which is a simplified version of FTP that allows files to be transferred over a network. It uses UDP communications rather than TCP.

D6.4 traceroute

The `traceroute` program traces the route of an IP packet through the Internet. It uses the IP protocol time-to-live field and attempts to get an ICMP TIME_EXCEEDED response from each gateway along the path to a defined host. The default probe datagram length is 38 bytes (although the sample runs use 40 byte packets by default). Sample run D6.6 shows an example of `traceroute` from a PC (`pc419.eece.napier.ac.uk`). It can be seen that initially it goes through a bridge (`pcbridge.eece.napier.ac.uk`) and then to the destination (`miranda.eece.napier.ac.uk`).

Sample run D6.7 shows the route from a PC (`pc419.eece.napier.ac.uk`) to a destination node (`www.bath.ac.uk`). Initially, from the originator, the route goes through a gateway (`146.176.151.254`) and then goes through a routing switch (`146.176.1.27`) and onto EaSt-

MAN ring via `146.176.3.1`. The route then goes round the EaStMAN to a gateway at the University of Edinburgh (`smds-gw.ed.ja.net`). It is then routed onto the SuperJanet network and reaches a gateway at the University of Bath (`smds-gw.bath.ja.net`). It then goes to another gateway (`jips-gw.bath.ac.uk`) and finally to its destination (`jess.bath.ac.uk`). Figure D6.2 shows the route the packet takes.

Note that gateways 4 and 8 hops away either don't send ICMP 'time exceeded' messages or send them with time-to-live values that are too small to be returned to the originator.

🖥 Sample run D6.6: Example traceroute
```
www:~/www$ traceroute miranda
traceroute to miranda.eece.napier.ac.uk (146.176.144.14), 30 hops max,
40 byte packets
1  pcbridge.eece.napier.ac.uk (146.176.151.252)  2.684 ms  1.762 ms 1.725 ms
2  miranda.eece.napier.ac.uk (146.176.144.14)  2.451 ms  2.554 ms   2.357 ms
```

Sample run D6.8 shows an example route from a local host at Napier University, UK, to the USA. As before, it goes through the local gateway (`146.176.151.254`) and then goes through three other gateways to get onto the SMDS SuperJANET connection. The data packet then travels down this connection to University College London (`gw5.ulcc.ja.net`). It then goes onto high speed connections to the USA and arrives at a US gateway (`mcinet-2.sprintnap.net`). Next, it travels to `core2-hssi2-0.WestOrange.mci.net` before reaching the Microsoft Corporation gateway in Seattle (`microsoft.Seattle.mci.net`). It finally finds its way to the destination (`207.68.145.53`). The total journey time is just less than half a second.

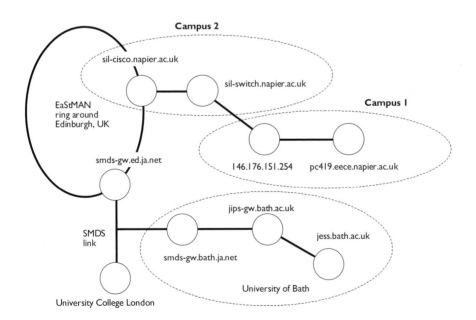

Figure D6.2   Route between local host and the University of Bath

```
www:~/www$ traceroute www.bath.ac.uk
traceroute to jess.bath.ac.uk (138.38.32.5), 30 hops max, 40 byte packets
1  146.176.151.254 (146.176.151.254)  2.806 ms  2.76 ms  2.491 ms
2  si1-switch.napier.ac.uk (146.176.1.27)  19.315 ms  11.29 ms  6.285 ms
3  si1-cisco.napier.ac.uk (146.176.3.1)  6.42 ms  8.40 ms  8.87 ms
4  * * *
5  smds-gw.ed.ja.net (193.63.106.129)  8.98 ms  30.30 ms  398.62 ms
6  smds-gw.bath.ja.net (193.63.203.68)  39.14 ms  46.83 ms  38.03 ms
7  jips-gw.bath.ac.uk (146.97.104.2)  32.90 ms  41.33 ms  42.42 ms
8  * * *
9  jess.bath.ac.uk (138.38.32.5)  41.05 ms  *  41.93 ms
```

```
> traceroute home.microsoft.com
1  146.176.151.254 (146.176.151.254)  2.931 ms  2.68 ms  2.658 ms
2  si1-switch.napier.ac.uk (146.176.1.27)  6.21 ms  8.81 ms  5.88 ms
3  si1-cisco.napier.ac.uk (146.176.3.1)  6.50 ms  6.63 ms  10.21 ms
4  * * *
5  smds-gw.ed.ja.net (193.63.106.129)  18.367 ms  9.242 ms  15.145 ms
6  smds-gw.ulcc.ja.net (193.63.203.33)  42.644 ms  36.794 ms  34.555 ms
7  gw5.ulcc.ja.net (128.86.1.80)  31.906 ms  30.053 ms  39.151 ms
8  icm-london-1.icp.net (193.63.175.53)  29.368 ms  25.42 ms  31.347 ms
9  198.67.131.193 (198.67.131.193)  119.195 ms  120.482 ms  67.479 ms
10 icm-pen-1-H2/0-T3.icp.net (198.67.131.25) 115.31 ms  126.15 ms
11 icm-pen-10-P4/0-OC3C.icp.net (198.67.142.69)  139.27 ms  197.953 ms  12
mcinet-2.sprintnap.net (192.157.69.48)  199.26 ms  267.44 ms 287.83 ms
13 core2-hssi2-0.WestOrange.mci.net (204.70.1.49)  216.00 ms  688.1 ms
14 microsoft.Seattle.mci.net (166.48.209.250) 310.44 ms  282.88 ms
15 * microsoft.Seattle.mci.net (166.48.209.250) 324.79 ms  309.51 ms
16 * 207.68.145.53 (207.68.145.53)  435.19 ms *
```

D6.5   nslookup

The nslookup program interrogates the local hosts file or a DNS server to determine the IP address of an Internet node. If it cannot find it in the local file then it communicates with gateways outside its own network to see if they know the address. Sample run D6.9 shows that the IP address of www.intel.com is 134.134.214.1.

```
C:\> nslookup
Default Server:  ees99.eece.napier.ac.uk
Address:  146.176.151.99
> www.intel.com
Server:  ees99.eece.napier.ac.uk
Address:  146.176.151.99
Name:    web.jf.intel.com
Address:  134.134.214.1
Aliases:  www.intel.com
230 % nslookup home.microsoft.com
Non-authoritative answer:
Name:    home.microsoft.com
Addresses:  207.68.137.69, 207.68.156.11, 207.68.156.14, 207.68.156.56
207.68.137.48, 207.68.137.51
```

D6.6   Windows programs

Microsoft Windows has seven main programs which can be used to diagnose network problems:

arp	Address resolution protocol (ARP) is used to determine the MAC address for a given IP address.
ipconfig	Displays the current TCP/IP settings for the host.
winipcfg	As ipconfig, but a Windows version.
netstat	Displays the status of all TCP/IP connections on the host.
nslookup	Determines the IP address for a given domain name (Windows NT only).
ping	Determines if a remote host is communicating using TCP/IP.
tracert	Traces the route from the current host to a remote host.

D6.6.1   Ping

The ping command is a standard program that can be used to determine if a host is responding to TCP/IP communications. Its format is:

```
Usage: ping [-t] [-a] [-n count] [-l size] [-f] [-i TTL] [-v TOS]
            [-r count] [-s count] [[-j host-list] | [-k host-list]]
            [-w timeout] destination-list

Options:
    -t              Ping the specified host until stopped.
    -a              Resolve addresses to hostnames.
    -n count        Number of echo requests to send.
    -l size         Send buffer size.
    -f              Set Don't Fragment flag in packet.
    -i TTL          Time To Live.
    -v TOS          Type Of Service.
    -r count        Record route for count hops.
    -s count        Timestamp for count hops.
    -w timeout      Timeout in milliseconds to wait for each reply.
```

Figure D6.3 shows that ping displays the IP address of the host for the entered domain name. In this case the www.napier.ac.uk host is contacted. It can be seen that its IP address is 146.176.1.8. Ping also displays the time delay for each time that it contacts the remote host. In the example in Figure D6.3 the delays are: 153 ms; 137 ms; 148 ms and 152 ms. It also displays the value of the TTL (time-to-live) field, which, in this case, is 115.

The ping command is run from a Command window, which is typically selected by either:

- Clicking on MS-DOS prompt on the Desktop. **MS**
- Selecting the MS-DOS prompt option in the Start menu.
- Typing command.com in the Start→Run option, as shown next.

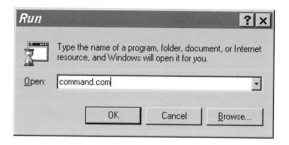

D6.6.2 Tracert

The traceroute (`tracert`) program can be used to determine the route from the local host to a remote host. Its usage is:

```
Usage: tracert [-d] [-h maximum_hops] [-j host-list] [-w timeout] target_name
Options:
    -d                  Do not resolve addresses to hostnames.
    -h maximum_hops     Maximum number of hops to search for target.
    -j host-list        Loose source route along host-list.
    -w timeout              Wait timeout milliseconds for each reply.
```

D6.6.3 Netstat/IPConfig

The netstat (`netstat`) program can be used to determine TCP/IP protocol statistics and the current TCP/IP network connections. Its format is:

```
NETSTAT [-a] [-e] [-n] [-s] [-p proto] [-r] [interval]
  -a        Displays all connections and listening ports.
  -e        Displays Ethernet statistics.
  -n        Displays addresses and port numbers in numerical form.
  -p proto  Shows connections for the protocol specified by proto; proto
            may be TCP or UDP.  If used with the -s option to display
            per-protocol statistics, proto may be TCP, UDP, or IP.
  -r        Displays the routing table.
  -s        Displays per-protocol statistics.  By default, statistics
            are shown for TCP, UDP and IP; the -p option may be used to
            specify a subset of the default.
  Interval  Redisplays selected statistics, pausing interval second
            between each display.  Press CTRL+C to stop redisplaying
            statistics.  If omitted, netstat will print the current
            configuration information once.
```

Examples of its usage are:

```
C:\WINDOWS>netstat -a
Active Connections
   Proto  Local Address      Foreign Address              State
   TCP    bill-s:1060        csunt1.napier.ac.uk:80       CLOSE_WAIT
```

```
TCP     bill-s:1061       csunt1.napier.ac.uk:80              CLOSE_WAIT
TCP     bill-s:1062       csunt1.napier.ac.uk:80              CLOSE_WAIT
TCP     bill-s:1063       csunt1.napier.ac.uk:80              CLOSE_WAIT
TCP     bill-s:1097       artemis.dcs.napier.ac.uk:ftp        ESTABLISHED
TCP     bill-s:1106       www.eece.napier.ac.uk:telnet        CLOSE_WAIT

C:\WINDOWS>netstat -s
Active Connections
   Proto  Local Address          Foreign Address        State
   TCP    62.136.29.56:1060      146.176.1.24:80        CLOSE_WAIT
   TCP    62.136.29.56:1061      146.176.1.24:80        CLOSE_WAIT
   TCP    62.136.29.56:1062      146.176.1.24:80        CLOSE_WAIT
   TCP    62.136.29.56:1063      146.176.1.24:80        CLOSE_WAIT
   TCP    62.136.29.56:1097      146.176.161.5:21       ESTABLISHED
   TCP    62.136.29.56:1106      146.176.151.139:23     CLOSE_WAIT
```

The Ipconfig program can be used to determine the IP configuration (otherwise WINIPCFG can be used). For example, to determine the IP address of the host computer:

```
C:\WINDOWS>ipconfig
0 Ethernet adapter :
     IP Address. . . . . . . . . : 62.136.29.56
     Subnet Mask . . . . . . . . : 255.0.0.0
     Default Gateway . . . . . . : 62.136.29.56

C:\WINDOWS>ipconfig /all
     Host Name . . . . . . . . . : BILL'S
     DNS Servers . . . . . . . . : 195.92.193.8
                                   194.152.64.35
     Node Type . . . . . . . . . : Broadcast
     NetBIOS Scope ID. . . . . . :
     IP Routing Enabled. . . . . : No
     WINS Proxy Enabled. . . . . : No
     NetBIOS Resolution Uses DNS : No

0 Ethernet adapter :
     Description . . . . . . . . : PPP Adapter.
     Physical Address. . . . . . : 44-45-53-54-00-00
     DHCP Enabled. . . . . . . . : Yes
     IP Address. . . . . . . . . : 62.136.29.56
     Subnet Mask . . . . . . . . : 255.0.0.0
     Default Gateway . . . . . . : 62.136.29.56
     DHCP Server . . . . . . . . : 255.255.255.255
     Primary WINS Server . . . . :
     Secondary WINS Server . . . :
     Lease Obtained. . . . . . . : 01 01 80 00:00:00
     Lease Expires . . . . . . . : 01 01 80 00:00:00
```

D6.6.4 arp

The arp command shows and modifies the IP address to MAC address translation tables.
The format is:

```
ARP -s inet_addr eth_addr [if_addr]
ARP -d inet_addr [if_addr]
ARP -a [inet_addr] [-N if_addr]
```

-a	Displays current ARP entries by interrogating the current protocol data. If inet_addr is specified, the IP and Physical addresses for only the specified computer are displayed. If more than one network interface uses ARP, entries for each ARP table are displayed.
-g	Same as -a.
inet_addr	Specifies an internet address.
-N if_addr	Displays the ARP entries for the network interface specified by if_addr.
-d	Deletes the host specified by inet_addr. inet_addr may be wildcarded with * to delete all hosts.
-s	Adds the host and associates the Internet address inet_addr with the Physical address eth_addr. The Physical address is given as 6 hexadecimal bytes separated by hyphens. The entry is permanent.
eth_addr	Specifies a physical address.
if_addr	If present, this specifies the Internet address of the interface whose address translation table should be modified. If not present, the first applicable interface will be used.

```
Example:
 > arp -s 157.55.85.212   00-aa-00-62-c6-09  .... Adds a static entry.
 > arp -a                                    .... Displays the arp table.
```

D7 Socket programming

D7.1 Introduction

The Windows Sockets specification describes a common interface for networked Windows programs. WinSock uses TCP/IP communications and provides for binary and source code compatibility for different network types.

The Windows Sockets API (WinSock API) is a library of functions that implement the socket interface by the Berkley Software Distribution of UNIX. WinSock augments the Berkley socket implementation by adding Windows-specific extensions to support the message-driven nature of Windows system.

D7.2 WinSock using C++

The Windows sockets specification describes a common interface for networked Windows programs. WinSock uses TCP/IP communications and provides for binary and source code compatibility for different network types.

The Windows sockets API (WinSock application programming interface or WSA) is a library of functions that implement the socket interface by the Berkley Software distribution of UNIX. WinSock augments the Berkley socket implementation by adding Windows-specific extensions to support the message-driven nature of Windows system.

The basic implementation normally involves:

- Opening a socket – this allows for multiple connections with multiple hosts. Each socket has a unique identifier. It normally involves defining the protocol suite, the socket type and the protocol name. The API call used for this is `socket()`.
- Naming a socket – this involves assigning location and identity attributes to a socket. The API call used for this is `bind()`.
- Associate with another socket – this involves either listening for a connection or actively seeking a connection. The API calls used in this are `listen()`, `connect()` and `accept()`.
- Send and receive between sockets – the API calls used in this are `send()`, `sendto()`, `recv()` and `recvfrom()`.
- Close the socket – the API calls used in this are `close()` and `shutdown()`.

D7.2.1 Windows sockets

The main WinSock API calls are:

`socket()`	Creates a socket.
`accept()`	Accepts a connection on a socket.
`connect()`	Establishes a connection to a peer.
`bind()`	Associates a local address with a socket.
`listen()`	Establishes a socket to listen for incoming connection.
`send()`	Sends data on a connected socket.
`sendto()`	Sends data on an unconnected socket.

`recv()`	Receives data from a connected socket.
`recvfrom()`	Receives data from an unconnected socket.
`shutdown()`	Disables send or receive operations on a socket.
`closesocket()`	Closes a socket.

Figure D7.1 shows the operation of a connection of a client to a server. The server is defined as the computer which waits for a connection, the client is the computer which initially makes contact with the server.

On the server the computer initially creates a socket with the `socket()` function, and this is bound to a name with the `bind()` function. After this, the server listens for a connection with the `listen()` function. When the client calls the `connect()` function the server then accepts the connection with `accept()`. After this the server and client can send and receive data with the `send()` or `recv()` functions. When the data transfer is complete the `closesocket()` is used to close the socket.

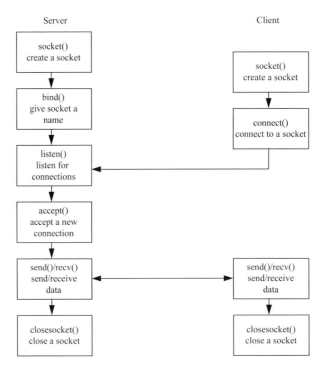

Figure D7.1   WinSock connection

D7.2.1.1   socket()

The `socket()` function creates a socket. Its syntax is

```
SOCKET socket (int af,  int type,   int protocol)
```

where

af A value of `PF_INET` specifies the ARPA Internet address format specification (others include `AF_IPX` for SPX/IPX and `AF_APPLETALK` for AppleTalk).

type Socket specification, which is typically either `SOCK_STREAM` or `SOCK_DGRAM`. The `SOCK_STREAM` uses TCP and provides a sequenced, reliable, two-way, connection-based stream. `SOCK_DGRAM` uses UDP and provides for connectionless datagrams. This type of connection is not recommended. A third type is `SOCK_RAW`, for types other than UDP or TCP, such as for ICMP.

protocol Defines the protocol to be used with the socket. If it is zero then the caller does not wish to specify a protocol.

If the `socket` function succeeds then the return value is a descriptor referencing the new socket. Otherwise, it returns `SOCKET_ERROR`, and the specific error code can be tested with `WSAGetLastError`. An example creation of a socket is given next:

```
SOCKET s;

    s=socket(PF_INET,SOCK_STREAM,0);
    if (s == INVALID_SOCKET)
    {
        cout << "Socket error"
    }
```

D7.2.1.2   bind()

The `bind()` function associates a local address with a socket. It is called before the `connect` or `listen` function. When a socket is created with `socket`, it exists in a name space (address family), but it has no name assigned. The `bind` function gives the socket a local association (host address/port number). Its syntax is:

```
int bind(SOCKET s, const struct sockaddr FAR * addr, int namelen)
```

where

s	A descriptor identifying an unbound socket.
namelen	The length of `addr`.
addr	The address to assign to the socket. The `sockaddr` structure is defined as follows:

```
struct sockaddr
{
    u_short     sa_family;
    char        sa_data[14];
};
```

In the Internet address family, the `sockadd_in` structure is used by Windows Sockets to specify a local or remote endpoint address to which to connect a socket. This is the form of the `sockaddr` structure specific to the Internet address family and can be cast to `sockaddr`. This structure can be filled with the `sockaddr_in` structure which has the following form:

```
struct SOCKADDR_IN
{
    short             sin_family;
    unsigned short    sin_port;
    struct            in_addr  sin_addr;
    char              sin_zero[8];
}
```

where

sin_family   must be set to AF_INET.
sin_port   IP port.
sin_addr   IP address.
sin_zero   padding to make structure the same size as sockaddr.

If an application does not care what address is assigned to it, it may specify an Internet address equal to INADDR_ANY, a port equal to 0, or both. An Internet address equal to INADDR_ANY causes any appropriate network interface be used. A port value of 0 causes the Windows sockets implementation to assign a unique port to the application with a value between 1024 and 5000.

If no error occurs then it returns a zero value. Otherwise, it returns INVALID_SOCKET, and the specific error code can be tested with WSAGetLastError. If an application needs to bind to an arbitrary port outside of the range 1024 to 5000 then the following outline code can be used:

```
#include    <windows.h>
#include    <winsock.h>
int main(void)
    {
    SOCKADDR_IN    sin;
SOCKET          s;
s = socket(AF_INET,SOCK_STREAM,0);

if (s == INVALID_SOCKET)
{
    // Socket failed
}

sin.sin_family = AF_INET;
sin.sin_addr.s_addr = 0;

sin.sin_port = htons(100); // port=100

if (bind(s, (LPSOCKADDR)&sin, sizeof (sin)) == 0)
{
    // Bind failed
}
return(0);
}
```

The Windows sockets htons function converts an unsigned short (u_short) from host byte order to network byte order.

D7.2.1.3 connect()

The `connect()` function establishes a connection with a peer. If the specified socket is unbound then unique values are assigned to the local association by the system and the socket is marked as bound. Its syntax is

```
int connect (SOCKET s, const struct sockaddr FAR * name,   int namelen)
```

where

              s   Descriptor identifying an unconnected socket.
              name   Name of the peer to which the socket is to be connected.
              namelen Name length.

If no error occurs then it returns a zero value. Otherwise, it returns SOCKET_ERROR, and the specific error code can be tested with WSAGetLastError.

D7.2.1.4 listen()

The `listen()` function establishes a socket which listens for an incoming connection. The sequence to create and accept a socket is:

- `socket()` – Creates a socket.
- `listen()` – this creates a queue for incoming connections and is typically used by a server that can have more than one connection at a time.
- `accept()` – these connections are then accepted with accept.

The syntax of `listen()` is

```
int listen (SOCKET s, int backlog)
```

where

        s   Describes a bound, unconnected socket.
        backlog Defines the queue size for the maximum number of pending connections may grow (typically a maximum of 5).

If no error occurs then it returns a zero value. Otherwise, it returns SOCKET_ERROR, and the specific error code can be tested with WSAGetLastError.

```
#include <windows.h>
#include <winsock.h>

int main(void)
{

SOCKADDR_IN    sin;
SOCKET         s;

    s = socket(AF_INET,SOCK_STREAM,0);
    if (s == INVALID_SOCKET)
    {
        // Socket failed
```

```
        }

        sin.sin_family = AF_INET;
        sin.sin_addr.s_addr = 0;

        sin.sin_port = htons(100); // port=100

        if (bind(s, (struct sockaddr FAR *)&sin, sizeof (sin))==SOCKET_ERROR)
        {
            // Bind failed
        }

        if (listen(s,4)==SOCKET_ERROR)
        {
            // Listen failed
        }
        return(0);
}
```

D7.2.1.5   accept()

The `accept()` function accepts a connection on a socket. It extracts any pending connections from the queue and creates a new socket with the same properties as the specified socket. Finally, it returns a handle to the new socket. Its syntax is

```
SOCKET accept(SOCKET s, struct sockaddr FAR *addr, int FAR   *addrlen )
```

where

s	Descriptor identifying a socket that is in listen mode.
addr	Pointer to a buffer that receives the address of the connecting entity, as known to the communications layer.
addrlen	Pointer to an integer which contains the length of the address addr.

If no error occurs then it returns a zero value. Otherwise, it returns INVALID_SOCKET, and the specific error code can be tested with WSAGetLastError.

```
#include <windows.h>
#include <winsock.h>

int main(void)
{

SOCKADDR_IN     sin;
SOCKET          s;
int             sin_len;

    s = socket(AF_INET,SOCK_STREAM,0);
    if (s == INVALID_SOCKET)
    {
        // Socket failed
    }

    sin.sin_family = AF_INET;
    sin.sin_addr.s_addr = 0;
    sin.sin_port = htons(100); // port=100

    if (bind(s, (struct sockaddr FAR *)&sin, sizeof (sin))==SOCKET_ERROR)
    {
```

```
    // Bind failed
    }

    if (listen(s,4)<0)
    {
        // Listen failed
    }
    sin_len = sizeof(sin);
    s=accept(s,(struct sockaddr FAR *) & sin,(int FAR *) &sin_len);
    if (s==INVALID_SOCKET)
    {
        // Accept failed
    }
    return(0);
}
```

D7.2.1.6   send()

The `send()` function sends data to a connected socket. Its syntax is:

```
int send (SOCKET s, const char FAR *buf, int len, int flags)
```

where

s	Connected socket descriptor.
buf	Transmission data buffer.
len	Buffer length.
flags	Calling flag.

The *flags* parameter influences the behaviour of the function. These can be

MSG_DONTROUTE	Specifies that the data should not be subject to routing.
MSG_OOB	Send out-of-band data.

If `send()` succeeds then the return value is the number of characters sent (which can be less than the number indicated by `len`). Otherwise, it returns `SOCKET_ERROR`, and the specific error code can be tested with `WSAGetLastError`.

```
#include <windows.h>
#include <winsock.h>
#include <string.h>
#define  STRLENGTH 100

int main(void)
{

SOCKADDR_IN     sin;
SOCKET          s;
int sin_len;
char  sendbuf[STRLENGTH];

    s = socket(AF_INET,SOCK_STREAM,0);
    if (s == INVALID_SOCKET)
    {
        // Socket failed
    }
```

```
    sin.sin_family = AF_INET;
    sin.sin_addr.s_addr = 0;
      sin.sin_port = htons(100); // port=100
    if (bind(s, (struct sockaddr FAR *)&sin, sizeof (sin))==SOCKET_ERROR)
    {
        // Bind failed
    }

    if (listen(s,4)<0)
    {
        // Listen failed
    }
    sin_len = sizeof(sin);

    s=accept(s,(struct sockaddr FAR *) & sin,(int FAR *) &sin_len);

    if (s<0)
    {
        // Accept failed
    }

    while (1)
    {
        // get message to send and put into sendbuff
        send(s,sendbuf,strlen(sendbuf),80);
    }
    return(0);
}
```

D7.2.1.7   recv()

The recv() function receives data from a socket. It waits until data arrives and its syntax is:

```
int recv(SOCKET s, char FAR *buf, int len, int flags)
```

where

s	Connected socket descriptor.
buf	Incoming data buffer.
len	Buffer length.
flags	Specifies the method by which the data is received.

If recv() succeeds then the return value is the number of bytes received (a zero identifies that the connection has been closed). Otherwise, it returns SOCKET_ERROR, and the specific error code can be tested with WSAGetLastError.

The flags parameter may have one of the following values:

MSG_PEEK	Peek at the incoming data. Any received data is copied into the buffer, but not removed from the input queue.
MSG_OOB	Process out-of-band data.

```
#include <windows.h>
#include <winsock.h>

#define  STRLENGTH 100

int main(void)
```

```
{
SOCKADDR_IN     sin;
SOCKET          s;
int             sin_len,status;
char            recmsg[STRLENGTH];

   s = socket(AF_INET,SOCK_STREAM,0);

   if (s == INVALID_SOCKET)
   {
      // Socket failed
   }

   sin.sin_family = AF_INET;
   sin.sin_addr.s_addr = 0;

   sin.sin_port = htons(100); // port=100

   if (bind(s, (struct sockaddr FAR *)&sin, sizeof (sin))==SOCKET_ERROR)
   {
       // Bind failed
   }

   if (listen(s,4)<0)
   {
      // Listen failed
   }
   sin_len = sizeof(sin);

   s=accept(s,(struct sockaddr FAR *) & sin,(int FAR *) &sin_len);

   if (s<0)
   {
      // Accept failed
   }
   while (1)
   {
      status=recv(s,recmsg,STRLENGTH,80);

      if (status==SOCKET_ERROR)
      {
         // no socket
         break;
      }
      recmsg[status]=NULL; // terminate string
      if (status)
      {
         // szMsg contains received string
      }
      else
      {
         break;
         // connection broken
      }
   }
   return(0);
}
```

D7.2.1.8 shutdown()

The shutdown() function disables send or receive operations on a socket and does not close any opened sockets. Its syntax is

```
int shutdown(SOCKET s, int how)
```

where

       s   Socket descriptor.

how   Flag that identifies operation types that will no longer be allowed. These are:
                0 – Disallows subsequent receives.
                1 – Disallows subsequent sends.
                2 – Disables send and receive.

If no error occurs then it returns a zero value. Otherwise, it returns INVALID_SOCKET, and the specific error code can be tested with WSAGetLastError.

D7.2.1.9   closesocket()

The closesocket() function closes a socket. Its syntax is:

```
int closesocket (SOCKET s);
```

where

    s   Socket descriptor.

If no error occurs then it returns a zero value. Otherwise, it returns INVALID_SOCKET, and the specific error code can be tested with WSAGetLastError.

D7.3   Visual Basic socket implementation

Visual Basic supports a WinSock control and allows the connection of hosts over a network. It supports both UDP and TCP. Figure D7.2 shows a sample Visual Basic screen with a WinSock object (in this case, it is named Winsock1). To set the protocol used then either select the properties window on the WinSock object, click protocol and select sckTCPProtocol, or sckUDPProtocol. Otherwise, within the code it can be set to TCP with:

```
Winsock1.Protocol = sckTCPProtocol
```

The WinSock object has various properties, such as:

    obj.RemoteHost   Defines the IP address or domain name of the remote host.
    obj.LocalPort   Defines the local port number.

The methods that are used with the WinSock object are:

    obj.Connect   Connects to a remote host (client invoked).
    obj.Listen   Listens for a connection (server invoked).
    obj.GetData   Reads data from the input steam.
    obj.SendData   Sends data to an output stream.

The main events are:

`ConnectionRequest`   Occurs when a remote host wants to make a connection with a server.

`DataArrival`   Occurs when data has arrived from a connection (data is then read with GetData).

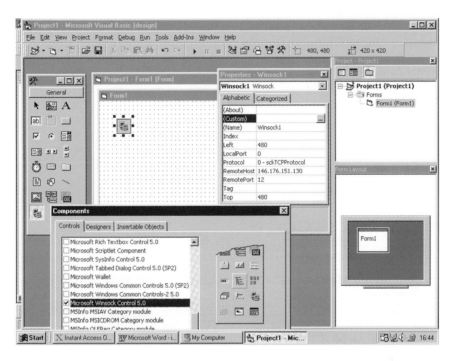

Figure D7.2   WinSock object

D7.3.1   Creating a server

A server must listen for connection. To do this, do the following:

1   Create a new standard EXE project.
2   Change the name of the default form to myServer.
3   Change the caption of the form to 'Server Application' (see Figure D7.3).
4   Put a WinSock control on the main form and change its name to myTCPServer.
5   Add two TextBox controls to the form. Name the first SendTxtData, and the second ShowText (see Figure D7.3).
6   Add the code given below to the form.

```
Private Sub Form_Load()
    ' Set the local port to 1001 and listen for a connection
    myTCPServer.LocalPort = 1001
```

```
    myTCPServer.Listen
    myClient.Show
End Sub

Private Sub myTCPServer_ConnectionRequest (ByVal requestID As Long)
    ' Check state of socket, if it is not closed then close it.
    If myTCPServer.State <> sckClosed Then myTCPServer.Close
    ' Accept the request with the requestID parameter.
    myTCPServer.Accept  requestID
End Sub

Private Sub SendTxtData_Change()
    ' SendTextData contains the data to be sent.
    ' This data is setn using the SendData method
    myTCPServer.SendData = SendTextData.Text
End Sub

Private Sub myTCPServer_DataArrival (ByVal bytesTotal As Long)
    ' Read incoming data into the str variable,
    ' then display it to ShowText
    Dim str As String
    myTCPServer.GetData str
    ShowText.Text = str
End Sub
```

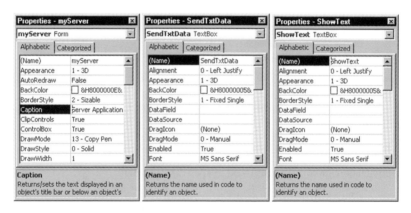

Figure D7.3   Server set-ups

Figure D7.4 shows the server set up.

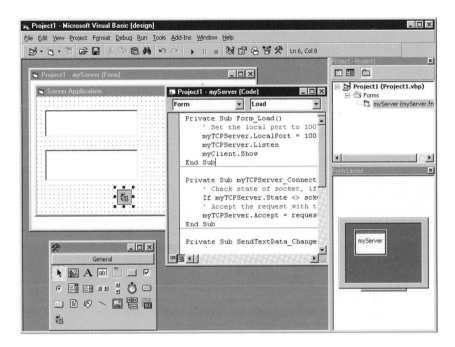

Figure D7.4   Server form

D7.3.2   Creating a client

The client must actively seek a connection. To create a client, do the following:

1   Add a new form to the project, and name it myClient.
2   Change the caption of the form to 'Client Application'.
3   Add a WinSock control to the form and name it myTCPClient.
4   Add two TextBox controls to the form. Name the first SendTxtData, and the second ShowText.
5   Draw a CommandButton control on the form and name it cmdConnect.
6   Change the caption of the CommandButton control to Connect.
7   Add the code given below to the form.

```
Private Sub Form_Load()
    ' In this case it will connect to 146.176.151.130
    ' change this to the local IP address or DNS of the local computer
    myTCPClient.RemoteHost = "146.176.151.130"
    myTCPClient.RemotePort = 1001
End Sub

Private Sub cmdConnect_Click()
    ' Connect to the server
    myTCPClient.Connect
End Sub
```

```
Private Sub SendTxtData_Change()
    myTCPClient.SendData SendTxtData.Text
End Sub

Private Sub tcpClient_DataArrival (ByVal bytesTotal As Long)
    Dim str As String
    myTCPClient.GetData str
    ShowText.Text = str
End Sub
```

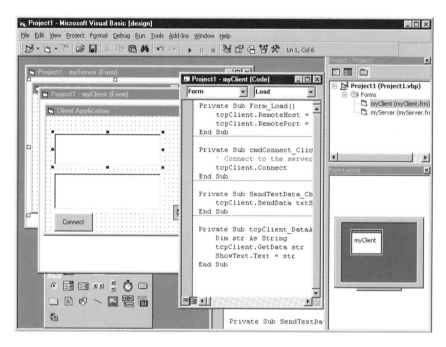

Figure D7.5   Client form

The program, when it is run, will act as a client and a server. Any text typed in the SendTxtData TextBox will be sent to the ShowText TextBox on the other form.

D7.3.3   Multiple connections

In Visual Basic, it is also possible to create multiple connections to a server. This is done by creating multiple occurrences of the server object. A new one is created every time there is a new connection (with the Connection_Request event). Each new server accepts the incoming connection. The following code, which has a WinSock control on a form called multServer, is given below.

```
Private ConnectNo As Long

Private Sub Form_Load()
```

```
      ConnectNo = 0
      multServer(0).LocalPort = 1001
      multServer(0).Listen
End Sub

Private Sub multServer_ConnectionRequest _
                        (Index As Integer, ByVal requestID As Long)
   If Index = 0 Then
      ConnectNo = ConnectNo + 1
      Load multServer(ConnectNo)
      multServer(ConnectNo).LocalPort = 0
      multServer(ConnectNo).Accept requestID
      Load txtData(ConnectNo)
   End If
End Sub
```

D7.3.4 Connect event

The Connect event connects to a server. If an error occurs then a flag (ErrorOccurred) is set to True, else it is False. Its syntax is

```
Private Sub object.Connect(ErrorOccurred As Boolean)
```

D7.3.5 Close event

The Close event occurs when the remote computer closes the connection. Applications should use the Close method to correctly close their connection. Its syntax is

```
object_Close()
```

D7.3.6 DataArrival event

The DataArrival event occurs when new data arrives, and returns the number of bytes read (bytesTotal). Its syntax is

```
object_DataArrival (bytesTotal As Long)
```

D7.3.7 Bind method

The Bind method specifies the local port (LocalPort) and the local IP address (LocalIP) to be used for TCP connections. Its syntax is

```
object.Bind LocalPort, LocalIP
```

D7.3.8 Listen method

The Listen method creates a socket and goes into listen mode (for server applications). Its stays in this mode until a ConnectionRequest event occurs, which indicates an incoming connection. After this, the Accept method should be used to accept the connection. Its syntax is:

object.Listen

D7.3.9 Accept method

The Accept method accepts incoming connections after a ConnectionRequest event. Its syntax is

object.Accept requestID

The requestID parameter is passed into the ConnectionRequest event and is used with the Accept method.

D7.3.10 Close method

The Close method closes a TCP connection. Its syntax is

object.Close

D7.3.11 SendData method

The SendData methods sends data (Data) to a remote computer. Its syntax is

object.SendData *Data*

D7.3.12 GetData method

The GetData method gets data (Data) from an object. Its syntax is

object.GetData data, [type,] [maxLen]

D7.4   Client/server VB program

Visual Basic contains a Winsock control, which can be used to provide TCP or UDP communications. When it is added to a form it is invisible to the user.

D7.4.1 Client operation

To create a client the following properties are set:

RemoteHost Set the IP address or the name of the server
RemotePort Set the remote port on which the server is listening

After this the client uses the Connect method.

D7.4.2 Server operation

LocalPort   Set the local port on which the server is listening

Next the server is set into the listen mode with the Listen method.

When a connection is made a ConnectionRequest event is caused. If the connection is to be accepted the Accept method is used.

D7.4.3 Communication

After the connection has been set-up the SendData method is used to send data and the GetData is used to read data. The client or server knows that data has arrived with the DataArrival method.

The code for the client form is:

```
Private Sub about_Click()
    frmAbout.Show
End Sub
Private Sub show_status()

    If (myTCPClient.State = sckClosed) Then
        status.Text = "CLOSED"
    ElseIf (myTCPClient.State = sckOpen) Then
        status.Text = "OPEN"
    ElseIf (myTCPClient.State = sckListen) Then
        status.Text = "LISTENING..."
    ElseIf (myTCPClient.State = sckConnecting) Then
        status.Text = "CONNECTING"
    ElseIf (myTCPClient.State = sckConnected) Then
        status.Text = "CONNECTED"
    ElseIf (myTCPClient.State = sckError) Then
        status.Text = "ERROR"
    Else
        status.Text = myTCPClient.State
    End If
End Sub

Private Sub cmdConnect_Click()
    If (myTCPClient.State <> sckClosed) Then myTCPClient.Close ' close existing
connection
    'Connect to the server
    myTCPClient.Connect
    server_address.Text = AddressIP.Text
    Call show_status
End Sub

Private Sub cmdDisConnect_Click()
    'Disconnect from the server
    myTCPClient.Close
    myTCPClient.RemoteHost = AddressIP.Text
    myTCPClient.RemotePort = AddressPort.Text
    Call show_status
End Sub

Private Sub Command1_Click()
    Call show_status
End Sub

Private Sub Form_Load()
    portnamec.AddItem ("Test")
    portnamec.AddItem ("Echo")
    portnamec.AddItem ("Daytime")
    portnamec.AddItem ("FTP")
    portnamec.AddItem ("SMTP")
    portnamec.AddItem ("Telnet")
```

> Method used to make a connection.

> Parameters used to set the remote host and the remote port.

```
        portnamec.AddItem ("Char. gen.")
        portnamec.AddItem ("Port 37")
        portnamec.AddItem ("WWW")
        portnamec.Text = "Test"
        AddressIP.AddItem "127.0.0.1"
        AddressPort.Text = "1001"
        localipaddress.Text = myTCPClient.LocalIP
        Call show_status
End Sub

Private Sub HelpClient_Click()
    If (myTCPClient.State <> sckClosed) Then myTCPClient.Close
    myTCPClient.RemoteHost = "www.dcs.napier.ac.uk"
    AddressIP.Text = "www.dcs.napier.ac.uk"
    AddressPort.Text = "13"
    portnamec.Text = "Daytime"
    myTCPClient.Connect
End Sub

Private Sub PortNameC_Click()
    'Choice of the port (name)
    If portnamec.Text = "Test" Then AddressPort.Text = "1001"
    If portnamec.Text = "Echo" Then AddressPort.Text = "7"
    If portnamec.Text = "Daytime" Then AddressPort.Text = "13"
    If portnamec.Text = "FTP" Then AddressPort.Text = "21"
    If portnamec.Text = "Telnet" Then AddressPort.Text = "23"
    If portnamec.Text = "SMTP" Then AddressPort.Text = "25"
    If portnamec.Text = "Char. gen." Then AddressPort.Text = "19"
    If portnamec.Text = "Port 37" Then AddressPort.Text = "37"
    If portnamec.Text = "WWW" Then AddressPort.Text = "80"
End Sub

Private Sub myTCPClient_DataArrival(ByVal bytesTotal As Long)
    'Display incoming data
    Dim str1 As String, str2 As String, str As String   'declare old, new, to-
tal data
    str1 = ShowText.Text      'old data
    myTCPClient.GetData str2    'incoming data (new data)
    str = str1 + str2    'total data to display
    ShowText.Text = str 'display to ShowText
End Sub

Private Sub myTCPClient_Close()
    If (myTCPClient.State = sckClosed) Or (myTCPClient.State = sckClosing) Then
        Call show_status
    Else
        myTCPServer.Close  ◄---------------------┤ Method used to close
    End If                                         the current connec-
                                                   tion.
End Sub

Private Sub AddressIP_Click()
    If (myTCPClient.State <> sckClosed) Then myTCPClient.Close ' close exist-
ing connection
    'Choose IP Address
    myTCPClient.RemoteHost = AddressIP.Text
End Sub

Private Sub AddressIP_Change()
    If (myTCPClient.State <> sckClosed) Then myTCPClient.Close ' close exist-
ing connection
    'Enter IP or DNS address
    myTCPClient.RemoteHost = AddressIP.Text
End Sub
```

```
Private Sub AddressPort_Change()
    If (myTCPClient.State <> sckClosed) Then myTCPClient.Close ' close exist-
ing connection
    'Change port number directly in the AddressPort box (manually)
    myTCPClient.RemotePort = AddressPort.Text
End Sub

Private Sub CloseC_Click()
    'Return to main menu
    End

End Sub

Private Sub SendTextData_KeyPress(KeyAscii As Integer)
    'When you press the ENTER key the contain of the top box is sent
    If KeyAscii = 13 Then
    myTCPClient.SendData SendTextData.Text + vbCrLf
    show_text_sent = show_text_sent + SendTextData.Text + vbCrLf
    SendTextData.Text = ""
    End If
End Sub
```

and the server code is:

```
Private Sub About_Click()
    frmAbout.Show
End Sub

Private Sub exit_Click()
    End
End Sub

Private Sub Form_Load()
    ' Set the local port to 1001 and listen for a connection
    listenport.Text = "1001"
    localipaddress.Text = myTCPServer.LocalIP ' Show local IP address
    Call show_status
End Sub
Private Sub show_status()

    If (myTCPServer.State = sckClosed) Then
        status.Text = "CLOSED"
    ElseIf (myTCPServer.State = sckOpen) Then
        status.Text = "OPEN"
    ElseIf (myTCPServer.State = sckListening) Then
        status.Text = "LISTENING..."
    ElseIf (myTCPServer.State = sckConnecting) Then
        status.Text = "CONNECTING"
    ElseIf (myTCPServer.State = sckConnected) Then
        status.Text = "CONNECTED"
    ElseIf (myTCPServer.State = sckError) Then
        status.Text = "ERROR"
    Else
        status.Text = myTCPServer.State
    End If
End Sub

Private Sub listenport_Change()
    If myTCPServer.State <> sckClosed Then myTCPServer.Close
    myTCPServer.LocalPort = listenport.Text
    myTCPServer.Listen
    Call show_status
```

> Method used to determine the state of the connection.

> Set local port, and set the server into listen mode.

```
End Sub

Private Sub myTCPServer_Close()
    If myTCPServer.State <> sckClosed Then myTCPServer.Close
    myTCPServer.LocalPort = listenport.Text
    myTCPServer.Listen
    ipaddress.Text = ""
    iphost.Text = ""
    remoteport.Text = ""
    Call show_status
End Sub

Private Sub myTCPServer_ConnectionRequest(ByVal requestID As Long)
    ' Check state of socket, if it is not closed then close it.
    If myTCPServer.State <> sckClosed Then myTCPServer.Close
    ' Accept the request with the requestID parameter.
    myTCPServer.Accept requestID
    ipaddress.Text = myTCPServer.RemoteHostIP
    If (myTCPServer.Protocol = 0) Then
        iphost.Text = "TCP"
    Else
        iphost.Text = "UDP"
    End If
    remoteport.Text = myTCPServer.remoteport
    Check1.Value = 1 ' show that remote has connected
    Call show_status
End Sub

Private Sub myTCPServer_DataArrival(ByVal bytesTotal As Long)
    ' Read incoming data into the str variable,
    ' then display it to ShowText
    Dim str As String
    myTCPServer.GetData str
    ShowText.Text = ShowText.Text + str
    Call show_status
End Sub

Private Sub SendTextData_KeyPress(KeyAscii As Integer)
    Call show_status
    If (KeyAscii = 13) Then
        myTCPServer.SendData SendTextData.Text + vbCrLf
        show_text_sent = show_text_sent + SendTextData.Text + vbCrLf
        SendTextData.Text = ""
    End If
End Sub
```

> Event caused when the client connects to the server.

> Event caused when data arrives from the client.

> Method used to get the data which has just arrived.

> Method used to send data to the client.

Screen shots from development system are given in Figure D7.6. In this case a remote computer is set to listen for a connection. The client then connects into it by connecting to the server's IP address. The server will then show the connection. After this the user on the client machine and the user on the server can communicate using the text windows. In this case they connect using port 1001.

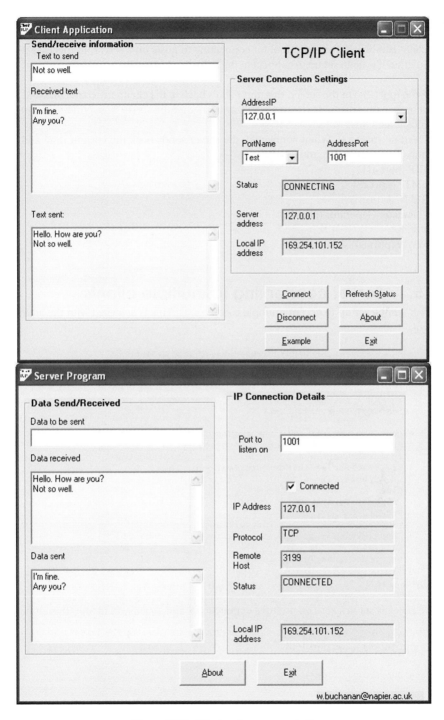

Figure D7.6 Client and server programs

D7.4.4 Testing server connections

The client can be used as a test tool for connecting to ports on a server. In this case the client program has been set up to connect to the following ports:

- Echo (port 7). On the server, this port echo's back to the client any characters that it has sent. It is thus useful for testing a link, and whether the server is responding to communications.
- Daytime (port 13). When connected, the server sends back the current time and date, and disconnects the connection.
- FTP (port 21).
- SMTP (port 25).
- TELNET (port 23).
- Character Generator (port 19).
- Port 37.
- WWW (port 80).

D7.5   Server connecting to multiple clients

A server can be set up to accept multiple connections. This is achieved with the additional code of:

```
Private Sub myTCPServer_ConnectionRequest(Index As Integer,
                                    ByVal requestID As Long)
    If Index = 0 Then

        intMax = intMax + 1
        Load myTCPServer(intMax)

    ' Accept the request with the requestID parameter.
        myTCPServer(intMax).Accept requestID
        ipaddress.Text = myTCPServer(intMax).RemoteHostIP
        If (myTCPServer(intMax).Protocol = 0) Then
            iphost.Text = "TCP"
        Else
            iphost.Text = "UDP"
        End If
        remoteport.Text = myTCPServer(Index).remoteport
        Check1.Value = 1 ' show that remote has connected
        Call show_status
        no_connections.Text = intMax
    End If
End Sub
```

where `Index` is set to a zero on multiple connections, and `requestID` defines the connection ID.

```
Dim intMax As Long

Private Sub About_Click()
    frmAbout.Show
End Sub

Private Sub exit_Click()
    End
End Sub
```

```
Private Sub Form_Load()
    intMax = 0
    ' Set the local port to 1001 and listen for a connection
    listenport.Text = "1001"
    localipaddress.Text = myTCPServer(0).LocalIP ' Show local IP address
    Call show_status
End Sub

Private Sub show_status()
' Shows the state of first server connection
    If (myTCPServer(0).State = sckClosed) Then
        status.Text = "CLOSED"
    ElseIf (myTCPServer(0).State = sckOpen) Then
        status.Text = "OPEN"
    ElseIf (myTCPServer(0).State = sckListening) Then
        status.Text = "LISTENING..."
    ElseIf (myTCPServer(0).State = sckConnecting) Then
        status.Text = "CONNECTING"
    ElseIf (myTCPServer(0).State = sckConnected) Then
        status.Text = "CONNECTED"
    ElseIf (myTCPServer(0).State = sckError) Then
        status.Text = "ERROR"
    Else
        status.Text = myTCPServer(0).State
    End If
End Sub

Private Sub listenport_Change()
    If myTCPServer(0).State <> sckClosed Then myTCPServer(0).Close
    myTCPServer(0).LocalPort = listenport.Text
    myTCPServer(0).Listen
    Call show_status
End Sub

Private Sub myTCPServer_Close(Index As Integer)
    If myTCPServer(Index).State <> sckClosed Then myTCPServer(Index).Close
    myTCPServer(Index).LocalPort = listenport.Text
    myTCPServer(Index).Listen
    ipaddress.Text = ""
    iphost.Text = ""
    remoteport.Text = ""
    Call show_status
End Sub

Private Sub myTCPServer_ConnectionRequest(Index As Integer, _
                                          ByVal requestID As Long)

    If Index = 0 Then

        intMax = intMax + 1
        Load myTCPServer(intMax)

    ' Accept the request with the requestID parameter.
        myTCPServer(intMax).Accept requestID
        ipaddress.Text = myTCPServer(intMax).RemoteHostIP
        If (myTCPServer(intMax).Protocol = 0) Then
            iphost.Text = "TCP"
        Else
            iphost.Text = "UDP"
        End If
        remoteport.Text = myTCPServer(Index).remoteport
        Check1.Value = 1 ' show that remote has connected
        Call show_status
        no_connections.Text = intMax
```

```
        End If
End Sub

Private Sub myTCPServer_DataArrival(Index As Integer, ByVal requestID As Long)
    ' Read incoming data into the str variable,
    ' then display it to ShowText
    Dim str As String
    myTCPServer(Index).GetData str
    ShowText.Text = ShowText.Text + str
    Call show_status
End Sub

Private Sub SendTextData_KeyPress(KeyAscii As Integer)
    Call show_status
    If (KeyAscii = 13) Then
        myTCPServer(0).SendData SendTextData.Text + vbCrLf
        show_text_sent = show_text_sent + SendTextData.Text + vbCrLf
        SendTextData.Text = ""
    End If
End Sub
```

A sample run of the server, with two connections, is shown in Figure D7.7.

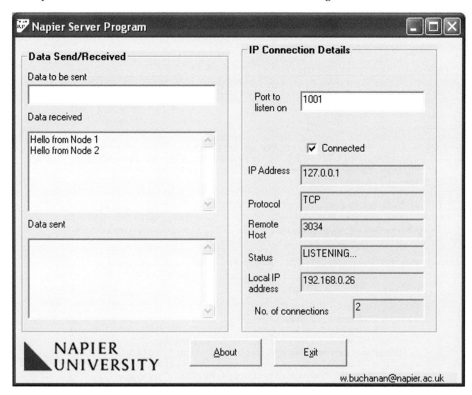

Figure D7.7   Server accepting two connections

D7.6   Java sockets

Figure D7.8 shows the operation of a connection of a client to a server. The server is defined as the computer which waits for a connection, the client is the computer which initially makes contact with the server.

On the server the computer initially creates a socket with `ServerSocket()` method, and then listens for a connection. The client creates a socket with the `Socket()` method. When the server receives this connection it accepts it with the `accept()` method. Streams can then be set up on these sockets with the `getInputStream()` and `getOutputStream()` methods, and the `readUTF()` and `writeUTF()` methods can be used to read and write data to/from the stream. When the data transfer is complete the `close()` method is used to close any open sockets.

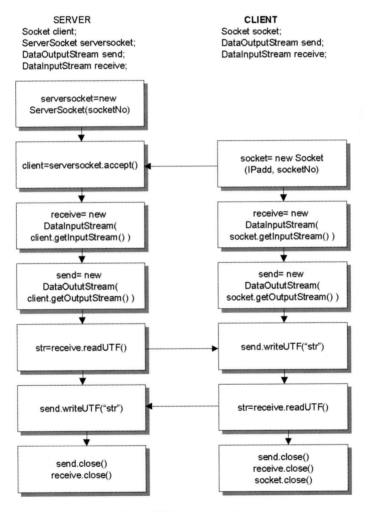

Figure D7.8 Socket connection

Data is received using:

```
try
 {
  DataOutputStream send=new DataOutputStream(client.getOutputStream());
  send.writeUTF(str);
 }
 catch (IOException e)
 {
   //something
 }
```

and transmitted with:

```
try
 {
   DataInputStream receive=new DataInputStream(client.getInputStream());
   str=receive.readUTF();
 }
 catch (IOException e)
 {    //something  }
```

D7.6.1   class java.net.Socket

The TCP protocol links two computers using sockets and ports. The constructors for `java.net.Socket` are:

`public Socket(InetAddress address, int port)`	Creates a stream socket and connects it to the specified address (`address`) on the specified port (`port`).
`public Socket(String host, int port)`	Creates a stream socket and connects it to the specified port (`port`) on the specified host (`host`).

The methods are:

`public synchronized void close()`	Closes the socket.
`public InetAddress getInetAddress()`	Returns the address to which the socket is connected.
`public InputStream getInputStream()`	Returns the `InputStream` for this socket.
`public int getLocalPort()`	Returns the local port to which the socket is connected.
`public OutputStream getOutputStream()`	Returns an `OutputStream` for this socket.
`public int getPort()`	Returns the remote port to which the socket is connected.
`public String toString()`	Converts the Socket to a String.

D7.6.2 Creating a socket

Java applet D7.1 constructs a socket for `www.eece.napier.ac.uk` using port 19 (`Socket re-mote = new Socket("www.eece.napier.ac.uk",19)`). After this the data stream is created and assigned to `DataIn`. The `readUTF()` method is then used to get the text from the stream.

📖 Java applet D7.1

```
import java.io.*;
import java.net.*;
import java.awt.*;
import java.applet.*;

public class client1 extends Applet
{
    TextArea tarea = new TextArea(5,50);

    public void init()
    {
    String          Instr;
    InputStream     Instream;
    TextArea        tarea;

        add(tarea);
        try
        {
            Socket remote = new Socket("www.eece.napier.ac.uk",19);

            Instream = remote.getInputStream();
            DataInputStream DataIn = new DataInputStream(Instream);
            do
            {
                Instr = DataIn.readUTF();
                if (Instr!=null)  tarea.setText(Instr);
            } while (Instr!=null);
        }
        catch (UnknownHostException err)
        {
            tarea.setText("UNKNOWN HOST: "+err);
        }
        catch (IOException err)
        {
            tarea.setText("Error" + err); }
        }
    }
}
```

Java program 2 contacts a server on a given port and returns the local and remote port. It uses command line arguments, and the program is run in the form:

```
java client2 host port
```

where `java` is the Java interpreter, `client2` is the name of the class file, *host* is the name of the host to contact and *port* is the port to use. The `args.length` parameter is used to determine the number of command line options. Anything other than two will display the following message:

```
Usage : client2 host port
```

📖 Java program D7.2

```
import java.net.*;
import java.io.*;
public class client2
{
    public static void main (String args[])
    {
        if (args.length !=2)
            System.out.println(" Usage : client2 host port");
        else
        {
            String inp;
            try
            {
                Socket sock = new Socket(args[0],
                            Integer.valueOf(args[1]).intValue());
                DataInputStream is =
                            new DataInputStream(sock.getInputStream());
                System.out.println("address : " +  sock.getInetAddress());
                System.out.println("port : " +  sock.getPort());
                System.out.println("Local address : " +
                                            sock.getLocalAddress());
                System.out.println("Localport : " + sock.getLocalPort());

                while((inp = is.readUTF()) != null)
                { System.out.println(inp);}
            }
            catch (UnknownHostException e)
            {
                System.out.println(" Known Host : " + e.getMessage());
            }
            catch (IOException e)
            {
                System.out.println("error I/O : " + e.getMessage());
            }
            finally
            {
                System.out.println("End of program");
            }
        }
    }
}
```

Sample run D7.1 shows a sample run which connects to port 13 on www.eece.napier.ac.uk. It can be seen that the connection to this port causes the server to return back the current date and time. Sample run D7.2 connects into the same server, in this case on port 19. It can be seen that a connection to this port returns a sequence of characters. Typical port values are: echo (7), null (9), daytime (13), character test (19), ftp (21), telnet (23), SMTP (25), TIME (37), DNS (53), HTTP (80) and POP3 (110).

💻 Sample run D7.1

```
>> java client2 www.eece.napier.ac.uk 13
Host and IP address : www.eece.napier.ac.uk/146.176.151.139
port : 13
Local address :pc419.eece.napier.ac.uk
Localport : 1393
Fri May  8 13:19:59 1998
End of program
```

```
>> java client2 www.eece.napier.ac.uk 19
Host and IP address : www.eece.napier.ac.uk/146.176.151.139
port : 19
Local IP address :pc419.eece.napier.ac.uk
Localport : 1403
 !"#$%&'()*+,-./0123456789:;<=>?@ABCDEFGHIJKLMNOPQRSTUVWXYZ[\]^_`abcdefg
!"#$%&'()*+,-./0123456789:;<=>?@ABCDEFGHIJKLMNOPQRSTUVWXYZ[\]^_`abcdefgh
"#$%&'()*+,-./0123456789:;<=>?@ABCDEFGHIJKLMNOPQRSTUVWXYZ[\]^_`abcdefghi
#$%&'()*+,-./0123456789:;<=>?@ABCDEFGHIJKLMNOPQRSTUVWXYZ[\]^_`abcdefghij
$%&'()*+,-./0123456789:;<=>?@ABCDEFGHIJKLMNOPQRSTUVWXYZ[\]^_`abcdefghijk
%&'()*+,-./0123456789:;<=>?@ABCDEFGHIJKLMNOPQRSTUVWXYZ[\]^_`abcdefghijkl
&'()*+,-./0123456789:;<=>?@ABCDEFGHIJKLMNOPQRSTUVWXYZ[\]^_`abcdefghijklm
'()*+,-./0123456789:;<=>?@ABCDEFGHIJKLMNOPQRSTUVWXYZ[\]^_`abcdefghijklmn
()*+,-./0123456789:;<=>?@ABCDEFGHIJKLMNOPQRSTUVWXYZ[\]^_`abcdefghijklmno
)*+,-./0123456789:;<=>?@ABCDEFGHIJKLMNOPQRSTUVWXYZ[\]^_`abcdefghijklmnop
*+,-./0123456789:;<=>?@ABCDEFGHIJKLMNOPQRSTUVWXYZ[\]^_`abcdefghijklmnopq
+,-./0123456789:;<=>?@ABCDEFGHIJKLMNOPQRSTUVWXYZ[\]^_`abcdefghijklmnopqr
```

D7.6.3 Client/server program

A server is a computer which runs a special program which passively waits for another computer (a client) to connect to it. This server normally performs some sort of special operation, such as FTP, Telnet or WWW service.

Java program D7.3 acts as a server program and waits for a connection on port 1111. When a connection is received on this port it sends its current date and time back to the client. This program can be run with Java program D7.2 (which is running on a remote computer) with a connection to the server's IP address (or domain name) and using port 1111. When the client connects to the server, the server responds back to the client with its current date and time.

📖 Java program D7.3

```java
import java.net.*;
import java.io.*;
import java.util.*;

class server
{
   public static void main( String arg[])
   {
      try
   {
      ServerSocket sock = new ServerSocket(1111);
         Socket sock1 = sock.accept();

         System.out.println(sock1.toString());
         System.out.println("address : " +     sock1.getInetAddress());
         System.out.println("port    : " +     sock1.getPort());

         DataOutputStream out =
             new DataOutputStream(sock1.getOutputStream());

         out.writeUTF("Welcome "+ sock1.getInetAddress().getHostName()+
             ". We are "+ new Date()+ "\n");

         sock1.close();
         sock.close();
```

```
        }
        catch(IOException err)
        {
                System.out.println(err.getMessage());
        }
        finally
        {
                System.out.println("End of the program");
        }
        }
}
```

D7.7   Java networking methods

Java directly supports TCP/IP communications and has the following classes:

java.net.ContentHandler	Class which reads data from a URLConnection and also supports MIME (Multipurpose Internet Mail Extension).
java.net.DatagramPacket	Class representing a datagram packet which contains packet data, packet length, Internet addresses and the port number.
java.net.DatagramSocket	Class representing a datagram socket class.
java.net.InetAddress	Class representing Internet addresses.
java.net.ServerSocket	Class representing Socket server class.
java.net.Socket	Class representing Socket client classes.
java.net.SocketImpl	Socket implementation class.
java.net.URL	Class URL representing a Uniform Reference Locator (URL) which is a reference to an object on the WWW.
java.net.URLConnection	Class representing an active connection to an object represented by a URL.
java.net.URLEncoder	Converts strings of text into URLEncoded format.
java.net.URLStreamHandler	Class for opening URL streams.

When an error occurs in the connection or in the transmission and reception of data it causes an exception. The classes which handle these are:

java.io.IOException	To handle general errors.
java.net.MalformedURLException	Malformed URL.
java.net.ProtocolException	Protocol error.
java.net.SocketException	Socket error.
java.net.UnknownHostException	Unknown host error.
java.net.UnknownServiceException	Unknown service error.

D7.7.1   class java.net.InetAddress

This class represents Internet addresses. The methods are:

`public static synchronized InetAddress[] getAllByName(String host)`	This returns an array with all the corresponding InetAddresses for a given host name (`host`).
`public static synchronized InetAddress getByName(String host)`	This returns the network address of an indicated host. A hostname of null returns the default address for the local machine.
`public String getHostAddress()`	This returns the IP address string (WW.XX.YY.ZZ) in a string format.
`public byte[] getAddress()`	This returns the raw IP address in network byte order. The array position 0 (addr[0]) contains the highest order byte.
`public String getHostName()`	Gets the hostname for this address. If the host is equal to null, then this address refers to any of the local machine's available network addresses.
`public static InetAddress getLocalHost()`	Returns the local host.
`public String toString()`	Converts the InetAddress to a String.

Java applet D7.4 uses the `getAllByName` method to determine all the IP addresses associated with an Internet host. In this case the host is named `www.microsoft.com`. It can be seen from the test run that there are 18 IP addresses associated with this domain name. It can be seen that the applet causes an exception error as the loop tries to display 30 such IP addresses. When the program reaches the 19th InetAddress, the exception error is displayed (`ArrayIndexOutOfBoundsException`).

📖 Java applet D7.4

```
import java.net.*;
import java.awt.*;
import java.applet.*;
public class http1 extends Applet
{
InetAddress[] address;
int i
   public void start()
   {
      System.out.println("Started");
      try
      {
         address=InetAddress.getAllByName("www.microsoft.com");
         for (i=0;i<30;i++)
         {
            System.out.println("Address " + address[i]);
         }
      }
      catch (Exception e)
      {
         System.out.println("Error :" + e);
      }
   }
}
```

🖥 Sample run D7.3

```
Started
Address www.microsoft.com/207.68.137.59
Address www.microsoft.com/207.68.143.192
Address www.microsoft.com/207.68.143.193
Address www.microsoft.com/207.68.143.194
Address www.microsoft.com/207.68.143.195
Address www.microsoft.com/207.68.156.49
Address www.microsoft.com/207.68.137.56
Address www.microsoft.com/207.68.156.51
Address www.microsoft.com/207.68.156.52
Address www.microsoft.com/207.68.137.62
Address www.microsoft.com/207.68.156.53
Address www.microsoft.com/207.68.156.54
Address www.microsoft.com/207.68.137.65
Address www.microsoft.com/207.68.156.73
Address www.microsoft.com/207.68.156.61
Address www.microsoft.com/207.68.156.16
Address www.microsoft.com/207.68.156.58
Address www.microsoft.com/207.68.137.53
Error :java.lang.ArrayIndexOutOfBoundsException: 18
```

Java applet D7.5 overcomes the problem of the displaying of the exception. In this case the exception is caught by inserting the address display within a `try {}` statement then having a catch statement which does nothing. Sample run D7.4 shows a sample run.

📖 Java applet D7.5

```java
import java.net.*;
import java.awt.*;
import java.applet.*;

public class http2 extends Applet
{
InetAddress[] address;
int i;
   public void start()
   {
       System.out.println("Started");
       try
       {
           address=InetAddress.getAllByName("www.microsoft.com");
           try
           {
               for (i=0;i<30;i++)
               {
                   System.out.println("Address " + address[i]);
               }
           }
           catch(Exception e)
           { / * Do nothing about the exception, as it
                 is not really an error */
           }
       }
       catch (Exception e)
       {
           System.out.println("Error :" + e);
       }
   }
}
```

```
Started
Address www.microsoft.com/207.68.137.59
Address www.microsoft.com/207.68.143.192
Address www.microsoft.com/207.68.143.193
Address www.microsoft.com/207.68.143.194
Address www.microsoft.com/207.68.143.195
Address www.microsoft.com/207.68.156.49
Address www.microsoft.com/207.68.137.56
Address www.microsoft.com/207.68.156.51
Address www.microsoft.com/207.68.156.52
Address www.microsoft.com/207.68.137.62
Address www.microsoft.com/207.68.156.53
Address www.microsoft.com/207.68.156.54
Address www.microsoft.com/207.68.137.65
Address www.microsoft.com/207.68.156.73
Address www.microsoft.com/207.68.156.61
Address www.microsoft.com/207.68.156.16
Address www.microsoft.com/207.68.156.58
Address www.microsoft.com/207.68.137.53
```

Java applet D7.6 shows an example of displaying the local host name (getLocalHost), the host name (getHostName) and the host's IP address (getHostAddress). Test run D7.5 shows a sample run.

📖 Java applet D7.6

```java
import java.net.*;
import java.awt.*;
import java.applet.*;

public class http3 extends Applet
{
InetAddress host;
String str;
int i;
    public void start()
    {
        System.out.println("Started");
        try
        {
            host=InetAddress.getLocalHost();
            System.out.println("Local host " + host);
            str=host.getHostName();
            System.out.println("Host name: " + str);
            str=host.getHostAddress();
            System.out.println("Host address: " + str);
        }
        catch (Exception e)
        {
            System.out.println("Error :" + e);
        }
    }
}
```

```
Started
Local host toshiba/195.232.26.125
Host name: toshiba
Host address: 195.232.26.125
```

The previous Java applets have all displayed their output to the output terminal (with `Sys-tem.out.println`). Java applet D7.7 uses the `drawString` method to display the output text to the Applet window. Figure D7.9 shows a sample run.

📖 Java applet D7.7

```java
import java.net.*;
import java.awt.*;
import java.applet.*;

public class http4 extends Applet
{
InetAddress[] address;
int i;
   public void paint(Graphics g)
   {
      g.drawString("Addresses for WWW.MICROSOFT.COM",5,10);
      try
      {
         address=InetAddress.getAllByName("www.microsoft.com");

         for (i=0;i<30;i++)
         {
            g.drawString(" "+ address[i].toString(),5,20+10*i);
         }
      }
      catch (Exception e)
      {
         System.out.println("Error :" + e);
      }
   }
}
```

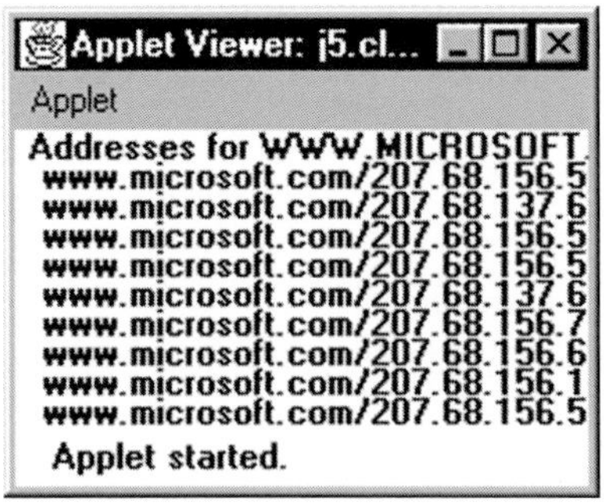

Figure D7.9 Sample run

D7.7.2 class java.net.URL

The URL (Uniform Reference Locator) class is used to reference to an object on the World Wide Web. The main constructors are:

`public URL(String protocol, String host, int port, String file)`	Creates an absolute URL from the specified protocol (`protocol`), host (`host`), port (`port`) and file (`file`).
`public URL(String protocol, String host, String file)`	Creates an absolute URL from the specified protocol (`protocol`), host (`host`) and file (`file`).
`public URL(String spec)`	Creates a URL from an unparsed absolute URL (`spec`)
`public URL(URL context, String spec)`	Creates a URL from an unparsed absolute URL (`spec`) in the specified context.

The methods are:

`public int getPort()`	Returns a port number. A return value of –1 indicates that the port is not set.
`public String getProtocol()`	Returns the protocol name.
`public String getHost()`	Returns the host name.
`public String getFile()`	Returns the file name.
`public boolean equals(Object obj)`	Compares two URLs, where `obj` is the URL to compare against.
`public String toString()`	Converts to a string format.
`public String toExternalForm()`	Reverses the URL parsing.
`public URLConnection openConnection()`	Creates a URLConnection object that contains a connection to the remote object referred to by the URL.
`public final InputStream openStream()`	Opens an input stream.
`public final Object getContent()`	Gets the contents from this opened connection.

D7.7.3   class java.net.URLConnection

Represents an active connection to an object represented by a URL. The main methods are:

`public abstract void connect()`	URLConnection objects are initially created and then they are connected.
`public URL getURL()`	Returns the URL for this connection.
`public int getContentLength()`	Returns the content length, a –1 if not known.

`public String getContentType()`	Returns the content type, a null if not known.
`public String getContentEncoding()`	Returns the content encoding, a null if not known.
`public long getExpiration()`	Returns the expiration date of the object, a 0 if not known.
`public long getDate()`	Returns the sending date of the object, a 0 if not known.
`public long getLastModified()`	Returns the last modified date of the object, a 0 if not known.
`public String getHeaderField` `    (String name)`	Returns a header field by name (name), a null if not known.
`public Object getContent()`	Returns the object referred to by this URL.
`public InputStream getInputStream()`	Used to read from objects.
`public OutputStream getOutputStream()`	Used to write to objects.
`public String toString()`	Returns the String URL representation.

D7.7.4   class java.net.URLStreamHandler

Abstract class for URL stream openers. Subclasses of this class know how to create streams for particular protocol types.

`protected abstract URLConnection` `    openConnection(URL u)`	Opens an input stream to the object referenced by the URL (u).
`protected void parseURL(URL u, String` `    spec, int start, int limit)`	Parses the string (spec) into URL (u), where start and limit refer to the range of characters in spec that should be parsed.
`protected String toExternalForm(URL u)`	Reverses the parsing of the URL.

`protected void setURL(URL u,  String`
`    protocol, String host, int port,`
`    String file, String ref)`
	Calls the (protected) set method out of the URL given.

D7.7.5   java.applet.AppletContext

The AppletContext can be used by an applet to obtain information from the applet's environment, which is usually the browser or the applet viewer. Related methods are:

`public abstract void showDocument(URL url)`	Shows a new document.
`public abstract void showDocument(URL url,` `    String target)`	Show a new document in a target window or frame.

D7.7.6 Connecting to a WWW site

Java applet D7.8 shows an example of an applet that connects to a WWW site. It allows the user to enter a URL and it also shows a status window (`status`).

📖 Java applet D7.8

```java
import java.net.*;
import java.awt.*;
import java.applet.*;

public class j1 extends Applet
{
URL       urlWWW;
Button    btn;
Label     label = new Label("Enter a URL:");
TextField inURL = new TextField(30);
TextArea status = new TextArea(3,30);

    public void init()
        {
            add(label);
            add(inURL);
            btn = (new Button("Connect"));
            add(btn);
            add(status);
        }

        public void getURL()//Check for valid URL
        {
            try
            {
                String str;
                str=inURL.getText();
                status.setText("Site: " + str);
                urlWWW  = new URL(str);
            }
            catch (MalformedURLException e)
            {
                status.setText("URL Error: " + e);
            }
        }

        public boolean action(Event evt, Object obj)
        {
            if (evt.target.equals(btn))
            {
                status.setText("Connecting...\n");
                getURL();
                getAppletContext().showDocument(urlWWW);
                return true;
            }
            return false;
        }
}
```

D7.8 Delphi sockets

D7.8.1 Delphi sockets (client)

Delphi has a ClientSocket component which supports a client connection to a server. This is contained in the Internet palette. An example of a client socket added to a form is shown in Figure D7.10.

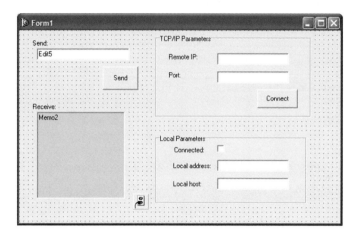

Figure D7.10 Adding a client socket to a form

In the example in Figure D7.10 the following code can be used to make a connection to a server:

```
procedure TForm1.Button1Click(Sender: TObject);
var port:integer;
begin
        port:=StrToInt(edit4.text);
        ClientSocket.Port:=port;
        ClientSocket.Host:=edit3.text;
        ClientSocket.ClientType:=ctNonBlocking;
        ClientSocket.Active:=true;
end;
```

Initially the properties are set for the socket connection, such as the port, and the server address. Finally the active property is set, which causes the client to connect to the server. When the client detects a connection, the Connection event occurs:

```
procedure TForm1.ClientSocketConnect(Sender: TObject;
                                        Socket: TCustomWinSocket);
begin
        Checkbox1.Checked:=true;
        Edit1.Text:=Socket.LocalAddress;
        Edit2.Text:=Socket.LocalHost;
        Memo2.Lines.Clear;
        edit5.Text:='';
end;
```

The Socket variable contains the information on the connection, such as the LocalAddress,

LocalHost, LocalPort, RemoteAddress, RemoteHost and RemoteAddress.

When the code is ready to be send the:

```
ClientSocket.Socket.SendText(edit5.text + chr(13)+chr(10));
```

The SendText method is used to send the text over the connected socket. Figure D7.11 shows an example of some of the properties and routines associated with sockets. In addition, in this example, the ASCII characters for Line Feed (10) and Carriage Return (13) are sent to force a new line on the server.

When data arrives over the socket, the Read event is called (with the information on the socket passed in the Socket parameter). The ReceiveText property can then be used to read the data from the socket (as illustrated in Figure D7.12):

```
procedure TForm1.ClientSocketRead(Sender: TObject;
                                  Socket: TCustomWinSocket);
begin
  Memo2.Lines.Add(Socket.ReceiveText);
end;
```

Program D7.1 lists an outline of the code.

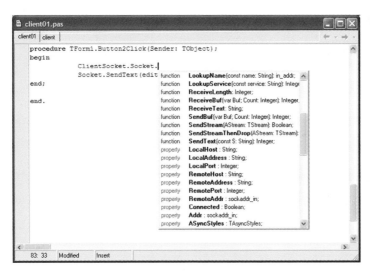

Figure D7.11 Some of the properties and routines associated with the socket

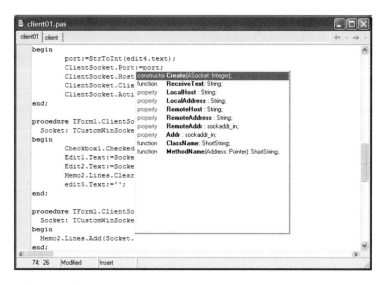

Figure D7.12 Some of the properties and routines associated with the socket

---

📋 **Delphi program D7.1**

```
unit client01;

interface

uses
  Windows, Messages, SysUtils, Variants, Classes, Graphics, Controls,
  Forms,Dialogs, ScktComp, StdCtrls;

type
  TForm1 = class(TForm)
    ClientSocket: TClientSocket;
    Label1: TLabel;
    Label2: TLabel;
    GroupBox1: TGroupBox;
    Edit3: TEdit;
    Label3: TLabel;
    Label5: TLabel;
    Edit4: TEdit;
    Button1: TButton;
    Memo2: TMemo;
    GroupBox2: TGroupBox;
    CheckBox1: TCheckBox;
    Label4: TLabel;
    Label6: TLabel;
    Edit1: TEdit;
    Edit2: TEdit;
    Label7: TLabel;
    Edit5: TEdit;
    Button2: TButton;

    procedure ClientSocketRead(Sender: TObject;
                                              Socket: TCustomWinSocket);
    procedure Button1Click(Sender: TObject);
    procedure ClientSocketConnect(Sender: TObject;
```

```
                                                     Socket: TCustomWinSocket);

    procedure Button2Click(Sender: TObject);

  private
    { Private declarations }
  public
    { Public declarations }
  end;

var
  Form1: TForm1;


implementation

{$R *.dfm}

procedure TForm1.Button1Click(Sender: TObject);
var port:integer;
begin
        port:=StrToInt(edit4.text);
        ClientSocket.Port:=port;
        ClientSocket.Host:=edit3.text;
        ClientSocket.ClientType:=ctNonBlocking;
        ClientSocket.Active:=true;
end;

procedure TForm1.ClientSocketConnect(Sender: TObject;
  Socket: TCustomWinSocket);
begin
        Checkbox1.Checked:=true;
        Edit1.Text:=Socket.LocalAddress;
        Edit2.Text:=Socket.LocalHost;
        Memo2.Lines.Clear;
        edit5.Text:='';
end;

procedure TForm1.ClientSocketRead(Sender: TObject;
                                                     Socket: TCustomWinSocket);
begin
  Memo2.Lines.Add(Socket.ReceiveText);
end;

procedure TForm1.Button2Click(Sender: TObject);
begin
      ClientSocket.Socket.SendText(edit5.text + chr(13)+chr(10));
end;

end.
```

A sample run is given in Figure D7.13.

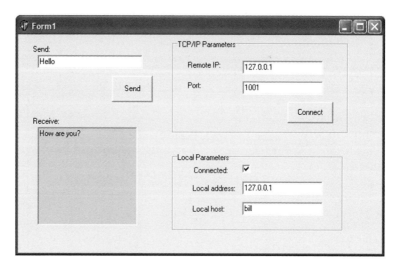

Figure D7.13 Sample run of the client

D7.8.2 Delphi sockets (Server)

A server differs for a client in that it waits for a connection from a client. When a client and server are used together, it is known as a client-server architecture. A sample design with the server component is given in Figure D7.14. Initially the server goes into a listening mode with the following:

```
procedure TForm1.FormCreate(Sender: TObject);
var port:integer;
begin
        port:=StrToInt(Edit1.Text);
        ServerSocket1.Port:=port;
        ServerSocket1.Active:=True;
        edit4.text:='Listening ...';
end;
```

This will listen on the port defined by the `port` variable. When a client connects the Accept event is called. Example code for this is:

```
procedure TForm1.ServerSocket1Accept(Sender: TObject;
  Socket: TCustomWinSocket);
begin
        Checkbox1.Checked:=true;
        edit2.text:=Socket.RemoteAddress;
        edit3.Text:=Socket.RemoteHost;
        edit5.text:=Socket.LocalAddress;
        edit4.text:='Connected';
end;
```

which displays that the connection has been made.

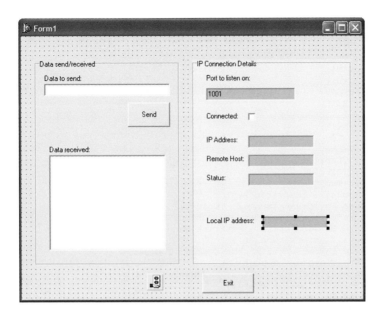

Figure D7.14 Sample design for a server

The ClientWrite event is called when the client sends data to the server. An example of the code is:

```
procedure TForm1.ServerSocket1ClientWrite(Sender: TObject;
  Socket: TCustomWinSocket);
begin
  Memo1.Lines.Add(Socket.ReceiveText);
end;
```

and the server can send data to the server using the following:

```
ServerSocket1.Socket.Connections[0].SendText(edit6.text);
```

An example program (which should work with the client from the previous section) is:

Delphi program D7.2

```
unit server01;

interface

uses
  Windows, Messages, SysUtils, Variants, Classes, Graphics, Controls, Forms,
  Dialogs, StdCtrls, ScktComp;

type
  TForm1 = class(TForm)
    GroupBox1: TGroupBox;
    Label1: TLabel;
    Edit1: TEdit;
    Label2: TLabel;
    CheckBox1: TCheckBox;
```

```
      Label3: TLabel;
      Label4: TLabel;
      Label5: TLabel;
      Label6: TLabel;
      Edit2: TEdit;
      Edit3: TEdit;
      Edit4: TEdit;
      Edit5: TEdit;
      GroupBox2: TGroupBox;
      Edit6: TEdit;
      Button1: TButton;
      Memo1: TMemo;
      Label7: TLabel;
      Label8: TLabel;
      Button2: TButton;
      ServerSocket1: TServerSocket;
      procedure FormCreate(Sender: TObject);
      procedure Button1Click(Sender: TObject);
      procedure ServerSocket1ClientWrite(Sender: TObject;
        Socket: TCustomWinSocket);
      procedure ServerSocket1Accept(Sender: TObject;
        Socket: TCustomWinSocket);
      procedure ServerSocket1ClientRead(Sender: TObject;
        Socket: TCustomWinSocket);
      procedure Button2Click(Sender: TObject);
    private
      { Private declarations }
    public
      { Public declarations }
    end;

var
  Form1: TForm1;

implementation

{$R *.dfm}

procedure TForm1.FormCreate(Sender: TObject);
var port:integer;
begin
        port:=StrToInt(Edit1.Text);
        ServerSocket1.Port:=port;
        ServerSocket1.Active:=True;
        edit4.text:='Listening ...';
end;

procedure TForm1.Button1Click(Sender: TObject);
begin
        ServerSocket1.Socket.Connections[0].SendText(edit6.text);
        edit6.text:='';
end;

procedure TForm1.ServerSocket1ClientWrite(Sender: TObject;
  Socket: TCustomWinSocket);
begin
  Memo1.Lines.Add(Socket.ReceiveText);
end;

procedure TForm1.ServerSocket1Accept(Sender: TObject;
  Socket: TCustomWinSocket);
begin
        Checkbox1.Checked:=true;
        edit2.text:=Socket.RemoteAddress;
```

```
        edit3.Text:=Socket.RemoteHost;
        edit5.text:=Socket.LocalAddress;
        edit4.text:='Connected';
end;

procedure TForm1.ServerSocket1ClientRead(Sender: TObject;
   Socket: TCustomWinSocket);
begin
   Memo1.Lines.Add(Socket.ReceiveText);
end;

procedure TForm1.Button2Click(Sender: TObject);
begin
        close;
end;

end.
```

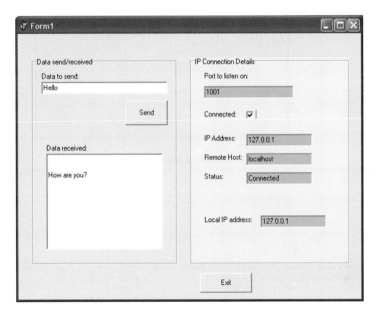

Figure D7.15 Sample run

The client and server can be tested by running each of them on the same machine, and using the address of 127.0.0.1 (which specifies the local address). Once the program is working, the client can be run on one machine and the server on another. The client must know the IP address (or host name) of the server. This address can be viewed from the server application (as shown in Figure D7.16).

D7.8.3 Connecting to standard ports

There are many standard ports which a client can cannot to a server. The most used are 80 (for HTTP, which gives WWW access), 23 (for TELNET access, which gives remote login), 25 (for SMTP, for email access) and 21 (for FTP, for remote file transfer). The client can be used to connect to these ports, by adding a combo box where the user can select the port. The code added can be:

Figure D7.16 Sample run

```
procedure TForm1.FormCreate(Sender: TObject);
begin
        ComboBox1.items.add('Echo');          // Port 7
        ComboBox1.items.add('Daytime');       // Port 13
        ComboBox1.items.add('Char gen');      // Port 19
        ComboBox1.items.add('FTP');           // Port 21
        ComboBox1.items.add('Telnet');        // Port 23
        ComboBox1.items.add('STMP');          // Port 25
        ComboBox1.items.add('WWW');           // Port 80
        ComboBox1.items.add('Test (1001)');   // Port 1001
end;

procedure TForm1.ComboBox1Change(Sender: TObject);
var val:integer;
begin
        val:=ComboBox1.ItemIndex;
        if (val=0) then ClientSocket.Port:=7
        else if (val=1) then ClientSocket.Port:=13
        else if (val=2) then ClientSocket.Port:=19
        else if (val=3) then ClientSocket.Port:=21
        else if (val=4) then ClientSocket.Port:=23
        else if (val=5) then ClientSocket.Port:=25
        else if (val=6) then ClientSocket.Port:=80
        else  ClientSocket.Port:=1001
end;
```

Figure D7.17 and Figure D7.18 shows two sample runs. In this case the WWW server is running on the local computer, and is accessed with the local address (127.0.0.1).

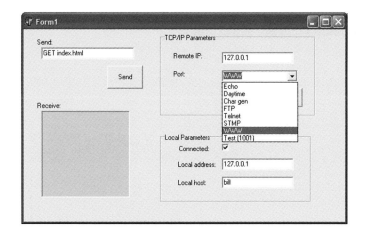

Figure D7.17 Sample run

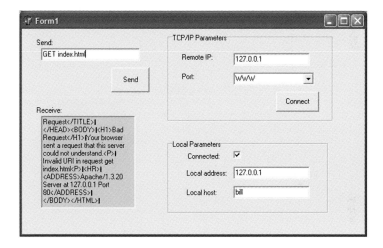

Figure D7.18 Sample run

E1   Routers

E1.1   Introduction

Routers are key elements of the Internet, and without routers there would be no Internet. They are highly secure and complex systems which run their own operating systems, and if operated correctly they can significantly improve the performance of interconnected networks. Their main function is to examine the network address of the data packets and decide the route that the data packet should take. To be able to determine the best route that the data packets should take they require routing protocols, such as RIP and EGP. These routing protocols allow routers to intercommunicate with other routers so that they can determine the structure of the interconnected networks. A routed protocol is one that is routed through interconnected networks, such as IP.

Internet is a complex infrastructure with devices with varying requirements, as illustrated in Figure E1.1. At the core there are organizational and Internet backbones. The connections to these come from organizational hosts (typically running from Ethernet-based networks), or from high-speed host connection provided by telecommunications companies (such as from ADSL or cable connections). At the outer layer of the Internet there are mobile devices. These can have relatively high transmission rates of over 1MBps, or from low-speed ones. Routers require to interconnect all these devices.

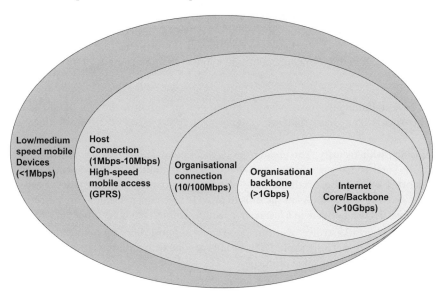

Figure E1.1   Internet infrastructure

E1.2   Router types

There are many different types of routers, with differing specifications. Figure E1.2 shows the different types of routers and switches which are used at differing requirement levels:

- **Core layer**. This layer requires fast switching with low delays. To enhance reliability users should not get direct access to the core of the system. There will be very little filtering and processing of the traffic at this layer, as this would slow down the flow of traffic. This there will be very little access list processing or address translation. The Cisco 7000, 7200 and 7500 are aimed at enterprise cores, while the 12000 series router is aimed an ISPs. These routers have large chassis, which allow a great deal of interfaces can be connected (possibly with differing types of connection media). This allows for easily scaleable networks. Typically, at the core level, there will be redundant links, to other connected routers. These redundant links typically have the same cost value, as load sharing can be applied. Figure E1.1 shows the connected to two other sites (B and C, from A). It can be seen that there are redundant links set-up so that one of the links can fail, and there is still a link between the sites. At the core level it can be expensive to add redundant links between sites, thus a less expensive approach is to use a dial-up connection, such as for frame relay or ISDN. At this level, too, routers have dual power supplies; so that they can be swapped or replaced without bring down the router.

- **Distribution layer**. At this layer, there is a great of security filter. As apposed to the core layer, distribution-layer routers typically require fewer interfaces and will typically have a slower switching speed. The routers used at this layer have interfaces which can be added and removed, but there is less capacity for this than at the core layer. Typical routers are 4000, 4500, and 3600 series routers. These are strong on apply security filter, with ACLs (Access Control Lists), and use techniques such as router summarization, route maps and distribution lists to enhance the flow of traffic.

- **Access layer**. At this layer, the routers provide access to the network. These typically have a few interfaces that at the other two layer. Typical devices are 1600, 1700, 2500, and 2600 series. Typical interfaces are for Ethernet connections, to connect to a local area network, or with serial connections, to connect to other routers, or an ISDN connection.

Networks have traditionally grown generally grown in size, with little thought of how scaleable the network is. Some basic rules are:

- **Accessibly, with security.** The greater the types of connections that are provided to a network, such as dial-up, wireless, and so on, the more difficult it can become to make the network secure. There is thus a trade-off between providing differing types of access against security problems. A key factor is to provide mechanisms which can bar certain types of access to a network in a fast response time, without effecting other parts of it.

- **Adaptable**. Networks evolve over time, and must support differing networking types, and protocols. The network should thus be able to cope with different types of networking equipment, and associated protocols.

- **Efficient**. A key factor of a network is to be efficient at all times, especially over peak loadings. It should thus try to eliminate any unwanted traffic at an early stage and more resources so that their traffic is optimized across the network.

- **Reliable**. Most networks require 24 hour, 7 day a week access, so reliability is an important factor.

- **Responsive**. Most networks must provide a defined Quality of Service (QoS) for response times, minimum delivery times, and so on.

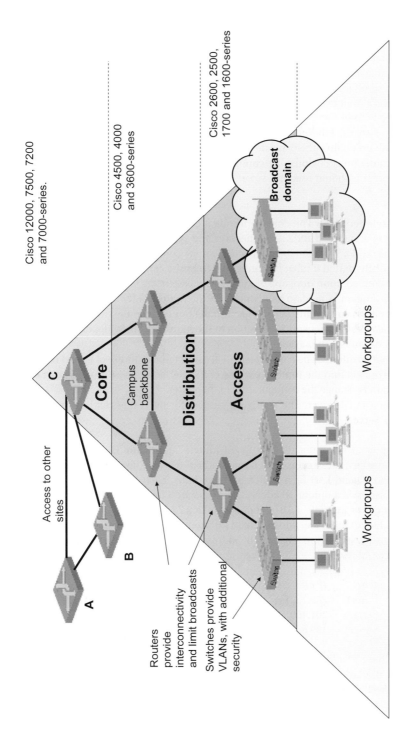

Cisco 12000, 7500, 7200 and 7000-series.

Cisco 4500, 4000 and 3600-series

Cisco 2600, 2500, 1700 and 1600-series

Access to other sites

Routers provide interconnectivity and limit broadcasts

Switches provide VLANs, with additional security

A

B

C

Core

Campus backbone

Distribution

Access

Broadcast domain

Workgroups

Workgroups

Figure E1.2 Router/switch attachments for each layer

E1.3   Router specifications

Each router has a number of interfaces; a data packet received on one interface is examined to determine if the destination address is on another subnet. If it is then it is routed to one of the other interfaces, if not then the data packet will not be routed onto another port. Figure E1.1 shows a router with four interfaces: Ether0, Ether1, Serial0 and Serial1. Serial interfaces are typically used for WANs, whereas Ethernet-type interfaces are typically used in LANs. Typically, also, the Ethernet interface is via a 15-pin D-type connector which interfaces to a transceiver unit onto either a twisted-pair or a coaxial connector.

The router must obviously be configured for the IP addresses of its connected networks, the protocols it should use, and so on. The router itself can be configured in a number of ways, such as:

- **Console terminal.** The console terminal connects to the router via the console port. This is a standard RS-232 connection and typically uses an RJ-45 connector on the router, and a 9-pin D-type connection on the console (typically a PC). When the router is initially started it must be configured from the console terminal, which can then initiate configuration from one of the following methods.
- **Via a modem.** A modem can connect to the router via the auxiliary port on the router. This allows an administrator to log into the router remotely via a telephone line. This is useful when the network connection to the router becomes inoperable, and only a telephone connection is available.
- **Virtual terminals.** The console terminal can set up a number of virtual terminals which can connect into the router from one of its interfaces. These typically use a telnet connection to change the configuration of the router.
- **From a TFTP server.** The configuration files for the router can be downloaded from a TFTP server.

This chapter includes practical setups of routers, and Figure E1.2 shows the setup of the system on which these setups are based on. The network uses five routers (LAB-A, LAB-B, LAB-C, LAB-D and LAB-E), a switch and two hubs. Each link that the routers connect to must be assigned a unique IP address. As these are Class C network addresses they all end with a zero. For example, LAB-A connects to 205.7.5.0 (from its Ether1 interface), 192.5.5.0 (from its Ether0 interface) and 201.100.11.0 (from its Serial0 interface). Each of the ports of the routers must be given a unique IP address. Thus the ports on LAB-A and LAB-B are assigned as follows:

Router	Port	IP address	Router	Port	IP address
LAB-A	Ether1	205.7.5.1	LAB-A	Ether0	192.5.5.1
LAB-A	Serial0	201.100.11.1	LAB-B	Serial1	201.100.11.2
LAB-B	Serial0	199.6.13.1	LAB-B	Ether0	219.17.100.1

Each of these IP addresses relates to the networks that it connects to, such as Ether1 connects to the 205.7.5.0 network. All the computers which connect to the switch on this network will have the same network part of their address, and will range from 205.7.5.2 to 205.7.5.254 (as 205.7.5.255 is used for a broadcast address to the 205.7.5.0 network). As all of the addresses are Class C addresses, the subnet mask will be 255.255.255.0 in all cases.

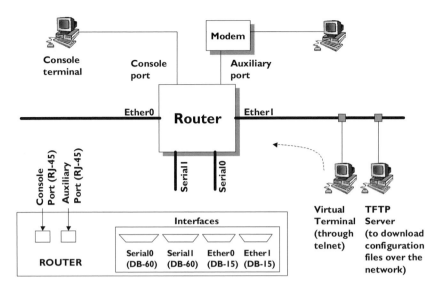

Figure E1.3 Router interfaces and configuration methods

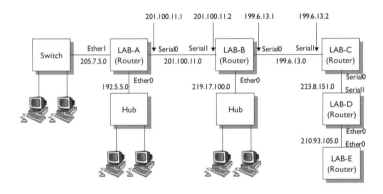

Figure E1.4 Sample interconnect network

E1.4   Router configuration and start-up

The router must be started in an orderly manner, so that it can operate correctly. The first step is to run a power-up, self-test. After this is successful, the router goes through the following steps:

- **The bootstrap loader** is loaded from ROM and run on the processor.
- **The operation system** (Cisco IOS – Internetwork Operating System) is then loaded from the boot field of a configuration register (which specifies either boot from flash memory, boot from the network or manual boot). The lower four bits of the configuration register define the boot field. A value of 0000 defines ROM monitor mode, where the user can manually boot the router with a b command at the prompt, a value of 0001b

defines that the boot should occur automatically from ROM, while any other value (from 0010b to 1111b) defines that the system is booted from the configuration defined in the NVRAM (Non-volatile RAM). Normally these binary values are defined in hexadecimal, thus 0x00 defines a manual boot, 0x01 defines an automatic boot from ROM and 0x02 defines that the system should boot from the commands given in NVRAM.

- The operating system is then **booted**, and it determines the hardware and the software on the system, and displays these to the console terminal.
- The operating system then loads the **configuration file** from NVRAM and executes it one line at a time. These lines start different processes, and define addresses and protocol types.
- If there is no configuration file in NVRAM, the router automatically goes into user **setup mode**, where the router asks the user questions about the router configuration. Once these have been specified the router saves these to NVRAM, so that the settings will be saved. Once saved, the router should automatically boot, without going into user setup mode. As much as possible the router tries to discover its environment, and tries to minimize the settings that the user has to add. Typically, values are given in squared brackets, which are defaults that the user can choose if the return key is pressed at the option.

Each router has memory which stores information on the setup of the router, and also the operating system of the router. The configuration file stores important information on the setup of the interfaces that is specific to the router. The configuration and other processes are stored in memory. The different types and uses of memory are:

- **NVRAM.** This type of memory does not lose its contents when the power is withdrawn, but can be written to. It is used to store the router's backup/startup configuration file. One of the options in the configuration is where the operating system image is loaded from, typically either from flash memory, or from a TFTP server.
- **Flash.** This is erasable, reprogrammable ROM, which keeps its contents when the power is taken away. It is used in the router to contain one or more copies of the operating system image and microcode. Flash memory allows for easy updates to the operating system software, without having to replace any parts of the hardware.
- **ROM.** This is a permanent type of memory, which cannot be changed, and does not lose its contents when the power is withdrawn. On the router it contains power-on diagnostics, a bootstrap program, and operating system software. Upgrades to ROM require a change of a ROM integrated circuit.
- **RAM.** This is the main memory of the router and stores running programs and the current running configuration file. Along with this, the RAM stores routing tables, ARP cache, packet buffering and packet hold queues. The contents of the RAM are lost when the power is withdrawn.

The configuration file stores information on the global configuration, processes and interface information for the router and its interface ports. Initially, when the system is booted, a bootstrap program is executed from the ROM, which then loads the operating system image in the RAM, as illustrated in Figure E1.3. The operating system then starts a number of routines which operate on the different protocols that are associated with the ports. This includes updating routing tables, buffering data packets and moving data, as well as executing user commands.

To be able to login into a router the user must have a password. This gets the user into the User EXEC mode, which allows the user to view the configuration of the router, and perform simple operations. As the router could be breached by an external hacker, a further password is required to enter into the Privileged EXEC mode, in which the user can actually change the configuration of the router, and perform extensive operations. Figure E1.3 shows the other modes that the router can be put into. For example, the RXBOOT mode allows the user to recover corrupted passwords, and a setup mode allows the router to be initially configured when it is first powered-on. The global configuration mode allows for simple, one-line, configuration tasks.

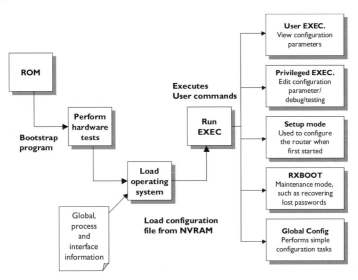

Figure E1.5 Router start-up and router modes

E1.5   Router commands

The router has a whole series of commands which can be used to determine the status of the router, and to change its configuration. There are two main modes that can be used: User Exec mode and Privileged Exec mode. Initially the user logs into the User Exec mode, and then uses a further secret password to get into the Privileged Exec mode. The enable command is used to go from User Exec mode into Privileged Exec mode. The prompt for User Exec is > and the prompt for Privileged Exec mode is #. Session run E1.1 shows an example of a user logging into a router and then logging into the Privileged mode. The ? character is used to give help on commands (with ? on its own) or with subcommands (such as show ?, as illustrated in Session run E1.17). A complete list of User Exec and Privileged Exec commands is given in Session run E1.15 and Session run E1.16.

⌨ Session run E1.1

```
LAB-A con0 is now available
Press RETURN to get started.
User Access Verification
Password:  *******
LAB-A>   ?
Exec commands:
  access-enable    Create a temporary Access-List entry
  access-profile   Apply user-profile to interface
  clear            Reset functions
  connect          Open a terminal connection
   ::::::::
LAB-A>   enable
Password:  **********
LAB-A#   ?
Exec commands:
  access-enable    Create a temporary Access-List entry
  access-profile   Apply user-profile to interface
  access-template  Create a temporary Access-List entry
  cd               Change current directory
   ::::::::
```

E1.5.1 Router status commands

The show command in user or privileged mode can be used to display the status of the router. These include:

- **show arp.** Displays the current status of router's ARP tables, which map IP addresses to MAC address. Session run E1.6 gives an example of this command.
- **show buffers.** This command shows detailed statistics on the buffers within the router. Session run E1.2 gives an example of this command. In this case, the memory buffers split into small buffers (104 bytes), middle buffers (600 bytes), big buffers (1524 bytes), very big buffers (4520 bytes), large buffers (5024 bytes) and huge buffers (18024 bytes).
- **show flash.** This command displays information on the data stored in the flash memory. An example is given in Session run E1.8.
- **show hosts.** This command displays a lists of connected hosts and their IP addresses.
- **show interfaces.** This command displays statistics for all interfaces configured on the router. Session run E1.10 shows an example.
- **show mem.** This command displays the usage of the routers memory. Session run E1.3 shows an example.
- **show processes.** This command shows the active processes.
- **show protocols.** This command displays the status of currently running protocols (such as IP, IPX, AppleTalk and DECnet). It can be seen from Session run E1.9 that there are three active interfaces (Ethernet0, Serial0 and Serial1), and that each of the interfaces is operating ('they are up'). For example the IP address of Ethernet0 interface is 219.17.100.1/24, which specifies that it has an IP address of 219.17.100.1 and that 24 bits are used to define the network part of the address (as expected as it is a Class C address).
- **show running-config.** This command displays the active configuration file.
- **show stacks.** This command displays the usage of stacks within the router. Session run E1.4 shows an example.

- **show startup.** Displays the startup configuration file.
- **show version.** This command display information on the hardware, software version, configuration file name, and the boot image. Session run E1.7 shows an example for a Cisco 2500-series router.

⌨ Session run E1.2

```
LAB-A#   show buffers
Buffer elements:
     500 in free list (500 max allowed)
     2026 hits, 0 misses, 0 created
Public buffer pools:
Small buffers, 104 bytes (total 50, permanent 50):
     49 in free list (20 min, 150 max allowed)
     669 hits, 0 misses, 0 trims, 0 created
  :::::::::
Huge buffers, 18024 bytes (total 0, permanent 0):
     0 in free list (0 min, 4 max allowed)
     0 hits, 0 misses, 0 trims, 0 created
     0 failures (0 no memory)
Interface buffer pools:
Ethernet0 buffers, 1524 bytes (total 32, permanent 32):
     8 in free list (0 min, 32 max allowed)
     24 hits, 0 fallbacks
     8 max cache size, 8 in cache
  :::::::::
Serial0 buffers, 1524 bytes (total 32, permanent 32):
     7 in free list (0 min, 32 max allowed)
     102 hits, 0 fallbacks
     8 max cache size, 8 in cache
```

⌨ Session run E1.3

```
LAB-A#   show memory
              Head    Total(b)    Used(b)    Free(b)    Lowest(b)  Largest(b)
Processor     84D10   1549040     1537528    11512          0      4560
     I/O      200000  2097152      437652    1659500    1463544    1463544
          Processor memory
  Address  Bytes Prev.   Next    Ref   PrevF   NextF   Alloc PC  What
  84D10    1064  0        85164   1                    31A6070   List Elements
  85164    2864  84D10    85CC0   1                    31A6070   List Headers
  85CC0    3992  85164    86C84   1                    3148B48   TTY data
```

⌨ Session run E1.4

```
LAB-A#   show stacks
Minimum process stacks:
 Free/Size    Name
 3528/4000    Router Init
 2380/4000    Init
 3468/4000    RADIUS INITCONFIG
 3380/4000    DHCP Client

Interrupt level stacks:
Level     Called Unused/Size   Name
  3            3  2772/3000     Serial interface state change interrupt
  4         1440  2612/3000     Network interfaces
  5        32703  2888/3000     Console Uart
```

E1.5.2 Show hosts

The show hosts command displays the hosts that are connected to the local router and their IP addresses. Session 18.5 shows an example session.

🖥 Session run E1.5

```
LAB-A>    show hosts
Default domain is not set
Name/address lookup uses domain service
Name servers are 255.255.255.255
Host            Flags       Age Type    Address(es)
LAB-B           (perm, OK) 17    IP     201.100.11.2   219.17.100.1
                                                       199.6.13.1
LAB-C           (perm, OK) 18    IP     199.6.13.2   223.8.151.1
                                                     204.204.7.1
LAB-D           (perm, OK) 19    IP     204.204.7.2   210.93.105.1
LAB-E           (perm, OK) 18    IP     210.93.105.2
LAB-A           (perm, OK) 19    IP     192.5.5.1   205.7.5.1   201.100.11.1
```

E1.5.3   Show arp

Arp tables are very important in that they allow a host to determine the MAC address of a host with a given IP address. To complete the table a host sends out ARP requests on the network and the host which has the IP address defined in the ARP request replies back with its MAC address. Session run E1.6 shows an example of an ARP table, which has four entries in it. In this case (see Figure E1.2), router LAB-A has four connected Ethernet adaptors, two of its own (205.7.5.1 and 192.5.5.1), a switch (205.7.5.254) and a hub (192.5.5.12). Figure E1.4 illustrates the layout of the connections. It can be seen that each Ethernet interface port has an associated IP address, and a unique IP address.

🖥 Session run E1.6

```
LAB-A#    show arp
Protocol   Address            Age (min)   Hardware Addr   Type   Interface
Internet   205.7.5.254            108     0030.8071.9f40  ARPA   Ethernet1
Internet   192.5.5.1               -      0010.7b81.1d72  ARPA   Ethernet0
Internet   192.5.5.12              1      0000.b430.b332  ARPA   Ethernet0
Internet   205.7.5.1               -      0010.7b81.1d73  ARPA   Ethernet1
```

E1.5.4   Show version

The show version command gives information on the operating system version, the hardware and the amount of on-board memory. It can be seen from Session run E1.7 that the amount of on-board flash memory is 8 MB, with 32 KB of NVRAM, and there are four interfaces (Serial0, Serial1, Ethernet0 and Ethernet1).

Flash memory (EEPROM) contains the operating system image, which can be upgraded electronically with an operating system update. In this case, the current flash file is c2500-d-l.120-4 (which defines that the image is for a Cisco 2500-series router-special features, and so on). The NVRAM is updated with a startup configuration file, and can be updated by the user at any time. It should be noted that the show version command also displays the 32-bit configuration register value, which, in this case, is 0x2102. The last four bits define the boot location, which, in this case, is 0010b (which causes the boot to occur from the location defined in NVRAM).

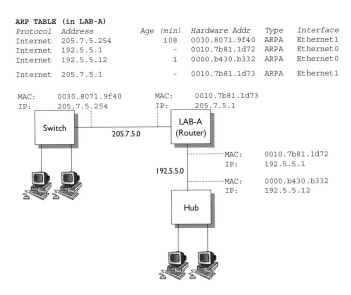

```
ARP TABLE (in LAB-A)
Protocol  Address        Age (min)  Hardware Addr   Type   Interface
Internet  205.7.5.254         108   0030.8071.9f40  ARPA   Ethernet1
Internet  192.5.5.1             -   0010.7b81.1d72  ARPA   Ethernet0
Internet  192.5.5.12            1   0000.b430.b332  ARPA   Ethernet0

Internet  205.7.5.1             -   0010.7b81.1d73  ARPA   Ethernet1
```

```
MAC:    0030.8071.9f40       MAC:    0010.7b81.1d73
IP:     205.7.5.254          IP:     205.7.5.1
```

```
                                        MAC:   0010.7b81.1d72
                                        IP:    192.5.5.1

                                        MAC:   0000.b430.b332
                                        IP:    192.5.5.12
```

Figure E1.6 Example of an ARP table

💻 Session run E1.7

```
LAB-A#   show version
Cisco Internetwork Operating System Software
IOS (tm) 2500 Software (C2500-D-L), Version 12.0(4), RELEASE SOFTWARE (fc1)
Copyright (c) 1986-1999 by cisco Systems, Inc.
Compiled Wed 14-Apr-99 21:21 by ccai
Image text-base: 0x03037C88, data-base: 0x00001000
ROM: System Bootstrap, Version 11.0(10c)XB2, PLATFORM SPECIFIC RELEASE SOFTWARE
(fc1)
BOOTFLASH: 3000 Bootstrap Software (IGS-BOOT-R), Version 11.0(10c)XB2, PLATFORM
SPECIFIC RELEASE SOFTWARE (fc1)
LAB-A uptime is 5 minutes
System restarted by reload
System image file is "flash:c2500-d-l.120-4"
cisco 2500 (68030) processor (revision L) with 2048K/2048K bytes of memory.
Processor board ID 13583483, with hardware revision 00000000
Bridging software.
X.25 software, Version 3.0.0.
2 Ethernet/IEEE 802.3 interface(s)
2 Serial network interface(s)
32K bytes of non-volatile configuration memory.
8192K bytes of processor board System flash (Read ONLY)
Configuration register is 0x2102
```

E1.5.5 Show flash

The show flash command displays important configuration information. It can be seen that, in Session run E1.8, the hostname is LAB-A, and that it connects to four interfaces (Ethernet0, Ethernet1, Serial0 and Serial1). Each of these interfaces has an associated IP address (such as 192.5.5.1 for Ethernet0), and a subnet mask (255.255.255.0). It can also be seen that the IP addresses of each of the interfaces of the other routers has been defined. For example:

```
ip host LAB-B 201.100.11.2 219.17.100.1 199.6.13.1
```

defines that LAB-B connects has three interface ports, which have IP addresses of
201.100.11.2, 219.17.100.1 and 199.6.13.1.

It can be seen from the initial information from the command that there is a total of
8 MB of memory in the flash memory (8192 KB), of which over 6 MB of memory has been
used. If there is enough memory, more than one operating system image can be stored. In
this case there is possibly not enough memory for another image. If more than one image
was to be stored, the user would have to upgrade the flash memory. When downloading a
new image from a TFTP server, the following should be done: check the size, name and
pathname of the new image on the TFTP server (using DIR or ls commands on an FTP session) and if there is enough flash memory for the new image. Note also that there can be
different passwords setup for each of the configuration sources, these are defined from:

- Line con 0. The console terminal. In the example, the password is Cisco.
- Line aux. The auxiliary terminal.
- Line vty 0 4. Defines a password from incoming Telnet sessions.

Session run E1.8
```
LAB-A#   show flash
System flash directory:
File  Length    Name/status
  1   6788464   c2500-d-l.120-4
[6788528 bytes used, 1600080 available, 8388608 total]
8192K bytes of processor board System flash (Read ONLY)
Current configuration:
!
version 12.0
service timestamps debug uptime
service timestamps log uptime
no service password-encryption
!
hostname LAB-A
!
enable secret 5 $1$EHcO$ro5NY5aMGtbyViNE/m7VG1      ◄——— Encrypted secret
enable password cisco                                      password
!
ip subnet-zero
ip host LAB-B 201.100.11.2 219.17.100.1 199.6.13.1
ip host LAB-C 199.6.13.2 223.8.151.1 204.204.7.1
ip host LAB-D 204.204.7.2 210.93.105.1
ip host LAB-E 210.93.105.2
ip host LAB-A 192.5.5.1 205.7.5.1 201.100.11.1
!
interface Ethernet0
 ip address 192.5.5.1 255.255.255.0
 no ip directed-broadcast
 no mop enabled
!
interface Ethernet1
 ip address 205.7.5.1 255.255.255.0
 no ip directed-broadcast
!
interface Serial0
 ip address 201.100.11.1 255.255.255.224
```

```
 no ip directed-broadcast
 no ip mroute-cache
 no fair-queue
 clockrate 56000
!
interface Serial1
 no ip address
 no ip directed-broadcast
 shutdown
!
router rip
 network 192.5.5.0
 network 201.100.11.0
 no ip directed-broadcast
 shutdown
!
router rip
 network 192.5.5.0
 network 201.100.11.0
 network 205.7.5.0
!
no ip classless
!
snmp-server community public RO
!
line con 0
 password cisco
 login
 transport input none
line aux 0
line vty 0 4
 password cisco
 login
!
end
```

In the privileged mode, the user can copy the contents of the flash memory to another file or to a TFTP server. This can be used to create a backup copy of the operating system before it is overwritten by a new version, or in case it is corrupted. The command to copy the flash memory to a TFTP server is (the default options are given in square brackets):

```
LAB-A#   copy flash tftp
IP address of remote TFTP server [201.10.30.3]?
Source filename [c2500-d-1.120-4]?
Writing c2500-d-1.120-4  !!!!!!!!!!!!!!!!!!!!!!!!!
successful tftp write
```

to copy the file back from the TFTP requires the following command:

```
LAB-A#   copy tftp flash tftp
IP address of remote TFTP server [201.10.30.3]?
Source filename []?c2500-d-1.120-5
Copy c2500-d-1.120-4 from 201.10.30.3 into flash memory? [confirm]
erase before writing? [confirm]
Clearing and initializing flash memory
[Ok]
```

E1.5.6 Show protocols

The show protocols command is important as it shows the interfaces that are connected, and their status. In Session run E1.9 it can be seen that the LAB-B router has three interfaces (Ethernet0, Serial0 and Serial1). It shows that each of these interfaces is currently connected, and that their protocol is operating (in this case the protocol used is IP).

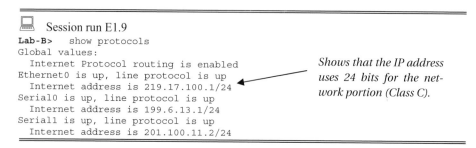

Session run E1.9
```
Lab-B>    show protocols
Global values:
  Internet Protocol routing is enabled
Ethernet0 is up, line protocol is up
  Internet address is 219.17.100.1/24
Serial0 is up, line protocol is up
  Internet address is 199.6.13.1/24
Serial1 is up, line protocol is up
  Internet address is 201.100.11.2/24
```
Shows that the IP address uses 24 bits for the network portion (Class C).

E1.5.7 Show interfaces

The show protocols shows some basic information on the interfaces that the router uses, whereas the show interfaces command in Session run E1.10 gives a detailed view of any, or all, of the interfaces on the router. It defines whether its link is currently operating, the IP and MAC address of the Ethernet adaptors (for example, Ethernet0 has a MAC address of 0010.7b81.1d72 and an IP address of 192.5.5.1). The counters can be cleared with the clear counters command. By resetting the counters the user can get a better idea of the current status of the network. The show interfaces command also displays:

- Bit rate on interface. It can be seen that the bit rate for Ethernet0 is 10 Mbps (BW 10000 Kbit).
- Error rate. Along with all this information, the show interfaces gives information on the number of errors that have occurred on an interface. In this case there are no errors, and defines the number of data packets that have been received.
- Time since last reboot. In this case the amount of up time is 5 minutes.
- Delay. In this case the delay is 1 ms (1000 usec).
- Keep-alive time. In this case it is once every 10 seconds.
- Number of collisions. In this case there have been no collisions.
- Input/output rate. In packets per second and bits per second.

Session run E1.10
```
LAB-A#   show interfaces
Ethernet0 is up, line protocol is up
  Hardware is Lance, address is 0010.7b81.1d72 (bia 0010.7b81.1d72)
  Internet address is 192.5.5.1/24
  MTU 1500 bytes, BW 10000 Kbit, DLY 1000 usec, rely 255/255, load 1/255
  Encapsulation ARPA, loopback not set, keepalive set (10 sec)
  ARP type: ARPA, ARP Timeout 04:00:00
  Last input 00:00:43, output 00:00:00, output hang never
  Last clearing of "show interface" counters never
  Queueing strategy: fifo
  Output queue 0/40, 0 drops; input queue 0/75, 0 drops
  5 minute input rate 0 bits/sec, 0 packets/sec
  5 minute output rate 0 bits/sec, 0 packets/sec
```

```
        62 packets input, 6425 bytes, 0 no buffer
        Received 50 broadcasts, 0 runts, 0 giants, 0 throttles
        0 input errors, 0 CRC, 0 frame, 0 overrun, 0 ignored, 0 abort
        0 input packets with dribble condition detected
        261 packets output, 31216 bytes, 0 underruns
        0 output errors, 0 collisions, 2 interface resets
        0 lost carrier, 0 no carrier
Ethernet1 is up, line protocol is up
   Hardware is Lance, address is 0010.7b81.1d73 (bia 0010.7b81.1d73)
   Internet address is 205.7.5.1/24   ... and so on.
```

E1.5.8   Running-config and startup-config

Two important commands are show running-config and show startup-config, as these show the current settings (with running-config), and the settings which are used at boot (startup-config). These settings can differ if the user has made a change to the settings of the router. Session run E1.11 show an example configuration from the Lab-B router. It can be seen that the Lab-B router has three interfaces (Ethernet0, Serial0 and Serial1). It uses the show running-config (the show startup-config can be used to display the backup configuration). It can be seen from Session run E1.11, that the hostname is Lab-B (hostname Lab-B), and that the networks it connects to are: 199.6.13.0, 201.100.11.0 and 219.17.100.0.

The copy running-config startup-config command is useful in storing any changes that a user has made to the setup of the router, so that the router will use the updated settings when the router has been rebooted. This should only be done when the user is sure that the changes that have been made are correct.

The erase startup-config command deletes the backup configuration file in NVRAM, and the reload command causes the system to reload the startup-configuration and reconfigure the system, as it was when the system was booted. This allows the user to undo any updates to the running configurations. Note that these commands can only be run from Privileged EXEC mode (which requires the secret password).

The running-config file can be transferred to the TFTP server with copy tftp running-config and copied back with copy running-config tftp.

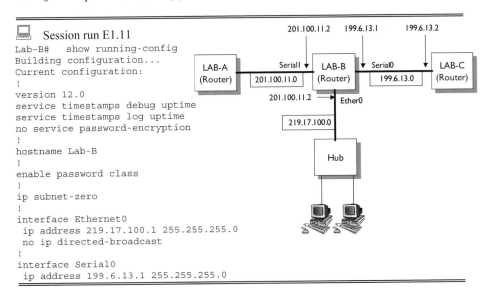

Session run E1.11

```
Lab-B#   show running-config
Building configuration...
Current configuration:
!
version 12.0
service timestamps debug uptime
service timestamps log uptime
no service password-encryption
!
hostname Lab-B
!
enable password class
!
ip subnet-zero
!
interface Ethernet0
 ip address 219.17.100.1 255.255.255.0
 no ip directed-broadcast
!
interface Serial0
 ip address 199.6.13.1 255.255.255.0
```

```
 ip directed-broadcast
 no ip mroute-cache
 no fair-queue
 clockrate 56000
!
interface Serial1
 ip address 201.100.11.2 255.255.255.0
 no ip directed-broadcast
!
router rip
 network 199.6.13.0
 network 201.100.11.0
 network 219.17.100.0
!
no ip classless
!
line con 0
 password cisco
 login
 transport input none
line aux 0
line vty 0 4
 password cisco
 login
!
end
```

E1.6   Cisco discovery protocol

Cisco routers are a foundation part of the Internet. To aid the testing and configuration of routing systems, Cisco have developed a protocol called the Cisco Discovery Protocol (CDP). It operates above the data link layer, and below the upper network-layer protocols, which allows CDP devices (running Cisco IOS Release 10.3 or later) to intercommunicate with each other and automatically discover other neighboring Cisco devices. The great advantage of this protocol is that it can support any network and transport layer protocols, and not just TCP and IP, such as SPX/IPX and AppleTalk.

The show cdp command allows a user to view the configuration of other neighboring routers. Session run E1.12 shows an example show cdp from the Lab-A router. It displays the device ID (in this case, it shows that the neighbors are Lab-B and 003080718F40), the type of device (in this case, Lab-B is a router (R) and 003080719F0 is an Ethernet switch T/S), the port which it connects to (Lab-B connects via Ser 1 port, and 003080719F40 connects from the AUI port), the port which it connects from (Lab-B connects from Ser 0 port, and 003080719F40 connects from the Eth 1 port) and the type of devices it is (in this case, the router connects to a Cisco 2500-series and a Cisco Catalyst 1900-series switch).

Session run E1.12

```
LAB-A>    show cdp neighbors
Capability Codes: R - Router, T - Trans Bridge, B - Source Route Bridge
                  S - Switch, H - Host, I - IGMP, r - Repeater
Device ID      Local Intrfce    Holdtme    Capability  Platform   Port ID
Lab-B          Ser 0            141           R         2500       Ser 1
003080719F40   Eth 1            157          T S        1900       AUI
```

It is also possible to get detailed information on neighbors with the show cdp neighbors detail command, as outlined in Session run E1.13. There are default values for the time between CDP updates and for aging CDP entries. Typically these are set at 60 seconds and 180 seconds, respectively. Old updates are automatically deleted when new updates arrive. Holdtime defines the amount of time (in seconds) since a CDP frame arrived with the required information.

Session run E1.13

```
LAB-A>   show cdp neighbors detail
------------------------
Device ID: Lab-B
Entry address(es):
  IP address: 201.100.11.2
Platform: cisco 2500,  Capabilities: Router
Interface: Serial0,  Port ID (outgoing port): Serial1
Holdtime : 171 sec

Version :
Cisco Internetwork Operating System Software
IOS (tm) 2500 Software (C2500-D-L), Version 12.0(4), RELEASE SOFTWARE (fc1)
Copyright (c) 1986-1999 by cisco Systems, Inc.
Compiled Wed 14-Apr-99 21:21 by ccai

------------------------
Device ID: 003080719F40
Entry address(es):
  IP address: 205.7.5.254
Platform: cisco 1900,  Capabilities: Trans-Bridge Switch
Interface: Ethernet1,  Port ID (outgoing port): AUI
Holdtime : 127 sec

Version : V8.01
```

To check other neighbors, and their connections, the Telnet command is used to log into the neighboring devices. Session run E1.14 shows an example of login into Lab-B and the switch.

Session run E1.14

```
Lab-A>   telnet 201.100.11.2


Lab-B>   show cdp neighbors
Capability Codes: R - Router, T - Trans Bridge, B - Source Route Bridge
                  S - Switch, H - Host, I - IGMP, r - Repeater

Device ID       Local Intrfce      Holdtme    Capability  Platform  Port ID
LAB-C           Ser 0              148        R           2500      Ser 1
LAB-A           Ser 1              144        R           2500      Ser 0
Lab-B>  telnet 205.7.5.254
        Catalyst 1900 - IP Configuration
        Ethernet Address:  00-30-80-71-9F-40
        --------------------- Settings -----------------------------------
    [I] IP address                             205.7.5.254
    [S] Subnet mask                            255.255.255.0
    [G] Default gateway                        205.7.5.1
    [M] IP address of DNS server 1             0.0.0.0
    [N] IP address of DNS server 2             0.0.0.0
    [D] Domain name                            dcs.napier.ac.uk
    [R] Use Routing Information Protocol       Enabled
```

```
--------------------- Actions -----------------------------------
   [P] Ping
   [C] Clear cached DNS entries
   [X] Exit to previous menu
Enter Selection:
```

E1.7   Cisco router commands

The User Exec commands include:

🖳 Session run E1.15

```
access-enable     Create a temporary Access-List entry
access-profile    Apply user-profile to interface
clear             Reset functions
connect           Open a terminal connection
disable           Turn off privileged commands
disconnect        Disconnect an existing network connection
enable            Turn on privileged commands
exit              Exit from the EXEC
help              Description of the interactive help system
lock              Lock the terminal
login             Log in as a particular user
logout            Exit from the EXEC
mrinfo            Request neighbor and version information from a
                   multicast router
mstat             Show statistics after multiple multicast traceroutes
mtrace            Trace reverse multicast path from destination to source
name-connection   Name an existing network connection
pad               Open a X.29 PAD connection
ping              Send echo messages
ppp               Start IETF Point-to-Point Protocol (PPP)
resume            Resume an active network connection
```

The Privileged EXEC commands include:

🖳 Session run E1.16

```
access-enable     Create a temporary Access-List entry
access-profile    Apply user-profile to interface
access-template   Create a temporary Access-List entry
bfe               For manual emergency modes setting
cd                Change current directory
clear             Reset functions
clock             Manage the system clock
configure         Enter configuration mode
connect           Open a terminal connection
copy              Copy from one file to another
debug             Debugging functions (see also 'undebug')
delete            Delete a file
dir               List files on a filesystem
disable           Turn off privileged commands
disconnect        Disconnect an existing network connection
enable            Turn on privileged commands
erase             Erase a filesystem
exit              Exit from the EXEC
help              Description of the interactive help system
lock              Lock the terminal
login             Log in as a particular user
```

```
logout              Exit from the EXEC
more                Display the contents of a file
mstat               Show statistics after multiple multicast traceroutes
mtrace              Trace reverse multicast path from destination to source
name-connection     Name an existing network connection
no                  Disable debugging functions
pad                 Open a X.29 PAD connection
ping                Send echo messages
ppp                 Start IETF Point-to-Point Protocol (PPP)
pwd                 Display current working directory
reload              Halt and perform a cold restart
resume              Resume an active network connection
rlogin              Open an rlogin connection
rsh                 Execute a remote command
send                Send a message to other tty lines
set                 Set system parameter (not config)
setup               Run the SETUP command facility
show                Show running system information
slip                Start Serial-line IP (SLIP)
systat              Display information about terminal lines
telnet              Open a telnet connection
terminal            Set terminal line parameters
test                Test subsystems, memory, and interfaces
traceroute          Trace route to destination
tunnel              Open a tunnel connection
undebug             Disable debugging functions (see also 'debug')
undelete            Undelete a file
verify              Verify a file
where               List active connections
write               Write running configuration to memory, network, or
                    terminal
```

Session run E1.17

```
LAB-A#   show ?
access-expression  List access expression
access-lists       List access lists
accounting         Accounting data for active sessions
aliases            Display alias commands
appletalk          AppleTalk information
arap               Show Appletalk Remote Access statistics
arp                ARP table
async              Information on terminal lines used as router interfaces
backup             Backup status
bridge             Bridge Forwarding/Filtering Database [verbose]
buffers            Buffer pool statistics
cdp                CDP information
clock              Display the system clock
compress           Show compression statistics
configuration      Contents of Non-Volatile memory
controllers        Interface controller status
debugging          State of each debugging option
decnet             DECnet information
dhcp               Dynamic Host Configuration Protocol status
dialer             Dialer parameters and statistics
dnsix              Shows Dnsix/DMDP information
entry              Queued terminal entries
file               Show filesystem information
flash:             display information about flash: file system
flh-log            Flash Load Helper log buffer
frame-relay        Frame-Relay information
history            Display the session command history
hosts              IP domain-name, nameservers, and host table
```

```
interfaces        Interface status and configuration
ip                IP information
ipx               Novell IPX information
key               Key information
line              TTY line information
location          Display the system location
logging           Show the contents of logging buffers
memory            Memory statistics
modemcap          Show Modem Capabilities database
ntp               Network time protocol
ppp               PPP parameters and statistics
printers          Show LPD printer information
privilege         Show current privilege level
processes         Active process statistics
protocols         Active network routing protocols
queue             Show queue contents
queueing          Show queueing configuration
registry          Function registry information
reload            Scheduled reload information
rhosts            Remote-host+user equivalences
rif               RIF cache entries
rmon              rmon statistics
route-map         route-map information
running-config    Current operating configuration
sessions          Information about Telnet connections
smds              SMDS information
smf               Software MAC filter
smrp              Simple Multicast Routing Protocol (SMRP) information
snapshot          Snapshot parameters and statistics
snmp              snmp statistics
spanning-tree     Spanning tree topology
stacks            Process stack utilization
standby           Hot standby protocol information
startup-config    Contents of startup configuration
subscriber-policy
                  Subscriber policy
subsys            Show subsystem information
tcp               Status of TCP connections
terminal          Display terminal configuration parameters
traffic-shape     traffic rate shaping configuration
users             Display information about terminal lines
version           System hardware and software status
whoami            Info on current tty line
x25               X.25 information
```

E2   Routing protocols

E2.1   Introduction

Routers filter network traffic so that the only internetwork traffic flows into and out of a network. In many cases, there are several possible routes that can be taken between two nodes on different networks. Consider the network in Figure E2.1. In this case, the upper network shows the connection between two nodes A and B through routers 1 to 6. It can be seen from the lower diagram that there are four routes that the data can take. To stop traffic taking a long route or even one that does not exist, each router must maintain a routing table so that it knows where the data must be sent when it receives data destined for a remote node.

For routers to find the best route they must communicate with their neighbors to find the best way through the network. This measure can be defined in a number of ways, such as the number of router hops to the remote node, the bandwidth on each link, latency, average error rates, current network traffic, and so on. Many routers use the number of router hops to determine the route, which is not always the best measure, as it may include a congested route. As with road traffic, it is often better to take the freeway (which is equivalent to a high-bandwidth route) than it is to take a route which has lower speed limits, or has a great deal of traffic congestion and/or traffic lights.

Each router communicates with its neighbors to build-up a routing table. For example in Figure E2.1 the routing table for router 1 could be:

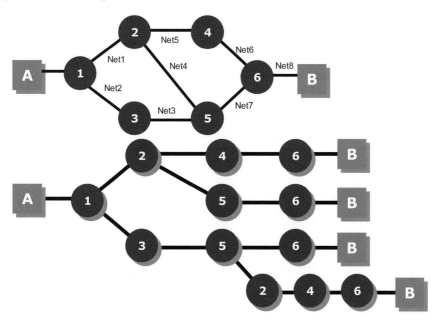

Figure E2.1   Example routing

Destination	Distance (hops)	Next router	Output port
Net5	1	2	(Net1)
Net7	2	3	(Net2)
Net8	3	2	(Net1)
Net3	1	3	(Net2)
And so on.			

It can be seen that the best route (measured by hops) from node A to Net8 is to go via Net1. This is the only information that the router needs to store. When the data gets to router 2 it has the choice of whether to send it to Net4 or Net5, as both routes get to Net8 in two hops.

A better method of determining the best route is to have some measure of the delay. For this routers pass delay information about their neighbors. For example, if the relative delay in Net5 was 1.5 and in Net6 it was 1.25, and the relative delay in Net4 was 1.1 and in Net7 was 1.3, then the relative delay between router 2 and router 6 can be calculated as:

$$\text{Route}(2,4,6) = 1.5 + 1.25 = 2.75 \qquad \text{Route}(2,5,6) = 1.1 + 1.3 = 2.4$$

Thus the best route is via router 5.

Another technique used to determine the best route is error probability. In this case, the probability of an error is multiplied to give the total probability. The route with the lowest error probability will be the most reliable route. For example:

$$P_e(2-5) = 0.01 \qquad P_e(5-6) = 0.15$$
$$P_e(2-4) = 0.05 \qquad P_e(4-6) = 0.1$$

Thus,

$$P_{noerror}(2,5,6) \quad = (1 - 0.01) \times (1 - 0.15)$$
$$= 0.8415$$
$$P_{noerror}(2,4,6) \quad = (1 - 0.05) \times (1 - 0.1)$$
$$= 0.855$$

Thus, the route via router 4 is the most reliable.

E2.2   Routing fundamentals

Layer 3 of the OSI model covers the network layer. There are two types of protocol at this level. These are:

- **Routing protocols.** A routing protocol provides a mechanism for routers to share routing information. These protocols allow routers to pass information between themselves, and update their routing tables. Examples of routing protocols are Routing Information Protocol (RIP), Interior Gateway Routing Protocol (IGRP), Enhanced Interior Gateway Routing Protocol (EIGRP), and Open Shortest Path First (OSPF).
- **Routed protocols.** These protocols are any network layer protocol that allows for the addressing of a host and a destination on a network, such as IP and IPX. Routers are re-

sponsible for passing a data packet onto the next router in, if possible, an optimal way, based on the destination network address. The definition of an optimal way depends on many things, especially its reachability. With IP, routers on the path between a source and a destination, examine the network part of the IP address to achieve their routing. Only the last router, which is connected to the destination node network, examines the host part of the IP address.

A route can either use static or dynamic routing. These are:

- **Dynamic routing.** In dynamic routing, the routers monitor the network, and can change their routing tables based on the current network conditions. The network thus adapts to changing conditions. Unfortunately, this method tends to reveal everything known about an internetwork to the rest of the network. This may be inappropriate for security reasons.
- **Static routing.** In static routing, a system administrator sets up a manual route when there is only one route to get to a network (a stub network). This type of configuring reduces the overhead of dynamic routing. Static routing also allows the internetwork administrator to specify the information that is advertised about restricted parts of a network.
- **Default routing.** These are manually defined by the system administrator and define the path that is taken if there is not a known route for the destination.

In order to achieve dynamic routing, each router uses a metric for a route to a destination. The route with the lowest metric wins and the router sends the data packet onto the next router in the best path. There are many ways to define the best route, these include:

- **Bandwidth.** The data capacity of a link, which is typically defined in bps.
- **Delay.** The amount of time that is required to send a packet from the source to a destination.
- **Load.** A measure of the amount of activity on a route.
- **Reliability.** Relates to the error rate of the link.
- **Hop count.** Defined by the number of routers that it takes between the current router and the destination.
- **Ticks.** Defines the delay of a link by a number of ticks of a clock.
- **Cost.** An arbitrary value which defines the cost of a link, such as financial expense, bandwidth, and so on.

Routers can use a single metric (such as hop count with RIP) or multiple metrics, where the updates in routing information can be sent by:

- **Broadcast.** In broadcast, routers transmit their information to other routers at regular intervals. A typical broadcast routing protocol is RIP, in which routers send their complete routing table once every few minutes, to all of their neighbors. This technique tends to be wasteful in bandwidth, as changes in the route do not vary much over short amounts of time.
- **Event-driven.** In event-driven routing protocols, routing information is only sent when there is a change in the topology or state of the network. This technique tends to be more efficient than broadcast, as it does not use up as much bandwidth.

Routing protocols suffer from several problems. The main problem with dynamic routing protocols is the amount of time that a network will take to change its routing to take into account changes in topology, whether it is due to failure, growth or reconfiguration. The knowledge that is passed between routers must be accurate and represent the true nature of any changes. This is known as convergence, and occurs when all of the routers on an inter-network have the same knowledge. An efficient network should have fast convergence, as it reduces the time that routers use outdated information, which would be used to send data packets on an incorrect route, or is sent over an inefficient route.

E2.3   Classless interdomain routing, route summarization and supernetting

Routers can use classless interdomain routing (CIDR), where a router determines the class of an IP address and uses this to identify the network and host parts of the address. With CIDR, the router uses a bitmask to identify the network and the host parts of the address, Also the usage of this bitmask is not restricted to multiples of octets. This bitmask allows the router to summarize routing information, where an address and a mask can represent multiple networks.

```
168.        32.         0.          0           /16
1010 1000   0010 0000   0000 0000   0000 0000
168.        33.         0.          0           /16
1010 1000   0010 0001   0000 0000   0000 0000
168.        34.         0.          0           /16
1010 1000   0010 0010   0000 0000   0000 0000
168.        35.         0.          0           /16
1010 1000   0010 0011   0000 0000   0000 0000
168.        36.         0.          0           /16
1010 1000   0010 0100   0000 0000   0000 0000
```

It can be seen from the above addresses that they have the first 12 bits in common. For a CIDR-based router the router can summarize these routes using a 12-bit prefix, with the value of:

```
1010 1000 0010
```

The subnet mask can then be set to 255.240.0.0, and the routes would be summarized with:

```
168.32.0.0/12
```

This method make routing more efficient, in terms of processing of the routing table, and also reduces the memory requirements.

Supernetting, or route aggregation, uses a bitmask to group multiple classful networks as a single network address, and can be thought of as the inverse of subnetting, as subnetting splits networks into subnetworks, whereas supernetting builds them back up into a complete network.

For example, if an organisation required 1000 hosts on a network. They could be granted a Class B address, but this would be wasteful, as a Class B address allows for 2^{16}-2 hosts (65534). An alternative approach would be for them to be granted four contiguous Class C address, which had a common part, which could be aggregated. For example, if they were granted the address:

```
200.          10.          188.           0
1100 1000.    0000 1010.   1011 1100.     0000 0000
200.          10.          189.           0
1100 1000.    0000 1010.   1011 1101.     0000 0000
200.          10.          190.           0
1100 1000.    0000 1010.   1011 1110.     0000 0000
200.          10.          191.           0
1100 1000.    0000 1010.   1011 1111.     0000 0000
```

There now 10 bits which can be used for hosts which gives 2^{10}-2 (1022) hosts, which is enough for all the hosts in the organisation. This address can be aggregated as they have a common address part. The subnet mask will thus be:

```
255.255.252.0
```

and the address can be aggregated with:

```
200.10.188.0/22
```

This type of approach allows ISPs to simplify their routing by allocated grouping addresses.

E2.4   Variable-length subnet masks

Variable-length subnet masks (VLSM) allows for different subnet masks to be used within an organization. For example, using the previous example

```
200.          10.          188.           0           /22
1100 1000.    0000 1010.   1011 1100.     0000 0000
```

It is possible to subnet the network within this address space to create six subnets (001, 011, 011 ... 110), by

```
200.          10.          189.           32          /27
1100 1000.    0000 1010.   1011 1101.     0010 0000
200.          10.          189.           64          /27
1100 1000.    0000 1010.   1011 1101.     0100 0000
200.          10.          189.           96          /27
1100 1000.    0000 1010.   1011 1101.     0110 0000
200.          10.          189.           128         /27
1100 1000.    0000 1010.   1011 1101.     1000 0000
    ::::
```

```
200.            10.           189.          192           /27
1100 1000.      0000 1010.    1011 1101.    1100 0000
```

Figure E2.2 illustrates this, where one side of the router is using on size of subnet mask, whereas the other side uses another size.

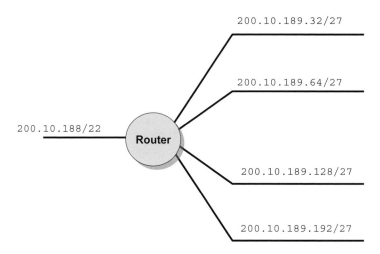

Figure E2.2 Example of VSLM

E2.5 Routing protocol techniques

There are three main types of routing protocols (as illustrated in Figure E2.3):

- **Distance-vector.** Distance-vector routing uses a distance-vector algorithm (such as the Bellman-Ford routing algorithm), which uses a direction (vector) and distance to any link in the internetwork to determine the best route. Each router periodically sends information to each of its neighbors on the cost that it takes to get to a distance node. Typically, this cost relates to the hop count (as with RIP). The main problem with distance-vector is that updates to the network are step-by-step, and it has high bandwidth requirements as each router sends its complete routing table to all of its neighbors at regular intervals.
- **Link-state.** Link-state involves each router building up the complete topology of the entire internetwork (or at least of the partition on which the router is situated), thus each router contains the same information. With this method, routers only send information to all of the other routers when there is a change in the topology of the network. Link-state is also known as shortest path first. Typical link-state protocols are OSPF, BGP and EGP. With OSPF, each router builds a hierarchical topology of the internetwork, with itself at the top of the tree. The main problem with link-state is that routers require much more processing power to update the database, and more memory as routers require to build a database with details of all the routers on the network.
- **Hybrid.** A mixture of distance-vector and link-state. Typical hybrid routing protocols are IS-IS and Enhanced IGRP.

An outline of the main techniques used in routing protocols is outlined in Figure E2.3.

E2.5.1 Distance-vector

In the distance-vector routing protocol, each router initially identifies each of its neighbors. Next, it defines each of its ports which connect to a network as having a distance of zero. The discovery process continues by communicating with each of its neighbors. A typical distance-vector algorithm is RIP, which uses a hop count as a metric, but other algorithms can use different cost metrics (such as bandwidth or delay).

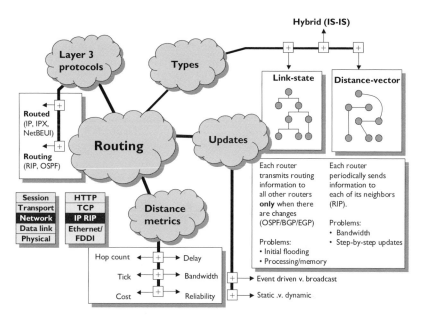

Figure E2.3   Example routing

An example network is shown in Figure E2.4. In this case, Router Z communicates with Router W and Router Y and receives their routing tables. Each router will maintain a routing table which defines the number of hops that it takes to get to a destination and the port of the router that the router should use. An example sequence may be:

- All routers communicate to determine their neighbors. For example, Router X knows that its neighbors are Router Y and Router W.
- All routers set the 'count to network' that they connect to, at zero.
- Router X then tells Router Y and Router W that it takes zero hops to get to Network A. Router Y will add one hop for the destination to Network A (hop count to A is one), and Router W will add one hop for the destination to Network A (hop count to A is one).
- Router Y then tells Router X and Router Z that it takes zero hops to get to Network B. Router X will add one hop for the destination to Network B (hop count to B is one), and Router Z will add one hop for the destination to Network B (hop count to B is one).
- Router Z then tells Router W and Router Y that it takes zero hops to get to Network C. Router W will add one hop for the destination to Network C (hop count to C is one), and

Router Y will add one hop for the destination to Network C (hop count to C is one).
- Router X sends its new updated routing table to W and Y, and informs them that it takes one hop to get to Network B. Router Y will not change its entry for Network B as it currently has a hop count of zero, but Router W will update its routing table for Network B to two hops.

... and so on. After the convergence time, the routers will then build up the tables shown in Figure E2.4. If a router gets information that it can reach the route from more than one path, it will take the lowest hop count for its table entry. In the example in Figure E2.4, there are two equal paths to get to Network B from Router W, each with a hop count of two. The router can thus use any one of these.

It should be noted that distance-vector is inefficient, as each router will send out its entire routing table at regular intervals. This is inefficient when there are no updates in the topology of the network. Updates also take some time, as they must be passed from router-to-router.

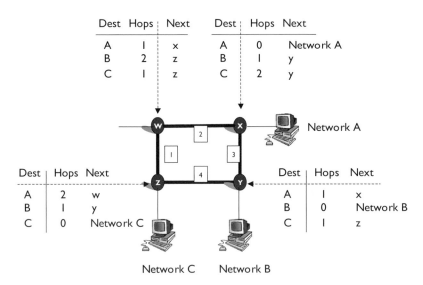

Figure E2.4 Example routing

Problems with distance-vector routing protocols

The major problems with distance-vector routing protocols (such as RIP) are:

- **Routing Loops.** These occur when slow convergence causes inconsistent routing entities when a new configuration occurs (Figure E2.5). In this case, Network A becomes unavailable. Router V will report this to Router Y, which will then report to Router Z and Router X. Both Routers X and Z will stop routing to Network A. Unfortunately Router W still thinks it can reach Network A with 3 hops, thus Router Z will receive information that says that Router W can get to Network A in 3 hops, and that it is unreachable from Router Y. Thus Router Z updates its routing table so that Network A is reachable in 4 hops, and that the next router to the destination is Router W. Router Z will then send its updated information to Router Y which informs it that there is a path to Network A from

Router Z to Router W, and so on. Router Y will then inform Router X, and so on. Thus, any data packet which is destined for Network A will now loop around the loop from Router Z to Router W to Router X to Router Y to Router Z, and so on.

- **Counting to Infinity.** As has been seen in Figure E2.5, data packets can loop around forever, because of incorrect routing information. In this loop, the distance-vector of the hop count will increment each time the packet goes through a router.

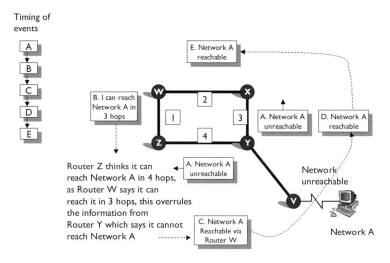

Figure E2.5 Routing loops

There are several solutions to the count-to-infinity and routing loop problems. These are:

- **Setting infinity values.** The count-to-infinity will eventually resolve itself when the routers have counted to infinity (as infinity will be constrained with the maximum definable value), but while the network is counting to this value, the routing information will be incorrect. To reduce the time that it takes to get to this maximum, a maximum value is normally defined. In RIP this value is set at 16 hops for hop-count distance-vectors, thus the maximum number of hops that can occur is **15.** This leads to a problem in that a destination which has a distance of more than 15 hops is unreachable, as a value of 16 or more defines that the network is unreachable.
- **Split horizon.** This method tries to overcome routing loops. With this routers do not update their routing table with information on a destination if they know that the network is already connected to the router (that is, the router knows more about the state of the network than any other router, as it connects to it). Thus in Figure E2.4, Router Z and Router X will not send routing information on Network B to Router Y, as they know that Network B is connected to Router Y.
- **Hold-Down Timers.** This method overcomes the count-to-infinity problem. With a hold-time time, a router starts a hold-time timer when it receives an update from a neighbor indicating that a previously accessible network is now inaccessible. It also marks the route as inaccessible. There are then three possible situations:

- If, at any time before the hold-down timer expires, an update is sent from the same neighbor which alerted the initial problem saying that it is now accessible, the router marks the network as accessible and removes the hold-down timer.
- If an update arrives from a different neighboring router with a better metric than the original metric, the router marks the network as accessible and removes the hold-down timer.
- If, at any time before the hold-down timer expires, an update is sent from a different neighbor which alerted the initial problem saying that it is accessible, but has a poorer metric than the previously recorded metric, the update is ignored. Obviously after the timer has expired the network will still be prone to looping routes, but the timer allows for a longer time for the network to settle down and recover the correct information.

E2.5.2   Link-state concepts

The link-state algorithm (known as shortest path first) maintains a complex database on the topology of a network. Each router thus has the complete picture of the whole of the network and has knowledge of distant routers, and how they interconnect. The distance-vector, on the other hand, has nonspecific information on distant networks, and no knowledge of distant routers.

The link-state algorithm uses link-state advertisements (LSAs) to advertise routing information from routers. From this each router build-up a topological database with themselves at the top of the tree, and uses a shortest path first (SPF) algorithm to determine the best route to get to a destination. A typical implementation is Open Shortest Path First (OSPF), which is defined in RFC1583, and uses Dijkstra's algorithm to determine the best path. An outline of it is given in Figure E2.6. Initially, on start-up, each router must discover the routes which it connects to. Next, each router advertises its connection to all the other routers on the network. From this, it builds up a topology database with the information. There may be multiple routes to get to a destination, thus the SPF algorithm is used to determine the best route. It is this route that is then used in the topological database. All the routers on the network will thus have the same information. The distance-vector approach uses constant updates of routing tables between neighbors, whereas the link-state approach only sends routing information when there is a change in the topology of the network. This information floods to all the routers on the network (the discovery process), thus all routers are updated with the new information.

In order for the link-state algorithm to work, a router must keep communicating with its neighbors to determine if they are still responding to communications, and if they have any changes in their link metrics. Each router only uses the most up-to-date information from LSA packets to build up the topological database.

The main problem with link-state, as apposed to distance-vector, is that the algorithm requires much more processing power, and also increased amount of memory to store up-to-date LSAs and the complete topological database. With Dijkstra's algorithm the processing task is proportional to the number of links in the internetwork multiplied by the number of routers in the internetwork.

Link-state routing is much more efficient in bandwidth, though, as the routing information is only passed when there is a change in the topology of the internetwork. Initially, though, there is a high requirement for bandwidth, as each of the routers must flood routing information through the internetwork. After the internetwork has converged, there is a reduced requirement for bandwidth, as apposed to the distance-vector method which has a constant demand on bandwidth.

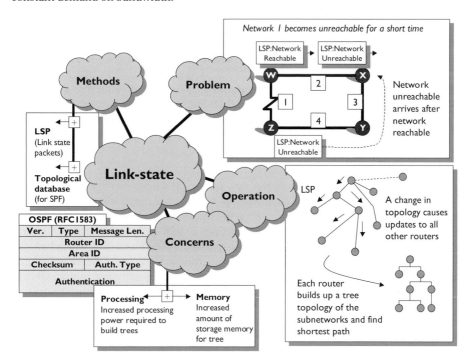

Figure E2.6 Link-state overview

The main problems with link-state are:

- **Link-state updates.** This problem is illustrated in Figure E2.6. In this case, Network link 1 becomes unavailable for a short time. Thus Router W and Router Z transmit the information that this link is unavailable to the rest of the network. In this case the information will be received by Router X and Router Y. If the network then becomes available from Router W, Router W will send out Network Reachable advertisement. If Router X receives this before it receives the Network Unreachable then Router X thinks that the network is still unavailable, even though it is available via Router W. This problem can cause whole sections of a network to become unavailable.
- **Scaling.** A problem with link-state occurs when scaling-up large internetworks when one network comes up before other parts of the network. This causes a timing problem where differing reachability information is sent between routers, thus routers might learn about different versions of the topology before they construct their SPF trees and routing tables. On a large internetwork, parts that update more quickly can cause problems for parts that update more slowly.

E2.5.3 Hybrid routing

An important third classification of routing algorithm is hybrid routing, which is a combination of both distance-vector and link-state routing, and is named balanced-hybrid routing.

These routing protocols use distance-vectors for more accurate metrics to determine the best paths to destination networks, and report routing information only when there is a change in the topology of the network. The event-driven nature of hybrid routing allows for rapid convergence (as with link-state protocols), but it requires much less processing power and memory than a link-state protocol would require. Examples of hybrid protocols are Intermediate System-to-Intermediate System (IS-IS) routing and Enhanced Interior Gateway Routing Protocol (EIGRP). The IS-IS routing protocol has been defined OSI link-state hierarchical routing protocol which is based on DECnet Phase V routing whereby ISs (routers) exchange routing information based on a single metric to determine network topology.

E2.6   RIP

Most routers support RIP and EGP. In the past, RIP was the most popular router protocol standard. Its widespread use is due, in no small part, to the fact that it was distributed along with the Berkeley Software Distribution (BSD) of UNIX (from which most commercial versions of UNIX are derived), and was originally defined in RFC 1058. Unfortunately, it suffers from several disadvantages and has been largely replaced by OSFP and EGB, which have the advantage over RIP in that they can handle large internetworks, as well as reducing routing table update traffic. By default, in RIP, each router transmits its complete routing table to their neighbor once every 30 seconds (although this time is configurable in most routers).

RIP uses a distance-vector algorithm which measures the number of network jumps (known as hops), up to a maximum of 16, to the destination router. This has the disadvantage that the smallest number of hops may not be the best route from source to destination. The OSPF and EGB protocols use a link state algorithm that can decide between multiple paths to the destination router, which are based, not only on hops, but also on other parameters such as delay, capacity, reliability and throughput.

With distance-vector routing each router maintains tables by communicating with neighboring routers. The number of hops in its own table is then computed, as it knows the number of hops to local routers. Unfortunately, the routing table can take some time to be updated when changes occur, because it takes time for all the routers to communicate with each other (known as slow convergence).

RIP packets, which use TCP **port 520**, generally add to the general network traffic as each router broadcasts its entire routing table every 30–60 seconds. Figure E2.7 outlines the RIP packet format. The fields are:

- **Operation** (2 bytes) – this field gives an indication that the RIP packet is either a request or a response. The first 8 bits of the field give the command/request name and the next 8 bits give the version number.
- **Network number** (4 bytes of IP addresses) – this field defines the assigned network address number to which the routing information applies (note that, although 4 bytes are shown, there are in fact 14 bytes reserved for the address. In RIP version 1 (RIPv1), with IP traffic, 10 of the bytes were unused; RIPv2 uses the 14-byte address field for other purposes, such as subnet masks.
- **Number of router hops** (2 bytes) – this field indicates the number of routers that a packet must go through in order to reach the required destination. Each router adds a single hop, the minimum number is 1 and the maximum is 16. The maximum number of hops to a destination is thus limited to 15.
- **Number of ticks** (2 bytes) – this field indicates the amount of time (in 1/18 second) it will

take for a packet to reach a given destination. Note that a route which has the fewest hops may not necessarily be the fastest route.

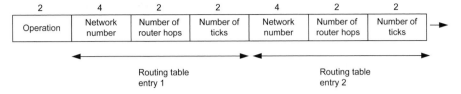

Figure E2.7 RIP packet format

E2.7 OSPF

The OSPF (Open Shortest Path First) is an open, non-proprietary standard which was created by the IETF (Internet Engineering Task Force), a task force of the IAB. It is a link state routing protocol and is thus able to maintain a complete and more current view of the total internetwork, than distance-vector routing protocols. Link state routing protocols have these features:

- They use link state packets (**LSPs**) which are special datagrams that determine the names of and the cost or distance to any neighboring routers and associated networks.
- Any information learned about the network is then passed to all known routers, and not just neighboring routers, using LSPs. Thus all routers have a fuller knowledge of the entire internetwork than the view of only the immediate neighbors (as with distance-vector routing).

OSPF adds to these features with:

- **Additional hierarchy.** OSPF allows the global network to be split into areas. Thus, a router in a domain does not necessarily have to know how to reach all the networks with a domain, it simply has to send to the right area.
- **Authentication of routing messages** using an 8-byte password. This length is not long enough to stop unauthorized users from causing damage. Its main purpose is to reduce the traffic from misconfigured routers. Typically, a misconfigured router will inform the network that it can reach all nodes with no overhead.
- **Load balancing.** OSPF allows multiple routes to the same place to be assigned the same cost and will cause traffic to be distributed evenly over those routes.

Figure E2.8 shows the OSPF header. The fields in the header are:

- **A version number** (1 byte) which, in current implementations, has the version number of 2.
- **The type field** (1 byte) which can range from 1 to 5. Type 1 is the Hello message and the others are to request, send and acknowledge the receipt of link state messages. Nodes, to convince their neighbors that they are alive and reachable, use hello messages. If a router fails to receive these messages from one of its neighbors for a period of time, it assumes that the node is no longer directly reachable and updates its link state

information accordingly.

- **Router ID** (4 bytes) identifies the sender of the message.
- **Area ID** (4 bytes) is an identifier to the area in which the node is located.
- **Authentication field** can either be set to 0 (none) or 1. If it is set to 1 then the authentication contains an 8-byte password.

The Hello packet is used to establish and maintain a connection. It is used to determine the routers that are connected to the current router. The connected routers then agree on HelloInterval and RouterDeadInterval values. The HelloIntervalue defines the number of seconds between Hello packets. The smaller the value, the faster the detection of topological changes. For example, X.25 typically uses 30 sec and LANs use 10 sec. The RouterDeadInterval defines the number of seconds before a router assumes that a route is down. It should be a multiple of HelloInterval (such as four times).

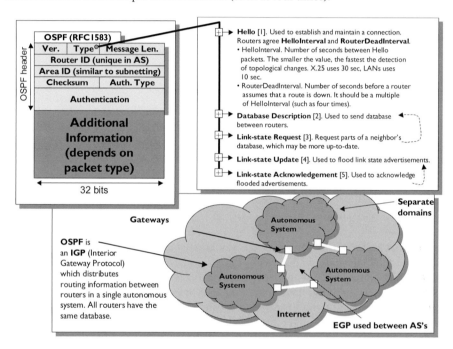

Figure E2.8   OSPF overview

When a router thinks that it does not have the correct information on a part of a route it sends Link-state Request, which request parts of a neighbor's database. The requested neighbor then sends back a Database Description which describes the requested part of its database.

When a router detects a change in its connections it sends a Link-state Update message, which is then flooded to all the routers on the internetwork. Routers return back a Link-state Acknowledgement to acknowledge the flooded advertisements.

It would of course be impossible for every router in the world to know about every other router and every link, thus each internetwork is segmented into Automomous Systems (ASs), which are bounded by a gateway. In these each router knows the complete topology

of the AS. An interior routing protocol (such as OSPF) is used to transmit routing information within the AS, and an exterior routing protocol (such as EGP) is used to route between
ASs, as illustrated in Figure E2.8. The Network Information Center (NIC) assigns a unique
16-bit number to enterprises for ASs.

The usage of ASs provides for a similar architecture for the Internet, where data packets
are routed from one domain into another. For example, all the universities in France could
define one domain. Anyone communicating with them will be routed in a defined domain
through a designated gateway. The routers within the domain would then have a complete
picture of all the internetworks within the domain. ASs also help to hide the architecture of
the interior network from other routers outside the AS.

E2.8   IGRP

IGRP (Interior Gateway Routing Protocol) is a distance-vector routing protocol (as RIP),
which is used as an interior routing within an AS. Like RIP, it transmits routing information
at regular intervals, but unlike RIP, it uses a much better measure of the metric, these include:

- Bandwidth.
- Delay.
- Load.
- Reliability.
- Maximum transmission unit (MTU), which defines the maximum data packet size that
  an interface can handle.

It advertises routing information every 90 seconds. The key points of IGRP are:

- Handles complex networks, as the metric can define problems (rather than the basic
  hop count used in RIP).
- It allows for more efficient routing, as the network can cope with different delays and
  bandwidths.
- Scaleable for very large networks.

E2.9   EGP/BGP

The two main interdomain routing protocols in recent history are **EGP** and **BGP**. EGP suffers from several limitations, and its principal one is that it treats the Internet as a tree-like
structure, as illustrated in Figure E2.9. This assumes that the structure of the Internet is
made up of parents and children, with a single backbone. A more typical topology for the
Internet is illustrated in Figure E2.10. BGP is now one of the most widely accepted exterior
routing protocol, and has largely replaced EGP.

BGP is an improvement on EGP (the fourth version of BGP is known as BGP-4), and is
defined in RFC1772. Unfortunately it is more complex than EGP, but not as complex as
OSPF. BGP assumes that the Internet is made up of an arbitrarily interconnected set of
nodes. It then assumes the Internet connects to a number of **AANs** (autonomously attached
networks), as illustrated in Figure E2.11, which create boundaries around organizations,
Internet service providers, and so on. It then assumes that, once they are in the AAN, the

packets will be properly routed.

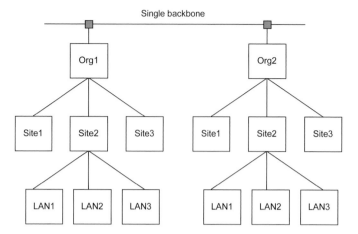

Figure E2.9   Tree-like topology

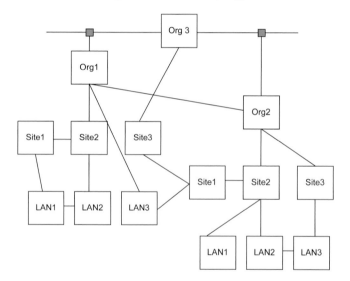

Figure E2.10   Network with multiple backbones

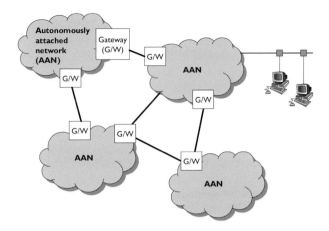

Figure E2.11 Autonomously attached networks

Most routing algorithms try to find the quickest way through the network, whereas BGP tries to find any path through the network. Thus, the main goal is reachability instead of the number of hops to the destination. So finding a path which is nearly optimal is a good achievement. The AAN administrator selects at least one node to be a BGP speaker and also one or more border gateways. These gateways simply route the packet into and out of the AAN. The border gateways are the routers through which packets reach the AAN.

The speaker on the AAN broadcasts its reachability information to all the networks within its AAN. This information states only whether a destination AAN can be reached; it does not describe any other metrics. An important point is that BGP is not a distance-vector or link state protocol because it transmits complete routing information instead of partial information.

The BGP update packet also contains information on routes which cannot be reached (withdrawn routes), and the content of the BGP-4 update packet is:

- **Unfeasible routes length** (2 bytes).
- **Withdrawn routes** (variable length).
- **Total path attribute length** (2 bytes).
- **Path attributes** (variable length).
- **Network layer reachability information** (variable length). This can contain extra information, such as 'use AAN 1 in preference to AAN 2'.

Routers within AS's share similar routing policies, and thus operate as a single administrative unit. All the routers outside the AS treat the AS as a single unit. The AS identification number is assigned by the Internet Assigned Numbers Authority (IANA) in the range of 1 to 65,535, where 64,512 to 65,535 are reserved for private use. The private numbers are only used within private domain, and must be translated to registered numbers when leaving the domain.

E2.9.1 BGP and routing loops

BGP uses TCP segments on port 179 to send routing information (whereas RIP uses port 520). BGP overcomes routing loops by constructing a graph of autonomous systems, based on the information provided by exchanging information between neighbors. It can thus build up a wider picture of the entire interconnected ASs. A keep-alive message is send between neighbours, which allows the graph to be kept up-to-date.

E2.9.2 Single-homed systems

ASs which have only one exit point are defined as single-homed systems, and are often referred to as stub networks. These stubs can use a default route to handle all the network traffic destined for non-local networks.

There are three methods that an AS can use so that the outside world can learn the addresses within the AS:

- **Static configuration**. For this, an Internet access provider could list the customer's networks as static entries within its own router. These would then be advertised to other routers connected to its Internet core. This approach could also be used with a CIDR approach which aggregates the routes.
- **Use an Interior Gateway Protocol** (IGP) on the link. For this, an Internet access provider could run a IGP on the single connection, this can then be used to advertise the connected networks. This method allows for a more dynamic approach, than static configuration. A typical IGP is OSPF.
- **Use an Exterior Gateway Protocol** (EGP) on the link. An EGP can be used to advertise the networks. If the connected AS does not have a registered AS, the Internet access provider can assign it from a private pool of AS numbers (64,512 to 65,535), and then strip off the numbers when advertising the AS to the core of the Internet.

E2.9.3 Multihomed system

A multi-homed system has more than one exit point from the AS. As it has more than one exit point, it could support the routing of data across the exit points. A system which does not support the routing of traffic through the AS is named a non-transit AS. Non-transit ASs thus will only advertise its own routes to the Internet access providers, as it does not want any routing through it. One Internet provider could force traffic through the AS if it knows that routing through the AS is possible. To overcome this, the AS would setup filtering to stop any of this routed traffic.

Multi-homed transit systems have more than one connection to an Internet access provider, and also allow traffic to be routed through it. It will route this traffic by running BGP internally so that multiple border routers in the same AS can share BGP information. Along with this, routers can forward BGP information from one border router to another. BGP running inside the AS is named Internet BGP (IBGP), while it is known as External BGP (EBGP) if it is running outside AS's. The routers which define the boundary between the AS and the Internet access provider is known as border routers, while routers running internal BGP are known as transit routers.

E2.10   BGP specification

Border Gateway Protocol (**BGP**) is an inter-Autonomous System routing protocol (exterior routing protocol), which builds on EGP. The main function of a BGP-based system is to communicate network reachability information with other BGP systems. Initially two systems exchange messages to open and confirm the connection parameters, and then transmit the entire BGP routing table. After this, incremental updates are sent as the routing tables change.

Each message has a fixed-size header and may or may not be followed a data portion. The fields are:

- **Marker.** Contains a value that the receiver of the message can predict. It can be used to detect a loss of synchronization between a pair of BGP peers, and to authenticate incoming BGP messages. 16 bytes.
- **Length.** Indicates the total length, in bytes, of the message, including the header. It must always be greater than 18 and no greater than 4096. 2 bytes.
- **Type.** Indicates the type of message, such as 1 – OPEN, 2 – UPDATE, 3 – NOTIFICATION and 4 – KEEPALIVE.

E2.10.1 OPEN message

The OPEN message is the first message sent after a connection has been made. A KEEPALIVE message is sent back confirming the OPEN message. After this the UPDATE, KEEPALIVE, and NOTIFICATION messages can be exchanged.

Figure E2.12 shows the extra information added to the fixed-size BGP header. It has the following fields:

- **Version.** Indicates the protocol version number of the message. Typical values are 2, 3 or 4. 1 byte.
- **My Autonomous System.** Identifies the sender's Autonomous System number. 2 bytes.
- **Hold Time.** Indicates the maximum number of seconds that can elapse between the receipt of successive KEEPALIVE and/or UPDATE and/or NOTIFICATION messages. 2 bytes.
- **Authentication Code.** Indicates the authentication mechanism being used. This should define the form and meaning of the Authentication Data and the algorithm for computing values of Marker fields.
- **Authentication Data.** The form and meaning of this field is a variable-length field which depends on the Authentication Code.

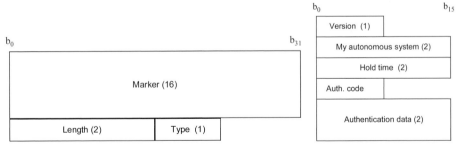

Figure E2.12 BGP message header and BGP OPEN message data

E2.10.2 UPDATE message format

The UPDATE message is used to transfer routing information between BGP peers. This information is used to construct a graph describing the relationships of the various Autonomous Systems. The extra information added to the fixed-size BGP header is as follows:

- **Total Path Attribute Length.** Indicates the length of the Path Attributes field in bytes. Its value must allow the number of Network fields to be determined as specified below. 2 bytes.
- **Path Attributes.** A variable length sequence of path attributes. Each path contains the attributes for attribute type, attribute length and attribute value. These are:

  - Attribute Type. Consists of the Attribute Flags byte (b_0–b_7) followed by the Attribute Type Code byte (b_8–b_{15}). 2 bytes. The format of the Attribute flags are:

    b_0 Optional bit. Defines whether the attribute is optional (if set to 1) or well-known (if set to 0).

    b_1 Transitive bit. Defines whether an optional attribute is transitive (if set to 1) or non-transitive (if set to 0).

    b_2 Partial bit. Defines whether the information contained in the optional transitive attribute is partial (if set to 1) or complete (if set to 0). For well-known attributes and for optional non-transitive attributes the Partial bit must be set to 0.

    b_3 Extended Length bit. Defines whether the Attribute Length is one byte (if set to 0) or two bytes (if set to 1).

    b_4–b_7 Unused and set to zero.

  - Attribute Type Code. Contains the Attribute Type Code.

- **Network.** Each Internet network number indicates one network whose Inter-Autonomous System routing is described by the Path Attributes. 4-byte.

The total number of Network fields in the UPDATE message can be determined by the formula:

$$\text{Message\_Length} = 19 + \text{Total\_Path\_Attribute\_Length} + 4 \times \text{No\_of\_networks}$$

E2.10.3 KEEPALIVE and NOTIFICATION message format

The KEEPALIVE message consists of only the message header (and is thus only 19 bytes long) and is used to determine if peers are reachable. Unlike other routing protocols, such as RIP, BGP does not continually poll its peers to determine if they are still reachable, instead peers exchange KEEPALIVE messages (which must be less than the hold time of the OPEN message). A typical maximum time between KEEPALIVE messages is one-third of the hold time period.

E2.10.4 Path attributes

Path attributes in the UPDATE message fall into four separate categories:

- **Well-known mandatory.**
- **Well-known discretionary.**
- **Optional transitive.**
- **Optional non-transitive.**

Attributes which are well known must be recognized by all BGP implementations. If they are mandatory they must be included in every UPDATE message. Discretionary attributes may or may not be sent in an UPDATE message. Table E2.1 defines the well-known attributes.

Table E2.1 Well-known attributes

Attribute Name	Type code	Length	Attribute category	Description
ORIGIN	1	1	Well-known, mandatory	Defines the origin of the path information. Values are: 0 IGP – network(s) are interior to the originating AS. 1 EGP – network(s) learned via EGP. 2 INCOMPLETE – network(s) learned by some other means.
AS_PATH	2	variable	Well-known, mandatory	AS_PATH attribute enumerates the ASs that must be traversed to reach the networks listed in the UPDATE message.
NEXT_HOP	3	4	Well-known, mandatory	Defines the IP address of the border router that should be used as the next hop to the networks listed in the UPDATE message.
UNREACHABLE	4	0	Well-known, discretionary	Used to notify a BGP peer that some of the previously advertised routes have become unreachable.
INTER-AS METRIC	5	2	Optional, non-transitive	May be used on external (inter-AS) links to discriminate between multiple exit or entry points to the same neighboring AS.

E2.10.5 BGP state transitions and actions

BGP states are:
1 – Idle;   2 – Connect;
3 – Active;   4 – OpenSent;
5 – OpenConfirm;   6 – Established.

The events are:

1 – BGP Start;
3 – BGP Transport connection open;
5 – BGP Transport connection open failed;
7 – ConnectRetry timer expired;
9 – KeepAlive timer expired;
11 – Receive KEEPALIVE message;
13 – Receive NOTIFICATION message.

2 – BGP Stop;
4 – BGP Transport connection closed;
6 – BGP Transport fatal error;
8 – Holdtime timer expired;
10 – Receive OPEN message;
12 – Receive UPDATE messages;

The following defines the state transitions of the BGP FSM and the actions that occur.

EVENT	ACTIONS	MESSAGE_SENT	NEXT_STATE
Idle (1)			
1	Initialize resources Start ConnectRetry timer Initiate a transport connection	none	2
Connect (2)			
1	none	none	2
3	Complete initialization Clear ConnectRetry timer	OPEN	4
5	Restart ConnectRetry timer	none	3
7	Restart ConnectRetry timer Initiate a transport connection	none	2
Active (3)			
1	none	none	3
3	Complete initialization Clear ConnectRetry timer	OPEN	4
5	Close connection Restart ConnectRetry timer		3
7	Restart ConnectRetry timer Initiate a transport connection	none	2
OpenSent (4)			
1	none	none	4
4	Close transport connection Restart ConnectRetry timer	none	3
6	Release resources	none	1
10	Process OPEN is OK Process OPEN failed	KEEPALIVE NOTIFICATION	5 1
OpenConfirm (5)			
1	none	none	5
4	Release resources	none	1
6	Release resources	none	1
9	Restart KeepAlive timer	KEEPALIVE	5
11	Complete initialization Restart Holdtime timer	none	6
13	Close transport connection Release resources		1
Established (6)			
1	none	none	6
4	Release resources	none	1
6	Release resources	none	1
9	Restart KeepAlive timer	KEEPALIVE	6

11	Restart Holdtime timer	KEEPALIVE	6
12	Process UPDATE is OK	UPDATE	6
	Process UPDATE failed	NOTIFICATION	1

E2.11   BGP configuration

BGP configuration commands are similar to those used for RIP. To configure the router to support BGP the following commands is used:

```
RouterA # config t
RouterA(config)#router bgp AS-number
```

With IGP's, such as RIP, the `network` command defined the networks on which routing table update are sent. For BGP a different approach is used to define the relationship between networks. This is:

```
RouterA # config t
RouterA(config) #router bgp AS-number
Router(config-router)#network network-number [mask network-mask]
```

where the `network` command defines where to advertise the locally learnt networks. These networks could have been learnt from other protocols, such as RIP. An optional `mask` can be used with the `network` command to specify individual subnets. With the BGP protocol neiphbors must establish a relationship, for this the following is used:

```
RouterA # config t
RouterA(config) #router bgp AS-number
Router(config-router)#network network-number [mask network-mask]
Router(config-router)# neighbor ip-address remote-as AS-number
```

which defines the IP address of a connected BGP-based router, along with its AS number.

E3   Security

E3.1   Introduction

An organization may experience two disadvantages in having a connection to the WWW and the Internet:

- The possible usage of the Internet for non-useful applications (by employees).
- The possible connection of non-friendly users from the global connection into the organization's local network.

For these reasons, many organizations have shied away from connection to the global network and have set up intranets. These are in-house, tailor-made internets for use within the organization and provide limited access (if any) to outside services and also limit the external traffic into the intranet (if any). An intranet might have access to the Internet but there will be no access from the Internet to the organization's Intranet.

Organizations which have a requirement for sharing and distributing electronic information normally have three choices:

- Use a propriety groupware package, such as Lotus Notes.
- Set up an intranet.
- Set up a connection to the Internet.

Groupware packages normally replicate data locally on a computer whereas intranets centralize their information on central servers which are then accessed by a single browser package. The stored data is normally open and can be viewed by any compatible WWW browser. Intranet browsers have the great advantage over groupware packages in that they are available for a variety of clients, such as PCs, UNIX workstations, Macs, and so on. A client browser also provides a single GUI interface which offers easy integration with other applications, such as electronic mail, images, audio, video, animation, and so on.

The main elements of an intranet are:

- Intranet server hardware and software.
- TCP/IP stack software on the clients and server.
- WWW browsers.
- A firewall.

Typically the intranet server consists of a PC running the Linux (PC-based UNIX-like) operating system. The TCP/IP stack is software installed on each computer and allows communications between a client and a server using TCP/IP.

A firewall is the routing computer which isolates the intranet from the outside world. Another method is to use an intermediate system which isolates the intranet from the external Internet. These intermediate systems include:

- A proxy. This connects to a number of clients; it acts on behalf of clients and sends requests from the clients to a server. It thus acts as a client when it communicates with a server, but as a server when communicating with a client. A proxy is typically used for security purposes where the client and server are separated by a firewall. The proxy connects to the client side of the firewall and the server to the other side of the firewall. Thus the server must authenticate itself to the firewall before a connection can be made with the proxy. Only after this has been authenticated will the proxy pass requests through the firewall. A proxy can also be used to convert between different versions of the protocols that use TCP/IP, such as HTTP.

- A gateway.
- A tunnel.

Each intermediate system is connected by TCP and acts as a relay for the request to be sent out and returned to the client. Figure E3.1 shows the set-up of the proxies and gateways.

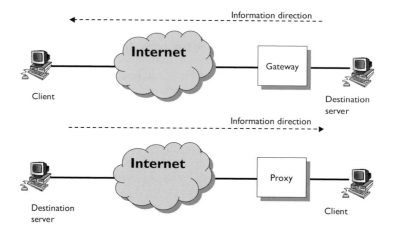

Figure E3.1   Usage of proxies and gateways

E3.2 Firewalls

A firewall (or security gateway) protects a network against intrusion from outside sources. They tend to differ in their approach, but can be characterized either as firewalls which block traffic or firewalls which permit traffic. They can be split into three main types:

- **Network-level firewalls** (packet filters). This type of firewall examines the parameters of the TCP/IP packet to determine if it should be dropped or not. This can be done by ex-amining the destination address, the source address, the destination port, the source port, and so on. The firewall must thus contain a list of barred IP addresses or allowable IP addresses. Typically a system manager will determine IP addresses of sites which are barred and add them to the table. Certain port numbers will also be barred, typically TELNET and FTP ports are barred and SMTP is allowed, as this allows mail to be routed into and out of the network, but no remote connections.
- **Application-level firewalls.** This type of firewall uses an intermediate system (a proxy server) to isolate the local computers from the external network. The local computer communicates with the proxy server, which in turn communicates with the external network, the external computer then communicates with the proxy which in turn

communicates with the local computers. The external network never actually communicates directly with the local computers. The proxy server can then be set-up to be limited to certain types of data transfer, such as allowing HTTP (for WWW access), SMTP (for electronic mail), outgoing FTP, but blocking incoming FTP.

- **Circuit-level firewalls.** A circuit-level firewall is similar to an application-level firewall but it does not bother about the transferred protocol.

E3.2.1 Network-level firewalls

The network-level firewall (or packet filter) is the simplest form of firewall and is also known as a screen router. It basically keeps a record of allowable source and destination IP addresses, and deletes all packets which do not have them. This technique is known as address filtering. The packet filter keeps a separate source and destination table for both directions, that is, into and out of the intranet. This type of method is useful for companies which have geographically spread sites, as the packet filter allows incoming traffic from other friendly sites, but blocks other non-friendly traffic. This is illustrated by Figure E3.2.

Unfortunately, this method suffers from the fact that IP addresses can be easily forged. For example, a hacker might determine the list of good source addresses and then add one of them to any packets which are addressed to the intranet. This type of attack is known as address spoofing and is the most common method of attacking a network.

E3.2.2 Application-level firewall

The application-level firewall uses a proxy server to act as an intermediate system between the external network and the local computer. Normally the proxy only supports a given number of protocols, such as HTTP (for WWW access) or FTP. It is thus possible to block certain types of protocols, typically outgoing FTP (Figure E3.3).

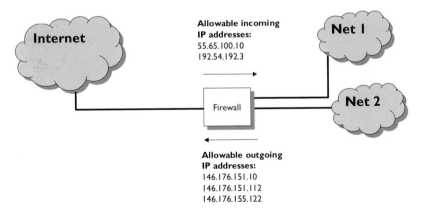

Figure E3.2 Packet filter firewalls

The proxy server thus isolates the local computer from the external network. The local computer communicates with the proxy server, which in turn communicates with the external network, the external computer then communicates with the proxy, which in turn, communicates with the local computer. The external network never actually communicates directly with the local computer. The left-hand window of Figure E3.4 shows a WWW browser set up to communicate with a proxy server to get its access. In the advanced options (right-hand side of Figure E3.4) different proxy servers can be specified. In this case, for HTTP (WWW access), FTP, Gopher, Secure and Socks (Windows Sockets). It can also be seen that a proxy server can be bypassed by specifying a number of IP addresses (or DNS).

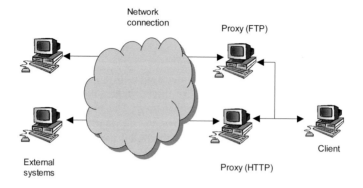

Figure E3.3   Application-level firewall

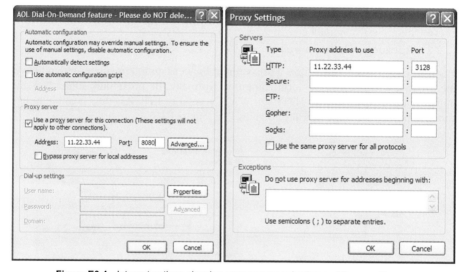

Figure E3.4   Internet options showing proxy server selection and Proxy settings

E3.3 Application-level gateways

Application-level gateways provide an extra layer of security when connecting an intranet to the Internet. They have three main components:

- A gateway node.
- Two firewalls which connect on either side of the gateway and only transmit packets which are destined for or to the gateway.

Figure E3.5 shows the operation of an application level-gateway. In this case, Firewall A discards anything that is not addressed to the gateway node, and discards anything that is not sent by the gateway node. Firewall B similarly discards anything from the local network that is not addressed to the gateway node, and discards anything that is not sent by the gateway node.

Thus, to transfer files from the local network into the global network, the user must do the following:

- Log onto the gateway node.
- Transfer the file onto the gateway.
- Transfer the file from the gateway onto the global network.

To copy a file from the network, an external user must:

- Log onto the gateway node.
- Transfer from the global network onto the gateway.
- Transfer the file from the gateway onto the local network.

A common strategy in organizations is to allow only electronic mail to pass from the Internet to the local network. This specifically disallows file transfer and remote login. Unfortunately, electronic mail can be used to transfer files. To overcome this problem the firewall can be designed specifically to disallow very large electronic mail messages, so it will limit the ability to transfer files. This tends not to be a good method as large files can be split up into small parts, then sent individually.

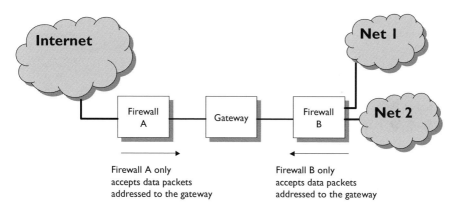

Figure E3.5 Application-level gateway

E3.4 Ring-fenced firewalls

Many large organizations have several sites which are spread over a geographically large area. This causes a major problem for security, as the different sites would have to be administered separately. Any small breaches on a single site could cause the whole organizational network to become threatened. One solution is to centralize the gateway into and out of the organization network. An example is given in Figure E3.6 where the three sites each have a firewall which protects security breaches between each of the sites. These then connect to a common router, which then connects to a strong firewall. At the gateway to each of the sites and at the gateway to the entire organization network, there is an audit-monitoring computer, which will log all the incoming and outgoing traffic over time. This could monitor incoming and outgoing IP addresses, domain names, transport protocols, and so on. Any security breaches can be easily detected by examining these logs. The audit monitor could also be used against staff if it shows that employees have been acting incorrectly, such as copying files from the organizational network to an external network, or accessing inappropriate WWW sites.

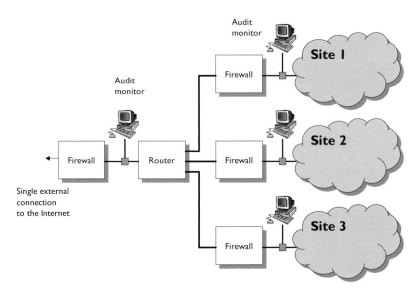

Figure E3.6 Ring-fenced firewall

E3.5 Encrypted tunnels

Packet filters and application-level gateways suffer from insecurity, which can allow non-friendly users into the local network. Packet filters can be tricked with fake IP addresses and application-level gateways can be hacked into by determining the password of certain users of the gateway then transferring the files from the network to the firewall, onto the gateway, onto the next firewall and out. The best form of protection for this type of attack is to allow only a limited number of people to transfer files onto the gateway.

The best method of protection is to encrypt the data leaving the network then to decrypt it on the remote site. Only friendly sites will have the required encryption key to receive and send data. This has the extra advantage that the information cannot be easily tapped into. Only the routers which connect to the Internet need to encrypt and decrypt, as illustrated in Figure E3.7.

Typically, remote users connect to a corporation intranet by connecting over a modem which is connected to the corporation intranet, and using a standard Internet connection protocol, such as Point-to-Point Protocol (PPP). This can be expensive in both phone calls or in providing enough modems for all connected users. These costs can be drastically reduced if the user connects to an ISP, as they provide local rate charges. For this a new protocol, called Point-to-Point Tunnelling Protocol (PPTP) has been developed to allow remote users connections to intranets from a remote connection (such as from a modem or ISDN). It operates as follows:

- The data sent to the ISP, using PPTP, is encrypted before it is sent into the Internet.
- The ISP sends the encrypted data (wrapped in an IP packet) to the intranet.
- Data is passed through the firewall, which has the software and hardware to process PPTP packets.
- Next, the user logs in using Password Authentication Protocol (PAP) or Challenge Handshake Authentication (CHAP).
- Finally, the intranet server reads the IP packet and decrypts the data.

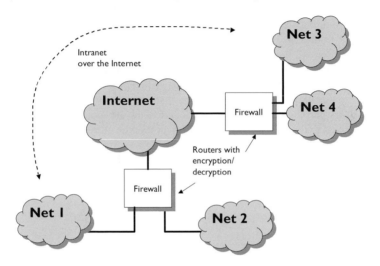

Figure E3.7   Encryption tunnels

E3.6 Filtering routers

Filtering routers run software which allows many different parameters of the incoming and outgoing packets to be examined, as illustrated in Figure E3.8, such as:

- **Source IP address.** The router will have a table of acceptable source IP addresses. This will limit the access to the external network as only authorized users will be granted IP addresses. This unfortunately is prone to IP spoofing, where a local user can steal an authorized IP address. Typically, it is done by determining the IP address of a computer and waiting until there is no-one using that computer, then using the unused IP address. Several users have been accused of accessing unauthorized material because other users have used their IP address. A login system which monitors IP addresses and the files that they are accessing over the Internet cannot be used as evidence against the user, as it is easy to steal IP addresses.
- **Destination IP address.** The router will have a table of acceptable outgoing destination IP addresses, addresses which are not in the table are blocked. Typically, this will be used to limit the range of destination addresses to the connected organizational intra-

net, or to block certain addresses (such as pornography sites).

- **Protocol.** The router holds a table of acceptable protocols, such as TCP and/or UDP.
- **Source port.** The router will have a table of acceptable TCP ports. For example, electronic mail (SMTP) on port 25 could be acceptable, but remote login on port 543 will be blocked.
- **Destination port.** The router will have a table of acceptable TCP ports. For example, FTP on port 21 could be acceptable, but TELNET connections on port 23 will be blocked.
- **Rules.** Other rules can be added to the system which define a mixture of the above. For example, a range of IP addresses can be allowed to transfer on a certain port, but another range can be blocked for this transfer.

Filter routers are either tightly bound when they are installed and then relaxed, or are relaxed and then bound. The type depends on the type of organization. For example, a financial institution will have a very strict router which will allow very little traffic, apart from the authorized traffic. The router can be opened up when the systems have been proved to be secure (they can also be closed quickly when problems occur).

An open organization, such as an education institution will typically have an open system, where users are allowed to access any location on any port, and external users are allowed any access to the internal network. This can then be closed slowly when internal or external users breach the security or access unauthorized information. For example, if a student is accessing a pornographic site consistently then the IP address for that site could be blocked (this method is basically closing the door after the horse has bolted).

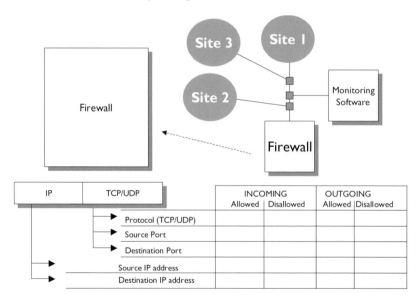

Figure E3.8 Filtering router

To most users the filtering router is an excellent method of limited traffic access, but to the determined hacker it can be easily breached, as the hacker can fake both IP addresses and also port addresses. It is extremely easy for a hacker to write their own TCP/IP driver software to address whichever IP address, and port numbers that they want.

E3.7 Security

Security involves protecting the system hardware and software from both internal attack and from external attack (hackers). An internal attack normally involves uneducated users causing damage, such as deleting important files, crashing systems. Another attack can come from internal fraud, where employees may intentionally attack a system for their own gain, or through some dislike for something within the organization. There are many cases of users who have grudges against other users, causing damage to systems, by misconfiguring systems. This effect can be minimized if the system manager properly protects the system. Typical actions are to limit the files that certain users can access and also the actions they can perform on the system.

Most system managers have seen the following:

- Users sending a file of the wrong format to the system printer (such as sending a binary file). Another typical one is where there is a problem on a networked printer (such as lack of paper), but the user keeps re-sending the same print job.
- Users deleting the contents of sub-directories, or moving files from one place to another (typically, these days, with the dragging of a mouse cursor). Regular backups can reduce this problem.
- Users deleting important system files (in a PC, these are normally AUTOEXEC.BAT and CONFIG.SYS). This can be overcome by the system administrator protecting important system files, such as making them read-only or hidden.
- Users telling other people their user passwords or not changing a password from the initial default one. This can be overcome by the system administrator forcing the user to change their password at given time periods.

Security takes many forms, such as:

- **Data protection.** This is typically where sensitive or commercially important information is kept. It might include information databases, design files or source code files. One method of reducing this risk is to encrypt important files with a password, and another is to encrypt data with a secret electronic key (files are encrypted with a commonly known public key, and decrypted with a secret key, which is only known by user who has the rights to access the files).
- **Software protection.** This involves protecting all the software packages from damage or from being misconfigured. A misconfigured software package can cause as much damage as a physical attack on a system, because it can take a long time to find the problem.
- **Physical system protection.** This involves protecting systems from intruders who might physically attack the systems. Normally, important systems are locked in rooms and then within locked rack-mounted cabinets.
- **Transmission protection.** This involves a hacker tampering with a transmission connection. It might involve tapping into a network connection or total disconnection. Tapping can be avoided by many methods, including using optical fibres which are almost impossible to tap into (as it would typically involve sawing through a cable with hundreds of fibre cables, which would each have to be connected back as they were

connected initially). Underground cables can avoid total disconnection, or its damage can be reduced by having redundant paths (such as different connections to the Internet).

- **Using an audit log file.** Many secure operating systems, such as Windows NT/2000, have an audit file, which is a text file that the system maintains and updates daily. This is a text file that can record all of the actions of a specific user, and is regularly updated. It can include the dates and times that a user logs into the system, the files that were accessed, the programs that were run, the networked resources that were used, and so on. By examining this file the system administrator can detect malicious attacks on the system, whether it is by internal or external users.

E3.2.3 Hacking methods

The best form of protection is to disallow hackers into the network in the first place. Organizational networks are hacked for a number of reasons and in a number of ways. The most common methods are:

- **IP spoofing attacks.** This is where the hacker steals an authorized IP address, as illustrated in Figure E3.9. Typically, it is done by determining the IP address of a computer and waiting until there is no-one using that computer, then using the unused IP address. Several users have been accused of accessing unauthorized material because other users have used their IP address. A login system which monitors IP addresses and the files that they are accessing over the Internet cannot be used as evidence against the user, as it is easy to steal IP addresses.
- **Packet-sniffing.** This is where the hacker listens to TCP/IP packets which come out of the network and steals the information in them. Typical information includes user logins, e-mail messages, credit card number, and so on. This method is typically used to steal an IP address, before an IP spoofing attack. Figure E3.10 shows an example where a hacker listens to a conversation between a server and a client. Most TELNET and FTP programs actually transmit the user name and password as text values; these can be easily viewed by a hacker, as illustrated in Figure E3.11.
- **Passwords attacks.** This is a common weak-point in any system, and hackers will generally either find a user with an easy password (especially users which have the same password as their login name) or will use a special program which cycles through a range of passwords. This type of attack is normally easy to detect. The worst nightmare of this type of attack is when a hacker determines the system administrator password (or a user who has system privileges). This allows the hacker to change system set-ups, delete files, and even change user passwords.

- **Sequence number prediction attacks.** Initially, in a TCP/IP connection, the two computers exchange a start-up packet which contains sequence numbers (Section D2.8). These sequence numbers are based on the computer's system clock and then run in a predictable manner, which can be determined by the hacker.
- **Session hi-jacking attacks.** In this method, the hacker taps into a connection between two computers, typically between a client and a server. The hacker then simulates the connection by using its IP address.

- **Shared library attacks.** Many systems have an area of shared library files. These are called by applications when they are required (for input/output, networking, graphics, and so on). A hacker may replace standard libraries for ones that have been tampered with, which allows the hacker to access system files and to change file privileges. Figure E3.12 illustrates how a hacker might tamper with dynamic libraries (which are called as a program runs), or with static libraries (which are used when compiling a program). This would allow the hacker to possibly do damage to the local computer, send all communications to a remote computer, or even view everything that is viewed on the user screen. The hacker could also introduce viruses and cause unpredictable damage to the computer (such as remotely rebooting it, or crashing it at given times).
- **Technological vulnerability attack.** This normally involves attacking some part of the system (typically the operating system) which allows a hacker to access the system. A typical one is for the user to gain access to a system and then run a program which re-boots the system or slows it down by running a processor intensive program. This can be overcome in operating systems such as Microsoft Windows and UNIX by granting re-boot rights only to the system administrator.
- **Trust-access attacks.** This allows a hacker to add their system to the list of systems which are allowed to log into the system without a user password. In UNIX this file is the *.rhosts* (trusted hosts) which is contained in the user's home directory. A major problem is when the trusted hosts file is contained in the root directory, as this allows a user to log in as the system administrator.

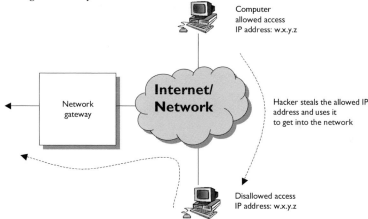

Figure E3.9   IP spoofing

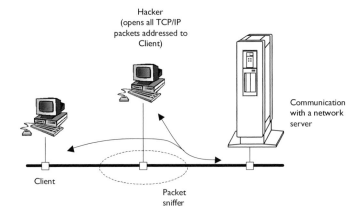

Figure E3.10   Packet sniffing

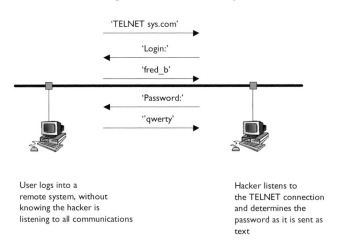

Figure E3.11   Packet sniffing on a TELNET connection

- **Social engineering attacks.** This type of attack is aimed at users who have little under-standing of their computer system. A typical attack is where the hacker sends an e-mail message to a user, asking for their password. Many unknowing users are tricked by this attack. A few examples are illustrated in Figure E3.13. From the initial user login, the hacker can then access the system and further invade the system. In one research study it was found that when telephoned by an unknown person and asked what their pass-word was, 90% of users immediately gave it, without asking any questions.

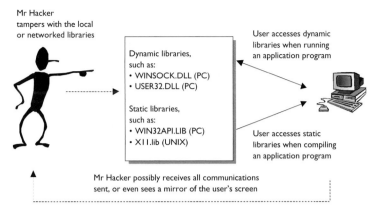

Figure E3.12 Shared library attack

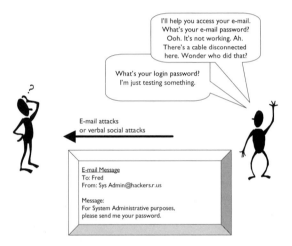

Figure E3.13 Social engineering attack

E3.2.4 Security policies

A well-protected system depends mainly on the system manager. It is up to the manager to define security policies which define how users can operate the system. A good set of policies would be:

- **Restrictions on users who can use a given account.** The system administrator needs to define the users who can login on a certain account.
- **Password requirements and prohibitions.** This defines the parameters of the password, such as minimum password size, time between password changes, and so on.
- **Internet access/restrictions.** This limits whether or not a user is allowed access to the Internet.
- **User account deletion.** The system administrator automatically deletes user accounts which are either not in use or users have been moved to another system.

- **Application program rules.** This defines the programs which a user is allowed to run (typically games can be barred for some users).
- **Monitoring consent.** Users should be informed about how the system monitors their activities. It is important, for example, to tell users that their Internet accesses are being monitored. This gives users no excuse when they are found to be accessing restricted sites.

E3.2.5 Passwords

Passwords are normally an important part of any secure network. They can be easily hacked with the use of a program which continually tries different passwords within a given range (normally called directory-based attacks). These can be easily overcome by only allowing a user three bad logins before the system locks the user out for a defined time. Novell Net-Ware and Windows NT/2000 both use this method, but UNIX does not. The system manager, though, can determine if an attack has occurred with the BADLOG file. This file stores a list of all the bad logins for a user and the location of the user.

Passwords are a basic system for providing security on a network, and they are only as secure as the user makes them. Good rules for passwords are:

- Use slightly unusual names, such as *vinegarwine, dancertop* or *helpcuddle*. Do not use names of a wife, husband, child or pet. Many users, especially ones who know the user, can easily guess the user's password.
- Use numbers after the name, such as *vinedrink55* and *applefox32*. This makes the password difficult to crack as users are normally only allowed a few chances to login correctly before they are logged out (and a bad login event written to a bad login file).
- Have several passwords which are changed at regular intervals. This is especially important for system managers. Every so often, these passwords should be changed to new ones.
- Make the password at least six characters long. This stops 'hackers' from watching the movement of the user's fingers when they login, or from running a program which tries every permutation of characters. Every character added multiplies the number of combinations by a great factor (for example, if just the characters from 'a' to 'z' and '0' to '9' are taken then every character added increases the number of combinations by a factor of 36).
- Change some letters for numbers, or special characters. Typically, 'o' becomes a 0 (zero), 'i' becomes 1 (one), 's' becomes 5 (five), spaces become '$', 'b' becomes '6', and so on. So a password of 'silly password' might become '5illy$pa55w0rd' (the user makes a rule for 's' and 'o'). The user must obviously remember the rule that has been used for changing the letters to other characters. This method overcomes the technique of hackers and hacker programs, where combinations of words from a dictionary are hashed to try and make the hashed password.

The two main protocols used are:

- **Password Authentication Protocol** (PAP). This provides for a list of encrypted passwords.
- **Challenge Handshake Authentication Protocol** (CHAP). This is a challenge-response system which requires a list of unencrypted passwords. When a user logs into the sys-

tem a random key is generated and sent to the user for encrypting the password. The user then uses this key to encrypt the password, and the encrypted password is sent back to the system. If it matches its copy of the encrypted password then it lets the user login. The CHAP system then continues to challenge the user for encrypted data. If the user gets these wrong then the system disconnects the login.

E3.2.6 Hardware security

Passwords are a simple method of securing a system. A better method is to use a hardware-restricted system which either bars users from a specific area or even restricts users from login into a system. Typical methods are:

- **Smart cards**. With this method a user can only gain access to the system after they have inserted their personal smart card into the computer and then entered their PIN code.
- **Biometrics**. This is a better method than a smart card where a physical feature of the user is scanned. The scanned parameter requires to be unchanging, such as finger-prints or retina images.

E3.2.7 Hacker problems

Once a hacker has entered into a system, there are many methods which can be used to further penetrate into the system, such as:

- **Modifying search paths.** All systems set up a search path which the system looks into to find the required executable. For example, in a UNIX system, a typical search path is /bin, /usr/bin, and so on. A hacker can change the search paths for a user and then replace standard programs with ones that have been modified. For example, the hacker could replace the e-mail program for one that sends e-mails directly to the hacker or any directory listings could be sent to the hacker's screen.
- **Modifying shared libraries.** As discussed previously.
- **Running processor intensive tasks** which slows the system down; this task will be run in the background and will generally not be seen by the user. The hacker can then further attack the system by adding the processor intensive task to the system start-up file (such as the rc file on a UNIX system).
- **Running network intensive tasks** which will slow the network down, and typically slow down all the connected computers. As with the processor intensive task, the networking intensive task can be added to the system start-up file.
- **Infecting the system with a virus or worm.**

Most PCs now have virus scanners which test the memory and files for viruses. This makes viruses easy to detect. A more sinister virus is spread over the Internet, such as the Internet worm which was released in November 1988.

E3.2.8 Internet problems

The Internet can cause a great deal of problems as it can allow open access for external users. Typical attacks include:

- **E-mail bombing**. This is where an external user(s) continually send an identical e-mail message to a particular address. E-mail spamming is a variant of this, where the same message is sent to many users, at a single time. This is made worse if the recipient actually responds back to the e-mail spamming message using all the recipients on the address list, as this will also flood the network with unwanted e-mail messages. E-mail bombing without the permission of the user is illegal in many countries and there should always be a message on the e-mail message which identifies the method that can be used to delete a user's name from an e-mail bombing database.

- **E-mail spoofing**. This is where external users setup incorrect e-mail addresses, and then send e-mails to other users. This could either be to cloak the identity of the person, or to try and pretend to be another known person. On a personal level, when pretending to be another person, this can be particularly disturbing, as many users think that the e-mail address in the From: field is always from that person. The cloaking is typically used with e-mail bombing, where a false user name is used to send e-mail bombs.
- **Denial of service** (DOS) attacks. These are severe attaches where external users continually try and access a server, typically a WWW server, an email server or network routers, and try and slow it down to the point that no-one else can get access to it. Unlike many other attacks there is very little that can be done about it, apart from tracing the source, and trying to block the transmissions.

E3.8 Viruses

Before the advent of LANs and the Internet, the most common mechanism for spreading a virus was through floppy disks and CD-ROM disks. Anti-virus programs can easily keep up to date with the latest viruses, and modify their databases. This is a relatively slow method of spreading a virus and will take many months, if not years, to spread a virus over a large geographical area. Figure E3.14 illustrates the spread of viruses.

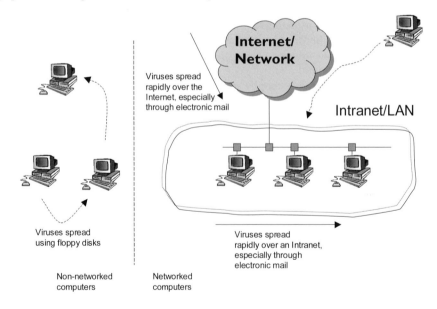

Figure E3.14   Spread of viruses

LANs and the Internet have changed all this. A virus can now be transmitted over a LAN in a fraction of a second, and around the world in less than a second. Thus a virus can be created and transmitted around the world before an anti-virus program can even detect that it is available.

A worm is a program which runs on a computer and creates two threads. A thread in a program is a unit of code that can get a time slice from the operating system to run concurrently with other code units. Each process consists of one or more execution threads that identify the code path flow as it is run on the operating system. This enhances the running of an application by improving throughput and responsiveness. With a worm, the first thread searches for a network connection and when it finds a connection it copies itself, over the network, to that computer. Next, the worm makes a copy of itself, and runs it on the system. Thus, a single copy will become two, then four, eight, and so on. This continues until the system, and the other connected systems, will be shutdown. The only way to stop the worm is to shutdown all the affected computers at the same time and then restart them. Figure E3.15 illustrates a worm virus.

E3.2.9 Boot sector viruses

The boot sector resides on the first sector of a partition on a hard disk, or the first sector on a floppy disk. On starting, the PC reads from the active partition on the hard disk (identified by C:) or tries to read from the boot sector of the floppy disk. Boot sector viruses replace the boot sector with new code and moves, or deletes the original code.

Non-bootable floppy disks have executable code in their boot sector, which displays the message 'Not bootable disk' when the computer is booted from it. Thus any floppy disk, whether it is bootable or non-bootable, can contain a virus, and can thus infect the PC.

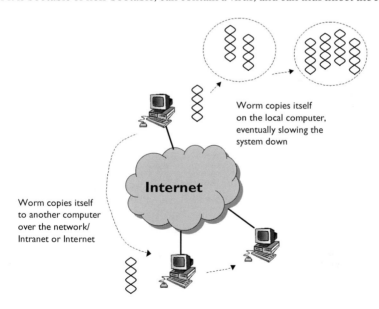

Worm copies itself on the local computer, eventually slowing the system down

Worm copies itself to another computer over the network/ Intranet or Internet

Internet

Figure E3.15 Worm viruses

E3.2.10 Partition viruses

When starting PCs, the system automatically reads the partition sector and executes the code it finds there. The partition sector (or Master Boot Record) is the first sector on a hard disk and it contains system start-up information, such as:

- Number of sectors in each partition.
- The start of the DOS partition starts.
- Small programs.

Viruses, which attach themselves to the partition sector, modify the code associated with the partition section. The system must be booted from a clean boot virus to eradicate this type of virus. Partition viruses only attack hard disks, as floppy disks do not have partition sectors. A partition is created with the FDISK program. Hard disks cannot be accessed unless they have a valid partition.

E3.2.11 File viruses

File viruses append or insert themselves into/onto executable files, such as .COM and .EXE programs. An indirect-action file virus installs itself into memory when the infected file is run, and infects other files when they are subsequently accessed.

E3.2.12 Overwriting viruses

Overwriting viruses overwrite all, or part, of the original program. They are easy to detect as missing files are easily detected.

E3.2.13 Macro viruses

One of the most common viruses is the macro virus, which attacks macro or scripting facilities which are available in word processors (such as Microsoft Word), spreadsheets (such as Microsoft Excel), and remote transfer programs. An example virus is the WM/CAP virus which modifies macros within Microsoft Word Version 6.0. When a macro is executed it can cause considerable damage, such as deleting files, corrupting files, and so on.

The greatest increase in macro viruses is the number of viruses which use Microsoft Visual Basic for Applications (VBA) as this integrates with Microsoft Office (although recent releases have guarded against macro viruses). A macro virus in Word 6.0 is spread by:

- The file is either transmitted over e-mail, over a LAN or from floppy disk.
- The infected file is opened and the `normal.dot` main template file is modified so that it contains the modified macros. Any files that are opened or created will now have the modified macros. The WM/CAP macro virus does not do much damage and simply overwrites existing macros.
- VBA is made to be event-driven, so operations, such as File Open or File Close, can have an attached macro. This makes it easy for virus programmers to write new macros.

Newer viruses are typically spread through e-mail clients, where the virus is run as a script, or is run as an e-mail attachment, which then infects other computers by sending itself to addresses in the user's e-mail address book.

Figure E3.16 shows an example of a macro created by Visual Basic programming. The developed macro (`Macro1()`) simply loads a file called AUTHOR.doc, selects all the text, converts the text to bold, and then saves the file as AUTHOR.rtf. It can be seen that this macro is associated with `normal.dot`.

These types of viruses typically exploit weaknesses in the security on the system. Fortunately, in most cases, these gaps can be plugged with software patches when they are found. Newer viruses, such as the Code Red worm have caused great panic, but it is typically their modified form that causes the most damage, as the original virus can be patched with new software, but a new version can spread quickly as virus programmers modify the virus code.

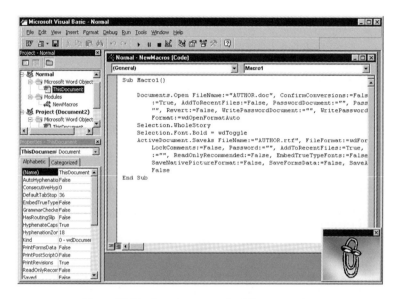

Figure E3.16 Sample macro using VB programming

E3.9   AAA

Major elements of security are **authentication**, **authorization**, and **accounting** (AAA). These allow for enhanced security for who is allowed to log into a network, what they are allowed to do, and logs the things that they have done. Typically this security is applied at the edge of a network, using a network access server (NAS). These servers must use a secure protocol in order for a host to communicate with a specialized security server. This server contain a database of the users and their associated passwords, and any other configurations. On routers there are three main security protocols:

- **TACACS+** - This system uses a centralized validation of users. It maintains a database which is a TACACS+ daemon running on a host computer, and provides for individual configuration of authentication, authorization, and accounting.
- **RADIUS** – This is a distributed client/server system. It is an open-standard and is specified in RFCs 2865, 2866, and 2868. With RADIUS, a client typically runs on a router, which sends authentication requests to a centralized RAUDIS server.
- **Kerberos** – This uses a secret-key encryption authentication method, but does not al-

low for authorization or accounting. It was designed to provide authentication, where a third party authenticates each of the parties to the other. For this, a trusted Kerberos server provides authentication tickets to users, which have a limited life.

On a router, AAA is enabled with:

```
Router(config)#aaa new-model
```

For a **TACACS+**, the IP address of the TACACS+ server must be specified with:

```
Router(config)#tacacs-server host ip-network-address
```

Next, the encryption key is specified with:

```
Router(config)#tacacs-server key encryption_word
```

For example, if the server is defined at 192.168.20.10, and using the shared key of mypass:

```
Router(config)#tacacs-server host 192.168.20.10
Router(config)#tacacs-server key mypass
```

For RADIUS, the IP address of the RADIUS server must be specified with:

```
Router(config)#radius-server host ip-address
```

Next, the encryption key is specified with:

```
Router(config)#radius-server key word
```

For example, if the server is defined at 192.168.20.10, and using the shared key of mypass:

```
Router(config)#radius-server host 192.168.20.10
Router(config)#radius-server key mypass
```

E4   Router programming and ACLs

E4.1   Router programming

Routers must be carefully programmed so that they operate correctly, and securely. This chapter defines some of the main tasks. These include:

- **Set-up a hostname**. This uses the `hostname` command.
- **Set-up IP addresses and subnet masks for each of the ports**. This uses the `ip address` command.
- **Set-up an executive password**. This uses the `enable secret` command.
- **Set-up login (console) and telnet (vty) passwords**. This uses the `password` and `login` commands.
- **Set-up a routing protocol**. This uses the `network` command.
- **Set-up a hosts name table**. This uses the `ip host` command.
- **Show the status of the ports, and the running configuration**. The command used for these are `show protocols` and `show running-config`.

E4.1.1 Getting in privileged mode
The router has two main modes:

- **User mode**. This is the initial mode that the user goes into when they log onto the router. In this mode it is not possible to configure the router, and it is only possible to perform simple commands such as telnet and ping.
- **Executive mode**. In this mode the full range of commands can be used, and the router can be programmed.

The command which is used to go from user mode into executive mode is `enable`. If a password is set for the executive mode, the user must enter this before they can enter into the executive mode. The prompt should change from a '>' to a '#'. The following gives an example:

```
Router> enable
Router#
```

If at any time you cannot remember the syntax of a command type-in the command and then press the '?' key.

E4.1.2 Setting hostname
The hostname is set using the `hostname` command. This name is reflected in the prompt of the router, and makes it easier to identify the current router. For example to set the host of LAB_A to LAB_A:

```
Router# config t
Enter configuration commands, one per line. End with END.
Router (config)# hostname LAB_A
LAB_A (config)#
```

E4.1.3 Setting the secret password
The secret password is used to enter into the executive mode. In the following case the password is defined as class.

```
LAB_A (config)# enable secret class
LAB_A (config)# exit
LAB_A# exit
LAB_A> enable
Password: ccc
Password: class
LAB_A#
```

E4.1.4 Setting the IP addresses on the ports
One of the most important things to set on the router is the IP address of each of the ports. These ports will be used as gateways out of the network segment to which they connect to. The interface command (or int for short) programs each of the interfaces. In the following example, the three ports on the router are programmed with the required IP addresses, and subnet masks. The ports will not automatically come on-line, and will start in a shutdown mode. Thus the no shutdown command is used to start them up.

```
LAB_A# config t
LAB_A (config)# int e0
LAB_A (config-if)# ip address 192.5.5.1 255.255.255.0
LAB_A (config-if)# no shutdown
LAB_A (config-if)# exit
LAB_A (config)# int e1
LAB_A (config-if)# ip address 205.7.5.1 255.255.255.0
LAB_A (config-if)# no shutdown
LAB_A (config-if)# exit
LAB_A (config)# int s0
LAB_A (config-if)# ip address 201.100.11.1 255.255.255.0
LAB_A (config-if)# clock rate 56000
LAB_A (config-if)# no shutdown
LAB_A (config-if)# exit
```

E4.1.5 Setting a routing protocol
The router will not be able to connect to other routers unless it runs a routing protocol which is the same as the other routers. This allows the routers to determine the best path to a remote device. In this case the RIP protocol is set-up with the router rip command, and then each of the networks in which the router will broadcast its routing table are defined (using the network command):

```
LAB_A (config)# router rip
LAB_A (config-router)# network 192.5.5.0
LAB_A (config-router)# network 205.7.5.0
LAB_A (config-router)# network 201.100.11.0
LAB_A (config-router)# exit
LAB_A (config)#
```

E4.1.6 Setting the line console password
Passwords are important in providing a degree of security to the router. There are three main passwords to set: the executive password, the console password, and the remote login (vty) password. The vty password defines the telnet password, and the console password defines the initial login password.

```
LAB_A (config)# Line con 0
LAB_A (config-line)# password cisco
```

```
LAB_A (config-line)# login
LAB_A (config-line)# exit
LAB_A (config)# exit
LAB_A # exit
User Access Verification
Password: cisco
LAB_A> enable
Password: class
LAB_A # config t
LAB_A (config)#
```

The telnet password is set with:

```
LAB_A (config)# Line vty 0
LAB_A (config-line)# password cisco
LAB_A (config-line)# login
LAB_A (config-line)# exit
LAB_A (config)# exit
```

E4.1.7 Setting the hostnames table

It is often difficult to remember the IP address of each of the ports, thus a router can be setup with its own hosts table, as shown next:

```
LAB_A (config)# ip host LAB_A 192.5.5.1 205.7.5.1
201.100.11.1
LAB_A (config)# ip host LAB_B 201.100.11.2 219.17.100.1
199.6.13.1
LAB_A (config)# ip host LAB_C 223.8.151.1 204.204.7.1
199.6.13.1
LAB_A (config)# ip host LAB_D 210.93.105.1 204.204.7.2
LAB_A (config)# ip host LAB_E 210.93.105.2
LAB_A (config)# exit
LAB # show running-config
```

E4.1.8 Determining if the ports are operating

To see if the ports are up, and if they are connected to the other routers, the show protocols command is used. For example:

```
LAB_A# show protocols
E0 is up, line protocol is up
Internet address is 192.5.5.1
E1 is up, line protocol is up
Internet address is 205.7.5.1
S0 is up, line protocol is up
Internet address is 201.100.11.1
```

The hosts table can also be viewed with show hosts.

E4.2   ACLs

A major concern in networking and the Internet is security. Firewalls are one of the most widely used methods of filtering network traffic. A firewall is basically a router running special filtering software which tests parts of the IP packet and the TCP segment (see Figure E4.1). Typically, the firewall will check:

• **Source IP address.** The address that the data packet was sent from.

- **Destination IP address**. The address that the data packet is destined for.
- **Source TCP port**. The port that the data segment originated from. Typical ports which could be blocked are FTP (port 21), TELNET (port 23), and WWW (port 80).
- **Destination TCP port**. The port that the data segment is destined for.
- **Protocol type**. This filters for UDP or TCP traffic.

The firewall can also filter for IPX/SPX traffic on a Novell NetWare network and AppleTalk, although these are more secure types of protocols, as they do not travel over the Internet, unless they are wrapped in an IP packet.

Firewalls can be quickly programmed so that they can react quickly to changing events. For example a denial-of-service attack can be caused by data packets continually being sent to a WWW server. In this case the firewall can be setup to quickly block the offending data packet, from as near to the source as possible. In many networks now, the firewall bars many types of traffic, and only lets through a limited range of data. E-mail (on ports 25 for SMTP or 110 for POP-3) is one type of traffic which is typically allowed through a firewall. Unfortunately email can carry viruses, which can infect the whole network.

The Cisco Internetwork Operating System (IOS) allows for each data packet to be filtered, with a set of deny or permit conditions. These are called Access Control Lists (ACLs). Each router can filter on each of its ports, for incoming or outgoing traffic. The incoming traffic, which is traffic which is entering a port, is defined as IN, and the outgoing traffic, the traffic leaving a port, is defined as OUT.

The firewall checks the ACL statements in a sequential order. If a condition match is true, the packet is either permitted or denied, and it does not check the rest of the ACL statements. If none of the ACL statements are matched, the data packet is dropped (known as an implicit *deny any*).

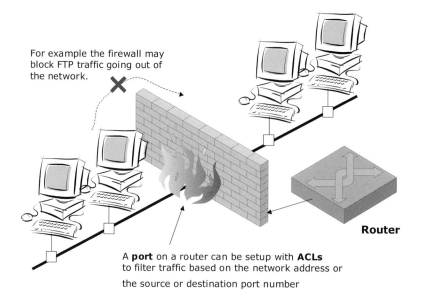

For example the firewall may block FTP traffic going out of the network.

Router

A **port** on a router can be setup with **ACLs** to filter traffic based on the network address or the source or destination port number

Figure E4.1: Router program

E4.2.1 Standard ACLs

Standard ACLs filter for a source IP address, and are grouped with an access-list number (as this allows one or more condition to be grouped into a single condition, which can then be applied to one or more ports). The format of the command is:

```
Router# access-list access-list-value {permit | deny} source source-mask
```

where the `source` is the source address, and `source-mask` defines the bits which are checked. For example is we had a network address of 156.1.1.0 with a subnet mask of 255.255.255.0. We could bar all the traffic from the host 156.1.1.10 from gaining access to the external network with:

```
Router# access-list 1 deny 156.1.1.10 0.0.0.0
```

where the `0.0.0.0` part defines that all the parts of the address are checked. The source-mask is know as the wild-card mask, where a 0 identifies that the corresponding bit in the address field should be check, and a 1 defines that it should be ignored. Thus if we wanted to bar all the hosts on the 156.1.1.0 subnet then we could use:

```
Router# access-list 1 deny 156.1.1.0 0.0.0.255
```

Finally we must allow all other traffic with:

```
Router# access-list 1 deny 156.1.1.0 0.0.0.255
Router# access-list 1 permit ip any any
```

Once the access-list is created it can then be applied to a number of ports with the command, such as:

```
Router (config)# interface Ethernet0
Router (config-if)# ip address 156.1.1.130 255.255.255.0
Router (config-if)# ip access-group 1 in
```

which will bar all the access from the 156.1.1.0 subnet from the Ethernet0 port on incoming traffic.

E4.2.2 Extended ACLs

Extended ACLs are a natural extension to ACLs, and allow source **and** destination address to be specified. Standard ACLs uses the access-list-values from 0 to 99, whereas extended ACLs use the values above 100. The format of the command is:

```
Router# access-list access-list-value {permit | deny} {test-conditions}
```

For example:

```
Router(config)#access-list 100 deny ip host 156.1.1.134 156.70.1.1 0.0.0.0
Router(config)#access-list 100 permit ip any any
```

This creates an access-list group with a value of 100. The first line has the syntax which defines that the source host of `156.1.1.134` is not allowed to access the destination of `156.70.1.1`, and the last part (`0.0.0.0`) defines that the firewall should match all of the bits in the destination address. Thus, in this case, the host with an IP address of `156.1.1.134` is not allowed to access the remote computer of `156.70.1.1`. It can access any other computer thought, as the second line allows all other accesses.

We can expand this to be able to check a whole range of bits in the address. This is achieved by defining a wild-card mask. With this we use 0's in the positions of the address that we want to match, and 1's in the parts which are not checked. Thus if we wanted to bar all the hosts on the `156.1.1.0` subnet from accessing the `156.70.1.0` subnet we would use the following:

```
Router(config)#access-list 100 deny ip 156.1.1.0 0.0.0.255 156.70.1.0 0.0.0.255
Router(config)#access-list 100 permit ip any any
```

Thus an address from `156.1.1.1` to `156.1.1.254` will not be able to access any address from `156.70.1.0` network.

If we have a Class B address with a subnet in the third field (such as 156.1.1.0) and we define that we shall allow all **odd** IP addresses to pass though to a given destination (such as `156.70.1.1`), and bar all **even** IP addresses we could implement the following:

```
Router(config)#access-list 100 deny ip 156.1.1.0 0.0.0.254 host 156.70.1.1
Router(config)#access-list 100 permit ip any any
```

This will allow any host with an odd number (such as 1, 3, 5, and so on), to access the `156.70.1.1` host, but as we check the least significant bit of the address (with the wildcard mask of 0000 0000 0000 0000 0000 0000 1111 1110) and if it is a 0 then the condition passes, and we will deny traffic from the even numbered hosts to `156.70.1.1`.

We can also bar access to complete parts of destination addresses. For example, if we wanted to bar all **odd** addresses from access the `156.70.1.0` subnet:

```
Router(config)#access-list 100 deny ip 156.1.1.1 0.0.0.254 156.70.1.0 0.0.0.255
Router(config)#access-list 100 permit ip any any
```

Once the access-list is created it can then be applied to a number of ports with the command, such as:

```
Router (config)# interface Ethernet0
Router (config-if)# ip address 156.1.1.130 255.255.255.192
Router (config-if)# ip access-group 100 in
```

which allows the access-list of a value of 100 to port E0 on incoming traffic (that is, traffic which is coming into this router port).

The firewall can also filter on TCP/UDP ports, and is defined with the TCP or UDP It has a similar syntax.

```
Router(config)#access-list access-list-value { permit | deny } {tcp | udp |
igrp} source source-mask destination destination-mask {eq | neq | lt | gt}
port
```

For example:

```
access-list 101 deny tcp 156.1.1.0 0.0.0.254 eq telnet host 156.70.1.1 eq telnet
access-list 101 permit ip any any
```

Denies telnet traffic from even addresses from the `156.1.1.0` subnet to the `156.70.1.1`
host, with is also destined for the telnet port (port 23).

E4.2.3 ACL examples

Figure E4.2 shows an example router running-configuration. It can be seen that the
Ethernet0 port has the access-list for 104 applied to its input port (`ip access-group 104
in`). This denies all the even IP address on the 182.2.1.0 subnet (`180.2.1.0` with a wild card of
`0.0.0.254`) access to the telnet port on 180.70.1.1 (`host 180.70.1.1 eq telnet`). It is thus
barring all the nodes on its own subnet from accessing the `180.70.1.1` server, as traffic
from the nodes enters this port (the `in` direction).

The Serial0 port has the 102 access-list applied to it, on the input to the port. This denies
WWW access for IP addresses from (`deny tcp 180.2.1.128 0.0.0.63 180.70.1.0
0.0.0.255 eq www`):

180.2.1.10 xxx xxxb

as the wildcard mask is:

0.0.0. 00 11 1111b

and the address to check against is:

182.2.1.128

which is:

182.2.1.1000 0000b

Thus if we compare the two:

Address	10110110b	0000 0010b	0000 0001b	1000 0000b
Wild-card	0000 0000b	0000 0000b	0000 0000b	0011 1111b
Resulting range	182	2	1	128 (1000 0000b) to 191 (10 11 1111b)

The range of barred address will thus be from 182.2.1.128 to 182.2.1.191. These will be
barred WWW access on the 180.70.1.0 subnet (from 180.70.1.0 to 180.70.1.255 – using
`180.70.1.0 0.0.0.255 eq www`)

Line no.	Router program
1	`version 12.0`
2	`service timestamps debug uptime`
3	`service timestamps log uptime`
4	`no service password-encryption`
5	`!`

```
 6    hostname my-router
 7    !
 8    enable secret 5 $1$op7P$LCHOURx5hc4Mns741ORvl/
 9    !
10    ip subnet-zero
11    !
12    interface Ethernet0
13     ip address 180.2.1.130 255.255.255.192
14     ip access-group 104 in
15    !
16    interface Serial0
17     ip address 180.70.1.2 255.255.255.0
18     ip access-group 102 in
19     encapsulation ppp
20    !
21    router igrp 111
22     network 180.2.0.0
23     network 180.70.0.0
24    !
25    access-list 100 deny   ip host 180.2.1.134 host 180.70.1.1
26    access-list 100 permit ip any any
27
28    access-list 101 deny   tcp 180.2.1.128 0.0.0.63 host 180.70.1.1 eq www
29    access-list 101 permit ip any any
30
31    access-list 102 deny   tcp 180.2.1.128 0.0.0.63 180.70.1.0 0.0.0.255 eq www
32    access-list 102 permit ip any any
33
34    access-list 103 deny   ip 180.70.1.0 0.0.0.255 180.2.1.128 0.0.0.63
35    access-list 103 permit ip any any
36
37    access-list 104 deny   tcp 180.2.1.0 0.0.0.254 host 180.70.1.1 eq telnet
38    access-list 104 permit ip any any
39    !
40    line con 0
41     transport input none
42    line aux 0
43    line vty 0 4
```

Figure E4.2: Router program

Another example is given in Figure E4.3. It can see that in this case the Serial0 port is using PPP encapsulation, with CHAP. The subnet mask on this port is 255.255.255.252, and the address is 192.168.10.65, which means that we have a Class C address, with 6 bits used for the subnet (as 252 is 1111 1100b). The port is thus on the 192.168.10.64 subnet, and has been assigned the first address.

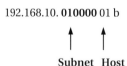

The ACL applied on this port is 101, which deny access for the addresses 160.10.3.0 to 160.10.3.244 which carry telnet traffic (`access-list 101 deny tcp any 160.10.3.0 0.0.0.255 eq telnet`).

Line no.	Router program
1	hostname myRouter

```
  2      !
  3      enable secret 5 AB$1$tA1$9437T32ab9DT33GmAch1
  4      !
  5      username mylogin password 7 11200B044813
  6      !
  7      interface Ethernet0
  8      ip address 160.10.2.1 255.255.255.0
  9      !
 10      interface Serial0
 11      ip address 192.168.10.65 255.255.255.252
 12      ip access-group 101 in
 13      encapsulation ppp
 14      no fair-queue
 15      ppp authentication chap
 16      !
 17      interface Serial1
 18      ip address 160.10.1.1 255.255.255.0
 19      !
 20      router igrp 10
 21      network 160.10.0.0
 22      !
 23      ip host Satellite_connection 160.10.1.2
 24      ip local-dns-server 160.10.2.10
 26      no ip classless
 27      !
 28      ip route 0.0.0.0 0.0.0.0 192.168.10.66
 29      !
 30      access-list 101 deny tcp any 160.10.3.0 0.0.0.255 eq telnet
 31      access-list 101 permit ip any any
 32      !
 33      line aux 0
 34      line vty 0 4
 35      password cisco
         login
         !
         end
```

E4.2.4 Placing ACLs

ACLs should be placed in the optimal place, so that they reduce the amount of unwanted traffic on the network/Internet. There are two main conditions:

- **Standard ACLs.** As a standard ACL cannot determine the destination address, it should be places as near as the **destination** that is barred, as possible. If it was placed at the source it would block other traffic, which is not barred.
- **Extended ACLs.** As an extended ACL allows us to check the source and the destination, the extended ACL should be placed as near as possible to the **source** of the traffic.

E4.2.5 Open and closed firewalls

Typically firewalls can defined as an open or closed firewall. An open firewall will generally allow most traffic through, but bar ceRouterAin addresses or ports. The typical style will be to deny traffic, and then permit everything else, such as;

```
access-list 100 deny    ip host 180.2.1.134 host 180.70.1.1
access-list 100 permit ip any any
```

Whereas a closed firewall will restrict traffic, and only allow ceRouterAin network addresses and/or ports, such as:

```
access-list 100 permit ip host 180.2.1.134 host 180.70.1.1
```

```
access-list 100 deny ip any any
```

E4.3 Network address translation

Network address translation (NAT) is defined in RFC1631, and swaps one network address with another. This allows private networks (RFC1918) to be created, which are then translated to public address when they access the Internet. A router can operate at the border of a domain and translate addresses from private to public, and vice-versa. For example, a node could be given a private address of 192.168.10.12. The NAT could then translate this to a public address of 168.10.34.31. The NAT table would then have the mapping of:

Private   **Public**
192.168.10.12   168.10.34.21

If a host from outside the domain sends a data packet back to the domain, the NAT will translate the public address back into the private address. These translations can be statically assigned, such as where it is setup with a permanent mapping, or dynamically, where the tables can change as the network requires. Figure E4.3 gives an example, where the destination address is 11.22.33.44. The address in this case is changed from 192.168.10.12 to 168.10.34.21, as the data packet goes out of the domain, and is changed back when it comes back into the domain.

NAT routers can use port address translation (PAT), which allows many internal address to be mapped to the same global address. This is also named as a *many-to-one* NAT, or address overloading. With PAT, the NAT router keeps a track of the connections, and the TCP/UDP ports that are being used. The NAT router then changes the global address back into a private address based on these.

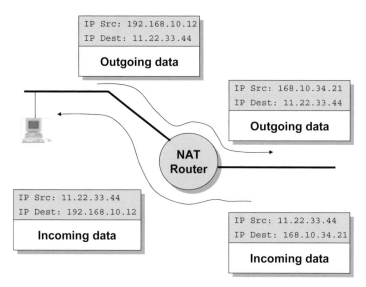

Figure E4.1 Example of NAT

E4.3.1 IP address unnumbered

An IP address unnumbered approach allows a port to borrow an IP address from an unused address on the network which it connects to. This is typically used when two routers connect to each other, and will typically be assigned a whole subnet for the single connection. Using IP address unnumbered allows the two interfaces to use there own IP addresses, such as shown in Figure E4.4.

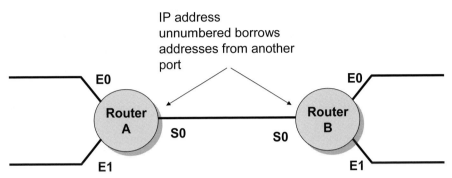

Figure E4.2   IP address unnumbered

The following shows how the unnumbered IP address is assigned:

```
RouterA # config t
RouterA (config) # int e0
RouterA (config-if) # ip address 168.10.34.1 255.255.255.0
RouterA (config-if) # int s0
RouterA (config-if) # ip unnumbered e0
```

And on the other router:

```
RouterB # config t
RouterB (config) # int e0
RouterB (config-if) # ip address 168.10.35.1 255.255.255.0
RouterB (config-if) # int s0
RouterB (config-if) # ip unnumbered e0
```

The serial ports will borrow from other ports on that the router connections. Typically IP address unnumbered are only really be applied to a point-to-point serial link. Unfortunately, with IP unnumbered it is not possible to ping the unnumbered ports. In addition, security cannot be applied to them.

E4.4   Programming dynamic NAT

Network address translation allows private IP address to be translated to public address. This can either be achieved statically, where the translation is fixed by a translation table, or can be dynamic, where the translation table is set-up as required by the network. Typically, a global address pool is used from which the public addresses are taken. The command for this has the format of:

```
RouterA# config t
```

```
RouterA(config)#ip nat pool name start-ip end-ip {netmask netmask | pre-
fix-length prefix-length}
```

where the submask length is defined by the optional netmask agument (such as
255.255.255.0), or by a length using prefix-length (or 24 for the 255.255.255.0 subnet
mask). After this, the types of packets which will be translated will be defined. This is
achieved with the access-list command, and has the form:

```
RouterA# config t
RouterA(config)#access-list access-list-number permit source      [source-
wildcard]
```

A dynamic translation uses the ip nat inside source list command, such as:

```
Router(config)#ip nat inside source list access-list-number pool name
```

where the access list number is defined. This is then applied to one of the interfaces using
the command (for s0):

```
RouterA# config t
RouterA (config) # int s0
RouterA(config-if)#ip nat inside
```

This will translate data packets which are coming into the port. To translate outgoing one,
the ip nat outside command is used.

For example, to define a pool of addresses from 180.10.11.1 to 180.10.11.254:

```
RouterA(config)#ip nat pool org_pool 180.10.11.1 180.10.11.254 netmask
255.255.255.0
```

which defines the global addresses as org_pool. This will be used to send translated data
packets out in the Internet. An access-list command is then used to match the translation
addresses:

```
RouterA(config)#access-list 2 permit 192.168.10.0 0.0.0.255
RouterA(config)#ip nat inside source list 2 pool org_pool
```

which applies the access-list number 2 to the IP NAT pool of org_pool. This can then be
applied to the interfaces with:

```
RouterA(config)#interface e0
RouterA(config-if)#ip nat inside
RouterA(config-if)#interface s0
RouterA(config0if)#ip nat outside
```

Thus if a host with an address of 192.168.10.10 sends a data packet out of the network, it will
have one of the addresses from the pool, such as 180.10.11.1. All the hosts outside the network will use the address from the pool to communicate with the node. By default, these
entries remain in the table for up to 24 hours (in order to allow communications to return).
The time-out can be changed using the command:

```
RouterA(config)#ip nat translation timeout seconds
```

This is an important factor, especially when there is a large number of hosts which can only use a limited pool of addresses. A lower time-out will allow an address to be released, so that another node can use it.

NAT also enhances security as it limits external users in their connection to local network, as the translations of addresses will not be permanent (unless a static translation is implemented). NAT thus hides the topology of the network.

Static translation uses a fixed lookup table to translate the addresses, where each address which requires an Internet address has a corresponding public IP address. If it is used on its own, it cannot thus preserve IP address. Thus, typically the two methods are used, where important nodes, such as servers, will have a static entry, as this guarantees them an address, while other nodes, which are less important, will be granted a dynamic translation. This also aids security as the important devices can run enhanced security and monitoring software, which might not be possible on lower-level devices, which are typically administered on a daily basis by non-IT personnel.

Static addresses are also useful in translating network topologies from one network address structure to another, or even when individual nodes are moved from one subnet to another.

An example of configuring for static addresses of a node of 192.168.10.10 to the address of 180.10.11.1:

```
RouterA(config)#ip nat inside source static 192.168.10.10 180.10.11.1
```

This can this be applied to the inside and outside interfaces with:

```
RouterA(config)#interface e0
RouterA(config-if)#ip nat inside
RouterA(config-if)#interface s0
RouterA(config-if)#ip nat outside
```

NAT allows organisations to quickly remap their addresses, as conditions require, such as changing Internet access provider, or to respond to a network breach.

One of the advanced features of NAT routers is their ability to use Port Address Translation (PAT), which allows multiple inside addresses to map to the same global address. This is sometimes called a *many-to-one* NAT, or *address overloading*. With address overloading, man private addressed nodes can access the Internet using a single global address. The NAT router keeps track of the different conversations by mapping TCP and UDP port numbers in the translation table. A translation entry is one which maps one IP address and port pair to another, and is called an extended *table entry*. This table will match internal private IP addresses and ports, to the global address.

The NAT command is used to configure PAT with:

```
RouterA(config)#ip nat inside source list access-list-number pool name overload
```

For example, if a network has 20 IP global addresses from 180.10.11.1 to 180.10.11.20, then the router could be configured with:

```
RouterA(config)#ip nat pool org_pat_pool 180.10.11.1 180.10.11.20 netmask
255.255.255.0
```

```
RouterA(config)#access-list 2 permit 10.1.1.0 0.0.0.255
RouterA(config)#ip nat inside source list 2 pool org_pat_pool overload
RouterA(config)#interface e 0
RouterA(config-if)#ip nat inside
RouterA(config-if)#interface s 0
RouterA(config-if)#ip nat outside
```

This creates an access-list with a label of 2, which is applied using the overload method, to provide PAT. This method is obviously important in a home network, where users are granted an IP address for their router. The home network can then be setup with private addresses.

E5   Encryption

E5.1   Introduction

The increase in electronic mail has also increased the need for secure data transmission. An electronic mail message can be easily intercepted as it transverses the world's communication networks. Thus there is a great need to encrypt the data contained in it. Traditional mail messages tend to be secure as they are normally taken by a courier or postal service and transported in a secure environment from source to destination. Over the coming years more individuals and companies will be using electronic mail systems and these must be totally secure.

Data encryption involves the science of cryptographics (note that the word *crytopgraphy* is derived from the Greek words which means hidden, or secret, writing). The basic object of cryptography is to provide a mechanism for two people to communicate without any other person being able to read the message.

Encryption is mainly applied to text transmission as binary data can be easily scrambled so it becomes almost impossible to unscramble. This is because text-based information contains certain key pointers:

- Most lines of text have the words 'the', 'and', 'of' and 'to'.
- Every sentence has a full stop.
- Words are separated by a space (the space character is the most probable character in a text document).
- The characters 'e', 'a' and 'i' are more probable than 'q', 'z' and 'x'.

Thus to decode a message an algorithm is applied and the decrypted text is then tested to determine whether it contains standard English (or the required language).

E5.2   Encryption and the OSI model

It is possible to encrypt data at any level of the OSI model, but typically it is encrypted when it is passed from the application program. This must occur at the presentation layer of the model, as illustrated in Figure E5.1. Thus, an external party will be able to determine the data at the session, transport, network and data link layer, but not the originally transmitted application data. Thus encryption is useful in hiding data from external parties, but cannot be used (with standard protocols) to hide:

- The session between the two parties. This will give information on the type of session used (such as FTP, TELNET or HTTP).
- The transport layer information. This will give information on the data packets, such as, with TCP, port and socket numbers, and acknowledgements.
- The network address of the source and the destination (all IP packets can be examined and the source and destination address can be viewed).
- The source and destination MAC address. The actually physical addresses of both the source and the destination can be easily examined.

Most encryption techniques use a standard method to encrypt the message. This method is normally well known and the software which can be used to encrypt or decrypt the data is widely available. The thing that makes the encryption process different is an electronic key, which is added into the encryption process. This encryption key could be private so that both the sender and receiver could use the same key to encrypt and decrypt the data. Unfortunately this would mean that each conversation with a user would require a different key. Another disadvantage is that a user would have to pass the private key through a secret channel. There is no guarantee that this channel is actually secure, and there is no way of knowing that an external party has a secret key. Typically public keys are changed at regular intervals, but if the external party knows how these change, they can also change their own keys. These problems are overcome with public-key encryption.

Most encryption is now public-key encryption (as illustrated in Figure E5.1). This involves each user having two encryption keys. One is a public-key which is given to anyone that requires to send the user some encrypted data. This key is used to encrypt any data that is sent to the user. The other key is a private-key which is used to decrypt the received encrypted data. No one knows the private-key (apart from the user who is receiving data encrypted with their public-key).

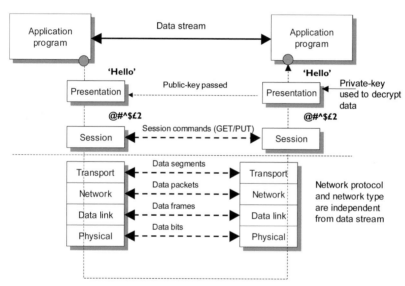

Figure E5.1 Encryption and the OSI model

E5.3   Legal issues

Patent laws and how they are implemented vary around the world. Like many good ideas, patents cover most of the cryptographic techniques. The main commercial techniques are:

- DES (Data Encryption Standard) which is patented but royalty-free.
- IDEA (International Data Encryption Algorithm) which is also patented and royalty-free for the non-commercial user.

Access to a global network normally requires the use of a public key. The most popular public-key algorithm is one developed at MIT and is named RSA (after its inventors Rivest,

Shamir and Adleman). All public-key algorithms are patented, and most of the important patents have been acquired by Public Key Partners (PKP). As the US government funded much of the work, there are no license fees for US government use. RSA is only patented in the US, but Public Key Partners (PKP) claim that the international Hellman-Merkle patent also covers RSA. The patent on RSA runs out in the year 2000. Public keys are generated by licensing software from a company called RSA Data Security Inc. (RSADSI).

The other widely used technique is Digital Signature Standard (DSS). It is freely licensable but in many respects it is technically inferior to RSA. The free licensing means that it is not necessary to reach agreement with RSADSI or PKP. Since it was announced, PKP have claimed the Hellman-Merkle patent covers all public-key cryptography. It has also strengthened its position by acquiring rights to a patent by Schnorr which is closely related to DSS.

E5.4   Random number generators

One way to crack a code is to exploit a weakness in the generation of the encryption key. The hacker can then guess which keys are more likely to occur. This is known as a statistical attack.

Many programming languages use a random number generator which is based on the current system time (such as `rand()`). This method is no good in data encryption as the hacker can simply determine the time that the message was encrypted and the algorithm used.

An improved source of randomness is the time between two keystrokes (as used in PGP – pretty good privacy). However this system has been criticized as a hacker can spy on a user over a network and determine the time between keystrokes. Other sources of true randomness have also been investigated, including noise from an electronic device and noise from an audio source.

E5.5   Cryptography

The main object of cryptography is to provide a mechanism for two (or more) people to communicate without anyone else being able to read the message. Along with this it can provide other services, such as:

- Giving a reassuring integrity check – this makes sure the message has not been tampered with by non-legitimate sources.
- Providing authentication – this verifies the sender identity.

Initially plaintext is encrypted into ciphertext, it is then decrypted back into plaintext, as illustrated in Figure E5.2. Cryptographic systems tend to use both an algorithm and a secret value, called the key. The requirement for the key is that it is difficult to keep devising new algorithms and also to tell the receiving party that the data is being encrypted with the new algorithm. Thus, using keys, there are no problems with everyone having the encryption/decryption system, because without the key it is very difficult to decrypt the message.

Figure E5.2
Encryption/decryption process

E5.5.1 Public key versus private key

The encryption process can either use a public key or a secret key. With a secret key the key is only known to the two communicating parties. This key can be fixed or can be passed from the two parties over a secure communications link (perhaps over the postal network or a leased line). The two most popular private key techniques are DES (Data Encryption Standard) and IDEA (International Data Encryption Algorithm).

In public-key encryption, each user has both a public and a private key. The two users can communicate because they know each other's public keys. Normally in a public-key system, each user uses a public enciphering transformation which is widely known and a private deciphering transform which is known only to that user. The private transformation is described by a private key, and the public transformation by a public key derived from the private key by a one-way transformation. The RSA (after its inventors Rivest, Shamir and Adleman) technique is one of the most popular public-key techniques and is based on the difficulty of factoring large numbers.

E5.5.2 Computational difficulty

Every code is crackable and the measure of the security of a code is the amount of time it takes persons not addressed in the code to break that code. Normally to break the code a computer tries all the possible keys until it finds a match. Thus a 1-bit code would only have 2 keys, a 2-bit code would have 4 keys, and so on. Table E5.1 shows the number of keys as a function of the number of bits in the key. For example it can be seen that a 64-bit code has 18 400 000 000 000 000 000 different keys. If one key is tested every 10 μs then it would take 1.84×10^{14} seconds (5.11×10^{10} hours or 2.13×10^{8} days or 5 834 602 years). So, for example, if it takes 1 million years for a person to crack the code then it can be considered safe. Unfortunately the performance of computer systems increases by the year. For example if a computer takes 1 million years to crack a code, then assuming an increase in computing power of a factor of 2 per year, then it would only take 500 000 years the next year. Table E5.2 shows that after almost 20 years it would take only 1 year to decrypt the same message.

The increasing power of computers is one factor in reducing the processing time; another is the increasing usage of parallel processing. Data decryption is well suited to parallel processing as each processor or computer can be assigned a number of keys to check the encrypted message. Each of them can then work independently of the other (this differs from many applications in parallel processing which suffer from interprocess(or) communication). Table E5.3 gives typical times, assuming a doubling of processing power each year, for processor arrays of 1, 2, 4 … 4096 elements. It can be seen that with an array of 4096 processing elements it takes only seven years before the code is decrypted within two years. Thus an organization which is serious about deciphering messages will have the resources to invest in large arrays of processors or networked computers. It is likely that many governments have computer systems with thousands or tens of thousands of processors operating in parallel. A prime use of these systems will be in decrypting messages.

Table E5.1 Number of keys related to the number of bits in the key

Code size	Number of keys	Code size	Number of keys	Code size	Number of keys
1	2	12	4 096	52	4.5×10^{15}
2	4	16	65 536	56	7.21×10^{16}
3	8	20	1 048 576	60	1.15×10^{18}
4	16	24	16 777 216	64	1.84×10^{19}

5	32	28	2.68×10^{8}	68	2.95×10^{20}
6	64	32	4.29×10^{9}	72	4.72×10^{21}
7	128	36	6.87×10^{10}	76	7.56×10^{22}
8	256	40	1.1×10^{12}	80	1.21×10^{24}
9	512	44	1.76×10^{13}	84	1.93×10^{25}
10	1 024	48	2.81×10^{14}	88	3.09×10^{26}

Table E5.2 Time to decrypt a message assuming an increase in computing power

Year	Time to decrypt (years)	Year	Time to decrypt (years)
0	1 million	10	977
1	500 000	11	489
2	250 000	12	245
3	125 000	13	123
4	62 500	14	62
5	31 250	15	31
6	15 625	16	16
7	7 813	17	8
8	3 907	18	4
9	1 954	19	2

Table E5.3 Time to decrypt a message with increasing power and parallel processing

Processors	Year 0	Year 1	Year 2	Year 3	Year 4	Year 5	Year 6	Year 7
1	1 000 000	500 000	250 000	125 000	62 500	31 250	15 625	7 813
2	500 000	250 000	125 000	62 500	31 250	15 625	7 813	3 907
4	250 000	125 000	62 500	31 250	15 625	7 813	3 907	1 954
8	125 000	62 500	31 250	15 625	7 813	3 907	1 954	977
16	62 500	31 250	15 625	7 813	3 907	1 954	977	489
32	31 250	15 625	7 813	3 907	1 954	977	489	245
64	15 625	7 813	3 907	1 954	977	489	245	123
128	7 813	3 907	1 954	977	489	245	123	62
256	3 906	1 953	977	489	245	123	62	31
512	1 953	977	489	245	123	62	31	16
1 024	977	489	245	123	62	31	16	8
2 048	488	244	122	61	31	16	8	4
4 096	244	122	61	31	16	8	4	2

E5.6 Government pressure

Many institutions and individuals read data which is not intended for them; they include:

- Government departments. Traditionally governments around the world have reserved the right to tap into any communications which they think may be against the national interest.
- Spies who tap into communications for industrial or governmental information.
- Individuals who like to read other people's messages.
- Individuals who 'hack' into systems and read secure information.
- Criminals who intercept information in order to use it for crime, such as intercepting PIN numbers on bankcards.

Governments around the world tend to be against the use of encryption as it reduces their chances to tap into information and determine messages. It is also the case that governments do not want other countries to use encryption because it also reduces their chances of reading their secret communications (especially military maneuvers). In order to reduce this threat they must do either of the following:

- Prevent the use of encryption.
- Break the encryption code.
- Learn everyone's cryptographic keys.

Many implementations of data encryption are in hardware, but increasingly it is implemented in software (especially public-key methods). This makes it easier for governments to control their access. For example the US government has proposed to beat encryption by trying to learn everyone's cryptographic key with the Clipper chip. The US government keeps a   record of all the serial numbers and encryption keys for each Clipper chip manufactured.

E5.7   Cracking the code

A cryptosystem converts plaintext into ciphertext using a key. There are several methods that a hacker can use to crack a code, including:

- **Known plaintext attack.** Where the hacker knows part of the ciphertext and the corresponding plaintext. The known ciphertext and plaintext can then be used to decrypt the rest of the ciphertext.
- **Chosen-ciphertext.** Where the hacker sends a message to the target, this is then encrypted with the target's private-key and the hacker then analyses the encrypted message. For example, a hacker may send an e-mail to the encryption file server and the hacker spies on the delivered message.
- **Exhaustive search.** Where the hacker uses brute force to decrypt the ciphertext and tries every possible key.
- **Active attack.** Where the hacker inserts or modifies messages.
- **Man-in-the-middle.** Where the hacker is hidden between two parties and impersonates each of them to the other.
- **The replay system.** Where the hacker takes a legitimate message and sends it into the network at some future time.
- **Cut and paste.** Where the hacker mixes parts of two different encrypted messages and, sometimes, is able to create a new message. This message is likely to make no sense, but may trick the receiver into doing something that helps the hacker.
- **Time resetting.** Some encryption schemes use the time of the computer to create the key. Resetting this time or determining the time that the message was created can give some useful information to the hacker.
- **Time attack.** This involves determining the amount of time that a user takes to decrypt the message; from this the key can be found.

E5.8   Letter probabilities

The English language has a great deal of redundancy in it, thus common occurrences in text can be coded with short bit sequences. The probability of each letter also varies. For example the letter 'e' occurs many more times than the letter 'z'. Program E5.7 in Section E5.12 gives a simple C program which determines the probability of letters within a text file. This program can be used to determine typical letter probabilities. Sample run E5.1 shows a sample run using some sample text. It can be seen that the highest probability is with the letter 'e', which occurs, on average, 94.3 times every 1000 letters. Table E5.4 lists the letters in order of their probability. Notice that the letters which are worth the least in the popular board game Scrabble (such as, 'e', 't', 'a', and so on) are the most probable and the letters with the highest scores (such as 'x', 'z' and 'q') are the least probable.

Sample run E5.1

Char.	Occur.	Prob.	Char.	Occur.	Prob.
a	1963	0.0672	b	284	0.0097
c	914	0.0313	d	920	0.0315
e	2752	0.0943	f	471	0.0161
g	473	0.0162	h	934	0.0320
i	1680	0.0576	j	13	0.0004
k	96	0.0033	l	968	0.0332
m	724	0.0248	n	1541	0.0528
o	1599	0.0548	p	443	0.0152
q	49	0.0017	r	1410	0.0483
s	1521	0.0521	t	2079	0.0712
u	552	0.0189	v	264	0.0090
w	383	0.0131	x	57	0.0020
y	278	0.0095	z	44	0.0015
.	292	0.0100	SP	4474	0.1533
,	189	0.0065			

E5.8.1   Frequency analysis

Frequency analysis involves measuring the occurrences of the letters in the ciphertext. This can give many clues as the English language contains certain key features for decypering, such as:

- Determine the probabilities of ciphertext letters. The least probable should be 'j', 'k', 'x' and 'z'. These have an accumulated occurrence of less than 1 per cent. One of the letters, an 'e', should have an occurrence of more than 10 per cent. Next the ciphertext letter probabilities should be measured against standard English language letter probabilities. If the two do not tie-up, it is likely that the text was written in another language.
- If the single letters do not yield the code, then two letter occurrences of the same letter should be examined. The most common ones are: ss, ee, tt, ff, ll, mm and oo. If the ciphertext contains repeated letters, it may relate to one of these sequences.
- If there are spaces between the words, the two letter words can be examined. The most popular two letter words are: an, as, at, am, be, by, do, of, to, in, it, is, so, we, he, or, on, if, me, up, go, no and us (see Section E5.13).
- If possible, the list of letter probabilities should be related to the type of message that is being sent. For example, military communications tend to omit pronouns and articles

(excluding words like he, a and I).
- Try and identify whole phrases, such as 'Hello who are you'. This can be used as a crow-bar to get the rest of the code.
- If the ciphertext corresponds to correct letter probabilities, but the deciphered text is still unreadable, it may be that the code is a transpositional cipher, where the letters have had their positions changed. For example, every two cipher characters have been swapped around.

Table E5.4 Letters and their occurrence in a sample text file

Character	Occurrences	Probability	Character	Occurrences	Probability
SPACE	4 474	0.1533	g	473	0.0162
e	2 752	0.0943	f	471	0.0161
t	2 079	0.0712	p	443	0.0152
a	1 963	0.0672	w	383	0.0131
i	1 680	0.0576	.	292	0.0100
o	1 599	0.0548	b	284	0.0097
n	1 541	0.0528	y	278	0.0095
s	1 521	0.0521	v	264	0.0090
r	1 410	0.0483	,	189	0.0065
l	968	0.0332	k	96	0.0033
h	934	0.0320	x	57	0.0020
d	920	0.0315	q	49	0.0017
c	914	0.0313	z	44	0.0015
m	724	0.0248	j	13	0.0004
u	552	0.0189			

E5.9   Basic encryption principles

Encryption codes have been used for many centuries. They have tended to be used in military situations where secret messages have to be sent between troops without the risk of them being read by the enemy.

E5.9.1   Alphabet shifting (Caesar code)

A simple encryption code is to replace the letters with a shifted equivalent alphabet. For example moving the letters two places to the right gives:

```
abcdefghijklmnopqrstuvwxyz
YZABCDEFGHIJKLMNOPQRSTUVWX
```

Thus a message:

```
the boy stood on the burning deck
```

would become:

```
RFC ZMW QRMMB ML RFC ZSPLGLE BCAI
```

This code has the problem of being reasonably easy to decode, as there are only 26 different code combinations. The first documented use of this type of code was by Julius Caesar who used a 3-letter shift.

E5.9.2 Vigenère code

A Caesar-type code shifts the alphabet by a number of places (as given in Table E5.5). An improved code was developed by Vigenère, but as a shifted alphabet is not very secure. In this code, a different row is used for each encryption. The way that the user moves between the rows must be agreed before encryption. This can be achieved with a code word, which defines the sequence of the rows. For example the codeword GREEN could be used which defined that the rows used were: Row 6 (G), Row 17 (R), Row 4 (E), Row 4 (E), Row 13 (N), Row 6 (G), Row 17 (R), and so on.

Table E5.5 Character-shifted alphabets

Plain	a b c d e f g h i j k l m n o p q r s t u v w x y z
1	B C D E F G H I J K L M N O P Q R S T U V W X Y Z A
2	C D E F G H I J K L M N O P Q R S T U V W X Y Z A B
3	D E F G H I J K L M N O P Q R S T U V W X Y Z A B C
4	E F G H I J K L M N O P Q R S T U V W X Y Z A B C D
5	F G H I J K L M N O P Q R S T U V W X Y Z A B C D E
6	G H I J K L M N O P Q R S T U V W X Y Z A B C D E F
7	H I J K L M N O P Q R S T U V W X Y Z A B C D E F G
8	I J K L M N O P Q R S T U V W X Y Z A B C D E F G H
9	J K L M N O P Q R S T U V W X Y Z A B C D E F G H I
10	K L M N O P Q R S T U V W X Y Z A B C D E F G H I J
11	L M N O P Q R S T U V W X Y Z A B C D E F G H I J K
12	M N O P Q R S T U V W X Y Z A B C D E F G H I J K L
13	N O P Q R S T U V W X Y Z A B C D E F G H I J K L M
14	O P Q R S T U V W X Y Z A B C D E F G H I J K L M N
15	P Q R S T U V W X Y Z A B C D E F G H I J K L M N O
16	Q R S T U V W X Y Z A B C D E F G H I J K L M N O P
17	R S T U V W X Y Z A B C D E F G H I J K L M N O P Q
18	S T U V W X Y Z A B C D E F G H I J K L M N O P Q R
19	T U V W X Y Z A B C D E F G H I J K L M N O P Q R S
20	U V W X Y Z A B C D E F G H I J K L M N O P Q R S T
21	V W X Y Z A B C D E F G H I J K L M N O P Q R S T U
22	W X Y Z A B C D E F G H I J K L M N O P Q R S T U V
23	X Y Z A B C D E F G H I J K L M N O P Q R S T U V W
24	Y Z A B C D E F G H I J K L M N O P Q R S T U V W X
25	Z A B C D E F G H I J K L M N O P Q R S T U V W X Y

Thus the message:

Keyword	GREENGREENGREEN
Plaintext	hellohowareyou
Ciphertext	NVPPBNFAEEKPSY

The great advantage of this type of code is that the same plaintext character will be encrypted with different values, depending on the position of the keyword. For example, if the keyword is GREEN, 'e' can be encrypted as 'K' (for G), 'V' (for R), 'I' (for E) and 'R' (for N). The greater the size of the code word, the more the rows that will be included in the encryption process. It is not possible to decipher the code by a frequency analysis, as letters will change their coding depending on the current position of the keyword. It is also safe from analysis of common two- and three-letter occurrences. For example 'ee' could be encrypted with 'KV' (for GR), 'VI' (for RE), 'II' (for EE), 'IR' (for EN) and 'RK' (for NG). A longer keyword would generate more combinations.

The Vigenère code is *polyalphabetic*, as it uses a number of cipher alphabets.

E5.9.3   Homophonic substitution code

A homophonic substitution code overcomes the problems of frequency analysis of code, as it assigns a number of codes to a character which relates to the probability of the characters. For example the character 'e' might have 10 codes assigned to it, but 'z' would only have one. An example code is given in Table E5.6.

Each of the codes is assigned at random to each of the letters, with the number of codes assigned related to the probability of their occurrence. Thus, using the code table in Table E5.6, the code mapping would be:

Plaintext	h	e	l	l	o	e	v	e	r	y	o	n	e
Ciphertext:	19	25	42	81	16	26	22	28	04	55	30	00	32

In this case there are four occurrences of the letter 'e', and each one has a different code. As the number of codes depends on the number of occurrences of the letter, each code will roughly have the same probability, thus it is not possible to determine the code mapping from the probabilities of codes. Unfortunately the code isn't perfect as the English language still contains certain relationships which can be traced. For example the letter 'q' normally is represented by a single code, and three codes represent a 'u'. Thus, if the ciphertext contains a code followed by one of three codes, then it is likely that the plaintext is a 'q' and a 'u'.

Table E5.6   Example homophonic substitution

a	b	c	d	e	f	g	h	i	j	k	l	m	n	o	p	q	r	s	t	u	v	w	x	y	z
07	11	17	10	25	08	44	19	02	18	41	42	40	00	16	01	15	04	06	05	13	22	45	12	55	47
31	64	33	27	26	09	83	20	03			81	52	43	30	62		24	34	23	14		46		93	
50		49	51	28			21	29			86		80	61			39	56	35	36					
63		76		32			54	53			95		88	65			58	57	37						
66				48			70	68					89	91			71	59	38						
77				67			87	73						94			00	90	60						
84				69										96					74						
				72															78						
				75															92						
				79																					
				82																					
				85																					

A homophonic cipher is a monoalphabetic code, as it only uses one translation for the code mappings (even though several codes can be used for a single plaintext letter). This alphabet remains constant, whereas a polyalphabet can change its mapping depending on a variable keyword.

E5.9.4 Code mappings

Code mappings can have no underlying mathematical relationship and simply use a code-book to represent the characters. This is known as a *monoalphabetic* code, as only one cipher alphabet is used. An example could be:

Input: abcdefghijklmnopqrstuvwxyz
Encrypted: MGQOAFZBCDIEHXJKLNTQRWSUVY

Program E5.1 shows a C program which uses this code mapping to encrypt entered text and Sample run E5.3 shows a sample run.

The number of different character maps can be determined as follows:

- Take the letter 'A' then this can be mapped to 26 different letters.
- If 'A' is mapped to a certain letter then 'B' can only map to 25 letters.
- If 'B' is mapped to a certain letter then 'C' can be mapped to 24 letters.
- Continue until the alphabet is exhausted.

Thus, in general, the number of combinations will be:

$$26 \times 25 \times 24 \times 23 \dots 4 \times 3 \times 2 \times 1$$

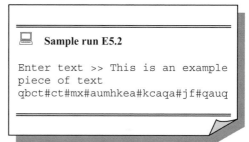

Sample run E5.2

```
Enter text >> This is an example
piece of text
qbct#ct#mx#aumhkea#kcaqa#jf#qauq
```

Thus the code has 26! different character mappings (approximately 4.03×10^{26}). It suffers from the fact that the probabilities of the mapped characters will be similar to those in normal text. Thus if there is a large amount of text then the character having the highest probability will be either an 'e' or a 't'. The character with the lowest probability will tend to be a 'z' or a 'q' (which is also likely be followed by the character map for a 'u').

Program E5.1

```c
#include <stdio.h>
#include <ctype.h>
int   main(void)
{
int   key,ch,i=0,inch;
char  text[BUFSIZ];
char  input[26]="abcdefghijklmnopqrstuvwxyz";
char  output[26]="mgqoafzbcdiehxjklntqrwsuvy";
   printf("Enter text >>");
   gets(text);
   ch=text[0];
   do
   {
```

```
        if (ch!=' ') inch=output[(tolower(ch)-'a')];
        else inch='#';
        putchar(inch);
        i++;
        ch=text[i];
    } while (ch!=NULL);
    return(0);
}
```

A code mapping encryption scheme is easy to implement but unfortunately, once it has been 'cracked', it is easy to decrypt the encrypted data. Normally this type of code is implemented with an extra parameter which changes its mapping, such as changing the code mapping over time depending on the time of day and/or date. Only parties which are allowed to decrypt the message know the mappings of the code to time and/or date. For example, each day of the week could have a different code mapping.

E5.9.5 Applying a key

To make it easy to decrypt, a key is normally applied to the text. This makes it easy to decrypt the message if the key is known, but difficult to decrypt the message if the key is not known. An example of a key operation is to take each of the characters in a text message and then exclusive-OR (XOR) the character with a key value. For example the ASCII character 'A' has the bit pattern:

    100 0001

and if the key had a value of 5 then 'A' exclusive-OR'ed with 5 would give:

'A'	100 0001
Key (5)	000 0101
Ex-OR	100 0100

The bit pattern 100 0100 would be encrypted as character 'D'. Program E5.3 is a C program which can be used to display the alphabet of encrypted characters for a given key. In this program the ^ operator represents exclusive-OR. Sample run E5.4 shows a sample run with a key of 5. The exclusive-OR operator has the advantage that when applied twice it results in the original value (it thus changes a value, but does not lose any information when it operates on it).

📄 **Program E5.2**
```
#include <stdio.h>

int  main(void)
{
int  key,ch;

    printf("Enter key value >>");
    scanf("%d",&key);

    for (ch='A';ch<='Z';ch++)
        putchar(ch^key);
```

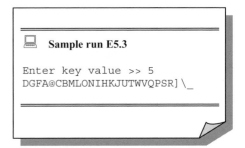

Sample run E5.3

```
Enter key value >> 5
DGFA@CBMLONIHKJUTWVQPSR]\_
```

```
        return(0);
}
```

Program E5.3 is an encryption program which reads some text from the keyboard, then encrypts it with a given key and saves the encrypted text to a file. Program E5.4 can then be used to read the encrypted file for a given key; only the correct key will give the correct results.

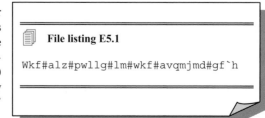

Program E5.3
```
/* Encryt.c */
#include <stdio.h>

int   main(void)
{
FILE *f;
char
   fname[BUFSIZ],str[BUFSIZ]
;
int   key,ch,i=0;

   printf("Enter output file name >>");
   gets(fname);

   if ((f=fopen(fname,"w"))==NULL)
   {
      puts("Cannot open input file");
      return(1);
   }
   printf("Enter text to be save to file>>");
   gets(str);

   printf("Enter key value >>");
   scanf("%d",&key);

   ch=str[0];
   do
   {
      ch=ch^key; /* Exclusive-OR character with itself */
      putc(ch,f);
      i++;
      ch=str[i];
   } while (ch!=NULL); /* test if end of string */
   fclose(f);
   return(0);
}
```

Sample run E5.4

```
Enter output filename >> out.dat
Enter text to be saved to file>> The
boy stood on the burning deck
Enter key value >> 3
```

File listing E5.1 gives a file listing for the saved encrypted text. One obvious problem with this coding is that the SPACE character is visible in the coding. As the SPACE character is 010 0000, the key can be determined by simply XORing 010 0000 with the '#'

File listing E5.1

```
Wkf#alz#pwllg#lm#wkf#avqmjmd#gf`h
```

character, thus:

SPACE	010 0000
'#'	010 0011
Key	000 0011

Thus the key is 000 0011 (decimal 3).

Program E5.4

```c
/* Decryt.c */
#include <stdio.h>
#include <ctype.h>
int   main(void)
{
FILE  *f;
char  fname[BUFSIZ];
int   key,ch;

   printf("Enter encrypted filename >>");
   gets(fname);
   if ((f=fopen(fname,"r"))==NULL)
   {
      puts("Cannot open input file");
      return(1);
   }

   printf("Enter key value >>");
   scanf("%d",&key);

   do
   {
      ch=getc(f);
      ch=ch^key;
      if (isascii(ch)) putchar(ch); /* only print ASCII char */
   } while (!feof(f));
   fclose(f);
   return(0);
}
```

Program E5.5 uses the exclusive-OR operator and reads from an input file and outputs to an output file. The format of the run (assuming that the source code file is called key.c) is:
key *infile.dat outfile.enc*

where *infile.dat* is the name of the input file (text or binary) and *outfile.enc* is the name of the output file.

The great advantage of this program is that the same program is used for encryption and for decryption. Thus:

key *outfile.enc newfile.dat*

converts the encrypted file back into the original file.

📄 Program E5.5

```c
#include <stdio.h>

int main(int argc, char *argv[])
{
FILE *in,*out;
char fname[BUFSIZ],key,ch,fout[BUFSIZ],fext[BUFSIZ],*str;

    printf("Enter key >>");
    scanf("%c",&key);

    if ((in=fopen(argv[1],"rb"))==NULL)
    {
        printf("Cannot open");
        return(1);
    }

    out=fopen(argv[2],"wb");

    do
    {
        fread(&ch,1,1,in); /* read a byte from the file */
        ch=((ch & 0xff) ^ (key & 0xff)) & 0xff;
        if (!feof(in)) fwrite(&ch,1,1,out); /* write a byte */

    } while (!feof(in));

    fclose(in); fclose(out);
}
```

E5.9.6 Applying a bit shift

A typical method used to encrypt text is to shift the bits within each character. For example ASCII characters only use the lower 7 bits of an 8-bit character. Thus, shifting the bit positions one place to the left will encrypt the data to a different character. For a left shift a 0 or a 1 can be shifted into the least significant bit; for a right shift the least significant bit can be shifted into the position of the most significant bit. When shifting more than one position a rotate left or rotate right can be used. Note that most of the characters produced by shifting may not be printable, thus a text editor (or viewer) cannot be used to view them. For example, in C the characters would be processed with:

```c
ch=ch << 1;
```

which shifts the bits of ch one place to the left, and decrypted by:

```c
ch=ch >> 1;
```

which shifts the bits of ch one place to the right.

Program E5.6 gives an example of a program that reads in a text file (or any file), and reads it one byte at a time. For each byte the program rotates the bits 2 places to the left (with rot_left) and saves the byte.

📄 **Program E5.6**
```c
#include <stdio.h>

unsigned char rot_left(unsigned char ch);
unsigned char rot_right(unsigned char ch);

int main(int argc, char *argv[])
{
unsigned char ch;
int i;
FILE *in,*out;
char fname[BUFSIZ],fout[BUFSIZ],fext[BUFSIZ],*str;
   if ((in=fopen(argv[1],"rb"))==NULL)
   {
      printf("Cannot open");
      return(1);
   }
   out=fopen(argv[2],"wb");

   do
   {
      fread(&ch,1,1,in);    /* read a byte from the file */
      ch=rot_left(ch);      /* perform two left rotates */
      ch=rot_left(ch);
      if (!feof(in)) fwrite(&ch,1,1,out); /* write a byte */
   } while (!feof(in));
   fclose(in); fclose(out);
}

// rotate bits to the left
unsigned char rot_left(unsigned char ch)
{
unsigned char bit8;

   bit8=(ch & 0x80) & 0x80;
   ch=ch << 1;
   ch = ch | ((bit8>>7) & 0x01);
   return(ch);
}
/* rotate bits to the right */
unsigned char rot_right(unsigned char ch)
{
unsigned char bit1;
   bit1=(ch & 1) & 0x01;
   ch=ch >> 1;
   ch = ch | ((bit1<<7) & 0x80);
   return(ch);
}
```

For example the text:

Hello. This is some sample text.

Fred.

becomes:

```
!•±±½,□Q¡¥Í□¥Í□Í½µ•□Í…µÃ±•□Ñ•áÑ¸4(4(□É•`¸
```

This can then be decrypted by changing the left rotates (rot_left) to right rotates (rot_right).

E5.10   Message hash

A message hash is a simple technique which basically mixes up the bits within the message, using exclusive-OR operations, bit-shifts or character substitutions.

- **Base-64 encoding.** This is used in electronic mail, and is typically used to change a binary file into a standard 7-bit ASCII form. It takes 6-bit characters and converts them to a printable character, as given in Section F1.6.4.
- **MD5.** This is used in several encryption and authentication methods. An example conversion is from:

```
Hello, how are you?
Are you feeling well?

Fred.
```
to:

```
518bb66a80cf187a20e1b07cd6cef585
```

E5.11   Private-key

Encryption techniques can use either public keys or secret keys. Secret-key encryption techniques use a secret key which is only known by the two communicating parties, as illustrated in Figure E5.3. This key can be fixed or can be passed from the two parties over a secure communications link (for example over the postal network or a leased line). The two most popular private-key techniques are DES (Data Encryption Standard) and IDEA (International Data Encryption Algorithm) and a popular public-key technique is RSA (named after its inventors, Rivest, Shamir and Adleman). Public-key encryption uses two keys, one private and the other public.

E5.11.1 Survey of private-key cryptosystems

The main private-key cryptosystems include:

- **DES.** DES (Data Encryption Standard) is a block cipher scheme which operates on 64-bit block sizes. The private key has only 56 useful bits as eight of its bits are used for parity. This gives 2^{56} or 10^{17} possible keys. DES uses a complex series of permutations and substitutions, the result of these operations is XOR'ed with the input. This is then repeated 16 times using a different order of the key bits each time. DES is a very strong code and has never been broken, although several high-powered computers are now available which, using brute force, can crack the code. A possible solution is 3DES (or triple DES) which uses DES three times in a row. First to encrypt, next to decrypt and finally to encrypt. This system allows a key-length of more than 128 bits.

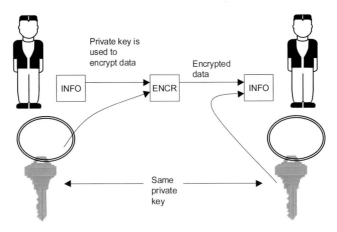

Figure E5.3 Private key encryption/decryption process

- **MOSS.** MOSS (MIME object security service) is an Internet RFC and is typically used for sound encryption. It uses symmetric encryption and the size of the key is not specified. The only public implementation is TIS/MOSS 7.1, which is basically an implementation of 56-bit DES code with a violation.
- **IDEA.** IDEA (International Data Encryption Algorithm) is similar to DES. It operates on 64-bit blocks of plaintext, uses a 128-bit key, and has over 17 rounds with a complicated mangler function. During decryption this function does not have to be reversed and can simply be applied in the same way as during encryption (this also occurs with DES). IDEA uses a different key expansion for encryption and decryption, but every other part of the process is identical. The same keys are used in DES decryption but in the reverse order. The key is devised in eight 16-bit blocks; the first six are used in the first round of encryption the last two are used in the second run. It is free for use in non-commercial version and appears to be a strong cipher.
- **RC4/RC5.** RC4 is a cipher designed by RSA Data Security, Inc and was a secret until information on it appeared on the Internet. The Netscape secure socket layer (SSL) uses RC4. It uses a pseudo random number generator where the output of the generator is XOR'ed with the plaintext. It is a fast algorithm and can use any key-length. Unfortunately the same key cannot be used twice. Recently a 40-bit key version was broken in eight days without special computer power. RC5 is a fast block cipher designed by Rivest for RSA Data Security. It has a parameterized algorithm with a variable block size (32, 64 or 128 bits), a variable key size (0 to 2048 bits) and a variable number of rounds (0 to 255). It has a heavy use of data dependent rotations and the mixture of different operations. This assures that RC5 is secure. Kaliski and Yin found that RC5 with a 64-bit block size and 12 or more rounds gives good security.
- **SAFER.** SAFER (Secure and Fast Encryption Routine) is a non-proprietary block-cipher developed by Massey in 1993. It operates on a 64-bit block size and has a 64-bit or 128-bit key size. SAFER has up to 10 rounds (although a minimum of 6 is recommended). Unlike most recent block ciphers, SAFER has a slightly different encryption and decryption procedure. The algorithm operates on single bytes at a time and it thus can be

implemented on systems with limited processing power, such as on smart-cards applications. A typical implementation is SAFER K-64 which uses a 40-bit key and has been
shown that it is immune from most attacks when the number of rounds is greater than
six.

- **SKIPJACK.** Skipjack is a new block cipher which operates on 64-bit blocks. It uses an
  80-bit key and has 32 rounds. The NSA has classified details of Skipjack and its algorithm is only available in hardware implementation called Clipper Chips. The name
  Clipper derives from an earlier implementation of the algorithm. Each transmission
  contains the session key encrypted in the header. The licensing of Clipper chips allows
  US government to decrypt all SKIPJACK messages.

E5.11.2 Data Encryption Standard (DES)

In 1977, the National Bureau of Standards (now the National Institute of Standards and
Technology) published the DES for commercial and unclassified US government applications. DES is based on an algorithm known as the Lucifer cipher designed by IBM. It maps a
64-bit input block to a 64-bit output block and uses a 56-bit key. The key itself is actually 64
bits long but as 1 bit in each of the 8 bytes is used for odd parity on each byte, the key only
contains 56 meaningful bits.

DES overview

The main steps in the encryption process are as follows:

- Initially the 64-bit input is permutated to obtain a 64-bit result (this operation does little to the security of the code).
- Next, there are 16 iterations of the 64-bit result and the 56-bit key. Only 48 bits of the
  key are used at a time. The 64-bit output from each iteration is used as an input to the
  next iteration.
- After the 16th iteration, the 64-bit output goes through another permutation, which is
  the inverse of the initial permutation.

Figure E5.4 shows the basic operation of DES encryption.

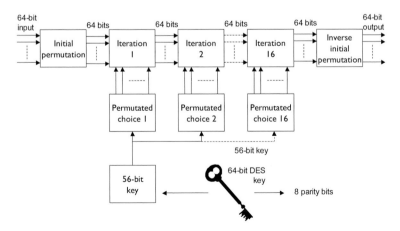

Figure E5.4 Overview of DES operation

Permutation of the data

Before the first iteration and after the last iteration, DES performs a permutation on the data. The permutation is as follows:

Initial permutation:

```
58 50 42 34 26 18 10 2   60 52 44 36 28 20 12 4   62 54 46 38 30 22 14 6
64 56 48 40 32 24 16 8   57 49 41 33 25 17 9  1   59 51 43 35 27 19 11 3
61 53 45 37 29 21 13 5   63 55 47 39 31 23 15 7
```

Final permutation:

```
40 8  48 16 56 24 64 32 39 7   47 15 55 23 63 31 38 6   46 14 54 22 62 30
37 5  45 13 53 21 61 29 36 4   44 12 52 20 60 28 35 3   43 11 51 19 59 27
34 2  42 10 50 18 58 26 33 1   41 9  49 17 57 25
```

These numbers specify the bit numbers of the input to the permutation and the order of the numbers corresponds to the output bit position. Thus, input permutation:

- Input bit 58 moves to output bit 1 (58 is in the 1st bit position).
- Input bit 50 moves to output bit 2 (50 is in the 2nd bit position).
- Input bit 42 moves to output bit 3 (42 is in the 3rd bit position).
- Continue until all bits are exhausted.

In addition, the final permutation could be:

- Input bit 58 moves to output bit 1 (1 is in the 58th bit position).
- Input bit 50 moves to output bit 2 (2 is in the 50th bit position).
- Input bit 42 moves to output bit 3 (3 is in the 42nd bit position).
- Continue until all bits are exhausted.

Thus, the input permutation is the reverse of the output permutation. Arranged as blocks of 8 bits, it gives:

```
58 50 42 34 26 18 10 2
60 52 44 36 28 20 12 4
62 54 46 38 30 22 14 6
 :              :
61 53 45 37 29 21 13 5
63 55 47 39 31 23 15 7
```

It can be seen that the first byte of input gets spread into the 8th bit of each of the other bytes. The second byte of input gets spread into the 7th bit of each of the other bytes, and so on.

Generating the per-round keys

The DES key operates on 64-bit data in each of the 16 iterations. The key is made of a 56-bit key used in the iterations and 8 parity bits. A 64-bit key of:

$$k_1 \, k_2 \, k_3 \, k_4 \, k_5 \, k_6 \, k_7 \, k_8 \, k_9 \, k_{10} \, k_{11} \, k_{12} \, k_{13} \, ... \, k_{64}$$

contains the parity k_8, k_{16}, k_{32} ... k_{64}. The iterations are numbered I_1, I_2, ... I_{16}. The initial permutation of the 56 useful bits of the key is used to generate a 56-bit output. It divides into two 28-bit values, called C_0 and D_0. C_0 is specified as:

$$k_{57} \, k_{49} \, k_{41} \, k_{33} \, k_{25} \, k_{17} \, k_9 \, k_1 \, k_{58} \, k_{50} \, k_{42} \, k_{34} \, k_{26} \, k_{18} \, k_{10} \, k_2 \, k_{59} \, k_{51} \, k_{43} \, k_{35} \, k_{27} \, k_{19} \, k_{11} \, k_3 \, k_{60} \, k_{52} \, k_{44} \, k_{36}$$

And D_0 is:

$$k_{63} \, k_{55} \, k_{47} \, k_{39} \, k_{31} \, k_{23} \, k_{15} \, k_7 \, k_{62} \, k_{54} \, k_{46} \, k_{38} \, k_{30} \, k_{22} \, k_{14} \, k_6 \, k_{61} \, k_{53} \, k_{45} \, k_{37} \, k_{29} \, k_{21} \, k_{13} \, k_5 \, k_{28} \, k_{20} \, k_{12} \, k_4$$

Thus the 28-bit C_0 key will contain the 57th bit of the DES key as the first bit, the 49th as the second bit, and so on. Notice that none of the 28-bit values contains the parity bits.

Most of the rounds have a 2-bit rotate left shift, but rounds 1, 2, 9 and 16 have a single-bit rotate left (ROL). A left rotation moves all the bits in the key to the left and the bit which is moved out of the left-hand side is shifted into the right-hand end.

The key for each iteration (K_i) is generated from C_i (which makes the left half) and D_i (which makes the right half). The permutations of C_i that produces the left half of K_i is:

$$c_{14} \, c_{17} \, c_{11} \, c_{24} \, c_1 \, c_5 \, c_3 \, c_{28} \, c_{15} \, c_6 \, c_{21} \, c_{10} \, c_{23} \, c_{19} \, c_{12} \, c_4 \, c_{26} \, c_8 \, c_{16} \, c_7 \, c_{27} \, c_{20} \, c_{13} \, c_2$$

and the right half of K_i is:

$$d_{41} \, d_{52} \, d_{31} \, d_{37} \, d_{47} \, d_{55} \, d_{30} \, d_{40} \, d_{51} \, d_{45} \, d_{33} \, d_{48} \, d_{44} \, d_{49} \, d_{39} \, d_{56} \, d_{34} \, d_{53} \, d_{46} \, d_{42} \, d_{50} \, d_{36} \, d_{29} \, d_{32}$$

Thus the 56-bit key is made up of:

$$c_{14} \, c_{17} \, c_{11} \, c_{24} \, c_1 \, c_5 \, c_3 \, c_{28} \, c_{15} \, c_6 \, c_{21} \, c_{10} \, c_{23} \, c_{19} \, c_{12} \, c_4 \, c_{26} \, c_8 \, c_{16} \, c_7 \, c_{27} \, c_{20} \, c_{13} \, c_2 \, d_{41} \, d_{52} \, d_{31} \, d_{37} \, d_{47} \, d_{55} \, d_{30} \, d_{40} \, d_{51} \, d_{45} \, d_{33} \, d_{48} \, d_{44}$$
$$d_{49} \, d_{39} \, d_{56} \, d_{34} \, d_{53} \, d_{46} \, d_{42} \, d_{50} \, d_{36} \, d_{29} \, d_{32}$$

Figure E5.5 illustrates the process (note that only some of the bit positions have been shown).

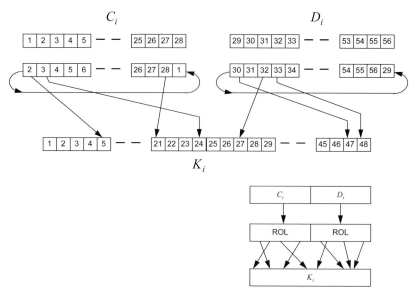

Figure E5.5 Generating the iteration key

Iteration operations

Each iteration takes the 64-bit output from the previous iteration and operates on it with a 56-bit per iteration key. Figure E5.6 shows the operation of each iteration. The 64-bit input is split into two parts, L_i and R_i. R_i is operated on with an expansion/permutation (E-table) to give 48 bits. The output from the E-table conversion is then exclusive-OR'ed with the permutated 48-bit key. Next a substitute/choice stage (S-box) is used to transform the 48-bit result to 32 bits. These are then XOR'ed with L_i to give the resulting R_{i+1} (which is R_i for the next iteration). The operation of expansion/XOR/substitution is often known as the mangler function. The R_i input is also used to produce L_{i+1}.

The mangler function takes the 32-bit R_i and the 48-bit K_i and produces a 32-bit output (which when XORed with L_i produces R_i+1). It initially expands R_i from 32 bits to 48 bits. This is done by splitting R_i into eight 4-bit chunks and then expanding each of the chunks into 6 bits by taking the adjacent bits and concatenating them onto the chunk. The leftmost and rightmost bits of R are considered adjacent. For example, if R_i is:

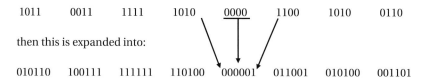

then this is expanded into:

010110   100111   111111   110100   000001   011001   010100   001101

The output from the expansion is then XOR'ed with K_i and the output of this is fed into the S-box. Each 6-bit chunk of the 48-bit output from the XOR operation is then substituted with a 4-bit chunk using a lookup table. An S-box table for the first 6-bit chunk is given in Table E5.7. Thus, for example, the input bit sequence of:

000000 000001 *XXXXXX* ...

would be converted to:

1110 0000 *xxxx* ...

Table E5.7 S-box conversion for first 6-bit chunk

Input	*Output*	*Input*	*Output*	*Input*	*Output*	*Input*	*Output*
000000	1110	010000	0011	100000	0100	110000	1111
000001	0000	010001	1010	100001	1111	110001	0101
000010	0100	010010	1010	100010	0001	110010	1100
000011	1111	010011	0110	100011	1100	110011	1011
000100	1101	010100	0100	100100	1110	110100	1001
000101	0111	010101	1100	100101	1000	110101	0011
000110	0001	010110	1100	100110	1000	110110	0111
000111	0100	010111	1011	100111	0010	110111	1110
001000	0010	011000	0101	101000	1101	111000	0011
001001	1110	011001	1001	101001	0100	111001	1010
001010	1111	011010	1001	101010	0110	111010	1010
001011	0010	011011	0101	101011	1001	111011	0000
001100	1011	011100	0000	101100	0010	111100	0101
001101	1101	011101	0011	101101	0001	111101	0110
001110	1000	011110	0111	101110	1011	111110	0000
001111	0001	011111	1000	101111	0111	111111	1101

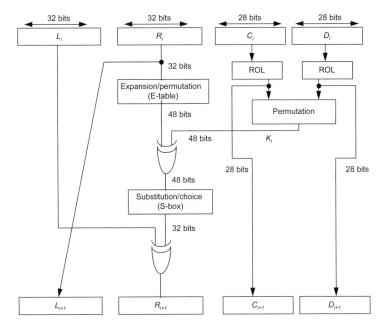

Figure E5.6 Iteration step

The design of the DES scheme was constructed behind closed doors so there are few pointers to the reasons for the construction of the encryption. One of the major weaknesses of the scheme is the usage of a 56-bit key, which means there are only 2^{56} or 7.2×10^{16} keys. Thus, as the cost of hardware reduces and the power of computers increases, the time taken to exhaustively search for a key becomes smaller each year.

In the past, there was concern about potential weaknesses in the design of the eight S-boxes. This appears to have been misplaced as no one has found any weaknesses yet. Indeed several researchers have found that swapping the S-boxes significantly reduces the security of the code.

A new variant, called Triple DES, has been proposed by Tuchman and has been standardized in financial applications. The technique uses two keys and three executions of the DES algorithm. A key, K_1, is used in the first execution, then K_2 is used and finally K_1 is used again. These two keys give an effective key length of 112 bits, that is 2×64 key bits minus 16 parity bits. The Triple DES process is illustrated in Figure E5.7.

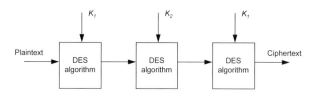

Figure E5.7 Triple DES process

E5.11.3 IDEA

IDEA (International Data Encryption Algorithm) is a private-key encryption process which is similar to DES. It was developed by Xuejia Lai and James Massey of ETH Zuria and is intended for implementation in software. IDEA operates on 64-bit blocks of plaintext; using a 128-bit key, it converts them into 64-bit blocks of ciphertext. Figure E5.8 illustrates the basic encryption process.

IDEA operates over 17 rounds with a complicated mangler function. During decryption this function does not have to be reversed and can simply be applied in the same way as during encryption (this also occurs with DES). IDEA uses a different key expansion for encryption and decryption, but every other part of the process is identical. The same keys are used in DES decryption but in the reverse order.

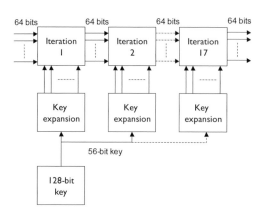

Figure E5.8 IDEA encryption

Operation

Each primitive operation in IDEA maps two 16-bit quantities into a 16-bit quantity. IDEA uses three operations, all easy to compute in software, to create a mapping. The three basic operations are:

- Exclusive-OR ($\oplus$).
- Slightly modified add (+), and ignore any bit carries.
- Slightly modified multiply ($\otimes$) and ignore any bit carries. Multiplying involves first calculating the 32-bit result, then taking the remainder when divided by $2^{16}+1$ (mod $2^{16}+1$).

Key expansions

The 128-bit key is expanded into fifty-two 16-bit keys, K_1, K_2, ... K_{52}. The key is generated differently for encryption than for decryption. Once the 52 keys are generated, the encryption and decryption processes are the same.

The 52 encryption keys are generated as follows:

- Keys 1–8: write out the 128-bit key and, starting from the left, chop off 16 bits at a time. This generates eight 16-bit keys. Thus the 128-bit key of *AAAAAAAAAAAAAAAA*... *HHHHHHHHHHHHHHHH* will generate eight keys of *AAAAAAAAAAAAAAAA*, *BBBBBBBBBBBBBBBB*, and so on.
- Keys 9–16: the next eight keys are generated at bit 25, and wrapped around to the beginning when at the end.
- Keys 17–24: the next eight keys are generated at bit 50, and wrapped around to the beginning when at the end.
- The rest of the keys are generated by offsetting by 25 bits and wrapped around to the beginning until the end.

The 64-bit (or 32-bit) per round, keys used are made up of 4 (or 2) of the encryption keys:

Key 1: $K_1K_2K_3K_4$	Key 2: K_5K_6	Key 3: $K_7K_8K_9K_{10}$
Key 4: $K_{11}K_{12}$	Key 5: $K_{13}K_{14}K_{15}K_{16}$	Key 6: $K_{17}K_{18}$
Key 7: $K_{19}K_{20}K_{21}K_{22}$	Key 8: $K_{23}K_{24}$	Key 9: $K_{25}K_{26}K_{27}K_{28}$
Key 10: $K_{29}K_{30}$	Key 11: $K_{31}K_{32}K_{33}K_{34}$	Key 12: $K_{35}K_{36}$
Key 13: $K_{37}K_{38}K_{39}K_{40}$	Key 14: $K_{41}K_{42}$	Key 15: $K_{43}K_{44}K_{45}K_{46}$
Key 16: $K_{47}K_{48}$	Key 17: $K_{49}K_{50}K_{51}K_{52}$	

Iteration

Odd rounds have a different process to even rounds. Each odd round uses a 64-bit key and even rounds use a 32-bit key.

Odd rounds are simple; the process is:

If the input is a 64-bit key of $I_1I_2I_3I_4$, where the I_1 is the most significant 16 bits, I_2 is the next most significant 16 bits, and so on. The output of the iteration is also a 64-bit key of $O_1O_2O_3O_4$ and the applied key is $K_aK_bK_cK_d$. The iteration for the odd iteration is then:

$$O_1 = I_1 \otimes K_a \qquad O_2 = I_3 + K_c$$

$$O_3 = I_2 + K_b \qquad\qquad O_4 = I_4 \otimes K_d$$

An important feature is that this operation is totally reversible: multiplying O_1 by the inverse of K_a gives I_1, and multiplying O_4 by the inverse of K_d gives I_4. Adding O_2 to the negative of K_c gives I_3, and adding O_3 to the negative of K_b gives I_2.

Even rounds are less simple, the process is as follows. Suppose the input is a 64-bit key of $I_1 I_2 I_3 I_4$, where I_1 is the most significant 16 bits, I_2 is the next most significant 16 bits, and so on. The output of the iteration is also a 64-bit key of $O_1 O_2 O_3 O_4$ and the applied key is 32 bits of $K_a K_b$. The iteration for the even round performs a mangler function of:

$$A = I_1 \otimes I_2 \qquad\qquad\qquad B = I_3 \otimes I_4$$
$$C = ((K_a \otimes A) + B)) \otimes K_b) \qquad D = (K_a \otimes A) + C$$

$$O_1 = I_1 \oplus C \qquad\qquad\qquad O_2 = I_2 \oplus C$$
$$O_3 = I_3 \oplus D \qquad\qquad\qquad O_4 = I_4 \oplus D$$

The most amazing thing about this iteration is that the inverse of the function is simply the function itself. Thus, the same keys are used for encryption and decryption (this differs from the odd round, where the key must be either the negative or the inverse of the encryption key).

IDEA security

There are no known methods that can be used to crack IDEA, apart from exhaustive search. Thus, as it has a 128-bit code it is extremely difficult to break, even with modern high-performance computers.

E5.12   Letter probability program

📄 **Program E5.7**

```c
#include <stdio.h>
#include <string.h>
#include <ctype.h>

#define   NUM_LETTERS 29

int    get_occurances(char c, char txt[]);

int    main(void)
{
char   ch, fname[BUFSIZ];
int    occ[NUM_LETTERS]={0,0,0,0,0,0,0,0,0,0,0,0,0,0,0,0,
                         0,0,0,0,0,0,0,0,0,0,0,0,0};
unsigned int    total,i;
FILE            *in;
   printf("Enter text file>>");
   gets(fname);
   if ((in=fopen(fname,"r"))==NULL)
   {
      printf("Can't find file %s\n",fname);
      return(1);
   }
   do
   {
```

```
        ch=tolower(getc(in));
        if (isalpha(ch))
        {
            (occ[ch-'a'])++;
            total++;
        }
        else if (ch=='.') { occ[NUM_LETTERS-3]++; total++; }
        else if (ch==' ') { occ[NUM_LETTERS-2]++; total++; }
        else if (ch==',') { occ[NUM_LETTERS-1]++; total++; }
    } while (!feof(in));

    fclose(in);
    puts("Char. Occur. Prob.");
    for (i=0;i<NUM_LETTERS;i++)
    {
        printf("  %c  %5d %5.4f\n",'a'+i,occ[i],(float)occ[i]/(float)total);
    }
    return(0);
}

int  get_occurances(char c, char txt[])
{
int  occ=0,i;
    for (i=0;i<strlen(txt);i++) if (c==txt[i]) occ++;
    return(occ);
}
```

E5.13   Occurrences of English letters, digrams, trigrams and words

Letters (%)		Digrams (%)		Trigrams (%)		Words (%)	
E	13.05	TH	3.16	THE	4.72	THE	6.42
T	9.02	IN	1.54	ING	1.42	OF	4.02
O	8.21	ER	1.33	AND	1.13	AND	3.15
A	7.81	RE	1.30	ION	1.00	TO	2.36
N	7.28	AN	1.08	ENT	0.98	A	2.09
I	6.77	HE	1.08	FOR	0.76	IN	1.77
R	6.64	AR	1.02	TIO	0.75	THAT	1.25
S	6.46	EN	1.02	ERE	0.69	IS	1.03
H	5.85	TI	1.02	HER	0.68	I	0.94
D	4.11	TE	0.98	ATE	0.66	IT	0.93
L	3.60	AT	0.88	VER	0.63	FOR	0.77
C	2.93	ON	0.84	TER	0.62	AS	0.76
F	2.88	HA	0.84	THA	0.62	WITH	0.76
U	2.77	OU	0.72	ATI	0.59	WAS	0.72
M	2.62	IT	0.71	HAT	0.55	HIS	0.71
P	2.15	ES	0.69	ERS	0.54	HE	0.71
Y	1.51	ST	0.68	HIS	0.52	BE	0.63
W	1.49	OR	0.68	RES	0.50	NOT	0.61
G	1.39	NT	0.67	ILL	0.47	BY	0.57
B	1.28	HI	0.66	ARE	0.46	BUT	0.56
V	1.00	EA	0.64	CON	0.45	HAVE	0.55
K	0.42	VE	0.64	NCE	0.43	YOU	0.55
X	0.30	CO	0.59	ALL	0.44	WHICH	0.53
J	0.23	DE	0.55	EVE	0.44	ARE	0.50
Q	0.14	RA	0.55	ITH	0.44	ON	0.47
Z	0.09	RO	0.55	TED	0.44	OR	0.45

E6   Public-key encryption

E6.1   Introduction

Public-key algorithms use a secret element and a public element to their code. One of the main algorithms is RSA. Compared with DES it is relatively slow but it has the advantage that users can choose their own key whenever they need one. The most commonly used public-key cryptosystems are covered in the next sections.

Private-key systems are not feasible for large-scale networks, such as the Internet or electronic commerce, as this would involve organizations creating hundreds or thousands of different private keys. Each conversation with an organization or even an individual within a company would require a separate key. Thus, public-key methods are much better suited to the Internet and, therefore, Intranets.

Figure E6.1 shows that a public-key system has two keys, a private key and a public key. The private key is secret to the user and is used to decrypt messages that have been encrypted with the user's public key. The public key is made available to anyone who wants to send an encrypted message to the person. Someone sending a message to the user will use the user's public key to encrypt the message and it can only be decrypted using the user's private key (as the private and public keys are linked in a certain way). Once the message has been encrypted not even the sender can decrypt it.

Typical public-key methods are:

- **RSA.** RSA stands for Rivest, Shamir and Adelman, and is the most commonly used public-key cryptosystem. It is patented only in the USA and is secure for key-length of over 728 bits. The algorithm relies on the fact that it is difficult to factorize large numbers. Unfortunately, it is particularly vulnerable to chosen plaintext attacks and a new timing attack (spying on keystroke time) was announced on the 7 December 1995. This attack would be able to break many existing implementations of RSA.
- **Elliptic curve.** Elliptic curve is a new kind of public-key cryptosystem. It suffers from speed problems, but this has been overcome with modern high-speed computers.
- **DSS.** DSS (digital signature standard) is related to the DSA (digital signature algorithm). This standard has been selected by the NIST and the NSA, and is part of the Capstone project. It uses 512-bit or 1024-bit key size. The design presents some lack in key-exchange capability and is slow for signature-verification.
- **Diffie-Hellman.** Diffie-Hellman is commonly used for key-exchange. The security of this cipher relies on both the key-length and the discrete algorithm problem. This problem is similar to the factorizing of large numbers. Unfortunately, the code can be cracked and the prime number generator must be carefully chosen.
- **LUC.** Peter Smith developed LUC which is a public-key cipher that uses Lucas functions instead of exponentiation. Four other algorithms have also been developed, these are: LUCDIF (a key-negotiation method); LUCELG PK (equivalent to EL Gamel encryption); LUCELG DS (equivalent to EL Gamel data signature system) and LUCDSA (equivalent to the DSS).

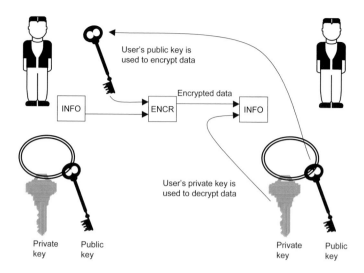

Figure E6.1   Overview of public-key systems

E6.1.1   RSA

The RSA encryption algorithm uses a one-way function, which is relatively easy to calculate in one direction, but extremely difficult to reverse the calculation. For example it is relatively simple for someone to calculate the square of a value using a pencil and paper, but it is difficult to find the square root of a value. Most of us could calculate the square of 63 as 3969, but what is the square root of 6889? The answer is 93.

Public-key encryption is the best way to secure data. With this method a user generates two electronic keys, typically with hundreds or thousands of bits. These keys are special number and relate to extremely large prime numbers (as it is difficult to factorize large prime numbers. For example, if a user had selected two prime numbers (small ones), and when I multiple them together I get the value of:

1,354,657

What was the original prime numbers [*1487 and 911*]? With public key encryption these numbers typically have thousands of bits, which gives values from 1 to 1,797,693,134,862, 315,907,729,305,190,789, ... (in total, it has 309 digits).

RSA is a public-key encryption/decryption algorithm and is much slower than IDEA and DES. The key length is variable and the block size is also variable. A typical key length is 512 bits. RSA uses a public-key and a private key, and uses the fact that large prime numbers are extremely difficult to factorize. The following steps are taken to generate the public and private keys:

1. Select two large prime numbers, p and q (each will be roughly 256 bits long). The factors p and q remain secret and n is the result of multiplying them together. Each of the prime numbers is of the order of 10^{100}.
2. Next, the public-key is chosen. To do this a number e is chosen so that e and $(p-1) \times (q-1)$ are relatively prime. Two numbers are relatively prime if they have no common factor greater than 1. The public-key is then $<e, n>$ and results in a key which is 512 bits long.

3. Next the private key for decryption, d, is computed so that:

$$d = e^{-1} \bmod [(p-1) \times (q-1)]$$

This then gives a private key of $<d, n>$. The values a and b can then be discarded (but should never be disclosed to anyone).

The encryption process to ciphertext, c, is then defined by:

$$c = m^e \bmod n$$

The message, m, is then decrypted with:

$$m = c^d \bmod n$$

It should be noted that the message block m must be less than n. When n is 512 bits then a message which is longer than 512 bits must be broken up into blocks of 512 bits.

Encryption/decryption keys

When two parties, P_1 and P_2, are communicating they encrypt data using a pair of public/private key pairs. Party P_1 encrypts its message using P_2's public-key. Then party P_2 uses its private key to decrypt this data. When party P_2 encrypts a message it sends to P_1 using P_1's public-key and P_1 decrypts this using its private key. Notice that party P_1 cannot decrypt the message that it has sent to P_2 as only P_2 has the required private key.

A great advantage of RSA is that the key has a variable number of bits. It is likely that, in the coming few years, powerful computer systems will determine all the factors to 512-bit values. Luckily the RSA key has a variable size and can easily be changed. Many users are choosing keys with 1024 bits.

Simple RSA example

Initially PARTY1 picks two prime numbers. For example:

$$p = 11 \text{ and } q = 3$$

Next, the n value is calculated. Thus:

$$n = p \times q = 11 \times 3 = 33$$

Next *PHI* is calculated by:

$$PHI = (p-1)(q-1) = 20$$

The factors of PHI are 1, 2, 4, 5, 10 and 20. Next the public exponent e is generated so that the greatest common divisor of e and *PHI* is 1 (e is relatively prime with PHI). Thus, the smallest value for e is:

$$e = 3$$

The factors of e are 1 and 3, thus 1 is the highest common factor of them. Thus n (33) and the e (3) values are the public keys. The private key (d) is the inverse of e modulo *PHI*.

$$d = e^{-1} \bmod [(a-1) \times (b-1)]$$

This can be calculated by using extended Euclidian algorithm, to give the private key, d of 7.

Thus $n = 33$, $e = 3$ and $d = 7$.

The PARTY2 can be given the public keys of e and n, so that PARTY2 can encrypt the message with them. PARTY1, using d and n can then decrypt the encrypted message.

For example, if the message value to decrypt is 4, then:

$$c = m^e \bmod n = 4^3 \bmod 33 = 31$$

Therefore, the encrypted message (c) is 31.

The encrypted message (c) is then decrypted by PARTY1 with:

$$m = c^d \bmod n = 31^7 \bmod 33 = 4$$

which is equal to the message value.

Simple RSA program

An example program which has a limited range of prime numbers is given next.

```
#include     <stdio.h>
#include     <math.h>

#define   TRUE   1
#define   FALSE  0

void  get_prime( long *val);
long  getE( long PHI);
long  get_common_denom( long e, long PHI);
long  getD( long e,   long PHI);
long  decrypt(long c,long n,  long d);

int    main(void)
{
long   a,b,n,e,PHI,d,m,c;

    get_prime(&a);
    get_prime(&b);
    n=a*b;
    PHI=(a-1)*(b-1);
    e=getE(PHI);

    d= getD(e,PHI);
    printf("Enter input value >> "); scanf("%ld",&m);

    printf("a=%ld b=%ld n=%ld PHI=%ld\n",a,b,n,PHI);
```

```c
    c=(long)pow(m,e) % n; /* note, this may overflow with large numbers */
                          /* when e is relatively large */

    printf("e=%ld d=%ld c=%ld\n",e,d,c);

    m=decrypt(c,n,d); /* this function required as c to      */
                      /*the power of d causes an overflow    */
    printf("Message is %ld ",m);
    return(0);
}

long  decrypt(long c,long n, long d)
{
long  i,g,f;

if (d%2==0) g=1; else g=c;

    for (i=1;i<=d/2;i++)
    {
        f=c*c % n;
        g=f*g % n;
    }
 return(g);
}

long getD( long e,  long PHI)
{
long u[3]={1,0,PHI};
long v[3]={0,1,e};
long q,temp1,temp2,temp3;

    while (v[2]!=0)
    {
        q=floor(u[2]/v[2]);
        temp1=u[0]-q*v[0];
        temp2=u[1]-q*v[1];
        temp3=u[2]-q*v[2];
        u[0]=v[0];
        u[1]=v[1];
        u[2]=v[2];
        v[0]=temp1;
        v[1]=temp2;
        v[2]=temp3;
    }
    if (u[1]<0) return(u[1]+PHI);
    else return(u[1]);
}

long  getE( long PHI)
{
 long great=0, e=2;

    while (great!=1)
    {
        e=e+1;
        great = get_common_denom(e,PHI);
    }
    return(e);
}

long get_common_denom(long e, long PHI)
{
long great,temp,a;
```

```
   if (e >PHI)
   {
      while (e % PHI != 0)
      {
         temp= e % PHI;
         e =PHI;
         PHI = temp;
      }
      great = PHI;
   } else
   {
      while (PHI % e != 0)
      {
         a = PHI % e;
         PHI = e;
         e = a;
      }
      great = e;
   }
   return(great);
}

void  get_prime( long *val)
{
#define NO_PRIMES 11
long  primes[NO_PRIMES]={3,5,7,11,13,17,19,23,29,31,37};
long  prime,i;
   do
   {
      prime=FALSE;
      printf("Enter a prime number >> ");
      scanf("%ld",val);
      for (i=0;i<NO_PRIMES;i++)
         if (*val==primes[i]) prime=TRUE;
   } while (prime==FALSE);
}
```

A sample run of the program is given next.

```
Enter a prime number >> 11
Enter a prime number >> 3
Enter input value >> 4
a=11 b=3 n=33 PHI=20
e=3 d=7 c=31
Message is 4
```

E6.1.2 PGP

PGP (Pretty Good Privacy) uses the RSA algorithm with a 128-bit key. It was developed by Phil Zimmermann and gives encryption, authentication, digital signatures and compression. Its source code is freely available over the Internet and its usage is also free of charge, but it has encountered two main problems:

- The source code is freely available on the Internet causing the US government to claim that it violates laws which relate to the export of munitions. Current versions have since been produced outside of the US to overcome this problem.
- It uses algorithms which have patents, such as RSA, IDEA and MD5.

Figure E6.2 shows the basic encryption process. The steps taken are:

A. Sender hashes the information using the MD5 algorithm.
B. Hashed message is then encrypted using RSA with the sender's private key (this is used to authenticate the sender as the sender's public key will be used to decrypt this part of the message).
C. Encrypted message is then concatenated with the original message.
D. Message is compressed using LZ compression.
E. A 128-bit IDEA key (K_M) is generated by some random input, such as the content of the message and the typing speed.
F. K_M is then used with the IDEA encryption. K_M is also encrypted with the receiver's public key.
G. Output from IDEA encryption and the encrypted K_M key are concatenated together.
H. Output is encoded as ASCII characters using Base-64 (Section F1.6.4 on Electronic Mail).

To decrypt the message the receiver goes through the following steps:

A. Receiver reverses the Base-64 conversion.
B. The receiver decrypts the K_M key using its own private RSA key.
C. The K_M key is then used with the IDEA algorithm to decode the message.
D. The message is then decompressed using an UNZIP program.
E. The two fragments produced after decompression will be the plaintext message and an MD5/RSA encrypted message. The plaintext message is the original message, whereas the MD5/RSA encrypted message can be used to authenticate the sender. This is done by applying the sender's public key to the decompressed encrypted part of the message. This should produce the original plaintext message.

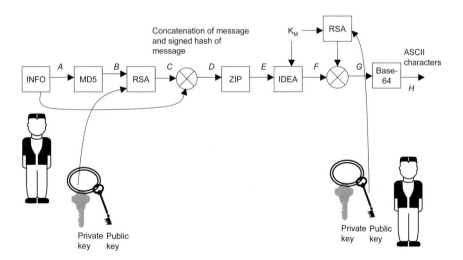

Figure E6.2 PGP encryption

PGP allows for three main RSA key sizes. There are:

- 384 bits. This is intended for the casual user and can be decoded by serious crackers.
- 512 bits. This is intended for the commercial user and can only be decoded by organizations with a large budget and extensive computing facilities.
- 1024 bits. This is intended for military uses and, at present, cannot be cracked by anyone. This is the recommended key size for most users of reasonably powerful computers (386/486/Pentium/*etc*). In the future, a 2048-bit code may be used.

E6.1.3   Example PGP encryption

The Pretty Good Privacy (PGP) program developed by Philip Zimmermann is widely available over the WWW. It runs as a stand-alone application, and uses various options to use the package. Table E6.1 outlines some of the options.

To produce output in ASCII for e-mail or to publish over the Internet, the –a option is used with other options. Table E6.2 shows the key management functions.

Table E6.1   PGP options

Option	Description
pgp -e textfile her_userid [other userids]	Encrypts a plaintext file with the recipient's public key. In this case, it produces a file named textfile.pgp.
pgp -s textfile [-u your_userid]	Sign a plaintext file with a secret key. In this case, it produces a file named textfile.pgp.
pgp -es textfile her_userid [other userids] [-u your_userid]	Signs a plaintext file with the sender's secret key, and then encrypt it with recipient's public key. In this case, it produces a file named textfile.pgp.
pgp -c textfile	Encrypt with conventional encryption only.
pgp ciphertextfile [-o plaintextfile]	Decrypt or check a signature for a ciphertext (.pgp) file.

Table E6.2   PGP key management options

Option	Description
pgp –kg	Generate a unique public and private key.
pgp –ka keyfile [keyring]	Adds key file's contents to the user's public or secret key ring.
pgp –kr userid [keyring]	Removes a key or a user ID from the user's public or secret key ring.
pgp –ke your_userid [keyring]	Edit user ID or pass phrase.
pgp –kx userid keyfile [keyring]	Extract a key from the public or secret key ring.
pgp –kv[v] [userid] [keyring]	View the contents of the public-key ring.
pgp –kc [userid] [keyring]	Check signatures on the public-key ring.
pgp –ks her_userid [–u your_userid] [keyring]	Sign someone else's public-key on your public-key ring.
pgp –krs userid [keyring]	Remove selected signatures from a userid on a keyring.

RSA Key Generation

Both the public and the private keys are generated with:

```
pgp -kg
```

Initially, the user is asked about the key sizes. The larger the key the more secure it is. A 1024 bit key is very secure.

```
C:\pgp> pgp -kg
Pretty Good Privacy(tm) 2.6.3i - Public-key encryption for the masses.
(c) 1990-96 Philip Zimmermann, Phil's Pretty Good Software. 1996-01-18
International version - not for use in the USA. Does not use RSAREF.
Current time: 1998/12/29 23:13 GMT
Pick your RSA key size:
    1)    512 bits- Low commercial grade, fast but less secure
    2)    768 bits- High commercial grade, medium speed, good security
    3)   1024 bits- "Military" grade, slow, highest security
Choose 1, 2, or 3, or enter desired number of bits: 3
Generating an RSA key with a 1024-bit modulus.
```

Next, the program asks for a user ID, which is normally the user's name and his/her password. This ID helps other users to find the required public key.

```
You need a user ID for your public key.  The desired form for this
user ID is your name, followed by your E-mail address enclosed in
<angle brackets>, if you have an E-mail address.
For example:  John Q. Smith <12345.6789@compuserve.com>
Enter a user ID for your public key:
Fred Bloggs <fred_b@myserver.com>
```

Next PGP asks for a pass phrase, which is used to protect the private key if another person gets hold of it. No person can use the secret key file, unless they know the pass phrase. Thus, the pass phase is like a password but is typically much longer. The phase is also required when the user is encrypting a message with his/her private key.

```
You need a pass phrase to protect your RSA secret key.
Your pass phrase can be any sentence or phrase and may have many
words, spaces, punctuation, or any other printable characters.
Enter pass phrase: fred bloggs
Enter same pass phrase again: fred bloggs
Note that key generation is a lengthy process.
```

The public and private keys are randomly derived by measuring the intervals between keystrokes. For this, the software asks for the user to type a number of keys.

```
We need to generate 384 random bits.  This is done by measuring the
time intervals between your keystrokes.  Please enter some random text
on your keyboard until you hear the beep:

We need to generate 384 random bits.  This is done by measuring the
time intervals between your keystrokes.  Please enter some random text
on your keyboard until you hear the beep:
<keyboard typing>
```

```
    0 * -Enough, thank you.
..................................****
..................................****
Pass phrase is good.  Just a moment....
Key signature certificate added.
Key generation completed.
```

This has successfully generated the public and private keys. The public-key is placed on the public key ring (PUBRING.PGP) and the private key is place on the user's secret key ring (SECRING.PGP).

```
C:\pgp> dir *.pgp
SECRING   PGP           518   12-29-98 11:20p secring.pgp
PUBRING   PGP           340   12-29-98 11:20p pubring.pgp
```

The –kx option can be used to extract the new public key from the public-key ring and place it in a separate public key file, which can be sent to people who want to send an encrypted message to the user.

```
C:\pgp> pgp -kx fred_b
Extracting from key ring: 'pubring.pgp', userid "fred_b".
Key for user ID: Fred Bloggs <fred_b@myserver.com>

1024-bit key, key ID CD5AE745, created 1998/12/29
Extract the above key into which file? mykey
Key extracted to file 'mykey.pgp'.
```

The public-key file (`mykey.pgp`) can be sent to other users, and can be added to their public key rings. Care must be taken never to send anyone a private key, but even if it is sent then it is still protected by the pass phase.

Often a user wants to publish their public key on their WWW page or transmit it by e-mail. Thus, it requires to be converted into an ASCII format. For this the –kxa option can be used, such as:

```
C:\pgp> pgp -kxa fred_b
Extracting from key ring: 'pubring.pgp', userid "fred_b".
Key for user ID: Fred Bloggs <fred_b@myserver.com>
1024-bit key, key ID CD5AE745, created 1998/12/29

Extract the above key into which file? mykey
Transport armor file: mykey.asc
Key extracted to file 'mykey.asc'.

Extract the above key into which file? mykey
Transport armor file: mykey.asc
Key extracted to file 'mykey.asc'.
```

The file `mykey.asc` now contains an ASCII form of the key, such as:

```
Type Bits/KeyID     Date        User ID
pub  1024/CD5AE745 1998/12/29 Fred Bloggs <fred_b@myserver.com>
-----BEGIN PGP PUBLIC KEY BLOCK-----
Version: 2.6.3i
```

```
mQCNAzaJY84AAAEEAK0nvnuYcwGEaNdeqcDGXD6IrMFwX3iKtdGkZgyPyiENLb+C
bGX7P2zSG0z1d8c4f5OKYR/RgxzN4ILsAKthGaweGD0FJRgeIvn6FHJxEzmdBWIh
ME/8h2HZfegSXta8hFAMc8o9ASamolk5KBL0YWfsQlDNbR+dMJpPqQ7NWudFAAUT
tCFGcmVkIEJsb2dncyA8ZnJlZF9iQG15c2VydmVyLmNvbT6JAJUDBRA2iWPOmk+p
Ds1a50UBAfkoA/4gO5DllYko4DfjPnq4ItDtN55SgoE3upPWL52R5RQZF1BoJEF6
eLT/kejD5b7gli/yP1S456bh/k8ifi9RwSPUFN/zFUsVVYrSjZKD3kzClV1/QgTy
YmlDHHHgou6rYFXk7mGEtWc4g4D1rzds+ppc/UjN8uNp5KQUg1FsVatvPA==
=X5Xx
-----END PGP PUBLIC KEY BLOCK-----
```

Now, someone's public-key can be added to Fred's public-key ring. In this case, Fred Bloggs wants to send a message to Bert Smith. Bert's public key, in an ASCII form, is:

```
Type Bits/KeyID      Date        User ID
pub  1024/770CA60D 1998/12/30 Bert Smith <Bert_s.otherserver.com>
-----BEGIN PGP PUBLIC KEY BLOCK-----
Version: 2.6.3i
mQCNAzaKE5AAAAEEAN+5td9acGlPcTKp5J42UpwbDqz6mHOaxcO1lp6CoPE3+AXT
jfREEQ+TC0ZxMP6cCcwtEMnjVqu2M7F6li3v/AVqQIRZZkFsEOZ+8hlseHB0FR8Y
f8FDpmgld6wNpp8ocOyVul/sBQl549u0C/KnVQ6LtXo7UlsBtnbua9J3DKYNAAUR
tCNCZXJ0IFNtaXRoIDxCZXJ0X3Mub3RoZXJzZXJ2ZXIuY29tPokAlQMFEDaKE5B2
7mvSdwymDQEB2xkEANLMEDncVrFjR71abUIWHqquEFK+sqnOHPbHyIBni18x03UM
jeQJM1WA9/uIPqzeABJdD6anX4oK3yiByQjI5CT5+OdmU0y4e2+k1ab5mxxUWs7S
Tib3K5LLvPGxsOInOdunjFKaBLkrfU/L+zid3iW9FV6Zy8P07yDL2SmobRbh
=6rTj
-----END PGP PUBLIC KEY BLOCK-----
```

Fred can add Bert's key onto his public-key ring with the –ka option:

```
C:\pgp> pgp -ka bert.pgp

Looking for new keys...
pub  1024/770CA60D 1998/12/30  Bert Smith <Bert_s.otherserver.com>

Checking signatures...
pub  1024/770CA60D 1998/12/30 Bert Smith <Bert_s.otherserver.com>
sig!      770CA60D 1998/12/30  Bert Smith <Bert_s.otherserver.com>

Keyfile contains:
  1 new key(s)

One or more of the new keys are not fully certified.
Do you want to certify any of these keys yourself (y/N)?
```

Bert's key has been added to Fred's public-key ring. This ring can be listed with the –kv, as given next:

```
C:\pgp> pgp -kv

Key ring: 'pubring.pgp'
Type Bits/KeyID      Date        User ID
pub  1024/770CA60D 1998/12/30 Bert Smith <Bert_s.otherserver.com>
pub  1024/CD5AE745 1998/12/29 Fred Bloggs <fred_b@myserver.com>
2 matching keys found.
```

Next, a message can be sent to Bert, using his public-key.

```
C:\pgp>edit message.txt
```
Bert,

This is a secret message. Please
delete it after you have read it!

Fred.

```
C:\pgp>pgp -e message.txt

Recipients' public key(s) will be used to encrypt.
A user ID is required to select the recipient's public key.
Enter the recipient's user ID: bert smith
Key for user ID: Bert Smith <Bert_s.otherserver.com>
1024-bit key, key ID 770CA60D, created 1998/12/30

WARNING:  Because this public key is not certified with a trusted
signature, it is not known with high confidence that this public key
actually belongs to: "Bert Smith <Bert_s.otherserver.com>".

Are you sure you want to use this public key (y/N)? y
.
Ciphertext file: message.pgp
```

If the message needs to be transmitted by electronic mail or via a WWW page, it can be converted into text format with the –ea option, as given next:

```
C:\pgp>pgp -ea message.txt

Recipients' public key(s) will be used to encrypt.
A user ID is required to select the recipient's public key.
Enter the recipient's user ID: bert smith

Key for user ID: Bert Smith <Bert_s.otherserver.com>
1024-bit key, key ID 770CA60D, created 1998/12/30

WARNING:  Because this public key is not certified with a trusted
signature, it is not known with high confidence that this public key
actually belongs to: "Bert Smith <Bert_s.otherserver.com>".
But you previously approved using this public key anyway.
.
Transport armor file: message.asc
```

The `message.asc` file is now in a form which can be transmitted in ASCII characters. In this case, it is:

```
-----BEGIN PGP MESSAGE-----
Version: 2.6.3i

hIwDdu5r0ncMpg0BBAC7jOUx74vLb701lOCO0/5Fkc6pDJinqpA7isJH+JYbFkDj
wSv6vF/jAEonEPL8RVtqWncNDwjjwwV9OVPEZeaZ0qgZTWdbdSUilfqxZsaBo8Uz
dmmbzxd7CDTpnSYEyFWosPyzdxJqlsICig79Loh7l1BdJXEhKnMy+1VMieNYtKYA
AABrB8LTMj2lkk9t6JfS2yOc1t9EfpVMLX+rxtPZ+Tq1aCOwfid4E77FyiKN260N
APzF8J6elXhBgNM3zesA8fR8KdEnrI2BYC2XsBzTxOiKnpqoLMwWl0A7TTyhv24L
1PhwFi/YQ2SPhemdpqY=
=ooNT
-----END PGP MESSAGE-----
```

Bert can now simply decrypt the received message.

```
C:\pgp\bert> pgp message.pgp

File is encrypted.  Secret key is required to read it.
Key for user ID: Bert Smith <Bert_s.otherserver.com>
1024-bit key, key ID 770CA60D, created 1998/12/30

You need a pass phrase to unlock your RSA secret key.
Enter pass phrase: Bert Smith
Pass phrase is good.  Just a moment......
Plaintext filename: message
```

Or Bert can convert the ASCII form into a binary format with the –da option, and decrypt the message as before.

```
C:\pgp\bert> pgp -da message.asc
Stripped transport armor from 'message.asc', producing 'message.pgp'.
```

E6.2   Authentication

It is obviously important to encrypt a transmitted message, but how can it be proved that the user who originally encrypted the message sent the message. This is achieved with message authentication. The two users who are communicating are sometimes known as the principals. It should be assumed that an intruder (hacker) could intercept and listen to messages at any part of the communication, whether it is the initial communication between the two parties and their encryption keys or when the encrypted messages are sent. The intruder could thus playback any communications between the parties and pretend to be the other.

E6.2.1   Shared secret-key authentication

With this approach a secret key, K_{12} (between Fred and Bert) is used by both users. This would be transmitted through a secure channel, such as a telephone call, personal contact, mail message, and so on. The conversation will then be:

- The initiator (Fred) sends a challenge to the responder (Bert) which is a random number.
- The responder transmits it back using a special algorithm and the secret key. If the initiator receives back the correctly encrypted value then it knows that the responder is allowed to communicate with the user.

The random number should be large enough so that it is not possible for an intruder to listen to the communication and repeat it. There is little chance of the same 128-bit random number occurring within days, months or even years.

This method has validated Bert to Fred, but not Fred to Bert. Thus, Bert needs to know that the person receiving his communications is Fred. Thus, Bert initiates the same procedure as before, sending a random number to Fred, who then encrypts it and sends it back. After Bert has successfully received this, encrypted communications can begin.

E6.2.2 Diffie-Hellman key exchange

In the previous section, a private key was passed over a secure line. The Diffie-Hellman method allows for keys to be passed electronically. For this, Fred and Bert pick two large prime numbers:

a = Prime Number 1
b = Prime Number 2

where:

$(a–1)/2$ is also prime. The values of a and b are public keys. Next, Fred picks a private key (c) and Bert picks a private key (d). Fred sends the values of:

$(a, b, b^c \bmod a)$

Bert then responds by sending:

$(b^d \bmod a)$

For example:

a = 43 (first prime number), b = 7 (second prime number), c = 9 (Fred's private key), d = 8 (Bert's private key). Note, that the value of a (43) would not be used as $(a–1)/2$ is not prime (21).
   Thus, the values sent by Fred will be:

(43, 7, 42)

The last value is 42 as 7^9 is 40,353,607, and 40,353,607 mod 43, is 42. Bert will respond back with:

(6)

as 7^8 is 5,764,801, and 5,764,801 mod 43 is 6.
   Next Fred and Bert will calculate:

$b^{cd} \bmod a$

and both use this as their secret key. Figure E6.3 shows an example of the interchange. It is difficult for an intruder to determine the values of c and d, when the values of a, b, c and d are large.
   Unfortunately, this method suffers from the man-in-the-middle attack, where the intruder incepts the communications between Fred and Bert. Figure E6.4 shows an interceptor (Bob) who has chosen a private key of e. Thus, Fred thinks he is talking to Bert, and vice-versa, but Bob is acting as the man-in-the-middle. Bob then uses two different keys when talking with Fred and Bert.

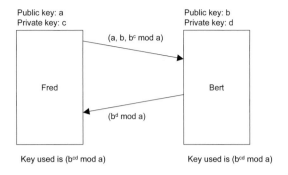

Figure E6.3   Diffie-Hellman key exchange

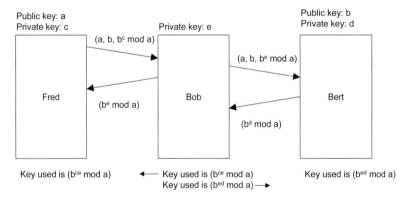

Figure E6.4   Man-in-the-middle attack

E6.2.3   Key distribution center

The Diffie-Hellman method suffers from the man-in-the-middle attack; it also requires a separate key for each communication channel. A KDC (key distribution center) overcomes these problems with a single key and a secure channel for authentication. In a KDC, the authentication and session keys are managed through the KDC. One method is the wide-mouth protocol, which does the following:

- Fred selects a session key (K_{SESS}).
- Fred sends an encrypted message which contains the session key. The message is encrypted with K_{KDC1}, which is the key that Fred uses to pass messages to and from the KDC.
- The KDC decrypts this encrypted message using the K_{KDC1} key. It also extracts the session key (K_{SESS}). This session key is added to the encrypted message and then encrypted with K_{KDC2}, which is the key that Bert uses to pass messages to and from the KDC.

This method is relatively secure as there is a separate key used between the transmissions of Fred and the KDC, and Bert and the KDC. These keys are secret to Fred and the KDC, and between Bert and the KDC. The drawback with the method is that if the intruder determines secret key used for Fred to communicate with the KDC then it is possible to trick the KDC that it is communicating with Fred. As the key is unchanging, the theft of a key may take some time to discover and the possible damage widespread. The intruder can simply choose a new session key each time there is a new session.

E6.2.4 Digital signatures

Digital signatures provide a way of validating an electronic document, in the same way as a hand-written signature does on a document. It must provide:

- Authentication of the sender. This is important as the recipient can verify the sender of the message.
- Authentication of the contents of the message. This is important, as the recipient knows that a third party has not modified the original contents of the message. Normally, this is also time-stamped.
- Authentication that the contents have not been changed by the recipient. This is important in legal cases where the recipient can prove that the message was as the original.

Secret-key signatures

The secret-key signature involves a user selecting a secret key which is passed to a central authority, who keeps the key private. When Fred wants to communicate with Bert, he passes the plaintext to the central authority and encrypts it with a secret key and the time-stamp. The central authority then passes an encrypted message to Bert using the required secret key. A time-stamp is added to the message that is sent to Bert. This provides for a legal verification of the time the message was sent, and also stops intruders from replaying a transmitted message. The main problem with this method is that the central authority (typically, banks, government departmental or legal professionals) must be trustworthy and reliable. They can also read all of the transmitted messages.

Message digests

Public- and private-key signatures provide for both authentication and secrecy, but in many cases, all that is required is that a text message is sent with the required authentication. A method of producing authentication is a message digest, which generates a unique message digest for every message. The most common form of message digest is MD5 (RFC1321, R.Rivest). It is designed to be relatively fast to compute and does not require any large substitution tables. In summary, its operation is:

- It takes as input a message of arbitrary length.
- Produces a 128-bit 'fingerprint' (or message digest) of the input.
- It is not possible to produce two messages which have the same message digest, or to produce any message from a prespecified target message digest.

MD5 algorithm

Initially, the message with b bits is arranged as follows:

$$m_0\, m_1\, m_2\, m_3\, m_4\, m_5\, m_6\, ...\, m_{b-1}$$

Next five steps are performed:

- Adding padding bits. The message is padded so that its length is 64 bits less than being a multiple of 512 bits. For example, if the message is 900 bits long, then an extra 60 bits will be added so that it is 64 bits short of 1024 bits. The padded bits are a single '1' bit followed by '0' bits. At least one bit must be added and, at the most, 512 bits are added.

- Append Length. A 64-bit representation of b (the length of the message before the padding bits were added) is appended to the result of the previous step. The resulting message will thus be a multiple of 512 bits, or:

  $$m_0\, m_1\, m_2\, m_3\, m_4\, m_5\, m_6\, \dots\, m_{n-1}$$

  where n is a multiple of 512.

- MD Buffer initialized. A four-word buffer (A, B, C, D) is used to compute the message digest. These are initialized to the following hexadecimal values (low-order bytes first):

  A: 01 23 45 67h   (0000 0001 0010 ... 0111) B: 89 ab cd efh
  C: fe dc ba 98h   (1111 1110 1101 ... 1000) D: 76 54 32 10h

- Message processed in 16-word blocks. Next four auxiliary functions are defined which operate on three 32-bit words and produce a single 32-bit word. These are:

$$F(x, y, z) = X.Y + \overline{X}.Z$$
$$G(x, y, z) = X.Z + Y.\overline{Z}$$
$$H(x, y, z) = X \oplus Y \oplus Z$$
$$I(x, y, z) = Y \oplus \left(X + \overline{Z}\right)$$

This step also involves a 64-element table T[1 ... 64] which is made of a function, where T[i] is equal to the integer part of 4 294 967 296 times abs(sin(i)), where i is in radians.

The algorithm is as follows:

```
/* Process each 16-word block. */
For i = 0 to N/16-1 do
      /* Copy block i into X. */
      For j = 0 to 15 do
            Set X[j] to M[i*16+j].
      end /* of loop on j */

      /* Save A as AA, B as BB, C as CC, and D as DD. */
      AA = A    BB = B
      CC = C    DD = D

      /* Round 1. */
      /* Let [abcd k s i] denote the operation  a = b + ((a + F(b,c,d) + X[k] + T[i]) <<< s). */
      /* Do the following 16 operations. */
      [ABCD 0 7 1] [DABC 1 12 2] [CDAB 2 17 3] [BCDA 3 22 4]
```

[ABCD 4 7 5] [DABC 5 12 6] [CDAB 6 17 7] [BCDA 7 22 8]
[ABCD 8 7 9] [DABC 9 12 10] [CDAB 10 17 11] [BCDA 11 22 12]
[ABCD 12 7 13] [DABC 13 12 14] [CDAB 14 17 15] [BCDA 15 22 16]

/* Round 2. */
/* Let [abcd k s i] denote the operation   a = b + ((a + G(b,c,d) + X[k] + T[i]) <<< s). */

/* Do the following 16 operations. */
[ABCD 1 5 17] [DABC 6 9 18] [CDAB 11 14 19] [BCDA 0 20 20]
[ABCD 5 5 21] [DABC 10 9 22] [CDAB 15 14 23] [BCDA 4 20 24]
[ABCD 9 5 25] [DABC 14 9 26] [CDAB 3 14 27] [BCDA 8 20 28]
[ABCD 13 5 29] [DABC 2 9 30] [CDAB 7 14 31] [BCDA 12 20 32]

/* Round 3. */
/* Let [abcd k s t] denote the operation   a = b + ((a + H(b,c,d) + X[k] + T[i]) <<< s). */

/* Do the following 16 operations. */
[ABCD 5 4 33] [DABC 8 11 34] [CDAB 11 16 35] [BCDA 14 23 36]
[ABCD 1 4 37] [DABC 4 11 38] [CDAB 7 16 39] [BCDA 10 23 40]
[ABCD 13 4 41] [DABC 0 11 42] [CDAB 3 16 43] [BCDA 6 23 44]
[ABCD 9 4 45] [DABC 12 11 46] [CDAB 15 16 47] [BCDA 2 23 48]

/* Round 4. */
/* Let [abcd k s t] denote the operation   a = b + ((a + I(b,c,d) + X[k] + T[i]) <<< s). */
/* Do the following 16 operations. */
[ABCD 0 6 49] [DABC 7 10 50] [CDAB 14 15 51] [BCDA 5 21 52]
[ABCD 12 6 53] [DABC 3 10 54] [CDAB 10 15 55] [BCDA 1 21 56]
[ABCD 8 6 57] [DABC 15 10 58] [CDAB 6 15 59] [BCDA 13 21 60]
[ABCD 4 6 61] [DABC 11 10 62] [CDAB 2 15 63] [BCDA 9 21 64]

/* Then perform the following additions */

A = A + AA   B = B + BB   C = C + CC   D = D + DD
end

Note that the <<< symbol represents the rotate left operation, where the bits are rotated to the left.

- Output. The message digest is produced from A, B, C and D, where A is the low-order byte and D the high-order byte.

Standard test results give the following message digests:

Message	Message digest
""	d41d8cd98f00b204e9800998ecf8427e
"a"	0cc175b9c0f1b6a831c399e269772661
"abc"	900150983cd24fb0d6963f7d28e17f72

"abcdefghijklmnopqrstuvwxyz"	`f96b697d7cb7938d525a2f31aaf161d0`
"ABCDEFGHIJKLMNOPQRSTUVWX YZabcdefghijklmnopqrstuvwxyz012345 6789"	`c3fcd3d76192e4007dfb496cca67e13b`
"1234567890123456789012345678901234567890 1234567890123456789012345678901234567890"	`57edf4a22be3c955ac49da2e2107b67a`

E6.2.5 PGP authentication

As well as encryption, PGP provides for a digital signature. This public-key method is an excellent way of authentication as it does not require the exchange of keys over a secure channel. In PGP, the sender's own private key is used to encrypt the message, thus signing it. This digital signature is then checked by the recipient by using the sender's public key to decrypt it. As previously mentioned, the advantages are:

- Authenticates the sender.
- Authentication of the contents of the message.
- Authentication that the message has not been modified by the recipient or any third party.
- Sender cannot undo a signature, once applied (there are no erasers with digital signatures).
- Message integrity.
- Allows signatures to be stored separately from messages, without actually revealing the contents of the message.

Thus, encryption is achieved by encrypting the message with the recipient's public key, and authentication by signing the message with the sender's private key. To make a digital signature, PGP encrypts using the secret key. It does not encrypt the whole message, only a message digest, which is a 128-bit extract of the message (a bit like a checksum). The MD5 algorithm is used for this, and provides a fingerprint that is extremely difficult to forge.

The MD5 algorithm is a standard algorithm and can be easily replicated, thus the senders private key is used to provide authentication, as the sender encrypts the message digest with his secret key. The steps are:

- Sender uses the message to determine the message digest.
- Sender's secret key encrypts the message digest and an electronic timestamp, forming a digital signature, or signature certificate.
- Sender sends the digital signature along with the message.
- Recipient reads the message and the digital signature. The message is decrypted by the receiver using the recipient's private key.
- Recipient recovers the original message digest from the digital signature by decrypting it with the sender's public key.
- Recipient calculates a new message digest from the message, and then checks this against the recovered message digest from the received information. If they are the same then it authenticates the message and the sender.

A hacker, if they tried to modify the message in any way, would have to do the following:

- Recreate another identical message digest (which is not really possible)

- Produce an altered message which produces an identical message digest (which again is not really possible).
- Create a new message with a different message digest (which is not really possible without knowing the sender's private key).

With the PGP program, the –sa option can be used to generate the digital signature. For example:

```
C:\pgp\bert> pgp -sa message.txt
A secret key is required to make a signature.
You specified no user ID to select your secret key,
so the default user ID and key will be the most recently
added key on your secret keyring.

You need a pass phrase to unlock your RSA secret key. bert smith
Key for user ID: Bert Smith <Bert_s.otherserver.com>
1024-bit key, key ID 770CA60D, created 1998/12/30

Enter pass phrase: Pass phrase is good.  Just a moment....
Output file 'message.asc' already exists.  Overwrite (y/N)? y

Transport armor file: message.asc
```

The encrypted digital signature, in this case, is:

```
-----BEGIN PGP MESSAGE-----
Version: 2.6.3i

owHrZJjKzMpg1jVtTdm77EvlPMt4GRn/KDP/Yr7JWPN8/Zani1pkBBmWznvTsdl4
g1yN9+WoRz+WqFb9L3vC1jElv3xZ1v45jLdMCuTqdz5ZyKe5WFV06/yfTbu7ZZ78
nP93yhIb4XW8qSu2sdrHfbhjr9TNY+Om/6FzveeigymfyzZvcOT/l2PKky3iqCGi
WC2+4jnjbLUXKVNfWc7NfPbr4ZqMJO7c1OLixPRUvZKKEgYgcEotKtHh5eLlCsnI
LFYAokSF4tTkotQSBZhChYCc1MTiVF6ulNSc1JJUhcwShcS0ktQihcr8UoWMxLJU
haLUxBSgsCLIGLei1BQ9Xi4A
=iGfx
-----END PGP MESSAGE-----
```

The message and the digital signature can be produced using the –sea option. In this case, it produces the file:

```
-----BEGIN PGP MESSAGE-----
Version: 2.6.3i

hIwDdu5r0ncMpg0BBACF3bP4h0vt9ajaD3Vgf4aSUds03jfB9xXzZY9YjzjHyFBX
dO8IzMyDB6KdeX2cJk1pdPWhHi0cRQ2ddxoEBdS38XCJtjuTf0DYkwid+0dClt69
ntkwy0Lc4Y6QoDk9BHnVtDTkUu8J12KJrkoRx4DikumVbGB+CCAfCTOcr1U2vqYA
AAEMsURzRPLqwXDToFkzXA11EAfQ5ECJPFbsejBJhkbZAZ0aswVMYgX52wEnWxcI
MRmz0IdRLDtXtZ9SJvFzWMpPzVygOmOMDKhiDuEOI89D/HOomMlBaRH41Zx6xqf4
8LuhtJSwNdgHE07jiGAmvKkxRobUeOmZoEqs6BrU8hveJwGE4n0OVwWIzXbqH2BL
GTD8nAMFgqbh1LGfc3SV6bIst7z13HdFMSg1ZonbQj39i/ZTv8qzHY5rqN7uBPJb
eHU02wjCo3Dyc1atohPApcNEYmgkzaSQYkKeL9Zo3JRlk9xGbjZdtSk6+fxYU2WF
BQrW/AQheT5lM68uDLe7OJ2+ny9m4nNEnwwDGqNaWg==
=f4f8
-----END PGP MESSAGE-----
```

The file can then be validated and decrypted as follows:

```
C:\pgp> pgp message
File has signature.  Public key is required to check signature.
.
Good signature from user "Bert Smith <Bert_s.otherserver.com>".
Signature made 1998/12/30 21:08 GMT using 1024-bit key, key ID 770CA60D

WARNING:  Because this public key is not certified with a trusted
signature, it is not known with high confidence that this public key
actually belongs to: "Bert Smith <Bert_s.otherserver.com>".
But you previously approved using this public key anyway.
Plaintext filename: message
```

E6.3   Internet security

As more information is stored on the Internet, and the amount of secure information, such as credit transfers and database transfers, increases, the need for a secure transmission mechanism also increases. The Internet has outgrown its founding protocol, HTTP. There thus has to be increased security in:

- Data encryption of WWW pages. This provides for secret information to be encrypted with a secret key.
- Message integrity. This provides a method of validating that the transmitted message is valid and has not been changed, either in transmission or in storage.
- Server authentication. This provides a method in which a server is authenticated to a client, to stop hackers pretending that they are the accessed server.
- Client authentication. This provides a method in which the client is authenticated to the server, to stop hackers from accessing a restricted server.

The main methods used are Secure Socket Layer (SSL) which was developed by Netscape, and Secure-HTTP (S-HTTP) which was developed by Enterprise Integration Technologies. Both are now being considered as International standards.

Two main problems are:

- Protection of transmitted information. For example, a person could access a book club over the Internet and then send information on the book and also credit-card information. The Book Club is likely to be a reputable company but criminals who can simply monitor the connection between the user and the Book Club could infiltrate the credit-card information.
- Protection of the client's computer. The Internet has little inherent security for the programs which can be downloaded from it. Thus, with no security, programs could be run or files can be download which could damage the local computer.

E6.3.1   Secure Socket Layer (SSL)

Many WWW sites now state that they implement SSL. SSL was developed by Netscape and has now been submitted to the W3 Consortium for its acceptance as an International standard.

SSL allows the information stored and the server to be authenticated. Its advantages are:

- Open and non-propriety protocol.
- Data encryption, server authentication and message integrity.
- Firewall compatibility.
- Tunneling connections.
- Supports S-MIME (Secure-MIME).

Figure E6.5 shows how SSL fits into the OSI model. It can be seen that it interfaces directly to TCP/IP. This thus has the advantage that it makes programs and high-level protocols   secure, such as ftp, telnet, SMTP and HTTP. Most browsers now support SSL, and many servers also support it. Figure E6.6 shows that the current browser supports SSL Version 2 and also Version 3.

Digital certificates

SSL supports independent certificate publishing authorities for server certificate authentication. These certificates have been validated by a reputable body and verify that the site is secure and genuine. These certificates can include Network server authentication, Network client authentication, Secure e-mail and Software Publishing, and can be viewed when connecting to the server. Typical certifying authorities are:

- ATT Certificate Services and ATT Directory Services.
- GTE Cyber Trust Root.
- internetMCI.
- Keywitness Canada.
- Microsoft Authenticode
- Thawte Personal.
- VeriSign.

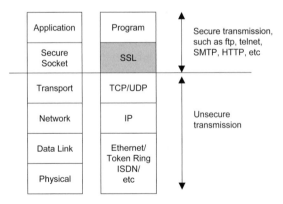

Figure E6.5   SSL and the OSI model

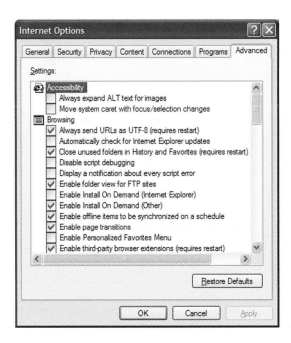

Figure E6.6 Security options

The WWW browser checks the certificate to see if it is valid. This includes checking the date that the certificate was issued, the site fingerprint (as show in Figure E6.7). The current date should be later than the issue date of the certificate. There is also an expiry date. If any of the information is not current and valid, the browser displays a warning.

Figure E6.7 shows an example of the properties for a VeriSign certificate.

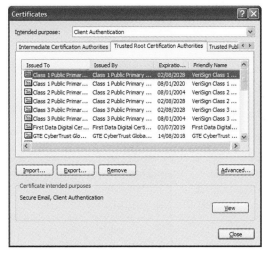

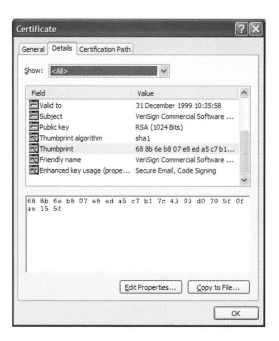

Figure E6.7 Thumbprint

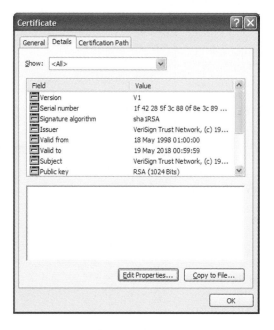

Figure E6.8 VeriSign certificate

E6.3.2 S-HTTP

HTTP supports the communication of multimedia information, such as audio, video, graphics and text. Unfortunately, it is not a secure method of transmission and an external person can tap it into. To overcome this, S-HTTP has been developed to provide improved security. Its features are:

- It is an extension to HTTP and uses HTTP-style headers.
- It incorporates encryption.
- It supports digital signatures for authentication.
- It supports certificates and key signing.

The Internet Engineering Task Force (IETF) is now considering S-HTTP for a standard method of transmitting secure HTTP over the Internet.

Message creation

An HTTP message contains both the message header and the message body. The header defines the type coding used in the body, its format, and so on. S-HTTP uses an encrypted message body and a message header, which includes the method that can be used to decrypt the message body. The process is as follows:

- The S-HTTP server (such as a WWW server) obtains the plain-text message of the information to send to the client (either locally or via a proxy). The message is either an HTTP message or some other data object (such as, a database entry or a graphical image).
- The server then encrypts the message body using the client's cryptographic preferences and the key provided by the client. The preference and key is passed in the initial handshake connection. This preference must also match the server's supported encryption techniques. The client normally sends a list of supported techniques and the server picks the most preferred one.
- The server sends the encrypted message to the client, in the same way as an HTTP transaction would occur, from which the client recovers the original message.

Message recovery

The encrypted file S-HTTP message is transmitted to the client, who then reads the message header to determine encryption technique. The client then decrypts it using the required private key, as shown in Figure E6.9. After this, the client displays the encapsulated HTTP or other data within the client's browser.

Normally in an HTTP transaction, the server terminates the connection after the transmission of the HTTP data. In S-HTTP this does not occur,

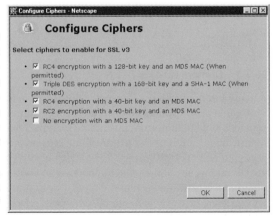

the server does not terminate the connection until the browser tells it so. This is because there is no need to perform a handshake, and thus the encryption key remains valid.

Browser and servers

SSL supports server authentication and also secure connections. This is achieved with:

- Secure transmission. Secure sites have URLs which begins with `https://`, where the `s` stands for secure. Other secure protocols are:

  - HTTPS (for HTTP).   FTPS (for FTP).
  - NNTPS (NNTP, news server).   UUCPS (UUCP).

Netscape Navigator and Microsoft Internet Explorer both show the connection to secure sites. Navigator shows it with key at the bottom of the window (a broken key shows a non-secure site), and Netscape Communicator and Internet Explorer displays a padlock. The figure on the right-hand side shows the configuration for SSL Version 3.

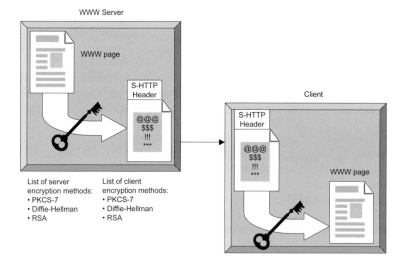

Figure E6.9 Encryption of WWW page

E6.3.3 Content advisor

A major problem with the Internet is the access to an almost unlimited amount of information, some of which may be unsuitable for certain users. An important consideration is the protection of children from unsuitable material, especially those of a violent or sexual content. Content advisors, which are built into browsers, allow a method of controlling the access to certain WWW pages. The ratings of WWW pages include four content types: language, nudity, sex and violence. The level of content can also be set and Table E6.3 gives different levels within each of the types. For example, language is split into five levels: Inoffensive slang (least likely to offend), mild expletives, moderate expletives, obscene gestures and explicit or crude language (most likely to offend). These ratings are industry-standards and have been defined independently by the Platform for Internet Content Selection (PICS) committee. It should be noted that not all Internet content is rated, although hopefully, in the future, all the material from certified sites will have a rating. This is the only true way to protect users from objectionable content. Every parent whose child has access to the Internet, and site managers (especially in schools) should have knowledge of these ratings and set the system up so that it protects innocent minds. Children should not be left to decide what they can, and what they cannot view. National laws cannot properly legislate against the content of material which is located in a foreign country.

Methods, which can be used to reduce the problem, are:

- Restrict access of WWW browsers to certified sites and set the content ratings for these sites.
- Log all DNS access. Many sites have a local DNS which tries to resolve IP addresses to domain names. Many of these programs allow a log to be kept to log DNS enquires and the IP address of the computer which accessed the site. The system manager can occasionally view the file to determine if certain users are abusing their privileges. A real-time trace can then be applied to catch these users (often a warning is the best medicine, followed by formal procedures if the accesses continue).
- Issue clear statements to all users, normally with large typed notices, which clearly state the sites and the type of content which should not be accessed. This is important from a legal point of view, and could be used as evidence that the organization has a clear statement on Internet access. Organizations who fail to do this are in danger of being held responsible for objectionable accesses.

The best policing policy is one of trust and of educating users. Unfortunately, a minority of users are tempted by the ease of access to objectionable information.

Table E6.3 Content advisor level settings

Level	Language	Nudity	Sex	Violence
0	Inoffensive slang	None	No sexual activity portrayed/ romance.	No aggressive violence; No natural or accidental violence.
1	Mild expletives. Or mild terms for body functions.	Revealing attire	Passionate kissing	Creatures injured or killed; damage to realistic objects.
2	Expletives; non-sexual anatomical references.	Partial nudity	Clothed sexual touching	Humans or creatures injured or killed. Rewards injuring non-threatening creatures.
3	Strong, vulgar language; obscene gestures. Use of epithets.	Frontal nudity	Non-explicit sexual touching	Humans injured or killed.
4	Extreme hate, speech or crude language. Explicit sexual references.	Provocative nudity	Explicit sexual actual	Wanton and gratuitous violence

E6.3.4 Security zones

Security zones support different levels of security for different areas of the Web to protect your computer. Each zone has a suitable security level; this is shown on the right-hand side of the Internet Explorer status bar. The browser checks the WWW sites zone when a page is opened or downloaded. The four zones are (Figure E6.11):

- **Local Intranet.** This is any address that does not require a proxy server. The default security level for this zone is Medium.
- **Trusted Sites.** This defines the sites that are most trusted, in which files can be run or downloaded without worrying about damaging the computer. The default security level for this zone is Low.
- **Restricted Sites.** This defines the sites that cannot be trusted. The default security level for this zone is High.
- **Internet.** This zone contains anything that is not on your computer or an intranet, or assigned to any other zone. The default security level for this zone is Medium.

Sites with a low security rate will generally be safe to run or download programs, whereas, they should be avoided in restricted sites. The security ratings are:

- High (most secure). Exclude content that could damage the local computer.
- Medium (more secure). Warn before running potentially damaging content.
- Low. Do not warn before running potentially damaging content.
- Custom. Allows users to set site security.

Security settings include (Figure E5.10):

- Active X controls and plug-ins. Active X plugs-ins and controls can run within a browser. These could possibly gain access to the resources of the computer, such as interrogating its resources and sending information about them over the network. Typically in a highly-secure environment, no Active X controls will be allowed to run within the browser.
- Java. Sets Java permissions. Some Java applets can cause security breaches.
- Downloads. Enable file downloads (enable or disable) and font downloads (enable, disable or prompt).
- User authentication. Logon details, such as Automatic logon, Anonymous login, Prompt for user name and password and Automatic Logon with current user name and password.
- Miscellaneous. Such as drag-and-drop and installation of desktop files.

Figure E6.10   Internet zone

Figure E6.11   Internet options

E6.4 VB RSA program

The equivalent VB program for the RSA algorithm is given next:

```
Function check_prime(ByVal val As Long) As Boolean
Dim primes
    primes = Array(1, 2, 3, 5, 7, 11, 13, 17, 19, 23, 29, 31, 37, 41, 43, 47,
        53, 59, 61, 67, 71, 73, 79, 83, 89, 97, 101, 103, 107, 109, 113, 127, 131,
        137, 139, 149, 151, 157, 163, 167, 173, 179, 181, 191, 193, 197, 199, 211,
        223, 227, 229, 233, 239, 241, 251, 257, 263, 269, 271, 277, 281, 283, 293,
        307, 311, 313, 317, 331, 337, 347, 349, 353, 359, 367, 373, 379, 383, 389,
        397)
    check_prime = False

    For i = 0 To 78
        If (val = primes(i)) Then
            prime = True
        End If
    Next i
    check_prime = prime
End Function

Function decrypt(ByVal c, ByVal n, ByVal d As Long)

Dim i, g, f As Long

On Error GoTo errorhandler

If (d Mod 2 = 0) Then
    g = 1
Else
    g = c
End If

    For i = 1 To d / 2

        f = c * c Mod n
        g = f * g Mod n
    Next i
 decrypt = g

 Exit Function
errorhandler:
    Select Case Err.Number   ' Evaluate error number.
        Case 6
            status.Text = "Calculation overflow, please select smaller values"
        Case Else
            status.Text = "Calculation error"
    End Select

End Function

Function getD(ByVal e As Long, ByVal PHI As Long) As Long
Dim u(3) As Long
Dim v(3) As Long
Dim q, temp1, temp2, temp3 As Long

u(0) = 1
u(1) = 0
u(2) = PHI
v(0) = 0
v(1) = 1
v(2) = e
```

```
    While (v(2) <> 0)
        q = Int(u(2) / v(2))
        temp1 = u(0) - q * v(0)
        temp2 = u(1) - q * v(1)
        temp3 = u(2) - q * v(2)
        u(0) = v(0)
        u(1) = v(1)
        u(2) = v(2)
        v(0) = temp1
        v(1) = temp2
        v(2) = temp3
    Wend
    If (u(1) < 0) Then
        getD = (u(1) + PHI)
    Else
        getD = u(1)
    End If
End Function

Function getE(ByVal PHI As Long) As Long
Dim great, e As Long

    great = 0
    e = 2

    While (great <> 1)
        e = e + 1
        great = get_common_denom(e, PHI)
    Wend
    getE = e
End Function

Function get_common_denom(ByVal e As Long, ByVal PHI As Long)
Dim great, temp, a As Long

    If (e > PHI) Then
        While (e Mod PHI <> 0)
            temp = e Mod PHI
            e = PHI
            PHI = temp
        Wend
        great = PHI
    Else
        While (PHI Mod e <> 0)
            a = PHI Mod e
            PHI = e
            e = a
        Wend
        great = e
    End If
    get_common_denom = great
End Function

Private Sub show_primes()
    status.Text = "1"
    no_primes = 1
    For i = 2 To 400
        prime = True
        For j = 2 To (i / 2)
            If ((i Mod j) = 0) Then
                prime = False
            End If
        Next j
```

```
            If (prime = True) Then
                no_primes = no_primes + 1
                status.Text = status.Text + ", " + Str(i)
            End If
      Next i
      status.Text = status.Text + vbCrLf + "Number of primes found:" +
Str(no_primes)
End Sub

Private Sub Command1_Click()
Dim p, q, n, e, PHI, d, m, c As Long

      p = Text1.Text
      q = Text2.Text
      If (check_prime(p) = False) Then
          status.Text = "p is not a prime or is too large, please re-enter"
      ElseIf (check_prime(q) = False) Then
          status.Text = "q is not a prime or is too large, please re-enter"
      Else
          n = p * q
          Text3.Text = n

          PHI = (p - 1) * (q - 1)
          e = getE((PHI))
          d = getD((e), (PHI))
          Text4.Text = PHI
          Text5.Text = d
          Text6.Text = e
          m = Text7.Text

          c = (m ^ e) Mod n
          Text8.Text = c
          m = decrypt(c, n, d)
          Text9.Text = m
          Label12.Caption = "Decrypt key =<" + Str(d) + "," + Str(n) + ">"
          Label13.Caption = "Encrypt key =<" + Str(e) + "," + Str(n) + ">"
      End If
End Sub

Private Sub Command2_Click()
      End
End Sub

Private Sub Command3_Click()
    frmBrowser.Show
End Sub

Private Sub Command4_Click()
    Call show_primes
End Sub

Private Sub Form_Load()

End Sub
```

Two sample runs are shown next.

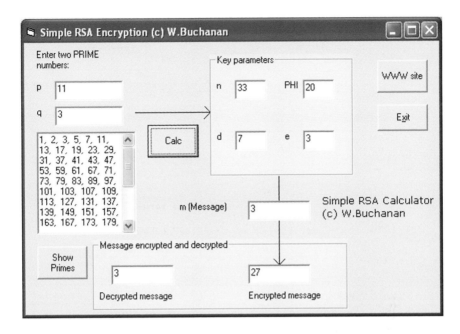

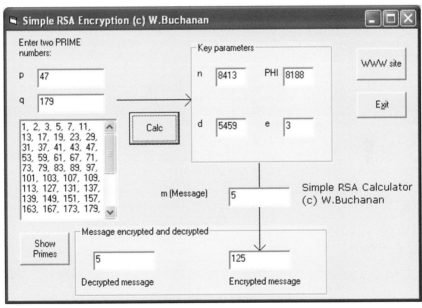

F1 Electronic mail

F1.1 Introduction

Electronic mail (e-mail) is one use of the Internet which, according to most businesses, improves productivity. Traditional methods of sending mail within an office environment are inefficient, as it normally requires an individual requesting a secretary to type the letter. This must then be proof-read and sent through the internal mail system, which is relatively slow and can be open to security breaches.

A faster, and more secure, method of sending information is to use electronic mail, where messages are sent almost in an instant. For example, a memo with 100 words will be sent in a fraction of a second. It is also simple to send to specific groups, various individuals, company-wide, and so on. Other types of data can also be sent with the mail message such as images, sound, and so on. It may also be possible to determine if a user has read the mail. The main advantages are:

- It is normally much cheaper than using the telephone (although, as time equates to money for most companies, this relates any savings or costs to a user's typing speed).
- Many different types of data can be transmitted, such as images, documents, speech, and so on.
- It is much faster than the postal service.
- Users can filter incoming e-mail easier than incoming telephone calls.
- It normally cuts out the need for work to be typed, edited and printed by a secretary.
- It reduces the burden on the mailroom.
- It is normally more secure than traditional methods.
- It is relatively easy to send to groups of people (traditionally, either a circulation list was required or a copy to everyone in the group was required).
- It is usually possible to determine whether the recipient has actually read the message (the electronic mail system sends bac   k an acknowledgement).

> E-mail standards:
>
> - **RFC821.** SMTP. Simple Mail Transfer Protocol. Defines the transfer of an e-mail message from one system to another.
> - **RFC822.** Defines the format of an e-mail message, with heading to define the sender and the recipient.
> - **RFC1521/1522.** MIME. Multipurpose Internet Mail Extensions. Defines a mechanism for supporting multiple attachments and for differing content types.
> - **RFC1939.** POP-3. Post Office Protocol – Version 3. Creation of a standard and simple mechanism to access e-mail messages on a mail server. As it is simple it allows for many different types of programs to download e-mail messages.

The main disadvantages are:

- It stops people using the telephone.
- It cannot be used as a legal document.
- Electronic mail messages can be sent impulsively and may be later regretted (sending by traditional methods normally allows for a rethink). In extreme cases, messages can be sent to the wrong person (typically when replying to an e-mail message, where a message is sent to the mailing list rather than the originator).

- It may be difficult to send to some remote sites. Many organizations have either no electronic mail or merely an intranet. Large companies are particularly wary of Internet connections and limit the amount of external traffic.
- Not everyone reads their electronic mail on a regular basis (although this is changing as more organizations adopt e-mail as the standard communications medium).

The main standards that relate to the protocols of e-mail transmission and reception are:

- Simple Mail Transfer Protocol (SMTP) – which is used with the TCP/IP protocol suite. It has traditionally been limited to the text-based electronic messages.
- Multipurpose Internet Mail Extension (MIME) – which allows the transmission and reception of mail that contains various types of data, such as speech, images and motion video. It is a newer standard than SMTP and uses much of its basic protocol.
- S/MIME (Secure MIME). RSA Data Security created S/MIME which supports encrypted e-mail transfers and digitally signed electronic mail.

F1.2   Shared-file approach versus client/server approach

An e-mail system can use either a shared-file approach or a client/server approach. In a shared-file system, the source mail client sends the mail message to the local post office. This post office then transfers control to a message transfer agent which then stores the message for a short time before sending it to the destination post office. The destination mail client periodically checks its own post office to determine if it has mail for it. This arrangement is often known as store and forward, and the process is illustrated in Figure F1.1. Most PC-based e-mail systems use this type of mechanism.

A client/server approach involves the source client setting up a real-time remote connection with the local post office, which then sets up a real-time connection with the destination, which in turn sets up a remote connection with the destination client. The message will thus arrive at the destination when all the connections are complete.

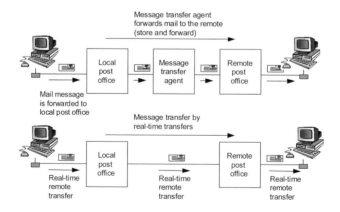

Figure F1.1   Shared-file versus client/server

F1.3 Using an e-mail client

E-mail clients, such as Microsoft Outlook, enables the user you to create and send e-mails, read and file. Microsoft Outlook contains a series of folders in which e-mails are stored. When an e-mail is written, it is placed in the **Outbox** where it will remain until a connection to the Internet, such as via an ISP. Likewise, when an e-mail is sent to your e-mail address, it is sent to the e-mail server, where it will stay in the **Inbox** of the server for your account. When you connect, the e-mails waiting for you will transfer to your computer and will be placed in the **Inbox** folder of the local computer. Typically, the e-mail message is then deleted from the server, as it is already stored on the local computer. Figure F1.2 and Figure F1.3 illustrates this principle.

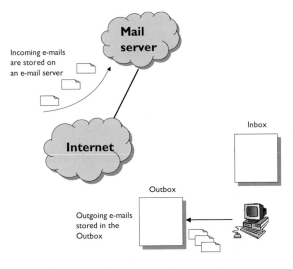

Figure F1.2 Before connecting to the Internet

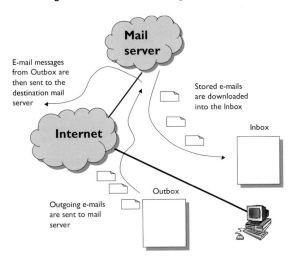

Figure F1.3 After connecting to the Internet

F1.4 Electronic mail overview

Figure F1.4 shows a typical e-mail architecture. It contains four main elements:

1. Post offices – where outgoing messages are temporally buffered (stored) before transmission and where incoming messages are stored. The post office runs the server software capable of routing messages (a message transfer agent) and maintaining the post office database.
2. Message transfer agents – for forwarding messages between post offices and to the destination clients. This software can either reside on the local post office or on a physically separate server.
3. Gateways – which provide part of the message transfer agent functionality. They translate between different e-mail systems, different e-mail addressing schemes and messaging protocols.
4. E-mail clients – normally the computer which connects to the post office. It contains three parts:

   - E-mail Application Program Interface (API), such as MAPI, VIM, MHS and CMC.
   - Messaging protocol. The main messaging protocols are SMTP or X.400. SMTP is defined in RFC 822 and RFC 821, whereas X.400 is an OSI-defined e-mail message delivery standard.
   - Network transport protocol, such as Ethernet, FDDI, and so on.

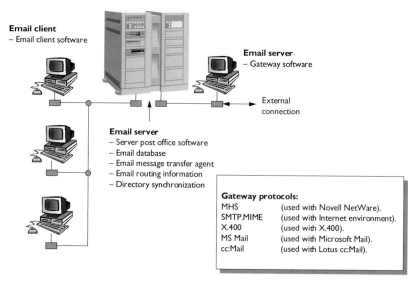

Figure F1.4   E-mail architecture

The main APIs are:

- MAPI (messaging API) – Microsoft part of Windows Operation Services Architecture.
- VIM (vendor-independent messaging) – Lotus, Apple, Novell and Borland derived e-mail API.
- MHS (message handling service) – Novell network interface which is often used as an

e-mail gateway protocol.
- CMC (common mail call) – E-mail API associated with the X.400 native messaging protocol.

Gateways translate the e-mail message from one system to another, such as from Lotus cc:Mail to Microsoft Mail. Typical gateway protocols are:

- MHS   (used with Novell NetWare).   SMTP.MIME (used with Internet environment).
- X.400 (used with X.400).   MS Mail (used with Microsoft Mail).
- cc:Mail (used with Lotus cc:Mail).

The Internet e-mail address is in the form of a name (such as f.bloggs), followed by an '@' and then the domain name (such as anytown.ac.uk). For example:

    f.bloggs@anytown.ac.uk

F1.5 SMTP

The IAB has defined the protocol SMTP in RFC821. This section discusses the protocol for transferring mail between hosts using the TCP/IP protocol. As SMTP is a transmission and reception protocol it does not actually define the format or contents of the transmitted message except that the data has 7-bit ASCII characters and that extra log information is added to the start of the delivered message to indicate the path the message took. The protocol itself is only concerned in reading the address header of the message.

F1.5.1   SMTP operation

SMTP defines the conversation that takes place between an SMTP sender and an SMTP receiver. Its main functions are the transfer of messages and the provision of ancillary functions for mail destination verification and handling.

Initially the user creates the message and a header is added which includes the recipient's e-mail address and other information. This message is then queued by the mail server, and when it has time, the mail server attempts to transmit it.

Each mail may have the following requirements:

- Each e-mail can have a list of destinations; the e-mail program makes copies of the messages and passes them onto the mail server.
- The user may maintain a mailing list, and the e-mail program must remove duplicates and replace mnemonic names with actual e-mail addresses.
- It allows for normal message provision, e.g. blind carbon copies (BCCs).

An SMTP mail server processes e-mail messages from an outgoing mail queue and then transmits them using one or more TCP connections with the destination. If the mail message is transmitted to the required host then the SMTP sender deletes the destination from the message's destination list. After all the destinations have been sent to, the sender then deletes the message from the queue.

If there are several recipients for a message on the same host, the SMTP protocol allows a single message to be sent to the specified recipients. In addition, if there are several messages to be sent to a single host, the server can simply open a single TCP connection and all the messages can be transmitted in a single transfer (there is thus no need to set up a connection for each message).

SMTP also allows for efficient transfer with error messages. Typical errors include:

- Destination host is unreachable. A likely cause is that the destination host address is incorrect. For example, `f.bloggs@toy.ac.uk` might actually be `f.bloggs@ toytown.ac.uk`.
- Destination host is out of operation. A likely cause is that the destination host has developed a fault or has been shut down.
- Mail recipient is not available on the host. Perhaps the recipient does not exist on that host, the recipient name is incorrect or the recipient has moved. For example, `fred.bloggs@toytown.ac.uk` might actually be `f.bloggs@toytown.ac.uk`. To overcome the problem of user names which are similar to a user's name then some systems allow for certain aliases for recipients, such as `f.bloggs`, `fred.bloggs` and `freddy.bloggs`, but there is a limit to the number of aliases that a user can have. If a user has moved then some systems allow for a redirection of the e-mail address. UNIX systems use the `.forward` file in the user's home directory for redirection. For example on a UNIX system, if the user has moved to `fred.bloggs@toytown.com` then this address is simply added to the `.forward` file.
- TCP connection failed on the transfer of the mail. A likely cause is that there was a time-out error on the connection (maybe due to the receiver or sender being busy or there was a fault in the connection).

SMTP senders have the responsibility for a message up to the point where the SMTP receiver indicates that the transfer is complete. This only indicates that the message has arrived at the SMTP receiver; it does not indicate that:

- The message has been delivered to the recipient's mailbox.
- The recipient has read the message.

Thus, SMTP does not guarantee to recover from lost messages and gives no end-to-end acknowledgement on successful receipt (normally this is achieved by an acknowledgement message being returned). Nor are error indications guaranteed. However, TCP connections are normally fairly reliable.

If an error occurs in reception, a message will normally be sent back to the sender to explain the problem. The user can then attempt to determine the problem with the message. SMTP receivers accept an arriving message and either place it in a user's mailbox or, if that user is located at another host, copies it to the local outgoing mail queue for forwarding. Most transmitted messages go from the sender's machine to the host over a single TCP connection. But sometimes the connection will be made over multiple TCP connections over multiple hosts. The sender specifying a route to the destination in the form of a sequence of servers can achieve this.

F1.5.2   SMTP overview

An SMTP sender initiates a TCP connection. When this is successful it sends a series of commands to the receiver, and the receiver returns a single reply for each command. All commands and responses are sent with ASCII characters and are terminated with the carriage return (CR) and line feed (LF) characters (often known as CRLF).

Each command consists of a single line of text; beginning with a four-letter command code followed by in some cases an argument field. Most replies are a single line, although multiple-line replies are possible. Table F1.1 gives some sample commands.

Table F1.1 SMTP commands

Command	Description
HELO *domain*	Sends an identification of the domain
MAIL FROM: *sender-address*	Sends identification of the originator (sender-address)
RCPT FROM: *receiver-address*	Sends identification of the recipient (receiver-address)
DATA	Transfer text message
RSEY	Abort current mail transfer
QUIT	Shut down TCP connection
EXPN *mailing-list*	Send back membership of mailing list
SEND FROM: *sender-address*	Send mail message to the terminal
SOML FROM: *sender-address*	If possible, send mail message to the terminal, otherwise send to mailbox
VRFY username	Verify user name (username)

SMTP replies with a three-digit code and possibly other information. Some of the responses are listed in Table F1.2. The first digit gives the category of the reply, such as 2*xx* (a positive completion reply), 3*xx* (a positive intermediate reply), 4*xx* (a transient negative completion reply) and 5*xx* (a permanent negative completion reply). A positive reply indicates that the requested action has been accepted, and a negative reply indicates that the action was not accepted.

Positive completion reply indicates that the action has been successful, and a positive intermediate reply indicates that the action has been accepted but the receiver is waiting for some other action before it can give a positive completion reply. A transient negative completion reply indicates that there is a temporary error condition which can be cleared by other actions and a permanent negative completion reply indicates that the action was not accepted and no action was taken.

F1.5.3   SMTP transfer

Figure F1.5 shows a successful e-mail transmission. For example if:

```
f.bloggs@toytown.ac.uk
```

is sending a message to:

```
a.person@place.ac.de
```

Then a possible sequence of events is:

- Set up TCP connection with receiver host.
- If the connection is successful, the receiver replies back with a 220 code (server ready). If it is unsuccessful, it returns back with a 421 code.
- Sender sends a HELO command to the hostname (such as HELO toytown.ac.uk).

- If the sender accepts the incoming mail message then the receiver returns a `250 OK` code. If it is unsuccessful then it returns a 421, 451, 452, 500, 501 or 552 code.
- Sender sends a `MAIL FROM:` *sender* command (such as `MAIL FROM: f.bloggs@ toytown.ac.uk`).
- If the receiver accepts the incoming mail message from the sender then it returns a `250 OK` code. If it is unsuccessful then it returns codes such as 251, 450, 451, 452, 500, 501, 503, 550, 551, 552 or 553 code.
- Sender sends an `RCPT TO:` *receiver* command (such as `RCPT TO: a.person@place.ac.de`).
- If the receiver accepts the incoming mail message from the sender then it returns a `250 OK` code.
- Sender sends a `DATA` command.
- If the receiver accepts the incoming mail message from the sender then it returns a `354` code (start transmission of mail message).
- The sender then transmits the e-mail message.
- The end of the e-mail message is sent as two LF, CR characters.
- If the reception has been successful then the receiver sends back a `250 OK` code. If it is unsuccessful then it returns a 451, 452, 552 or 554 code.
- Sender starts the connection shutdown by sending a `QUIT` command.
- Finally, the sender closes the TCP connection.

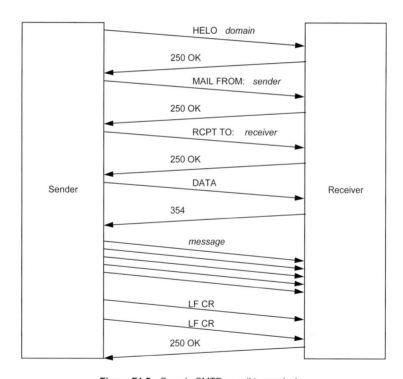

Figure F1.5 Sample SMTP e-mail transmission

Table F1.2 SMTP responses

CMD	Description	CMD	Description
211	System status	500	Command unrecognized due to a syntax error
214	Help message	501	Invalid parameters or arguments
220	Service ready	502	Command not currently implemented
221	Service closing transmission channel	503	Bad sequence of commands
250	Request mail action completed successfully	504	Command parameter not currently implemented
251	Addressed user does not exist on system but will forward to receiver-address	550	Mailbox unavailable, request action not taken
354	Indicate to the sender that the mail message can now be sent. The end of the message is identified by two CR, LF characters	551	The addressed user is not local, please try receiver-address
421	Service is not available	552	Exceeded storage allocation, requested mail action aborted
450	Mailbox unavailable and the requested mail action was not taken	553	Mailbox name not allowed, requested action not taken
451	Local processing error, requested action aborted	554	Transaction failed
452	Insufficient storage, requested action not taken		

The following text shows some of the handshaking that is used in transmitting an electronic mail message (the UNIX mail –v command is used to show the handshaking. The commands sent to the mail server are highlighted in bold. It can be seen that the responses are 220 (Service ready), 221 (Request mail action completed successfully), 250 (Request mail action completed successfully) and 354 (Indicate to the sender that the mail message can now be sent).

```
> mail -v w.buchanan@napier.ac.uk
Subject: Test
This is a test message. Hello, how are you.
Fred.
EOT

w.buchanan@napier.ac.uk... Connecting to central.napier.ac.uk. (smtp)...
220 central.napier.ac.uk ESMTP Sendmail 8.9.1/8.9.1; Fri, 18 Dec 1998 15:55:45
GMT
>>> HELO www.eece.napier.ac.uk
```

```
250 central.napier.ac.uk Hello bill_b@www.eece.napier.ac.uk [146.176.151.139],
pleased to meet you
>>> MAIL From:<bill_b@www.eece.napier.ac.uk>
250 <bill_b@www.eece.napier.ac.uk>... Sender ok
>>> RCPT To:<w.buchanan@napier.ac.uk>
250 <w.buchanan@napier.ac.uk>... Recipient ok
>>> DATA
354 Enter mail, end with "." on a line by itself
>>> .
250 PAA24767 Message accepted for delivery
w.buchanan@napier.ac.uk... Sent (PAA24767 Message accepted for delivery)
Closing connection to central.napier.ac.uk.
>>> QUIT
221 central.napier.ac.uk closing connection
```

F1.5.4   RFC 822

SMTP uses RFC 822, which defines the format of the transmitted message. RFC 822 contains two main parts:

- A header – which is basically the mail header and contains information for the successful transmission and delivery of a message. This typically contains the e-mail addresses for sender and receiver, the time the message was sent and received. Any computer involved in the transmission can added to the header.
- The contents.

Normally the e-mail-reading program will read the header and format the information to the screen to show the sender's e-mail address; it splits off the content of the message and displays it separately from the header.

An RFC 822 message contains a number of lines of text in the form of a memo (such as To:, From:, Bcc:, and so on). A header line usually has a keyword followed by a colon and then followed by keyword arguments. The specification also allows for a long line to be broken up into several lines.

Here is an RFC 822 message with the header shown in italics and the message body in bold. Table F1.3 explains some of the RFC 822 items in the header.

```
From FREDB@ACOMP.CO.UK Wed Jul  5 12:36:49 1995
Received: from ACOMP.CO.UK ([154.220.12.27]) by central.napier.ac.uk
(8.6.10/8.6.10) with SMTP id MAA16064 for <w.buchanan@central.napier.ac.uk>;
Wed, 5 Jul 1995 12:36:43 +0100

Received: from WPOAWUK-Message_Server by ACOMP.CO.UK
    with Novell_GroupWise; Wed, 05 Jul 1995 12:35:51 +0000

Message-Id: <sffa8725.082@ACOMP.CO.UK >

X-Mailer: Novell GroupWise 4.1

Date: Wed, 05 Jul 1995 12:35:07 +0000
From: Fred Bloggs <FREDB@ACOMP.CO.UK>
To: w.buchanan@central.napier.ac.uk
Subject:   Technical Question
Status: REO
Dear Bill
    I have a big problem. Please help.
Fred
```

Table F1.3 Header line descriptions

Header line	Description
From FREDB@ACOMP.CO.UK Wed Jul 5 12:36:49 1995	Sender of the e-mail is FREDB@ ACOM.CO.UK
Received: from ACOMP.CO.UK ([154.220.12.27]) by central.napier.ac.uk (8.6.10/8.6.10) with SMTP id MAA16064 for <w.buchanan@central.napier.ac.uk>; Wed, 5 Jul 1995 12:36:43 +0100	It was received by CENTRAL.NAPIER.AC.UK at 12:36 on 5 July 1995
Message-Id: <sffa8725.082@ACOMP.CO.UK >	Unique message ID
X-Mailer: Novell GroupWise 4.1	Gateway system
Date: Wed, 05 Jul 1995 12:35:07 +0000	Date of original message
From: Fred Bloggs <FREDB@ACOMP.CO.UK>	Sender's e-mail address and full name
To: w.buchanan@central.napier.ac.uk	Recipient's e-mail address
Subject: Technical Question	Mail subject

F1.6 MIME

SMTP suffers from several drawbacks, such as:

- SMTP can only transmit ASCII characters and thus cannot transmit executable files or other binary objects.
- SMTP does not allow the attachment of files, such as images and audio.
- SMTP can only transmit 7-bit ASCII character thus it does not support an extended ASCII character set.

A new standard, Multipurpose Internet Mail Extension (MIME), has been defined for this purpose, which is compatible with existing RFC 822 implementations. It is defined in the specifications RFC 1521 and 1522. Its enhancements include the following:

- Five new message header fields in the RFC 822 header, which provide extra information about the body of the message.
- Use of various content formats to support multimedia electronic mail.
- Defined transfer encodings for transforming attached files.

The five new header fields defined in MIME are:

- MIME-version – a message that conforms to RFC 1521 or 1522 is MIME-version 1.0.
- Content-type – this field defines the type of data attached.
- Content-transfer-encoding – this field indicates the type of transformation necessary to

represent the body in a format which can be transmitted as a message.

- Content-id – this field is used to uniquely identify MIME multiple attachments in the e-mail message.
- Content-description – this field is a plain-text description of the object with the body. It can be used by the user to determine the data type.

These fields can appear in a normal RFC 822 header. Figure F1.6 shows an example e-mail message. It can be seen that the API has split the message into two parts: the message part and the RFC 822 part. The RFC 822 part is shown in Figure F1.7. It can be seen that, in this case, the extra MIME messages are:

```
From: "Bill Buchanan" <w.buchanan@napier.ac.uk>
To: <f.bloggs@napier.ac.uk>
Subject: ECBS 2000 Referee Database
Date: Wed, 24 Nov 1999 00:09:22 -0000
MIME-Version: 1.0
```

This defines it as MIME Version 1.0; the data that the e-mail was sent, the person who sent the mail message, and so on.

📖 **RFC 822 example file listing (refer to Figure F1.7)**

```
Received: from central.napier.ac.uk (146.176.2.3) by csumail1.napier.ac.uk
with SMTP  (IMA Internet Exchange 2.12 Enterprise) id 00232062; Wed, 24 Nov 99
04:35:35 +0000
Received: from mail6.svr.pol.co.uk (mail6.svr.pol.co.uk [195.92.193.212])
   by central.napier.ac.uk (8.9.1/8.9.1) with ESMTP id EAA03895;
   Wed, 24 Nov 1999 04:31:40 GMT
Received:from modem-111.doxycycline.dialup.pol.co.uk
([62.136.63.239]helo=bills)
   by mail6.svr.pol.co.uk with smtp (Exim 3.03 #0)
   id 11qQ0t-00069D-00; Wed, 24 Nov 1999 00:10:25 +0000
Reply-To: <w.buchanan@napier.ac.uk>
From: "Bill Buchanan" <w.buchanan@napier.ac.uk>
To: <w.buchanan@napier.ac.uk>
Subject: ECBS 2000 Referee Database
Date: Wed, 24 Nov 1999 00:09:22 -0000
Message-ID: <NDBBJGAHLDCDDONHKJEOMEBFCIAA.w.buchanan@napier.ac.uk>
MIME-Version: 1.0
Content-Type: multipart/mixed;    boundary="----
```

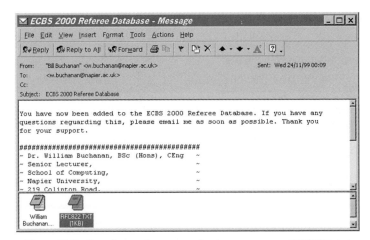

Figure F1.6 Sample e-mail message showing message and RFC822 part

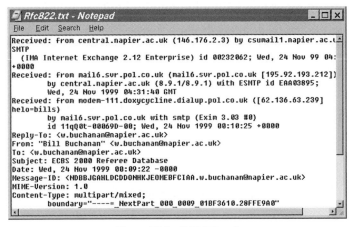

Figure F1.7 RFC 822 part

F1.6.1 MIME content types

Content types define the format of the attached files. There are a total of 16 different content types in seven major content groups. If the text body is pure text then no special transformation is required. RFC 1521 defines only one subtype, text/plain; this gives a standard ASCII character set.

A MIME-encoded e-mail can contain multiple attachments. The content-type header field includes a boundary which defines the delimiter between multiple attachments. A boundary always starts on a new line and has the format:

```
-- boundary name
```

The final boundary is:

```
-- boundary name --
```

For example, the following message contains two parts:

📖 **Example MIME file with 2 parts**

```
From: Dr William Buchanan <w.buchanan@napier.ac.uk>
MIME-Version: 1.0
To: w.buchanan@napier.ac.uk
Subject: Any subject
Content-Type: multipart/mixed; boundary="boundary name"
This part of the message will be ignored.
-- boundary name
Content-Type: multipart/mixed; boundary="boundary name"
This is the first mail message part.
-- boundary name
And this is the second mail message part.
-- boundary name --
```

Table F1.4   MIME content-types

Content type	Description
text/plain	Unformatted text, such as ASCII
text/richtext	Rich text format which is similar to HTML
multipart/mixed	Each attachment is independent from the rest and all should be presented to the user in their initial ordering
multipart/parallel	Each attachment is independent from the others but the order is unimportant
multipart/alternative	Each attachment is a different version of the original data
multipart/digest	This is similar to multipart/mixed but each part is message/rfc822
message/rfc822	Contains the RFC 822 text
message/partial	Used in fragmented mail messages
message/external-body	Used to define a pointer to an external object (such as an ftp link)
image/jpeg	Defines a JPEG image using JFIF file format
image/gif	Defines GIF image
video/mpeg	Defines MPEG format
audio/basic	Defines 8-bit μ-Law encoding at 8 kHz sampling rate
application/postscript	Defines postscript format
application/octet-stream	Defines binary format which consists of 8-bit bytes

The part of the message after the initial header and before the first boundary can be used to add a comment. This is typically used to inform users that do not have a MIME-compatible program about the method used to encode the received file. A typical method for converting binary data into ASCII characters is to use the programs UUENCODE (to encode a binary file into text) or UUDECODE (to decode a uuencoded file).

The four subtypes of multipart type can be used to sequence the attachments; the main subtypes are:

- multipart/mixed subtype – which is used when attachments are independent but need to be arranged in a particular order.
- multipart/parallel subtype – which is used when the attachments should be present at the same time; a typical example is to present an animated file along with an audio attachment.

tachment.

- multipart/alternative subtype – which is used to represent an attachment in a number of different formats.

F1.6.2   Example MIME

The following file listing shows the message part of a MIME-encoded e-mail message (i.e. it excludes the RFC 822 header part). It can be seen that the sending e-mail system has added the comment about the MIME encoding. In this case the MIME boundaries have been defined by:

```
-- IMA.Boundary.760275638
```

📖 **Example MIME file**

```
This is a Mime message, which your current mail reader
may not understand. Parts of the message will appear as
text. To process the remainder, you will need to use a Mime
compatible mail reader. Contact your vendor for details.

--IMA.Boundary.760275638

Content-Type: text/plain; charset=US-ASCII
Content-Transfer-Encoding: 7bit
Content-Description: cc:Mail note part

This is the original message .....

--IMA.Boundary.760275638—
```

F1.6.3   Mail fragments

A mail message can be fragmented using the content-type field of message/partial and then reassembled back at the source. The standard format is:

```
Content-type: message/partial;
    id="idname"; number=x; total=y
```

where *idname* is the message identification (such as xyz@hostname, x is the number of the fragment out of a total of y fragments. For example, if a message had three fragments, they could be sent as:

📖 **Example MIME file with 3 fragments (first part)**

```
From: Fred Bloggs <f.bloggs@toytown.ac.uk>
MIME-Version: 1.0
To: a.body@anytown.ac.uk
Subject: Any subject
Content-Type: message/partial;
    id="xyz@toytown.ac.uk"; number=1; total=3
Content=type: video/mpeg
```

First part of MPEG file

```
From: Fred Bloggs <f.bloggs@toytown.ac.uk>
MIME-Version: 1.0
To: a.body@anytown.ac.uk
Subject: Any subject
Content-Type: message/partial;
    id="xyz@toytown.ac.uk"; number=2; total=3
Content=type: video/mpeg
```

Second part of MPEG file

```
From: Fred Bloggs <f.bloggs@toytown.ac.uk>
MIME-Version: 1.0
To: a.body@anytown.ac.uk
Subject: Any subject
Content-Type: message/partial;
    id="xyz@toytown.ac.uk"; number=3; total=3
Content=type: video/mpeg
```

Third part of MPEG file

F1.6.4   Transfer encodings

MIME allows for different transfer encodings within the message body:

- 7bit – no encoding, and all of the characters are 7-bit ASCII characters.
- 8bit – no encoding, and extended 8-bit ASCII characters are used.
- quoted-printable – encodes the data so that non-printing ASCII characters (such as line feeds and carriage returns) are displayed in a readable form.
- base64 – encodes by mapping 6-bit blocks of input to 8-bit blocks of output, all of which are printable ASCII characters.

When the transfer encoding is:

```
Content-transfer-encoding: quoted-printable
```

then the message has been encoded so that all non-printing characters have been converted to printable characters. A typical transform is to insert =*xx* where *xx* is the hexadecimal equivalent for the ASCII character. A form feed (FF) would be encoded with '=0C',

A transfer encoding of base64 is used to map 6-bit characters to a printable character. It is a useful method in disguising text in an encrypted form and also for converting binary data into a text format. It takes the input bitstream and reads it six bits at a time, then maps this to an 8-bit printable character. Table F1.5 shows the mapping.

Thus if a binary file had the bit sequence:

```
101000101010010001010101010
```

It would first be split into groups of 6 bits, as follows:

```
101000    101010  100010  101010  000000
```

This would be converted into the ASCII sequence:

```
YsSqA
```

which is in a transmittable form.

Thus the 7-bit ASCII sequence 'FRED' would use the bit pattern:

```
1000110 1010010 1000101 1000100
```

which would be split into groups of 6 bits as:

```
100011 010100 101000 101100 010000
```

which would be encoded as:

```
jUosQ
```

Table F1.5 MIME base64 encoding

Bit value	Encoded character	Bit value	Encoded character	Bit value	Encoded character	Bit value	Encoded character
0	A	16	Q	32	g	48	w
1	B	17	R	33	h	49	x
2	C	18	S	34	i	50	y
3	D	19	T	35	j	51	z
4	E	20	U	36	k	52	0
5	F	21	V	37	l	53	1
6	G	22	W	38	m	54	2
7	H	23	X	39	n	55	3
8	I	24	Y	40	o	56	4
9	J	25	Z	41	p	57	5
10	K	26	a	42	q	58	6
11	L	27	b	43	r	59	7
12	M	28	c	44	s	60	8
13	N	29	d	45	t	61	9
14	O	30	e	46	u	62	+
15	P	31	f	47	v	63	/

F1.6.5 Example

The following parts of the RFC 822 messages.

(a)
```
Received: from publish.co.uk by ccmaill.publish.co.uk (SMTPLINK
V2.11.01)
Return-Path: <FredB@local.exnet.com>
Received: from mailgate.exnet.com ([204.137.193.226]) by
zeus.publish.co.uk with SMTP id <17025>; Wed, 2 Jul 1997 08:33:29
+0100
Received: from exnet.com (assam.exnet.com) by mailgate.exnet.com with
SMTP id AA09732 (5.67a/IDA-1.4.4 for m.smith@publish.co.uk); Wed, 2
Jul 1997 08:34:22 +0100
Received: from maildrop.exnet.com (ceylon.exnet.com) by exnet.com
with SMTP id AA10740 (5.67a/IDA-1.4.4 for <m.smith@publish.co.uk>);
Wed, 2 Jul 1997 08:34:10 +0100
```

```
Received: from local.exnet.com by maildrop.exnet.com (4.1/client-
1.2DHD)
    id AA22007; Wed, 2 Jul 97 08:25:21 BST
From: FredB@local.exnet.com (Arthur Chapman)
Reply-To: FredB@local.exnet.com
To: b.smith@publish.co.uk
Subject: New proposal
Date: Wed, 2 Jul 1997 09:36:17 +0100
Message-Id: <66322430.1380704@local.exnet.com>
Organization: Local College
```

(b)

```
Received: from central.napier.ac.uk by ccmailgate.napier.ac.uk
(SMTPLINK V2.11.01) Return-Path: <fred@singnetw.com.sg>
Received: from server.singnetw.com.sg (server.singnetw.com.sg
[165.21.1.15]) by central.napier.ac.uk (8.6.10/8.6.10) with ESMTP id
DAA18783 for <w.buchanan@napier.ac.uk>; Sun, 29 Jun 1997 03:15:27 GMT
Received: from si7410352.ntu.ac.sg (ts900-1908.singnet.com.sg
[165.21.158.60])
    by melati.singnet.com.sg (8.8.5/8.8.5) with SMTP id KAA08773
    for <w.buchanan@napier.ac.uk.>; Sun, 29 Jun 1997 10:14:59 +0800
(SST)
Message-ID: <33B5C33B.6CCC@singnetw.com.sg>
Date: Sun, 29 Jun 1997 10:06:51 +0800
From: Fred Smith <fred@singnetw.com.sg>
X-Mailer: Mozilla 2.0 (Win95; I)
MIME-Version: 1.0
To: w.buchanan@napier.ac.uk
Subject: Chapter 15
Content-Type: text/plain; charset=us-ascii
Content-Transfer-Encoding: 7bit
```

(c)

```
Received: from central.napier.ac.uk by ccmailgate.napier.ac.uk
(SMTPLINK V2.11.01)
Return-Path: <bertb@scms.scotuni.ac.uk>
Received: from master.scms.scotuni.ac.uk ([193.62.32.5]) by cen-
tral.napier.ac.uk (8.6.10/8.6.10) with ESMTP id MAA20373 for
<w.buchanan@napier.ac.uk>; Tue, 1 Jul 1997 12:25:38 GMT
Received: from cerberus.scms.scotuni.ac.uk (cer-
berus.scms.scotuni.ac.uk [193.62.32.46]) by master.scms.scotuni.ac.uk
(8.6.9/8.6.9) with ESMTP id MAA10056 for <w.buchanan@napier.ac.uk>;
Tue, 1 Jul 1997 12:24:32 +0100
From: David Davidson <bertb@scms.scotuni.ac.uk>
Received: by cerberus.scms.scotuni.ac.uk (SMI-8.6/Dumb)
    id MAA03334; Tue, 1 Jul 1997 12:23:17 +0100
Date: Tue, 1 Jul 1997 12:23:17 +0100
Message-Id: <199707011123.MAA03334@cerberus.scms.scotuni.ac.uk>
To: w.buchanan@napier.ac.uk
Subject: Advert
Mime-Version: 1.0
Content-Type: text/plain; charset=us-ascii
Content-Transfer-Encoding: 7bit
Content-MD5: TzKyk+NON+vy6Cm6uqy9Cg==
```

F1.7 Post Office Protocol (POP)

The Post Office Protocol was first defined in RFC918, but has since been replaced with POP-3, which is defined in RFC1939. The objective of POP is to create a standard method for users to access a mail server. E-mail messages are uploaded onto a mail server using SMTP, and then downloaded using POP. With POP the server listens for a connection, and when this occurs the server sends a greeting message, and waits for commands. The standard port reserved for POP transactions is 110. Like SMTP, it consists of case-insensitive commands

with one or more arguments, followed by the Carriage Return (CR) and Line Feed (LF) characters, typically represented by CRLF. These keywords are either three or four characters long.

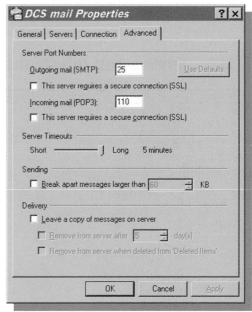

The client opens the connection by sending a USER and a PASS command, for the user name and password, respectively. If successful this will give access to the mailbox on the server. The client can then read the messages with the following commands:

- RDEL. Reads and deletes all the messages from the mailbox.
- RETR. Reads the messages from the mailbox, and keeps them on the server.

When transferring, the e-mail server locks the mailbox, and waits for the client to respond. The client then uses the RECV command to receive data from the mailbox. When complete the client sends a RCVD command. If the RDEL was initially sent, the server will delete the messages from the mailbox, otherwise the messages will stay on the server. A QUIT command terminates the session. After each command the e-mail server must respond back. The commands and responses for POP can be summarized by:

Command	Description	Possible responses
USER *name*	Defines the name of the user.	"+OK", "-ERR"
PASS *password*	Defines the password for the user	"+OK", "-ERR"
RETR *mailbox*	Begins a mail reading transaction, but does not delete the messages once they have been transferred.	"+*val*", "-ERR"
RDEL *mailbox*	Begins a mail reading transaction, and deletes the messages once they have been transferred. The messages are not deleted until a RCEV command.	"+*val*", "-ERR"
RVEC	Acknowledges the reception of the mail messages.	"+OK", or aborted connection
RCVD	Confirms that client has received the mail messages.	"+OK", "-ERR"
QUIT	Client wishes to end the session.	"+OK" then close

| NOOP | No operation but prompts the mail server for an OK response. | "+OK" |
| RSET | Sent by the client to inform the server to abort the current transaction. | "+OK" |

An important objective of POP is that messages are normally downloaded from the e-mail server, and then deleted. POP is a simple protocol, and allows for many different programs to access e-mail servers, without having to implement a complex protocol. Typically WWW browsers can be setup to access the POP-3 server.

F1.8   Smilies and acronyms

Smilie	Description	Smilie	Description
:-)	smile	:->	sarcastic
;-)	wink	:-)))	laughing or double chin
:.-)	laughing tears	;-)=)	grin
:-D	laughing	:-}	wry smile
:-P	tongue	:-(	sad, angry
:-<	sad	:-I	indifferent/sad
:.-(	weeping	:-II	angry
:-@	angry	}-)	evil
:-X	mute	:-()	talking
:-O	surprised/shocked	=:-)	shocked
O:-)	halo	:-3	has eaten a lemon
:-/	skeptical	:-Z	sleeping
:-x	kissing	:-*	sorry, I didn't want to say that
?-(	sorry, I don't know what went wrong	:*)	drunk (red nose)
%-)	stared too long at monitor	#-)	dead
X-)	unconscious	:-Q	smoking
(:-)	bald	.-)	one-eyed
-:-)	punk	<:-)	stupid question (donkey's hat)
<|-)	Chinese	@:-)	Arab
8:-)	little girl	:-)-8	big girl
[:-]	robot	::-)	wearing glasses
8-)	wearing glasses/wide-eyed grin	B-)	horn-rimmed glasses
B:-)	sunglasses on head	.^)	side view
:<)	moustache	_O-)	aquanaut
{:-)	wig	:-E	vampire
:-[	vampire	(-:	left-handed
:o)	boxer's nose	:)	happy
[:]	robot	:]	gleep, friendly
=)	variations on a theme	:}	(what should we call these?)
:>	(what?)	:@	(what?)
:D	laughter	:I	hmmm...
:(	sad		

Acronym	Description	Acronym	Description
2U2	to you, too	AAMOF	as a matter of fact
AFAIK	as far as I know	AFK	away from keyboard
ASAP	as soon as possible	BBL	be back later
BOT	back on topic	BRB	be right back
BTW	by the way	BYORL	bring your own rocket launcher
C4N	ciao for now	CFD	call for discussion
CFV	call for vote	CU	see you
CUL	see you later	CYA	see ya
DIY	do it yourself	EOD	end of discussion
EOT	end of transmission	F2F	face to face
FAI	frequently argued issue	FAQ	frequently asked questions
FOAF	friend of a friend	FWIW	for what it's worth
FYI	for your information	GAL	get a life
GFC	going for coffee	GRMBL	grumble
GTG	got to go	HAND	have a nice day
HTH	hope this helps	IAC	in any case
IC	I see	IDGI	I don't get it
IMHO	in my humble opinion	IMNSHO	in my not so humble opinion
IMO	in my opinion	IMPE	in my previous/personal experience
IMVHO	in my very humble opinion	IOW	in other words
IRL	in real life	KISS	keep it simple stupid
LOL	laughing out loud	NC	no comment
ONNA	oh no, not again!	OOTC	obligatory on-topic content
OTOH	on the other hand	REHI	hello again (re-Hi!)
ROFL	rolling on the floor laughing	RTDox	read the documentation
SHTSI	somebody had to say it	SO	significant other
THX	thanks	TIA	thanks in advance
TLA	three letter acronym	TOS	terms of service
TTFN	ta-ta for now	TTYL	talk to you later
WIIWD	what it is we do	WWDWIIWD	when we do what it is we do
YGWYPF	you get what you pay for		

F2 WWW and HTTP

F2.1 Introduction

The World-Wide Web (WWW) and the Internet have more jargon words and associated acronyms than anything else in modern life. Words, such as

> gopher, ftp, telnet, TCP/IP stack, intranets, Web servers, clients, browsers, hypertext, URLs, Internet access providers, dial-up connections, UseNet servers, firewalls

have all become common in the business vocabulary.

The WWW was initially conceived in 1989 by CERN, the European particle physics research laboratory in Geneva, Switzerland. Its main objective was:

to use the hypermedia concept to support the interlinking of various types of information through the design and development of a series of concepts, communications protocols, and systems

One of its main characteristics is that stored information tends to be distributed over a geographically wide area. The result of the project has been the worldwide acceptance of the protocols and specifications used. A major part of its success was due to the full support of the National Center for Supercomputing Applications (NCSA), which developed a family of user interface programs known collectively as Mosaic.

The WWW, or Web, is basically an infrastructure of information. This information is stored on the WWW on Web servers and it uses the Internet to transmit data around the world. These servers run special programs that allow information to be transmitted to remote computers which are running a Web browser, as illustrated in Figure F2.1. The Internet is a common connection in which computers can communicate using a common addressing mechanism (IP) with a TCP/IP connection.

The information is stored on Web servers and is accessed by means of pages. These pages can contain text and other multimedia applications such as graphic images, digitized sound files and video animation. There are several standard media files (with typical file extensions):

- **GIF/JPEG files for compressed images** (GIF or JPG).
- **QuickTime movies for video** (QT or MOV).
- **Audio** (AU, SND or WAV).
- **MPEG files for compressed video** (MPG).
- **MS video** (AVI).
- **Postscript files** (PS or EPS).
- **Compressed files** (ZIP, Z or GZ).
- **Java/JavaScript** (JAV or JS).

Each page contains text known as hypertext, which has specially reserved keywords to represent the format and the display functions. A standard language known as HTML (Hypertext Markup Language) has been developed for this purpose. Hypertext pages, when interpreted by a browser program, display an easy-to-use interface containing formatted text, icons, pictorial hot spots, underscored words, and so on. Each page can also contain links to other related pages.

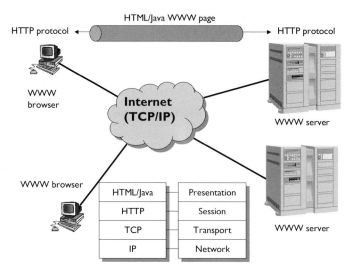

Figure F2.1 Web servers and browsers

The topology and power of the Web now allows for distributed information, where information does not have to be stored locally. To find information on the Web the user can use powerful search engines to search for related links. Figure F2.2 shows an example of Web connections. The user initially accesses a page on a German Web server, this then contains a link to a Japanese server. This server contains links to UK and USA servers. This type of arrangement leads to the topology that resembles a spider's web, where information is linked from one place to another.

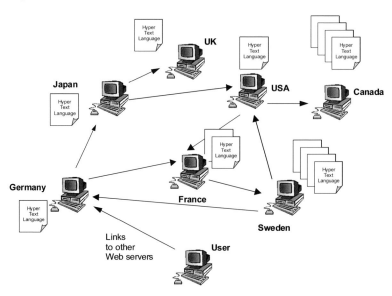

Figure F2.2 Example Web connections

F2.2 Advantages and disadvantages of the WWW

The WWW and the Internet tend to produce a polarization of views. Thus, before analysing the WWW for its technical specification, a few words must be said on some of the subjective advantages and disadvantages of the WWW and the Internet. It should be noted that some of these disadvantages could be seen as advantages to some people, and vice versa. For example, freedom of information will be seen as an advantage to a freedom-of-speech group but often a disadvantage to security organizations. Table F2.1 outlines some of the advantages and disadvantages.

Table F2.1 Advantages and disadvantages of the Internet and the WWW

	Advantages	*Disadvantages*
Global information flow	Less control of information by the media, governments and large organizations.	Lack of control on criminal material, such as certain types of pornography and terrorist activity.
Global transmission	Communication between people and organizations in different countries which should create the Global Village.	Data can easily get lost or state secrets can be easily transmitted around the world.
Internet connections	Many different types of connections are possible, such as dial-up facilities (perhaps over a modem or with ISDN) or through frame relays. The user only has to pay for the service and the local connection.	Data once on the Internet is relatively easy to tap into and possibly easy to change.
Global information	Creation of an ever-increasing global information database.	Data is relatively easy to tap into and possibly easy to change.
Multimedia integration	Tailor-made applications with good presentation tools.	Lack of editorial control leads to inferior material, which is hacked together.
Increasing WWW usage	Helps to improve its chances of acceptance into the home.	Increased traffic swamps the global information network and slows down commercial traffic.
WWW links	Easy to set up and leads users from one place to the next in a logical manner.	WWW links often fossilize where the link information is out of date or doesn't even exist.
Education	Increased usage of remote teaching with full multimedia education.	Increase in surface learning and lack of deep research. It may lead to an increase in time wasting (too much surfing and too little learning).

F2.3 Client/server architecture

The WWW is structured with clients and servers, where a client accesses services from the server. These servers can either be local or available through a global network connection. A local connection normally requires the connection over a local area network but a global connection normally requires connection to an Internet service provider. These providers are often known as Internet service providers (ISPs), sometimes as Internet connectivity providers (ICP). They provide the mechanism to access the Internet and have the required hardware and software to connect from the user to the Internet. This access is typically provided through one of the following:

- Connection to a client computer through a dial-up modem connection (typically at 28.8 kbps or 56 kbps).
- Connection to a client computer through a dial-up ISDN connection (typically at 64 kbps or 128 kbps).
- Connection of a client computer to a server computer which connects to the Internet through a frame relay router (typically 56 kbps or 256 kbps), or broadband communication, with ADSL.
- Connection of a client computer to a local area network which connects to the Internet through a T1, 1.544 Mbps router.

These connections are illustrated in Figure F2.3. A router automatically routes all traffic to and from the Internet whereas the dial-up facility of a modem or ISDN link requires a connection to be made over a circuit-switched line (that is, through the public telephone network). Home users and small businesses typically use modem connections (although ISDN connections are becoming more common). Large corporations which require global Internet services tend to use frame routers. Note that an IAP may be a commercial organization (such as CompuServe or America On-line) or a support organization (such as giving direct connection to government departments or educational institutions). A commercial IAP organization is likely to provide added services, such as electronic mail, search engines, and so on.

An Internet presence provider (IPP) allows organizations to maintain a presence on the Internet without actually having to invest in the Internet hardware. The IPPs typically maintain WWW pages for a given charge (they may also provide sales and support information).

F2.4 Web browsers

Web browsers interpret special hypertext pages which consist of the hypertext markup language (HTML) and JavaScript. They then display it in the given format. There are currently four main Web browsers:

- **Netscape Navigator** – Navigator is one of the most widely used WWW browsers and is available in many different versions on many systems. It runs on PCs (running Microsoft Windows), UNIX workstations and Macintosh computers, and has become the standard WWW browser and has many add-ons and enhancements. The basic package also has many compatible software plug-ins which are developed by third-party suppliers. These add extra functionality, such as video players and sound support.
- **NSCA Mosaic** – Mosaic was originally the most popular Web browser when the Internet

first started. It has now lost its dominance to Microsoft Internet Explorer and Netscape Navigator. NSCA Mosaic was developed by the National Center for Supercomputing Applications (NCSA) at the University of Illinois.

- **Lynx** – Lynx is typically used on UNIX-based computers with a modem dial-up connection. It is fast to download pages but does not support many of the features supported by Netscape Navigator or Mosaic.
- **Microsoft Internet Explorer** – Explorer now comes as a standard part of Microsoft Windows and as this has become the most popular computer operating system then so has this browser.

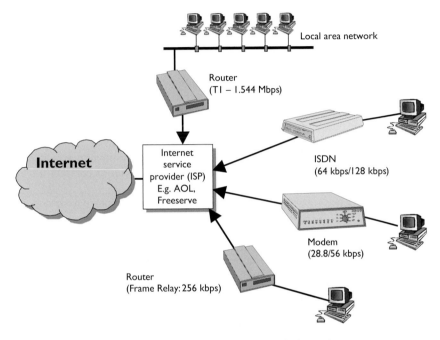

Figure F2.3 Example connections to the Internet

F2.5 Universal resource locators (URLs)

Universal resource locators (URLs) are used to locate a file on the WWW. They provide a pointer to any object on a server connected over the Internet. This link could give FTP access, hypertext references, and so on. URLs contain:

- The protocol of the file (the scheme).
- The server name (domain).
- The pathname of the file.
- The filename.

URL standard format is:

<scheme>:<scheme-specific-part>

and can be broken up into four parts. These are:

```
aaaa://bbb.bbb.bbb/ccc/ccc/ccc?ddd
```

where

`aaaa:` is the access method and specifies the mechanism to be used by the browser to communicate with the resource. The most popular mechanisms are:

> `http:`. HyperText Transfer Protocol. This is the most commonly used mechanism and is typically used to retrieve an HTML file, a graphic file, a sound file, an animation sequence file, a file to be executed by the server, or a word processor file.
> `https:`. HyperText Transfer Protocol. It is a variation on the standard access method and can be used to provide some level of transmission security.
> `file:`. Local file access. This causes the browser to load the specified file from the local disk.
> `ftp:`. File Transport Protocol. This method allows files to be downloaded using an FTP connection.
> `mailto:`. E-mail form. This method allows access to a destination e-mail address. Normally the browser automatically generates an input form for entering the e-mail message.
> `news:`. USENET news. This method defines the access method for a news group.
> `nntp:`. Local Network News Transport Protocol.
> `telnet:`. TELNET. The arguments following the access code are the login arguments to the telnet session as `user[:password]@host`.

`//bbb.bbb.bbb` is the Internet node and specifies the node on the Internet where the file is located. If a node is not given then the browser defaults to the computer which is running the browser. A colon may follow the node address and the port number (most browsers default to port 80, which is also the port that most servers use to reply to the browser).

`/ccc/ccc/ccc` is the file path (including subdirectories and the filename). Typically systems restrict the access to a system by allocating the root directory as a subdirectory of the main file system.

`?ddd` is the argument which depends upon the access method, and the file accessed. For example, with an HTML document a '#' identifies the fragment name internal to an HTML document which is identified by the A element with the NAME attribute.

An example URL is:

```
http://www.toytown.anycor.co/fred/index.html
```

where `http` is the file protocol (Hypertext Translation Protocol), `www.toytown.anycor.co` is the server name, `/fred` is the path of the file and the file is named `index.html`.

F2.5.1 Files

A file URL scheme allows files to be assessed. It takes the form:

```
file://<host>/<path>
```

where *<host>* is the fully qualified domain name of the system to be accessed, *<path>*   is
the full path name, and takes the form of a directory path, such as *<directory>/ <directory>/
.../ <name>*.
  For a file:

```
C:\DOCS\NOTES\NETWORKS\NET_CHAP13.DOC
```

would be accessed as from dummy.com with:

```
file://dummy.com/C|DOCS/NOTES/NETWORKS/NET_CHAP13.DOC
```

Note, that if the host is defined as localhost or is an empty string then the host is assumed
to be the local host. The general format is:

```
fileurl  =  "file://" [ host | "localhost" ] "/" fpath
```

F2.5.2 Electronic mail address

The mailto scheme defines a link to an Internet e-mail address. An example is:

```
mailto: fred.bloggs@toytown.ac.uk
```

When this URL is selected then an e-mail message will be sent to the e-mail address
fred.bloggs@toytown.ac.uk. Normally, some form of text editor is called and the user
can enter the required e-mail message. Upon successful completion of the text message it is
sent to the addressee.

F2.5.3 File Transfer Protocol (FTP)

The ftp URL scheme defines that the files and directories specified are accessed using the
FTP protocol. In its simplest form it is defined as:

```
ftp://<hostname>/<directory-name>/<filename>
```

The FTP protocol normally requests a user to log into the system. For example, many public
domain FTP servers use the login of:

```
anonymous
```

and the password can be anything (but it is normally either the user's full name or their
Internet e-mail address). Another typical operation is changing directory from a starting
directory or the destination file directory. To accommodate this, a more general form is:

```
ftp://<user>:<password>@<hostname>:<port>/<cd1>/<cd2>/ .../<cdn>/<filename>
```

where the user is defined by *<user>* and the password by *<password>*. The host name, *<hostname>*, is defined after the @ symbol and change directory commands are defined by the *cd* commands. The node name may take the form `//user [:password]@host`. Without a user name, the user `anonymous` is used.

For example the reference to the standard related to HTML Version 2 can be downloaded using the URL:

```
ftp://ds.internic.net/rfc/rfc1866.txt
```

and draft Internet documents from:

```
ftp://ftp.isi.edu/internet-drafts/
```

The general format is:

```
ftpurl    =  "ftp://" login [ "/" fpath [ ";type=" ftptype ]]
fpath     =  fsegment *[ "/" fsegment ]
fsegment  =  *[ uchar | "?" | ":" | "@" | "&" | "=" ]
ftptype   =  "A" | "I" | "D" | "a" | "i" | "d"
```

F2.5.4   Hypertext Transfer Protocol (HTTP)

HTTP is the protocol which is used to retrieve information connected with hypermedia links. The client and server initially perform a negotiation procedure before the HTTP transfer takes place. This negotiation involves the client sending a list of formats it can support and the server replying with data in the required format.

Users generally move from a link on one server to another server. Each time the user moves from one server to another, the client sends an HTTP request to the server. Thus the client does not permanently connect to the server, and the server views each transfer as independent from all previous accesses. This is known as a stateless protocol.

An HTTP URL takes the form:

```
http://<host>:<port>/<path>?<searchpart>
```

Note that, if the *<port>* is omitted, port 80 is automatically used (HTTP service), *<path>* is an HTTP selector and *<searchpart>* is a query string.

The general format is:

```
httpurl   =  "http://" hostport [ "/" hpath [ "?" search ]]
hpath     =  hsegment *[ "/" hsegment ]
hsegment  =  *[ uchar | ";" | ":" | "@" | "&" | "=" ]
search    =  *[ uchar | ";" | ":" | "@" | "&" | "=" ]
```

F2.5.5   News

UseNet or NewsGroup servers are part of the increasing use of general discussion news groups which share text-based news items. The news URL scheme defines a link to either a news group or individual articles with a group of UseNet news.

A news URL takes one of two forms:

```
news:<newsgroup-name>        news:<message-id>
```

where *<newsgroup-name>* is a period-delimited hierarchical name, such as 'news.inter', and *<message-id>* takes the full form of the message-ID, such as:

<message-ID>@<full_domain_name>

The general form is:
```
newsurl       = "news:" grouppart
grouppart     = "*" | group | article
group         = alpha *[ alpha | digit | "-" | "." | "+" | "_" ]
article       = 1*[ uchar | ";" | "/" | "?" | ":" | "&" | "=" ] "@" host
```

F2.6 Web browser design

The Web browser is a carefully engineered software package which allows the user to efficiently find information on the WWW. Most are similar in their approach, but differ in their presentation. Figure F2.4 shows the tool bar for Microsoft Internet Explorer. This has been designed to allow the user to move smoothly through the WWW.

Figure F2.4   Microsoft Explorer tool bar

 The Back and Forward options allow the user to traverse backwards and forwards through links. This allows the user to trace back to a previous link and possibly follow it.

 The Stop option is used by the user to interrupt the current transfer. It is typically used when the user does not want to load the complete page. This often occurs when the browser is loading a graphics image.

 The Web browser tries to reduce data transfer by holding recently accessed pages in a memory cache. This cache is typically held on a local disk. The Refresh forces the browser to reload the page from the remote location.

 Often a user wishes to restart a search and can use the Home option to return to it. The home page of the user is set up by one of the options.

 The Search option is used to connect to a page which has access to the search programs Microsoft Explorer typically connects to.

 Often a user has a list of favourite Web pages. This can be automatically called from the Favourites option. A new favourite can be added with the Add To Favourites ... option. These favourites can either be selected from the Favourites menu option (such as Internet Start) or from within folders (such as Channels and Links).

F2.7 HTTP

The foundation protocol of the WWW is the Hypertext Transfer Protocol (HTTP) which can be used in any client/server application involving hypertext. It is used on the WWW for transmitting information using hypertext jumps and can support the transfer of plaintext, hypertext, audio, images, or any Internet-compatible information. The most recently defined standard is HTTP 1.1, which has been defined by the IETF standard.

HTTP is a stateless protocol where each transaction is independent of any previous transactions. Thus when the transaction is finished the TCP/IP connection is disconnected, as illustrated in Figure F2.5. The advantage of being stateless is that it allows the rapid access of WWW pages over several widely distributed servers. It uses the TCP protocol to establish a connection between a client and a server for each transaction then terminates the connection once the transaction completes.

HTTP also supports many different formats of data. Initially a client issues a request to a server which may include a prioritized list of formats that it can handle. This allows new formats to be easily added and also prevents the transmission of unnecessary information.

A client's WWW browser (the user agent) initially establishes a direct connection with the destination server which contains the required WWW page. To make this connection the client initiates a TCP connection between the client and the server. After this is established the client then issues an HTTP request, such as the specific command (the method), the URL, and possibly extra information such as request parameters or client information. When the server receives the request, it attempts to perform the requested action. It then returns an HTTP response, which includes status information, a success/error code, and extra information. After the client receives this, the TCP connection is closed.

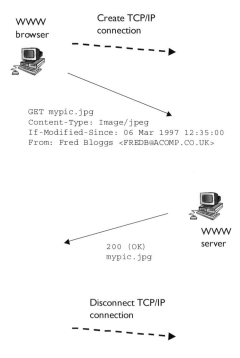

Figure F2.5 Example HTTP transaction

F2.7.1 Caches, tunnels and user agents

In a computer system, a cache is an area of memory that stores information likely to be accessed in a fast access memory area. For example, a cache controller takes a guess on which information the process is likely to access next. When the processor wishes to access the disk then, if it has guessed right, the cache controller will load from the electronic memory rather than loading it from the disk. A WWW cache stores cacheable responses so that there is a reduction in network traffic and an improvement in access times. Figure F2.6 shows an example use of a cache. Initially (1) the client sends out a request for a page, along with the date that it was last accessed. If the page has not changed then the server sends back a message saying that it has not been changed. The client will then use the page that is stored in the local cache.

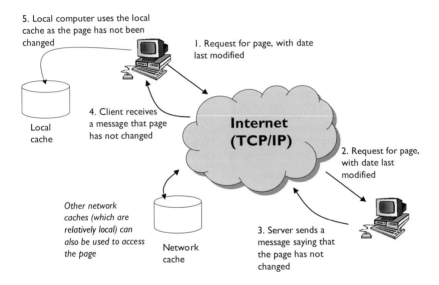

Figure F2.6 Using caches

Often Internet Service Providers use a network cache which stores pages that users have recently accessed. If a request is made for a page which has already been accessed, and is stored in the cache, the network cache can be used to provide the page to the requester. In the future, network caches could be used to considerably speed-up WWW page download. In this, popular pages would be regularly downloaded to the cache, and sent to the clients when required. An important factor is keeping the cache regularly updated. For this HTTP requests must still be sent with the date and time that the page was last updated. If there is a change, the new updated page should be sent (and obviously also stored in the cache).

Some WWW browsers can also be setup so that they do not re-access a previously loaded page, if it is re-requested within a given time. This can be annoying for the user, especially if the page is updating itself within a short interval (such as with a WWW camera). A Reload button is typically used to force the WWW browser to re-request the page.

Tunnels are intermediary devices which act as a blind relay between two connections. When the tunnel becomes active, it is not seen to be part of the HTTP communications.

When the connection is closed by both sides, the tunnel ceases to exit.

A user agent, in HTTP, is a client which initiates requests to a server. Typically this is a WWW browser or a WWW spider (an automated WWW trailing program).

F2.7.2   HTTP messages

HTTP messages are either requests from clients to servers or responses from servers to clients (Figure F2.7). The message is either a simple-request, a simple-response, full-request or a full-response. HTTP Version 0.9 defines the simple request/ response messages whereas HTTP Version 1.1 defines full requests/responses.

HTTP is a stateless protocol where each transaction is independent of any previous transactions. The advantage of being stateless is that it allows the rapid access of WWW pages over several widely distributed servers. It uses the TCP protocol to establish a connection between a client and a server for each transaction then terminates the connection once the transaction completes.

HTTP also supports many different formats of data. Initially a client issues a request to a server which may include a prioritized list of formats that it can handle. This allows new formats to be easily added and also prevents the transmission of unnecessary information.

A client's WWW browser (the user agent) initially establishes a direct connection with the destination server which contains the required WWW page.

To make this connection the client initiates a TCP connection between the client and the server. After this is established the client then issues an HTTP request, such as the specific command (the method), the URL, and possibly extra information such as request parameters or client information.

When the server receives the request, it attempts to perform the requested action.

It then returns an HTTP response, which includes status information, a success/error code, and extra information itself.

After the client receives this, the TCP connection is closed.

Figure F2.7   HTTP operation

Simple requests/responses

The simple request is a GET command with the requested URI such as:

```
GET   /info/dept/courses.html
```

The simple response is a block containing the information identified in the URI (called the entity-body).

Full requests/responses

Very few security measures or enhanced services are built into the simple requests/responses. HTTP Version 1.0/1.1 improves on the simple requests/responses by adding many extra requests and responses, as well as adding extra information about the data supported. Each message header consists of a number of fields which begin on a new line and consist of the field name followed by a colon and the field value. This follows the format of RFC822 (as shown in Section F1.5.4) and allows for MIME encoding. It is thus similar to MIME-encoded e-mail. A full request starts with a request line command (such as GET, MOVE or DELETE) and is then followed by one or more of the following:

- General-headers which contain general fields that do not apply to the entity being transferred (such as MIME version, date, and so on).
- Request-headers which contain information on the request and the client (e.g. the client's name, its authorization, and so on).
- Entity-headers which contain information about the resource identified by the request and entity-body information (such as the type of encoding, the language, the title, the time when it was last modified, the type of resource it is, when it expires, and so on).
- Entity-body which contains the body of the message (such as HTML text, an image, a sound file, and so on).

A full response starts with a response status code (such as OK, Moved Temporarily, Accepted, Created, Bad Request, and so on) and is then followed by one or more of the following:

- General-headers, as with requests, contain general fields which do not apply to the entity being transferred (MIME version, date, and so on).
- Response-headers which contain information on the response and the server (e.g. the server's name, its location and the time the client should retry the server).
- Entity-headers, as with request, which contain information about the resource identified by the request and entity-body information (such as the type of encoding, the language, the title, the time when it was last modified, the type of resource it is, when it expires, and so on).
- Entity-body, as with requests, which contains the body of the message (such as HTML text, an image, a sound file, and so on).

The following example shows an example request. The first line is always the request method; in this case it is GET. Next there are various headers. The general-header field is Content-Type, the request-header fields are If-Modified-Since and From. There are no entity parts to the message as the request is to get an image (if the command had been to PUT then there would have been an attachment with the request). Notice that a single blank line delimits the end of the message as this indicates the end of a request/response. Note that the headers are case sensitive, thus Content-Type with the correct types of letters (and GET is always in uppercase letters).

📖 **Example HTTP request**

```
GET mypic.jpg
Content-Type: Image/jpeg
If-Modified-Since: 06 Mar 1997 12:35:00
From: Fred Bloggs <FREDB@ACOMP.CO.UK>
```

Request messages
The most basic request message is to GET a URI. HTTP/1.1 (Figure F2.8) adds many more requests including:

COPY	DELETE	GET	HEAD	POST	LINK
MOVE	OPTIONS	PUT	TRACE	UNLINK	WRAPPED

As before, the GET method requests a WWW page. The HEAD method tells the server that the client wants to read only the header of the WWW page. If the If-Modified-Since field is included then the server checks the specified date with the date of the URI and verifies whether it has not changed since then.

A PUT method requests storage of a WWW page and POST appends to a named resource (such as electronic mail). LINK connects two existing resources and UNLINK breaks the link. A DELETE method removes a WWW page. The request-header fields are mainly used to define the acceptable type of entity that can be received by the client; they include (Figure F2.9):

```
Accept               Accept-Charset       Accept-Encoding
Accept-Language      Authorization        From
Host                 If-Modified-Since    Referer
Proxy-Authorization  Range
Unless               User-Agent
```

The Accept field is used to list all the media types and ranges that the client can accept. An Accept-Charset field defines a list of character sets acceptable to the server and Accept-Encoding is a list of acceptable content encodings (such as the compression or encryption technique). The Accept-Language field defines a set of preferred natural languages.

The Authorization field has a value which authenticates the client to the server. A From field defines the e-mail address of the user who is using the client (e.g. From: fred.blogg@anytown.uk) and the Host field specifies the name of the host of the resource being requested.

A useful field is the If-Modified-Since field, used with the GET method. It defines a date and time parameter and specifies that the resource should not be sent if it has not been modified since the specified time. This is useful when a client has a local copy of the resource in a local cache and, rather than transmitting the unchanged resource, it can use its own local copy.

The Proxy-Authorization field is used by the client to identify itself to a proxy when the proxy requires authorization. A Range field is used with the GET message to get only a part of the resource.

The Referer field defines the URI of the resource from which the Request-URI was obtained and enables the server to generate lists of back-links. An Unless field is used to make a comparison based on any entity-header field value rather than a date/time value (as with GET and If-Modified-Since).

Method types

GET. Retrieves the information that is defined in the Request-URI. If the request message includes an If-Modified-Since header field, the GET is conditional on the date and time that is defined in the If-Modified-Since header. Conditional GETs allow cached system to be refreshed only when resources have been updated.

HEAD. Identical to GET, but the server should not return any Entity-Body in the response. It can be used for obtaining information on the resource without actually receiving the Entity-Body. It can be used to test links for the accessibility, validity, and so on.

POST. Used to request that the destination server accepts the entity enclosed in the request as a subordinate of a resource. Typical applications are annotating existing resources and posting messages to bulletin boards, newsgroups, and so on.

PUT. Requests that the enclosed entity is stored under the supplied Request-URI. If the Request-URI is an existing resource, the enclosed entity is considered as a modified version of the existing resource, else it is treated as a new resource.

DELETE. Requests that the server deletes the resource identified by the Request-URI.

Content-encoding:
```
GET mypic.jpg
Content-Type: Image/jpeg
If-Modified-Since: 06 Mar 1997 12:35:00
From: Fred Bloggs <FREDB@ACOMP.CO.UK>
```

Sent from WWW browser to the WWW server

Figure F2.8   Messages sent from WWW browser to WWW server

Content-language:
The Language field defines the language of the resource. Its format is *Language-tag*, where *Language* is the language (such as en for English), and *tag* is the dialect. For example:

    Content-type: audio/basic
    Content-Language: en-scottish

Content-encoding
The Content-Encoding field describes the type of encoding used in the entity. It indicates the additional content coding that has been applied to the resource. In most cases the encoding is 'gzip' or 'x-compress' (or 'x-gzip' and 'compress'). The Content-Type header field defines the underlying content. An example of this field is:

    Content-Encoding: x-gzip
    Content-Type = text/plain

where the content type is plain text, which has been zipped with gzip (a Lempel-Ziv based compression program). The x-compress program uses Lempel-Ziv-Welsh (LZW) compression.

From:
The From field contains an Internet e-mail address of the owner of the requesting user agent, such as:

    From: fred_b@myserver.com

It is typically used for logging purposes.

Last modified:
The Last-Modified indicates the date and time the resource was last modified. An example of the field is:

    Last-Modified: Wed, 23 Dec 1998 03:20:25 GMT

Content-type:
The Content-Type field defines the media type of the Entity-Body sent to the recipient.
An example of the field is:

    Content-type: text/plain; charset = ISO-8859-1

Content-Types are of the format *type/subject*. Typical types are 'application', 'image', 'text', 'audio' and 'video', and example content types are:

    text/plain text/enriched image/gif
    image/jpeg audio/basic   video/mpeg
    application/postscript   application/msword

Figure F2.9   HTTP header types

The User-Agent field contains information about the user agent originating this request.

Response messages
In HTTP/0.9 the response from the server was either the entity or no response. HTTP/1.1 includes many other responses (Figure F2.10). These include:

Accepted	Bad Gateway
Bad Request	Conflict
Continue	Created
Forbidden	Gateway Timeout
Gone	Internal Server Error
Length Required	Method Not Allowed
Moved Permanently	Moved Temporarily
Multiple Choices	No Content
Non-Authoritative Info	None Acceptable
Not Found	Not Implemented
Not Modified	OK
Partial Content	Payment Required
Proxy Authorization Required	Request Timeout
Reset Content	See Other
Service Unavailable	Switching Protocols
Unauthorized	Unless True
Use Proxy	

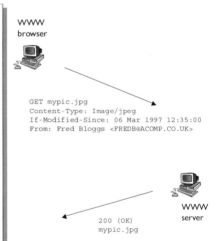

2xx SUCCESSFUL
200 (OK) Request succeeded. Information returned depends on the method used. With GET, the requested entity is sent in the response.
201 (Created) New resource has been created. The new created resource is defined in the URI returned in the entity of the response.
202 (Accepted) Request has been accepted for processing, but the processing is continuing.
204 (No Content) Successful implementation, but there is no new information to be sent back.
3xx REDIRECTION
300 (Multiple choices) Request resource is available from one or more locations. If the server has a preference it adds a Location field with the preferred URL.
301 (Moved Permanently) Requested resource has been assigned a new permanent URL. Future references should be made to the specified URL, which is located in the Location field.
302 (Moved Temporarily) Requested resource has temporarily moved to another URL. The calling agent should still use the URI given in the Request-URI.
304 (Not Modified) This is sent when the client issues a GET request with the If-Modified-Since field is set to a given time, and the document has not modified since the time specified.
4xx CLIENT ERROR
5xx SERVER ERROR

WWW browser

GET mypic.jpg
Content-Type: Image/jpeg
If-Modified-Since: 06 Mar 1997 12:35:00
From: Fred Bloggs <FREDB@ACOMP.CO.UK>

WWW server

200 (OK)
mypic.jpg

Figure F2.10 HTTP responses

These responses can be put into five main groupings:

- Client error – Bad Request, Conflict, Forbidden, Gone, Payment required, Not Found, Method Not Allowed, None Acceptable, Proxy Authentication Required, Request Timeout, Length Required, Unauthorized, Unless True.
- Informational – Continue, Switching Protocol.
- Redirection – Moved Permanently, Moved Temporarily, Multiple Choices, See Other, Not Modified, User Proxy.
- Server error – Bad Gateway, Internal Server Error, Not Implemented, Service Unavailable, Gateway Timeout.
- Successful – Accepted, Created, OK, Non-Authoritative Info. The OK field is used when the request succeeds and includes the appropriate response information.

The response header fields are:

```
Location           Proxy-Authenticate      Public
Retry-After        Server                  WWW-Authenticate
```

The Location field defines the location of the resource identified by the Request-URI. A Proxy-Authenticate field contains the status code of the Proxy Authorization Required response.

The Public field defines non-standard methods supported by this server. A Retry-After field contains values which define the amount of time a service will be unavailable (and is thus sent with the Service Unavailable response).

The WWW-Authenticate field contains the status code for the Unauthorized response.

General-header fields

General-header fields are used either within requests or within responses; they include:

```
Cache-Control    Connection      Date     Forwarded
Keep-Alive       MIME-Version    Pragma   Upgrade
```

The Cache-Control field gives information on the caching mechanism and stops the cache controller from modifying the request/response. A Connection field specifies the header field names that apply to the current TCP connection.

The Date field specifies the date and time at which the message originated; this is obviously useful when examining the received message as it gives an indication of the amount of time the message took to arrive at its destination. Gateways and proxies use the Forwarded field to indicate intermediate steps between the client and the server. When a gateway or proxy reads the message, it can attach a Forwarded field with its own URI (this can help in tracing the route of a message).

The Keep-Alive field specifies that the requester wants a persistent connection. It may indicate the maximum amount of time that the sender will wait for the next request before closing the connection. It can also be used to specify the maximum number of additional requests on the current persistent connection.

The MIME-Version field indicates the MIME version (such as MIME-Version: 1.0). A Pragma field contains extra information for specific applications.

In a request the Upgrade field specifies the additional protocols that the client supports and wishes to use, whereas in a response it indicates the protocol to be used.

Entity-header fields
Depending on the type of request or response, an entity-header can be included:

```
Allow               Content-Encoding        Content-Language
Content-Length      Content-MD5             Content-Range
Content-Type        Content-Version         Derived-From
Expires             Last-Modified           Link
Title               Transfer-encoding
URI-Header          extension-header
```

The Allow field defines the supported methods supported by the resource identified in the Request-URI. A Content-Encoding field indicates content encodings, such as ZIP compression, that have been applied to the resource (Content-Encoding: zip).

The Content-Language field identifies natural language(s) of the intended audience for the enclosed entity (e.g. Content-language: German) and the Content-Length field defines the number of bytes in the entity.

The Content-Range field designates a portion of the identified resource that is included in this response, while Content-Type indicates the media type of the entity body (such as Content-Type=text/html, Content-Type=text/plain, Content-Type=image/gif or Content-type=image/jpeg). The version of the entity is defined in the Content-Version field.

The Expires field defines the date and time when the entity is considered stale. The Last-Modified field is the date and time when the resource was last modified.

The Link field defines other links and the Title field defines the title for the entity. A Transfer-Encoding field indicates the transformation type that is applied so the entity can be transmitted.

F2.8   HTTP reference

F2.8.1   Method definitions

The main methods are:

- **GET.** Retrieves the information that is defined in the Request-URI. If the request message includes an If-Modified-Since header field, the GET is conditional on the date and time that is defined in the If-Modified-Since header. Conditional GETs allow cached system to be refreshed only when resources have been updated.
- **HEAD.** Identical to GET, but the server should not return any Entity-Body in the response. It can be used for obtaining information on the resource without actually receiving the Entity-Body. It can be used to test links for the accessibility, validity, and so on.
- **POST.** Used to request that the destination server accept the entity enclosed in the re-

quest as a subordinate of a resource. Typical applications are annotating existing resources and posting message to bulletin boards, newsgroups, and so on.

- **PUT.** Requests that the enclosed entity is stored under the supplied Request-URI. If the Request-URI is an existing resource, the enclosed entity is considered as a modified version of the existing resource, else it is treated as a new resource.
- **DELETE.** Requests that the server deletes the resource identified by the Request-URI.
- **LINK.** Establishes one or more links between the existing resources and resources identified by the Request-URI.
- **UNLINK.** Opposite of LINK.

F2.8.2   HTTP message

HTTP messages are text-based and are either requests from the client to the server, or are responses from the server to the client. They can either be Simple-Requests/Responses (HTTP/0.9), such as:

GET   <SPACE>   Request-URI   <CRLF>
or Full-Requests/Responses (HTTP/1.0 or HTTP/1.1), such as:

GET <SPACE> Request-URI <SPACE> HTTP-Version <CRLF>
HEAD <SPACE> Request-URI <SPACE> HTTP-Version <CRLF>
POST <SPACE> Request-URI <SPACE> HTTP-Version <CRLF>

Simple-Request format is discouraged as it prevents a server from identifying the media type of the returned entity. Both types can include optional header fields and an entity body.   Entity bodies are separated from the headers by a null line.
HTTP header fields consist of a name followed by a colon (':'), then a space followed by the field values. They include:

General-Headers.	These are applicable for both request and response messages, but they do not apply to the entity being transferred.
Request-Header.	These allow clients to pass extra information about the request, and about itself, to the server. They act as request modifiers.
Entity-Header.	These define optional metainformation about the Entity-Body.
Response-Header.	These allow the server to pass additional information about the response which cannot be placed in the Status-Line.

The Date field represents the date and time of the transmitted message (in the same format as RFC822). An example is:

Date: Wed, 30 Dec 1998 15:22:15 GMT

The Pragma field allows a client to refresh a cached copy which is known to be corrupted or stale and is used to include implementation-specific directives that may apply to any recipient along the request/response chain. An example is:

pragma-directive = no-cache

The Authorization field authenticates a user agent to a server. The server sends a challenge to the user agent, based on a user-ID and a password for each realm (a sting). The user agent must return back a valid user-ID and password for the Request-URI (this is the basic authentication scheme).

When the server receives an unauthorized request for a URI, the server responds with a challenge, such as:

WWW-Authenticate: Basic realm = "FredServer"

where "FredServer" is the realm to identify the protection space of the Request-URI. The client must then send back its user-ID and password, separated by a single colon character, and using base64 encoded (see Section F2.6.4). An example may be:

Authorization: Basic A = IYaacZZP===GSpKQarcc31pacbu

The From field is typically used for logging purposes and contains an Internet e-mail address of the owner of the requesting user agent, such as:

From: fred_b@myserver.com

The If-Modified-Since field is used with the GET to define that a GET is conditional on the date that the resource was last modified. If it was not modified since the specified date then the resource is not sent in the Entity-Body and a 304 response (Not Modified) is sent. An example of this field is:

If-Modified-Since: Wed, 30 Dec 1998 15:22:15 GMT

The Referer field allows the client to specify the address (URI) from which the Request-URI was obtained. This allows the server to trace referenced links. An example of this field is:
    Referer: http://www.w3.org/hypertext/DataSources/Overview.html

The Location field defines the resource location that was specified in the Request-URI. An example of this field is:

Location: http://www.myserver.com/test/newlink.html

The Server field contains information about the software which is used by the origin server to handle the request. An example of this field is:

Server: CERN/3.0 libwww/2.17

The Content-Encoding field describes the type of encoding used in the entity. It indicates the additional content coding has been applied to the resource. In most cases the encoding is 'gzip' or 'x-compress' (or 'x-gzip' and 'compress'). The Content-Type header field defines the underlying content. An example of this field is:

Content-Encoding: x-gzip
Content-Type = text/plain

where the content type is plain text, which has been zipped with gzip (a Lempel-Ziv based compression program). The x-compress program uses Lempel-Ziv-Welsh (LZW) compression.

The Content-Length field defines the number of bytes in the Entity-Body. An example is:

Content-Length: 4095

The Content-Type field defines the media type of the Entity-Body sent to the recipient. An example of the field is:

Content-type: text/plain; charset=ISO-8859-1

Content-Types are of the format *type/subject*. Typical types are 'application', 'image', 'text', 'audio' and 'video', and example content types are:

```
text/plain                text/enriched          image/gif
image/jpeg                audio/basic            video/mpeg
application/octet-stream  application/postscript
application/msword        application/rtf
```

The Expires field defines the date and time after which the entity should be considered as stale. An example of the field is:

Expires: Wed, 30 Dec 1998 15:22:15 GMT

The Last-Modified field indicates the date and time the resource was last modified. An example of the field is:

Last-Modified: Wed, 23 Dec 1998 03:20:25 GMT

The Language field defines the language of the resource. Its format is *Language-tag*, where *Language* is the language (such as en for English), and *tag* is the dialect. For example:

Content-type: audio/basic
Content-Language: en-scottish

F2.8.3 Status codes

Informational 1xx

The Informational status codes indicate a provisional response. They are typically used for experimental purposes.

Successful 2xx

The successful status codes indicate that a client's request has been successful. These include:

200 (OK)	Request succeeded. Information returned depends on the method used. With GET, the requested entity is sent in the response.
201 (Created)	New resource has been created. The new created resource is defined in the URI returned in the entity of the response.
202 (Accepted)	Request has been accepted for processing, but the processing is continuing.
204 (No Content)	Successful implementation, but there is no new information to be sent back.

Redirection 3xx

The redirection status code indicates that further action is required to service the request. These include:

300 (Multiple Choices)	Request resource is available from one or more locations. If the server has a preference it adds a Location field with the preferred URL.
301 (Moved Permanently)	Requested resource has been assigned a new permanent URL. Future references should be made to the specified URL, which is located in the Location field.
302 (Moved Temporarily)	Requested resource has temporarily moved to another URL. The calling agent should still use the URI given in the Request-URI.
304 (Not Modified)	This is sent when the client issues a GET request with the If-Modified-Since field is set to a given time, and the document has not modified since the time specified.

Client Error 4xx

The client error status codes indicate that an error has occurred on the client. These include:

400 (Bad Request)	Request cannot be understood by the server due to bad syntax.
401 (Unauthorized)	Request requires user authentication. A response includes the WWW-Authenticate header field, which contains a challenge for the requested resource. The client must then repeat the request with a suitable Authorization header field.
403 (Forbidden)	Server will not service the request. It is typically used when the server does not want to reveal the reason why it is not servicing the request.
404 (Not Found)	Server did not find the required Request-URI.

Server Error 5xx

The server error status codes indicate that there is an error with the server.

500 (Internal Server Error)	Unexpected server condition in servicing the request.
501 (Not Implemented)	Server does not support the request.
502 (Bad Gateway)	Server, while acting as a gateway or proxy, received an invalid response from the upstream server it accessed in attempting to service the request.

503 (Service Unavailable)	Server is currently unavailable, possibly because of server maintenance or overloading.

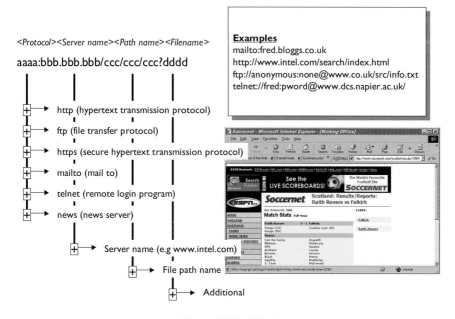

Figure F2.11   URL format

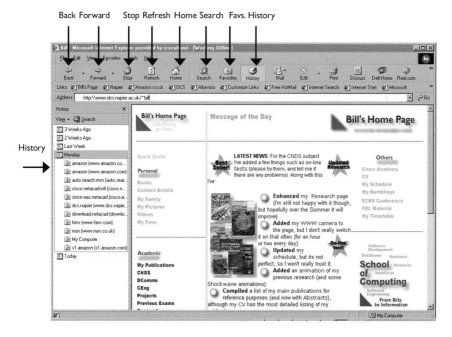

Figure F2.12   WWW Browser design

F2.9   Example conversation

It is possible to listen to both WWW client and WWW server discussions using the WinSock client, and the WinSock server. For example the following screen shows the information sent from a WWW client to a WWW server:

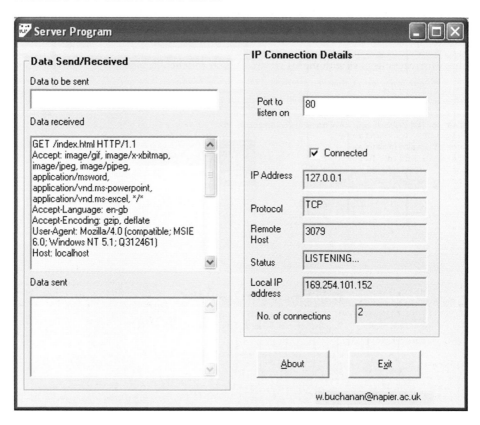

It can be seen that the local server port is 80, and that the client is using port 3078. A Microsoft Internet Explorer client which requires to access the index.html page will request it with:

```
GET /index.html HTTP/1.1
Accept: image/gif, image/x-xbitmap, image/jpeg, image/pjpeg, applica-
tion/msword, application/vnd.ms-powerpoint, application/vnd.ms-excel, */*
Accept-Language: en-gb
Accept-Encoding: gzip, deflate
User-Agent: Mozilla/4.0 (compatible; MSIE 6.0; Windows NT 5.1; Q312461)
Host: localhost
Connection: Keep-Alive
```

and a NetScape 4.7 client will access it with:

```
GET /index.html HTTP/1.0
Connection: Keep-Alive
User-Agent: Mozilla/4.77 [en] (Windows NT 5.0; U)
```

```
Host: localhost
Accept: image/gif, image/x-xbitmap, image/jpeg, image/pjpeg, image/png, */*
Accept-Encoding: gzip
Accept-Language: en
Accept-Charset: iso-8859-1,*,utf-8
```

If we issue the command from a WWW client (and press RETURN twice):

```
GET /index.html HTTP/1.0
```

The sever responds back with the HTTP information and the WWW page:

```
HTTP/1.1 200 OK
Date: Sun, 20 Jan 2002 21:44:17 GMT
Server: Apache/1.3.14 (Win32)
Last-Modified: Thu, 17 Jan 2002 10:58:22 GMT
ETag: "0-67c6-3c46ae4e"
Accept-Ranges: bytes
Content-Length: 26566
Connection: close
Content-Type: text/html

<!DOCTYPE HTML PUBLIC "-//W3C//DTD HTML 4.0 Transitional//EN">
<HTML><HEAD><TITLE>Bill Buchanan Home Page</TITLE>
<META http-equiv=Content-Type content="text/html; charset=windows-1252">
<META etc ....
```

As shown next:

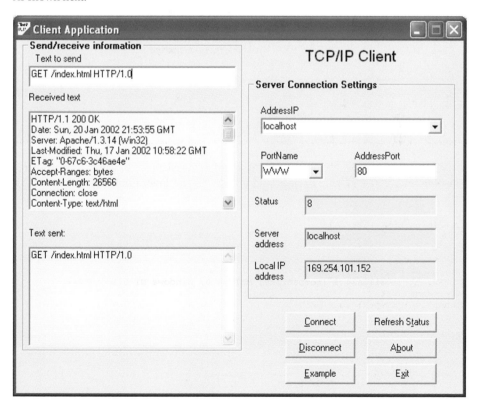

F3 SNMP, Wins, Bootp, DNS and DHCP

F3.1 Introduction

SNMP (Simple Network Management Protocol) is a well-supported standard which can be used to monitor and control devices. It typically runs of hubs, switches and bridges. Many SNMP devices provides both general network management and device management through a serial cable, modem, or over the network from a remote computer. It involves a primary management station communicating with different management processes. Figure F3.1 shows an outline of an SNMP-based system. A SNMP agent runs SNMP management software. An SNMP server sends commands to the agent which responses back with the results. In this figure the server asks the agent for its routing information and the agent re-sponds with its routing table. These responses can either be polled (the server sends a request for information) or interrupt-driven (where the agent sends its information at given events). A polled system tends to increase network traffic as the agent may not have any updated information (and the server must re-poll for the information).

The SNMP (Simple Network Management Protocol) protocol is initially based in the RFC1157 document. It defines a simple protocol which gives network element management information base (MIB). There are two types of MIB: MIB-1 and MIB-2. MIB-1 was defined in 1988 and has 114 table entries, divided into two groups. MIB-2 is a 1990 enhancement which has 171 entries organized into 10 groups (RFC 1213). Most devices are MIB-1 compli-ant and newer one with both MIB-1 and MIB-2.

The database contains entries with four fields:

- Object type. Defines the name of the entry.
- Syntax. Gives the actual value (as string or an integer).
- Access field. Defines whether the value is read-only, read/write, write-only and not ac-cessible.
- Status field. Contains an indication on whether the entry in the MIB is mandatory (the managed device must implement the entry), optional (the managed device may im-plement the entry) or obsolete (the entry is not used).

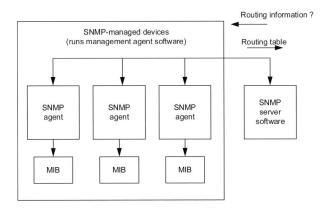

Figure F3.1 SNMP architecture

SNMP is a very simple protocol but suffers from the fact that it is based on connectionless, unreliable, UDP. The IAB have recommended that the Common Management Information Services (CMIS) and Common Management Information Protocol (CMIP) be accepted as standard for future TCP/IP systems. The two main version of SNMP are SNMP Ver1 and SNMP Ver2. SNMP has added security to stop intruders determining network loading or the state of the network.

F3.2   SNMP

The SNMP architecture is based on a collection of:

- Network management stations. These execute management applications which monitor and control network elements.
- Network elements. These are devices such as hosts, gateways, terminal servers, and so on and have management agents which perform network management functions replying to requests from network management stations.

The SNMP management information represented by a subset of the ASN.1 language. SNMP models all management agent functions as alterations or inspections of variables. Thus, a protocol entity on a logically remote host interacts with the management agent resident on the network element in order to retrieve (get) or alter (set) variables.

SNMP determines the current state of the network by polling for appropriate information from monitoring center(s).

F3.2.1   Protocol specification

The network management protocol operates by inspecting or altering variables on an agent's MIB (management information base). They communicate by exchanging messages within UDP datagrams. These messages are defined using ASN.1 and are specified in listing F3.1. They consist of:

- A Version identifier (`version`). An integer value defining the version number.
- SNMP community name (`community`). An eight character string defining the community name.
- A protocol data unit (`data`). All SNMP implementations five PDUs: `GetRequest-PDU`, `GetNextRequest-PDU`, `GetResponse-PDU`, `SetRequest-PDU`, and `Trap-PDU`.

The protocol receives messages from:

- UDP port 161. For all messages apart from report traps (Trap-PDU).
- UDP port 162. Report trap Messages

📄 **Listing F3.1**
```
RFC1157-SNMP DEFINITIONS ::= BEGIN
IMPORTS
   ObjectName, ObjectSyntax, NetworkAddress, IpAddress, TimeTicks
      FROM RFC1155-SMI;
```

```
-- top-level message
    Message ::=
        SEQUENCE {
            version       -- version-1 for this RFC
              INTEGER {
                version-1(0)
              },
            community    -- community name
              OCTET STRING,
            data         -- e.g., PDUs if trivial
              ANY        -- authentication is being used
        }

-- protocol data units
    PDUs ::=
        CHOICE {
            get-request          GetRequest-PDU,
            get-next-request     GetNextRequest-PDU,
            get-response         GetResponse-PDU,
            set-request          SetRequest-PDU,
            trap                 Trap-PDU
            }
-- the individual PDUs and commonly used
-- data types will be defined later
END
```

Common constructs

Listing F3.2 defines the ANS.1 constructs used in the PDUs. RequestID distinguishes between outstanding requests. ErrorStatus is an integer (0-5) which defines the error level,
a zero indicates no error, a 1 indicates tooBig, and so on. When an error occurs, the ErrorIndex parameter is typically used to indicate which variable in a list caused the error.

The VarBind parameter (variable binding) refers to the link between the name of a variable and the variable's value, and VarBindList is a list of variable names and their
corresponding values.

📄 **Listing F3.2**
```
-- request/response information
    RequestID ::=
        INTEGER
    ErrorStatus ::=
        INTEGER {
            noError(0), tooBig(1), noSuchName(2),
            badValue(3), readOnly(4), genErr(5)
        }
    ErrorIndex ::=
        INTEGER

    -- variable bindings
    VarBind ::=
        SEQUENCE {
            name    ObjectName,
            value   ObjectSyntax
        }
```

```
VarBindList ::=
        SEQUENCE OF
        VarBind
```

GetRequest-PDU

GetRequest-PDU gets objects the MIB of the receiptiant. These objects are defined in the variable binding field. On no errors, the receiptiant sends back `GetResponse-PDU`, with:

- Each object named in the variable-bindings field of the received message.
- Corresponding component of the `GetResponse-PDU` representing by the name.
- Value of each of the variables.

If all the objects are found, the value of the error-status field and the error-index field of the `GetResponse-PDU` must be `noError` and zero, respectively. The request-id field will be the same as the received message.

If any of the objects cannot be found in the DIB then the receiptiant sends to the originator a `GetResponse-PDU` with an error-status field value of is `noSuchName`. The value of error-index is set to the value of the error-index field of the object name component in the received message.

Listing F3.3 defines the general form of the `GetRequest-PDU`.

📄 **Listing F3.3**
```
GetRequest-PDU ::= [0]
        IMPLICIT SEQUENCE {
            request-id            RequestID,
            error-status          ErrorStatus,
            error-index           ErrorIndex,
            variable-bindings     VarBindList
        }
```

GetNextRequest-PDU

GetNextRequest-PDU is sent when the protocol entity makes a request of its SNMP application entity. If no error occurs then the receiving protocol entity sends the GetResponse-PDU containing noError in the error-status field and a zero value in the errorindex field. The value of the request-id field of the GetResponse-PDU is that of the received message.

Listing F3.4 defines the format in ASN.1 language. The only difference between this PDU and the GetRequest-PDU is defined with type value of 0 (rather than 1).

📄 **Listing F3.4**
```
GetNextRequest-PDU ::=
IMPLICIT SEQUENCE {
            request-id            RequestID,
            error-status          ErrorStatus,
            error-index           ErrorIndex,
            variable-bindings     VarBindList
        }
```

GetResponse-PDU

GetResponse-PDU occurs after a protocol entity receives a GetRequest-PDU, GetNextRequest-PDU, or a SetRequest-PDU. After it is received the receiving protocol entity sends its contents to its SNMP application entity. Listing F3.5 defines the format in ASN.1 language.

 Listing F3.5

```
GetResponse-PDU ::=
    IMPLICIT SEQUENCE {
        request-id              RequestID,
        error-status            ErrorStatus,
        error-index             ErrorIndex,
        variable-bindings       VarBindList
    }
```

The SetRequest-PDU

The protocol entity sends a SetRequest-PDU at the request of its SNMP application entity. When received the receiving entity sends the corresponding value is assigned to the variable for each object named in the variable-bindings field of the received message. Listing F3.6 defines the format in ASN.1 language.

 Listing F3.6

```
SetRequest-PDU ::=
IMPLICIT SEQUENCE {
        request-id              RequestID,
        error-status            ErrorStatus,
        error-index             ErrorIndex,
        variable-bindings       VarBindList
    }
```

Trap-PDU

Trap-PDU occurs when the protocol entity receives a request from a SNMP application entity. When received, the receiving protocol entity sends its contents to its SNMP application entity. The variable-bindings component of the Trap-PDU is implementation-specific, these are:

- coldStart (0). Sending protocol entity is reinitializing itself, thus the agent's configuration may be altered.
- warmStart (1). Sending protocol entity is reinitializing itself, so that neither the agent configuration nor the protocol entity implementation will be altered.
- linkDown (2). Sending protocol entity recognizes a failure in one of the communication links represented in the agent's configuration.
- linkUp (3). Sending protocol entity recognizes that one of the communication links represented in the agent's configuration has come up.
- authenticationFailure (4). Sending protocol entity is the addressee of a protocol message that is not properly authenticated.
- egpNeighborLoss (5). EGP neighbor for whom the sending protocol entity was an EGP peer no longer exists.
- enterpriseSpecific (6). Sending protocol entity recognizes an enterprise-specific event.

The form of the Trap-PDU is:

```
Trap-PDU ::=     [4]
   IMPLICIT SEQUENCE {
      enterprise     -- type of object generating type

        OBJECT IDENTIFIER,
      agent-addr          -- address of object generating
        NetworkAddress,   -- trap
      generic-trap        -- generic trap type
        INTEGER {
          coldStart(0), warmStart(1),
          linkDown(2),  linkUp(3),
          authenticationFailure(4),  egpNeighborLoss(5),
          enterpriseSpecific(6)
        },
      specific-trap  -- specific code, present even
        INTEGER,     -- if generic-trap is not
                     -- enterpriseSpecific
      time-stamp     -- time elapsed between the last
      TimeTicks,     -- (re)initialization of the network
               -- entity and the generation of the trap
      variable-bindings  -- "interesting" information
        VarBindList
   }
```

MIB-2 added a number of groups, include system, interfaces, at, ip, icmp, tcp, udp, egp, transmission and snmp.

F3.2.2   system

These include:

- sysObjectID. Identifies object ID.
- sysUpTime. Identifies system up time.
- sysContact. Identifies the system contact.
- sysName. Identifies the system name.
- sysLocation. Identifies the location of the system.
- sysServices. Identifies the system services.

F3.2.3   interfaces

The interfaces table includes:

- ifNumber. Number of interfaces.
- ifTable. List of interface entities:
  - ifIndex. Interface index value.
  - ifDescr. Interface description.
  - ifType. Interface type: other(1), regular1822(2), hdh1822(3), ddn-x25(4), rfc877-x25(5), ethernet-csmacd(6), iso88023-csmacd(7), iso88024-tokenBus(8), iso88025-tokenRing(9), iso88026-man(10), starLan(11), proteon-10Mbit(12), proteon-80Mbit(13), hyperchannel(14), fddi(15), lapb(16), sdlc(17), ds1(18), e1(19), basicISDN(20), primaryISDN(21), ppp(23), softwareLoopback(24), eon(25), ethernet-3Mbit(26))
  - ifSpeed. Speed of interface, in bits per second.

o ifPhysAddress.
o ifAdminStatus. Administration status is Up (1), down (2) or testing (3).
o ifOperStatus. Operational status is Up (1), down (2) or testing (3).
o ifLastChange. Time since last change.
o ifInUcastPkts.
o ifInNUcastPkts.
o ifInDiscards.
o ifInErrors.
o ifInUnknownProtos.
o ifOutOctets.
o ifOutUcastPkts.
o ifOutNUcastPkts.
o ifOutDiscards.
o ifOutErrors.
o ifOutQLen.
o ifSpecific.

F3.2.4   at

The address translations table includes:

- atTable. This defines the addresses translations table, and each interface contains one network address to physical address translation:
    o atIfIndex. Interface interface.
    o atPhysAddress. Physical address of the interface.
    o atNetAddress. Network address of the interface.

F3.2.5   ip

This ip table include information on IP traffic, such as:

- ipForwarding. Defines whether the node is a gateway or not. It can be set to: forwarding (for a gateway) or not-forwarding.
- ipDefaultTTL. IP Time-to-live.
- ipInReceives. The total number of IP packets (including ones in error).
- ipInHdrErrors. Discarded IP packets, due to header problems.
- ipInAddrErrors . Discarded IP packets, due to incorrect addresses (such as 0.0.0.0).
- ipForwDatagrams. Number of IP packets which were forwarded.
- ipInUnknownProtos. Number of IP packets with an unknown protocol.
- ipInDiscards. Discarded packets due to processing problems, such as lack of buffer memory.
- ipInDelivers. Number of successfully IP packets.
- ipOutRequests.
- ipOutDiscards.
- ipOutNoRoutes. Discarded IP packets, due to no router for the packets.
- ipFragOKs. Number of completed fragments.
- ipFragFails. Number of unsuccessful fragments.
- ipFragCreates. Number of fragments created.
- ipAddrTable.
- ipAddrEntry:

    ○ ipAdEntAddr. Network address.
    ○ ipAdEntIfIndex. Address index.
    ○ ipAdEntNetMask. Subnet mask.
    ○ ipAdEntBcastAddr. Broadcast address.
    ○ ipAdEntReasmMaxSize.
- ipRoutingTable:
    ○ ipRouteDest. Destination address. A value of 0.0.0.0 is defined as a default route.
    ○ ipRouteIfIndex Route index.
    ○ ipRouteMetric1. Route metric 1. If it is not using the value is set to -1.
    ○ ipRouteMetric2.
    ○ ipRouteMetric3.
    ○ ipRouteMetric4.
    ○ ipRouteNextHop.
    ○ ipRouteType. Route types are: other, invalid, direct and indirect.
    ○ ipRouteProto. Protocol types are: other, local, netmgmt, icmp, egp, ggp, hello, rip,
     is-is, es-is, ciscoIGRP. bbnSpfIgp, ospf and bgp.
    ○ ipRouteAge.
    ○ ipRouteMask.
    ○ ipRouteMetric5.
- ipRouteInfo:
    ○ ipNetToMediaIfIndex. Route index.
    ○ ipNetToMediaPhysAddress. Physical address.
    ○ ipNetToMediaNetAddress. Network address.
    ○ ipNetToMediaType. Set to other, invalid, dynamic or static.

F3.2.6 icmp

The ICMP table includes:

- icmpInMsgs.
- icmpInErrors.
- icmpInDestUnreachs.
- icmpInTimeExcds
- icmpInParmProbs
- icmpInSrcQuenchs.
- icmpInRedirects.
- icmpInEchos.
- icmpInEchoReps.
- icmpInTimestamps.
- icmpInTimestampReps.
- icmpInAddrMasks.
- icmpInAddrMaskReps.
- icmpOutMsgs.
- icmpOutErrors.
- icmpOutDestUnreachs.
- icmpOutTimeExcds.
- icmpOutParmProbs.
- icmpOutSrcQuenchs.
- icmpOutEchos.

- icmpOutEchoReps.
- icmpOutTimestamps.
- icmpOutTimestampReps.
- icmpOutAddrMasks.
- icmpOutAddrMaskReps.

F3.2.7   Tcp

The TCP table includes:

- tcpRtoAlgorithm. This is used to determine the time-out for unacknowledged segments. This can be: other, constant, rsre or vanj (Van Jacobson's)
- tcpRtoMin. Minimum retransmission time-out (in milliseconds).
- tcpRtoMax Maximum retransmission time-out (in milliseconds).
- tcpMaxConn. Maximum number of TCP connections.
- tcpActiveOpens. Number of active TCP connections.
- tcpPassiveOpens. Number of passive TCP connection.
- tcpAttemptFails.
- tcpEstabResets.
- tcpCurrEstab.
- tcpInSegs. Number of input segments.
- tcpOutSegs. Number of output segments.
- tcpRetransSegs. Number of retransmitted segments.
- tcpConnTable:
    o tcpConnState. The state can be: closed, listen, synSent, synReceived, established, finWait1, finWait2, closeWait, lastAck, closing, timeWait or deleteTCB.
    o tcpConnLocalAddress. Local address.
    o tcpConnLocalPort. Local port.
    o tcpConnRemAddress. Remote address.
    o tcpConnRemPort. Remote port.

F3.2.8   Udp

The Udp table includes:

- udpInDatagrams.
- udpNoPorts.
- udpInErrors.
- udpOutDatagrams
- udpTable:
    o udpLocalAddress
    o udpLocalPort

F3.2.9   Egp

The Egp table includes:

- egpInMsgs.
- egpInErrors.
- egpOutMsgs.

- egpOutErrors.
- egpNeighTable:
  - egpNeighState.
  - egpNeighAddr.
  - egpNeighAs.
  - egpNeighInMsgs.
  - egpNeighInErrs.
  - egpNeighOutMsgs.
  - egpNeighOutErrs.
  - egpNeighInErrMsgs.
  - egpNeighOutErrMsgs.
  - egpNeighStateUps.
  - egpNeighStateDowns.
  - egpNeighIntervalHello.
  - egpNeighIntervalPoll.
  - egpNeighMode.
  - egpNeighEventTrigger.

F3.2.10 Transmission

This defines a table of the underlying media for the interfaces, and is typically an experimental portion of the database.

F3.2.11 snmp

The snmp table includes information on SNMP:

- snmpInPkts.
- snmpOutPkts.
- snmpInBadVersions.
- snmpInBadCommunityNames.
- snmpInBadCommunityUses.
- snmpInASNParseErrs.
- snmpInTooBigs.
- snmpInNoSuchNames.
- snmpInBadValues.
- snmpInReadOnlys.
- snmpInGenErrs.
- snmpInTotalReqVars.
- snmpInTotalSetVars.
- snmpInGetRequests.
- snmpInGetNexts.
- snmpInSetRequests.
- snmpInGetResponses.
- snmpInTraps.
- snmpOutTooBigs.
- snmpOutNoSuchNames.
- snmpOutBadValues.
- snmpOutGenErrs.
- snmpOutGetRequests.

- snmpOutGetNexts.
- snmpOutSetRequests.
- snmpOutGetResponses.
- snmpOutTraps.
- snmpEnableAuthenTraps.

F3.3   SNMP for Windows

Windows can run an SNMP agent which responds to a management system requests for information (Figure F3.2). Agents respond to messages, and generally do not originate them. A trap message is the only SNMP-initiated message, and is used to enhance security. Traps are alarm conditions which are caused by network events, such as a system reboot or a change in network conditions, such as coldStart, warmStart, linkDown and linkup.

Management hosts and agents build into an SNMP community, which are managed as a single administrative entity. For security purposes, only agents and management systems within the same community are allowed to communicate with each other.

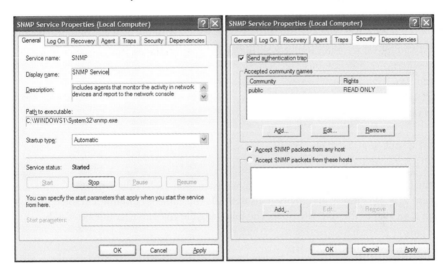

Figure F3.2   SNMP agent for Windows

F3.4   RMON (Remote Monitoring)

In addition to SNMP, many systems support two additional types of network management: EASE (Embedded Advanced Sampling Environment) and RMON. RMOS is SNMP MIB that specifies the types of information listed in a number of special MIB groups that are commonly used for traffic management. Typical groups are Statistics, History, Alarms, Hosts, Hosts Top N, Matrix, Filters, Events, and Packet Capture. The information can be gathered by dedicated hardware devices or by software built in to data communications equipment, such as routers, bridges, or switches (often known as an embedded agent).

F3.5 EASE (Embedded Advanced Sampling Environment)

EASE is a Hewlett-Packard developed system which samples LAN data to build traffic matrices and monitor users of the network. It can be used standard network types (such as 10BASE-2 and Token Ring) and to high speed networks (such as 100VG-AnyLAN, 100Base-T and FDDI)

F3.6 Bootp protocol

The bootp protocol allocates IP addresses to computers based on a table of network card MAC addresses. When a computer is first booted, the bootp server interrogates its MAC address and then looks up the bootp table for its entry. The server then grants the corresponding IP address to the computer. The computer then uses it for connections. This is one method of limiting access to the Internet.

F3.6.1 Bootp program

The bootp program is typically run on a Lynx-based PC with the `bootp` program. The following shows that the `bootp` program is currently running on a computer:

```
$ ps -ax
   PID TTY STAT  TIME COMMAND
     1 con S    0:06 init
    31 con S    0:01 /usr/sbin/inetd
 14142 con S    0:00 bootpd -d 1
    35 con S    0:00 /usr/sbin/lpd
    49 p 3 S    0:00 /sbin/agetty 38400 tty3
 14155 pp0 R    0:00 ps -ax
 10762 con S    0:18 /usr/sbin/named -b /usr/local/adm/named/named.boot
```

For the bootp system to operate then it must use a table to reconcile the MAC addresses of the card to an IP address. In the previous example this table is contained in the bootptab file which is located in the /etc directory. The following file gives an example bootptab:

📄 Contents of bootptab file

```
# /etc/bootptab: database for bootp server
# Blank lines and lines beginning with '#' are ignored.
#
# Legend:
#  first field -- hostname
#        (may be full domain name and probably should be)
#
#  hd -- home directory
#  bf -- bootfile
#  cs -- cookie servers
#  ds -- domain name servers
#  gw -- gateways
#  ha -- hardware address
#  ht -- hardware type
#  im -- impress servers
#  ip -- host IP address
#  lg -- log servers
```

```
#  lp -- LPR servers
#  ns -- IEN-116 name servers
#  rl -- resource location protocol servers
#  sm -- subnet mask
#  tc -- template host (points to similar host entry)
#  to -- time offset (seconds)
#  ts -- time servers
#
#hostname:ht=1:ha=ether_addr_in_hex:ip=ip_addr_in_dec:tc=allhost:
.default150:\
   :hd=/tmp:bf=null:\
   :ds=146.176.151.99 146.176.150.62 146.176.1.5:\
   :sm=255.255.255.0:gw=146.176.150.253:\
   :hn:vm=auto:to=0:
.default151:\
   :hd=/tmp:bf=null:\
   :ds=146.176.151.99 146.176.150.62 146.176.1.5:\
   :sm=255.255.255.0:gw=146.176.151.254:\
   :hn:vm=auto:to=0:
pc345:  ht=ethernet: ha=0080C8226BE2:  ip=146.176.150.2: tc=.default150:
pc307:  ht=ethernet: ha=0080C822CD4E:  ip=146.176.150.3: tc=.default150:
pc320:  ht=ethernet: ha=0080C823114C:  ip=146.176.150.4: tc=.default150:
pc331:  ht=ethernet: ha=0080C823124B:  ip=146.176.150.5: tc=.default150:
 :         :
pc460:  ht=ethernet: ha=0000E8C7BB63:  ip=146.176.151.142: tc=.default151:
pc414:  ht=ethernet: ha=0080C8246A84:  ip=146.176.151.143: tc=.default151:
pc405:   ht=ethernet:  ha=0080C82382EE:  ip=146.176.151.145:
tc=.default151:
```

The format of the file is:

```
#hostname:ht=1:ha=ether_addr_in_hex:ip=ip_addr_in_dec:tc=allhost:
```

where `hostname` is the hostname, the value defined after `ha=` is the Ethernet MAC address, the value after `ip=` is the IP address and the name after the `tc=` field defines the host information script. For example:

```
pc345:  ht=ethernet:  ha=0080C8226BE2:   ip=146.176.150.2:
tc=.default150:
```

defines the hostname of `pc345`, indicates it is on an Ethernet network, and shows its IP address is 146.176.150.2. The MAC address of the computer is `00:80:C8: 22:6B:E2` and it is defined by the script `.default150`. This file defines a subnet of 255.255.255.0 and has associated DNS of

```
146.176.151.99 146.176.150.62 146.176.1.5
```

and uses the gateway at:

```
146.176.150.253
```

F3.7 DHCP

Dynamic Host Configuration Protocol (DHCP) allows for the transmission of configuration information over a TCP/IP network. Microsoft implemented Dynamic Host Configuration Protocol (DHCP) on their Windows NT operating system and many other vendors are incorporating it into the systems. It is based on the Bootstrap Protocol (BOOTP) and adds additional services, such as:

- Automatic allocation of reusable IP network addresses.
- Additional TCP/IP configuration options.

It has two components:

- A protocol for delivering host-specific configuration parameters from a DHCP server to a host
- A mechanism for allocation of network addresses to hosts.

DHCP has been fully defined in the following RFCs:

RFC1533. DCHP options and Bootp vendor extensions.
RFC1534. Interoperation between DHCP and BOOTP.
RFC1541. DHCP.
RFC1542. Clarifications and Extensions for Bootstrap Protocol.
RFC2131. DHCP.
RFC2240. DHCP for Novell.

DHCP uses a client-server architecture, where the designated DHCP server hosts (servers) allocate network addresses and deliver configuration parameters to dynamically configured hosts (clients).

The three techniques that DHCP uses to assign IP addresses are:

- Automatic allocation. DHCP assigns a permanent IP address to a client.
- Dynamic allocation. DHCP assigns an IP address to a client for a limited period of time or when the client releases the address. It allows for automatic reuse of IP addresses that are no longer used by clients. It is typically used when there is a limited pool of IP addresses (which is less than the number of hosts) so that a host can only connect when it can get one of the IP addresses from the pool.
- Manual allocation. DHCP is used to convey an IP address which has been assigned by the network administrator. This allows DHCP to be used to eliminate assigning an IP address to a host through its operating system.

Networks can use several of these techniques.

DHCP messages are based on BOOTP messages, this allows DHCP to listen to a BOOTP relay agent and to allow integration of BOOTP clients and DHCP servers. A BOOTP relay agent or relay agent is an Internet host or router that passes DHCP messages between DHCP clients and DHCP servers. DHCP uses the same relay agent behavior as the BOOTP protocol specification. BOOTP relay agents are useful because it eliminates the need of having a DHCP server on each physical network segment.

Some of the objectives of DHCP are:

- DHCP should be a mechanism rather than a policy. DHCP must allow local system administrators control over configuration parameters where desired.
- No requirements for manual configuration of clients.
- DHCP does not require a server on each subnets and should communicate with routers and BOOTP relay agents and clients.
- Ensure that the same IP address cannot be used use by more than one DHCP client at a time.
- Restore DHCP client configuration when the client is rebooted.
- Provide automatic configuration for new clients.
- Support fixed or permanent allocation of configuration parameters.

F3.7.1   Host configuration parameters

The host configuration parameters are:

Be a router	on/off
Non-local source routing	on/off
Policy filters for non-local source routing	(list)
Maximum reassembly size	integer
Default TTL	integer
PMTU aging timeout	integer
MTU plateau table	(list)

IP-layer parameters are:

IP address	(address)
Subnet mask	(address mask)
MTU	integer
All-subnets-MTU	on/off
Broadcast address flavor	00000000h / FFFFFFFFh
Perform mask discovery	on/off
Be a mask supplier	on/off
Perform router discovery	on/off
Router solicitation address	(address)
Default routers, list of:	
router address	(address)
preference level	integer
Static routes, list of:	
destination	(host/subnet/net)
destination mask	(address mask)
type-of-service	integer
first-hop router	(address)
ignore redirects	on/off
PMTU	integer
perform PMTU discovery	on/off

Link-layer parameters, per interface:

Trailers	on/off
ARP cache timeout	integer

Ethernet encapsulation   (RFC 894/RFC 1042)

TCP parameters, per host:
    TTL   integer
    Keep-alive interval   integer
    Keep-alive data size   0/1

Where MTU is Path MTU Discovery and RD is Router Discovery.

F3.7.2   Protocol outline

Figure F3.3 defines the format of a DHCP message. The numbers in parentheses indicate the size of each field in octets.

- Op. Defines message code/ op code (1 for BOOTREQUEST and 2 for BOOTREPLY). 1 byte.
- Htype. Defines hardware address type, such as, 1 for 10 Mbps Ethernet. 1 byte.
- Hlen. Hardware address length such as 6 for Ethernet. 1 byte.
- Hops. Client sets to 0, optionally used by relay agents when booting through a relay agent. 1 byte.
- Xid. Transaction ID which is a random number chosen by the client and used by the client and the server to associate messages and responses. 4 bytes.
- Secs. Sets by client for the number of seconds elapsed since client began address acquisition. 2 bytes.
- Flags. Flags, the format is BRRR...R where R bits are reserved for future use (and must always be zero) and B defines the broadcast bit which overcomes the problem where some clients that cannot accept IP unicast datagrams before the TCP/IP software is configured. 2 bytes.
- Ciaddr. Defines the client's IP address. It is only addressed when the client is in the BOUND, RENEW or REBINDING state and can respond to ARP requests. 4 bytes.
- Yiaddr. Clients IP address. 4 bytes.
- Siaddr. IP address of next server to use in bootstrap; returned in DHCPOFFER, DHCPACK by server. 4 bytes.
- Giaddr. Relay agent IP address and is used in booting through a relay agent. 4 bytes.
- Chaddr. Clients MAC address. 16 bytes.
- Sname. Optional null terminated server host name string. 64 bytes.
- File. Boot null-terminated file name string. 128 bytes.
- Options. Optional parameters field. Variable number of bytes.

F3.7.3   Allocating a network address

The protocol between clients and server is defined by DHCP messages, these are:

- DHCPDISCOVER. The client broadcasts this to locate available servers. When a client initially is started it binds with an address of 0.0.0.0. It then sends out the DHCPDISCOVER message in a UDP packet to port 67 (which is the DHCP/BOOTP server port).
- DHCPNAK. Sent by the server to the client indicating that the clients network address is wrong (for example, client has moved and does not have the correct subnet) or the time

allocation for its network address has expired. On receiving a DHCPNAK message, the client restarts the configuration process.

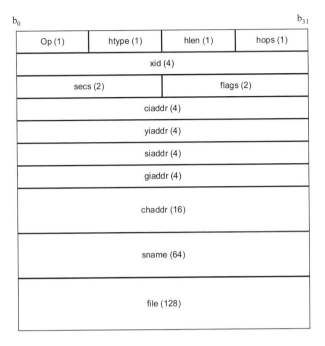

Figure F3.3 DHCP message format

- DHCPOFFER. After a DHCPDISCOVER message, a server may response to a client with a DHCPOFFER message that includes an available network address in the 'yiaddr' field. When allocating a new address, servers normally check that the offered network address is not already in use. Sending out an ICMP Echo Request to the new address can do this. If the client receives one or more DHCPOFFER messages from one or more servers then the client may choose to wait for multiple responses. It chooses the server based on the configuration parameters offered in the DHCPOFFER messages. The server sends out the DHCPOFFER message in a UDP packet to port 68 (which is the DHCP/BOOTP client port). This is send as a broadcast as the client does not currently have an IP address.
- DHCPREQUEST. Sent by clients to servers when either requesting offered parameters from one server and implicitly declining offers from all others, confirming parameter allocation (such as after a system boot), or extending the time on a particular network address. The server selected in the DHCPREQUEST message responds with a DHCPACK message containing the configuration parameters for the requesting client. The 'client identifier' ('chaddr') and assigned network address define a unique identifier for the client's and are used by both the client and server to identify the lease. Servers not selected by the DHCPREQUEST message use the message as notification that the client has declined that server's offer.
- DHCPACK. Sent by the server to a client with configuration parameters, including committed network address. The client receives the DHCPACK message with configu-

ration parameters, after which the client is setup. If the client detects that the address is already in use then the client sends back a DHCPDECLINE message to the server and restarts the configuration process.

- DHCPDECLINE. Sent by a client to the server indicating network address is already in use.
- DHCPRELEASE. Sent by a client to the server relinquishing network address. It identifies the lease to be released with its client identifier (chaddr) and network address in the DHCPRELEASE message.
- DHCPINFORM. Sent by a client to the server, asking only for local configuration parameters.

F3.7.4   Time allocations

Client acquires the lease of a network time for specified time (either finite or infinite time). The units of time are unsigned integer value in seconds, although the value FFFFFFFFh is used to represent infinity. This gives a range of between 0 and approximately 100 years.

When a client cannot contact the local DHCP server and has knowledge of a previous network address then it may continue to use the previous assigned network address until the lease expires. If the lease expires before the client can contact a DHCP server then the client immediately stops using the previous network address and informs local users of the problem.

F3.8   Domain name server

Each institution on the Internet has a host that runs a process called the domain name server (DNS). The DNS maintains a database called the directory information base (DIB) which contains directory information for that institution. On adding a new host, the system manager adds its name and its IP address. After this, it can then access the Internet. An example of DNS is given in Figure F3.4.

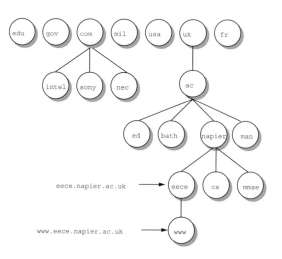

Figure F3.4   Example domain naming

Each registered domain on the Internet is responsible for running a DNS server on its own site. This must define the names and corresponding IP address for the nodes in its domain. When a local DNS server does not know the IP address for a specific node, it will contain another DNS and asks it if it knows the IP address. This then continues until a DNS server is found which knows the IP address. All the DNS servers along the way will update their tables, so that if they are asked for the entry, within a given time, they will respond back with its address, without contacting other DNS servers. The definitive DNS server will be the one which administers the domain. DNS server must thus age-out addresses, and refresh their tables at given periods. This will be done by contacting the domain DNS controllers. This aging-out of entries allows for a dynamic Internet, where nodes can change their location, and address, while retaining their name. They also allow new nodes to be added and deleted from a domain.

F3.8.1 DNS program

The DNS program is typically run on a Linux-based PC with a program called named (located in /usr/sbin) with an information file of named.boot. To run the program the following is used:

```
/usr/bin/named -b /usr/local/adm/named/named.boot
```

The following shows that the DNS program is currently running.

```
$ ps -ax
  PID TTY STAT   TIME COMMAND
  295 con  S     0:00 bootpd
   35 con  S     0:00 /usr/sbin/lpd
  272 con  S     0:00 /usr/sbin/named -b /usr/local/adm/named/named.boot
  264 p 1  S     0:01 bash
  306 pp0  R     0:00 ps -ax
```

In this case the data file named.boot is located in the /usr/local/adm/named directory. A sample named.boot file is:

```
/usr/local/adm/named - soabasefile
            eece.napier.ac.uk -main record of computer names
            net/net144   -reverse look-up database
            net/net145      "      "
            net/net146      "      "
            net/net147      "      "
            net/net150      "      "
            net/net151      "      "
```

This file specifies that the reverse look-up information on computers on the subnets 144, 145, 146, 147, 150 and 150 is contained in the net144, net145, net146, net147, net150 and net151 files, respectively. These are stored in the net subdirectory. The main file which contains the DNS information is, in this case, eece.napier.ac.uk. Whenever a new computer is added onto a network, in this case, the eece.napier.ac.uk file and the net/net1** (where ** is the relevant subnet name) are updated to reflect the changes. Finally, the serial number at the top of these data files is updated to reflect the current date, such as 19970321 (for 21st March 1997).

The DNS program can then be tested using `nslookup`. For example:

```
$ nslookup
Default Server:  ees99.eece.napier.ac.uk
Address:  146.176.151.99

> src.doc.ic.ac.uk
Server:  ees99.eece.napier.ac.uk
Address:  146.176.151.99

Non-authoritative answer:
Name:     swallow.doc.ic.ac.uk
Address:  193.63.255.4
Aliases:  src.doc.ic.ac.uk
```

F3.9   WINS

The Windows Internet Naming Service (WINS) is an excellent companion to DHCP. WINS provides a name registration and resolution on TCP/IP. It extends the function of DNS which will only map static IP addresses to TCP/IP host names. WINS is designed to resolved NetBIOS names on TCP/IP to dynamic network addresses assigned by DHCP. As it resolves NetBIOS names it is obviously aimed at Microsoft Windows-based (and DOS) networks.

F3.9.1   Name registration

The WINS server stores a WINS database which maps IP addresses to NetBIOS names. The operation is as follows:

1. Startup. WINS client send a Name Registration Request in a UDP packet to the WINS server to registers its NetBIOS name and IP address. When the WINS server receives it then it checks its stored database to make sure that the requested name is not already in use on the network.
2. Unsuccessful registration. When a client tries to register a name that is currently in use then the server sends the client a Denial message. The user of the client will then be informed that the computer's name is already in use on that network.
3. Successful registration. On successful name registration, the server sends a Name Registration Acknowledgement to the client. It fills the Time-to-Live (TTL) field to define the amount of time that the name registration will be active, after this time the server will cancel it
4. Initially re-registering name. The WINS client must send a Name Refresh Request a given time interval so that its name will not expire. The first request is made after one-eight of the TTL time, and then if unsuccessful after periods of one-eight of the TTL time. It has not been able to contact the primary WINS server after half the time defined in the TTL field, then the client tries to contact the secondary WINS server (if there is one).

5. Re-registering a name. After the first registration, the following registration will be made a 50 percent of the TTL time (instead of one-eight of the time).
6. Client shutdown. When a WINS client shuts down, it sends a Name Release Request to the WINS server, releasing its name from the WINS database.

F3.9.2 Name resolution

A client that requires the resolution of a NetBIOS name to an IP will go through the following:

1. Check the name is actually the local computer then looks in its own name resolution cache for a match.
2. Sends a required for a directed name lookup from the WINS server. If it finds one the WINS server sends its IP address to the client.
3. If the WINS server does not find a match then the client broadcasts to the network for help.
4. If there is no response from a broadcast then the client looks into its local LMHOSTS file, else it will look in its local HOSTS file.

F3.9.3 WINS proxy agents

Many older Windows systems do not support WINS clients. To allow them to communicate with a WINS server a WINS proxy agent can be used. This agent listens to the network for clients broadcasting for NetBIOS names resolution. The WINS proxy agent then redirects then to the WINS server, which will then pass the IP address resolution to the proxy agent, which in turn will pass it onto the client.

F4 FTP/HTTP/Telnet set up and programming

F4.1 FTP

FTP (File Transfer Protocol) is one of the most popular TCP/IP programs, and can be used to transfer files between an FTP server and an FTP client. The basic commands used are:

ABOR	Abort previous command	**ACCT**	Specify account
ALLO	Allocate storage	**APPE**	Append to a file
CDUP	Go to directory above	**CWD**	Change working directory
DELE	Delete a file	**HELP**	Show help information
LIST	List directory (ls -l)	**MKD**	Make directory
MDTM	Show last modification time	**MODE**	Specify data transfer mode
NLST	Give name of list of files	**NOOP**	No operation (to prevent disconnection)
PASS	Specify password	**PASV**	Prepare for server-to-server transfer
PORT	Specify port	**PWD**	Display current working directory
QUIT	Quit session	**REST**	Restart incomplete session
RETR	Retrieve a file	**RMD**	Remove a directory
RNFR	Specify rename-from filename	**RNTO**	Spread rename-to filename
SITE	Non-standard commands	**SIZE**	Return size of file
STOR	Store a file	**STOU**	Store a file with a unique name
STRU	Specify data transfer structure	**SYST**	Show operation system type
TYPE	Specify data transfer type	**USER**	Specify user name
XCUP	Change of parent of current working directory	**XCWD**	Change working directory
XMKD	Make a directory	**XPWD**	Print a directory
XRMD	Remove a directory		

The `ftpd` daemon is run from the Internet daemon (`inetd` and `inetd.conf`). It is automatically run when there is a request from the ftp port which is specified in the `/etc/services` file (typically port 21). Users who use ftp must have an account in the `/etc/password` file and any users who are barred from ftp access should be listed in the `/etc/ftpusers` file.

Anonymous FTP logins are where the user logs in as `anonymous` (typically using their e-mail address as the password). The user then uses the `~ftp` directory for all transfers. Typically the structure is:

`~ftp/bin`	Contains a copy of the `/bin/ls` file.
`~ftp/etc`	Contains the `passwd`, `group` and `logingroup` files for the users which own files within ~ftp.
`~ftp/etc/passwd`	Defines users who own files within `~ftp`.
`~ftp/etc/group`	Defines groups who own files within `~ftp`.
`~ftp/pub`	General area where files can be uploaded to or downloaded from.

Note that anonymous FTP is inherently dangerous to system security. To protect against damage the `-l` option in the `ftpd` daemon can be used to log all accesses to the system log. The `-t` option in the `ftpd` daemon defines the timeout time for a session.

In order to permit anonymous FTP, a line similar to the following must be added to the `/etc/password` file:

```
ftp:*:400:10:anonymousFTP:/user/ftp:/bin/false
```

where, in this case, 400 is the unique user ID for the ftp login, 10 is the group ID number for the guest group and `/user/ftp` specifies the home directory for the anonymous ftp account.

F4.2   Telnet

Telnet allows for a client to make a remote connection to a Telnet server. This connection occurs from the users port (U) to the server's port (L). Normally L is port 23, and, as a TCP connection is identified by a pair of ports, there can be several connections with different user ports. Telnet basically defines certain characters which are used for control purposes so that standard characters can be sent between the client and the server. It has keys which define the 128 standard ASCII characters. In addition to these characters there are addition codes which have special functions. All Telnet commands have at least two bytes, which are the IAC (Interrupt As Command) byte (Code = 255), followed by the command character, these include:

- Synch. This key allows one of the hosts to cleat the data path of the other host. Code = 242.
- Break (BRK). This key indicates that the Break key was pressed.   Code =2 43.
- Interrupt Process (IP). This key suspends, interrupts, aborts or terminates the process to which the Telnet terminal is connected. Code = 244.
- Erase Character (EC). Erases a character. Code = 247.
- Erase Line (EL). Erases a line of text. Code = 248.

A typical emulation for Telnet is VT220, of which the basic character sequences are:

FIND=200	INSERT HERE=201	REMOVE=202
SELECT=203	PREV SCREEN=204	NEXT SCREEN=205
UP ARROW=206	DOWN ARROW=207	RIGHT ARROW=208
LEFT ARROW=209	NUM 0=210	NUM 1=211
NUM 2=212	NUM 3=213	NUM 4=214
NUM 5=215	NUM 6=216	NUM 7=217
NUM 8=218	NUM 9=219	NUM DASH=220
NUM COMMA=221	NUM PERIOD=222	NUM ENTER=223
PF1=224	PF2=225	PF3=226
PF4=227	F6=228	F7=229
F8=230	F9=231	F10=232
F11=233	F12=234	F13=235
F14=236	F15=237	F16=238
F17=239	F18=240	F19=241
F20=242	HELP KEY=258	DO KEY=259
CCH=^[T	EPA=^[W	ESA=^[G
HTJ=^[I	HTS=^[H	IND=^[D
MW=^[U	NEL=^[E	OSC=^[]
PLD=^[K	PLU=^[L	PM=^[6
PU1=^[Q	PU2=^[R	RI=^[M

SPA=^[V	SS2=^[N	SSA=^[F
STS=^[S	VTS=^[J	

Along with these there are various generic key definitions:

SCROLL PAGE DOWN=0	SCROLL LINE DOWN=1	SCROLL PAGE UP=2
SCROLL LINE UP=3	SCROLL PAGE LEFT=4	SCROLL LINE LEFT=5
SCROLL PAGE RIGHT=6	SCROLL LINE RIGHT=7	
NEW SESSION=8	PREVIOUS SESSION=9	NEXT SESSION=10
SCROLL LOCK=11	COPY=12	PASTE=13
CLEAR SCREEN=14	PRINT SCREEN=15	LOGGING=16
NULL=^@	SOH=^A	STX=^B
ETX=^C	EOT=^D	ENQ=^E
ACK=^F	BEL=^G	BS=^H
HT=^I	LF=^J	VT=^K
FF=^L	CR=^M	SO=^N
SI=^O	DLE=^P	DC1=^Q
DC2=^R	DC3=^S	DC4=^T
NAK=^U	SYN=^V	ETB=^W
CAN=^X	EM=^Y	SUB=^Z
ESC=^[	FS=^\	GS=^]
RS=^^	US=^	DEL=\x7F
SS3=\x8F	DCS=\x90	CSI=\x9B
APC=\x9F	ST=\x9C	

F4.2.1 Telnet daemon

The Internet daemon (inetd) starts the telnetd daemon when there is a request from the telnet port which is specified in the /etc/services files (typically port 23). To start the telnetd the /etc/inetd.conf file must contain the line:

```
telnet stream tcp nowait root /etc/telnetd telnetd -b/etc/issue
```

/etc/inetd.conf

The /etc/inetd.conf is called from the Internet daemon (inet). Its general format is:

<service_name> <sock_type> <proto> <flags> <user> <server> <args>

where
service_name	Name of the specified service and is defined in the /etc/services file.
sock_type	Defines whether it is connection oriented (stream) or connectionless (datagram).
proto	Defines the protocol (TCP or UDP) and is defined in the /etc/protocols.
flags	Defines the action which should be taken upon detection of a connection. nowait defines that there should be no wait in starting up the service daemon, whereas wait informs it that it should wait for the service to start.
user	Defines the owner of the service.
server	Defines the name of the service.
arg	Defines addition arguments.

For example:

```
ftp     stream  tcp   nowait  root    /etc/ftpd ftpd
telnet  stream  tcp   nowait  root    /etc/telnetd telnetd
finger  stream  tcp   nowait  guest   /etc/fingerd fingerd
login   stream  tcp   nowait  root    /etc/login logind
```

/etc/inittab

The /etc/inittab file is called when the system is initially started. Its general format is:

label : *run_level* : *action* : *process*

where

label	Specified name.
run_level	Defines run level, such as: 0 (power down), 1 (administratively down), s (single user), 2 (multi-user), 3 (remote file sharing), 4 (unused), 5 (firmware) and 6 (system restart).
action	Control method that init uses over the execution of the process, such as boot (start up the specified process), bootwait (start up the pro-cess, but wait until the process has started before parsing the configuration file), initdefault (set the run level that init enters at system start up), off (if process is not running, ignore this line), once (start process once, and then leave it to run to its end), respawn (restart the process, if it has stopped) and wait (wait until the process completes before continuing).
process	Program that should be used.

An example is given next:

```
mess: 2:bootwait:/bin/cat /etc/message_of_the_day > /dev/console
r0: 1:wait:/etc/rc1
r1: 2: wait:/etc/rc2
go1:2:off:/etc/getty tty1
```

F4.2.2   Telnet client commands

The Telnet client command prompt accepts a number of command, these are:

open	Open hostname port number to establish a Telnet connection (open hostname [port]).
close	Close an existing Telnet connection.
display	Show current settings.
quit	Exits from the Telnet session.
set	Sets the terminal type for the connection.
unset	Turn off local echoes.
status	Shows whether there is a connection.
Ctrl-]	Go to the command mode

An example session is shown below:

```
C:> telnet
Telnet> ?
Commands may be abbreviated. Supported commands are:

c    - close              close current connection
d    - display            display operating parameters
o    - open hostname [port] connect to hostname (default port 23).
q    - quit               exit telnet
set  - set                set options (type 'set ?' for a list)
sen  - send               send strings to server
st   - status             print status information
u    - unset              unset options (type 'unset ?' for a list)
?/h  - help               print help information

Telnet> display
Escape Character is 'CTRL+]'
Will auth(NTLM Authentication)
Local echo off
New line mode - Causes return key to send CR & LF
Current mode: Console
Will term type
Preferred term type is ANSI

Telnet>
```

The NTLM authentication allows clients and servers to authenticate themselves to each other. In a normal mode the user name and password are sent in plaintext format. Anyone who listens to the network traffic between the client and server can then read these. NTLM uses encryption to encrypt the username and password.

F4.2.3   Telnet server (Windows)

Previous to Windows 2000 Server and XP Professional, Windows did not directly support a Telnet session on a computer. With the Telnet server program is login.cmd file is executed whenever a user logins into the Telnet server. This file can be used to display a special message, or to run other programs. An example login.cmd file (which will be stored in the %SystemRoot%\system32 folder) is:

```
@echo off
rem
rem  Default global logon script
rem
echo
*=======================================================
echo
Welcome to My Telnet Server
echo
*=====================================================
cd /d %HOMEDRIVE%\%HOMEPATH%
```

To increase user-level security, only NTFS partitions should be accessible. Also a TelnetUsers group can be created, and all the Telnet users are added to it. File and directory permissions can then be assigned to control the access that members have to the files and directories.

Often code page mapping must be setup so that the session can display extended character. This can be achieved by running the chcp command with the appropriate page. For example, to support English and Western European UNIX, add the command **chcp 1252**.

An example of the server startup program is shown in Figure F4.1. The program that is run is tlntsvr.exe.

Figure F4.1   Telnet server properties

F4.3   FTP programming

Most programming language have FTP components which implement most of the FTP protocol, and allow the programmer to make simple calls to the component. In VB the main component is Inet. It has the following properties, events and methods.

F4.3.1   Properties

AccessType	This set sets or returns a value which is used to determine whether a proxy is used (icNamedProxy) or not (icDirect). If the default setting is set in the register then the property is set to icUseDefault.
Document	This sets or returns the name of the file or document that will be used with the Execute method. When it is not set, the default document is returned from the FTP server.
Name	This returns the name that is used in the code to identify the FTP object.
Proxy	This sets or returns the name of the proxy server used to communicate with the Internet.
RequestTimeOut	This sets or returns or sets the time length, in seconds, to wait before a time-out expires.

ResponseCode   This returns the error code from an icError state occurs in the State-Changed event. More information is stored in the ResponseInfo property.

ResponseInfo   This return the text message for the last known error.

URL   This sets or returns URL that is used by the Execute or OpenURL methods.

UserName   This sets or returns the name that is sent with requests to remote computers.

F4.3.2   Methods

The main methods used in FTP programming are:

Cancel   This method cancels the current transaction, and closes down any opened connections.

Execute   This method executes a request on the server. In FTP, typical requests are GET, PWD, and so on.

OpenURL   This method returns or opens and returns a document at the specified URL.

The format of the Execute method is:

object.Execute url, operation, data

The main operations are:

Operation	Description
CD dir1	Change directory (dir1).
CDUP	Change to parent directory.
CLOSE	Closes current FTP connection.
DELETE file	Deletes file.
DIR	List directory command.
GET file1 file2	Gets a remote file (file1), and creates as a new local file (file2).
LS	List directory
MKDIR dir1	Creates a directory (dir1).
PUT file1 file2	Puts a local file (file1) to the remote host (file2).
PWD	Shows the current working directory.
QUIT	Quit the session
RECV file1 file2	Retrieves the remote file (file1), and creates a new local file (file2).
RENAME file1 file2	Renames the remote file (file1) to the new name (file2).
RMDIR dir1	Remove a directory (dir1).
SEND file1 file2	Same as PUT.
SIZE dir1	Returns the size of the directory (dir1).

F4.3.3   Event

The only event associated with the Inet object is StateChanged. It is called with:

object_StateChanged(ByVal State As Integer)

Its setting are:

Constant	Value	Description
icNone	0	No state to report.
icHostResolvingHost	1	Resolving the IP address of the host
icHostResolved	2	Resolved the IP address of the host
icConnecting	3	Connecting to the host.
icConnected	4	Successfully connected to the host.
icRequesting	5	Sending a request to the host.
icRequestSent	6	Successfully sent the request.
icReceivingResponse	7	Receiving a response from the host.
icResponseReceived	8	Successfully received a response from the host.
icDisconnecting	9	Disconnecting from the host computer.
icDisconnected	10	Successfully disconnected from the host computer.
icError	11	Error occurred in communicating with the host.
icResponseCompleted	12	Request has completed and all data has been received.

For example for an Inet1 object, the following could be used:

```
Private Sub Inet1_StateChanged(ByVal State As Integer)
   Dim Msg As String

   Select Case State
   Case icNone
      ' Ignore, no error
   Case icHostResolvingHost
      Msg = "Resolving Host... "

   ' Other settings are inserted here

   Case icError   ' 11
      Msg = "ErrorCode: "&Inet1.ResponseCode&" : "&Inet1.ResponseInfo
   End Select
End Sub
```

F4.3.4   Example program

Program F4.2 gives a basic FTP client. A connection is initially made with:

```
Inet1.AccessType = icUseDefault
Inet1.URL = text1.Text
Inet1.UserName = Text2.Text
Inet1.Password = Text3.Text
```

and when a connection is made the reply from the FTP server causes a StateChanged event. If the response from the server has been successful, the State is defined as icResponseCompleted. The data is read with the getChunk() method, with:

```
Case icResponseCompleted
     Dim data As Variant
         data = Inet1.GetChunk(1024, icString)
         Do While LenB(data) > 0
             status.Text = status.Text + data
             data = Inet1.GetChunk(1024, icString)
```

```
            Loop
            status.Text = status.Text + vbCrLf
    End Select
```

A command is sent to the server is defined as:

```
    Inet1.Execute , "Command"
```

which sends Command to the server.

📄 Program F4.1
```
Private Sub button_connect_Click()
    Inet1.AccessType = icUseDefault
    Inet1.URL = text1.Text
    Inet1.UserName = Text2.Text
    Inet1.Password = Text3.Text
End Sub

Private Sub button_help_Click()
    frmBrowser.Show
End Sub

Private Sub button_exit_Click()
    End
End Sub

Private Sub button_dir_Click()
    Inet1.Execute , "LS"
    command_window.Text = command_window.Text + "LS:" + vbCrLf
End Sub

Private Sub button_close_Click()
    Inet1.Execute , "CLOSE"
    command_window.Text = command_window.Text + "CLOSE:" + vbCrLf
End Sub

Private Sub button_pwd_Click()
    Inet1.Execute , "PWD"
    command_window.Text = command_window.Text + "PWD:" + vbCrLf
End Sub

Private Sub button_size_Click()
    Inet1.Execute , "SIZE ."
    command_window.Text = command_window.Text + "SIZE:" + vbCrLf
End Sub

Private Sub button_mkdir_Click()
    Inet1.Execute , "MKDIR TEMP"
    command_window.Text = command_window.Text + "Mkdir temp:" + vbCrLf
End Sub

Private Sub button_rmdir_Click()
    Inet1.Execute , "RMDIR TEMP"
    command_window.Text = command_window.Text + "Rmdir temp:" + vbCrLf
End Sub

Private Sub button_status_Click()
    status.Text = ""
End Sub
```

```
Private Sub Form_Load()
End Sub

Private Sub Inet1_StateChanged(ByVal State As Integer)
    Select Case State
    Case icNone
        ' Ignore, no error
    Case icHostResolvingHost
        status.Text = status.Text + "Resolving host... " + vbCrLf
    Case icHostResolved
        status.Text = status.Text + "Resolved host... " + vbCrLf
    Case icConnecting
        status.Text = status.Text + "Connecting to host... " + vbCrLf
    Case icConnected
        status.Text = status.Text + "Connected to host... " + vbCrLf
    Case icError
        status.Text = status.Text + "ErrorCode: " & Inet1.ResponseCode & " : "
            & Inet1.ResponseInfo
    Case icResponseCompleted
        Dim data As Variant
            data = Inet1.GetChunk(1024, icString)
            Do While LenB(data) > 0
                status.Text = status.Text + data
                data = Inet1.GetChunk(1024, icString)
            Loop
            status.Text = status.Text + vbCrLf
    End Select

End Sub

Private Sub text_ftp_command_Change()
    Inet1.Execute , text_ftp_command.Text
    command_window.Text = command_window.Text + Text4.Text
End Sub
```

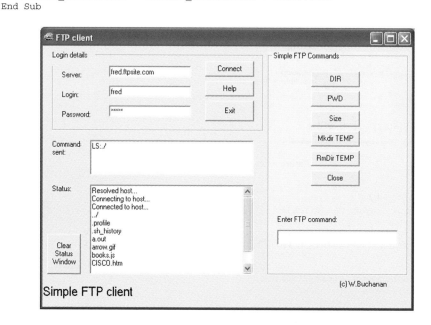

Figure F4.2   FTP client sample run

F4.4   HTTP programming

The Inet object can be used to access the HTTP protocol. The basic command are:

GET url   Gets a URL.
HEAD   Retries the header information for a URL
POST   Provides additional information for request to an HTTP server.
PUT   Replaces data at the URL.

An example of the GET is:

```
Execute "http://www.myserver.com" & "/index.htm", "GET"
```

A sample run is shown in Figure F4.3.

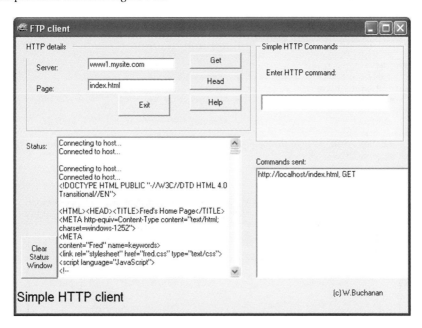

Figure F4.3   HTTP client sample run

📄 **Program F4.2**

```
Private Sub button_get_Click()
    Inet1.AccessType = icUseDefault
    Inet1.Execute "http://" + text_url.Text + "/" + text_file.Text, "GET"
    command_window.Text ="http://"+ text_url.Text + "/" + text_file.Text + ", GET"
End Sub

Private Sub button_clear_Click()
    status.Text = ""
End Sub

Private Sub button_head_Click()
    Inet1.AccessType = icUseDefault
```

```
        Inet1.URL = "http://" + text_url.Text + "/" + text_file.Text
        Inet1.Execute Inet1.URL, "HEAD"
End Sub

Private Sub button_help_Click()
    frmBrowser.Show
End Sub

Private Sub button_exit_Click()
    End
End Sub

Private Sub http_command_text_box_Change()
    Inet1.Execute , http_command_text_box.Text
    command_window.Text = command_window.Text + Text4.Text
End Sub

Private Sub Inet1_StateChanged(ByVal State As Integer)
    Select Case State
    Case icNone
        ' Ignore, no error
    Case icHostResolvingHost
        status.Text = status.Text + "Resolving host... " + vbCrLf
    Case icHostResolved
        status.Text = status.Text + "Resolved host... " + vbCrLf
    Case icConnecting
        status.Text = status.Text + "Connecting to host... " + vbCrLf
    Case icConnected
        status.Text = status.Text + "Connected to host... " + vbCrLf
    Case icError
        status.Text = status.Text + "ErrorCode: " & Inet1.ResponseCode & " : " &
Inet1.ResponseInfo

    Case icResponseCompleted
        Dim data As Variant
            data = Inet1.GetChunk(1024, icString)
            Do While LenB(data) > 0
                status.Text = status.Text + data
                data = Inet1.GetChunk(1024, icString)
            Loop
            status.Text = status.Text + vbCrLf
    End Select
End Sub
```